Understanding Poverty

EDITED BY

Abhijit Vinayak Banerjee
Roland Bénabou
Dilip Mookherjee

OXFORD
UNIVERSITY PRESS

2006

OXFORD
UNIVERSITY PRESS

Oxford University Press, Inc., publishes works that further
Oxford University's objective of excellence
in research, scholarship, and education.

Oxford   New York
Auckland   Cape Town   Dar es Salaam   Hong Kong   Karachi
Kuala Lumpur   Madrid   Melbourne   Mexico City   Nairobi
New Delhi   Shanghai   Taipei   Toronto

With offices in
Argentina   Austria   Brazil   Chile   Czech Republic   France   Greece
Guatemala   Hungary   Italy   Japan   Poland   Portugal   Singapore
South Korea   Switzerland   Thailand   Turkey   Ukraine   Vietnam

Copyright © 2006 by Oxford University Press, Inc.

Published by Oxford University Press, Inc.
198 Madison Avenue, New York, New York 10016

www.oup.com

Oxford is a registered trademark of Oxford University Press

Library of Congress Cataloging-in-Publication Data
Understanding poverty / [edited by] Abhijit Vinayak Banerjee, Roland Bénabou,
Dilip Mookherjee.
    p. cm.
Includes bibliographical references and index.
ISBN-13: 978-0-19-530519-7; 978-0-19-530520-3 (pbk.)
ISBN: 0-19-530519-1; 0-19-530520-5 (pbk.)
1. Poverty.   2. Poor.   I. Banerjee, Abhijit V.   II. Bénabou, Roland.   III. Mookherjee, Dilip.
HC79.P6U533   2006
362.5—dc22   2005018492

9 8 7 6 5 4 3 2 1

Printed in the United States of America
on acid-free paper

UNDERSTANDING POVERTY

Contents

Contributors

Daron Acemoglu
Department of Economics
Massachusetts Institute of
Technology

Philippe Aghion
Department of Economics
Harvard University

Beatriz Armendáriz de Aghion
Department of Economics
Harvard University

Abhijit Vinayak Banerjee
Department of Economics
Massachusetts Institute of
Technology

Pranab Bardhan
Department of Economics and
Institute of International
Studies
University of California at
Berkeley

Kaushik Basu
Department of Economics
Cornell University

Roland Bénabou
Department of Economics and
Woodrow Wilson School
Princeton University

Timothy Besley
Department of Economics
London School of Economics

Anne Case
Department of Economics and
Woodrow Wilson School
Princeton University

Angus Deaton
Department of Economics and
Woodrow Wilson School
Princeton University

Esther Duflo
Department of Economics
Massachusetts Institute of
   Technology

Stanley L. Engerman
Department of Economics
University of Rochester

Mukesh Eswaran
Department of Economics
University of British Columbia

Maitreesh Ghatak
Department of Economics
London School of Economics

Simon Johnson
Sloan School of Management
Massachusetts Institute of
   Technology

Ashok Kotwal
Department of Economics
University of British Columbia

Michael Kremer
Department of Economics
Harvard University

Jean-Jacques Laffont
   in memoriam
Institut d'Économie Industrielle
   (IDEI)
University of Social Sciences,
   Toulouse

Glenn C. Loury
Department of Economics
Brown University

Edward Miguel
Department of Economics
University of California at
   Berkeley

Dilip Mookherjee
Department of Economics and
   Institute for Economic
   Development
Boston University

Jonathan Morduch
Wagner Graduate School of
   Public Service
New York University

Sendhil Mullainathan
Department of Economics
Harvard University

Kaivan Munshi
Department of Economics
Brown University

Thomas Piketty
Fédération Paris-Jourdan and
   CEPREMAP
École Normale Supérieure

Martin Ravallion
World Bank

Debraj Ray
Department of Economics
New York University

James Robinson
Department of Government
Harvard University

Emmanuel Saez
Department of Economics
University of California at
   Berkeley

T. Paul Schultz
Department of Economics and
   Economic Growth Center
Yale University

Kenneth L. Sokoloff
Department of Economics
University of California at Los
    Angeles

Jean Tirole
Institut d'Économie Industrielle
    (IDEI)
University of Social Sciences,
    Toulouse

Robert M. Townsend
Department of Economics
University of Chicago

Christopher Udry
Department of Economics and
    Economic Growth Center
Yale University

Introduction and Overview

Abhijit Vinayak Banerjee, Roland Bénabou, &
Dilip Mookherjee

Poverty is one of the central problems of economics. A staggeringly large number of people in the world live on less than $1 a day—almost one in five, amounting to over a billion people. If the poverty line is raised to $2 a day, over half the world's population is poor. Even by this definition, someone who is poor still consumes less in one month than what most people in the developed world consume in a single day, often in a single meal. Though these consumption measures represent material standards of living—food, clothing, shelter, transportation, fuel, school tuition, and so on—they also correlate closely with wider notions of capabilities and well-being. The poor are not just cold and hungry; they are also frequently malnourished, illiterate, prone to sickness, unemployment, alcoholism, and depression; they are excluded from many markets and social groups, and are vulnerable to natural disasters and predation by organized crime and rapacious officials. Poverty limits awareness of their rights and their ability to access legal institutions to protect those rights. Worse still, they are often trapped in this situation for most of their lives, with little hope of release for themselves and their children. The problem is particularly acute in developing countries, but is by no means restricted to them: substantial pockets of poverty exist in many rich countries. Poverty is a tragedy not only for the individuals concerned but also for the world at large, being intimately linked with some of the most pressing social and political problems of our time: crime, violence, broken families, loss of communities, public health crises, overpopulation, environmental degradation, corruption, poor governance, and ethnic conflict.

Since the mid-1980s there has been a large amount of exciting research by economists on poverty. Much of this work has been inspired by the combination of a body of theory that takes market failures and institutional failures seriously with access to a world of new data directly relevant to poverty, often collected in the field by the researchers themselves. Unfortunately, much of the knowledge generated by this research is not available to a wider public, unless they are willing to delve into the pages of specialized journals. This has the unfortunate consequence that broader political attitudes of the educated public and policy makers toward antipoverty policies have remained largely uninformed by what economists have learned since the mid-1980s in the last twenty years.

Some of this ignorance reflects the fact that researchers have few opportunities, and even fewer incentives, to venture into the public arena. Speaking out in public is never easy, because so much depends getting the tone right. One has to know how to avoid the Scylla of oversimplifying advocacy without getting caught in the Charybdis of an evenhandedness that leaves everything unresolved. It is therefore no surprise that the average economist is often reluctant to air his views in public, preferring to remain on the more familiar terrain of scholarly debate. This is particularly true on politically polarized issues such as those relating to poverty, globalization, underdevelopment, or child labor. To speak out is to risk misunderstanding, caricature, and opprobrium, with being ignored the most likely outcome.

This volume came out of the feeling that something important was getting lost as a result of this state of affairs. We felt it would be useful to put together a body of critical essays, written primarily for non-economists, and written well, that would take on different aspects of the problem of poverty. We also felt that there should be a particular emphasis on developing countries, where the issue is most critical. The ideal essay would be one that would lead the reader through its own reasoning process, from the basic facts through the methodology and all the way to a conclusion of practical relevance on some important issue. This, we thought, would be the most effective way of communicating to a broad audience the essence of what has been learned about poverty and some of the policies that can most effectively combat it.

With this goal in mind we solicited contributions from a diverse group of economists currently doing some of the leading research related to poverty, broadly construed. Rather than a traditional survey, we asked each of them to write an essay that would convey to an audience of serious non-specialists their own views of what the most important insights on a given topic are, and how these can inform policy. We also encouraged them to lay out what economists do not yet know but would like to know, since this will presumably define the research agenda and subsequent policy design in the years ahead.

There were also methodological considerations in putting together the volume. First, we focused primarily on what economists call "micro" issues, those involving the circumstances of specific households, enterprises, communities, or markets. We were also keen to bring in some of the recent work on the role of institutions and the influence of politics on economic outcomes. Another objective was to include contributions dealing with some of the global issues that loom large today, such as globalization and intellectual property rights. Left out are important macroeconomic issues such as deficits, monetary policy, and exchange rates, largely on the ground that those share a distinct methodology and set of concerns only indirectly connected with poverty. They could conceivably form the subject of another volume.

Second, in the (very rough) dichotomy between well-established knowledge and principles and "new" approaches and results, we privileged the second. This is of course not to say that the standard economic recommendations of enforcing secure property rights, liberalizing agricultural markets, eliminating major price distortions, and promoting competition or openness to trade are not also relevant for development and poverty reduction. Indeed, many of them are discussed in various chapters of this volume. But the arguments that go with many of these are quite familiar, almost to the point where they constitute the stereotype of "economist-speak."

By contrast, most new developments since the mid-1980s in this area have stemmed from economists' having to grapple with, model, and devise solutions for breakdowns in the functioning of certain markets. The most pervasive of these "market failures" are those that impede the ability of the poor to make the private or collective "investments" they need to escape poverty. The problem is particularly acute in the financial sector, where the poor are frequently excluded from credit and insurance markets.

Recognizing the central role played by market imperfections in the genesis and persistence of poverty does not, however, translate into a blind faith in government intervention. Indeed, a second major line of research during this period has focused on the failures of government interventions and collective action to deliver what the poor need. Several chapters of the volume thus focus on topics such as corruption, rent-seeking or capture by an elite, public sector reform, optimal incentives, and institutional design.

Third, we gave a preeminent place to empirically oriented research: presenting the facts themselves, which often are not well known by the general public, as well as explaining the frequently novel methods by which these facts were uncovered. We did, however, include a number of purely theoretical contributions that we felt would help the reader think about these facts and their implications. Taken together, the essays in this volume are representative of the constant cycle of interchange between theory, field-based empirical studies, and policy design that is the hallmark of modern development economics.

The impetus for putting together a book of this kind originated from the MacArthur Foundation-sponsored Research Network on Inequality and Economic Performance, in which the three of us are participants. We owe a special debt to the network for this role, and more fundamentally for bringing together an interdisciplinary group of economists, political scientists, and sociologists with a shared interest in inequality, poverty, and economic development. In particular, we thank the leaders of this network, Pranab Bardhan and Samuel Bowles, for their active encouragement of the production of this book. We did not, however, restrict ourselves to members of this network in inviting contributions, and cast a much wider net.

The essays are organized into three main sections. The first deals broadly with the origins and determinants of poverty, including the roles of historical legacies of colonialism versus geography and culture, of legal and political institutions, of government policy, and of globalization. The second section deals with the design of antipoverty policy in a number of specific areas, such as tax and welfare systems, child labor regulations, education, microcredit, intellectual property rights, and alternative mechanisms for delivering public services. The last section deals with new directions for thinking about poverty, particularly those that deviate from the conventional approaches used by economists and impinge upon areas traditionally covered by psychology and sociology.

The rest of this introductory chapter is organized as follows. The following section lays out some broad facts concerning poverty and discusses issues surrounding the measurement of poverty, an issue addressed in the first essay, by Angus Deaton. This is followed by three sections, each providing a commentary on the collection of essays in each of the three main sections of the volume.

THE FACTS: HOW MUCH POVERTY? WHERE IS IT?
IS IT GETTING WORSE?

Everyone is aware that there is a lot of poverty in the world, irrespective of how economists choose to measure it, and that it is disproportionately concentrated in Asia and Africa. Nevertheless, it is useful to confirm these impressions with careful measurement. It is even more useful to identify relevant correlates of poverty, as a first step in diagnosing the problem. Has poverty grown over the past century, or the past few decades? How does it relate to growth, globalization, overpopulation, or any other possible cause or symptom that we care about? What are the Millenium Development Goals with respect to poverty reduction? Do the facts suggest anything about suitable policies?

The first essay in the volume, by Angus Deaton, introduces some of the key issues concerning poverty measurement. As he argues, poverty is a multidimensional phenomenon encompassing lack of access to various basic necessities, such as nutrition, health, education, housing, security, and opportunity for future improvement. Yet there is a need for measures simple enough to grasp and remember that can be compared across space and time; otherwise it is easy to get lost in a morass of statistical detail. This is the idea that the poverty line serves. It sets a standard for what it means to be poor, usually defined in terms of the amount of money needed to achieve some accepted standard of consumption. This, obviously, still leaves a lot that is open to disagreement: Should the standard be met on the basis of nutritional requirements? Or on the basis of some vision of what people ought to have? How does one adjust for differences in the cost of living, or the variations in the exchange rates? Should one simply count the number of people below the poverty line, or should one give more weight to the depth of poverty?

The measure of poverty most frequently used and reported (for instance, by policy makers, multilateral institutions, or the media) is the number of people living below (i.e., with consumption below) a poverty line of either $1 or $2 per day, expressed in terms of 1993 U.S. dollars, adjusting for differences in purchasing power across different currencies. This corresponds quite closely to the poverty lines used in the poorest countries. In terms of these measures, there is indeed a lot of poverty. Approximately 1.2 billion people—about a fifth of the world's population—fell below the extreme poverty line of $1 a day in the late 1990s. If we use the $2 line, this number rises to 2.8 billion, more than half the world's population.

Most global poverty is concentrated in South Asia and sub-Saharan Africa, where the proportions of people in extreme poverty were 40% and 46%, respectively, in 1998. Of the 1.2 billion, over 800 million were located in these two regions, and another 280 million in East Asia (including China). One therefore has to focus particularly on Asia and sub-Saharan Africa when thinking of problems of global poverty.

Using other dimensions of basic needs points to the same general pattern. The 2004 *Human Development Report* shows that of the 831 million people who were undernourished in the year 2000, sub-Saharan Africa, East Asia, and South Asia, respectively, accounted for 185 million, 212 million, and 312 million. Of the 104 million primary school-age children not in school, they included 44, 14, and 32 million, respectively. Of the 11 million children under the age of five dying each year, 5, 1, and 4 million of them were in these three regions. They also had 273 million, 453 million, and 225 million people without access to improved water sources, out of a global total of 1.2 billion.[1] The crude method of using a simple consumption threshold of $1 or $2 thus appears to capture many other relevant dimensions of poverty as well.

The Millenium Development Goals, adopted by a United Nations summit of representatives of 189 countries in September 2000, consist of eight objectives to be achieved by 2015, covering poverty, hunger, primary education, gender equality, child mortality, and access to water and sanitation. The measure of extreme poverty (proportion below $1 a day) is sought to be reduced by half of the 1990 levels by the year 2015. Most projections show that these goals are unlikely to be met on the basis of current performance in sub-Saharan Africa, as well as in countries in Central and Eastern Europe and the CIS. The goals for universal primary education and for reducing child mortality by two-thirds are expected to be at least one hundred years away in sub-Saharan Africa, and no dates can be set for achievement of the goals concerning hunger, poverty, and access to sanitation, because performance in these areas is currently worsening in sub-Saharan Africa rather than improving.[2]

There has been some recent controversy concerning poverty estimates and projections into the future, not just among different academics but also spilling over to the pages of *The Economist*.[3] The estimates reported above have been calculated by the World Bank, on the basis of consumption surveys of households in different countries. *The Economist* reported much lower levels of poverty—only 7% of the world's population below $1 a day in 1998, rather than one fifth—using a different methodology (in which country incomes are calculated on the basis of national accounts data, and the breakup of this total across different groups is inferred from inequality estimates obtained from the consumption surveys).

Whatever the relative merits of the different methodologies, the main differences they give rise to concern mainly the *level* of poverty. There is much less disagreement over *changes* in global poverty. Between the early 1980s and 2001, both sets of estimates show that poverty rates fell by almost half: approximately 400 million people crossed the $1 threshold during this time. This amounts to a fairly dramatic reduction in poverty. There is thus no basis for views, often expressed by protesters against globalization and privatization, that these trends have coincided with a rise in global poverty. Most of the poverty reduction happened in Asia, and particularly in China, which has experienced growing integration into the world economy and a rise in market forces. On the other hand, the geographic distribution of global poverty changed dramatically. The number of poor people roughly doubled in Africa: in the early 1980s this continent housed one in ten of the world's poorest, a proportion that rose to one in three by 2001.[4]

Longer-term trends in poverty also show a secular decline over the past two centuries. Table 0.1 shows the best currently available estimates (from Bourguignon and Morrisson 2002) of the extreme poverty rate (proportion of world population under the $1 a day threshold in 1985 U.S. dollars, corrected for differences in prices across countries), along with average life expectancy, world per capita income, and measures of inequality. The poverty rate dropped from 84% in 1820 to 66% in 1910, then to 55% in 1950, and to 24% in 1992. The second half of the twentieth century thus witnessed a dramatic reduction that had little historical precedent. Patterns of life expectancy showed a similar improvement, rising from 27 years in 1820 to 33 years in 1910, then to 50 years in 1950, and to 61 years in 1992. These reductions in poverty coincided with rising per capita incomes, which doubled in the course of the nineteenth century, and more than trebled in the twentieth century.

This positive association between growth and poverty reduction has been observed more generally, not only across countries but also within countries over varying periods of time. For instance, over the course of a business cycle, poverty rates in any given country typically drop during upswings and

Table 0.1: World Distribution of Income and Life Expectancy Since 1820

	1820	1870	1910	1950	1992
Extreme Poverty (% under $1/day 1990 PPP)	84	75	66	55	4
Life Expectancy (average years)	27	n.a.	33	50	61
Per capita income (US 1990 Purchasing Power Parity $)	659	890	1460	2146	4912
Inequality: Gini Coefficient	.50	.56	.61	.64	.66
Inequality: Theil Index	.52	.67	.74	.81	.86
Income Share: Bottom 20%	4.7	3.8	3.0	2.4	2.2
Income Share: Top 10%	43	48	51	51	53
Within-Country-Group Inequality (Theil index)	.46	.48	.50	.32	.34
Across-Country-Group Inequality (Theil Index)	.06	.19	.30	.48	.51

PPP = Purchasing Power Parity dollars
Source: F. Bourguignon and C. Morrisson (2002).

rise during recessions. Such patterns obtain throughout different regions of the world, in both developed and developing countries, with few exceptions.[5] While this is frequently viewed as a manifestation of the saying that "a rising tide raises all boats," or of the "trickle down" view that the only effective way to reduce poverty is to promote growth, Deaton (among many others in this volume) cautions against reading too much into these facts. In particular, he notes that growth at the bottom of the income distribution has generally not been as rapid as overall growth, particularly in recent decades. Table 0.1 shows that the income share of the bottom fifth of the world's population has more than halved since the early nineteenth century.

More important, one should not infer from these facts that raising growth alone is *sufficient* to ensure reduction of poverty, and therefore that policy makers can afford to ignore distributional matters. Such a view imputes a particular direction of causation, from growth to poverty reduction, as well as the implicit assumption that policies cannot effectively reduce poverty via any other channel. Yet the facts point only to a positive correlation. They

are equally consistent with the reverse flow of causation—that poverty reduction drives growth instead of the other way around. In that case, the
appropriate lesson for policy makers also gets turned on its head: policy
makers should focus primarily on reducing poverty, and growth will take
care of itself. As it stands, the fact of a positive correlation does not settle
the direction of causation, or whether there is any causal connection at all—
perhaps some third factor is correlated with growth, on the one hand, and
with poverty, on the other. We shall return to these issues later on.

Deaton's concern with the failure of the bottom of the income distribution
to grow on par with the rest reflects a more general pattern of rising income
inequality. The Bourguignon-Morrisson estimates reported in Table 0.1 show
that income inequality grew substantially over the course of the past two
centuries. This means that a larger proportion of the benefits of growth
flowed to the rich: for instance, the share of the top 10% grew from 43% to
53% between 1820 and 1992, while that of the bottom 20% fell from 4.7%
to 2.2%. Hence, while the poor do not become poorer, the benefits of growth
tend to be skewed in favor of the rich.

The last two rows in Table 0.1 provide an interesting perspective on this
pattern of rising inequality. They show the part of overall inequality that
results from inequality within different country groups, contrasted with that
arising from inequality across country groups [where the world is grouped
into six regions: Africa; Japan, Korea, and Taiwan; Asia (excluding Japan,
Korea, and Taiwan]; Latin America; Eastern Europe; and Western Europe
and its offshoots). In 1820 the bulk of inequality was accounted for by disparities within country groups. Over time, within-country group inequality
has become smaller, while between-country group inequality has risen markedly, and now accounts for the dominant share of overall world inequality.
In other words, inequality in the world today is largely inequality between
regions rather than inequality within regions. Two centuries ago nearly all
countries were uniformly poor; nowadays only some are. This reinforces
what we noted above regarding the geographic concentration of the world's
poor. And, combined with the facts noted above concerning the correlation
of growth rates with reductions in poverty, it implies that we cannot ignore
macroeconomic issues in discussions of poverty: The factors that tend to
keep growth rates low in the poorest countries of the world therefore become
germane to discussions of world poverty.

THE CAUSES OF POVERTY

The quest for the "ultimate" causes of poverty is understandably one of the
holiest of Holy Grails among economists. What makes some wealthy and
others poor has been the subject of many of the classical texts of economics
(going back at least to Adam Smith). Not surprisingly, views on the ultimate
causes of poverty vary over a wide spectrum, particularly with respect to the
appropriate role of market forces and state interventions.

For instance, an influential policy approach in recent times emphasizes the need to promote market forces at the expense of state-led development in poor and middle-income countries. Commonly referred to as the "Washington Consensus" and traditionally advocated by representatives of international institutions in Washington, D.C.—including the International Monetary Fund (IMF), the World Bank, and the InterAmerican Development Bank—with the backing of the U.S. Treasury, the typical policy package combines opening countries to foreign trade and investment flows, privatizing state-owned enterprises, deregulating businesses and industries, and implementing restrictive fiscal and monetary policies. In the words of John Williamson, the World Bank economist who coined the term, the Washington Consensus reflected an approach "contemptuous of equity issues" popular in Washington, D.C., policy circles in the 1980s (Birdsall and de la Torre 2001). Indeed, conspicuous by their absence are policies that attack poverty directly. The underlying view is that the only effective way to reduce poverty is to promote growth via "trickle-down." Nevertheless, this consensus has weakened recently, in particular with the disappointing performance of many Latin American countries that had followed this approach since the mid-1980s, resulting in a growing interest in equity issues among these same institutions.[6]

Despite this weakening, however, the "orthodox" approach continues to hold sway in policy circles (e.g., at the IMF).[7] A rejoinder called "Washington Contentious" has recently been put forward by Nancy Birdsall and Augusto de la Torre on behalf of the Carnegie Endowment for International Peace, arguing for a package of policy measures that directly confronts poverty: better social safety nets, schools for the poor, progressive taxes, promotion of small businesses, protecting workers' rights, antidiscrimination policies, land reforms, improvements in public services, and reducing protectionism in rich countries. Others, including the World Development Report 2004 of the World Bank and academic economists, have also begun to advocate a wider set of political and institutional reforms, including promoting democracy, the rule of law, property rights (especially for the poor), reducing corruption, enhancing government accountability, and strengthening the role of civil society.

Implicit in any given policy approach is a view of the ultimate causes of poverty. At one extreme, some may argue that trying to do anything about poverty is fruitless, because it is ultimately rooted in immutable characteristics of personality, culture, or geography. Somewhat less extreme is the Washington Consensus view that economic growth is the only significant determinant of poverty, and market-friendly policies are the only effective way of raising growth. Also implicit in this view is the notion that the distribution of income is somehow a natural constant, or that distributional or institutional policies can never be successful in raising the share of the poor in the overall social pie without significantly reducing the size of the pie itself. Each of these views can be tested against what we have learned from research about growth and poverty reduction around the world.

The next two essays in this volume, by Daron Acemoglu, Simon Johnson, and James Robinson, and by Stanley Engerman and Kenneth Sokoloff examine some of the historical origins of modern-day underdevelopment, with a view to disentangling the role of historical institutions and inequality, on the one hand, from that of geography or culture-based factors, on the other. Both essays argue for the view that historical inequities in the design of colonial institutions since the fifteenth century constitute the most important source of current disparities in living standards across countries in the world. Specifically, these institutional differences are more fundamental than differences in geography, religion, or culture. The essays thus press the view that the roots of poverty at the macroeconomic level lie in man-made factors rather than in immutable circumstances beyond the control of social planners, and moreover, that there are powerful historical forces that cause inequality and backwardness to be perpetuated over long spans of time.

Although the arguments of those emphasizing the role of geography (operating through the effect of climate on work effort or disease) receive some statistical corroboration in cross-country correlations between living standards and geographical variables, Acemoglu, Johnson, and Robinson point out that geography is unable to account for the remarkable reversals of fortune in the relative living standards of different countries that occurred around the eighteenth and nineteenth centuries. Countries with high levels of urbanization and population density (two variables that correlate closely with per capita income) in the fifteenth century tend to have lower per capita incomes in the twentieth century. They argue that this reversal can be accounted for by the pattern of European colonial settlements between the fifteenth and the seventeenth centuries. In countries that were more prosperous and densely populated in the fifteenth century, colonial settlers tended to set up more "extractive" institutions intended to extract a higher surplus from the native population. These institutions were inimical to the development of a system of property rights and rule of law, essential prerequisites for successful industrialization in the eighteenth and nineteenth centuries. The authors buttress their argument with examples from the twentieth century, such as Korea and Germany, countries with a homogeneous culture and geography that were split into two parts with differing institutions, resulting in wide disparities in living standards within a few decades. Acemoglu, Johnson, and Robinson argue that geography may at best have played an indirect role in accounting for living standards disparities today, by influencing historical patterns of colonial settlement.

The essay by Stanley Engerman and Kenneth Sokoloff makes a similar point. They focus on disparities in living standards between different countries in North America and Latin America, and argue that these are rooted in the historical evolution of colonial institutions between the fifteenth and seventeenth centuries. Geography played only an indirect role, by influencing the original patterns of these institutions. In the fifteenth century, the key to prosperity was suitability for plantation agriculture in a few cash crops (especially sugarcane) based on large supplies of cheap labor. Where these conditions prevailed, the early Spanish and Portuguese settlers set up highly extractive institutions, in striking contrast to patterns of settlement in North America (characterized by subsistence agriculture and a scarcity of labor relative to land), which were considerably poorer and more egalitarian. Sokoloff and Engerman also explain the sources of high persistence of these institutional inequalities and their subsequent importance in retarding industrialization in the eighteenth and nineteenth centuries. Huge inequalities in suffrage, land, education, and access to finance resulted from early institutions in Latin America, in contrast with North America, thus limiting the spread of markets, entrepreneurial opportunities, and technological advances that formed the basis of nineteenth-century industrialization.

These two chapters thus deny any natural tendency for societies to gravitate toward superior institutions—there is no invisible hand, it seems, that leads countries toward better institutions. Societies that inherit poor institutions may be stuck with them for long spans of time, mainly because there is some powerful group in society (usually an economic elite) that receives benefits from those institutions and hence has a stake in fighting to preserve them. Many of these institutional failures involve denial of essential inputs and services to the poor, such as voting rights, education, land, or finance, so that they have neither the resources nor the skills—or, indeed, the social status—to be full participants in the economy. The result is that these economies never get to take advantage of the talents of much of their populace and, as a result, grow slowly. In this view, then, low growth is the result of high levels of inequality and poverty, rather than the other way around. The direction of causation is precisely the opposite of the theory implicitly underlying the Washington Consensus. The historical record also suggests that inequality is highly mutable, susceptible in particular to distributional policies (e.g., taxation, land reform, public education, or provision of finance to small entrepreneurs).

The next chapter, by Thomas Piketty, examines the historical record with respect to changes in inequality during the twentieth century. This analysis takes place against the backdrop of the classic hypothesis advanced by Simon Kuznets concerning the evolution of inequality along paths of economic development. Kuznets suggested that inequality would follow an inverted U with the level of development: rising in the early stages, then falling in later ones. The Kuznets curve has thus often been associated with the view that rising inequality is an inevitable by-product of early stages of economic development, and one just has to wait for enough development to occur for inequality to fall. It is one of the arguments often invoked for the view that policy makers seeking to reduce poverty may as well focus on growth as the primary mechanism and push the economy beyond the hump of the inverted U, so that inequality can subsequently begin to decline along the process of development.

Kuznets based his hypothesis on a rather casual comparison of inequality across a cross section of countries in the first half of the twentieth century. Moreover, the sources of data for income distribution that he used were of questionable quality and comparability across countries. And, in any case, there is a considerable gap between the statistical evidence itself and the inference that has tended to be made on the basis of that evidence. The evidence pertains to the correlation between inequality and the level of development across countries, rather than changes in inequality along the path of development for a given country or group of countries. In the half-century that has elapsed since Kuznets proposed his hypothesis, researchers have generally been unable to find a similar pattern (or any discernible pattern at all) between inequality and development when looking at changes over time.[8] Moreover, if we had found such a pattern, it would only have indicated the presence of suitable correlations, which do not imply anything about patterns of causation. One would need much more detailed information concerning the nature of changing inequality to infer that the causation runs from development to falling inequality.

In order to gain a better understanding of the dynamics of inequality, Piketty examines the historical record over the twentieth century of a number of currently developed countries (France, the United Kingdom, and the United States) that experienced significant reductions in inequality during this period, using sources of data (such as tax records) not previously used by researchers for this purpose. He argues that the observed reductions resulted primarily from a decline in the concentration of capital incomes arising during the great upheavals of the two world wars and the Great Depression of the 1930s. And since World War II, an increase in inequality has been actively limited by progressive taxation of income and wealth. Piketty also argues that there is little evidence that these policies harmed growth. Indeed, it is possible that they supported growth by financing a welfare state that widened access of the poor to human capital and entrepreneurial finance. Such a mechanism, he suggests, is consistent with modern theories of economic development in which capital markets are imperfect and the cause of underdevelopment is limited access of the poor to education and finance.

Piketty goes on to note that, contrary to the Kuznets view, there has been an upturn in inequality since the mid-1980s in developed countries. While a large literature has argued that this has been caused in large part by increasing demand for skills, he argues that supply-side factors, operating through an inadequate supply of schooling or an unwillingness to raise minimum wages have had a significant role as well. Lax regulation of corporate governance in the United States has also permitted a spectacular rise in executive compensation. Piketty's essay thus undermines the basic theory underlying the Washington Consensus: that inequality or poverty is impervious to distributional policies, as well as the "Kuznetsian" view that inequality has a natural, inexorable tendency to decline once the economy gets rich enough per capita.

The next few essays dwell further on the role of government policy in reducing poverty, in the context of the more recent experience of developing countries. Philippe Aghion and Beatriz Armendáriz de Aghion examine the causes of poverty and underdevelopment from the standpoint of modern growth theory. Using the example of Indian growth experience since the mid-1980s, they argue that innovation and productivity improvement have been substantially responsible for poverty reduction in that country. Moreover, these improvements depend on a range of factors that reflect both institutions and government policies. These include the supply of educated labor, property rights protection, government subsidies to innovation, macroeconomic stability, financial development, and product market competition. Modern growth theory predicts that the salutary effects of increased competition (caused by trade or industrial liberalization, for instance) on the productivity of different firms in any given industry will be higher, the closer they are to the technological frontier and the less they are bound by pro-worker regulations.

Aghion and Armendáriz de Aghion argue that detailed research on the recent Indian growth experience bears out these theoretical predictions. In particular, variations in the initial institutional settings and the level of technology across different Indian states can explain why the effects of market-friendly reforms have varied substantially within India, resulting in growing regional inequality. They go on to suggest that this kind of view can explain why similar market-friendly deregulation reforms have generated less satisfactory results in Latin America, compared with India or East Asia.

The next pair of essays, by Abhijit Banerjee and Pranab Bardhan, respectively, explore in more detail the role of government policies promoting globalization, defined as the liberalization of international flows of trade and investment, on poverty in poor countries. Banerjee starts by reviewing the historical evidence in favor of the traditional prediction of conventional trade economics that trade liberalization ought to reduce poverty in labor-abundant developing countries, while increasing poverty in labor-scarce developed ones. This follows from the idea that trade will allow each side to specialize in what it is best situated to produce, which in the case of labor-abundant countries happens to be labor-intensive goods. Since that ought to raise the demand for labor, laborers in poor countries should end up better off after trade liberalization. While the historical evidence from the middle of the nineteenth century to the mid-twentieth century does seem broadly supportive of this view, more recent developments (since the 1980s) appear to be inconsistent with it. Specifically, there is evidence of growing inequality in Latin America and Asia occurring at the same time as growing liberalization of trade and investment regimes.

Banerjee argues that one important reason why traditional trade theory fails to apply is the growing role of *reputation* (brand names and/or trust between buyers and suppliers) in trading arrangements. This means that it is not enough to have a cost advantage in order to be successful in global trade: one also needs to convince buyers that they can trust what you are selling them. Since poor countries often do not have producers who are automatically trusted, it takes them a long time to expand their production in the sectors where they can be successful after globalization; and because these sectors do not expand fast enough, they cannot absorb the laborers from the industries that are shutting down because of liberalization. This is why many people in poor countries end up getting hurt by globalization, at least in the short run. Despite these problems, Banerjee argues that developing countries should not jettison trade liberalization policies, since they are essential for these countries to gain access to expanding foreign markets, critical imports, and new technology. He argues for a policy approach that combines friendliness to foreign trade and investment with a strong commitment to helping the losers from trade liberalization, and with ways of taxing the international brain drain of skilled personnel from poor to rich countries.

The next essay, by Pranab Bardhan, confronts the certitudes and oversimplifications that run through the usual rhetoric of globalization debates, and explains the complexity of the effect of globalization on the poor in developing countries. Drawing on recent empirical research, his essay considers the validity of views commonly expressed in public arenas concerning different channels by which trade and investment flows affect poverty. In some contexts, he points out, greater globalization would benefit the poor. For instance, expanding the access of producers in poor countries to Western markets for food and garments is likely to raise the wages of unskilled workers and the earnings of self-employed farmers or small enterprise owners. Greater international competition among trade intermediaries can also lower the profit margins of middlemen, so that poor producers get a better price for their products. In other contexts, globalization can hurt the poor: since capital is more mobile than labor, workers can lose bargaining power, an effect accentuated by the increasing use of labor-saving technologies. With respect to child labor or environmental standards, the effects of freer trade may go either way; Bardhan describes contexts where trade liberalization has reduced the incidence of child labor, contrary to the claims of globalization opponents.

In the context of trade-related intellectual property rights, however, Bardhan agrees with most of the arguments advanced by opponents of globalization: he finds little justification for increasing drug prices in poor countries to provide incentives to Western pharmaceutical firms, and points to the manner in which Western governments balk at paying high prices for drugs when confronted with public health crises in their own countries. In other contexts, such as labor and environmental standards, Bardhan argues for the need for new forms of international cooperation and public–private partnerships. Overall, the main emphasis of his essay is to argue that globalization debates have suffered from misplaced emphasis; greater attention needs to be devoted to institutional reforms, both *within* and across developing countries, that are targeted toward poverty alleviation.

In the next essay of this section, Mukesh Eswaran and Ashok Kotwal stress the role of agricultural productivity in reducing poverty. Their argument is based on the fact that unskilled labor power is the sole asset available to the poor, so improvements in wages of unskilled workers are essential to reduce poverty. These wages, in turn, depend on the level of agricultural productivity for a variety of reasons. A higher availability of complementary assets such as land, livestock, or implements raises the productivity of unskilled workers and their wages directly. Moreover, it allows the subsistence food requirements of society to be met with fewer workers engaged in agriculture, thus releasing labor for industrial occupations where productivity growth tends to outstrip that of agriculture. Finally, agricultural surpluses generate exports, which permit the technology imports that are essential to early stages of industrialization.

Despite these factors, many countries have adopted development strategies with an urban bias that have prevented rapid growth in agricultural productivity by imposing controls on prices and trades of agricultural commodities. Eswaran and Kotwal agree with the previous authors in their assessment that deregulation and trade liberalization will reduce poverty in developing countries, particularly if OECD countries agree to allow them greater market access. They also argue for government policies that would encourage the adoption and diffusion of high-yield crop varieties, and provide complementary public investments in irrigation and transport.

In summary, the essays in this section emphasize the key role of domestic institutions in reducing poverty, relative to the effects of relatively immutable societal characteristics such as geography or culture, or the alleged adverse role of globalization or market integration. The historical analyses lay the emphasis on institutions that encourage and promote property rights, and widen political participation of the poor and their access to key assets such as land, education, and finance. The more contemporary analyses add to this the importance of improving public delivery of health and education to the poor, providing complementary public investments that would raise agricultural productivity, and entering into trade agreements that would expand the access of poor producers in developing countries to world markets.

Some Commonly Alleged "Cultural" Causes of Poverty: Overpopulation, Corruption, and Ethnic Conflict

Among the various alleged "cultural" causes of poverty are overpopulation, corruption, and ethnic conflict. Poorer countries are indeed more prone to these three major problems. It is tempting, then, to conclude that these are important structural causes of poverty. Combined with the view that fertility, corruption, and factional conflict are immutable cultural attributes not particularly capable of being influenced by government policies, it is easy to adopt a fatalistic attitude that little can be done to alleviate global poverty.

Such views are based on a number of implicit beliefs that deserve a critical examination. The first one is that the causation runs from fertility, corruption, or ethnic conflict to poverty. Yet one observes only that poverty tends to coexist with these problems. This correlation could equally well reflect a causation that runs in the opposite direction: overpopulation, corruption, or civil wars may be outcomes rather than causes of poverty. If so, the ultimate causes of poverty lie elsewhere. Moreover, if the causation does indeed run in the reverse direction, it would add greater urgency to the need for reducing poverty, since that would also contribute to reducing problems of overpopulation, corruption, and civil conflict.

Even if poverty were the effect of these broader social problems, the fatalist position requires a second article of faith: that high fertility, corruption, and social conflict are determined by immutable cultural factors which are impervious to the actions of policy makers. Otherwise, policies could be chosen to influence these broader social problems, which would then contribute to lessening poverty.

The next two essays, by Paul Schultz and Mukesh Eswaran, provide an overview of research findings concerning the connection between fertility and poverty that casts considerable doubt on both of these beliefs. Schultz surveys much of the evidence from studies of the relationship between fertility and income at the level of individual households. As he explains in detail, the existence of a significant positive correlation between fertility and poverty does not establish anything about direction of causation. Having to take care of a large number of children may push a family into poverty; alternatively, it is possible that more affluent families choose to have fewer children. Or there may not be any direct relationship between fertility and poverty at all, with the observed correlation resulting instead from other factors, such as the education level of parents, the level of insecurity they face over care in their old age, or absence of a well-developed financial sector. To examine whether there is any causal link from fertility to poverty, researchers use the method of comparing families who have twins with those who do not, while controlling for various family characteristics. Having twins is tantamount to a random, unexpected increase in the number of children, so studying the effect of this demographic "shock" is a "clean" test of whether fertility indeed causes poverty. Schultz reports the results of a large study in Kenya in which these fertility shocks were found to have no effect on subsequent consumption per capita within the family, indicating the absence of any such causal link.

What, then, accounts for the tendency for poorer families to have more children? Comparing households with differing incomes and education profiles, one observes that those with higher labor earnings and mother's education have fewer children, while those with higher income from agricultural land rents have more. Hence the composition of income sources matters considerably, which is consistent with the predictions of economic theory. These results suggest that fertility levels can be influenced by policies that promote women's education, urbanization, and the dissemination of subsidized birth control procedures.

Mukesh Eswaran widens the scope of this discussion by describing a range of institutional features of poor countries that encourage families to have a large number of children. Apart from a lack of women's education, these include the reliance of parents on children for old-age support and, before the parents reach old age, for income from child labor; high levels of infant mortality; gender inequality within households; and a preference for male children. Many of these features can be influenced by policy choices, such as public schooling, health, and social insurance. The empowerment of women within households can be enhanced by widening opportunities for them to obtain education, work outside the home, receive loans, and be entitled to own land or other assets on par with males. Overall, there seems to be little basis for the fatalistic notion that nothing can be done about problems of overpopulation: instead, all the evidence points in the opposite direction. There are numerous examples of countries or states, such as Sri Lanka, Costa Rica, and the state of Kerala in India, that have achieved significant reductions in fertility rates by investing in widespread education of women and in public health.

The next essay, by Jean-Jacques Laffont, addresses the question of why corruption tends to be a particular problem for developing countries. He sketches a theory of three successive stages of development, in each of which the extent of corruption is determined by the pattern of specialization of tasks within the government, along with the resources it has available for combating corruption. Traditional societies tend to be characterized by relatively low levels of corruption owing to the smallness, simplicity, and high levels of monitoring of the decisions of leaders by the society's members. Developing societies, characterized by an increasing size and complexity of public decision-making, tend to involve more delegation of authority by political leaders to bureaucrats, which leads to the emergence of corruption. The scope for such corruption grows initially with the level of development, while the means available to the government for combating it are limited. At later stages of development, political leaders have greater resources available, while bureaucrats become wealthier and thus more responsive to incentives. Provided that political leaders have the requisite will to combat corruption (which depends in turn on whether the society in question is a democracy), corruption can thereafter decline with further development.

Laffont argues that the empirical evidence concerning reported levels of corruption across countries with differing per capita incomes is supportive of the idea of corruption first going up and then coming down with development. He also argues that, besides the level of development, other variables that are correlated with corruption include the extent of openness to trade and foreign investment, the importance of natural resources in exports, and the county's legal origins. Specifically, everything else remaining the same, countries that are less open, that rely more on natural resource exports, or that have a legal system originating in the French system are more corrupt. Countries that follow a Scandinavian-style legal system are substantially less corrupt than French-law countries and exhibit a stronger tendency for corruption to decline as development proceeds. On the basis of the evidence, it is hard to stick to the view that corruption is primarily "culturally" determined. It seems more plausible that corruption is a product of the level of development, as well as specific policy and institutional choices. Especially in societies in the process of developing, limiting corruption is a challenge that requires considerable political will, and in which political institutions have a key role to play.

In the next essay, Edward Miguel focuses on the challenge posed by ethnic diversity for successful public action aiming to alleviate poverty. The fractionalization of ethnic identity has tended to generate violent conflict and limit collective action, particularly in sub-Saharan Africa. It is common to believe these conflicts to be the legacy of tribal divisions within these countries and of the way national boundaries were drawn at the time of their independence from colonial rule. Yet Miguel argues that there is considerable scope for governments to pursue a wider policy of "nation-building" that promotes a sense of national identity, in order to reduce the extent of such conflicts. He illustrates his argument by presenting evidence from recent field studies that such a policy of nation-building allowed ethnically diverse communities in rural Tanzania to achieve considerable success in local fundraising for primary schools, while ethnically diverse Kenyan communities just on the other side of the border largely failed. Policies of nation-building include encouraging the development of a common national language and of curricula in schools that promote a shared sense of identity. Miguel criticizes the Washington Consensus approach for being excessively preoccupied with short-term economic growth and, for this reason, treating with suspicion initiatives to promote strong central governments in poor countries.

HOW SHOULD WE GO ABOUT FIGHTING POVERTY?

The essays in the first section establish compelling arguments for an activist policy approach toward poverty reduction. The second section of articles proceeds to examine the design of such policies in a broad range of areas that include tax and welfare systems, child labor regulations, education, public service delivery mechanisms, microcredit, and intellectual property rights.

Redistributive Policy

The standard framework within which economists and policy makers have traditionally thought about redistribution is that of an "equity-efficiency trade-off" in which society's redistributive goals must be weighed against the supply-side distortions that taxes and transfers create in labor supply, savings, and other economic decisions. The canonical formalization of this trade-off is the theory of Mirrlees (1971), which has three main implications for the structure of the optimal redistributive policy: (1) redistribution should be (mostly) in cash rather than in kind; (2) it should combine a relatively high level of guaranteed income with a steep phaseout rate (the rate at which benefits are reduced as earnings increase); and (3) marginal rates at the top should be very low (i.e., the highest marginal incomes should not be taxed).

Many of the recent advances in the analysis and practice of redistribution involve major departures from these recommendations, reflecting in part the growing recognition that once dynamics (i.e., the investment decisions that determine the evolution of individual productivities) and a host of market imperfections—particularly acute in less-developed countries—are taken into account, the (in)famous trade-off often vanishes. The chapters of this section thus provide arguments for why appropriately designed policies can have beneficial effects on *both* equity (and insurance) and efficiency (or growth), especially in the long run. These policies typically depart in important ways from the traditional prescription, involving, for instance, in-kind, geographically targeted, or non-income-tested benefits. They must also, however, confront at some point the basic incentive and informational issues that led Mirrlees to his conclusions. Moreover, as developing nations become more similar to advanced ones in terms of asset markets, education systems, and social safety nets, one can expect the policy design issues that come up in advanced "welfare states" to become increasingly relevant for developing countries as well.[9]

These "classical" issues of redistributive policy and the models used to analyze them thus represent a natural starting point for this section. There has, in fact, been a lot of action here as well: the essay by Emmanuel Saez provides an overview of how economists' thinking and government policy in developed countries have evolved in tandem since 1980, simultaneously responding to and stimulating a considerable amount of empirical work on how people respond to different redistributive schemes.

In the basic Mirrlees theory, individuals with disparate productive abilities choose how much to work, with the government observing only the income they earn as a result. Discouraging effort of more productive people is more costly than discouraging effort by the less able, in terms of both forgone earnings and taxes accruing to the government. Owing to this, the optimal tax scheme (as calculated by Saez, using U.S. data) guarantees everyone a substantial income (as welfare payment, for example) but a relatively rapid phaseout of the welfare benefits as labor earnings rise. As a result, under this scheme a substantial fraction of the poor work little or not at all, deriving most of their income from public assistance. Meanwhile, marginal rates near the top are low, since the presumption is that the rich work harder.

Against this background, two key shifts have occurred. First, concerns about incentive distortions "at the top" (reductions in labor supply or shifts to nontaxable forms of compensation by the most productive individuals) have proven to be somewhat overstated.[10] At the same time, concerns about distortions "at the bottom" have come to be seen as very important. The main concern is whether welfare recipients would work at all, rather than the decision of how much to work. Indeed, the empirical evidence consistently shows that the response of working hours to taxes is rather small, whereas that of labor force participation is much greater, especially for women (and second earners more generally).

These findings are important for several reasons. First, voters are strongly averse to the idea of decoupling income from work and attach very negative stereotypes of laziness and dishonesty to the idea of people "living off welfare." Second, prolonged nonparticipation in the labor force by parents tends to lead to the transmission of poverty to the next generation, both through an inability to accumulate assets at the family level and through the amplification mechanism of social spillovers: too many people living on welfare in a neighborhood results in a dearth of positive role models, contacts with potential employers, and other local inputs into the next generation's human capital.

Saez goes on to report recent research extending the Mirrlees framework to accommodate the distinction between the participation decision and the choice of hours. This significantly modifies the nature of the optimal policy, which turns out to resemble the earned income tax credit (EITC) in the United States. First, it is now preferable to have a much lower level of basic income support but complement it with a subsidy to poor people based on the number of hours worked. Second, this subsidy rate ultimately declines and turns back into a steep phaseout region, but only at much higher levels of income than in the traditional negative income tax scheme. Such a policy makes work pay for low-skill individuals, inducing some who would otherwise choose unemployment to start working, without tempting higher ability individuals to quit. It thus leaves the participation decision (where the discouragement effect can be quite large) relatively undistorted and concentrates the disincentives on people with relatively higher incomes, who are typically all going to be in the labor force anyway. For the latter group the discouragement effect of high taxes on the number of hours worked tends to be small, so it does not hurt incentives very much.

Following the United States, where EITC is now the largest cash transfer program for the poor, a number of industrialized countries have begun to move in this direction. Theoretical models calibrated using empirical estimates of the relevant elasticities, such as that of Saez, can be used to determine the optimal cutoffs and marginal rates. They also make clear predictions about other important issues, such as the desirability of making the scheme largely individual-based rather than household-based, lest the primary income push the secondary earners' participation decision into the phaseout range.

Among the many other aspects of redistributive policy discussed by Saez is the issue of time limits on welfare payments, especially unemployment benefits. Standard dynamic models predict that individuals can self-insure rather well through savings against temporary fluctuations in income, so that social insurance benefits should be fairly modest and limited in duration. The empirical evidence, however, shows that unemployment spells are associated with significant decreases in consumption. And this is not the only discrepancy between the theory of savings and what we see in the world. Saez therefore predicts that the next major shift in economists' thinking about redistributive policy will be toward the recognition and explicit modeling of certain important departures from full rationality in the behavior of economic agents. This thought is echoed in the essays by Duflo and Mullainathan in the last section of this volume.

The next essay, by Martin Ravallion, offers an extensive survey of the many reasons why, in the presence of imperfect markets, the traditional idea of an equity-efficiency trade-off might fail, making it possible to simultaneously promote equity *and* growth. For each of these mechanisms, Ravallion first briefly outlines the theoretical argument and underlying market failure, then offers a detailed and balanced discussion of the current state of empirical knowledge concerning the main assumptions and testable implications of these models. The most drastic (and most easily understandable) manifestation of these market failures takes the form of "poverty traps." Certain segments of the population are simply unable to accumulate the critical level of assets that would allow them or their offspring to achieve their productive potential, participate efficiently in economic activity, and ultimately escape poverty. However, even when it is sometimes possible to escape poverty, the same mechanism can lead to serious misallocations, resulting in large efficiency losses and making poverty a very persistent condition.

A first poverty-perpetuating mechanism arises when resources fall short of a basic nutrition- and health-related "efficiency wage" level below which workers cannot effectively function or children properly develop. Ravallion discusses evidence from both South Asia and Africa that malnutrition (triggered, for instance, by a drought) makes farmworkers less productive and has long-lasting detrimental effects on children's learning and future incomes. The economic costs of high infection rates for (treatable or preventable) debilitating diseases such as malaria in much of the developing world, and now AIDS in several African countries, are also all too visible.

A second mechanism, which has featured prominently in much of the theoretical literature on inequality and development, is that of imperfections in credit markets that impede efficient investment by the poor in both human and physical capital. If the investment technology features decreasing returns, so that a unit of capital is less productive when it is in the hands of the rich, a redistribution of resources from richer to poorer households (not necessarily the poorest, if there is some initial phase of increasing returns) can improve the efficiency of aggregate investment and raise growth. Such patterns are found in empirical studies of the returns to education: for instance, as explained in the essay by Anne Case, returns fall when moving from primary to secondary to tertiary education. In agriculture, similarly, output per acre decreases with landholding size, suggesting that a more equal distribution of ownership must be impeded by some constraint that prevents poor peasants from borrowing to finance the purchase of additional land (or associated inputs). Ravallion reports results from studies of the dynamics of income and wealth at the level of individual families in Hungary, Russia, and rural China, where there is evidence for decreasing returns.

On the other hand, these longitudinal studies do not yield any evidence of thresholds that would indicate the presence of (household-level) poverty traps at low income levels. The data suggest instead that people ultimately bounce back from transitory income shocks (accidents, sickness, drought, etc.), but this can take a long time, especially for the poor. This finding probably reflects that fact that household members can, to some degree, either hold savings or insure each other as a way of dealing with adverse shocks, as discussed in later essays by Chris Udry and Robert Townsend. However, the lack of access to a well-functioning financial system in developing countries means that these savings are often held in livestock (which is hardly the safest asset) or jewelry (which is not very productive). Many other decisions contribute to the perpetuation of poverty: in order to limit exposure to risk, farmers are reluctant to adopt cash crops or new high-yield crop varieties, and they often respond to adverse income shocks by pulling children out of school and sending them to work to make ends meet. So here again, it seems plausible that reducing income risk (and hence inequality) might also improve investment and efficiency. The essay by Jonathan Morduch later in this volume discusses how microinsurance may be a response to exactly these problems.

Another type of inequality-generating market failure involves neighborhood effects. Living in a difficult neighborhood makes it harder for children to learn the skills that society most values and resist the temptations of crime. In such cases, there is the possibility of local poverty traps (or low-growth traps). The example that is most often used in this context is the close connection between local housing values and access to quality education in the United States. Ravallion's work on China points to the existence of similar local poverty traps in rural areas.

In the last part of his essay, Ravallion turns to concrete policy implications, assessing the performance of several programs that incorporate some of the main lessons from the theoretical and empirical research. These policies are thus typically focused on promoting education and health, where some of the major market failures occur, and are often geographically targeted at poor areas. In assessing the impact of these policies, researchers are mindful not only of the benefits (such as increased school enrollment rates) but also of the costs (such as what people could have earned in those hours that they now spend in school). In line with the literature on political economy or redistribution, researchers are also wary of the possible capture of these programs by local elites and thus pay particular attention to the effects of different delivery channels on the effective distribution of benefits.

Leading examples of such "new" schemes are Bangladesh's Food for Education Program (FEP), Mexico's Progresa (now called Oportunidades), and Brazil's Bolsa Escola. The basic idea in each case is to offer subsidies to families in economically backward areas—both in cash and in kind (food, school supplies)—that are conditional on their keeping their children in school and taking them regularly for health care visits. The monetary component is often substantial, coming close to what the child would be earning by working full-time in the case of Progresa and somewhat less in the other cases. As reported from different perspectives by Ravallion, Udry, and Case in their respective essays, systematic and rigorous evaluations of these programs have so far yielded very positive results, showing significant gains in school enrollment and child health and concomitant reductions in child labor. Ravallion also discusses policy options that provide some insurance against income losses, such as workfare and other subsidized employment programs, like Trabajar in Argentina and the Employment Guarantee Scheme of the state of Maharashtra in India. Such schemes are generally quite effective at providing insurance in times of crises, although in more "normal" times the regular labor income forgone by participants can offset a substantial fraction of the benefits (up to half in the Trabajar program). Clearly, we are now back to issues closely related to those covered by Saez, and there is likely to be scope for fruitful applications of such models to the developing world. Another interesting idea discussed by Ravallion is that of concentrating the work performed by workfare participants on selected poor areas, since this yields a "double dividend" by helping remedy some of the deficiencies in public assets—such as roads, irrigation, infrastructure, or schools—that were among the main contributors to poverty in the first place.

Dilip Mookherjee also starts his essay by taking issue with the traditional view of the equity-efficiency trade-off, noting the limitations inherent in Mirrlees-type frameworks that result from their neglect of long-term considerations concerning the acquisition of assets by the poor and make them ill-suited to understanding the self-perpetuating nature of poverty. The "new" view of poverty, by contrast, is one in which a lack of appropriate *assets* (financial, human, and sometimes social) leads to the exclusion of certain segments of society from productive participation in normal economic activity, resulting both in a social loss and in the perpetuation of high inequality, within as well as across generations.

Mookherjee begins by describing an artificial world that illustrates some important features of the dynamic approach to poverty and its implications for the design of policy. He imagines a setting in which parents incur a fixed cost to educate their children, credit markets are absent, and both skilled and unskilled labor are essential inputs into production. In this context, the economy's long-run skill mix can take a wide range of values: history determines where it will end up. If an economy inherits a small fraction of skilled individuals, the resulting scarcity of skill causes skilled wages to be high. Conversely, unskilled households earn little and become poor; combined with their exclusion from credit markets, this prevents them from investing in their children's education. The high level of inequality and poverty and low level of skill in the economy then become self-perpetuating. In contrast, societies that start with a larger proportion of skilled households foster greater investment by unskilled households in their children's schooling, causing such societies to converge to permanently lower poverty and higher per capita income.

In this world, the traditional idea flowing out of the Mirrlees framework that the poor should be helped through income-tested cash transfers—as in negative income tax proposals—may not work particularly well. The problem with such a policy is that while the poor now have more money, their incentive to educate their children is lower: the higher social safety net will moderate the consequences of their children's failure to acquire skills, and this may breed a pattern of continued dependence on the welfare system. By contrast, a universal in-kind redistributive scheme, taking the form of an education subsidy (such as Mexico's Progresa or Bangladesh's FEP), will reduce poor families' costs of investment without directly dampening the benefit, and can thus lift the whole economy to both a more productive and a more egalitarian long-run equilibrium.

Child Labor

The essays by Christopher Udry and Kaushik Basu make the costs of self-perpetuating poverty quite vivid by starting off with statistics on child labor. It is estimated that in 2000, about one in ten (or 210 million) of the world's children between the ages of five and fourteen were working, with the proportion rising to one third in Africa. Even these figures are probably underestimates, especially for girls, since detailed case studies cited by Basu show that domestic work is often underreported.

The notion of child labor typically conjures up images of sweatshops, hazardous or forced labor, and other forms of abuse. These, in turn, often bring about an instinctive demand for across-the-board prohibitions on child work, to be enforced both by developing countries through their legal systems and by advanced countries through the threat of trade sanctions and consumer boycotts. There is no doubt that abusive forms of child labor exist and need to be vigorously combated. But, as the data cited by Udry show, the bulk of the problem really lies elsewhere. First, child labor is primarily a rural and agricultural phenomenon, with most children working either on the family land or as hired farm laborers; substantial numbers, primarily girls, also work in the household or as domestics. Second, the main cost involved is really the sacrifice of these children's human capital (and everything that it would bring, from higher earnings and better health to enhanced political participation) that results from their failure to attend school.

Udry distinguishes two main reasons why poor families may be led to sacrifice their children's future to current income needs, thereby perpetuating the cycle of asset deprivation and poverty into the next generation. The first reason is the lack of well-functioning credit markets. Even with free public education available, sending a child to school still entails a significant opportunity cost, namely, the labor earnings or domestic services (allowing another family member to work more) that the child could bring. Udry brings new evidence to bear on the subject, drawing on longitudinal studies that show how negative shocks to family income result in an increase in the children's labor force participation, at least until the household's financial situation has recovered. Such "buffering" of family fortunes through child work has been observed following a variety of adverse events, ranging from the father's loss of employment in Brazilian cities to losses caused by fires, insects, or rodents in African and Indian villages.

A second reason why children might get sent to work, despite the long-term cost this entails for their future, has to do with the nature of the family relationship. When parents invest in the health or education of minor children, they have no guarantee that the children will ever repay them. Therefore the investment reflects the priorities of the parents, which do not have to be what the child would want. As a result, if parents are shortsighted or if they do not think enough about their children's future relative to their own current predicament, or if one parent cares less about the children than the other and they fight about it, investment in children may suffer. In particular, a lot of recent research reviewed by Udry shows that mothers and fathers often evaluate children's welfare very differently: mothers typically have a much higher propensity to spend extra income on the nutrition, health, and education of their children, particularly girls. Partly as a result, several transfer programs, such as Progresa, channel their benefits to the children specifically through the mother.

How should the problem of child labor be addressed? Both Udry and Basu first explain why "popular" remedies such as outright bans, trade sanctions, and boycotts are at best ineffective and quite possibly counterproductive means of reducing child labor. Basu argues that the historical evidence from Great Britain and the United States in the nineteenth century does not support the idea that legislation and regulation can substantially reduce the extent of child labor. Seemingly sensible measures, such as fining or otherwise punishing employers found to employ children, could actually *increase* the amount of child labor. The reason is that the policy causes employers to decrease the wages offered to children by the expected value of the fines they may have to pay. When this happens, families who need to achieve a target level of total income to make ends meet will respond by having their children work more. Of course, a high enough fine combined with a high enough probability of detection would eventually drive children's market wage, and therefore also their labor supply, to zero. In practice, however, much of it would just shift to the underground and illegal sectors, where the activities children would engage in would be likely to be much more dangerous or abusive (such as crime and prostitution).

A second problem discussed by Udry is that even if child labor prohibitions can be enforced effectively and without perverse effects on either the level or the nature of children's work, they are likely to cause significant income and welfare losses to the families involved. This applies whether the children continue to work under the new policy (for a lower wage or in a more "underground" manner) or if they start to attend school, since without other interventions, the return on that investment was already judged to be too low by the families, given the dire constraints they face.[11]

In the emotion-laden public debate, such traditional "economists' arguments" often fall on deaf ears, perhaps in part because they are usually accompanied only by broad recommendations to rely on pro-growth economic strategies as the best way to gradually eliminate child labor. Fortunately, theoretical research, empirical studies, and controlled policy evaluations have now converged on a very concrete, economically sound, and faster-acting policy instrument that can be offered alongside good development strategies. This is the same class of conditional, locally monitored, education subsidy programs discussed earlier, in which parents (especially mothers) receive both cash transfers and in-kind benefits for sending their children to school and health clinics. The evidence surveyed by Udry shows remarkable gains on both the school attendance front (changes in enrollment rates of close to 20 percentage points) and the child labor front (reductions in participation rates ranging from 9% in Nicaragua to 20–30% under Bangladesh's FEP).

Education

Skeptics may, and perhaps should, ask at this point whether the central emphasis on education that emerges from so much of the theoretical and empirical work reviewed so far is really warranted. Indeed, when favorably assessing the significant gains in school enrollment and declines in child labor force participation obtained by programs such as those discussed earlier, there is an implicit presumption that the return to educational investment is high enough to justify both the direct expenditures and the opportunity cost represented by children's potential earnings from (say) farmwork or their contribution to household activities.[12] But is this presumption really justified? More generally, how large are the returns to education? In her essay, Anne Case explains why these critical questions are much more difficult to answer than one would think, and how a new kind of empirical studies, based on explicitly randomized or "natural" experiments, is overcoming these difficulties.

In every country there are strong correlations between a person's education, earnings, health, and, for women, lowered fertility. Isolating a causal effect of education is very difficult, however, since there is no doubt that there are also reverse channels of causality: healthier children, for example, are better able to study. Part of the correlation also comes from unobservable factors that affect both education and income. For example, genetically transmitted talents and social connections that children get from their parents raise a child's income both directly and through increased education.

Proper inference of causation requires that we find some variation in educational investment that has no direct connection with income, health, or fertility. Case's essay discusses a number of recent studies that have creatively exploited specific institutional changes which led to large shifts in educational investment without changing anything else. A first example arises from changes in compulsory schooling laws implemented by various U.S. states at different times in the early twentieth century. Linking the resulting exogenous variations in completed education to later mortality outcomes, Lleras-Muney finds a significant effect of education on longevity. A second example is the work of Duflo, who evaluates the effects of a massive program of building primary schools by the Indonesian government in the early 1970s. Linking the variations in educational achievement attributable to children's different exposures to the program with their earnings two decades later, she estimates a substantial return, on the order of 10% per year of additional primary schooling.

In the second part of her essay, Case turns to the question of which inputs into education (e.g., smaller classes, better-trained teachers, books, computers, etc.) yield the higher returns. Here again she argues forcefully for being very careful about causally interpreting correlations. She points out that if educators and administrators are pursuing *any kind* of systematic objective (whether efficiency related, equity related, or both) in allocating inputs across students, classes, or schools, those who access certain inputs will be different from those who do not. For instance, administrators may group more talented and less disruptive students into larger classes, generating a reverse correlation between class size and achievement. Alternatively, these groups may be assigned better teachers, which will cause the contribution of teacher quality to educational performance to be overstated. Case reports on studies that exploit discontinuities in the rules governing class size in Israel and plausibly exogenous variations in centrally allocated inputs across Black schools in South Africa during apartheid to circumvent these problems and clearly establish the existence of substantial returns to class size reductions.

The best kind of data, however, comes from true randomized experiments, where the level and nature of the interventions on different schools or villages is randomly chosen, as well as the order in which they receive these extra resources. This type of design, allowing for a perfectly clean comparison of "treatment group" and "control group" outcomes, is still relatively rare; examples include the implementation of Progresa in Mexico and the studies by Michael Kremer[13] and others on textbooks, uniforms, and school meals in African schools. One hopes with Case that, as agencies such as the World Bank, nongovernmental organizations (NGOs), local governments, and academic researchers continue to increasingly work together, it will become increasingly common.

Service Delivery Mechanisms

Market failures feature prominently in many of the poverty-generating mechanisms discussed in previous essays. There was a time when the presumption was that in such situations the government would simply step in to fill the void, providing funds and delivering essential goods and services in the manner of a benevolent and omniscient central planner. No longer. As the essay on public goods by Timothy Besley and Maitreesh Ghatak documents, economic researchers and development practitioners nowadays are acutely aware that government failures may be as severe as market failures, and sometimes even worse. For instance, in rural Indian villages the absenteeism rate of teachers in government schools is 25%, and that of nurses and medical personnel reaches 40%.

Poor government policy can first of all arise from an inadequate understanding of how markets function. The preceding essays provided several examples of how well-intended, plausible-sounding redistributive schemes or regulations that are implicitly based on the wrong economic model (or no model at all) can severely backfire.

Very often, however, government failure reflects *internal* agency problems, such as rent-seeking, corruption, capture by special interests, ethnic favoritism, and the like. These problems, which are considerably exacerbated in the developing world but clearly affect rich countries as well, have led to a new focus on incentives, governance, and institutional design for the public sector, together with a reevaluation of the proper division of labor between government agencies, nonprofit organizations, and the private sector. In the words of Besley and Ghatak, the question of *how* public goods should be provided is now seen as being at least as important as that of *how much* is provided.

Although voluntary provision of certain public goods by wealthy donors or through collective networks can be important, there are many constraints on the effectiveness of these alternatives to government provision. Provision through local or social networks, for example, is likely to entail discrimination against outsiders, which may well contribute to the persistence of inequalities, and be an important impediment to geographic or occupational mobility. Empirical study of farmer-run sugar cooperatives in India suggests that inequality in landholdings is associated with significantly lower levels of cooperation and efficiency (Banerjee et al. 2001). There are also certain tasks, such as public safety and the administration of justice, that governments are uniquely suited to carrying out. Even there, however, there are important issues of constitutional design, as well as the appropriate degree of decentralization between the national, state, and municipal levels.

Whatever functions the government retains in the delivery of public goods, the design of proper incentive schemes and systems of accountability for the concerned public servants is essential. As Besley and Ghatak explain, the fact that many of the missions involved are characterized by multiple dimensions of performance (think of education or health) and competing objectives (cost-effectiveness, quality, and equity) makes it difficult to use high-powered incentives. The fact that one may want to select civil servants who have a genuine intrinsic motivation for public service goes in the same direction, while the need to attract and retain individuals with high ability goes the opposite way. The balance needs to be determined through a careful, mission-by-mission analysis. But certainly the evidence on absenteeism, red tape, and corruption suggests that most government bureaucracies fall well short of the optimal use of incentives and accountability. A related important issue studied in recent work and summarized in the essay is the role of checks and balances, and in particular that of monitoring by the media.

The recognition of the importance of government failure and corruption in the developing world has, in recent years, led to a growing role for both domestic and foreign NGOs in the delivery of public services to the poor, as well to as victims of natural or man-made disasters. While this is an important and positive development, Besley and Ghatak issue a timely warning against the "angelic" vision of NGOs that seems to have replaced, in the public eye, the tarnished image of the government. They point out that the objectives of these entities are often multiple or ill-defined (e.g., doing good or spreading the faith), their governance structure opaque, their accountability minimal because they are unelected, and the opportunities for poor beneficiaries to see them compete extremely limited. On the other hand, many (but certainly not all) of them do compete for funding from private donors, international charities, and organizations. This offers the opportunity for the latter, particularly institutions such as the World Bank, to start requiring not only more financial transparency but also more systematic evaluations of these NGOs' interventions.

The devolution of traditionally public missions to the private sector through privatization, deregulation, or subcontracting involves similar issues. To what extent, or at what pace, should developing countries follow the lead of developed ones in allowing transportation, communication, or energy to be taken over by private actors? The example of schools, discussed by Besley and Ghatak, illustrates some of the issues involved. On one hand, there is evidence from the United States suggesting that competition from private (Catholic) schools may improve the performance of public schools in the same city. On the other hand, the effects of school voucher schemes are still vigorously debated by empirical researchers. A large-scale study of vouchers in Chile, for instance, suggests that they mostly led to increased cream-skimming and socioeconomic stratification with academic losses for students from less-advantaged families, gains for those from more affluent backgrounds, and a zero net effect on average test scores.[14] The general message of the essay by Besley and Ghatak is thus that the traditional line between the public and private (whether for profit or nonprofit) sectors' roles in the delivery of public goods is becoming increasingly blurred, perhaps even irrelevant. The attention of economists and policy makers should be refocused instead on core issues of incentives and mechanism design that are largely common to both sectors, as well as on the related role that should be played by the competition between them.

Intellectual Property Rights

The next two essays, by Jean Tirole and Michael Kremer, focus on the vexed issue of intellectual property rights. Writing in the shadow of the impending implementation of TRIPS (Agreement on Trade-Related Aspects of Intellectual Property), both Kremer and Tirole are acutely aware of the cruel dilemmas it poses. In particular, under TRIPS all countries would have to respect current product patents on medicines, which almost surely will substantially raise the prices of many lifesaving drugs for people in developing countries. However, as drug companies are never too shy to remind us, drug development is an enormously expensive and risky business that most firms would not undertake unless the promised rewards were commensurate. Patent protection has long been the accepted way to provide these rewards, in effect by offering the firms a guarantee of monopoly profits for a fixed period. The result is drug prices that are beyond the reach of a large part of the world's population.

The way to solve this problem, Tirole argues, is to ensure that drug prices are lower in poor countries. He suggests that this may do a better job of helping those who are genuinely in need than almost any other policy of global redistribution. However, while the pharmaceutical companies may want to set different prices in different countries, the prices they would want to set in poor countries will not be nearly low enough to be affordable for the average person. This is because cutting the price to the point where the poor in developing countries can afford to buy essential drugs would leave firms with almost no profit. They would do better by setting a high price and selling only to the rich. To get the prices down enough, public action is needed.

There are obviously many ways to get the prices down. Forcing the firm to give up its patent through compulsory licensing would do it, but at a substantial political (and perhaps economic) cost. Tirole favors a less radical option: buying out the patent for a particular country, using government or donor money, and then selling the drug there at an affordable price. One of his key points is that this need not be very expensive: the company targets only the elites in poor countries and therefore sets a relatively high price for the units it sells there, since no one else can really afford the drug. Since the elites tend to be small, it is unlikely that the firm is making very much money from that country, so buying out the patent should be reasonably cheap.

The idea that we should buy out patents and take them out of the hands of monopolists is taken a step further in the essay by Michael Kremer. Kremer argues that buyouts not only have the potential to bring existing drugs to those who need them, but they also provide an efficient way to reward the development of new drugs. This is especially important for the treatment and prevention of diseases such as malaria and tuberculosis, where there is very little new research, largely because they are seen as poor people's diseases. Drug companies do not put a lot of effort into developing drugs and vaccines for these diseases, simply because they do not expect to make a lot of money by selling them. To make matters worse, once there is a drug, it will be politically very difficult for the firm to not give it away if large numbers of people are dying from the disease.

To get around this problem, Kremer suggests that donors establish a fund to back up what he calls a purchase commitment. The fund would stand committed to help developing countries buy a certain minimum number of doses of the vaccine (or drug) at a price high enough to make it worthwhile for drug companies to develop it. Since developing countries would not be able to afford that price (this is why the commitment was necessary in the first place), the fund would top up the amount the host countries are able to pay. For units beyond the committed amount, the fund (or the country) would have the option of buying as much as it needs at cost. Since the firm would have already covered its costs through the commitment, it should have no grounds for objecting.

More generally, Kremer distinguishes between "push" programs that subsidize research itself—for example, through grants to researchers—and "pull" programs that reward research outputs, such as a purchase commitment. He feels that push programs are important for generating the core ideas that everyone builds on, but they do not really provide rewards for doing what it takes to turn successful research ideas into drugs and vaccines for everyday use: undertaking the trials, the approval process, the patenting process, the risks of lawsuits, and so on. These costs of developing a marketable drug can be as large as the cost of generating the original idea, or even larger. While research has its own rewards (publications, prizes, recognition), development costs pay off only if the drug gets to the market. Finding ways to reward firms for incurring these development costs is therefore crucial; pull programs have a lot to offer in this regard.

Both these essays offer a way forward from the simple opposition of human need and corporate greed. They recognize the need to reward innovation and the need to make drugs available to everyone, and argue that a limited amount (i.e., relative to the social benefits) of donor money can do a lot to help us reconcile these needs.

Economics, all too often, is about trade-offs: what you gain in one place, you tend to lose in another. What makes the above discussion of intellectual property rights different is that it is less about reconciling the irreconcilable and more about finding a way forward: in other words, innovation rather than accommodation.

Microfinance

The potential for innovation in economics is perhaps best exemplified by the project of microfinance. The next essay, by Jonathan Morduch, starts by arguing that poor people in developing countries are largely excluded from financial markets, a theme that also appears in the essays by Townsend and Udry. The poor cannot, for example, buy insurance against things that are palpably outside their control, such as rainfall. As a result, when there is crop failure resulting from a drought, farmers often deal with income shortfalls by cutting their consumption.

Morduch describes one of the key problems with providing insurance to poor people: it is very costly to keep track of and collect premium payments from them. In part this is because they tend to live in more remote places or places where insurance agents are reluctant to visit. In part it is because they are poor, and therefore what they can afford to pay is not worth the cost of collecting. Morduch mentions an example from burial societies among fishing communities in Cochin, India, where the premium paid for life insurance was 4 cents a week. And in part it is because the poor find it difficult to save: it is a lot easier to collect $2 once a year than 4 cents once a week, but that would require that the poor hold on to their weekly 4 cents until they have accumulated $2.

Despite this, the Cochin fishermen have not given up trying to get insurance. Instead, they have innovated: they now pay their 4 cents per week into a communal pot and then the claims are paid out from this pot. Since no one has to come from outside to collect, those costs are avoided.

What they have is, however, far from perfect. One problem is that the community is small, and the total amount of claims in a year is quite unpredictable. In order to make sure that it has enough money to cover all the claims in a bad year when many people step forward with claims, the fund has to collect more cash than it would need in a typical year, which imposes a significant burden for cash-strapped fishermen. Moreover, the community does not have the sophistication to tailor its insurance product to the needs of its clients: everyone gets the same deal, even though needs often vary dramatically. And once one moves from death to more complex sets of risks, the community is even less likely to be the best insurer, simply because it does not have the capacity to adjudicate the claims. How is the community supposed to know whether the rainfall was indeed as low as a rainfall insurance claimant insists, or whether a particular health problem was covered by the insurance?

To resolve these problems, a different innovation is needed, one that allows the advantages of community monitoring and collection to be combined with the know-how and scale of a large insurance company. This is what microinsurance, the insurance side of microfinance, is meant to do. Morduch's essay describes a number of important recent attempts in this direction, such as the development of rainfall insurance in Morocco. Nevertheless, he argues that these problems are nowhere near being solved entirely. Often, one solution creates new problems. For instance, rainfall insurance designed to protect the incomes of farmers pushes up grain prices in a drought, which ends up hurting the rural landless who are net buyers rather than sellers of grain.

The next essay, by Robert Townsend, evaluates microfinance from a different angle, asking what it has delivered rather than what it can deliver. His focus is on villages in Thailand, where financial markets generally work very imperfectly: the poorest cannot borrow at all, and even those who can, typically need to put up collateral worth many times the loan they are getting. Access to both formal and informal finance did improve considerably over the two decades between the mid-1970s and mid-1990s, the period covered by his study. Based on the observed correlations between credit, investment, and consumption, and a model that allows him to predict changes in people's decisions, Townsend tries to evaluate the effects of this expansion. He recognizes that this is a complicated exercise involving large amounts of guesswork, and therefore devotes a substantial part of his essay to explaining the underlying methodology and assumptions. With all the resulting caveats, his results suggest that some forms of microlending are much more effective than others. In particular, cash loans are much more valuable than loans in kind, and financial institutions that also provide savings services and training achieve the best outcomes. His estimates suggest that having the best institutions may raise the growth rate of incomes in the village by as much as 5–6% per annum.

This kind of result is of course part of the reason why microfinance has generated so much excitement in the development community. But it also underscores the importance of getting microfinance right, and the need for careful evaluations of what works and what does not, and being open to further innovations.

NEW WAYS OF THINKING ABOUT POVERTY

Modern development economics grew in part out of resisting culturalist explanations of underdevelopment. As evidenced by the essays by Schultz, Eswaran, Laffont, and Miguel in the first section of this book, the resistance still continues. This is not always how it was in development economics. In the 1950s and 1960s, many of the leading theorists of underdevelopment, such as Arthur Lewis, Walter Rostow, and Simon Kuznets, were comfortable with the idea that poor countries were not altogether ready for capitalism. From this standpoint, people in these countries were viewed as much too indolent, inclined to enjoy rather than accumulate; the goal of the development project was to instill in them the capitalist virtues of thrift and hard work.

This was, of course, entirely in the spirit of the broader paradigm of modernization theory that dominated sociological theory of that era. The idea that underdevelopment is rooted in essential differences between people is of course much older, often associated with theories of racial superiority or, in a different form, in the work of the great sociologist Max Weber, who emphasized the essential historicity of the culture that created capitalism. Modernization theory, a product of the optimistic postwar years, went a step beyond Weber: the conditions for capitalism were now subsumed in the broader condition of being modern; this condition was something that could be engineered by a judicious mixture of education and state intervention.

The work of Ted Schultz, Gary Becker, and others, starting in the 1950s, was explicitly intended to be in defiance of all this. Drawing on a range of evidence, Schultz argued that a peasant family in a poor country is no less rational in its use of its meager resources than its richer American counterparts. The fact that people in poor countries have many children, while those in richer countries have only one or two, Gary Becker argued, has nothing to do with their religiosity or their view of human agency. It has everything to do with what he called—with more than a touch of "épater la bourgeoisie"—the quantity/quality trade-off in children. Parents, he argued, have children in part as a way of ensuring that they are taken care of in old age. From this point of view, it would always be better to have more children, except that the more children you have, the less you invest in any one of them. This, however, matters only if you are investing a significant amount to start with. If you are not going to invest, say, because there are no jobs for educated children, you may as well have as many children as you can manage. On the other hand, if you do plan to invest quite a bit, having fewer children may be a good idea. The poor will stop having many children when they have reason to invest in their children. Until such time, it will be fruitless to try to persuade them to use contraception: Beckerian economists delighted in stories of condoms, distributed for free by well-meaning outsiders, that ended up being used by kids as balloons.

In a similar vein, though somewhat less controversially, Ted Schultz argued that the failure of the poor in developing countries to educate their children reflects the lack of economic opportunities for educated people in these countries. When there will be jobs for the educated, education will naturally follow. Government programs that try to encourage children to get more education are, at best, misguided and quite often harmful since they induce children to spend time in school that they could spend more profitably working.

These rather extreme recommendations, not surprisingly, have long been abandoned. Most economists today, more or less across the entire political spectrum, take the view that the government does have a role in promoting both education and birth control. The main disagreements are about the relative importance of outside interventions versus the internal dynamics of families. But in the arguments made to justify outside intervention, it continues to be taken as given that the goal is to help people do what they want but cannot achieve on their own because they lack resources or power or proper access to markets. Thus, the subsidization of education is justified on the grounds that people may not be able to afford the education they want, and the promotion of contraception is described as a way of helping women to avoid having more children than they want. In other words, there is no suggestion that poor people or people in poor countries want the "wrong" things. They simply cannot get what they want.

For development economists until very recently, this was something of an item of faith. A large body of evidence showing that people do have a hard time getting what they want—both because they lack resources and market access and because of the way families function—did little to undermine this faith. It was recognized, of course, that none of this rules out the possibility that poor people and people in poor countries also differ in what they want. But the available language within economics did not really encourage talking about these issues. *De gustibus non est disputandum*, Gary Becker and George Stigler famously declared—economists should not argue with taste. But if all tastes are equally "right," it is awkward to have to argue that many people, and indeed many nations, are doomed to poverty as a direct consequence of what they want. No wonder the literature has preferred to stress external constraints.

Conspiracies of silence, however tacit, are always at risk of being undermined by evidence. The essay by Esther Duflo tries to see how far one can go with external constraints. She describes a long line of evidence, which confirms the relevance of external constraints but also raises, with increasing urgency, the need to go beyond them. Her essay culminates with the description of a cumulative sequence of experiments that eventually force us to confront the limits of the received theory.

In these experiments, Duflo (along with her coauthors Michael Kremer and John Robinson) tried to understand why most farmers in Busia (in western Kenya) do not use fertilizers, despite being strongly encouraged to do so by government agronomists. The initial experiments, carried out in partnership with a Kenyan NGO, involved getting farmers to apply different combinations and quantities of fertilizers on randomly chosen small plots of their land. The first results confirmed one natural suspicion that one might have under these conditions. The government agronomists were wrong—the full package of fertilizers that they recommended using at planting did not pay, mainly because the seeds often failed to germinate and required replanting. On the other hand, the returns on using a small amount of fertilizer after the seeds had germinated, which is sometimes called top-dressing, seemed to be uniformly large and positive—the six-season average return was 231%—but the farmers need not have known about this. Knowledge is indeed an external constraint.

Once the farmers tried top-dressing and saw what it did, one might have imagined that they would need no more convincing. However, just so that nothing got left to chance, field officers from the project visited every one of these farmers, discussed their (profitable) experience with top-dressing, and told them that all their neighbors had had a similar experience. Yet in the second season only 37% of these farmers used any fertilizer, compared with 20% in the control group, and by the fourth season this was down to 29%.

When asked why they did not use fertilizer, all the farmers said that they did not have the money. The trouble is that this could only be the whole story if the farmers were literally penniless, since even a small amount of money invested in fertilizer would be very profitable (it would cover just a small amount of land). The experimenters were not convinced: they felt that farmers could certainly afford to save up a little bit to buy fertilizer.

This was confirmed when the NGO offered a random subset of these farmers the opportunity to buy fertilizers at harvest time and promised to deliver the fertilizer to them in top-dressing season. Fertilizer usage doubled, suggesting that these farmers both had the money and were willing to wait for the extra rewards that fertilizer would bring them. Yet they needed the NGO to do the saving for them: they were not prepared to try to hold on to the same amount of money on their own for the few months between harvesting and the next round of sowing. When they said that they did not have the money, they were acknowledging some internal constraint on their ability to save on their own, rather than an external constraint on their resources (though the fact that they had limited resources might play on their willingness to try harder to save).

The worry is whether one can talk about internal constraints without, in effect, blaming the poor for their poverty. The essay by Sendhil Mullainathan suggests a way out. He starts from the premise that these internal constraints are universal. Indeed, a lot of them, he suggests, are almost hardwired into us, and only the most stringent application of will can free us from their insidious control. As an example, he describes an experiment by Madrian and Shea, in which a U.S. firm made a small change in the form people fill out stating how much they will put into their 401(k) accounts, in which they save for retirement. Traditionally the default option on the form was to contribute nothing; in the experiment this was changed to a contribution of 3% of income. For anybody who was actively exercising the choice, this should not have made a difference, since both no contribution and 3% of income remained options both before and after the change. Yet the change in the form raised the fraction of 401(k) participants from 38% to 86%. All these people were happy to save more, but were incapable of the (small) act of will that would have let them do so. Actively choosing to do the right thing is very different from passively letting it happen.

It follows from this distinction between active and passive choices that the fact that some people make better choices than others is as much about the environment (especially the nature of the available default choices) as it is about the people themselves. Poor people and people in poor countries often suffer because the default options they are offered are not particularly well designed, perhaps for some of the same reasons that vaccines for poor people's diseases are undersupplied. Moreover, given the economic pressures they are under, the benefits from better default choices are likely to be bigger for these people than for middle-class people in rich countries. Mullainathan ends by describing an experiment by Ashraf, Gons, and Yin, in which poor subjects in the Philippines were offered the option of locking away their savings, which effectively changed their default option, and got an enormously enthusiastic response. In this context, the reader may also recall the essay by Morduch, earlier in this volume, which talks at length about how hard it is to get the poor to save.

This is not to say that the poor are entirely or even primarily passive in the way they respond to the fact that markets often do not do what they want or need. One way they deal with these problems is by making use of their social ties. This is the topic of the essay by Kaivan Munshi. He offers the example of the market for savings and credit. Many people in the developing world do not have access to a bank, and even where they are physically able to get there, the bank often finds it unprofitable to deal with them. As a result, the community serves as a "bank substitute." People come together to form rotating savings and credit associations (ROSCAs), called chit funds in India, *tontines* in Cameroon, and a multitude of other names all over the developing world. In these ROSCAs everyone puts in a fixed amount of money every month for several months, and one person among them gets the entire pool in each month. The order in which different members win the pool is decided either by lottery or through a bidding process. Those who win late are in effect lending to those who win early.

The problem with this kind of organization is that someone needs to make sure that the people who have already won the pot continue to pay their dues. This is where social ties come in. Most ROSCAs are organized around some kind of community-based network, and the power of the network over its members helps make sure that people do not default.

Relying on the community to deliver what the market does not also has its costs, however. The main concern is that it gives the community too much power over the lives of its individual members. Sometimes this is exercised purely as a way for the powerful to exploit the less powerful. Munshi offers the examples of sugar cooperatives in India, which were originally set up to protect sugar farmers from exploitation by the market, but in which the more powerful big farmers now exploit the smaller farmers. Munshi does not take a stand on whether this makes it worse than it would have been, had the market been allowed to operate. But he is clearly warning us against any expectation that the community will be able to entirely replace the formal institutions of capitalism. In a similar vein, he suggests that sometimes the community exerts its power by restricting the choices of its members in ways that harm their long-term interest. If the community disapproves of contraception, as it seems to have done in the parts of Bangladesh that Munshi describes in his essay, then people who value their community ties will not use contraceptives even if they personally prefer to have fewer children.

In the next essay, Glenn Loury expresses a similar concern about the power of the community. His specific focus is on discrimination and the persistence of poverty among African Americans in the United States. The pernicious form of discrimination in today's United States, he suggests, is not the open and crude discrimination that one found fifty years ago, but the more insidious kind that is rooted in the way society implicitly theorizes about race. What Loury calls *biased social cognition* happens because people have become used to thinking about social phenomena in terms of race. As he points out, people are troubled by the fact that girls are underrepresented in science and math classes in schools, but not by the fact that African American men are overrepresented in prisons. Loury argues that this is because our theory tells us to expect no differences between boys and girls in the first case, whereas in the second case society sees nothing that it did not expect. It is willing to use race as a category to explain behaviors that lead to imprisonment.

Moreover, Loury argues, even if the "theory" that race, rather than any other attribute of African Americans (such as poverty or a history of being mistreated), explains their greater proneness to crime, this could just be the result of how society thinks about race. If everyone suspects you of being a criminal because you are black, jobs will be hard to come by; then crime may well be the only alternative left to you as a means of survival.

Yet because other people usually are not conscious of the power of their own "theories," they see the problems of African Americans as an unfortunate but inevitable fact of life, which will remain that way until African Americans decide to take charge of their lives. This creates widespread resistance to social policies that focus on helping African Americans. The poverty trap is then rooted ultimately in the minds of others in society—on their conceptions and misconceptions.

This is obviously an important caveat to the discussion about internal versus external constraints. Loury is warning us that external constraints come in many variants, some more apparent than others. Poor people have to deal not only with their lack of resources but also with the prejudices of others, and, as the essay by Debraj Ray eloquently argues, their own prejudices about themselves.

Ray's essay deals with what he calls failures of aspiration. Aspirations, he argues, are what make people try hard to succeed, but only if they consciously or subconsciously perceive that success is within reach. In other words, what matters is what Ray calls the aspiration gap, the difference between the standard of living that people aspire to and the standard of living they have already achieved. He argues that they will try harder when this gap is neither very large nor very small. If it is too large, the goal seems too distant to be within reach; if it is too small, it is not worth the effort.

This, then, suggests a simple theory that might explain the findings reported in Duflo's essay, where the poor do not always grab every opportunity offered to them: their aspiration gap may be too large or too small. It may be too small because the poor may not be aware of certain possibilities, and therefore think that they have nothing to aspire to. This is possible, though perhaps unlikely in the modern world of television. The more worrying possibility is that the gap is too large: the poor see what they want, but believe, incorrectly, that they have no way of getting there. They might not have, for example, met anybody who made it there, and therefore mistakenly assume that it is beyond their own reach. This is most likely in economically polarized societies, where the poor may not know many people from their own milieu who have made it out of poverty. In caste- or race-structured societies, the social structure may have been frozen for so long that people in different social groups have come to believe that there are immutable differences between them.

Taken together, these essays presage what we feel is an important new trend in the economics of poverty: a willingness to take the social and psychological environment of the poor seriously. At the same time, however, economics is increasingly being taken over by a hard-nosed empiricism, which is skeptical about all ideas unless, as the expression goes, they "show up in the data." These two vectors are just beginning to cross. Where that encounter takes us will surely be interesting new terrain.

NOTES

1. See *Human Development Report 2004,* table 2, 129.
2. See *Human Development Report 2004,* 129ff.
3. See, for instance, "More or Less Equal?" *The Economist,* Mar. 11, 2004; "Pessimistic on Poverty?" *The Economist,* Apr. 7, 2004.
4. This is reported by Martin Ravallion in *The Economist,* Apr. 7, 2004.
5. For a review of the detailed evidence on this, see Fields (2001), chap. 5.
6. See Moises Naim, "Washington Consensus: A Damaged Brand." *Financial Times,* Oct. 28, 2002.
7. See, for instance, Anne O. Krueger, first deputy managing director, International Monetary Fund, "The Challenge of Poverty: How the IMF Can Help Africa." Keynote address to the African Economic Research Consortium, Nairobi, Kenya, Dec. 4, 2003, available at http://www.imf.org/external/np/speeches/2003/120403.htm.
8. For an introductory survey, see Fields (2001), chap. 3.
9. One can already see this in middle-income countries (say Brazil), which must confront redistributive issues of both the "classical" and "new" kinds.
10. One should be careful that this might not carry over to poorer countries, where the fiscal system is not as well developed and there are many more opportunities for tax evasion, capital flight, etc.
11. A welfare loss occurs unless parents suffer from present-bias (time-inconsistent) preferences or underestimate the returns to education. In such cases, "paternalistic" interventions may (but need not) raise family welfare.
12. The gains in children's health associated with such programs are of course intrinsically desirable, but health could be subsidized independently of education.
13. See Kremer (2003).
14. See Hsieh and Urquiola (2003).

BIBLIOGRAPHY

Banerjee, Ahijit, Dilip Mookherjee, Kaivan Munshi, and Debraj Ray. "Inequality, Control Rights and Efficiency: Sugar Cooperatives in Western Maharashtra." *Journal of Political Economy* 109 (1) (2001): 138–190.

Birdsall, Nancy, and Augusto de la Torre. *Washington Contentious: Economic Policies for Social Equity in Latin America*. Washington, D.C.: Carnegie Endowment for International Peace and Inter-American Dialogue, 2001.

Bourguignon, François, and Christian Morrisson. "Inequality Among World Citizens: 1820–1992." *American Economic Review* 92 (4) (2002): 727–744.

Chen, Shaohua, and Martin Ravallion. "How Did the World's Poorest Fare in the 1990's?" World Bank Discussion Paper, 2000.

Fields, Gary. *Distribution and Development*. Cambridge, Mass.: MIT Press, 2001.

Hsieh, Chang-Tsai, and Miguel Urquiola. "When Schools Compete, How Do They Compete? An Assessment of Chile's Nationwide School Voucher Program." Mimeo, University of California at Berkeley, 2003.

Human Development Report 2004: Cultural Liberty in Today's Diverse World. New York: United Nations Development Programme, 2004.

Kremer, Michael. "Randomized Evaluations of Educational Programs in Developing Countries: Some Lessons." *American Economic Review, Papers and Proceedings* 93 (2) (2003): 102–106.

Mirrlees, James A. "An Exploration in the Theory of Optimal Income Taxation." *Review of Economic Studies* 38 (2) (1971): 175–208.

UNDERSTANDING POVERTY

1

Measuring Poverty

Angus Deaton

As the name suggests, economic development was originally thought of as economic growth, but in recent years it has increasingly come to be thought of as poverty reduction. The World Bank proclaims that "Our dream is a world free of poverty," and increasingly works to direct all of its activities toward poverty reduction. In 2000 the General Assembly of the United Nations adopted a set of "Millennium Development Goals," the first of which is to eradicate extreme poverty and hunger—more specifically, to "reduce by half, between 1990 and 2015, the proportion of people whose income is less than $1 a day." How do we know who is poor and who is not? Is poverty the same as hunger? What is the relationship between economic growth and poverty reduction? How will we know whether the first Millennium Development Goal has been met, or whether world poverty is falling at all? These are some of the questions that I address in this essay.

LOCAL AND NATIONAL POVERTY

Everyone has some idea what poverty is, and most people have little difficulty answering the question "Do you consider yourself poor?," although some people need a moment or two to think about it. Nor do people find it hard to answer the same question about their neighbors or other people they know. Yet these simple ideas turn out to be hard to extend to countries, and harder still to the world as a whole.

A participatory rural assessment, usually known by its acronym PRA, is a procedure often used by researchers and by nongovernmental organizations (NGOs) working in villages in poor countries. The researchers sit with the

villagers at the local gathering place and find out about the village, mapping
its houses, the school, the water supply, its agricultural activities, and who
lives where. It is common to ask the villagers to say who is well off, who is
not so well off, and who is poor, and in most cases, villagers have no difficulty
in making the identification. No doubt there are some mistakes, and some
people conceal some assets from their neighbors, but the results usually make
sense. The poor are often people who cannot work because they are ill or
suffer from a long-term disability or are elderly. There are also poor and
vulnerable groups in specific locations, such as Indian widows who are unfortunate enough not to have sons to support them. Such information can
sometimes be used as part of poverty relief efforts. In India, one scheme, the
Antyodaya (Last Man First) food program, relies on local councils to identify
the very poorest of rural households, who receive subsidized food rations.
There is a similar scheme in Indonesia. But it is possible to push this local
poverty identification too far. If the sums to be distributed are large enough,
they become worth misappropriating, and there is an incentive for people to
identify their friends and relatives (or themselves) as poor. Similarly, some
NGOs have discovered that if they use the poverty identification to enroll
people in employment or training schemes, then after a few visits *everyone*
is reported to be poor.

National poverty counts are also used for allocating funds. In the United
States and many other countries, some government benefits are confined to
poor or near-poor people. In India, the central government subsidizes food
provision to state governments according to the fraction of the population
that is poor. The South African government transfers funds to municipalities
according to estimates of the fraction of their population that is poor. Thus
we can't always rely on a poverty measurement system in which people self-
identify their poverty. Even so, there is much to be learned from asking
people what constitutes poverty. For example, the Gallup Poll in the United
States has regularly asked people to report what is the smallest amount of
money a family of four, two adults and two children, would need "to get
along in this community." Although some people give fanciful answers, the
central tendency of these reports provides a sensible measure of the "poverty
line," the amount of income that is the border between poverty and non-
poverty. Yet if the national poverty line were to be set using the results of
such a poll, it is easy to imagine interest groups asking people to inflate their
answers with the expectation of higher benefits.

SCIENCE AND POLITICS

There is a long tradition of setting "scientific" poverty lines by calculating
the cost of a minimal standard of living, with a particular focus on having
enough to eat. The poorest people in poor countries spend most of their
money—in some places as much as three quarters—on food. For them, not
having enough money is much the same thing as not having enough food.

Yet even the poorest buy things other than food—clothing and housing, most obviously—as well as an increasing number of goods that are not usually classified as necessities. For example, the average household in rural India spent 70% of its budget on food in 1983, but only 62% in 1999–2000, by which time 31% of households owned a radio and 19% a television. As people become better off, and even while they are still poor by most standards, they spend a smaller fraction of their budgets on food—a regularity known as Engel's Law, after Ernst Engel, who first noted it in 1857—so that economic growth makes it increasingly difficult to think of poverty *entirely* in terms of food, certainly in rich countries such as the United States, where in 2001 the typical household spent only 13.5% of its budget on food, but also increasingly in poor countries that are becoming less poor, such as India.

Even so, the rhetorical link between hunger and poverty remains strong, and many countries calculate poverty lines by calculating how much it costs to obtain enough food, usually in terms of meeting a calorie norm of around 2,000 calories a day (as suggested by nutritional experts at the Food and Agricultural Organization of the United Nations), or by some local nutritional council or institute. Sometimes these norms are set differently for people doing agricultural labor, who typically need many more calories, perhaps 4,000 a day. Sometimes there are even separate standards for men and women (women apparently need less energy, though such distinctions are rarely made today) and for children. Although people need protein as well as calories, it is usually assumed that someone who is getting enough calories through a normal diet will automatically get enough protein. Even so, certain micronutrients remain a concern, and the lack of some of these trace elements can result in disease and disability; for example, iodine deficiency—often remedied through iodized salt—can result in mental retardation, goiters, and problems during pregnancy.

How is the cost of calories calculated? One way is to pose the question formally, in terms of the cost of subsistence. Given all the foods in the market, as well as the calorie content and prices of each, what is the smallest amount of money that is needed to buy a bundle containing 2,000 calories? This solution of this problem played a role in the development of the mathematical technique of linear programming. But when George Stigler first worked out the answer in 1945, he discovered a diet that was monotonous and uninteresting and that no one could reasonably be expected to eat. (Animal feed is another matter, and linear programming is often used to set cost-effective diets for animals in feedlots.) Such a mathematical solution takes no account of the fact that people care about other things than just nutrients, including variety and flavor, and that what people want to eat is affected by their preferences and by the society in which they live. To escape Stigler's conclusion, calories can be converted into money by looking at what people actually spend and finding the income (or total expenditure) level at which, on average, people get 2,000 calories. This can be done by plotting what is called the "calorie Engel curve," a graph with income or total expenditure along the horizontal axis and the average calories of households at that income or expenditure level on the vertical axis. The 2,000 calorie point on the vertical axis is then traced to the corresponding point on the horizontal axis, which becomes the income or expenditure poverty line. People living in households with less than this amount are classified as poor and people with more as nonpoor.

There are variants of the calorie method. In the United States, the poverty line was set by starting not from a calorie norm but from an economy food plan recommended by the Department of Agriculture, which was then multiplied by three to allow for goods other than food. (Though according to some accounts, the food plan was "adjusted" in order to ensure that the poverty line was close to a value already in use by the administration of the day, so that the science was at least partly window dressing for the politics.) Some allowance must also be made for the fact that different households contain different numbers of people. The simplest method is to do all of the calculations on a per capita basis, plotting calories per capita on the vertical axis and income or expenditure per capita on the horizontal axis. Alternately, as in the United States, different poverty lines can be drawn up for different household types.

Calorie-based poverty lines are widely used around the world. The association with food appears to be attractive, in part because poor people do indeed spend much of their budget on food, but perhaps also because there is more political support for antipoverty programs that involve food than for measures based on goods that are seen as less meritorious. The right to food is more compelling than the right to other consumer goods. The nutritional basis and the involvement of nutritional scientists in setting the norms also appear to add legitimacy to the lines and the counts that are based on them.

Even so, it is clear that the food rhetoric is mostly just that. In particular, even when a national poverty line is set using the calorie method, it is usually updated over time in a way that is inconsistent with the maintenance of the nutritional norm. In countries as widely different as the United States and India, the official poverty lines have never been updated so as to preserve the original link with food. Although there have been minor revisions, the lines have essentially been held constant in real terms, so that the poverty lines now are simply the original poverty lines updated for general inflation. At first blush, this sort of updating might be seen to preserve the original intent, and certainly, if price inflation is correctly calculated, a household at the poverty line in India in 2000 has the same purchasing power as a household at the poverty line when it was first drawn up in 1971. Yet people at the same level of living purchase fewer calories now than they used to, perhaps because fewer of them are engaged in manual labor in agriculture and thus need less energy, so that if one were really to believe in a fixed calorie standard, the poverty line would have to be revised upward. Such revision is something for which there is typically little political support, in India or in the United States, if only because raising the poverty line would increase the number of people designated as poor, which, in the absence of legislative changes, would trigger additional progressive redistribution.

There are similar problems in adapting poverty lines over space, as well as over time. Urban people are typically more sedentary than rural people, and so consume fewer calories at the same level of income. So if the same calorie standard is used for both urban and rural sectors, the urban poverty line will be higher. This sometimes leads to higher calculated poverty *rates* in cities than in the countryside, even when levels of living are clearly much lower in the latter and, indeed, when people are willingly migrating into the cities. Higher urban poverty lines make some sense because urban prices are usually higher, but once again the politics of "urban bias" often find it congenial to overstate the number of poor people in the cities to justify transfers to groups who are vocal and who live close to the seats of power. The problems of updating over time, and of different poverty lines for different places, could in principle be solved by the selection of separate calorie standards. Yet no one really knows how to set such standards, and better calorie standards would do nothing to deal with another deficiency of the measure, that it takes no explicit account of the nonfood part of consumption (should poverty lines be higher in colder places or in hilly places?), a part that is more important in cities than in the countryside and that becomes more important over time.

An alternative interpretation of national poverty lines recognizes that they are to some extent arbitrary, so that within a range, a number of different poverty lines could just as well serve the purpose. At any given time, people have an imprecise notion of what a decent minimum income is, so that a range of "scientific" lines is likely to be acceptable. But it is the science, not the notion, that will give way if there is a conflict. But once the line is set, it appears to be politically difficult to update for anything other than general price increases. Eventually, such lines move out of the range of acceptability, and there will be pressure for change. But because of the political issues involved in redistribution, lines survive beyond the time when they can be justified, either by considerations of food or as some average of what people think a poverty line ought to be. Poverty lines are as much political as scientific constructions.

THE MICAWBER PROBLEM

In Dickens's *David Copperfield*, the character Mr. Micawber has an eloquent understanding of a poverty line. As he frequently observes, "Income twenty shillings, expenses nineteen shillings and sixpence—result, happiness. Income twenty shillings, expenses twenty shillings and sixpence—result, misery." One of the reasons Mr. Micawber's observation is so memorable is that it is nonsense. Why should everything depend on such a tiny difference? And why do we say that someone who is just below the poverty line is poor, and thus a candidate for transfers and the special attention of the World Bank, while someone who is just above it, whether by sixpence or by six annas, needs no help and can be safely left to his or her own devices? Even if we could set the poverty line precisely, and even if we could precisely measure each person's income, neither of which conditions is close to being met, it makes no sense to treat such similar people so differently.

There is another good argument for not doing so. A government that cares not at all about poverty but is being held to a poverty reduction standard, or is keen to be seen to be reducing poverty, could do so by giving small amounts of money to those just below the line, just enough to lift them out of poverty. This money could even come from the very poor—once someone is poor, taking money away from him or her does nothing to add to the poverty count. This tactic is open to any government whose poverty record is judged by the fraction of people below the poverty line.

It is sometimes argued that Mr. Micawber was right after all, and that, if we think about it hard enough and do the supporting research, we will find some income level, or perhaps some combination of income and other things—an index of well-being—where there is a real observable jump in behavior. For example, for children at school, having a pair of shoes might make the difference between being accepted or being treated as a pariah, just as the possession of a particular brand of sneaker might have a similar effect in a better-off country. Yet decades of research into people's spending patterns and income levels has always failed to find any clear discontinuity in the data, a point at which behavior suddenly changes that we might use as the cutoff for a poverty line.

The Micawber problem can be remedied by going beyond a count of the poor and taking note of the *degree* of poverty. The *head count ratio* is the most familiar measure of poverty and is defined as the fraction of the population in poverty. We can add to this measure information about the average incomes (or expenditures) of the poor. A standard way of doing so is to compute the fraction by which each poor person is short of the poverty line, so that someone at half the poverty line would have a value of 0.5, while someone with nothing would have a value of 1.0. The *poverty gap* measure of poverty is then obtained by multiplying the head count ratio by the average value of this fractional shortfall among the poor. Someone just below the line now counts for less than someone a long way below it, and our malevolent government can no longer cook its books by taking money from the poorest and giving it to those just below the line. In practice, only academics and a few statistical agencies calculate such measures with any regularity. Their theoretical superiority seems to be outweighed by the difficulty of explaining these measures to the press or to the public, and in truth, it seems to be rare that poverty comparisons between two places, two countries, or two dates are different if we use the better measures. Yet it is always beneficial to keep the deficiencies of the head count ratio in mind.

POVERTY AND GROWTH

When there is economic growth, in the sense of an increase in average consumption and average income, what happens to poverty depends on what happens to the *distribution* of income and consumption. If everyone's incomes grow together, then growth at the mean goes straight into poverty reduction. If economic growth benefits only the rich, the distribution of income widens, and there will be no reduction in poverty in spite of the fact that growth among the rich means that average incomes are growing. It is sometimes argued that income distribution changes only very slowly, so that, at least in the short run, growth automatically reduces poverty. By the same argument, it is possible to *measure* poverty from data on *average* incomes or expenditures; with the distribution fixed, incomes at the bottom grow at the same rate as incomes at the mean.

These arguments are both dangerous and factually incorrect. In the 1990s, world poverty fell a good deal less than would have been expected from the relatively rapid rates of economic growth in some of the large countries such as India and China. Growth at the bottom of the income distribution was not as rapid as overall growth. There are good reasons to expect this to happen. Many countries in the world experienced increasing inequality in the 1990s, and in countries such as India, the rapid expansions in high-technology industries is likely to disproportionately benefit the well-educated, at least at first. Growth in agriculture, on which most poor people depend, has been less rapid. Beyond this, there is a general argument that, in poor countries that are growing, the growth in measured national income tends to overstate the true growth rate as more and more informal production is brought into the accounts. This informal production is better captured in the surveys used to measure poverty, if only because many of them rely on consumption, not income. I like to think of this as the "Al Capone effect"; the notorious gangster could never be convicted of murder or extortion but was brought to justice on tax evasion charges when prosecutors showed that his expenditures were wildly in excess of his income. The message here is that it is important to measure poverty directly by collecting data on the living standards of poor people and not to *assume* that the incomes of the poor grow at the same rate as the average. Making that assumption is effectively a refusal to confront one of the central questions of the day: whether growth around the world is good for the poor.

POVERTY AND CAPABILITIES

So far I have discussed poverty as a lack of income or of consumption. But this is only one aspect of poverty. Even if you have enough goods, they are worth little if you are not healthy enough to enjoy them. Children who live in an unsanitary environment will obtain little nutritional benefit from the food they eat if they continually suffer from diarrhea. More broadly, girls who are denied the opportunity to go to school experience yet another type of poverty, the poverty of not being able to read and to participate in activities that are open only to the literate. People are also poor in another sense if they lack the resources to participate fully—in Adam Smith's terms, "are afraid to appear in public"—in the society in which they live, even if their incomes would be sufficient in some other society. In recent years, Amartya Sen's has been an important voice urging that poverty needs to be seen more broadly than inadequacy of income. He argues that poverty is the absence of one or more of the basic capabilities that are needed to achieve minimal functioning in the society in which one lives. This includes not having enough income to ensure being adequately fed, clothed, or sheltered (income poverty) or being unhealthy (health poverty), as well as being denied access to education, political participation, or a full role in society. Sen also recognizes that poverty is sometimes *relative* to the norms and customs of the society in which someone lives; full participation in a wealthy society may require more money than participation in a poor one.

The aim is not to try to combine these different aspects of poverty into a single measure, and we are clearly not always concerned with every case of deprivation in all dimensions. Even so, if we confine ourselves to income-based measures, we risk missing important features of poverty. For example, a government that raises taxes to pay for better public services or better public health may *increase* income poverty while reducing poverty more broadly. Conversely, it is sometimes argued that rapid economic growth that favors the rich, although not reducing the incomes of the poor, may reduce the access of the poor to public services that are redirected toward the rich and perhaps also the democratic rights of the poor, if money influences the political process. In consequence, and even in the absence of an adequate measure that combines all aspects of poverty, the broader perspectives have had a major effect on the way that poverty is measured. International institutions such as the World Bank and the United Nations measure not only the number of people whose income is low but also pay attention to measures of health, such as infant and child mortality rates and life expectancy, and to participation in education. Five of the eight Millennium Development Goals are about promoting health and education. The United Nations Development Programme annually publishes a Human Development Index for each country that consists of an average of three measures: one for income, one for life expectancy, and one for literacy. And individual countries are increasingly assigning to these broader measures the prominence that was once reserved for national income alone.

It is important to note that these additional measures of well-being are not substitutes for one another, nor should it be supposed that they necessarily move together, so that one dimension can serve as a proxy for another. For example, improvements in public health, such as malaria eradication, vaccinations, and clean water, led to considerable improvements in life expectancy in many countries of Africa that were experiencing little or no income growth. There were great successes in income growth and poverty reduction in India in the 1990s, as there had been in the 1980s. Yet the reduction in infant mortality rates in India was less rapid in the 1990s than in the 1980s, with the opposite true for education, where school attendance rose rapidly, especially among girls. More generally, the rate of decline in child mortality throughout the poor world was slower in the 1990s than in the 1980s, in spite of higher rates of growth of GDP per capita. While it is true that income growth is often a powerful agent for the reduction in non-income poverty, it is neither necessary nor sufficient as we can see from the fact that health and educational poverty have been effectively eliminated in some poor places. Costa Rica, Cuba, China prior to the economic reforms, and the Indian state of Kerala are the most often cited examples. In at least some cases, public provision can reduce poverty even at low incomes.

The fact that income tends to be positively correlated with other aspects of well-being also alerts us to the fact that poor people in the world are poorer, and rich people richer, than we would recognize on the basis of their incomes alone. Africans not only have less money than Europeans and Americans, they also have lower life expectancy and less chance of ever going to school. Such associations also hold *within* countries; poorer people are more likely to lose their babies and can expect to have shorter lives, and this is as true in the rich countries of Europe and North America as it is in the poor countries of Asia and Africa. Taking a broader view of poverty gives us a more complete picture of deprivation and of the inequality within and between countries.

Thinking about poverty as the inability to participate in society leads to concepts of *relative* poverty, as opposed to the *absolute* poverty of not having enough to eat or not enjoying good health. Relative measures of poverty are often constructed by using poverty lines that move with average income, so that the minimum acceptable income is tied to what other people get. For example, the Council of Ministers of the European Community recognizes someone as poor if he or she lives in a household whose income is less than half of average household income. And although the U.S. government uses a poverty line that is fixed in real terms, the answers to the Gallup "get along" questions in the United States consistently track half of median income, so that this measure seems to correspond well to what Americans think the poverty line should be. But relative lines are not much used in poor countries, where the main concern seems to be absolute poverty, the inability to meet basic needs of health and nutrition. In rich countries, where meeting basic needs is no longer an issue for the vast majority of households, there is a greater emphasis on social inclusion and not being too far from the mainstream of other citizens. Even among countries that do not adjust their own poverty lines, there is a tendency for middle- and high-income countries to have higher poverty lines than poorer countries. The 2001 poverty line in the United States for a family of two adults and two children was $18,000 a year, more than ten times as much as the international "extreme poverty" line of $1 per person per day used by the World Bank and the United Nations.

MEASURING POVERTY IN THE WORLD

Measuring poverty at the local level is straightforward; at the national level it is hard but manageable; and at the level of the world as a whole it is extremely difficult, so much so that some people argue that it is not worth the effort. In particular, because there is no world political authority that can set a poverty line and use it in antipoverty policies, we lack the opportunities that exist at the national level to come to some sort of political agreement on what is a useful definition of poverty. Instead, we have a measure that is useful mainly for the international organizations and for First World NGOs that are arguing for greater resource flows to poor countries. Yet the recent debate on the costs and benefits of globalization has drawn new interest to the world poverty counts and has raised wildly differing claims and counterclaims. Those in favor of globalization point to recent high rates of growth among some of the world's poorest countries and argue that growth almost always means poverty reduction. Those who are against it argue that globalization has benefited mainly the rich countries, deepening poverty for most people and countries of the world. Are our poverty measures capable of providing an answer one way or the other? And, if so, who is right?

The obvious way to make a world poverty count is simply to add up the counts from each country. But such estimates would be of little interest. In the count for 2001, the U.S. Census Bureau estimated that there were 32.9 million poor people in the United States, while the Planning Commission of the Government of India estimated that there were 260.25 million poor people in India in 1999–2000. I think there are few people who take a strong enough relativist view of poverty to argue that these poverty counts are commensurate and simply add them up. The World Bank, in constructing the world poverty data, makes no attempt to do so; indeed, it excludes the rich countries altogether. For the low- and middle-income countries, instead of using the national poverty lines, which are higher the richer the country is, the World Bank uses a common international poverty line designed to be appropriate for extreme poverty, defined as poverty in the poorest countries. A good way to think about this is that the counts use a poverty line close to that of India, so that the basic idea is to count everyone in the world whose level of consumption is low enough for them to count as poor in India.

To put this idea into practice, we need to convert the Indian poverty line into the currency of other countries: Indonesian rupiahs, Thai bahts, Mexican pesos, Kenyan shillings, and so on. For nearly all of the countries, there are market exchange rates, although it is often convenient (especially for audiences in rich countries) to convert the Indian poverty line into U.S. dollars first, and then to convert from U.S. dollars into all the other currencies of the world. But it turns out that market exchange rates are not useful here.

In particular, market exchange rates make the poor countries appear too poor relative to the rich ones, compared with the real differences in their living standards. (For the same reason, it is a serious mistake to calculate measures of world inequality using official exchange rates.) The problem is that (to simplify matters a little) market exchange rates are determined by supply and demand of imports and exports; importers into India need dollars and euros, which are supplied by exporters selling Indian goods in the world market. The market exchange rate then ensures that goods that are traded into and out of India have prices in rupees that, when converted at the market exchange rate, are comparable with the world prices of those goods in dollars. But many goods that are important to poor people, including much of their food, all of their housing, and the services that they buy, are neither imported nor exported. Land, housing, and services that use cheap Indian labor (remember that India is poor) would be a great bargain in New York, but that does nothing to raise their prices, because they are in India, not New York, and it is impossible to ship such things from India to New York. The result is that an American dollar, converted into rupees at the market exchange rate, will buy a great deal more than a dollar's worth of goods in India. Equivalently, the Indian poverty line in 1999–2000, which for urban people was 454 rupees per person per month, is worth several multiples of the $9 per person per month that 454 rupees would have brought at the market exchange rate of 50 rupees to the dollar. Instead, it is necessary to use a different set of exchange rates, called *purchasing power parity* (PPP) exchange rates, which are designed to convert currencies in a way that preserves purchasing power, and which, for the comparison between India and the United States, coverts 454 rupees to around $50 per person per month. The Indian rural poverty line is 328 rupees, which converts to $38, a little more than one PPP dollar per person per day.

All of this is fine in theory, but the construction of PPP exchange rates is controversial and subject to substantial margins of error. Perhaps the most serious of the criticisms is that the PPP exchange rates that are used were not constructed for the purpose of measuring poverty, so that there is no guarantee that they will accurately convert the living standards of poor people from one country to another. Another problem is the low priority that many statistical offices give to providing numbers that have no domestic use. Perhaps in consequence, when the PPP numbers are revised or updated, there are wild swings in the poverty counts, even for broad regions of the world. PPP exchange rates are not calculated for every country, nor for every year in any country, so there is a good deal of reliance on interpolations and predictions, some of which are almost certainly quite inaccurate. So there are critics who doubt whether the PPP numbers have any value for measuring global poverty.

Even when the $1 a day has been converted to local currency, we have not come to the end of our difficulties. The poverty count in each country is the number of people living in households whose consumption per capita is less than the local version of the international poverty line. The information for that calculation comes from *household surveys*, in which a random sample of households in each country is visited and asked questions about their incomes and expenditures. There is a good deal of variability in the quality of these surveys. In some countries, such as India, where modern survey methodology was first developed, the statistical authorities are experienced and expert. But that is not always the case. And even when the surveys are well conducted, details of how the questions are asked—which are far from uniform across countries—can have large effects on the results. For example, some countries, such as most of Latin America and China, collect data on incomes, while others, such as India, Pakistan, and Indonesia, collect data on expenditures. There is no straightforward way of converting poverty counts based on one into poverty counts based on the other. Another important, although seemingly trivial, issue is the length of what is known as the reporting period. When respondents are asked how much they spent, for example on rice, the question must refer to a specific period, for example the last seven days, the last fourteen days, or the last month. In India, the statistical office has traditionally used a thirty-day reporting period for food, a choice that was based on experimental evaluations of different reporting periods carried out in the 1950s. Even so, the thirty-day period is unusually long by international standards, and an experimental survey was set up in which a randomly selected half of the households got a thirty-day reporting period, while the others got a seven-day reporting period. On average, households reported about 30% more food purchases on the seven-day questionnaire and only about 18% more on all expenditures including food—not such a large difference in itself, but enough to cut the measured number of poor in India by half! It seems that statistical poverty reduction is a good deal easier than substantive poverty reduction. While it might be argued that the choice of reporting period doesn't matter much for India itself, where everyone would adapt to the new measurement system and its associated poverty levels, the fact that reporting periods and other "details" are different in different countries undermines our ability to make comparable counts that can be added up across countries.

In spite of all the faults in the data, a fairly clear picture is now emerging of what has been happening to poverty around the world near the end of the millennium. The overall count of income-poor in the world is dominated by what has been happening in India and in China, where there has been a great deal of economic growth. Although the growth rates of income and consumption around the poverty line have been slower than growth at the mean—there has been a widening of income inequality—there has still been sufficient growth among the poor in both countries for there to be reductions not only in the fraction of people who are poor but also in the actual number of the very poorest people, those living on less than $1 a day. (However, the number of those who live on less than $2 a day is rising, according to the most recent estimates.) In spite of increased income poverty in much of

Africa, in the transition countries of Eastern Europe and the former Soviet Union, and most recently in some countries in Latin America, the huge weight of population in India and China dominates in the world counts. While it would be true to say that, apart from those two countries, poverty in the world is getting worse, it is also true that nearly half the world's population lives in places where poverty is falling. On the negative side, there is no progress or even negative progress in Africa, with increasing income poverty accompanied by falling life expectancy associated with HIV/AIDS. While few people would attribute the AIDS catastrophe to the effects of economic globalization, we must likewise be careful not to automatically attribute to globalization the success of reductions in income poverty. Indeed, the role of globalization in poverty reduction remains a hotly debated topic.

PART I

THE CAUSES OF POVERTY

2

Understanding Prosperity and Poverty: Geography, Institutions, and the Reversal of Fortune

Daron Acemoglu, Simon Johnson, & James Robinson

GEOGRAPHY, INSTITUTIONS, AND THE POVERTY OF NATIONS

There are tremendous differences in incomes and standards of living between the rich and the poor countries of the world. For example, average per capita income in sub-Saharan Africa today is less than one twentieth of per capita income in the United States—and this is after adjusting for differences in purchasing power, which helps African incomes. For those of us lucky enough to be living in North America or Western Europe, it is difficult even to imagine how people can survive at such income levels.

Explanations abound for these huge differences in the economic fortunes of countries. Poor countries, such as those in sub-Saharan Africa, Central America, and South Asia, usually lack functioning markets, have poorly educated populations, and possess outdated or nonexistent machinery and technology. These are, however, only *proximate* causes of poverty, in turn begging the question of why these places don't have better markets, human capital, machinery, and technology. There must be some *fundamental* causes of poverty leading to these outcomes and, through these channels, to poverty.

The two main contenders to explain the fundamental causes of cross-country differences in prosperity are geography and institutions. The *geography hypothesis*, which has a large following both in the popular imagination and in academia, maintains that the geography, climate, and ecology of a society's location shape both its technology and the incentives of its inhabitants. There are at least three main versions of the geography hypothesis, each emphasizing a different mechanism for how geography affects prosperity. First, climate may be an important determinant of work effort, incentives, and even productivity. Second, geography may determine the technology that a society develops, especially in agriculture. The third variant of the geography hypothesis, popular especially since the 1990s, links poverty to "disease burden": "The burden of infectious disease is similarly higher in the tropics than in the temperate zones" (Sachs 2000, p. 32).[1]

In this chapter, we argue that differences in institutions are more important than geography for understanding the divergent economic and social conditions of nations. While the geography hypothesis emphasizes forces of nature as a primary factor in the poverty of nations, the *institutions hypothesis* is about man-made influences. According to this view, some societies are organized in a way that upholds the rule of law, encourages investment of all kinds, facilitates broad-based participation by citizens, and supports market transactions. Loosely speaking, we can refer to these societies as having developed good institutions.

Three crucial elements of these good institutions are (1) enforcement of property rights for a broad cross section of society, so that a variety of individuals have incentives to invest and take part in economic life; (2) constraints on the actions of elites, politicians, and other powerful groups so these people cannot expropriate the incomes and investments of others or create a highly uneven playing field; and (3) some degree of equal opportunity for broad segments of the society, so that they can make investments, especially in human capital, and participate in productive economic activities. These good institutions—or *institutions of private property,* a term emphasizing the importance of the enforcement of rule of law and property rights— do not exist in many societies. In these countries, the rule of law is selectively applied and property rights are nonexistent for the vast majority of the population. Furthermore, the political and economic power of elites is unlimited, and only a small fraction of citizens has access to education, investment, and productive opportunities.

The institutions hypothesis goes back at least to John Locke, Adam Smith, and John Stuart Mill, and it features prominently in many current academic contributions and popular debates (e.g., Jones 1981). John Locke, for example, stressed the importance of property rights: "there must of necessity be a means to appropriate them some way or other, before they can be of any use, or at all beneficial to any particular man" ([1690] 1980, p. 10). He further argued that the main purpose of government was "the preservation of the property of . . . members of the society" (p. 47). More recently, Douglass North was awarded a Nobel Prize in part for articulating the role of institutions in understanding economic development.

It is perhaps surprising that some societies have dysfunctional institutions, despite the large economic and social costs that these bring. Our perspective in this essay is that there are no compelling reasons to think that societies will naturally gravitate toward good institutions. In fact, appreciating why this is so will be key to understanding why institutions vary across countries. Institutions not only affect the economic prospects of nations but also are central to the *distribution* of income among various individuals and groups in society—in other words, institutions affect both the size of the social pie and how it is distributed. This perspective implies that a potential change from dysfunctional and bad institutions toward better ones, which will increase the size of the social pie, may nonetheless be *blocked* when such a change significantly reduces the size of the slice that powerful groups receive and when they cannot be *credibly* compensated for this loss after the change in institutions.[2] By the same token, powerful groups will often opt for institutions that do not provide any rights to the majority of the population so that they can extract resources or labor from them, or monopolize the most lucrative businesses. Motivated by this reasoning, we will refer to bad and dysfunctional institutions as *extractive institutions,* emphasizing the fact that they are there, or were introduced in the first place, as a means of supporting the extraction of resources by one group at the expense of the rest of the society.

In the rest of this essay, we develop the case for the importance of institutions. To build this case, we will go back to the history of European colonization, which provides us with a natural laboratory where, while geography remained constant, European colonists radically transformed institutions in many of these societies. That institutions matter, naturally does not imply that geography is not important. The two explanations could be complementary rather than competing. Geographic and ecological factors, for example, have undoubtedly played a major role in determining where early civilizations located and where humans migrated during their early history. Nevertheless, the evidence we discuss in this essay also suggests that the role of geography is relatively limited in understanding the sources of prosperity and poverty today.

GEOGRAPHY VERSUS INSTITUTIONS: WHAT WE SEE TODAY

If you want to believe that geography matters, look at a world map. Locate the poorest places in the world, with per capita income levels less than one twentieth of that of the United States. You will find almost all of them close to the equator, in very hot regions with periodic torrential rains. If, following Montesquieu (1748), you believe that climate matters for economic activity, then this is supportive of that view.

Next, look at some recent writings on agricultural productivity. You will see many ecologists and economists claim that the tropical areas do not have enough frost to clean the soil and are suffering from soil depletion because of heavy rains. Here seems to be evidence that tropical agriculture is less productive than its temperate counterpart—as argued, for example, by Myrdal (1968).

Next turn to sources on tropical diseases, for example, the recent report by the World Health Organization (2001). Not surprisingly, given the term *tropical disease*, areas infested with these diseases are at the tropics and much poorer than the United States and Europe, where such diseases are entirely absent. Here seems to be evidence that the burden of disease condemns these places to poverty.

Does this evidence establish that geography is a first-order influence on prosperity? *No.* It is true there is *a correlation* between geography and prosperity, that is, a simple statistical association. But statistical association does not prove causation. Most important, there are often *omitted factors* driving the associations we observe in the data.

Consider an example from the history of malaria, the quintessential tropical disease, to illustrate this point. In the nineteenth century doctors did not understand what caused malaria. To make progress toward protecting European troops stationed in the tropics, they developed an "empirical theory" of malaria by observing that people who lived or traveled close to swamps caught malaria. In other words, they turned the association between the incidence of malaria and the presence of swamps into a causal relationship that the incidence of malaria was *caused* by swamps—and elaborated on this theory by arguing that malaria was transmitted by mists, bad airs, and miasmas emitted by swamps and bogs. Of course they were wrong, and in the late nineteenth century other scientists proved that this statistical association was caused by an omitted factor, mosquitoes. Malaria is caused by parasites transmitted by mosquito bites, primarily by the mosquitoes of the genus *Anopheles,* which breed well in swamps, explaining the statistical association between swamps and malaria infection.

In the same way, it is quite possible that an omitted factor, some institutional feature, is the root cause of the poverty of many tropical countries, and the statistical association between geography and poverty is a mere correlation and no more.

In fact, if you want to find a similar statistical association between institutions and prosperity, there is plenty of evidence for that as well. For example, we can measure institutions in terms of the protection for entrepreneurs' property rights—protection against expropriation risk. This is the result of assessments between 1985 and 1995 by Political Risk Services, an organization that collects and compiles this information and sells it to businesspeople contemplating investment in these places. A high score means a high degree of protection against expropriation. Figure 2.1 shows the correlation between this measure of institutions and income per capita today (more accurately, the logarithm of income per capita in 1995, adjusted for purchasing power parity differences across countries).

But, as was the case with geography, this statistical association does not prove causation. It could once again be omitted factors, or even reverse causality: the fact that richer countries can afford better institutions, better protection against arbitrary behavior, and better constitutions, which account for the association depicted in Figure 2.1.

How can we make progress in distinguishing between the roles of geog-

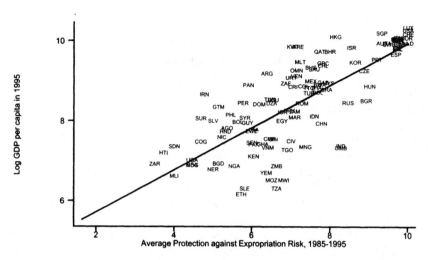

Figure 2.1 Log Income per Capita in 1995 versus Perceived Protection against Expropriation Risk, 1985–1995

raphy and of institutions as fundamental causes of prosperity and poverty? There is relatively little we can learn by looking at correlations, but a lot we can gather by going back in history and making use of the "experiments" that it offers us.

In the natural sciences, causal theories are tested by conducting controlled *experiments*. For example, to investigate whether Tylenol helps with headaches, we would randomly allocate a large number of otherwise similar subjects with headaches into one of two groups, either the treatment group, which will receive Tylenol, or the control group, which will receive a placebo, an apparently identical but actually inactive pill. We will then see whether there is an improvement in the headaches of the treatment group relative to the control group. If the answer is yes, subject to caveats related to statistical power, we can conclude that it is Tylenol that has the causal effect on headaches. This has to be so, since in our experiment all other conditions were kept the same between the two groups.

Controlled experiments are much harder to conduct in the social sciences. We cannot change a country's institutions and watch what happens to the incomes and welfare of its citizens (and that's fortunate!). However, even if we cannot use controlled experiments to test what determines prosperity, history may offer a *natural experiment*, in which we can convincingly argue that one factor changes while other potential determinants for the outcomes of interest remain constant. The remainder of this chapter looks in detail at this experiment.

THE REVERSAL OF FORTUNE

The global colonization by Europeans starting in the fifteenth century was a natural experiment. The colonization experience transformed the institutions in many lands conquered or controlled by Europeans but, by and large, had no effect on their geographies. Therefore, if geography is the key factor determining the economic potential of an area or a country, the places that were rich before the arrival of the Europeans should continue to be rich after colonization and, in fact, today as well. In other words, since the key determinant of prosperity remains the same, we should see a high degree of *persistence* in economic outcomes. If, on the other hand, it is institutions that are central, then those places where good institutions were introduced or developed should get richer compared with those where Europeans introduced or maintained extractive institutions.

Historical evidence suggests that Europeans indeed pursued very different colonization strategies with very different associated institutions in various colonies. At one extreme, Europeans set up extractive institutions, exemplified by the Belgian colonization of the Congo, slave plantations in the Caribbean, and forced labor systems in the mines of Latin America. These institutions introduced neither protection for the property rights of regular citizens nor constraints on the power of elites. This is not surprising, since these institutions were designed to facilitate Europeans' extraction of resources from the colonies.

At the other extreme, many Europeans settled in a number of colonies, creating societies replicating and often improving European forms of institutions protecting private property. Primary examples of this mode of colonization include Australia, New Zealand, Canada, and the United States. The settlers in these societies also managed to place significant constraints on elites and politicians, even if they had to fight to achieve this objective. In both North America and Australia, the plans of the British crown to develop a more hierarchical structure were thwarted by the protests, demonstrations, and migrations of the lower strata of European settlers (indentured servants in North America and descendants of convicts in Australia).

So what happened to economic development after colonization? Did places that were rich before colonization remain rich, as suggested by the geography hypothesis? Or was there a systematic change in economic fortunes associated with the changes in institutions?

The historical evidence shows no evidence of the persistence suggested by the geography hypothesis. On the contrary, there is a remarkable *reversal of fortune* in economic prosperity. Societies—such as the Mughals in India and the Aztecs and the Incas in the Americas—that were among the richest civilizations in 1500 are among the poorer societies of today. In contrast, countries occupying the territories of the less-developed civilizations in North America, New Zealand, and Australia are now much richer than those in the lands of the Mughals, Aztecs, and Incas.

The reversal of fortune is not confined to this comparison. Using proxies for prosperity before modern times, we can show that it is a much more widespread phenomenon. Two useful proxies for income per capita, especially in preindustrial societies, are urbanization rates and population density. Only societies with a certain level of productivity in agriculture and a relatively developed system of transport and commerce could sustain large urban centers and a dense population. Figure 2.2 shows the relationship between income per capita and urbanization (fraction of the population living in urban centers with more than 5,000 inhabitants) today and demonstrates that even in the current period there is a significant relationship between urbanization and prosperity. Naturally, high rates of urbanization do not mean that the majority of the population lived in prosperity. In fact, before the twentieth century urban centers were often highly unhealthy and unequal. Nevertheless, urbanization is a good proxy for average income per capita in society, which closely corresponds to the measure we are using to look at prosperity today.

Figures 2.3 and 2.4 depict the relationship between income per capita today and urbanization rates and (log) population density in 1500. We picked 1500 since it is before European colonization had an effect on any of these societies. A strong negative relationship, indicating a reversal in the rankings in terms of economic prosperity between 1500 and today, is clear in both figures. In fact, the figures show that in 1500 the temperate areas were generally less prosperous than the tropical areas.

This reversal is prima facie evidence against the most standard (simple) versions of the geography hypothesis discussed above: it cannot be that the climate, ecology, or disease environments of the tropical areas condemn them

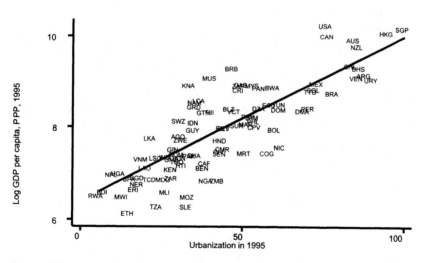

Figure 2.2 Log Income per Capita in 1995 versus Urbanization in 1995

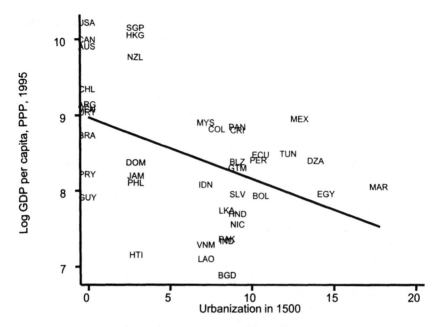

Figure 2.3 Log Income per Capita in 1995 versus Urbanization in 1500

to poverty today, since these areas, with the same climate, ecology, and disease environments, were *richer* than the temperate areas 500 years ago.

Nevertheless, it is possible to develop more sophisticated geography hypotheses predicting time-varying effects of climate, ecology, or disease environments. Perhaps certain geographic characteristics that were not useful, or were even harmful, for successful economic performance in 1500 turned out to be beneficial later on.

A possible example, which can be called "the latitude specific technology hypothesis," argues that areas in the tropics had an early advantage, but later agricultural technologies, such as the heavy plow, crop rotation systems, domesticated animals, and high-yield crops, have favored countries in the temperate areas.[3] However, the evidence is not consistent with this hypothesis. First, the reversal in relative incomes seems to have been related to population density and prosperity before Europeans arrived, not to any inherent geographic characteristics of the area. Furthermore, according to the latitude specific technology hypothesis, the reversal should have occurred when European agricultural technology spread to the colonies. Yet while the introduction of European agricultural techniques, at least in North America, took place earlier, as documented above, the reversal occurred mostly during the nineteenth century and was closely related to industrialization.

The timing and the nature of the reversal do not support other versions of the sophisticated geography hypothesis.[4] Overall, the evidence strongly

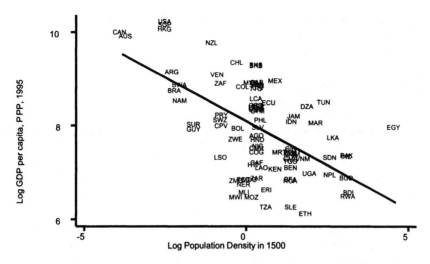

Figure 2.4 Log Income per Capita in 1995 versus Log Population Density in 1500

suggests that the reversal of fortune among the former European colonies is not consistent with theories in which geographic factors are the central determinants of cross-country income differences today.

INSTITUTIONS AND THE REVERSAL

Is the reversal of fortune consistent with the institutions hypothesis? The answer is yes. In fact, once we look at the variation in colonization strategies, we see that the reversal of fortune is exactly what the institutions hypothesis predicts.

European colonialism made Europeans the politically powerful group with the capability to influence institutions more than any indigenous group was able to at the time. As suggested by our discussion above, we expect Europeans to have done so not according to the interest of the society as a whole, but in order to maximize their benefits. And this is exactly what the historical evidence suggests happened.

In places where Europeans did not settle, and thus did not care much about aggregate output or welfare; in places where there was a large population to be coerced and employed cheaply in mines or in agriculture, or simply taxed; in places where there was a lot to be extracted, Europeans pursued the strategy of setting up extractive institutions. In those colonies, there were no constraints on the power of the elites (i.e., the Europeans and their allies), and no civil or property rights for the majority of the population; in fact, many of them were forced laborers or slaves. Contrasting with this pattern, in other colonies Europeans settled in large numbers and developed the laws and institutions of the society to ensure that they themselves were protected in both their political and their economic lives. In these settler colonies, the institutions were therefore much more conducive to investment and economic growth.

This discussion also suggests that Europeans were more likely to invest in the development of institutions of private property in areas that were sparsely settled and previously relatively poor. And this is what the data show. The relatively densely settled and highly urbanized colonies ended up with extractive institutions, while sparsely settled and nonurbanized areas received an influx of European migrants and developed institutions protecting property rights and constraining elites. European colonialism therefore led to an *institutional reversal,* in the sense that the richer places ended up with worse institutions.

To be fair, it is possible the Europeans did not actively introduce extractive institutions in many of these places. The structures of the Mughal, Aztec, and Inca empires were already very hierarchical and nondemocratic, with power concentrated in the hands of rulers. Perhaps the Europeans simply took over these institutions. Whether this is so is secondary for our focus. What matters is that in densely settled and relatively developed places, it was in the interests of Europeans to have extractive institutions, while in the sparsely settled areas it was in their interests to develop institutions of private property, thus leading to the institutional reversal.

The institutional reversal combined with the institutions hypothesis predicts the reversal of fortune: relatively rich places got worse institutions, and if these institutions were really important, we should see these places become relatively poor over time. This is exactly what we find with the reversal of fortune.[5]

We find further support for the view that the reversal of fortune is related to the institutional reversal, and the effect of this institutional reversal on long-run growth, in the fact that there appears to be no comparable reversal among countries not colonized by Europeans between 1500 and today, and nothing of the sort in the colonized or noncolonized samples between 1000 and 1500. Something special, most probably related to changes in institutions, took place in these lands after colonization.

The timing and the nature of the reversal are also consistent with the institutions hypothesis. The initially highly urbanized countries had higher levels of urbanization and prosperity until around 1800. At that time the initially low-urbanization countries started to grow much more rapidly, and a prolonged period of divergence began. There was more industry (per capita and total) in India in 1750 than in the United States. By 1860, the United States and colonies, such as Australia and New Zealand, with relatively good institutions began to move ahead rapidly, and by 1953 a huge gap had opened up.

Recall that the institutions hypothesis links incentives to invest in physical and human capital and in technology to institutions and argues that economic prosperity results from these investments. Therefore, institutions should become more important when there are major new investment opportunities. The opportunity to industrialize is the major investment opportunity of the era. In fact, it would not be an exaggeration to say that countries that are rich today, both among the former European colonies and other countries, are those that industrialized successfully during the nineteenth century.

Moreover, industrialization is precisely the type of process that requires investment from various segments of the society in new technology and commerce, market transactions supported by law and order, and a workforce investing in skills and human capital; in other words, a process that requires the protections offered by institutions of private property. In contrast, before industrialization, a country could be rich from agriculture, such as the relatively prosperous sugar colonies of Barbados, Cuba, Jamaica, and Saint-Domingue, which had highly extractive institutions that concentrated power in the hands of plantation owners. These institutions were probably costly for economic performance even in these largely agricultural societies, but less costly than they would have been if economic activity relied on more investment from a larger segment of society. The fact that former colonies with better institutions should industrialize and pull ahead of the rest during the nineteenth century is thus what the institutions hypothesis predicts.

Therefore, the institutions hypothesis is also consistent with the timing and nature of the reversal, which took place mainly in the nineteenth century and because societies with good institutions took advantage of the opportunity to industrialize, while those with extractive institutions failed to do so.

It is also useful to note that this evidence is not consistent with another hypothesis related to colonialism: that the reversal reflects the heavy plunder of the colonies by Europeans. This hypothesis would be an extension of the Marxist analyses of colonialism and of the development of the modern world economy.[6] But if plunder were the cause of the reversal, we would expect the reversal to happen shortly after colonization, the period of the most intense plunder. Instead, it took place mostly in the nineteenth century, at least for the Americas. This indicates that the reversal was not the direct consequence of colonization per se, but resulted from the institutions that were put in place by the colonial powers with the aim of extracting resources.

MORTALITY OF EUROPEAN SETTLERS: ANOTHER SOURCE OF DIVERGENCE IN INSTITUTIONS

So far we have seen that Europeans pursued different colonization strategies in different places, with very different associated institutions and that a key determinant of whether they set up good institutions or not is whether they settled in large numbers. One factor explains much of the variation in settlement rates of Europeans: the disease environment they faced in the colonies. Europeans, it turns out, had no immunity to the diseases of the tropics, particularly malaria and yellow fever.

Yellow fever is largely eradicated today, but malaria is still endemic in many parts of sub-Saharan Africa and, as discussed above, causes the deaths of millions of children every year. Nevertheless, the majority of the adult inhabitants of areas in which malaria is endemic have either genetic or (more often) acquired immunity, ensuring that they do not die or are not completely incapacitated by even the most deadly strain of malaria, falciparum malaria. In contrast, malaria infection meant almost certain death for Europeans, especially in the nineteenth century, before the causes and prevention of malaria were understood.[7]

As a result of the prevalence of yellow fever and malaria, potential European settlers and European troops faced very different mortality rates in the colonies. For example, before 1850, the annual mortality rates for a settlement size maintained at 1,000 (through replacement) ranged from 8.55 in New Zealand, which was lower than in Europe at that time, to 49 in India, 130 in Jamaica, and around 500 in West Africa. The widely differing mortality rates of settlers led to different settlement rates and to divergent institutional paths for various colonies.

Figure 2.5 shows a very strong association between (the log of) these mortality rates for European settlers and the measure of current institutions used in Figure 2.1, protection against expropriation risk between 1985 and 1995. Institutions today are much worse in places with higher settler mortality. Figure 2.6, in turn, shows a very strong association between these mortality rates and economic prosperity today, again as measured by income

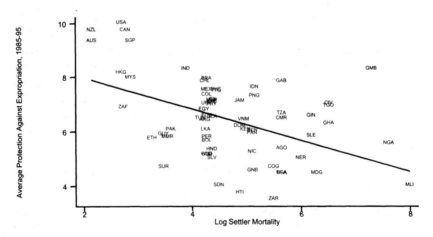

Figure 2.5 Perceived Protection against Expropriation Risk, 1985–1995 versus Log Settler Mortality

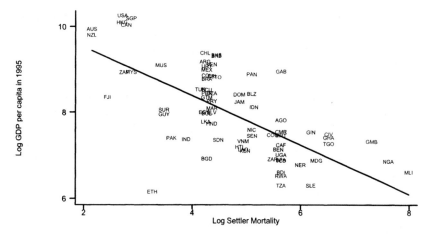

Figure 2.6 Log Income per Capita in 1995 versus Log Settler Mortality

per capita: countries that had lower mortality rates for European settlers are now richer. What explains this pattern?

In Acemoglu, Johnson, and Robinson (2001), we document that this pattern reflects neither the current prevalence of malaria, nor current general health conditions, nor various geographic factors ranging from temperature to humidity, from natural resources to soil quality.[8] Instead, we argue that the association shown in Figure 2.6 works through the effect of these mortality rates on European settlement and institutional development. In places where they faced high mortality rates, Europeans did not settle and typically introduced extractive institutions. Extractive institutions have a lot of staying power; for example, groups who benefit from using the power of the state to expropriate others will resist and attempt to block any move toward better institutions. As a result, in many cases extractive institutions have persisted from colonial times to today and still adversely affect economic growth.

The idea that Figure 2.6 captures the effect of European settler mortality rates working via institutional development, not the direct effect of these diseases, is also supported by the mortality rates of indigenous peoples in these areas. While Europeans faced very high death rates, the indigenous population had mortality rates similar to those of Europeans in their home countries. For example, the annual mortality rates of native troops serving in Bengal and Madras were respectively 11 and 13 in 1,000, similar to—in fact, lower than—the annual mortality rate of British troops serving in Britain, which was approximately 15 in 1,000. In contrast, the death rates of British troops serving in these colonies were much higher because of their lack of immunity to local disease. For example, death rates in Bengal and Madras for British troops were between 70 and 170 in 1,000.

That the relationship in Figure 2.6 does not reflect the direct effect of the disease environment is also consistent with the fact that using only information about the prevalence of yellow fever leads to similar results.[9] Since yellow fever is largely eradicated today, this is unlikely to reflect the direct effect of yellow fever.

The advantage of exploiting this source of variation in institutions is that we can both get a rough sense of how important institutions are in explaining current differences in economic performance, and also test for possible direct effects of various geographic characteristics. The results indicate that differences in institutions across countries today account for the bulk of the differences in economic outcomes. Moreover, once we take the influence of institutions into account, none of these geographic characteristics appear to have a significant effect on income per capita today.[10]

Overall, the evidence both from the reversal of fortune and from the divergent patterns of institutional development driven by differences in European settler mortality rates points to the same conclusion: institutions have a large and quantitatively important effect on economic prosperity today. What's more, once we recognize the importance of institutions for economic performance, geography seems to play a relatively small role in the large cross-country differences in prosperity today.

CONCLUSION: GEOGRAPHY VERSUS INSTITUTIONS

The evidence presented so far makes a fairly convincing case that institutional differences, not geographic factors, are at the root of the very large differences in economic prosperity we observe today. It is true that countries in or near the tropics are poorer than those in temperate areas. However, this does not reflect the effect of climate or ecology on economic outcomes, but simply the fact that a key determinant of prosperity—institutions—differs between these areas. Institutions differ, in turn, because institutions in many parts of the world today are shaped by the colonial history of these areas; Europeans were more likely to settle in the temperate areas and develop institutions encouraging investment and economic progress, and they were more likely to set up extractive institutions in tropical areas and in areas that at the time were more prosperous and densely settled, which were also typically the ones in or near the tropics.

Does all this mean that geography is unimportant? Yes and no. There is no evidence that geography plays a major (quantitatively large) *direct* role in the very large differences in income per capita and growth potential of countries today. But this does not mean that geography is unimportant. It is important in at least four major ways.

First, geography and diseases almost surely matter for economic outcomes. There can be no agriculture at the poles, and it is a truism that healthy individuals will be more productive and motivated in their work, in school, and in their lives. The statement here is that the effects of geography and diseases are not a major factor in explaining the tremendous cross-country differences in prosperity—not that geography and diseases have no economic effects at all.[11]

Second, because geography is not at the root of the tremendous differences in economic prosperity today does not mean that it was unimportant in history. It is quite possible that geographic differences shaped the reasons why some areas were richer than others more than 500 years ago. This must be the primary candidate for explaining why tropical areas among the colonies were more prosperous than temperate ones in 1500. Going even farther back, geographic characteristics must have been important in determining where settled agriculture developed and where humans migrated.

Third, geography could have an effect via institutions, especially during a particular historical juncture. After all, the disease environment is a geographic characteristic of many tropical areas. However, the major effect of disease environments was not direct, but indirect:[12] during the period of European colonization, they determined whether Europeans could settle and, therefore, which types of institutions developed.[13]

Finally, and most importantly, even if geography has no effect on income per capita, it does have significant effects on "social welfare," properly measured. Many parts of the world, especially many parts in the tropics, suffer from poorer health and higher mortality and morbidity than North America and Western Europe, partly because of their geographic characteristics (and partly because the corresponding diseases in North America and Europe have been eradicated as a result of the economic development of these societies!). It is important to understand the social and human costs of disease and act upon them. Many scholars, journalists, and commentators argue that the Western world should invest in the health of less-developed populations and try to reduce mortality and morbidity in these areas because of the economic benefits that these investments will create. Our perspective is that we should undertake such investments on humanitarian and social grounds. After all, we have as much reason to care about the lives of people as about their incomes.

NOTES

1. Due to space constraints, in this essay we cannot do full justice to the range of geography hypotheses. See Acemoglu, Johnson, and Robinson (2002) for more on these views.

2. See North (1981), Bates (1981), and Olson (1982) for a general discussion; Acemoglu and Robinson (2000, 2002) for why elites may block beneficial institutional change because they fear losing their politically privileged position; and Acemoglu (2003) for problems associated with the credibility of striking deals between powerful groups and the rest of the society so as to compensate the latter after institutional changes take place.

3. See, for example, Bloch (1967) or White (1962).

4. Again, see Acemoglu, Johnson, and Robinson (2002) for more discussion.

5. Acemoglu, Johnson, and Robinson (2002) show that the reversal of fortune can be statistically accounted for by the differences in institutions during or after colonial times, further supporting the conclusion in this paragraph.

6. See, for example, Frank (1978) or Wallerstein (1974–1980).

7. See Curtin (1989).

8. Controlling for these geographic characteristics has little effect on the relationship of interest, partly because prevalence of malaria and yellow fever is not related to any simple geographic characteristics.

9. See Acemoglu, Johnson, and Robinson (2001).

10. See Acemoglu, Johnson, and Robinson (2001); see also Easterly and Levine (2003).

11. Existing evidence from microdata on the effect of health on individual economic outcomes indicates significant effects, which are quantitatively at least one order of magnitude smaller than cross-country differences in income per capita, consistent with this conclusion. See, for example, the survey in Acemoglu, Johnson, and Robinson (2003).

12. Similarly, Engerman and Sokoloff (1997) have emphasized how the geography of the Caribbean, which made it an ideal place for sugar production, was a key factor in the development of a plantation economy based on slavery, thus having adverse long-term economic consequences, but through institutions rather than directly.

13. Therefore, not only did these characteristics not have a direct effect, but we should not expect them to have a *universal* effect on economic outcomes via their influence on institutions. Instead, they had an effect on institutional development in the context of European colonialism. If it had happened to be West Africans colonizing Europe and the rest of the world, rather than the other way around, the prevalence of malaria would not have been associated with the development of extractive institutions.

BIBLIOGRAPHY

Acemoglu, Daron. "Why Not a Political Coase Theorem? Social Conflict, Commitment and Politics." *Journal of Comparative Economics* 31 (2003): 620–652.

Acemoglu, Daron, Simon Johnson, and James A. Robinson. "Colonial Origins of Comparative Development: An Empirical Investigation." *American Economic Review* 91 (2001): 1369–1401.

Acemoglu, Daron, Simon Johnson, and James A. Robinson. "Reversal of Fortune: Geography and Institutions in the Making of the Modern World Income Distribution." *Quarterly Journal of Economics* 117 (Nov. 2002): 1231–1294.

Acemoglu, Daron, Simon Johnson, and James A. Robinson. "Disease and Development in Historical Perspective." *Journal of the European Economic Association* 1 (2003): 397–405.

Acemoglu, Daron, and James A. Robinson. "Political Losers as a Barrier to Economic Development." *American Economic Review* 90 (2000): 126–130.

Acemoglu, Daron, and James A. Robinson. "Economic Backwardness in Political Perspective." Working paper 8831, National Bureau of Economic Research, 2002.

Bates, Robert H. *Markets and States in Tropical Africa.* Berkeley: University of California Press, 1981.

Bloch, Marc. *Land and Work in Mediaeval Europe.* New York: Harper & Row, 1967.

Curtin, Philip D. *Death by Migration: Europe's Encounter with the Tropical World in the Nineteenth Century.* New York: Cambridge University Press, 1989.

Diamond, Jared M. *Guns, Germs and Steel: The Fate of Human Societies.* New York: Norton, 1997.

Easterly, William, and Ross Levine. "Tropics, Germs, and Crops: How Endowments Influence Economic Development." *Journal of Monetary Economics* 50 (2003): 3–39.

Engerman, Stanley L., and Kenneth L. Sokoloff. "Factor Endowments, Institutions, and Differential Paths of Growth Among New World Economies." In *How Latin America Fell Behind.* Edited by S. H. Haber. Stanford: Stanford University Press, 1997.

Frank, Andre Gunder. *Dependent Accumulation and Underdevelopment.* London: Macmillan, 1978.

Gurr, Ted Robert. "Polity II: Political Structures and Regime Change, 1800–1986." Unpublished paper, University of Colorado, 1997.

Jones, Eric L. *The European Miracle: Environments, Economies, and Geopolitics in the History of Europe and Asia.* New York: Cambridge University Press, 1981.

Locke, John. *Two Treatises of Government* [1690]. Indianapolis, Ind.: Hackett, 1980.

Maddison, Angus. *The World Economy: A Millennial Perspective.* Paris: Organization for Economic Cooperation and Development, 2001.

McEvedy, Colin, and Richard Jones. *Atlas of World Population History.* New York: Facts on File, 1978.

Montesquieu, Charles de Secondat. *The Spirit of the Laws* [1748]. New York: Cambridge University Press, 1989.

Myrdal, Gunnar. *Asian Drama: An Inquiry into the Poverty of Nations.* 3 vols. New York: Twentieth Century Fund, 1968.

North, Douglass C. *Structure and Change in Economic History.* New York: Norton, 1981.

Olson, Mancur. *The Rise and Decline of Nations: Economic Growth, Stagflation, and Economic Rigidities.* New Haven, Conn.: Yale University Press, 1982.

Sachs, Jeffrey D. "Notes on a New Sociology of Economic Development." In *Culture Matters: How Values Shape Human Progress.* Edited by Lawrence E. Harrison and Samuel P. Huntington. New York: Basic Books, 2000.

Sachs, Jeffrey D. "Tropical Underdevelopment." Working paper 8119, National Bureau of Economic Research, 2001.

Wallerstein, Immanuel M. *The Modern World-System.* 3 vols. New York: Academic Press, 1974–1980.

White, Lynn, Jr. *Medieval Technology and Social Change.* London: Oxford University Press, 1962.

World Health Organization. "Macroeconomics and Health: Investing in Health for Economic Development." 2001. http://www3.who.int/whosis/cmh.

3

Colonialism, Inequality, and Long-Run Paths of Development

Stanley L. Engerman & Kenneth L. Sokoloff

The study, if not the practice, of colonialism is again in fashion. Over the last few years, the institution, especially as pursued by Europeans, has enjoyed a revival in interest among both scholars and the general public. One reason for this reexamination may be sentimentality for a more simply ordered world, since a number of these new accounts cast colonial empires in a more favorable light than has generally been customary. Deepak Lal, for example, argues that those nations that established empires merit praise, because their creations normally brought about lower levels of conflict and costs of carrying out long-distance trade, and also promoted greater prosperity in the affected societies.[1] Niall Ferguson highlights progressive sides to Britain's oversight of her colonies, such as the introduction of efficient civil services and rule of law, as well as the prohibition of slavery.[2] The image of kinder and gentler imperial powers also has some foundation in the work of Lance Davis and Robert Huttenback, who in their meticulous and detailed estimates found that Britain was not nearly so aggressive or successful in extracting returns from its colonies as she could have been, and indeed that her empire generated little in the way of returns for the home country overall.[3]

Quite a different motivation, however, has been behind the recent proliferation of studies by economists of the European effort to colonize most of the rest of the world.[4] Inspired by the goal of improving understanding of the processes and institutions of economic growth, these scholars have been attracted by the quasi-natural experiment generated by a small number of countries establishing many colonies across a wide range of environments. The logic is that the historical record of these different societies can be analyzed to determine whether there were systematic patterns in how their institutions or economies evolved with respect to initial conditions. For example, have colonies with a British heritage, or those in a particular sort of physical environment, realized more economic progress over time than their counterparts have? In other words, the history of European colonization provides scholars with a rich supply of evidence, or a laboratory, that can be used to study economic performance and the evolution of institutions over the long run. Because some of the characteristics of the colonies were in place at or near the time of settlement, and thus can reasonably be treated as exogenous, many economists have been hopeful that the data generated by their later development can be used to get at causal relationships or mechanisms.

Inequality is one of the key variables that emerge from these studies as of great consequence to long-run paths of development. Moreover, not only does extreme inequality seem to have had a profound influence on societies so afflicted, but the dynamics of European settlement generated many colonies in that condition. Several research teams have arrived at similar conclusions, but perhaps the most direct examination of the impact of inequality has been the work we have done on the economies of the Americas. Our investigation began with a question: Why was it that for at least 250 years after the Europeans arrived to colonize the so-called New World, most observers regarded the English, French, Dutch, and Spanish settlements on the northern part of the North American continent as relative backwaters with limited economic prospects, and that the flows of resources to the Americas mirrored that view? The simple answer is that per capita incomes, especially for those of European descent, were higher in at least parts of the Caribbean and South America than they were in the colonies that were to become the United States and Canada well into the late eighteenth and early nineteenth centuries. Looking back from the vantage point of the early twenty-first century, however, it is clear that the real puzzle is why the first colonies established by Europeans in the Americas were those that fell behind—and, conversely, why the societies populated by those who came later and had to settle in areas considered less favorable have proved more successful economically over the long run.

A traditional and popular explanation for these intriguing patterns credits the success of the North American economies to the superiority of English institutional heritage, or to the better fit of Protestant beliefs with market institutions.[5] However, proponents of this interpretation generally neglect the implications of the fact that different British colonies in the New World evolved quite distinct societies and sets of economic institutions, despite beginning with roughly the same legal and cultural background and drawing immigrants from similar places and economic classes. British Guiana (now Guyana), Jamaica, and British Honduras (now Belize) are among the many whose records of development stand in stark contrast with those of the United States and Canada, but resemble those of neighboring societies of different national heritages. Impressed with how the evidence seemed inconsistent with the notions that British heritage or Protestantism was the key factor, we instead offered an alternative explanation of the divergent paths of development among the societies of the Americas. We highlighted how the great majority of European colonies in the New World came to be characterized early in their histories, primarily because of their factor endowments, by extreme inequality in the distributions of wealth, human capital, and political influence. We argued, moreover, that these initial differences in inequality were of major import, because societies that began with great inequality tended, as compared with the small number—including those that came to make up the United States and Canada—that began with relative equality and homogeneity of the population, to evolve institutions that contributed to the persistence of substantial inequality and generally poor records of development over the long run.[6]

What led to such substantial differences in inequality across colonies? Briefly put, extreme inequality arose in the colonies of the Caribbean and in Brazil because their soils and climates gave them a comparative advantage in growing sugar and other lucrative crops that were produced at lowest cost during the seventeenth, eighteenth, and nineteenth centuries on very large slave plantations. These colonies soon specialized heavily in their comparative advantage, and with the consequent importation of enormous numbers of slaves, their populations came to be composed of a small elite of European descent and a dominant share of the population (generally 85% or more) consisting of black slaves or (later) nonwhite freedmen and their descendants. Extreme inequality in wealth and human capital came to characterize much of Spanish America as well. The inequality here arose from the endowment of large populations of Native Americans and from the Spanish practices (which were influenced by preexisting Native American organizations in Mexico and Peru) of awarding claims on land, native labor, and rich mineral resources to members of the elite (whose number was limited by restrictive immigration policies). However, some societies, such as Argentina, Uruguay, and Costa Rica, were less affected. In contrast, the societies of the northern part of North America developed with relative equality and population homogeneity because there were relatively few Native Americans on the East Coast where the colonies were established, and the climates and soils favored a regime of mixed farming centered on grains and livestock that exhibited quite limited economies of scale in production.

Although the Americas provide a particularly well-suited context for the study of the impact of inequality on institutional and economic development, the patterns in that part of the world may well have important implications for the experience of societies established as European colonies elsewhere. With the exceptions of Australia and New Zealand, European settlements in other parts of the world were not based upon large numbers of European settlers who became the key productive laborers, but upon small numbers who remained on the perimeter of the country and exercised control through military power or political arrangements with the local rulers. For example,

the Portuguese, Dutch, British, and French sailed around the Cape of Good
Hope, at roughly the same time as they went to the Americas, to acquire
territories and control of large native populations in Asia. The numbers of
European settlers were few and they were generally involved in either political
administration or in operating very large agricultural units. As in the Caribbean, these settler populations were rarely directly employed in producing
commodities for sale in European markets, and their primary concern was
more with control than with the production of economic surpluses. As for
Africa, the early European settlements on the coast, mainly trading forts,
were not able to exercise control over the native population. Even when
Europeans were able to move inland during the 19th century, after the introduction of quinine, European domination was achieved with relatively few
settlers through arrangements with local powers or via military prowess. (The
main exception to this generalization is South Africa, but even here those of
European descent accounted for about 20% of the population.) The last to
be settled of the European colonies were the Pacific Ocean islands, including
Fiji and Hawaii. There too, and particularly where sugar could be grown,
Europeans accounted for only small proportions of the population. In virtually all of these colonies, suffrage was restricted and expenditures on education and other public services tended to be miniscule, reflecting (and
contributing to) the magnitude of the inequality that existed between those
of European descent and others.

Almost everywhere Europeans settled during their grand epoch of expansion across the globe, they did so with higher levels of wealth, human capital
(including literacy and familiarity with technology and markets), and political
influence or power than the natives enjoyed. Where the Europeans encountered large native populations who survived contact with Western diseases
and were colonized, as in Mexico, Peru, Indonesia, and India, their small
shares in the population, and the scarcity of their human capital, generally
meant that they did extremely well relative to the bulk of the natives and
that there was great inequality. Where they moved into fairly empty or de-
populated territories, however (as in Australia, New Zealand, Canada, and
the United States), relative equality tended to prevail.[7] Colonies in the former
category often had comparative advantages quite different from those of Europe (due to different climates and valuable natural resources), and since
free workers were motivated primarily by the prospects of economic returns,
they generally attracted the greater number of Europeans until the nineteenth
century, when the greater opportunities associated with industrialization
shifted attention to North America.[8] Overall, it seems likely that the phenomenon of European colonization generating many societies with very high,
and some with quite low, degrees of inequality was not confined to the
Americas.

INEQUALITY AND INSTITUTIONS

The stark contrasts in the degree of initial inequality across the European colonies in the Americas, if not elsewhere, present scholars with a wonderful opportunity to study whether and how inequality affects the processes and path of development. Whereas previous treatments of the impact of inequality on growth have often been concerned with how savings or investment rates might be affected, we and other scholars who have sought to use the natural experiment provided by colonization focus on the hypothesis that extreme differences in the extent of inequality across colonies gave rise to systematic differences in the ways institutions evolved, and in turn on paths of development.[9] The argument is that greater equality or homogeneity among the population led, over time, to more democratic political institutions, to more investment in public goods and infrastructure, and to institutions that offered relatively broad access to property rights and economic opportunities.[10] In contrast, where there was extreme inequality, political institutions were less democratic, investments in public goods and infrastructure were far more limited, and the institutions that evolved, tended to provide highly unbalanced (favoring elites) access to property rights and economic opportunities. The resulting differences in access to opportunities may be important in accounting for the disparate records of long-term growth, because where processes of early industrialization have been sustained (such as in Britain and the United States during the nineteenth century, and even East Asia in the twentieth), they have generally involved broad participation in the commercial economy. Economies that provided only narrow access to opportunities might have been, and might be, less capable of realizing sustained economic growth.

There are various mechanisms through which the extent of inequality in a society might affect the character of institutions that develop. The avenue that typically receives the most attention works through political inequality. When political power or influence is concentrated among a small segment of the population, that group is able to shape policies or institutions to its advantage. We expect members of such elites to act in their own interest, for example, by inducing the government to make investments and provide services they favor while being assessed for a less than proportionate share of the costs, or to define and enforce property and other sorts of rights in ways that treat them in a preferential manner. Some activity of this sort is present in all societies, because the distribution of political influence is never entirely equal, and those with more resources generally fare better in the competition over influencing the government. But the extent and ultimate impact of such activity can vary even across nominal democracies, especially when the right to vote depends on literacy or wealth (or other attributes), or where ballots are not secret. The absence of democracy, or a situation when one class of the population has the capability to impose its will by force if need be, is an extreme case of how political inequality can lead to institutions that favor a narrow range of the population.

The importance of political inequality (or military might) often figures prominently in discussions of how institutions are established in colonies. The presumption that those with a monopoly of force or a dominant share of the votes get their way does not seem unreasonable. Nevertheless, it is worth reflecting on the relevance of the modern adage: *you can't always get what you want.*[11] No matter how much inequality there is in political influence or in any other dimension, there are frequently constraints that inconveniently narrow the range of feasible possibilities for the fortunate individual or class. The initial objects of the colonies established in the Americas, and indeed elsewhere in the world, were generally the same—to generate economic returns for the respective European country. Although the goals may have been similar, the diverse environments in which the colonies were located led to a variety of economic structures and institutions as the colonizers sought to take best advantage of the different opportunities and challenges they faced. Miscalculations of the effects of various institutional designs, with resulting unintended consequences, were of course not uncommon. The colonists came with similar backgrounds and institutional heritages, but heterogeneity developed as they applied and adapted the technologies and institutional heritages they brought with them to conditions quite unlike those in the Old World. Moreover, the extent to which the metropolis, or any political authority, could effectively specify the institutions prevailing in any colony varied with the local circumstances.

It is well known that in many of the Spanish colonies in Latin America, especially where aboriginal populations were concentrated, a relatively small number of individuals were favored with large grants of land and long-enduring claims on labor and tribute from natives. Less fully appreciated, however, is that there were also efforts to implant a European-style organization of agriculture based on concentrated ownership of land combined with labor provided by tenant farmers or indentured servants in many of the colonies of North America, as when Pennsylvania, New York, Maryland, and Canada were established. (The same could be said for Australia.) But these attempts invariably failed; large landholdings unraveled because even men of ordinary means were able to set up and flourish as independent farmers where land was abundant and cheap, labor was scarce, and scale economies were absent. Despite William Penn having received the royal charter for Pennsylvania, and accordingly having initial control of the territory, such conditions frustrated the attempts of this fabulously wealthy member of the elite to replicate an English-style organization of agriculture in the New World. As much as wealthy men such as Penn might have liked, in an ideal world, to institute hierarchical institutions that greatly advantaged those of their class, their ability to attain that goal was tempered by the need to attract more labor, and more productive labor, to their respective colonies; that is, even landowners were desirous of taking steps that would attract more migrants from Europe and elsewhere. Similarly, the Puritans who settled in the Massachusetts Bay Colony might have liked to do as their brethren who chose to establish their early seventeenth-century colony on Providence Island (off the coast of Nicaragua) and rely on Native Americans, indentured servants, or slaves to perform their manual labor, but the cold, harsh climate in New England would not support such a commercial strategy.[12] Indeed, a century later New Englanders despaired of being able to afford the high prices slaves commanded in the international market.[13]

These cases suggest that political inequality alone was not sufficient for elites to obtain institutions that greatly advantaged them with respect to government policies or access to property rights and other kinds of economic opportunities. In some environments, even when political or military power was highly concentrated in their hands, elites may have voluntarily, and without threat of violent upheaval, found it in their interest to provide better conditions and treatment to the humble. Although a variety of factors might lead to such an evidently anomalous outcome and ways of characterizing them, the relative scarcity of labor seems, in the context of the European colonies, to have been a crucial one. Where labor was relatively scarce, as compared with land and other resources, political inequality was not accompanied by economic inequality. In such circumstances, the lack of economic inequality (or relative equality) circumscribed how far political elites could go in designing institutions to the advantage of their members. In a situation where there was relative political equality, however, economic inequality—as reflected in the relative scarcity of a factor in somewhat elastic supply—might lead to institutions that maximized the advantage of that scarce factor. Hence, economic inequality can sometimes, in the sorts of conditions that are not uncommon in colonies or less-developed countries (with an abundance of unskilled labor but a scarcity of capital and skilled labor), exert more of an influence on the way institutions evolve than political inequality per se can.

SUFFRAGE AND SCHOOLING

Comparative study of the record of the long-term development of the societies of the Americas supports our hypothesis that there were empirical regularities in the ways strategic institutions evolved, such that those that began as colonies with relatively extreme inequality were more restrictive in providing access to economic opportunities and less oriented toward investing in public goods and infrastructure than were those that began with relative equality or homogeneity among the population. This pattern contributed to the long-term persistence of extreme inequality among the former group, and may also help to explain why their long-term records of economic growth have been mediocre at best, relative to those of the latter and especially relative to expectations during the era of European colonization. The specific mechanisms that worked to produce the divergence in institutional and other developments are complex and difficult to discern, but it seems clear that they often involved factors other than differences in the political power of the elite.

It has long been recognized that the conduct of elections, including who holds the right to vote, is one of the most crucial institutions. Varying the rules or organization of how votes are cast and of who casts them can have a fundamental impact on the policy choices that the elected representatives— who in some sense constitute the collective government of the electors— make. Since governments generally have a monopoly of power over certain important activities, there are often major implications for how a society's resources or wealth is distributed across the population, as well as for the pace of economic growth. Given what is at stake, it should not be surprising that throughout history many have fought and died over both the design of the rules and the outcomes of elections. Most of the societies of the Americas had achieved independence from their colonial masters and were at least nominal democracies by the early nineteenth century, and thus our estimates (see Table 3.1) of how broadly the franchise was extended over time and of what fractions of respective populations actually voted in elections have a direct bearing on the extent to which elites based largely on wealth, human capital, race, and gender held disproportionate political power in their respective countries, and on whether and how initial differences in such power or influence persisted.

It was common in all countries to reserve the right to vote to adult males until the twentieth century (in the United States, white adult males until after the Civil War), but the estimates reveal that the United States and Canada were the clear leaders in doing away with restrictions based on wealth and literacy and much higher fractions of the populations voted in these countries than anywhere else in the Americas. Not only did the United States and Canada attain the secret ballot and extend the franchise even to the poor and illiterate much earlier (restrictions that were reintroduced in the United States at the expense of blacks and immigrants in the 1890s), but the evolution of the proportion of the population that voted was at least a half-century ahead of even the most democratic countries of South America (Uruguay, Argentina, and Costa Rica, which have generally been regarded as among the most egalitarian of Latin American societies and whose initial factor endowments most closely resembled those of the United States and Canada).

It is remarkable that as late as 1900, none of the countries in Latin America had the secret ballot or more than a minuscule fraction of the population casting votes.[14] The great majority of European nations, as well as the United States and Canada, achieved secrecy in balloting and universal adult male suffrage long before other countries in the western hemisphere, and the proportions of the populations voting in the former were always higher, often four to five times higher, than those in the latter. Although many factors may have contributed to the low levels of participation in South America

Table 3.1: Laws Governing the Franchise and the Extent of Voting in Selected Countries, 1840–1940

		Lack of Secrecy in Balloting	Wealth Requirement	Literacy Requirement	Proportion of the Population Voting (%)
1840–80					
Chile	1869	N	Y	Y	1.6
	1878	N	N	N[1]	—
Costa Rica	1880	Y	Y	Y	—
Ecuador	1848	Y	Y	Y	0.0
	1856	Y	Y	Y	0.1
Mexico	1840	Y	Y	Y	—
Peru	1875	Y	Y	Y	—
Uruguay	1840	Y	Y	Y	—
	1880	Y	Y	Y	—
Venezuela	1840	Y	Y	Y	—
	1880	Y	Y	Y	—
Canada	1867	Y	Y	N	7.7
	1878	N	Y	N	12.9
United States	1850[2]	N	N	N	12.9
	1880	N	N	N	18.3
1881–1920					
Argentina	1896	Y	Y	Y	1.8[3]
	1916	N	N	N	9.0
Brazil	1894	Y	Y	Y	2.2
	1914	Y	Y	Y	2.4
Chile	1881	N	N	N	3.1
	1920	N	N	Y	4.4
Colombia	1918[4]	N	N	N	6.9
Costa Rica	1912	Y	Y	Y	—
	1919	Y	N	N	10.6
Ecuador	1888	N	Y	Y	2.8
	1894	N	N	Y	3.3
Mexico	1920	N	N	N	8.6
Peru	1920	Y	Y	Y	—
Uruguay	1900	Y	Y	Y	—
	1920	N	N	N	13.8
Venezuela	1920	Y	Y	Y	—
Canada	1911	N	N	N	18.1
	1917	N	N	N	20.5
United States	1900	N	N	Y[5]	18.4
	1920	N	N	Y	25.1

continued

		Lack of Secrecy in Balloting	Wealth Require-ment	Literacy Require-ment	Proportion of the Population Voting (%)
1921–40					
Argentina	1928	N	N	N	12.8%
	1937	N	N	N	15.0
Bolivia	1951	?	Y	Y	4.1
Brazil	1930	Y	Y	Y	5.7
Colombia	1930	N	N	N	11.1
	1936	N	N	N	5.9
Chile	1931	N	N	Y	6.5
	1938	N	N	Y	9.4
Costa Rica	1940	N	N	N	17.6
Ecuador	1940	N	N	Y	3.3
Mexico	1940	N	N	N	11.8
Peru	1940	N	N	Y	—
Uruguay	1940	N	N	N	19.7
Venezuela	1940	N	Y	Y	—
Canada	1940	N	N	N	41.1
United States	1940	N	N	Y	37.8

[1]After eliminating wealth and education requirements in 1878, Chile instituted a literacy requirement in 1885, which seems to have been responsible for a sharp decline in the proportion of the population who were registered to vote.

[2]Three states, Connecticut, Louisiana, and New Jersey, still maintained wealth requirements at 1840, but eliminated them soon afterwards. All states except for Illinois and Virginia had implemented the secret ballot by the end of the 1840s.

[3]This figure is for the city of Buenos Aires, and likely overstates the proportion who voted at the national level.

[4]The information on restrictions refers to national laws. The 1863 Constitution empowered provincial state governments to regulate electoral affairs. Afterwards, elections became restricted (in terms of the franchise for adult males) and indirect in some states. It was not until 1948 that a national law established universal adult male suffrage throughout the country. This pattern was followed in other Latin American countries, as it was in the U.S. and Canada to a lesser extent.

[5]Eighteen states, 7 southern and 11 non-southern, introduced literacy requirements between 1890 and 1926. These restrictions were directed primarily at Blacks and immigrants.

Notes and Sources: Engerman, Haber, and Sokoloff 2000.

and the Caribbean, wealth and literacy requirements were serious binding constraints. Some societies, such as Barbados, maintained wealth-based suffrage restrictions until the mid-twentieth century, while most joined the United States and Canada in moving away from economic requirements in the nineteenth century. Whereas the states in the United States frequently adopted explicit racial limitations when they abandoned economic requirements, however, Latin American countries typically chose to screen by literacy.

The contrast between the United States and Canada, on the one hand, and the Latin American countries, on the other, was not so evident at the outset. Despite the sentiments popularly attributed to the Founding Fathers, voting in the United States was largely a privilege reserved for white men with significant amounts of property until early in the nineteenth century. By 1815, only four states had adopted universal white male suffrage, but as the movement to do away with political inequality gained strength, the rest of the country followed suit: virtually all new entrants into the Union extended voting rights to all white men (with explicit racial restrictions and very favorable definitions of residence for white immigrants generally introduced in the same state constitutions that did away with economic requirements), and older states revised their laws in the wake of protracted political debates. The rapid extension of access to the franchise in the frontier states, which were distinguished by both more equal distributions of wealth and labor scarcity, not coincidentally paralleled liberal policies toward public schools and access to land, as well as other policies that were expected to be attractive to potential migrants.[15] It is hard to avoid the conclusion that political equality was the result of economic equality rooted in labor scarcity, rather than the reverse. It is striking that pioneers in extending suffrage, such as new states of the United States, Argentina, and Uruguay, did so during periods in which they hoped to attract migrants, such that the rights to suffrage formed part of a package of policies thought to be attractive to those contemplating relocation.[16] When elites—such as holders of land or other assets—desire common men to locate in the polity, they thus may choose to extend access to privileges and opportunities even in the absence of threats of civil disorder; indeed, a polity (or one set of elites) may find itself competing with another to attract the labor or other resources.[17] Alternative explanations, such as the importance of national heritage, are not very useful in identifying why Argentina, Uruguay, and Costa Rica pulled so far ahead of their Latin American neighbors, or why other British colonies in the New World lagged behind Canada.

Schooling institutions provide yet another appropriate and important test of whether societies that began with extreme inequality exhibited different patterns of investment in public goods and of access to economic opportunities. Increases in a society's levels of schooling and literacy have been related both theoretically and empirically to many socioeconomic changes conducive to growth, including higher labor productivity, more rapid technological change, and higher rates of commercial and political participation.[18] Although many New World societies arising out of European colonization were so prosperous that they clearly had the material resources to support and attain leadership in literacy by establishing a widespread network of primary schools, only a few made such investments on a scale sufficient to serve the general population before the twentieth century. The exceptional societies, in terms of leadership in investing in institutions of primary education, were the United States and Canada (see Table 3.2). Virtually from the time of settlement, the populations of these countries seem generally to have been convinced of the value of providing their children with a basic education, including the ability to read and write. It was common for schools to be organized and funded at the village or town level, especially in New England. The United States probably had the most literate population in the world by the beginning of the nineteenth century, but the common school movement, which got under way in the 1820s (following closely after the movement to extend the franchise), put the country on an accelerated path of investment in educational institutions. Between 1825 and 1850, nearly every northern state that had not already done so, enacted a law strongly encouraging or requiring localities to establish free schools open to all children and supported by general taxes.[19] Schools were also widespread in early nineteenth-century Canada, and although this northernmost English colony lagged the United States by several decades in establishing tax-supported schools with universal access, its literacy rates were nearly as high.[20]

The rest of the hemisphere trailed far behind the United States and Canada in primary schooling and the attainment of literacy. Despite enormous wealth, the British colonies were very slow to organize schooling institutions that would serve broad segments of the population.[21] Similarly, even the most progressive Latin American countries, such as Argentina and Uruguay, were more than seventy-five years behind the United States and Canada in this regard. These societies began to boost their investments in public schooling at roughly the same time that they intensified their efforts to attract migrants from Europe, well before they implemented a general liberalization of the franchise. While this association might be interpreted as providing for the socialization of foreign immigrants, it also suggests that the elites may have been inclined to extend access to opportunities as part of an effort to attract the scarce labor for which they were directly or indirectly competing. The latter perspective is supported by the observation that major investments in primary schooling did not generally occur in any Latin American country until the national governments provided the funds; in contrast to the pattern in North America, local and state governments in Latin America were not willing or able to take on this responsibility on their own. Most of these societies did not achieve high levels of literacy until well into the twentieth century. Fairly generous support was made available, however, for universities and other institutions of higher learning that were more geared toward children of the elite.

Table 3.2: Literacy Rates in the Americas, 1850–1950

	Year	Ages	Rate (%)
Argentina	1869	+6	23.8
	1895	+6	45.6
	1900	+10	52.0
	1925	+10	73.0
Barbados	1946	+10	92.7
Bolivia	1900	+10	17.0
Brazil	1872	+7	15.8
	1890	+7	14.8
	1900	+7	25.6
	1920	+10	30.0
	1939	+10	57.0
British Honduras	1911	+10	59.6
(Belize)	1931	+10	71.8
Chile	1865	+7	18.0
	1875	+7	25.7
	1885	+7	30.3
	1900	+10	43.0
	1925	+10	66.0
	1945	+10	76.0
Colombia	1918	+15	32.0
	1938	+15	56.0
	1951	+15	62.0
Costa Rica	1892	+7	23.6
	1900	+10	33.0
	1925	+10	64.0
Cuba	1861	+7	23.8
			(38.5, 5.3)*
	1899	+10	40.5
	1925	+10	67.0
	1946	+10	77.9
Guatemala	1893	+7	11.3
	1925	+10	15.0
	1945	+10	20.0
Honduras	1887	+7	15.2
	1925	+10	29.0
Jamaica	1871	+5	16.3
	1891	+5	32.0
	1911	+5	47.2
	1943	+5	67.9
	1943	+10	76.1
Mexico	1900	+10	22.2
	1925	+10	36.0
	1946	+10	48.4

continued

Table 3.2: continued

	Year	Ages	Rate (%)
Paraguay	1886	+7	19.3
	1900	+10	30.0
Peru	1925	+10	38.0
Puerto Rico	1860	+7	11.8
			(19.8, 3.1)*
Uruguay	1900	+10	54.0
	1925	+10	70.0
Venezuela	1925	+10	34.0
Canada	1861	All	82.5
English-majority counties	1861	All	93.0
French-majority counties	1861	All	81.2
United States			
North Whites	1850	+10	96.9
South Whites	1850	+10	91.5
All	1870	+10	80.0
			(88.5, 21.1)*
	1890	+10	86.7
			(92.3, 43.2)*
	1910	+10	92.3
			(95.0, 69.5)*

*The figures for Whites and Non-Whites are reported respectively within parentheses.
Sources: Engerman, Haber, and Sokoloff 2000.

Two mechanisms help explain why extreme levels of inequality depressed investments in schooling. First, in settings where private schooling predominated or where parents paid user fees for their children's schooling, greater wealth or income inequality would generally reduce the fraction of the school-age population enrolled, holding per capita income constant. Second, greater inequality likely exacerbated the collective action problems associated with the establishment and funding of universal public schools, either because the distribution of benefits across the population was quite different from the incidence of taxes and other costs, or simply because the population's heterogeneity made it more difficult for communities to reach consensus on public projects. Where the wealthy enjoyed disproportionate political power, they were able to procure schooling services for their own children and to resist being taxed to underwrite or subsidize services to others.

Indeed, this sort of interpretation is supported by examination of the structures of public finance employed across the Americas over time. At the national government level, taxes on international trade were the principal source of tax revenue throughout the hemisphere after the wave of independence movements of the late eighteenth and early nineteenth centuries. In the United States, a 1789 law establishing the tariff was one of the first laws enacted by the federal government. Although the federal government had other sources of revenue, customs duties provided by far the dominant share of national government revenue up through the Civil War. In rough terms, these revenues amounted to 1 to 2% of GNP (except for spurts during war-time) and were primarily (over 80%) directed to defense, interest on debt, general government expenses, and other miscellaneous expenditures. The patterns were roughly the same in Latin America. In Mexico, for example, port taxes, income from the tobacco monopoly, and excise taxes yielded 75 to 85% of national government revenue over the latter half of the nineteenth century. In Colombia, customs duties and income from state monopolies on commodities such as tobacco and salt brought in nearly 80% of national revenues by the 1840s. Overall, although wars and other threats to the social order (such as the War of 1812, the U.S. Civil War, the war between Mexico and the United States, and various internal uprisings) sometimes stimulated the imposition of direct taxes that extended the reach of national govern-ments in progressive directions (the income tax in the United States during the Civil War, and the Mexican property tax that was introduced because of the war between that country and the United States), the general pattern throughout the hemisphere well into the twentieth century was reliance by national governments on tax structures that targeted commodities or trade rather than income or wealth.[22]

Stark differences existed across the societies of the Americas, however, in the size and revenue sources of state/provincial and local governments. Local governments were much smaller in Latin American nations than in the United States and Canada (see Table 3.3). They accounted for only about 10% of total government revenue in Brazil, Colombia, and Mexico through-out the nineteenth century (and in Chile, between 10 and 20% during the second decade of the twentieth century, despite the absence of state/provin-cial governments). The contrast with the neighboring societies in North America is dramatic. In both the United States and Canada, the local gov-ernments collected more than half of overall government revenue from the middle of the nineteenth century onward. Even as late as the 1930s, the share of local government revenue was near 40% in both the United States and Canada.

This predisposition of the North American populations to organize and support local governments was evident as early as the seventeenth century, despite the absence during that era of distinctively (as compared with other societies in the Americas) high per capita incomes. It is not entirely clear how substantial local governments were at the establishment of the United States, but local governments certainly grew very rapidly during the early decades of the nineteenth century as the common school movement pro-gressed, and as local governments were increasingly engaged in helping to organize new investments in roads and other infrastructure required as the economy began to industrialize. What is apparent is that, with a few brief

Table 3.3: Distribution of Tax Revenues Across Levels of Government during the 19th and 20th Centuries: Brazil, Chile, Colombia, Mexico, Canada, and the United States

	National Government (%)	Provincial Governments (%)	Municipalities or Other Local (%)
Brazil			
1826	30.8	69.2	0
1856	79.5	17.1	3.3
1860	78.2	18.2	3.5
1885/86	76.3	18.5	5.2
Chile			
1913	85.8	—	14.2
1915	82.7	—	17.3
1920	85.3	—	14.7
Colombia			
1839	88.4	2.9	8.7
1842	91.8	1.6	6.7
1850	85.4	8.7	5.8
1870	46.6	30.8	22.6
1894	60	32	8
1898	66.7	28.6	4.8
Mexico			
1882	69.1	19.5	11.5
1890	74.7	16.3	9
1900	67.3	19.8	12.9
1908	70.6	17.1	12.3
Canada			
1933	42.5	17.9	39.6
1950	68.7	18.7	12.6
1960	62.8	20.7	16.4
United States			
1855	25.5	17.4	57.1
1875	39.6	16.4	44.0
1895	36	14	50
1913	29.1	13.2	57.6
1927	35.5	18	46.5
1950	68.3	17.3	14.4

Sources and Notes: Sokoloff and Zolt 2004.

exceptions during and after major wars, local governments were the largest component of the overall government sector throughout the nineteenth century. This is especially striking because the aggregate pattern of expenditures by local governments was quite progressive, in that, well into the nineteenth century, their main priorities were schools, roads, and other infrastructure that generate broadly distributed social returns.[23] Moreover, their heavy reliance on the property tax, together with their large share of the government sector, made for a rather progressive tax structure at both the local and national (the aggregate of all levels of government together) levels.[24] This pattern, characterized by property and inheritance taxes accounting for the bulk of the revenue collected by governments at all levels, endured into the early decades of the twentieth century (a similar pattern holds in Canada).[25] In contrast, although the local governments in Latin America were somewhat like their North American counterparts in raising relatively more revenue from taxes on property and income than did the respective national or state/ provincial governments, they did so to a much lesser extent. This, together with the markedly smaller size of local governments in Latin American nations, resulted in radically different, and much less progressive, aggregate tax structures overall than in the United States or Canada.

Although there may be other explanations for these patterns in the evolution of tax institutions, the evidence is consistent with the hypothesis that initial differences in the extent of inequality across these societies contributed to the different decisions they made regarding how much revenue to raise, the relative use of different tax instruments, the nature and size of state and local governments, and the types and sizes of government expenditure programs. In general, the countries that began with more inequality developed structures of public finance that relied relatively more on indirect taxes and placed less of a tax burden on those with higher levels of wealth. This alone should have encouraged the persistence of extreme inequality, but the stunted local governments, the authorities most concerned with public schooling, transportation, water/sewer projects, and other types of investment projects that generate benefits for a broad spectrum of the population, also worked in the same direction. An explanation for this pattern is readily available. With a radically unequal distribution of resources, elites would bear most of any tax burden, especially one levied on wealth or income, and realize smaller than proportionate benefits, especially since they could privately procure many of the same services for themselves and their families. It was only in the twentieth century, when returns to schooling grew, when suffrage came to be extended, and when import-substitution policies sharply reduced the revenues that could be captured from imports, that the structures of public finance in Latin America began to change in more progressive directions.

Land policy offers a final example of the ways in which institutions may have contributed to the persistence of inequality over the long run. Virtually all the economies in the Americas had ample supplies of public lands well into the nineteenth century and beyond. Since the respective governments of each colony, province, or nation were regarded as the owners of this resource, they were able to influence the distribution of wealth, as well as the pace of settlement for effective production, by implementing policies to control the availability of land, set prices, establish minimum or maximum acreages, provide credit for the purchase of land, and design tax systems. Because agriculture was the dominant sector throughout the Americas, questions of how best to employ this public resource for the national interest, and how to make the land available for private use, were widely recognized as highly important and often became the subject of protracted political debates and struggles. Land policy was also used to affect the labor force, either by encouraging immigration through making land readily available or by influencing the regional distribution of labor (or supply of wage labor) through limiting access and raising land prices.

The United States never experienced major obstacles in this regard, and the terms of land acquisition became easier over the course of the nineteenth century.[26] The Homestead Act of 1862, which essentially made land free, in plots suitable for family farms, to all those who settled and worked the land for a specified period, was perhaps the culmination of this policy of promoting broad access to land. Canada pursued similar policies: the Dominion Lands Act of 1872 closely resembled the Homestead Act in both spirit and substance. Argentina and Brazil instituted similar changes in the second half of the nineteenth century as a means to encourage immigration, but these efforts were much less directed, and thus less successful at getting land to smallholders than the programs in the United States and Canada.[27] In Argentina, for example, a number of factors explain the contrast in outcomes. First, the elites of Buenos Aires, whose interests favored keeping scarce labor in the province if not in the capital city, were much more effective at weakening or blocking programs than were their urban counterparts in North America. Second, even those policies nominally intended to broaden access tended to involve large grants to land developers (with the logic that allocative efficiency could best be achieved through exchanges between private agents) or transfers to occupants who were already using the land (including those who were grazing livestock). They thus generally conveyed public lands to private owners in much larger and more concentrated holdings than did the policies in the United States and Canada. Third, the processes by which large landholdings might have broken up in the absence of scale economies may have operated very slowly in Argentina: once the land was in private hands, its potential value for grazing may have set too high a floor on land prices for immigrants and other ordinary would-be farmers. Such constraints were exacerbated by the underdevelopment of mortgage and financial institutions more generally.[28]

Argentina, Canada, and the United States had an extraordinary abundance of virtually uninhabited public lands to transfer to private hands in the interest of bringing this public resource into production and serving other general interests. In societies such as Mexico, however, the issues at stake in land policy were very different. Good land was relatively scarce, and labor was relatively abundant. Here the lands in question had long been controlled by Native Americans, but without individual private property rights. Mexico was not unique in pursuing policies, especially in the final decades of the nineteenth and the first decade of the twentieth century, that had the effect of conferring ownership of much of this land to large non-Native American landholders.[29] The 1856 Ley Lerdo and the 1857 Constitution had set down methods of privatizing these public lands in a manner that could originally have been intended to help Native American farmers enter a national land market and commercial economy. Under the regime of Porfirio Díaz, however, these laws became the basis for a series of new statutes and policies that between 1878 and 1908 effected a massive transfer of such lands (over 10.7% of the national territory) to large holders, such as survey and land development companies, either in the form of outright grants for services rendered by the companies or for prices set by decree.

In Table 3.4, we present estimates for these four countries of the fractions of household heads, or a near equivalent, that owned land in agricultural areas in the late nineteenth and early twentieth centuries. The figures indicate enormous differences across the countries in the prevalence of landownership among the adult male population in rural areas. On the eve of the Mexican Revolution, the figures from the 1910 census suggest that only 2.4% of household heads in rural Mexico owned land. The number is astoundingly low. The dramatic land policy measures in Mexico at the end of the nineteenth century may have succeeded in privatizing most of the public lands, but they left the vast majority of the rural population without any land at all. The evidence obviously conforms well with the idea that in societies that began with extreme inequality, such as Mexico, institutions evolved so as to greatly advantage the elite in access to economic opportunities, and they thus contributed to the persistence of that extreme inequality.

In contrast, the proportion of adult males who owned land in rural areas was quite high in the United States, at just below 75% in 1900. Although the prevalence of landownership was markedly lower in the South, where blacks were disproportionately concentrated, the overall picture is one of land policies, such as the Homestead Act, providing broad access to this fundamental type of economic opportunity. Canada had an even better record, with nearly 90% of household heads owning the agricultural lands they occupied in 1901. The estimates of landholding in these two countries support the notion that land policies made a difference, especially when compared with Argentina. The rural regions of Argentina constitute a set of frontier provinces, where one would expect higher rates of ownership than in Buenos Aires. The numbers, however, suggest a much lower prevalence of landownership than in the two North American economies.[30] Nevertheless, all of these countries were far more effective than Mexico in making landownership available to the general population. The contrast between the United States and Canada, with their practices of offering easy access to small units of

Table 3.4: Landholding in Rural Regions of Mexico, the United States, Canada, and Argentina during the Early 1900s

Country, Year, and Region	Proportion of Household Heads Who Own Land[a]
Mexico, 1910	
North Pacific	5.6
North	3.4
Central	2.0
Gulf	2.1
South Pacific	1.5
Total rural Mexico	2.4
United States, 1900	
North Atlantic	79.2
South Atlantic	55.8
North Central	72.1
South Central	51.4
Western	83.4
Alaska/Hawaii	42.1
Total United States	74.5
Canada, 1901	
British Columbia	87.1
Alberta	95.8
Saskatchewan	96.2
Manitoba	88.9
Ontario	80.2
Quebec	90.1
Maritime[b]	95.0
Total Canada	87.1
Argentina, 1895	
Chaco	27.8
Formosa	18.5
Missiones	26.7
La Pampa	9.7
Neuquén	12.3
Río Negro	15.4
Chubut	35.2
Santa Cruz	20.2
Tierra del Fuego	6.6

Sources: Engerman and Sokoloff 2002.
a. Landownership is defined as follows: in Mexico, household heads who own land; in the US, farms that are owner operated; in Canada, total occupiers of farm lands who are owners; and in Argentina, the ratio of landowners to the number of males between the ages of 18 and 50.
b. The Maritime region includes Nova Scotia, New Brunswick, and Prince Edward Island.

land, and the rest of the Americas (as well as the contrast between Argentina and Mexico), is consistent with the hypothesis that the initial extent of inequality influenced the way in which institutions evolved and, in so doing, helped foster persistence in the degree of inequality over time.

CONCLUSION

There has long been debate over the impact of the worldwide European establishment of colonies that took place over centuries, beginning in the 1400s. Much of the controversy has been concerned with issues such as the imbalance of military power and how the long-term performance of the colonized areas and the colonizing economies were affected by the exchange of resources and terms of trade between them. As we have argued here, however, one of the most fundamental consequences of European colonization may have been in altering the composition of the populations in the colonized societies. Because the efforts of the Europeans generally meant implanting communities that were greatly advantaged over natives in terms of human capital and legal status and because the trajectories of institutional development were sensitive to the incidence of extreme inequality that often followed, European colonial activity had long, lingering effects. Although more study is needed to identify all of the mechanisms at work, it seems clear that colonies in the Americas with extreme inequality, compared with those with relative equality, were systematically more likely to evolve institutions that restricted access to economic opportunities and to generate lower rates of public investment in schools and other infrastructure considered conducive to growth. These patterns of institutional development, which tend to yield persistence over time in economic performance, may be helpful in understanding why a great many of these societies that began with extreme inequality still suffer from the same condition.

NOTES

1. Lal (2004).
2. Ferguson (2003).
3. Davis and Huttenback (1986).
4. For examples of what has become a substantial literature, see Engerman and Sokoloff (1997, 2002); Acemoglu and Robinson (2001, 2002); and Easterly and Levine (2003).
5. For example, see North (1988) and Coatsworth (1993) for discussions of why the English institutional heritage helped Canada and the United States in realizing economic growth. For general discussions of the role of institutions in worldwide economic growth, see North (1981).
6. Engerman and Sokoloff (1997, 2002).
7. In those cases where the endowments were well suited to large-scale, labor-intensive production of staples, slaves or contract laborers were often brought in to provide a labor force. The importation of slaves into the Caribbean basin to grow sugar is the outstanding example of this, and the extensive use of contract labor from

South Asia to augment the labor force, especially where land was relatively abundant, after the emancipation of slaves provides another. See Engerman (1982, 1983, 1986).

8. Engerman and Sokoloff (2002).

9. For examples of the approach that highlights variation in savings rates with relative income or with rates of taxation, see Alesina and Rodrik (1994) and Persson and Tabellini (1994). For those investigating the impact of inequality on institutions more broadly, see Engerman and Sokoloff (1997, 2002); Acemoglu et al. (2001, 2002); and Easterly and Levine (2003).

10. There are of course some classic expositions of these and similar ideas. See, for example, Tocqueville ([1835] 1969) and Turner (1948).

11. Rolling Stones (1969).

12. Kupperman (1993).

13. As McManus (1973, p. 23) makes clear, those in the northern United States were priced out of the market for slaves by the 1760s: "By 1764 Thomas Rich, one of Philadelphia's leading traders noted that 'the time is over for the sale of Negroes here.' "

14. There is some controversy about whether Argentina had wealth and literacy requirements for suffrage. Whatever the case, the proportion of the population voting was very low in that country (1.8% in 1896) until the electoral reform law of 1912. Those who point to the absence of such electoral restrictions at the level of the national government suggest that the low voter participation was due to a failure of immigrants to change their citizenship and vote, as well as to the lack of a secret ballot. Others believe that restrictions on the franchise had, in fact, been enacted and were enforced at the provincial level until 1912. See the discussion in Engerman and Sokoloff (2005).

15. See the extended treatment of these and related issues in Engeman and So-koloff (2004).

16. For the concern with attracting immigrants to the United States and Argentina, for example, see Engerman and Sokoloff (2005); Castro (1971); and Adelman (1994).

17. See Acemoglu and Robinson (2000) for the argument that in many Western European countries, the franchise was extended under threat.

18. See the discussion in Easterlin (1981).

19. Cubberley (1920).

20. See, for example, Phillips (1957) and Wilson et al. (1970).

21. Indeed, significant steps were not taken in this direction until the British Colonial Office began promoting schooling in the 1870s. The increased concern for promoting education in the colonies may have been related to developments in Great Britain itself. Several important expansions of the public provision of elementary education occurred during the 1870s, including the 1870 Education Act and the 1876 passage of a law calling for compulsory schooling through the age of ten.

22. The income tax introduced during the Civil War was ultimately ruled unconstitutional, and thus it was not until a constitutional amendment was ratified by the states that such a tax could be permanently reinstituted.

23. By 1900, local governments seem to have obtained well over 90% of revenue from property taxes. For further discussion of how the importance of the property tax as a source of state revenue varied over the nineteenth century, see Wallis (2001).

24. Any conclusions about just how progressive or regressive any particular tax

structures are, must, of course, take into account the ultimate incidence of the taxes assessed. An analysis of incidence is beyond the scope of this essay. Nevertheless, we feel rather confident, especially for the nineteenth century, in following the convention of presuming that property taxes are more progressive in incidence than levies consisting of tariffs on imported goods and the revenues obtained from state monopolies on consumer commodities such as liquors and tobacco.

25. In 1902, property, death, and gift taxes accounted for more than 60% of total tax revenue to all levels of government in the United States combined. See Sokoloff and Zolt (2004, Table 7.1).

26. See Gates (1968) for a comprehensive overview of U.S. land policy. Discussions of Canadian land policy include Solberg (1987); Pomfret (1981, pp. 111–119); and Adelman (1994, chap. 2).

27. See Viotti da Costa (1985, chap. 4); Solberg (1987); Solberg's essay in Platt and di Tella (1985); and the excellent discussions in Adelman (1994).

28. Because the major crops produced in the expansion of the northern United States and Canada were grains, the land could be profitably worked on relatively small farms, given the technology of the times. This may help explain why such a policy of smallholding was implemented and effective. See Atack and Bateman (1987); and Danhof (1969). In Argentina, however, small-scale wheat production coincided with ownership of land in large units, thereby maintaining a greater degree of overall inequality in wealth and political power. See Solberg (1970, 1987). In addition to grains, livestock production on large landholdings also increased dramatically in the late nineteenth century, and scale economies in the raising of livestock may have helped maintain the large.

29. For further discussion of Mexico, see McBride (1923); Tannebaum (1929); and Holden (1994).

30. Our preliminary work with the data from the 1914 census yields the same qualitative results. It is worth noting that the proportion of families that owned land are exaggerated by the 1895 census figures. A close examination of the manuscripts indicates that double counting, in which both husband and wife were listed as landowners, was prevalent in many parts of Argentina.

BIBLIOGRAPHY

Acemoglu, Daron, Simon Johnson, and James A. Robinson. "The Colonial Origins of Comparative Development: An Empirical Investigation." *American Economic Review* 91 (Dec. 2001): 1369–1401.

Acemoglu, Daron, Simon Johnson, and James A. Robinson. "Reversal of Fortune: Geography and Institutions in the Making of the Modern World Income Distribution." *Quarterly Journal of Economics* 117 (Nov. 2002): 1231–1294.

Acemoglu, Daron, and James A. Robinson. "Why Did Western Europe Extend the Franchise?" *Quarterly Journal of Economics* 115 (Nov. 2000): 1167–1199.

Adelman, Jeremy. *Frontier Development: Land, Labour, and Capital on Wheatlands of Argentina and Canada. 1890–1914.* New York: Oxford University Press, 1994.

Alesina, Alberto F., and Dani Rodrik. "Distributive Politics and Economic Growth." *Quarterly Journal of Economics* 109 (May 1994): 465–490.

Atack, Jeremy and Fred Bateman. *To Their Own Soil: Agriculture in the Antebellum North.* Ames, Iowa: Iowa State University Press, 1987.

Castro, Donald. *The Development of Argentine Immigration Policy, 1852–1914.* Ann Arbor, Mich.: University Microfilms, 1971.

Coatsworth, John H. "Notes on the Comparative Economic History of Latin America and the United States." In *Development and Underdevelopment in America: Contrasts of Economic Growth in North and Latin America in Historical Perspective.* Edited by Walther L. Bernecker and Hans Werner Tobler. New York: Walter de Gruyter, 1993.

Cubberley, Ellwood P. *The History of Education.* Boston: Houghton Mifflin, 1920.

Danhof, Clarence H. *Change in Agriculture: The Northern United States, 1820–1870.* Cambridge, Mass.: Harvard University Press, 1969.

Davis, Lance E. and Robert A. Huttenback. *Mammon and the Pursuit of Empire: The Political Economy of British Imperialism, 1860–1912.* New York: Cambridge University Press, 1986.

Deininger, Klaus, and Lyn Squire. "A New Data Set and Measure of Income Inequality." *World Bank Economic Review* 10 (Sept. 1996): 565–591.

Easterlin, Richard A. "Why Isn't the Whole World Developed?" *Journal of Economic History* 41 (Mar. 1981): 1–19.

Easterly, William, and Ross Levine. "Tropics, Germs, and Crops: The Role of Endowments in Economic Development." *Journal of Monetary Economics* 50 (Jan. 2003): 3–39.

Engerman, Stanley L. "Economic Adjustments to Emancipation in the United States and the British West Indies." *Journal of Interdisciplinary History* 12 (Autumn 1982): 191–220.

Engerman, Stanley L. "Contract Labor, Sugar and Technology in the Nineteenth Century." *Journal of Economic History* 43 (Sept. 1983): 635–659.

Engerman, Stanley L. "Servants to Slaves to Servants: Contract Labour and European Expansion." In *Colonialism and Migration: Indentured Labour Before and After Slavery.* Edited by P. C. Emmer. Dordrecht: Martinus Nijhoff, 1986.

Engerman, Stanley L., Stephen Haber, and Kenneth L. Sokoloff. "Inequality, Institutions, and Differential Paths of Growth Among New World Economies." In *Institutions, Contracts, and Organizations.* Edited by Claude Menard. Cheltenham, U.K.: Edward Elgar, 2000.

Engerman, Stanley L., Elisa V. Mariscal, and Kenneth L. Sokoloff. "The Evolution of Schooling Institutions in the Americas, 1800–1925." Unpublished working paper, 2002. University of California, Los Angeles.

Engerman, Stanley L., and Kenneth L. Sokoloff. "Factor Endowments, Institutions, and Differential Paths of Growth Among New World Economies: A View from Economic Historians of the United States." In *How Latin America Fell Behind.* Edited by Stephen Haber. Stanford, Calif.: Stanford University Press, 1997.

Engerman, Stanley L., and Kenneth L. Sokoloff. "Factor Endowments, Inequality and Paths of Development Among New World Economies." *Economia* 3 (Fall 2002): 41–109.

Engerman, Stanley L., and Kenneth L. Sokoloff. "The Evolution of Suffrage Institutions in the Americas." *Journal of Economic History* 65 (December 2005): 891–921.

Ferguson, Niall. *Empire: The Rise and the Demise of the British World Order and the Lessons for Global Power.* New York: Basic Books, 2003.

Gates, Paul W. *History of Public Land Law Development.* Washington, D.C.: U.S. Government Printing Office, 1968.

Holden, Robert. *Mexico and the Survey of Public Lands: The Management of Modernization, 1876–1911.* Dekalb: Northern Illinois University Press, 1994.

Kupperman, Karen Ordahl. *Providence Island, 1630–1641: The Other Puritan Colony.* New York: Cambridge University Press, 1993.

Lal, Deepak. *In Praise of Empires: Globalization and Order.* New York: Palgrave Macmillan, 2004.

McBride, George McCutchen. *The Land Systems of Mexico.* New York: National Geographic Society, 1923.

McManus, Edgar J. *Black Bondage in the North.* Syracuse, N.Y.: Syracuse University Press, 1973.

North, Douglass C. *Structure and Change in Economic History.* New York: Norton, 1981.

North, Douglass C. "Institutions, Economic Growth and Freedom: An Historical Introduction." In *Freedom, Democracy, and Economic Welfare.* Edited by Michael Walker. Vancouver, B.C.: Fraser Institute, 1988.

Persson, Torsten, and Guido Tabellini. "Is Inequality Harmful for Growth? Theory and Evidence." *American Economic Review* 84 (June 1994): 600–621.

Phillips, Charles E. *The Development of Education in Canada.* Toronto: W. J. Gage, 1957.

Platt, D. C. M., and Guido di Tella, eds. *Argentina, Australia, and Canada: Studies in Comparative Development 1870–1965.* London: Macmillan, 1985.

Pomfret, Richard. *The Economic Development of Canada.* Toronto: Methuen, 1981.

Rolling Stones. "You Can't Always Get What You Want." In *Let It Bleed.* New York: Gideon Music, 1969.

Sokoloff, Kenneth L., and Eric M. Zolt. "Inequality and the Evolution of Institutions of Taxation in the Americas." In New *Perspectives on Latin American Economic History.* Edited by Sebastian Edwards, Gerardo Esquivel, and Graciela Marquez. Chicago: University of Chicago Press, forthcoming 2006.

Solberg, Carl E. *Immigration and Nationalism: Argentina and Chile, 1890–1914.* Austin: University of Texas Press, 1970.

Solberg, Carl E. "Land Tenure and Land Settlement: Policy and Patterns in the Canadian Prairies and the Argentine Pampas, 1880–1930." In *Argentina, Australia and Canada: Studies in Comparative Development, 1870–1965.* Edited by D.C.M. Platt and Guido di Tella. London: Macmillan, 1985.

Solberg, Carl E. *The Prairies and the Pampas: Agrarian Policy in Canada and Argentina 1880–1930.* Stanford, Calif.: Stanford University Press, 1987.

Tannebaum, Frank. *The Mexican Agrarian Revolution.* New York: Macmillan, 1929.

Tocqueville, Alexis de. *Democracy in America* [1835]. Translated by George Lawrence. Edited by J. P. Mayer. Garden City, N.Y.: Doubleday, 1969.

Turner, Frederick J. The *Frontier in American History.* New York: H. Holt, 1948.

Viotti da Costa, Emilia. *The Brazilian Empire: Myths and Histories.* Chicago: University of Chicago Press, 1985.

Wallis, John Joseph. "A History of the Property Tax in America." In *Property Taxation and Local Government Finance: Essays in Honor of C. Lowell Harriss.* Edited by Wallace E. Oates. Cambridge, Mass.: Lincoln Institute of Land Policy, 2001.

Wilson, J. Donald, Robert M. Stamp, and Louis-Philippe Audet. *Canadian Education: A History.* Scarborough, Ont.: Prentice-Hall, 1970.

4

The Kuznets Curve: Yesterday and Tomorrow

Thomas Piketty

Since the mid-1950s, the Kuznets curve hypothesis has been one of the most debated issues in development economics. And rightly so. In a nutshell, the hypothesis simply says that income inequality should follow an inverse-U shape along the development process, first rising with industrialization and then declining, as more and more workers join the high-productivity sectors of the economy (Kuznets 1955). This theory has strong—and fairly optimistic—policy consequences: if LDCs are patient enough and do not worry too much about the short-run social costs of development, they should soon reach a world where growth and inequality reduction go hand in hand, and where poverty rates drop sharply.

Today, the Kuznets curve is widely held to have doubled back on itself, especially in the United States, with the period of falling inequality during the first half of the twentieth century being followed by a sharp reversal of the trend since the 1970s. Consequently, most economists have now become fairly skeptical about universal laws relating development and income inequality. It would be misleading, however, to conclude that Kuznets's hypothesis is no longer of interest. First, a number of poor countries may not have passed what Kuznets identified as the initial industrialization stage. Thus it is still important to make sure that we understand why developed countries went through an initial inverse-U curve. Fifty years after Kuznets, what do we know about the reasons why inequality declined in the West during the first half of the twentieth century, and are there lessons to be drawn for today's poor countries?

Next, one could argue that what has been happening since the 1970s in developed countries is just a remake of the previous inverse-U curve: a new industrial revolution has taken place, thereby leading to rising inequality, and inequality will decline again at some point, as more and more workers benefit from the new innovations. In a sense, Kuznets's theory can be viewed as a sophisticated formulation of the standard, trickle-down view of development: innovations first benefit a few individuals and eventually trickle down to the mass of the people. Back in the 1950s, Kuznets stressed the rural/urban dimension of the process: in his view, development meant moving from a low-income, rural, agricultural sector to a high-income, urban, industrialized sector. But the same logic can obviously be applied to other two-sector models, such as a model with an "old economy" sector and a "new economy," IT-intensive sector. So the more general question I want to ask is the following: Looking at the most recent trends in both rich and poor countries, what evidence do we have in favor of this "technical change" view of inequality dynamics, whereby waves of technological innovations generate waves of inverse-U curves?

The rest of this essay is organized as follows. In the second section, I focus upon the inequality decline that took place in the West during the first half of the twentieth century. I argue that recent historical research is rather damaging for Kuznets's interpretation: the reasons why inequality declined in rich countries seem to be due to very specific shocks and circumstances that do not have much to do with the migration process described by Kuznets and that are very unlikely to occur again in today's poor countries (one hopes). In the third section, I take a broader perspective on the technical change view of inequality dynamics, drawing both from historical experience and from more recent trends. I argue that this view has proven to be excessively naïve to properly account for the observed facts and that country-specific institutions often play a role that is at least as important as technological waves. Although this essay focuses primarily on the impact of development on distribution (in the Kuznets tradition), I will occasionally refer to the reverse causality, from distribution to growth (an issue that has attracted a lot of attention since the mid-1990s).

WHY DID INEQUALITY DECLINE IN THE WEST?

At the time Kuznets gave his presidential address to the 1954 American Economic Association Annual Congress in Detroit, there were few data on distribution. For the most part, the address (which was to become his famous 1955 article) relied on the 1913–1948 series on U.S. top income shares that Kuznets had just constructed and published in a voluminous and path-breaking book (Kuznets 1953). Although income distribution had played a central role in economic thinking at least since the time of Ricardo and Marx, this was the very first time that an economist was able to produce a homogeneous distribution series covering a reasonably long time period. These series showed that a marked inequality decline had taken place in the United States between 1913 and 1948.[1] Kuznets had no data prior to the creation of the federal income tax in 1913, but the general presumption was that in-equality had been rising during the nineteenth century, with a turning point around 1900. In order to account for the turning point, Kuznets introduced the famous two-sector model. The theory of the inverse-U curve was born.

A large number of studies have attempted since the 1950s to test the inverse-U curve hypothesis in LDCs. However, as was noted in a recent survey, it is fair to say that the evidence is mixed and at best inconclusive (Kanbur 2000). In fact, data limitations make it very difficult to perform proper testing of Kuznets's hypothesis outside developed countries. In most LDCs, estimates of income distribution are scarce, and available for only a selected (and typically small) number of years. When time series are available, they are usually limited to the most recent decades, and never go back in time before the 1950s. This makes it almost impossible to conduct adequate longitudinal testing of the inverse-U curve theory in most countries.[2] One often needs to revert to cross-sectional testing, which raises serious issues of interpretation and reliability, especially given the poor quality and lack of homogeneity of available cross-country data sets on income distribution.[3] The sharp decline in inequality that occurred in developed countries during the first half of the twentieth century and that served as the basis for the 1954 AEA presidential address, remains the best available evidence in favor of the Kuznets curve hypothesis.

There are, however, important pieces of evidence that Kuznets was miss-ing in 1953–1954 and that contribute to explaining why he advocated such an overly optimistic and universal interpretation of what happened between 1900 and 1950. First, because existing data at the time ended in 1948, Kuznets was not able to see that the inequality decline in the United States and in most other developed countries stopped almost immediately after World War II. Next, and most important, available U.S. data did not allow him to de-compose income inequality trends into a labor income component and a capital income component. Fortunately, there are other countries (such as France) where administrative tax data make it possible to construct separate series for income inequality, wage inequality, and wealth inequality over the entire twentieth century. France is also an interesting testing ground regard-ing the impact of rural–urban migration on inequality dynamics: agricultural workers were particularly numerous at the beginning of the century in France (around 30% of all wage earners in 1900, down to 20% in 1930, 10% in 1950, and less than 1% in 2000), and very low wages were concentrated in that sector.

The key finding is that although top income shares declined substantially in France over the period 1900–1950 (even more so than in the United States), wage inequality—as measured by top wage shares and by broader indicators such as the 90–10 interdecile ratio—remained extremely stable (see Figure 4.1 and Piketty 2003). That is, the decline in income inequality was for the most part a capital income phenomenon. Holders of large for-tunes were badly hurt by major shocks during the 1914–1945 period (wars,

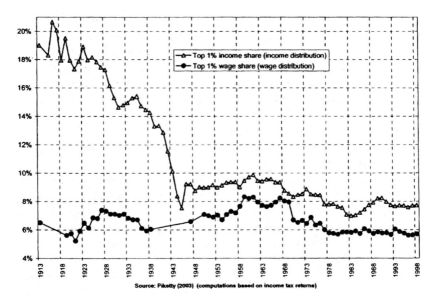

Figure 4.1 The Fall of Top Capital Incomes in France, 1913–1998

inflation, recessions), and this explains why top income shares fell. This interpretation is confirmed by myriad independent data sources (including estate tax data and macroeconomic series) and by the very peculiar timing of the fall: top capital incomes and income inequality at large did not start falling until World War I, partly recovered during the 1920s, then fell sharply during the years of the Great Depression, and even more so during World War II. The labor market and the rural–urban migration process played no role: low-wage rural workers slowly disappeared, but they were replaced by low-wage urban workers at the bottom of the distribution, so that overall wage inequality hardly changed.

Although existing data are not as complete as for France, newly constructed U.S. series (allowing for more detailed decompositions than the original Kuznets series) show that the same general conclusion also applies to the United States: wage inequality did not start declining before World War II, and the bulk of the 1913–1948 inequality decline can be accounted for by capital income shocks.[4] Recent research on the United Kingdom, Canada, and Germany also confirms the key role played by shocks in inequality dynamics during this period.[5]

Needless to say, the idea that capital owners were hurt by major shocks between 1914 and 1945, and that this contributed to the inequality decline is not new. What is new is that there was not much else going on. It is also interesting to note that Kuznets did stress in his 1955 article the key role played by wars, inflation, recessions, and the rise of progressive taxation—though this is not the part of the explanation that most economists chose to remember. It was only at the end of his presidential address that he suggested that an additional process (based upon the two-sector model) might also have played a role. Kuznets was fully aware that he had basically no empirical support in favor of this interpretation: "This is perhaps 5 percent empirical information and 95 percent speculation, some of it possibly tainted by wishful thinking" (Kuznets 1955, p. 26). But, as he himself put it quite bluntly, what was at the stake in the 1950s was nothing but "the future prospect of the underdeveloped countries within the orbit of the free world" (p. 24). To a large extent, the optimistic theory of the inverse-U curve is the product of the Cold War.

There are two other important lessons that can be drawn from historical research on income inequality in the West. First, the rise of progressive income and estate taxation probably explains (at least in part) why top capital incomes were not able to fully recover from the 1914–1945 shocks and why capital concentration never returned to its prewar level. That is, progressive taxation can have a substantial long-run impact on pretax income inequality, via its effects on future capital concentration. Although this view was fairly common early in the twentieth century, it has been overly neglected during recent decades. Cutting back on progressivity can have important long-run consequences on wealth inequality and the resurgence of rentiers, both in poor countries and in developed economies.

Next, it is interesting to note that the structural decline of capital concentration that took place between 1914 and 1945 in developed countries does not seem to have had a negative impact on their later growth performance—quite the contrary: per capita growth rates have been substantially higher in the postwar period than during the nineteenth century and all the more so in countries such as France and Germany, where the shocks incurred by capital owners were particularly severe. This is consistent with the theory of capital market imperfections: in the presence of credit constraints, excessive wealth inequality entails negative consequences for social mobility and growth. There are good reasons to believe that the 1914–1945 shocks allowed new generations of talented entrepreneurs to replace old-style capitalist dynasties at a faster pace than would have otherwise been the case.[6] At the very least, what we learn from these historical case studies is that high capital concentration was not a prerequisite for growth. Such a case studies approach to the inequality-growth relationship seems more promising than the reduced-form, cross-country regressions routinely run by economists during the 1990s, and from this it is fair to say that we did not learn very much (due in particular to the poor quality of ready-to-use cross-country data sets).[7]

TECHNICAL CHANGE VERSUS INSTITUTIONS

The fact that capital shocks played the leading role during the 1914–1945 period obviously does not imply that the technical change view of inequality dynamics has no relevance. After all, the idea that technological waves have a major impact on labor market inequality makes a lot of sense. The problem with this view is that it is excessively naïve and deterministic. In practice, the impact of technology on inequality depends on a large number of institutions, and these institutions vary a great deal over time and across countries. Chief among these are the institutions governing the supply and structure of skills, from formal schooling institutions to on-the-job training schemes. To a large extent, the dynamics of labor market inequality are determined by the race between the demand for skills and the supply of skills. New technologies tend to raise the demand for skills, but the impact on inequality depends on whether the supply of skills is rising at a faster or a slower rate. There is no general presumption that the race should go one way or the other.

One example might make the point more concrete. The supply of skills has been rising continuously since the Industrial Revolution, during both the nineteenth and the twentieth centuries. In a country such as France, in spite of the constant rise of literacy rates over the nineteenth century, substantial segments of the labor force (especially rural workers) were basically illiterate in 1900. They were slowly replaced by urban workers with basic skills during the twentieth century. Why is it that the end of rural backwardness and the diffusion of industrial technology did not lead to a compression of wage inequality, contrarily to what Kuznets had expected? Well, probably because the demand for new skills kept increasing, and the supply of new skills was just enough to prevent wage dispersion from rising. Had the schooling institutions managed to raise the supply of skilled workers at a faster pace, the outcome might have been different.

Another leading example is the rise of wage dispersion that has occurred in the United States since the 1970s. According to one popular theory, this dramatic evolution is simply due to skill-biased technical change. However, a number of economists have challenged this explanation. For instance, it has been noted that education-related wage gaps rose for younger workers, but not for older workers. What this suggests is that the slowdown in the rate of growth of educational attainment (number of college graduates, etc.) for the younger cohorts has been a key driving force behind the observed changes.[8] Whether or not wage dispersion will decline in the future probably depends a lot on the ability of educational institutions to deliver higher growth rates of skill supply.

It has also been noted that inequality between bottom wages and the middle ranks rose only during the 1980s and then stabilized during the 1990s, despite continuing advances in computer technology. This suggests that changes in the minimum wage (rather than market forces) played the dominant role (the minimum wage fell in the 1980s, and stabilized in the 1990s).[9] Minimum wage and other labor market institutions can in turn have an impact on the direction of technical change: for instance, more wage compression can encourage more investment in technologies increasing the productivity of less-skilled workers.[10]

There are many other institutions that play a key role in inequality dynamics. For instance, it is very hard to explain the dramatic rise of very top wages in the United States (which accounts for a disproportionate share of the rise of top wage shares observed since the 1970s) on the basis of technical change alone. Between 1970 and 2000, the average real compensation of the top 100 CEOs was multiplied by a factor of more than 30, while the average wage in the U.S. economy increased by about 10% (see Figure 4.2). There is a lot of evidence suggesting that such a phenomenal rise of executive compensation has more to do with bad governance and lack of control (perhaps due to very dispersed capital ownership) than with the rise of CEO efficiency and productivity.[11] Investors have recently started to realize that CEO compensation has gone out of control, but there is a long way to go before we come back to a more reasonable state of affairs. It is also quite likely that changing social norms and attitudes toward inequality have played an important role in this evolution. Short of that, it's difficult to understand why very top wages increased so much in the United States and not in Europe. The idea that social norms are an important factor in setting pay is particularly plausible for very top wages, given that it is virtually impossible for board members (as well as for economists) to measure precisely the productivity of a CEO.

Finally, government institutions and changing social norms can also be relevant for the analysis of rising income inequality in a number of LDCs. For instance, it is unclear whether one can account for the huge rise of very top incomes (and particularly top wages) observed in a country such as India during the 1990s on the basis of demand and supply alone (see Figure 4.3). There is today in many parts of the world a wider acceptance of inequality than was the case a few decades ago, and this probably has a strong impact

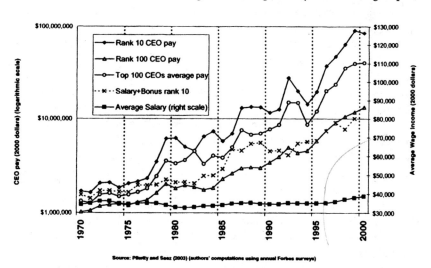

Source: Piketty and Saez (2003) (authors' computations using annual Forbes surveys)

Figure 4.2 CEO Pay versus Average Wage Income in the US, 1970–2000

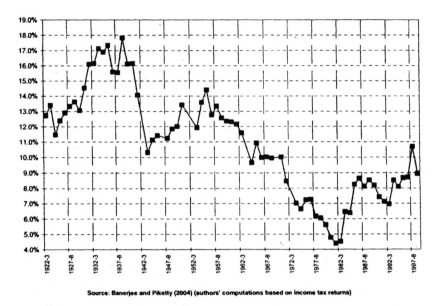

Source: Banerjee and Piketty (2004) (authors' computations based on income tax returns)

Figure 4.3 The Top 1% Income Share in India, 1922–2000

on actual inequality. Whether or not this will remain so in the near future is very much an open issue at this stage.

CONCLUDING COMMENTS

In this essay, I have attempted to provide a critical overview of recent research on the interplay between economic development and economic inequality. There are a number of important conclusions that emerge.

First, the reasons why inequality declined in industrialized countries during the first half of the twentieth century do not have much to do with the optimistic trickle-down process advocated by Kuznets in the 1950s. The compression of income distribution that took place during the 1914–1945 period was due, for the most part, to very specific capital shocks and circumstances that are very unlikely to happen again. Progressive income and estate taxation probably explains to a large extent why capital concentration did not return to the very high levels observed before the shocks. The historical experience of developed countries also shows that high wealth inequality is not necessary for growth, and that it can even be harmful.

Next, there are myriad country-specific institutions (from educational and labor market institutions to corporate governance and social norms) that play a key role in shaping the interplay between development and inequality. Rising dispersion of income is not the mechanical and largely unavoidable consequence of technical change. Nor is the trend going to reverse in a spontaneous fashion. Inequality dynamics depend primarily on the policies and institutions adopted by governments and societies as a whole.

NOTES

1. Kuznets also relied on disparate estimates available for Germany and the United Kingdom suggesting that a similar trend had taken place in these countries.

2. In countries where reasonably homogeneous series going back to the 1950s are available, one tends to observe a U-curve (with inequality falling until the 1970s and rising since the 1970s–1980s) rather than an inverse-U curve. See the case of Taiwan described by Kanbur (2000, pp. 808–811). See also the 1922–2000 top income shares series constructed by Banerjee and Piketty (2004) for India, which also depict a U-shaped curve.

3. See, e.g., Atkinson and Brandolini (2001).

4. See Piketty and Saez (2003).

5. See Atkinson (2003); Saez and Veall (2004); and Dell (2004). An international database offering homogeneous top shares series for over twenty countries is currently being compiled by Atkinson and Piketty (2005).

6. Research by Piketty, Postel-Vinay, and Rosenthal (2004) on wealth accumulation in pre-1914 France shows that the very high levels of wealth concentration observed on the eve of World War I were associated with retired rentiers rather than active entrepreneurs (i.e., wealth was getting older and older until the war), which is consistent with the credit constraints view.

7. See the references in note 3. One additional problem with ready-to-use data sets (such as the Deininger–Squire data set) is that they never offer any decomposition of income inequality into a wage inequality component and a wealth inequality component, which makes them particularly ill-suited for the study of the credit constraint channel. For a sharp critique of cross-country regressions on inequality and growth, see also Banerjee and Duflo (2001).

8. See Card and Lemieux (2001) and Card and DiNardo (2002).

9. See Lee (1999) and Card and DiNardo (2002).

10. See Acemoglu (2002).

11. See Bertrand and Mullainathan (2001). See also Krugman (2002).

BIBLIOGRAPHY

Acemoglu, Daron. "Cross-Country Inequality Trends." NBER Working Paper 8832, 2002.

Atkinson, Anthony Barnes. "Top Incomes in the United Kingdom over the Twentieth Century." Oxford: Nuffield College, 2003. Mimeo.

Atkinson, Anthony Barnes, and Andrea Brandolini. "Promise and Pitfalls in the Use of 'Secondary' Data-Sets: Income Inequality in OECD Countries as a Case Study." *Journal of Economic Literature* 39 (2001): 771–799.

Atkinson, Anthony Barnes, and Thomas Piketty. *Top Incomes over the Twentieth Century.* 2 vols. New York: Oxford University Press, 2005.

Banerjee, Abhijit, and Esther Duflo. "Inequality and Growth: What Can the Data Say?" Cambridge, Mass.: MIT, 2001. Mimeo.

Banerjee, Abhijit, and Thomas Piketty. "Top Indian Incomes, 1922–1998." CEPR discussion paper, 2004.

Bertrand, M., and Sendhil Mullainathan. "Do CEOs Set Their Own Pay? The Ones Without Principles Do." *Quarterly Journal of Economics* 116 (2001): 901–932.

Card, David, and John DiNardo. "Skill-Biased Technical Change and Rising Wage Inequality: Some Problems and Puzzles." NBER Working Paper 8769, 2002.

Card, David, and Thomas Lemieux. "Can Falling Supply Explain the Rising Return to College for Younger Men? A Cohort-Based Analysis." *Quarterly Journal of Economics* 116 (2001): 705–746.

Dell, F. "Income Inequality in Germany, 1880–2000." Paris-Jourdan, 2004. Mimeo.

Kanbur, Ravi. "Income Distribution and Development." In *Handbook of Income Distribution*, 791–841. Edited by A. B. Atkinson and F. Bourguignon. New York: Elsevier, 2000.

Krugman, Paul. "For Richer." *New York Times*, Oct. 20, 2002.

Kuznets, Simon. "Shares of Upper Income Groups in Income and Savings." National Bureau of Economic Research, 1953.

Kuznets, Simon. "Economic Growth and Economic Inequality." *American Economic Review* 45 (1955): 1–28.

Lee, David S. "Wage Inequality in the United States During the 1980s: Rising Dispersion or Falling Minimum Wage?" *Quarterly Journal of Economics* 114 (1999): 977–1023.

Piketty, Thomas. "Income Inequality in France, 1901–1998." *Journal of Political Economy* 111 (2003): 1004–1042.

Piketty, Thomas, Gilles Postel-Vinay, and Jean Laurent Rosenthal. "Wealth Concentration in a Developing Economy: Paris and France, 1807–1994." CEPR discussion paper, 2004.

Piketty, Thomas, and Nancy Qian. "Income Inequality and Progressive Income Taxation in China and India, 1986–2010." Paris-Jourdan and Camridge, Mass.: MIT, 2004. Mimeo.

Piketty, Thomas and Emmanuel Saez. "Income Inequality in the United States, 1913–1998." *Quarterly Journal of Economics* 118 (2003): 1–39.

Saez, Emmanuel, and Michael Veall. "The Evolution of High Incomes in Canada, 1920–2000." Berkeley: University of California, and Hamilton, Ont.: McMaster University, 2004. Mimeo.

5

New Growth Approach to
Poverty Alleviation

Philippe Aghion & Beatriz Armendáriz de Aghion

Growth theory has often been perceived by development economists as being orthogonal to their main concern, namely, that of understanding the sources of persistent poverty and stagnation in households and villages, and of designing policies aimed at overcoming them. Growth theory, they would argue, is a subdiscipline of macroeconomics: it features economies with representative producers and consumers; and it focuses on aggregate savings and the role of physical or human capital accumulation in long-run growth and convergence. In particular, growth theory is not so concerned with poverty and inequality between rich and poor individuals within a country.

Empirical growth studies have been equally perceived as being too aggregate: most often carried out at a cross-country level, they involve aggregate variables such as average per capita gross domestic product (GDP), average total factor productivity (TFP), average savings rate, average measures of financial development, or average education indicators. In contrast, by focusing directly on households and local institutions and infrastructure, and by using highly targeted control experiments to evaluate the effectiveness of such institutions in a particular community or village, development economists feel entitled to believe that they have found the right approach to deal with the issue of poverty alleviation, and of how to close the gap between rich and poor.

This essay is an attempt to break the divide between growth and development economics. Using the example of India over the past decades, we argue that innovation and/or productivity growth have been main engines of poverty reduction in that country. We also argue that new growth theories can shed light on this process. Moreover, these can also explain why growth and poverty reduction have not occurred in Latin America. The reminder of this essay is organized as follows. In the second section we summarize what is currently known about the evolution of growth and poverty indicators in India since the 1960s. In the third section, we provide a very brief presentation of new growth theory and of some of its main predictions. In the fourth section we use our description of new growth theory to analyze the reform process in India. In the fifth section, we show that the 1991 reforms have had unequalizing effects on productivity and profitability across industries and states. Finally, in the last section we reflect upon the contrasting experiences of Asia and Latin America with regard to productivity growth and poverty alleviation.

SOME RECENT FINDINGS ON GROWTH, POVERTY, AND INEQUALITY IN INDIA

It is a well-established fact that poverty started a pronounced and steady decline in India in the 1960s and 1970s (see Datt and Ravallion 1998). But meanwhile there was little growth in the manufacturing sector. So what explains this reduction in poverty? Here, the now well-established answer is that it was the green revolution, and the resulting boost to productivity in agriculture, that made it happen.[1] That is, the diffusion of a fundamental innovation to the entire agricultural sector, and its spillovers to the urban sector, via its effects on food prices and wages.[2] Somewhat surprisingly, this declining poverty trend was sustained in the 1980s and 1990s, even though the productivity impact of the green revolution had been largely exhausted. In their paper "Poverty and Inequality in India," Angus Deaton and Jean Drèze (2002) analyze the evolutions of inequality and poverty in India over the past decades. They employ survey data provided by three quinquennial rounds of questionnaires (conducted over the time intervals 1987–1988, 1993–1994, and 1999–2000) on households' consumption of a given set of durable and nondurable goods. This information in turn is used to evaluate the number of individuals who lie below the poverty line divided by the total population, or the "head-count ratio."

The first main finding reported by Deaton and Drèze (see Table 5.1) is that even after one adjusts for changes in the design of questionnaires from one round to the next (official methodology), or for changes in price indexes over time (adjusted methodology), poverty in both rural and urban areas has substantially declined since the 1980s.

Deaton and Drèze also find the same pattern when using poverty gap or agricultural wage measures instead of the head count. A second finding is that consumption inequality across individual households increased between the period 1993–1994 and the period 1999–2000, which in turn is consistent with Abhijit Banerjee and Thomas Piketty's (2001) finding of a substantial increase in income inequality among the highest income earners. Moreover,

Table 5.1: Poverty Reduction in India Headcount Ratios (Percentage)

	Official Methodology[a]			Adjusted Estimates[b]		
	1987–1988	1993–94	1999–00	1987–88	1993–94	1999–00
Rural	39.4	37.1	26.8	39.0	33.0	26.3
Urban	39.1	32.9	24.1	22.5	17.8	12.0

Source: Deaton and Drèze (2002)
a. Consumption data from the Planning Commission National Sample Survey
b. Consumption data adjusted for improved comparability and price indexes.

such findings are consistent with the result presented in the 2004 article by Philippe Aghion, Robin Burgess, Stephen Redding, and Fabrizio Zilibotti (hereafter referred to as "ABRZ"): that the variance of profits across registered manufacturing firms in India has increased dramatically since 1991.

What has happened to growth over the same period? Here, the most informative study is by Dani Rodrik and Arvind Subramanian (2004), who find (see Table 5.2) that after a prolonged stagnation, all productivity variables—real per capita GDP, real GDP per worker, and TFP—have taken off since the early 1980s and have kept growing at a sustained high rate ever since.

Thus, a very first look at the period since the 1960s suggests that the green revolution, and then the advent of sustained productivity growth in the manufacturing sector, explain this poverty alleviation phenomenon to a large extent. In both instances, technology and entrepreneurship in the rural and in the urban sectors have played a key role.

NEW GROWTH THEORY IN A NUTSHELL

Three main ideas underlie the new theories of endogenous technical progress.[3] First, productivity growth is driven primarily by the rate of technological innovations, in the form of new products, new processes, and new ways of organizing production. Second, most innovations are the result of entrepreneurial activities or investments, such as research and development investments, which involve risky experimentation and learning. Third, the incentive to engage in innovative investments is itself affected by the economic environment.

Here are five prime examples of institutions and/or policies that affect long-run productivity growth through their impact on entrepreneurs' incentives, or through their ability to make innovative investments:

1. An *effective education system* will have a positive effect on long-run productivity growth, both by increasing the efficiency of innovation technologies and investments (both are highly skill intensive) and

Table 5.2: Average Growth Rates in India (Percentage)

IMF Estimates	1960–1970	1970–1980	1980–1990	1990–1999
Output	3.75	3.16	5.64	5.61
Output per worker	1.77	0.86	3.69	3.30
Total Factor Productivity	1.17	0.47	2.89	2.44

Source: Table 1 in Rodrik—Subramanian (2004)

by reducing the cost of skilled labor, which in turn increases the profits that accrue to successful innovators. As shown by Benhabib and Spiegel (1994) and Krueger and Lindhal (2001), a higher stock of human capital increases countries' ability both to innovate at the frontier and to imitate more advanced technologies.[4]

2. A legal environment that allows entrepreneurs to *appropriate* a significant fraction of the revenues generated by their innovative investments. In particular, better *protection of* (intellectual) *property rights* or a *labor market* that is not too unfavorable to employers, will enhance the expected profits from innovation and thereby encourage innovative investments and productivity growth. That better property rights protection is growth-enhancing has been widely established since the nineteenth century, and it comes out very clearly in the recent work on the economics of institutions (e.g., see La Porta et al. 1998; Hall and Jones 1999; and Acemoglu et al. 2001). The role of labor market regulations is equally important, as we show in ABRZ (2004) and report in the section "The Unequalizing Effects of the Indian Liberalization Experience" (below).

3. *Macroeconomic stability* also tends to foster long-term productivity growth;[5] it reduces interest rates and therefore increases the present discounted value of rents to a successful innovator and, more generally, encourages entrepreneurs to be more forward-looking and emphasize R&D as well as other types of long-term innovative investments over time. As shown by Aghion, Angeletos, et al. (2004), the latter is particularly true in countries with lower levels of financial development.

4. As shown by Levine et al.,[6] *financial development* is of paramount importance for long-run productivity growth, because it makes it easier for entrepreneurs to finance their innovative investments. More recently, Aghion, Howitt, and Mayer (2004) show that financial development is a key variable explaining why some countries converge toward the technological frontier whereas other countries diverge. The same considerations can explain why, within a given country, some firms or sectors grow faster than others. They can also explain why productivity growth may increase inequality. This

in turn follows from the following considerations: (1) in an environment with credit constraints, firms cannot borrow more than a specified multiple of their current profits; (2) the current equilibrium profits of a firm are typically proportional to its current productivity; (3) the R&D cost of catching up with the technological frontier is typically proportional to the frontier productivity level. Thus, the lower the current productivity of a firm, the more costly it is for that firm to catch up with the technological frontier, and therefore the lower the probability of technological catch-up. Hence, in an economy with low financial development, firms that are initially closer to the technological frontier will tend to grow faster than firms initially farther below the frontier.

5. *Higher competition* among incumbent firms and/or a *higher entry threat* (e.g., as induced by trade liberalization or a reduction in entry or licensing costs) will tend to encourage innovations by incumbent firms aimed at escaping competition or entry by potential rivals. The incentive to react to higher entry threat or higher competition by increasing innovative investments will tend to be higher for firms technologically close to their competitors in the same industry or to potential entrants at the technological frontier. Those are indeed the most likely to escape competition or entry through innovating. On the other hand, higher competition or entry will have either no effect or a negative effect on backward firms that stand little chance of competing in the postliberalization environment.[7]

Our view is that the new growth approach outlined in this section provides good lenses with which to interpret the recent poverty reduction in India. While the relation between the new growth approach and the green revolution is well established,[8] in the next section we shall argue that this approach is equally relevant to understanding what has happened to growth and poverty since the 1980s.

TWO WAVES OF GROWTH-ENHANCING REFORMS IN INDIA

There is a debate on what triggered the Indian growth takeoff. On the one hand, ABRZ (2004) emphasize the importance of the 1991 reforms. They argue that up to this point, firms and industries were constrained both internally, by pervasive central government control through public ownership and a tight control over licensing, and externally, by high tariff and nontariff barriers and controls on foreign direct investment. As a response to the balance-of-trade crisis, the New Industrial Policy was introduced in 1991, pretty much in line with what the new growth theories outlined in the previous section might suggest: (1) trade liberalization, with a 51% reduction in tariffs on 97% of products, which increased competition and entry; (2) a boost to foreign direct investment, with the automatic approval of foreign technology agreements involving up to 51% of foreign equity participation in a large number of industries, which would both foster entry and allow the Indian enterprise sector to partly circumvent financial constraints; (3) deregulation, with a substantial easing of procedures to start up a new production unit or manufacture new products, and privatization, with a dramatic reduction in the number of sectors reserved for the public sector, which would further encourage innovation by incumbent firms and also stimulate entry; (4) further expansion of allowed production capacities and reductions in corporate income tax, which increased entrepreneurs' ability to appropriate the reward from their innovative investments.

However, Rodrik and Subramanian (2002) showed that the Indian takeoff predates the 1991 reforms as far back as the early 1980s. But if that is so, can we then really attribute the high growth rates since the 1990s to the liberalization reforms of 1991? Or did growth over the whole period result instead from other changes that occurred in 1980 or before, and would have much less to do with what new growth theories suggest?

In fact, Rodrik and Subramanian (2002) identify two phases in the Indian growth experience since the 1980s: there is first what they call the phase of "pro-business" reforms, starting in 1980 with the return of Indira Gandhi and the subsequent rise of Rajiv Gandhi. These two leaders sent a clear signal to the enterprise sector that the Congress Party and the Indian government would abandon its previous pro-socialism and pro-poor rhetoric and favor the expansion of *existing* private companies through pro-business measures such as the easing of restrictions on capacity expansion, the removal of price controls, and the reduction of corporate taxes. Though this reform package did not emphasize trade or entry liberalization, if we believe the new growth approach outlined above, all these measures should be expected to foster productivity growth by increasing incumbent entrepreneurs' ability to *appropriate* the rents from their innovative investments. And indeed, this policy shift by the Indian government was followed by a growth acceleration that in turn was due primarily to a continuous increase in productivity and, to a lesser extent, to factor accumulation. Rodrik and Subramanian demonstrate that the sequencing of the policy change and the growth takeoff was not spurious, but reflected a causal relationship, in two ways: (1) the growth upsurge was more pronounced in Indian states where members of the local government belonged to (or were allied with) the ruling Congress Party; (2) there was a significant shift in private investment from the household to the manufacturing sector, which in turn reflected a positive reaction of the private sector to what it perceived as an improved investment climate.

As explained above, it was not until 1991 that markets and trade were truly liberalized, and here the second phase of the Indian growth experience started. As argued in the previous section, higher competition and entry should be expected to further encourage innovative investments aimed at escaping them, which in turn would explain why growth continued at the same rate during the 1990s in spite of the balance-of-trade crisis. However, in contrast with the 1980s, poverty reduction in the 1990s appears to have slowed down, and poverty levels even fluctuated in the early 1990s. As we shall argue in the next section, such fluctuations might be explained by the fact that trade liberalization entails winners and losers, both within and across sectors.

THE UNEQUALIZING EFFECTS OF THE
INDIAN LIBERALIZATION EXPERIENCE

ABRZ (2004) analyze the impact of liberalization on the performance of registered manufacturing firms.[9] They run panel regressions of performance measures such as TFP growth or profitability in a particular industry in a particular state at a particular time. They regress these performance measures over (1) the prereform proximity of the state industry to the Indian technological frontier (defined as labor productivity in the three-digit state industry in 1990 divided by labor productivity in the most productive three-digit state industry in that year); (2) a dummy variable that captures the liberalization reform and is equal to zero before 1991 and to 1 thereafter; (3) labor market institutions at the state level, and in particular the extent to which labor regulations in the state are more "pro-employer" or more "pro-employee" relative to other states. To capture state-level institutions, ABRZ follow Besley and Burgess (2003), who use the number and direction (pro-employer or pro-employee) of the state-level amendments to the 1947 Industrial Disputes Act to measure the extent to which the labor regulations are more pro-employer or more pro-employees in the states of India. They look at both whether the direction of regulatory change over the 1980–1997 period affected industry performance and whether prereform labor market institutions affected postreform performance. ABRZ also control for state industry and year fixed effects, and the standard errors are adjusted for clustering by state to deal with problems of serial correlation.

The key empirical results from ABRZ (2004) can be summarized as follows. TFP, investment, and profitability respond more positively to the liberalization reform in industries that are initially closer to the technological frontier. Moreover, technological progress and the growth in profitability are slower in industries located in more pro-employee states; this is fully consistent with the view, put forward by new growth theories, that the institutional environment in which firms operate affects their investment incentives and, subsequently, their productivity growth performance. Finally, liberalization increases the negative impact of pro-worker regulations on productivity growth. Thus, greater rent extraction by workers reduces firms' incentives to fight entry through more intense innovative investments. That investments reacted in the same heterogeneous way as profitability and productivity across firms in different states, or at different distances from their industry frontier, is direct evidence that what happened during the 1990s amounted to more than a pure selection between firms that were intrinsically more performing, and therefore could better withstand the liberalization shock, and the less performing firms that such reforms would condemn to obsolescence. Rather, as predicted by the new growth theories, it is through their effects on firms' investment incentives in different states and industries that the liberalization reforms affected subsequent productivity growth. And it is because firms' incentives to innovate and respond to the increased entry threat differed across states, and across initial levels of technological development, that we observed a heterogeneous growth response to these reforms.

Thus, the liberalization reforms of 1991 increased average productivity and profitability over the subsequent decade, but they also increased inequality. And while poverty reduction slowed down, it nevertheless occurred, on average, over the whole period.

WHY DID POVERTY REDUCTION OCCUR IN ASIA AND NOT IN LATIN AMERICA?

In our discussion so far we have tried to argue that poverty alleviation and economic development should be addressed from a macro-growth perspective as well as from a pure micro-household viewpoint. However, someone critical of our way of thinking would bring up the example of Latin American countries where poverty indicators have deteriorated over the past decades even though (or perhaps because) these countries implemented a "Washington Consensus" type of package (price and trade liberalization, privatization, and stabilization). Interestingly, neither poverty nor growth indicators have improved in those countries during the recent period, so that Latin America is not a counterexample to begin with. Yet it is worth understanding why Latin American countries are not growing. Part of a possible answer to this question relies on the combination of three elements: inequality, education, and trade. First is inequality, which is higher in Latin America than in Asia.[10] As suggested by Alesina and Rodrik (1994) and Benabou (1996), too much inequality tends to be detrimental to growth, especially in less developed countries. Second is education, which is far more widespread in East Asian countries such as Korea and Hong Kong than in Latin America. Third is trade: East Asian countries, and more recently China, have followed more aggressive export promotion strategies combined with high investments of physical and human capital. Another part of the answer to the above question thus may lie in differences in growth strategies pursued by different countries and regions: through their export promotion policies, Asian countries have targeted their efforts on imitating the most innovative sectors in developed countries, whereas Latin American countries have followed import substitution policies driven by the local market and by a static view of comparative advantage.

The reasons why these growth-enhancing factors are missing in some parts of the world, and present in others, has been the subject of a fast-growing literature on the economics of institutions (see La Porta et al. 1997; Hall and Jones 2000; and Acemoglu et al. 2001). But this literature has not yet delivered recommendations on new mechanisms that might potentially help overcome legal and political obstacles to the implementation of more effective pro-education, pro-health, pro-private-sector growth policies. But here is precisely where, we believe, the growth and household approaches can be reconciled into a renewed theory of development. More specifically, to maximize the effectiveness of top-down growth-enhancing government programs, we see a role for nongovernmental organizations (NGOs) to monitor the implementation of these programs. For example, microfinance institutions, most of which are NGOs, have vested interests in monitoring household participation in health and education programs while monitoring the quality of these programs, in addition to promoting financial development and the banking sector. However, in the absence of top-down strategies, all that these microfinance institutions have achieved is to help people survive within poverty, not to grow out of it, as shown by recent empirical evidence (see Armendariz and Morduch 2004).

NOTES

1. As well explained in Todaro and Smith (2003), "After the green revolution of the late 1960s and early 1970s, agricultural production started increasing at an annual rate of 3%. This was largely due to improvements in agricultural technologies and irrigation systems. As a result, India became self-sufficient in grain production. It was able to increase its wheat production from 10 million tons in 1964 to over 45 million tons in 1985."

2. See Eswaran and Kotwal (1994). We thank Dilip Mookherjee for pointing out this reference to us.

3. See Romer (1990) and Aghion and Howitt (1992, 1998).

4. Vandenbussche et al. (2004) use similar cross-country panel data to show that the closer a country initially lies to the technological frontier, the greater the importance of higher education relative to primary/secondary education for productivity growth.

5. Cross-country evidence of a negative correlation between volatility and growth was first provided by Ramey and Ramey (1995). See also Aghion, Angeletos, et al. (2004).

6. In particular, see King and Levine (1993) and Levine et al. (2002).

7. See Aghion, Bloom, et al. (2005); Aghion, Burgess, et al. (2003); and Aghion, Blundell, et al. (2004).

8. See World Bank (1998), which offers a detailed description of the green revolution and of how its diffusion was facilitated by suitable government policy on education, intellectual property, foreign direct investment, technological licensing, and "vast programs to help focus public [research] laboratories on the needs of productive sector."

9. These correspond to firms with more than ten employees. Over the period 1980–1997, these firms accounted for 10% of GDP, twice as much as the unregistered sector.

10. World Bank (1998) estimated that the average Gini coefficients for Latin America and East Asia were, respectively, 0.49 and 0.40, which indeed reflects a higher level of inequality in Latin America compared with East Asia.

BIBLIOGRAPHY

Acemoglu, Daron, Philippe Aghion, and Fabrizio Zilibotti. "Distance to Frontier, Selection, and Economic Growth." NBER working paper 9066, 2002.

Acemoglu, Daron, Simon Johnson, and James Robinson. "The Colonial Origins of Comparative Development: An Empirical Investigation." *American Economic Review* 91 (2001): 1369–1401.

Aghion, Philippe, Marios Angeletos, Abhijit Banerjee, and Kalina Manova. "Volatility, R&D, and Growth." Mimeo, Harvard University, 2004.

Aghion, Philippe, Nicholas Bloom, Rachel Griffith, and Peter Howitt. "Competition and Innovation: An Inverted-U Relationship."*Quarterly Journal of Economics* 120 (2) (2005): 701–728.

Aghion, Philippe, Richard Blundell, Rachel Griffith, Peter Howitt, and Susan Prantl. "Entry, Innovation and Growth: Theory and Evidence." Mimeo, Harvard University, 2004.

Aghion, Philippe, Robin Burgess, Stephen Redding, and Fabrizio Zilibotti. "The Unequalizing Effect of Liberalization: Theory and Evidence from India." Mimeo, Harvard University and University College London, 2003.

Aghion, Philippe, and Peter Howitt. "A Model of Growth through Creative Destruction." *Econometrica* 60 (1992): 323–351.

Aghion, Philippe, and Peter Howitt. *Endogenous Growth Theory.* Cambridge, Mass.: MIT Press, 1998.

Aghion, Philippe, Peter Howitt, and David Mayer. "The Effect of Financial Development on Convergence: Theory and Evidence," *Quarterly Journal of Economics,* February 2005, 173–222.

Alesina, Alberto, and Dani Rodrik. "Distributive Politics and Economic Growth." *Quarterly Journal of Economics* 108 (1994): 465–490.

Armendáriz de Aghion, Beatriz, and Jonathan Morduch. *The Economics of Microfinance.* Cambridge, Mass.: MIT Press, 2005.

Banerjee, Abhijit, and Andrew Newman. "Occupational Choice and the Process of Development." *Journal of Political Economy* 101 (1993): 274–298.

Benabou, Roland. "Inequality and Growth." In *NBER Macroeconomics Annual,* vol. 11. Cambridge, Mass.: MIT Press, 1996.

Benhabib, Jess, and Mark Spiegel. "The Role of Human Capital in Economic Development: Evidence from Aggregate Cross-Country Data." *Journal of Monetary Economics* 34 (1994): 143–173.

Datt, Gaurav, and Martin Ravallion. "Farm Productivity and Rural Poverty in India." Food Consumption and Nutrition Division Paper no. 42, International Food Policy Research Institute, 1998.

Deaton, Angus, and Jean Drèze. "Poverty and Inequality in India: A Reexamination." Working paper 107, Princeton University, 2002.

Eswaran, Mukesh, and Ashok Kotwal. *Why Poverty Persists in India.* Delhi: Oxford University Press, 1994.

Galor, Oded, and Joseph Zeira. "Income Distribution and Macroeconomics." *Review of Economic Studies* 60 (1993): 35–52.

Hall, Robert, and Charles Jones. "Why Do Some Countries Produce So Much More

Output per Worker Than Others?" *Quarterly Journal of Economics* 114 (1999): 83–116.

King, Robert, and Ross Levine. "Finance, Entrepreneurship, and Growth." *Journal of Monetary Economics* 32 (1993): 513–542

Krueger, Alan, and Mikael Lindahl. "Education for Growth: Why and for Whom?" *Journal of Economic Literature* 34 (2001): 1101–1136.

Levine, Ross, Norman Loayza, and Thorsten Beck. "Financial Intermediation and Growth: Causality and Causes." *Journal of Monetary Economics* 22 (2000): 3–42.

Rodrik, Dani, and Arvind Subramanian. "From 'Hindhu Growth' to Productivity Surge: The Mystery of the Indian Growth Transition." Mimeo, Harvard University, 2004.

Romer, Paul. "Endogenous Technical Change." *Journal of Political Economy* 98 (1990): 71–102.

Todaro, Michael, and Stephen Smith. *Economic Development*. Harlow, Essex, U.K.: Pearson Education, 2003.

Vandenbussche, Jérome, Philippe Aghion, and Costas Meghir. "Distance to Frontier and Composition of Human Capital." Mimeo, Harvard University and University College London, 2004.

World Bank. *World Development Report*. Washington, D.C.: World Bank, 1998.

6

Globalization and All That

Abhijit Vinayak Banerjee

Globalization is one of those strange things that everyone is for or against but no one feels the need to define. It is, of course, all those things that are in the news these days—call centers in Accra, French farmers lying down on the highway, bebop nights in Bangladesh—but what do they all add up to?

It seems natural and tempting to try to define a globalized world as one where there is unrestricted flow of commodities and ideas across national boundaries, and globalization as the process of approaching that ideal. This would mean, however, that Canada would have to move toward U.S. gun laws and Dutch drug laws, which seems unfair. Perhaps we could allow countries to have their own laws about who can consume what (but not where it was made). The bigger problem, of course, is what to do with all the people from India who want to move across the U.S. boundary. Clearly, not even the most enthusiastic globalizer is talking about the unregulated movement of people.

Unrestricted migration is not an option, we are told, because of its potential for enormous displacement and damage to the social fabric. But is there not damage to the social fabric when cotton farmers in India end their lives because, with imports so much cheaper, no one wants their cotton anymore? In the first half of 2004, there were over 300 reported farmer suicides in the state of Andhra Pradesh alone, many of them by drinking the very pesticides that they had bought to protect their cotton crop.[1] The sad truth is that we have been taught to privilege the costs of migration by the sheer virulence of the racist reaction that it has sometimes engendered. The victims of freer trade are handicapped by their inability to effectively invoke the irresistible rhetoric of blood and honor.

There are, of course, many others who have reason to be grateful for what globalization has done for them. And this includes not only the millionaires in Bangalore and Beijing, but also their chauffeurs and cleaning ladies. The starvation of the cotton farmer ought to be weighed against the potential starvation of his sister, who, after being abandoned by her husband, found a bearable living cleaning dishes in the homes of the software rich.

Indeed, as David Ricardo explained almost exactly two centuries ago, since trade allows the country to specialize in what it does best, total income ought to go up when a country opens itself to trade, implying that the income gains to the winners should be larger than the income losses suffered by the losers. After all, we all understand the advantage of specializing in what we do best. This is the reason why most of us choose to rely on the baker for baking our bread and the potter for producing our pottery.

The past couple of centuries have given us a chance to appreciate the many ways in which this simple and powerful argument is not entirely complete, but it is a rare economist who fails to be compelled by its essential logic. He will concede that there are cases where trade might reduce total income, and accept that there are situations where that might justify protection, but for the most part, when an economist worries about globalization, he is worrying about the losers. He knows that the losers, especially if they happen to be poor to start with, cannot be especially comforted by the fact that there are winners and that these winners are winning big (indeed, it might grate all the more).

Economists have always had useful things to say about the distributional consequences of international trade. Indeed, some of the most important insights of that most creative era of modern economics, the thirty years starting around 1930, come from attempts to say something about who gains (and who loses) from trade. The theory that builds on these insights, what one might call high trade theory, is as elegant as anything economists have produced. Nevertheless, I will argue, in order to have a useful conversation about globalization today, we need to go beyond this way of looking at the world, not because the theory was wrong to start with, but because the world for which it was conceived is no longer the world in which we live. This is the point of departure of this essay. My hope is that it conveys a sense of why today's world is different from the world of high trade theory, and helps the reader in thinking about who are likely to be the winners and losers in today's world, and how one might try to help the losers.

THE WORLD OF HIGH TRADE THEORY

One of the most insightful results in modern economics is the Samuelson-Stolper Theorem: it tells us that if a labor-abundant country is opened to trade with a labor-scarce country, laborers in the first country and the employers in the second will profit at the expense of the workers in the second country and the employers in the first. The logic is simple: trade gives each country a bigger market for the goods it is best suited to produce, goods where it has comparative advantage. We would expect countries to have comparative advantage in goods that make greatest use of its abundant resources. Thus a labor-abundant country should see an expansion of its production of labor-intensive goods, with corresponding increases in the demand for labor and its price. Since nowadays labor-abundant countries also tend to be poor, and laborers are usually poorer than their employers, this implies that freeing up trade helps the poor in the poorer country. Their employers, of course, suffer for much the same reason—higher wages mean higher costs for them—and as a result, inequality in the poorer country ought to fall. And laborers in the rich country are hurt by the fact that their countrymen can go elsewhere for their labor-intensive goods, with the result that wages in the two countries are drawn closer—illustrating the famous link from free trade to what used to be called *factor price convergence*.[2]

According to the data we have, these heartening predictions seem to have held up rather well throughout the nineteenth century and until well into the twentieth. In the first half of the nineteenth century, international trade was, as it had always been, largely a matter of exchanging goods that had more value than weight and, as such, a marginal (albeit highly profitable) part of economic life. On the Atlantic rim this was a period of divergence. Wages were growing fastest in the richest countries—England and the United States—and some of the less favored countries, such as Spain and the Netherlands, were in a slump.[3] But in each case the driver was at home—U.S. wage growth was propelled by the growing realization of the nation's many natural advantages (the period ends with the California gold rush), and in England, workers were finally getting the benefits of decades of industrialization. Globalization was still a bit player.

Then, suddenly, the floodgates opened. In 1846, England repealed the Corn Laws, which allowed the government to restrict the import of wheat to protect domestic farmers, setting off a spate of unilateral and bilateral lowering of barriers to trade all across Western and Central Europe.[4] Transatlantic steam shipping was introduced in 1838, and by 1870 a series of innovations—the screw propeller, the compound engine, steel hulls, among others—had made transporting bulk freight by steamships practical. Railways, introduced in the 1830s, came of age after 1850—mileage all over the world grew by more than five times between 1850 and 1870—completing the integration of the interior with the ports that had begun with the canal revolution of the first half of the century. Also, mechanical refrigeration started being used in the transporting of meat across the Atlantic after 1870.

The combination of these forces led to rapid expansion of trade over the period 1870–1913, with the share of merchandise exports in 1913 across a set of sixteen OECD countries rising to levels that they typically did not exceed until well after 1950, and in some cases (such as the United Kingdom) not until the 1980s.[5] It meant that the price of grains and meat in the labor-abundant, land-scarce countries of Western and Central Europe fell to levels comparable with those in the labor-scarce, land-abundant countries in the New World—Argentina, Australia, Canada, and the United States. Wheat prices in Liverpool were 57.6% higher than wheat prices in Chicago in 1870, but only 17.8% higher in 1895, and the U.S.-British meat price gap shrank from nearly 100% in 1885 to less than 20% in 1913.[6]

If nothing else had changed, the fall in the price of food should, by itself, have shrunk the gap in the real (consumption) value of wages between Europe and the New World. And there is indeed some evidence of faster wage growth in Europe over this period. While there was almost no wage growth in Australia between 1870 and 1913, and U.S. wages grew by about 1% per year, wage growth was around 2.5% per year in Scandinavia and around 1.75% per year in Ireland and Italy. But there were also a number of anomalies. Wage growth in the richest European countries—Belgium, France, Germany, the Netherlands and the United Kingdom—was no higher than in the United States; and in the less developed countries in the New World, such as Argentina and Canada, wages actually grew considerably faster.

The same theory that tells us there should be convergence in wages also tells us that there should be convergence in the price of land, though the gains from trade here go to the landowners in the land-abundant countries. We do find that prices for agricultural land rose by almost 400% in land-abundant Australia between 1870 and 1913, nearly trebled in the United States over the same period, and declined in Britain, France, and Sweden. But in Denmark, Germany, and Spain, which were land-scarce countries, land prices went up.

Of course we are asking for a lot here. Quite so much fealty to a specific theory may be unreasonable to expect, given that there are many other reasons why wages and prices go up—capital accumulation and technological upgrading being the most obvious among them. A more modest goal would be to ask whether the ratio of wages to land prices became more similar in all these countries. If there was something (say political change) that made both wages and land prices go up in one country and down in another, neither wages nor land prices would converge, but their ratio might. And indeed, this is exactly what we find. Every Western and Central European country with the exception of Spain shows sharp growth in the ratio of wages to land prices, and every New World country for which we have data shows a decline.[7]

For labor-abundant Europe, the period of expanded trade that led up to the First World War was a period of growing equality within. The nervous years between the wars saw the reversal of all that. In these years of growing xenophobia and economic nationalism, tariff barriers were raised and borders were closed to immigrants. And, at least for Western Europe, inequality started to grow once again. Between 1870 and 1913, equality, measured by the ratio of the wages of unskilled workers to the output produced by an average worker, went up in the countries where wages were low and went down where wages were the highest. Between 1921 and 1938, we see exactly the opposite pattern—no one really did well, this being the era of the Great Depression, but the poor did the worst in Italy and France and the best in Canada, Australia, and the United States.[8]

It is not entirely obvious that we can interpret this evidence as support for trade theory. The problem, noted by the O'Rourke and Williamson study that is the source of most of our information about the nineteenth and early twentieth centuries, is that the pro-trade decades were also pro-immigration decades. Enormous numbers of people immigrated from all over Europe to the Americas, creating the melting pot that we know today. The U.S. labor force would have been smaller by about a quarter in 1910, were it not for the flow of immigrants over the previous four decades. This drove wages up in the countries they had left and down in the countries where they went. Indeed, O'Rourke and Williamson do a calculation that shows that immigration alone can explain all the changes in the income distribution in this period and more, though they are at pains to convince us that this cannot be right. Perhaps one day better data will reveal what really happened. In the meanwhile, the fans of trade theory must find the overall picture from this period rather comforting. The problems start later.

THE PROBLEM YEARS

After the brutal interlude of World War II, trade resumed, now under the supervision of the newly created guardians of the world trading system: the World Bank, the IMF, and the GATT. Decolonization followed, and suddenly the poorest countries in the world had a chance to make their own trade policies. Since the mid-1950s, trade barriers have been raised and brought down many times in every corner of the world (though perhaps today we live in a world that is more open to trade than at any time since 1930). What can we take away from this experience?

There have been a number of in-depth studies of what happened when specific countries liberalized. Adrian Wood studied the East Asian "tigers" and found that low-skilled workers did relatively well in Korea, Singapore, and Taiwan (but not in Hong Kong) in the decade that followed the lowering of trade barriers. This is as one might have expected, given everything we have been told about how they grew rich by exporting labor-intensive goods.

Things started going wrong with the Mexican liberalization of 1985–1987. Over this two-year period, Mexico massively reduced both the coverage of its import quota regime and the average duty on imports. Over the rest of the decade, blue-collar workers lost almost 15% of their wages while their white-collar counterparts gained in the same proportion, reversing the trend toward greater equality in the years leading up to the trade liberalization.[9] Argentina showed a similar pattern: trade barriers were massively lowered at the beginning of the 1990s, and between 1990 and 1998 the college premium, which is the ratio of wages for those who have a college degree to those of the average unskilled worker, almost doubled for men and almost trebled for women, in both cases reversing an equalizing trend that had started in 1980.[10] This meant that the lowest wage earners were effectively excluded from the wage growth that took place in this period. In Colombia, trade barriers were massively lowered between 1985 and 1992, leaving the economy more open than it had ever been. Between 1990 and 1998, the college premium went up by over 20%, which is small by Argentine standards, but not negligible. Similar patterns have also been found in Chile in the 1970s, Costa Rica in the late 1980s, and Uruguay in the 1990s.

Lest one think that this is some Latin American perversion, the same correlation between liberalization and increasing inequality showed up in the two Asian giants, China and India. Between 1980 and 1998, while China became increasingly open to the world economy, the income share of the poorest quintile went down from 8% to 7%, while the share of the richest quintile went up from about 30% to about 45%. And in India, all evidence points to an explosion of inequality in the urban areas over the post-liberalization years (1991–2000), after many decades when inequality went neither up nor down.

To check on what we are finding here, we could compare what happened over the last few decades in countries that were open to trade, with what happened in countries that were closed (or we could compare countries that *became open* with countries that did not). This is really what we were doing with the historical data, and now that we have data from a hundred countries and more, it is actually possible to be more precise and try to eliminate other sources of possible difference between these countries. A number of people have now tried this exercise. Most have found, sometimes to their surprise, that being open to trade either increases inequality or has no effect at all. And the one study that directly focuses on the well-being of the poor (defined as the bottom 40%) finds that their income grows more slowly when the economy is more open to trade, not just in comparison with the rich but in absolute terms.

Correlation, as social scientists never tire of reminding each other, is not causation, and none of this evidence is quite strong enough to entirely transcend that old divide. However, what these case studies do show is that, at the time when countries opened themselves to trade, something happened that was powerful enough to make the countries change course toward greater equality in the nineteenth and early twentieth centuries and toward greater *inequality* in the last decades of the twentieth. That something may not be the trade liberalization itself, but it is something that operates at a similar time scale; in other words, it cannot be confounded with those other, much more long-term, factors that also affect income distribution, such as the nature of technology and the norms of society.

The studies do offer some clues to what the confounding factors might be (if it is not the effect of trade liberalization) that we have been deliberately ignoring so far. Feenstra and Hanson (1997) argue that trade has very little to do with why inequality went up in Mexico, and they argue that it was largely driven by the foreign investment that came in with the liberalization. They suggest the following line of reasoning: when an American firm builds a factory in Mexico to make something it used to make at home, the demand for skilled labor should go up, simply because anything that used to be produced in the United States ought to be much more skill-intensive than most things Mexico used to produce. This is correct, but only if we accept the assumption that once production moves to Mexico, the firm would not switch to a very different (and less skill-intensive) way of doing things. This is perhaps the natural assumption in cases where the overall production process remains centered in the United States and just a few steps get sent to Mexico, but not necessarily when the entire production process is moved to Mexico. When Nike goes to Vietnam, given just how much cheaper un-skilled/semi-skilled labor is available in Vietnam compared with the United States, it would seem natural for Nike to try to reorganize production to use more of this kind of labor, thereby benefiting the low-skilled workers relative to everyone else.

On purely theoretical grounds, it seems that the impact of foreign in-vestment on inequality in a relatively poor country like Mexico could have gone either way. The evidence from the Mexican case, at least prima facie, seems to support the Feenstra-Hanson view: it does seem to be the case that skilled workers gained more where there was more foreign investment. Feen-stra and Hanson estimate that the impact of foreign investment alone can explain almost half of the rise in the wages of nonproduction workers (a proxy for white-collar workers). The fact remains, however, that half the increase is still unexplained and, in addition, it remains for us to explain why the *fall* in inequality predicted by trade theory did not happen.

A less interesting theory of why things did not work out the way they were supposed to argues that in Argentina, Colombia, and Mexico, it was the industries with a high concentration of low-skilled workers that had the highest tariffs to begin with and where the tariff cuts and the resulting fall in prices were the largest. But tariffs matter only if you are in an industry that is a net importer, and indeed most of these studies do find that prices fell more in industries where the tariff cut was deeper—confirming that the barriers to trade in these industries were actually blocking imports. It follows that these Latin American countries must have been importing all these labor-intensive goods, despite the fact that nearly 90% of Latin America's external trade is with rich, labor-scarce countries.

The puzzle deepens when we push this argument a step further. When these studies directly look at changes in employment across sectors, the strik-ing thing is the lack of correlation between changes in tariffs (or the resulting change in imports) and changes in employment. After all, our faith in the therapeutic qualities of trade comes from the belief that trade helps the coun-try specialize in what it is good at, and we might have expected that removing the barriers to trade would set off the process of reallocation of labor in that salubrious direction.

One might wonder, especially if one comes from a certain political persuasion, whether the absence of labor reallocation is a result of draconian labor regulations that make it impossible to fire anyone. As it turns out, manufacturing employment fell dramatically in Argentina, considerably in Colombia, and more modestly but still significantly in Mexico. It also does not seem to be true that people in what would have been shrinking sectors protected their jobs by taking huge pay cuts (say out of a love of their jobs). Wages did fall, but the correlation between the fall in wages and the changes in protection is never very large. The removal of protection hurt all workers and not just the workers in the protected industries.

It is not that trade theory cannot find a way around these new puzzles. One can always invoke special explanations, something that just happened to coincide with the shift in trade policy. But there is a general sense that things are not fitting together, that one has to do too much work these days to defend the view, dear to trade economists, that trade always helps the poor in poor countries. It looks like we might be missing something important.

RETHINKING TRADE THEORY

The key missing ingredient, I believe, is reputation. Reputation is an omnibus word that economists use to describe a range of things, from the expectation of quality associated with a brand name, to the trust that two people who have been doing business for a long time have in each other.

Brand names are clearly hugely important in today's trade. This makes perfect sense, given that the average buyer in the north (who has all the money), is rich enough today to afford to indulge his sense of quality. Clothes must not shrink or bleed; machines must not fall apart in a week; and software must be ready when promised. Consumers would rather pay something extra for a brand name because they feel assured of the quality.

Trust, less obviously, is also vital. Retailers are willing to pay more to trusted suppliers because they do not want to offend their customers by selling duds. And manufacturers want suppliers who are known to be reliable, because what they make and sell is only as good as its weakest link.

The obverse of quality being important is that the price is not quite as important as it used to be. In 1997, when the Indian software industry was just beginning to become a household name, I happened to be in the offices of one of the leading exporters of customized software. We were talking about the industry, and the CEO said, almost casually, "We just raised the price per line of code by 50%, and our clients did not seem to mind. I think we will raise it by another 50% in a few months." I happen to know that he was not bragging. Indian software in those days (we are now in the time scale of the software world) was so cheap that it did not make sense for the average overseas buyer to give up someone they knew and trusted for someone new, even at half the price. After all, the new supplier could be incompetent or worse, and chances were that the buyer would find out only after the software was ready, many months hence. For the typical buyer of customized software, a Fortune 500 company, the cost of the lost time was probably worth as much as it was paying for the software, or more.

The logic here applies as much to T-shirts as it does to software. The famous New York department store, Macy's, orders its T-shirts from its overseas suppliers in the fall of each year, but the T-shirts go on sale the next spring. If, when the T-shirts arrive in early spring, Macy's discovers that they are not what it had asked for, it would be too late to do much about it for that year. The loss of face vis-à-vis its customers could be enormous. It has to be worth paying extra to suppliers that it can trust.

Several consequences follow from recognizing the centrality of reputation. First, reputation is a bit like a fixed cost—the advantage it gives you is independent of how much you sell, though if you expand beyond the point where you are able to maintain quality, your reputation will eventually collapse. Over some range, however, it clearly pays for firms that have a reputation to keep expanding. It is no accident that Gucci now markets everything from perfumes to polo shirts, and Amazon.com is no longer just the bookseller to the world.

Second, when firms that have a brand name shift production to a Third World country, they are often reluctant to change the process of production, even though the local cost structure might favor reorganization. This is because they are worried about whether they will be able to exercise the same degree of control over quality when they change their processes, not necessarily because the new processes are inherently harder to control but because they are unfamiliar. Given that so much is riding on predictably delivering quality, experimenting with their processes is not something they do lightly.

This reluctance to change processes means that when a First World firm relocates to a Third World country, it demands the same kind of labor that it was using at home. This may be why foreign investment is associated with a rise in the skill premium.

Third, the urge to capitalize on their brand name is an important part of what drives multinationals to set up shop in LDCs that are willing to have them. And since services are where brand names count the most (would you trust your money to a bank that you have never heard of; or get advice from a consultant on his first day on the job?), a lot of multinationals are headed for the service sector. Since service industries tend to employ large numbers of white-collar workers, this is one more reason why the skill premium goes up when the multinationals come in.

Fourth, we would expect a great deal of inertia in the choice of from whom to buy. Combined with the fact that those who have a reputation will tend to want to grow, this implies that it could take a long time before cost advantages show up in the pattern of trade. This may explain why the Argentines and the Colombians import labor-intensive goods from the labor-scarce north. It also explains why so many domestic firms shrink or shut down when their countries are opened to trade—they cannot compete with the reputation of the best-established multinational suppliers. The firms that survive and expand, apart from the few that already have an established international reputation, will be the ones that are in sectors where reputation does not matter so much—manufacturers aimed at the lower end of the local market or exports to other Third World countries, for example. This may be one way to interpret the fact that in all the Latin American examples, the informal sector expanded following trade liberalization.

Finally, and perhaps most important, all this suggests that it may be some time before those who lose their livelihoods with the liberalization find comparable jobs in the industries that start to grow after the liberalization. In the long run, we would expect the country to broadly specialize in industries where its factor endowments give it a natural advantage, but success in building a reputation will clearly be crucial in determining exactly what it ends up exporting to the world. This process is likely to be slow because building a reputation takes time: Esther Duflo and I found that in the Indian software industry it took about five years to be really trusted by foreign buyers, and in software everything happens quickly.[11] It is likely to be doubly slow because capital markets in developing countries work very poorly, and even visibly successful firms have trouble getting enough capital to expand as fast as they want. In another joint project with Esther Duflo, we found that even firms in India, where the return on the extra dollar is 80 cents or more, cannot get enough capital.

This problem is made worse now by the fact that China and India are in the process of expanding their exports to the level that their enormous reserves of skilled manpower would justify. They have cheap wages, a large and wealthy émigré population that provides them with the necessary contacts, and a growing reputation. Most other countries would have to build their own reputations in competition with these two established players, just when they are gathering steam. It cannot be easy.

WHAT THEN?

If I am right in looking at the world in this way, where does it leave us? Relative to the benign vision of globalization offered by the Samuelson-Stolper Theorem, at least for the poor in poor countries, all this is obviously bad news, though recognizing the problem does help us control the damage. It tells us, for one thing, that countries need to think hard about reputation.

There are a number of steps that a country can take to make reputation acquisition less of an issue. More effective court systems make it easier to sue for damages if a supplier misbehaves, which encourages buyers to consider sellers who are yet to make a name for themselves. Developing trade relations with other developing countries has a similar effect, because poorer buyers may be more willing to trade off quality for low prices. It is perhaps no accident that Guido Porto found that Mercosur, which integrated the economies of Argentina, Brazil, Paraguay, and Uruguay into a single (almost) free trade zone, benefited the poor in Argentina.

A public scoring system for buyers and sellers, where buyers report their experiences with specific suppliers and vice versa (for example, on CNET .com or Dealtime.com), may be one way to speed the process of building up a reputation, simply by making it easier to identify malefactors. We do, however, have to careful about the possibility of abuse here. Sellers may try to blackmail buyers by threatening to give them a harsh report.

Creating an environment that is friendly toward multinational investors also helps, though most countries seem to trust domestic capitalists more than their foreign counterparts. My sense is that this is largely unwarranted (though perhaps politically necessary). The prima facie evidence seems to be that within any sector multinationals pay higher wages to people with the same observable qualities, compared with domestic firms. Indeed, the simple fact of being in the public eye probably makes them behave better.

Multinationals are useful because their reputations can intermediate between domestic sellers and foreign buyers, and also because they are better at negotiating with regulators in the north, who are often all too willing to protect domestic producers from cheaper imports, in the name of protecting the health of domestic consumers. Much of what China now exports is produced by nameless firms in China, but marketed under some global brand name. In the typical case, the Chinese firm sells to some other established firm, often based in Hong Kong, and it is this firm that sells to the eventual marketer. This double intermediation is useful because the firm in Hong Kong has a reputation in the world of other firms, not among the eventual buyers, while the firm that does the final sale does not need to learn all the nuances of Chinese supply chains. Indian customized software firms have a similar system. The firm will often have a U.S. front office that the buyers know and deal with, which in turn will pass on the actual work to Indian partners, whom the buyers know about only vaguely.

Finally, improving capital markets is yet another way to make building a reputation easier. Firms that have been doing well need to go to scale quickly, and inefficient capital markets slow their growth.

All this, of course, does not answer the really basic question: Is trade worth it? The conventional answer, at least among economists, is that trade is worth it as long as it makes the pie bigger. If the income gains to those who gain from trade are larger than the losses to those who lose, we should be in favor of trade, because we could always redistribute the gains to make everyone better off. On the other hand, if I am right in my diagnosis of what drives trade today, the losers will include large numbers of poor people in poor countries, and I very much doubt that they will all be compensated for their losses. The problem is that targeted redistribution is never easy. Identifying the losers is hard, taxing the winners is harder, and making sure that the money does not somehow get lost along the way is sometimes well nigh impossible. The best way to make sure that no one loses from liberalization is almost surely not to do it.

On the other hand, I know of no example of a labor-abundant developing country that has had sustained growth without being outwardly oriented in some broad sense of the term. The problem is that growing countries need technology and capital from abroad, and to pay for these imports and to take full advantage of what they are good at doing, they need markets abroad.

It is true that none of this directly requires being totally open to imports: China, after all, is only starting to get there. But it does require a credible commitment to remain open for the foreseeable future, to convince foreign investors that the country will earn enough foreign currency to repay what it is borrowing now. And it requires being sufficiently open to imports from the north to keep the WTO happy, if for no other reason than keeping the markets in the north open to its exports. In the end, the choice is between cutting oneself more or less completely off and giving up on fast growth, and accepting a very substantial degree of openness.

Having thought about it, I think I come out on the side of openness. We live in a world where people have come to see the good life as something to which they can legitimately aspire. There is no way to put that genie back in the bottle (even if we could, I do not know that I would want to). The explosion of ethno-religious conflict around the world since the 1980s, I believe, is a product of an era in which hopes were created and then denied. To go back and convince people that growth is not worth it, is to invite a bloodbath.

Given that, our job as economists should be to think of ways to make the whole process as painless for the many losers as it can be made to be. There seems to be broad agreement these days that openness should go with a strong commitment to an acceptable guaranteed minimum living for all. While I am certainly in favor, two remarks are in order. First, the popular view seems to be that the guarantee should primarily take the form of a right to education and health. This is in many ways very appealing, but my sense is that we know very little about how to deliver these services effectively to the poor in poor countries. An income support program, targeted toward the elderly and women with young children, combined with a negative income tax program targeted toward those who are working for low wages (modeled on the earned income tax credit in the United States), has the obvious advantage that we know it helps the poor. Second, many of the biggest losers will be the owners of very small firms and farms and workers in the organized sector, rather than the very poor. The minimum guarantees that are being discussed are clearly not going to compensate them for what they will have lost. While in some ways this is fair—after all, they do have more to start with—we should recognize that at the very least, they think that they have a right to be compensated. There is very little work that I know of that thinks hard about how to target the nondestitute.

Finally, there is the issue of how to share the benefits of trade fairly across countries. The economics of how the gains from trade get distributed across the trading partners is always subtle, and I have no way to say who gains more. The distribution of costs, on the other hand, seems clear enough. Every rich country has a well-established system of welfare that will automatically compensate its losers. Every poor country will have to set up new mechanisms to do so, and pay for them now. In addition, migration today is explicitly a system by which rich countries raid the poor countries for talent. With every engineer or doctor who settles in the north, a poor country loses a potential entrepreneur or a public servant, and it is hard for me to believe that the money they send back is compensation enough. Globalization, by the simple fact of increasing contact, can only make it easier for the north to pick off the people it wants. It is true that globalization has encouraged some of these people to take a second look at the opportunities in their own countries, but on balance I suspect it is still a cost (China and India may be exceptions here, though I would not be sanguine).

I therefore see no reason why the poor countries should not demand an explicit price from the rich for agreeing to remain open. There are many ways the price could be paid, but let me end by mentioning one that appeals very much to the economist in me. Given that rich countries are aging fast and need labor, why not a system of quotas for immigration to rich countries that are open to everyone (i.e., not just the doctors and engineers) in poor countries that agree to remain open.[12] The quota would be allocated by a lottery, and would allow one person between the ages of twenty and thirty-five to have a work permit in a rich country for a fixed period, say five years. His/her travel expenses and some resettlement costs would be paid for, and precautions would be taken to make sure that in most cases, he/she did go back, so that the home country would benefit from his/her savings and the skills he or she had acquired.

This will not be easy: It will require us to confront the forces of racism and xenophobia that will surely try to make the most of new opportunities. But in the end, if we cannot ask the rich democracies to do what is both just and economically rational, what is left for us to hope for?

NOTES

1. *http://www.indiatogether.org/2004/jun/psa-farmdie.htm.*
2. Because labor, land, and capital used to be called factors of production, and it is their prices that converge.
3. Kevin O'Rourke and Jeffrey Williamson, *Globalization and History* (Cambridge, Mass.: MIT Press, 2000).
4. Ibid.
5. Based on ibid., Table 3.1.
6. Ibid.
7. Ibid., Table 2.2.
8. Ibid.
9. Robert Feenstra and Gordon Hanson, "Foreign Direct Investment and Relative

Wages: Evidence from Mexico's Maquiladoras," *Journal of International Economics* 42 (1997): 371–394.

10. Sebastian Galliani and Pablo Sanguinetti, "The Impact of Trade Liberalization on Wage Inequality: Evidence from Argentina," mimeo, Universidad di Tella, Buenos Aires, 2002.

11. Abhijit Banerjee and Esther Duflo, "Reputation Effects and the Limits of Contracting," *Quarterly Journal of Economics* 115 (3) (2000): 989–1017.

12. I am certainly not the first person to think along these lines. See, for example, Jagdish Bhagwati, "Borders Beyond Control," *Foreign Affairs* 82 (1), (2003): 98–104; and Dani Rodrik, "How to Make the Trade Regime Work for Development," mimeo, Harvard University, 2004.

7

The Global Economy and the Poor

Pranab Bardhan

The majority of people I know outside the world of economics and business are opposed to globalization; in this they are often particularly swayed by their concerns for the world's poor. Economists who generally support globalization have to address these concerns. Of course, as in most contentious public debates, different people have different things in mind when they refer to globalization. A large part of the widespread opposition to globalization relates to three different aspects of its impact:

1. The fragility of valued local and indigenous cultures of masses of people in the world facing the onslaught of global mass production and cultural homogenization (through global brand-name products, movies, music, fast food, soft drinks, Internet, etc.)
2. The devastation caused to fragile economies by billions of dollars of volatile *short-term* capital stampeding around the globe in herd-like movements
3. The damage caused to jobs, wages, and incomes of poor people by the dislocations and competition of international trade and foreign investment, and the weakening of the ability of the state to compensate for this damage and in general to alleviate poverty.

While I am personally in favor of some restrictions on the full fury of globalization in connection with the first two and can even provide some economic justification for such restrictions, in this essay I shall confine myself to a discussion mainly of the third issue. Thus I shall interpret globalization to mean openness to foreign trade and *long-term* capital flows[1] and try to understand the possible difficulties that poverty alleviation policies in poor countries may face from such international economic integration. For this we need first to look at the processes by which globalization may affect the conditions of the poor and then analyze the ways in which the policies meant to relieve those conditions are hemmed in by global constraints. In general, I believe that globalization can cause many hardships for the poor, but it also opens up opportunities that some countries can utilize and others cannot, largely depending on their domestic political and economic institutions. The net outcome is often quite complex and almost always context-dependent, belying the glib pronouncements for or against globalization made in the opposing camps.

When we refer to poverty, we shall limit ourselves to absolute (as opposed to relative) poverty, measured by some absolute minimum living standards. Most of the general statements on the impact of globalization on such poverty, both in academic discussion and in the media, essentially concern correlations rather than causation. Pro-globalizers point to the large decline in poverty in China and India in the recent decades of international economic integration. However, we still lack convincing demonstrations that this decline is not to a large extent due to internal factors such as expansion of infrastructure or the massive 1978 land reforms or the relaxation of restrictions on rural-to-urban migration in China, or to the spread of the green revolution in agriculture, large antipoverty programs, or social movements in India. Those who are more dubious of global processes point out that in the same decades poverty has remained stubbornly high in sub-Saharan Africa. But this may have little to do with globalization, and more to do with unstable or failed political regimes, and wars and civil conflicts that have afflicted several countries in Africa. If anything, such instability only reduced their extent of globalization, because it scared off many foreign investors and traders.

Going beyond correlations, the causal processes through which international economic integration can affect poverty considered in this paper primarily involve the poor *in their capacity as workers* and *as recipients of public services* or *users of common property resources*. I will thus be ignoring the poor as consumers. Whether they gain as consumers from trade depends on whether they are net buyers of tradable goods—for example, the landless laborers in east or south India who are net buyers of rice may gain from imports of cheaper rice from Thailand, but may lose from higher prices of medicine as the Indian drug market becomes internationalized. Also, a monopolistic retail market structure often blocks the pass-through from border prices to domestic prices. For example, in Mexico after NAFTA, the cartelized tortilla sector largely maintained prices even with the availability of cheaper North American corn.

THE POOR AS SELF-EMPLOYED WORKERS

Let us first consider the case of *poor workers*. They are mainly either self-employed or wage earners. The self-employed work on their own tiny farms or as artisans and petty entrepreneurs in small shops and firms. The major constraints they usually face are in credit, storage, marketing, insurance, access to new technology, extension services, infrastructure (such as roads, power, ports, telecommunication, and irrigation), and government regulations (involving venal inspectors or policemen, insecure land rights, etc.). Relieving these constraints often requires substantive domestic policy changes, and foreign traders and investors are not directly to blame (in fact, they may sometimes help in relieving some of the bottlenecks in infrastructure and services and in the supply of essential parts, components, and equipment). If these changes are not made and the self-employed poor remain constrained, then of course it is difficult for them to withstand competition from large agribusiness companies or manufacturing firms (foreign or domestic).

When small producers are heavily involved in exports (for example, coffee producers in Uganda, rice growers in Vietnam, garment producers in Bangladesh or Cambodia), the major hurdle they face is often due not to more globalization but to *less*. As is by now well known, developed country protectionism and subsidization of farm and food products and simple manufactures (such as textiles and clothing) severely restrict the export prospects for poor countries.

Another increasingly important barrier to trade that many small farmers in developing countries face in world markets is that rich countries now shut out many of these imports under a host of safety and sanitary regulations (sometimes imposed under pressure from lobbyists of import-competing farms in those countries). This actually increases the importance of involving rich-country global companies in marketing poor-country products. These companies can deal with the regulatory and lobbying machinery in rich countries far better than the small producers in poor countries can, and at the same time can provide consumers with credible guarantees of quality and safety. Of course, these companies will charge hefty fees for this marketing service (usually much larger than the total production cost), but the small farmers will usually be better off with them rather than without.

Similarly, it may be very difficult, costly, and time-consuming for small producers of manufactures or services in developing countries to establish brand name and reputation in quality and timely delivery, which are absolutely crucial in marketing, particularly in international markets (much more than comparative costs of production that traditional trade theory emphasizes). This is where multinational marketing chains with global brand names, mediating between domestic suppliers and foreign buyers, can be very helpful for a long time, and paying the high marketing margin they charge may sometimes be worth it. At the same time, coordinated attempts by developing countries, with technical assistance from international organizations, to build international quality certification institutions for their products should be a high priority. Those who are justifiably outraged by the extremely high marketing margins the monopoly multinational companies currently charge the poor producers should agitate more for antitrust action, not antitrade action. There should also be more energetic international attempts to certify codes against international restrictive business practices and to establish an international antitrust investigation agency, possibly under WTO auspices.

It is also important to keep in mind that trade liberalization, even when increasing the mean incomes of the poor producers, may heighten their vulnerability, particularly by increasing the variance of prices or income sources. The evidence on this is mixed, but it is clear that the poor are less able to cope with adverse shocks than the rest of the population.[2]

THE POOR AS WAGE WORKERS

Turning to *poor wage earners,* the literature on how international trade affects the absolute level of the real wages or employment of unskilled workers is meager compared with the one on wage inequality (which, though an important issue, is not directly relevant to my concern with absolute poverty here). Empirically, it is hard to disentangle the effects of trade reform on wages from those flowing from macroeconomic policy changes or other ongoing deregulatory reforms and technological changes.

Traditional international trade theory suggests that the workers in a poor country (presumably with abundant supplies of unskilled labor) having a comparative advantage in products intensive in unskilled labor should benefit from trade liberalization. The improvement in wages and employment of garment workers in Bangladesh or Mauritius with expanding exports is an obvious example. The matter is, of course, complicated by the fact that developing countries (say, Brazil or Mexico or Turkey) may import labor-intensive products from even poorer countries (say, China, Indonesia, or Bangladesh), so that trade, consistent with the traditional theory, may lead to lower wages in the former set of developing countries, for which there seems to be some evidence.[3] Similarly, if a poor country has large supplies of other factors of production (such as land or mineral resources), trade liberalization may not benefit the labor-intensive sectors.

What about the presence in poor countries of large and powerful multinational companies that hire people with low bargaining power? There is little evidence that poor, unskilled workers get lower wages (or fewer jobs) in the presence of those companies, compared with what they will get in their absence, other things remaining the same.[4] Contrary to the impression created by the campaign in affluent countries against "sweatshops" run by multinational companies in poor countries, it can be pointed out that the poor are often banging at the gates of these sweatshops for a chance of entry, since these are far better than their current alternatives: working in occupations with inferior work conditions or no employment at all. This is not an argument against efforts to improve their work conditions (and certainly not in favor of the totally indefensible cases of forced labor or hazardous or unsafe work conditions).[5] But it does suggest that we should look at the reality of the severely limited opportunities faced by the poor and the unintended consequences of trying to restrict rich-country imports of "sweatshop" products because of the harm that may be caused to the displaced poor workers.

Of course, sometimes the large companies, instead of hiring labor themselves, outsource their activities to smaller firms and household enterprises, where the wages and overhead costs are lower, to the detriment of the formal sector employees. But the net effect on the workers of the country should take into account the resultant improvement in wages and employment among the usually much poorer informal sector workers.

There are, however, three important reasons why opening the economy may worsen the conditions of workers. One relates to the issue of mobility of workers or their ability to retool and relocate as the market conditions change. This often depends on the state of available credit, information, social networks, and infrastructural facilities. When the latter are absent or deficient, workers stuck in the declining sectors in an open economy get hurt.

A second reason has to do with the nature of technical change. Since much technical change in rich countries is biased against the services of unskilled labor, transplantation of those new techniques by multinational companies into poor countries will cause employment and wages of unskilled labor to go down. This has reportedly been the case, for example, with global tenders to construction companies, such as Bechtel or Mitsui, using labor-saving technology, which has rendered many construction workers unemployed in India.

The third reason has to do with collective bargaining. Globalization often leads to a weakening of unions. As foreign competition (or even the threat of it) lowers profit margins, the old rent-sharing arrangements between employers and unionized workers come under pressure. Rents decline for both capital and labor, but labor may have to take a larger cut as internationally less mobile labor faces more mobile capital. Companies can more credibly threaten substitution of foreign factors of production, including intermediate inputs, for domestic factors.[6] This may lead to lower wages and, sometimes more important, increased risk of unemployment.

Even when poor, unskilled workers lose as a result of international liberalization, it may be possible to combine a policy of liberalization with a domestic policy of compensating the losers at low cost. The main problem, of course, is that of credible commitment on the part of the ruling politicians that losers will be compensated. Recent history in many countries is full of governments' broken promises to displaced workers. Obviously, this is a particularly important matter in poor countries, where there is very little effective social protection available from the state. Rich countries have better social safety nets and some programs in place helping, however imperfectly, displaced workers to adjust (such as the federal adjustment assistance program in the United States). International organizations that preach the benefits of free trade should take the responsibility for funding and facilitating such adjustment assistance programs in poor countries that can help workers in coping with job losses and getting retrained and reemployed. There should be more income support programs, such as the Trabajar program in Argentina or programs to train and help the unemployed in finding new jobs, such as the Probecat in Mexico or the newly installed social safety net program for workers in sick public sector enterprises in West Bengal (funded by the U.K. Department of International Development and implemented by an NGO).

Until issues of general economic security for poor workers in developing countries are satisfactorily resolved, globalization is bound to raise anxiety and hostility among workers worried about their job security. If mass politics in a country is organized, as it usually is, in such a way that the nation-state is the primary political forum for demanding and getting the necessary redistributive and insurance functions of a society (rendered more important by the economics of international specialization), to the extent that the nation-state is weakened by forces of international economic integration, it is a matter of serious concern. Much depends, of course, on a society's institutions of conflict management and coordination. It is not a coincidence that countries that have a better record in building these institutions have coped better with the dislocations brought about by international trade. The major example is the Scandinavian countries, where in spite of a strong tradition of an organized labor movement and worker solidarity over many decades of the twentieth century, the unions in general have been in favor of an open economy and the worker dislocations have been better managed.

The general issue of the weakening of the nation-state is rather complex. There is a possible loss of national policy options brought about by a poor country's participation in international trade and investment and in the framework of global institutions and rules that govern them. I agree with the antiglobal protesters that many of the international organizations which define the rules of this order are accountable more to the corporate and financial community of rich countries than to the poor. The decision-making processes in these organizations need to be much more transparent and responsive to the lives of the people their decisions crucially affect.[7]

But the protesters' demand for the abolition of international organizations such as the WTO is, however, misplaced. If the alternative to a multilateral organization like the WTO is for a developing country to face the United States in bilateral trade negotiations, the United States is likely to be much more dominant and arbitrary in such negotiations than in the dispensations of the WTO (which in its arbitration decisions has sometimes ruled against the U.S. position). Of course, serious efforts are needed to strengthen the technical negotiation capacity of poor countries in international trade forums where they face the well-equipped and well-funded teams of lawyers and negotiators representing rich countries.

Turning now to the issue of a government's fiscal options in a global economy, many people are of the opinion that the scope for taxing capital to raise revenue is severely limited by the threat of capital flight in the long run, even if we ignore the problem of short-term speculative capital flows. While this limitation can be serious, one should not exaggerate its effects. Most countries collect only a small part of their revenues from capital taxation, even in relatively closed economies. In any case there are strong arguments for funding redistributive policies through progressive consumption taxes (say, VAT) rather than taxes on capital or labor. There is, however, a short-run problem in some developing countries whose public budgets are heavily dependent on customs duties, which decline with trade liberalization.

THE POOR AS USERS OF PUBLIC SERVICES AND COMMON RESOURCES

Let us now briefly turn to the case of the *poor as recipients of public services.* In the low-income developing countries the poor, particularly those who are in the preponderant informal sector, do not receive much effective social protection from the state. But the public sector is usually involved in basic services such as education, health, and public works programs. Cuts in public budgets on these basic services are often attributed to globalization, because the budget cuts to reduce fiscal deficits often come as part of a package of macroeconomic stabilization prescribed by international agencies such as the IMF. While there is a lot of scope for improvement in the stabilization programs to minimize the adverse impact on the poor, one should keep in mind that the fiscal deficits in these poor countries (except for the decline in customs revenue due to tariff cuts) are often brought about in the first place more by domestic profligacy in matters of subsidies to the rich, salaries for the bloated public sector, or military extravagance. Faced with mounting fiscal deficits, the governments often find it politically easier to cut the public expenditures for the voiceless poor. This is due primarily to the domestic political clout of the rich, who are disinclined to share in the necessary fiscal austerity. It is always convenient to blame an external agency for a problem that is essentially domestic in origin.

The low quality and quantity of public services such as education and health in poor countries is not just due to their relatively low share in the public budget. To a large extent even the limited amount of money allocated in the budget does not reach the poor because of all kinds of top-heavy administrative obstacles and bureaucratic and political corruption. Again this is a domestic institutional failure, not largely an external problem. The major effort required here is to strengthen the domestic institutions of accountability.

Apart from basic public services, the poor are also *users of common property resources,* the decline in which is not usually taken into account in standard estimates of poverty, based as they are on either household surveys of private consumer expenditure or national income accounts. Environmentalists argue that trade liberalization damages the poor by encouraging overexploitation of the fragile environmental resources (forests, fisheries, surface and groundwater irrigation, grazing lands, etc.) on which the daily livelihoods of the rural poor in particular crucially depend.

Here also the answers are actually complex, and mere trade restriction is not the solution. The environmental effects of trade liberalization on the rural economy depend on the crop pattern and the methods of production. Take, for example, an African rural economy where the exportable product is a capital-intensive tree crop (such as coffee or cocoa), the import substitute is a land-intensive crop (such as corn), and there is a labor-intensive subsistence (nontraded) crop (such as roots and tubers). The economy may have a comparative advantage in tree crops. In this case an increase in import substitution leads to an expansion of cultivated land under the land-intensive crop as well as a shortening of the fallow period, leading to depletion of natural vegetation and biomass. Trade liberalization in this context, through encouraging the production of the less land-intensive tree crop, can significantly improve the natural biomass, as has been shown by Lopez (2000) for Côte d'Ivoire in the latter part of the 1980s, using the data from the Living Standards Survey and remote sensing data from satellite images.

One reason why land-intensive crops may lead to overuse of land and depletion of natural vegetation (or that expansion of the agricultural frontier in general leads to deforestation) is the lack of well-defined property rights or lack of their enforcement on public or communal land. In such cases the private cost of expanding production is less than the social cost, and there is overuse and degradation of environmental resources. If the country exports such resource-intensive products, foreign trade may make this misallocation worse. International trade theorists point out that trade restriction is not the first-best policy in this situation; correcting the property rights regime is. But the latter involves large changes in the legal-regulatory or community institutional framework, which take a long time to implement. Given the threshold effects and irreversibilities in environmental degradation (a forest regeneration requires a minimum stock, for example), one may not be able to afford to wait. In that case, some program of (time-bound) trade restriction, coupled with serious attempts to overhaul the domestic institutional framework, may be necessary. In other cases, domestic policy changes can be implemented much more quickly, and restricting trade is unnecessary and undesirable. For example, administered underpricing of precious environmental resources (irrigation water in India, energy in Russia, timber concessions in

Indonesia, etc.) is a major cause of resource depletion, and correcting it should not take much time. Domestic vested interests, not globalization, are responsible for the prolongation of such socially damaging policies.

In the case of some resource-intensive exports it is difficult for a country to adopt environmental regulations if its international competitors do not adopt them at the same time and have the ability to undercut the country in international markets. Here there is an obvious need for coordination of environmental regulation policies in the countries concerned. Given the low elasticity of demand for many resource-intensive primary export commodities from developing countries in the world market, such coordinated policies need not lead to a decline in export revenue.

A common charge against multinational companies is that they flock to developing country "pollution havens" to take advantage of lax environmental standards. In one of the very few careful empirical studies on the question, Eskeland and Harrison (2003) examine the pattern of foreign investment in Mexico, Venezuela, Morocco, and Côte d'Ivoire. They find no evidence that foreign investment in these countries is related to pollution abatement costs in rich countries. They also find that within a given industry, foreign plants are significantly more energy-efficient and use cleaner types of energy compared with their local peers.

CONCLUSION

In general, debates on globalization often involve a clash of counterfactuals. On one side, those who are against the pace of business-as-usual global trade and investment are making a plea for doing something about the jobs and entrepreneurial opportunities for the poor and for small enterprises that are being wiped out; they also oppose the monopolistic practices of giant multinational companies and the environmental damage caused by their economic expansion. Thus their counterfactual is the world of more social justice and less dominant trading and investment companies, which gives some more breathing space to the poor producers and workers. On the other side, the counterfactual for pro-globalizers is the case when there is no (or limited) trade or foreign investment, a world that may be worse for the poor (as it is in the extreme cases of the closed economies of North Korea and Burma). The way out of this clash of counterfactuals is to insist that there are policies which may attempt to help the poor without necessarily undermining the forces of globalization. In this essay we have emphasized that in the medium-to-long run, globalization need not make the poor much worse off, *if* appropriate domestic policies and institutions are in place and appropriate coordination among the involved parties can be organized. If the institutional prerequisites can be managed, globalization opens the door for some new opportunities even for the poor. Of course, domestic institutional reform is not easy—it requires political leadership, popular participation, and administrative capacity that are often lacking in poor countries. One can only say that if we keep the focus on agitating against multinational companies and international organizations such as the WTO, attention in those countries often is deflected from the domestic institutional vested interests, and the day of politically challenging them is postponed. In fact, in some cases opening the economy may unleash forces for such a challenge.

As in the debates several decades ago around "dependency" theories in development sociology, there is often a tendency to attribute many of the problems of underdevelopment to the inexorable forces of the international economic and political order, ignoring the sway of domestic vested interests. In many countries poverty alleviation in the form of expansion of credit and marketing facilities, land reform, public works programs for the unemployed, and provision of education, vocational training, and health need not be blocked by the forces of globalization. This, of course, requires a restructuring of existing budget priorities and a better and more accountable political and administrative framework, but the obstacles to these are often largely domestic (particularly in countries where there are some coherent governance structures in place). In other words, for these countries, globalization is often not the main cause of their problems, contrary to the claim of critics of globalization—just as globalization is often not the main solution of these problems, contrary to the claim of some gung-ho free traders.

All this, of course, does not remove the responsibility of international organizations and entities to help the poor of the world by working toward a reduction of rich-country protection on goods produced by the poor, by energetic antitrust action to challenge the monopoly power of international (producing and trading) companies based in rich countries, by facilitating international partnerships in research and development of products (for example, drugs, vaccines, crops) suitable for the poor, by organizing more substantial (and more effectively governed) financial and technology transfers and international adjustment assistance for displaced workers, and by help in building (legal and technical) capacity for poor countries in international negotiations and quality certification organizations. Globalization should not be allowed to be used either by its critics or by its proponents as an excuse for inaction on the domestic as well as the international front when it comes to relieving the poverty that oppresses the life of billions of people in the world.

NOTES

1. I shall also ignore the substantial poverty-reducing potential of international (unskilled) labor flows from poor to rich countries.

2. For a brief summary of the empirical literature on this question, see Winters et al. (2004).

3. For detailed evidence from Colombia, see Goldberg and Pavcnik (2005).

4. See, for example, Aitken et al. (1996).

5. Conceptually, one should distinguish between unsafe or hazardous work conditions and forced labor, on the one hand, and low-wage jobs, on the other. Under

capitalism, just as workers willing to sell themselves as serfs are not permitted to do so, so unsafe work conditions that can cause bodily injury are to be strictly regulated. But the case for stopping workers from accepting low-wage jobs is much weaker.

6. See Currie and Harrison (1997); Rodrik (1997); Leamer (1998); and Scheve and Slaughter (2002). For some firm-level evidence that, controlling for firm characteristics, foreign-owned plants in Indonesia are associated with a larger probability of shutting down their operations than domestic plants, see Bernard and Sjoholm (2003).

7. It is also to be noted that in the WTO each member country has one vote (the convention is to reach decisions by "consensus"), whereas in the Bretton Woods institutions (IMF and the World Bank) voting is dollar-weighted. But there is no denying that the rich countries (and their large corporate lobbies) exercise a dominant effect on the agenda-setting and decision-making of the WTO, as they do in the Bretton Woods institutions.

BIBLIOGRAPHY

Aitken, Brian, Ann E. Harrison, and Robert Lipsey. "Wages and Foreign Ownership: A Comparative Study of Mexico, Venezuela, and the United States." *Journal of International Economics* 40 (3/4) (1996): 345–371.

Bernard, Andrew, and Fredrik Sjoholm. "Foreign Owners and Plant Survival." National Bureau of Economic Research working paper 10039, 2003.

Currie, Janet, and Ann E. Harrison. "Sharing the Costs: The Impact of Trade Reform on Capital and Labor in Morocco." *Journal of Labor Economics* 15 (3) (1997): S44–S71.

Eskeland, Gunnar, and Ann E. Harrison. "Moving to Greener Pastures? Multinationals and the Pollution Haven Hypothesis." *Journal of Development Economics* 70 (1) (2003): 1–24.

Goldberg, Penny, and Nina Pavcnik. "Trade, Wages, and the Political Economy of Trade Protection: Evidence from the Colombian Trade Reforms." *Journal of International Economics* 66 (1) (2005): 75–106.

Leamer, Edward E. "In Search of Stolper-Samuelson Linkages between International Trade and Lower Wages." In *Imports, Exports, and the American Worker,* edited by S. M. Collins, 141–202. Washington, D.C.: Brookings Institution Press, 1998.

Lopez, R. "Trade Reform and Environmental Externalities in General Equilibrium: Analysis for an Archetype Poor Tropical Country." *Environment and Development Economics* 4 (4) (2000): 337–404.

Rodrik, Dani. *Has Globalization Gone Too Far?* Washington, D.C.: Institute of International Economics, 1997.

Scheve, Ken F., and Mathew J. Slaughter. "Economic Insecurity and Globalization of Production." National Bureau of Economic Research working paper 9339, 2002.

Winters, Alan L., Neil McCulloch, and Andrew McKay. "Trade Liberalization and Poverty: The Evidence So Far." *Journal of Economic Literature* 42 (1) (2004): 72–115.

8

The Role of Agriculture
in Development

Mukesh Eswaran & Ashok Kotwal

All industrialized countries have an agrarian past. Two centuries ago, the vast majority of people in every country lived off agriculture, as they do today in much of the developing world. As countries develop, their labor force shifts to industry and services, and in the process the well-being of the people improves. The purpose of this essay is to shed some light on the economic logic that drives the process and on the important role that agricultural productivity plays in it. We will argue that agricultural productivity growth is the key to poverty alleviation and then discuss the policy implications for developing countries.

In the first section, we will show how the process of secular decline in poverty is inevitably associated with a movement of labor from agriculture to other sectors, and how agricultural productivity growth facilitates such a movement. In the second section, we will discuss the importance of international trade in this process. Both agricultural and trade policies tend to generate political battles because they redistribute incomes from one group to another. We will tackle this political economy question in the third section and discuss the causes (and also the consequences) of the observed policy bias against agriculture. In the fourth section, we will discuss the two main determinants of agricultural growth—technology and crop diversification—and reflect on the policy options available to poor countries to induce agricultural growth without causing domestic upheavals.

THE PROCESS OF POVERTY REDUCTION

The essential manner in which agricultural productivity growth improves our well-being is by reducing the amount of time and resources needed to meet

111

our subsistence needs. When people have enough left over in their budgets after satisfying their food requirements, they demand nonagricultural goods, and this is what creates markets for industrial goods and for services. What is responsible for creating such a surplus over their subsistence is also what is responsible for enabling a small part of the labor force to produce enough food for the whole society: growth in agricultural productivity. In other words, nothing that we associate with economic development—consumption of industrial goods and sophisticated services, specialization of labor, and technical progress—would have been possible if agricultural productivity had not reached a high enough level to release labor and other resources for other pursuits.

Let us now establish the relationship between agricultural productivity and the poverty within a country in a more systematic way. Before we start looking into the intricate links between these, we should note that small cultivators and workers comprise a significant proportion of the poor in developing countries. Clearly, an increase in agricultural productivity directly increases the family incomes of small cultivators. But it is not quite as easy to see how agricultural productivity growth determines the well-being of workers, especially in nonagricultural activities, and this is where we need a conceptual framework.

Consider workers in developing countries who own little or nothing by way of assets. For them, poverty is bound up with the magnitude of the wage rate relative to the price of the goods consumed. Any significant dent in their poverty, therefore, has to be made largely through its effect on the wage rate. Furthermore, the poorest countries have the highest proportions of their labor force employed in agriculture. There is an intimate connection between the poverty level and the size of the agricultural labor force. It is from this connection that agriculture draws its important—almost indispensable—role in the process of economic development.

In market economies, the remuneration of a production input (labor, land, capital, etc.) depends, of course, on its productivity. The productivity of an input such as labor, however, in general depends on how much of other, complementary inputs (such as land, capital, etc.) are concurrently employed. The greater the amounts of land (or capital) a worker has access to, the greater is his or her productivity. In developing countries, the land-to-labor ratio is thus a crucial determinant of the productivity of the poor in agriculture. Indeed, one reason they are poor is precisely because the land-to-labor ratio is low.

Poverty in the rural, agricultural sector implies poverty of workers in the urban sector as well. This is because urban wages are linked to rural wages. If rural wages are low, so are urban wages. If rural wages rise, urban industry is forced to raise urban wages in order to attract workers to industry. Thus the low productivity of agricultural workers in developing countries is responsible not only for rural poverty but also for urban poverty. Therefore, an important component of the fight against poverty in developing countries must be the attempt to raise the land-to-labor ratio in agriculture.

If increasing the inputs that are complementary to labor in the production process is one prong in the battle against poverty, increasing the efficiency of the production technology itself is another. Technical progress, which generates higher output levels from the same bundle of inputs, has played the dominant role in improving our standard of living since antiquity, but particularly since the advent of the Industrial Revolution. Given the link between poverty and agricultural productivity, improvements in agricultural technologies acquire a particularly important role in poverty alleviation.

In comparison with agriculture, industry uses hardly any land at all. If a low land-to-labor ratio in agriculture is a cause of rural and urban poverty, it might appear that a simple solution to this problem would be to move labor out of agriculture and into industry. Unfortunately, this avenue is not as open as it seems, since we are constrained by the manner in which consumers typically spend their incomes on agricultural and industrial goods. A market economy will produce only goods that people want to purchase.

The biological imperative of survival leads us to give priority to agricultural goods when our incomes are low. To someone who is starving, industrial goods would be deemed a luxury. To fix ideas, let us adopt a stark representation of the notion of biologically driven expenditures on goods.[1] Until a person has enough income to consume a certain amount of food, assume she spends all her income on food; after she has consumed this amount, she spends any extra available income entirely on industrial goods. This strictly hierarchical expenditure pattern is a reasonable enough approximation to reality that its adoption is merited by the simplification it affords in thinking. It is consistent with the well-known empirical fact called Engel's Law, which states that the proportion of a family's income spent on food declines as income rises.

Consider an economy that does not engage in international trade (a "closed economy") and in which there are potentially two sectors, one producing an agricultural good (grain) and another producing an industrial good (textiles). The production of grain requires land and labor, whereas the production of textiles requires only labor. The remuneration of the inputs (wages for labor and land rent on land) will depend on their productivities. There will be two classes of people in this economy: landlords and workers. Let us assume that all landlords also work. Thus landlords earn labor income and land rental income, whereas the workers have only labor income. Suppose the hierarchical expenditure pattern alluded to above dictates that a person requires G kilograms of grain per month before she will spend any of her income on textiles.

Each person earns income from her input(s) and, depending on whether she has enough income to purchase G kilograms of grain, she will spend all or part of her income on grain and the rest on textiles. A landlord will clearly consume at least as much grain and at least as much textiles as a worker. In such an economy, how will labor be allocated between the agricultural and industrial sectors? Its allocation across the two sectors must be such that, at the incomes determined by the productivities of the inputs, the total amounts demanded of grain and textiles must equal the total amounts supplied.

We can now see why the percentage of the labor force in the agricultural sector of a poor country tends to be high. Poor countries typically employ technologies that have low productivity. As a result, almost all the resources of the economy are needed to produce the food requirements of the population. Since whatever a closed economy consumes must be domestically produced, most of the labor force will be employed in agriculture. In fact, at very low levels of technical efficiency, there may be no demand at all for textiles, and the entire labor force will be employed in agriculture. Were such a country, in its zeal to emulate the developed countries, to attempt to jump-start industry through state intervention, its attempt would end in failure. Given the preferences for agricultural and industrial goods as dictated by biology, a country needs to be sufficiently rich in order to sustain a viable industrial sector.

Suppose the agricultural technology improves, either because it is domestically improved or because superior foreign technology is borrowed. Since the new technology renders labor and land more productive, their remuneration will increase. The demand for grain will increase, as will the supply. With substantial technical change, the landlord class will begin to demand textiles, and this very change in technology will also release workers from agriculture to produce the industrial good being demanded—marking the emergence of industry. Further increases in the productivity of the technology may even allow workers to begin consuming textiles. The important point is that improvement in the agricultural technology unambiguously betters the lot of the poor (workers) by allowing them to consume more grain and, possibly, more textiles. Furthermore, by siphoning off from agriculture the workers needed to produce the industrial good now being demanded, the improvement of technology has the additional salutary effect of raising the land-to-labor ratio in agriculture—which further increases the wage rate.

Will we get the same outcome if industry rather than agriculture experiences productivity improvement? To answer this, suppose the economy's population size and the supply of land are such that workers are consuming only grain, and landlords, being richer, are consuming both grain to satiation and textiles. This is a realistic scenario in most developing countries. Consider now the effect of technological change in industry, which enables each worker to produce more textiles. What benefit, if any, will the workers receive from this? The productivity increase will lower the price of textiles, since each meter of textiles now requires less labor. Workers, who are still not sated with grain, however, will not see any benefit from this price decline because they do not consume textiles. But there is another avenue through which productivity improvements can impinge on well-being. The wages of a worker may rise in purchasing power and enable her to buy more of the good she does consume, grain. A more productive computer scientist, for example, earns a higher income that she can spend on goods other than computers. Will a similar process operate here? No, and for the following reason.

Since, in this exercise, agricultural technology is not changing, the only way in which an agricultural (and, hence, industrial) worker's wage rate will increase is if there is a migration of workers from agriculture to industry, leaving each agricultural worker more land to work with. Were this to transpire, the total amount of food demanded would increase because workers would demand more grain while the landlords would demand the same amount as before. Since there are now fewer agricultural workers, however, the supply of food will decrease. This imbalance between the demand for and supply of grain would thwart the reallocation of labor to industry and prevent the wage rate from rising. As a result, technical progress in industry would have no effect at all on poverty. People would not be willing to substitute the now cheaper industrial good for the agricultural good. The increased output of textiles would be consumed entirely by landlords.

The hierarchical nature of consumer expenditures renders industrial progress useless as far as poverty alleviation is concerned. In reality, expenditures are not strictly hierarchical. Consumers are likely to have some small amount of substitutability between grain and textiles. The extent of this is quite limited, however, and so is the extent of the impact of industrial technical change on poverty. This is the essential argument underpinning our strong belief in the special role that agriculture plays in the alleviation of poverty.

IMPORTANCE OF INTERNATIONAL TRADE

The reasoning used above presumes that the developing country is a closed economy. But suppose that in a closed economy, the domestic cost of producing textiles is lower than its international price, and the country now opens up to trade. It will clearly export the industrial good, and from the foreign exchange proceeds of these exports, it will finance the import of at least some of its needs of the agricultural good. The export market available for textiles and the attendant imports of cheaper grain allow the industrial sector to absorb more labor than would have been possible in a closed economy.[2] By raising the land-to-labor ratio, industrial exports increase the wage rate of workers. Embarking on trade, in this case, would generate a one-time benefit to workers of this country. Further, if industrial technological progress in the developing country is proceeding at a faster rate than in its trading partners, the country will capture an ever-increasing share of the international textile market. Continuously absorbing labor from the agricultural sector will bestow a continuous benefit on the poor. First Taiwan and South Korea and later China have followed the strategy of aggressively expanding their industrial exports to the rest of the world and posting very high growth rates, earning the phenomenon the title "The East Asian Miracle." A rapid increase in their manufactured exports has led to a corresponding decline in agricultural employment.

But if a land-scarce and labor-abundant country could attain a competitive edge in industrial goods so that labor could be moved to industrial employment, there is an argument to be made that industrial investment should be favored at the expense of agricultural investment. Moreover, there are other arguments for favoring industrial investment. First, there are technological reasons. Typically, industry as a sector exhibits faster growth than agriculture. It is less handicapped by land, an input that is fixed in supply. Capital is the main input complementary to labor in industrial production, and unlike land, it can be accumulated over time. In addition, there is greater scope in industry than in agriculture to improve production efficiency through acquired experience ("learning by doing"). It is almost tempting to argue that an improvement in agricultural productivity may hurt a country in the long run if it entrenches a trade pattern that has a country importing rather than producing most of its industrial consumption. By doing so, it may give up on harnessing the industrial sector as an engine of growth. However, it would be unrealistic to presume that an agrarian economy with little experience in industry could suddenly transform itself into an industrial exporter.

How does an agrarian economy begin to industrialize? It must import equipment and technology from developed countries if it wants to get the benefit of the technological progress that has taken place in the developed world. But to import machinery, it must export something that it has an advantage in producing. Typically, developing countries started their industrialization programs by exporting agricultural products or minerals. For example, Japan's initial exports were silk and bamboo products; Taiwan's were rice and sugar; Malaysia's were rubber and timber. Even in Canada and the United States, the developmental process during their industrialization period was driven by the exports of staples such as wheat and beaver pelts. As incomes rise all over the world, consumers' preference for variety grows. American and European consumers demand tropical fruits and vegetables and flowers. A developing country with a productive and diversified agriculture is in a better position to take advantage of the technological progress and taste for variety in developed countries in order to initiate its own industrialization.

It should be noted that land-abundant countries such as the United States and Canada have been major food exporters in the world for a long time, and their comparative advantage in agriculture did not hamper their industrial growth. In 1900, the proportion of the labor force in agriculture in these countries was 38.9% and 40.2%, respectively. In 2000, these percentages had declined to 2.35% and 2.33%, respectively.[3] How did this happen? Interestingly, it was growth in agricultural productivity that spawned and sustained industrialization in these countries. It did so not only by generating agricultural exports that financed imports of machinery but also by generating linkages (spillovers) to other sectors. When a vast majority of people live off agriculture, productivity growth in that sector raises incomes across the country, creating demand for industrial goods and helping the industrial sector achieve higher productivity through learning by doing. What is implicitly assumed here is that the domestic industrial sector is protected from foreign competition until it can compete internationally.[4] But even when no such protection is provided, industrialization can proceed gradually through growth linkages generated by a rise in agricultural incomes.

But in order to capture an essential aspect of these growth linkages to the two sectors we have been considering thus far, we need to add a third sector: services.[5] Indeed, the service sector comprises a significant proportion of labor employment even in developing countries. Consumers as well as manufacturers demand services. Examples are construction, transportation, insurance, credit, repair services, and refrigeration. When agricultural productivity increases, consumers become richer and, apart from demanding industrial goods, they also demand services of various kinds. These services have to be domestically produced, since they are typically nontraded. With growing income, the domestic service sector expands, offering a greater variety of services and more of each kind.

The emergence and expansion of the service sector confers benefits on the (incipient) industrial sector, which can be more competitive when it has access to a wider variety of services. Thus an increase in agricultural productivity, by spawning a domestic service sector, enables the country to industrialize. Once industrial production begins, productivity can increase by the usual learning-by-doing route. Thus, even without protection from foreign competition in industry, growth in agricultural productivity is more likely to facilitate industrialization rather than forestall it. Just as in a closed economy, this productivity growth impinges on poverty by (ironically) moving labor off the land and into other activities.

POLICY BIAS AGAINST AGRICULTURE AND CONSEQUENCES FOR POVERTY

Despite all these good arguments in favor of agriculture, this sector has been much neglected in developing countries. Many previously colonial countries in Africa, South Asia, and Latin America regarded their lack of industrial development as the main reason for their subjugation, and concentrated on industrial development as soon as they became independent. Not only was far too small a share of total public investment allocated to agriculture, but policies were implemented that artificially rendered the industrial sector relatively more profitable than the agricultural. These diluted incentives for private investment at the same time that public investment in agriculture was being reduced. Let us see how.

Clearly, the profitability of any sector depends on the price of the output relative to the prices of inputs (the "terms of trade" for that sector). For example, the profitability of textiles will be raised if cloth is made artificially more expensive while cotton is made artificially cheaper. Not only will such a measure reduce cotton-producing farmers' incomes; it will also make clothes for their families more expensive. Protection of industry creates an urban class that can get better organized than farmers, since the former are concentrated in cities while the latter are diffused throughout the country-side. Policy makers are inevitably more responsive to the demands of the urban class, which gets used to making exorbitant claims on the public trea-sury. For example, unionized workers often strike for higher salaries while agitating for lower prices for food and public services (such as rail travel). This phenomenon, common in many developing countries, is called "urban bias."[6]

A consequence of urban bias is that organized urban groups (industrial unions, the chamber of commerce, consumer groups) pressure politicians to keep the prices of industrial goods high and those of agricultural goods low.[7] For example, urban consumers' groups agitate for export controls on food-stuffs such as rice and sugar; the textile sector contrives a ban on cotton exports. These policies result in low domestic prices for these farm products. Similarly, manufacturing firms as well as organized labor have a common interest in lobbying for protective tariffs, thus maintaining high domestic prices for their products. Some of these domestically produced goods are industrial inputs to agriculture, such as fertilizer, pesticides, and agricultural implements (e.g., water pumps). Farmers' incomes, and thus any returns they expect to make on investments in their farms, are squeezed. Urban bias reduces incentives to invest in agriculture. This is one reason why agricultural productivity is so low in many developing countries.

Liberalization of agricultural terms of trade has had significantly beneficial effects on the poor in the two most populous countries of the world. The recent economic liberalization in China started in 1979 with agricultural price liberalization (41% increase by 1980 in the prices at which the state procured agricultural produce), coupled with greater autonomy and incentives to com-munes. From 1978 through 1990, agricultural production doubled in China. Not only did the percentage of labor force in agriculture fall from 70% in 1979 to 60.1% in 1990, but the absolute amount of labor employed in ag-riculture fell by 31%.[8] This was a period of significant transformation in China. If agriculture did well, industry did almost twice as well. The index of industrial production went from 100 in 1978 to 388.7 in 1990 (according to Agricultural Department of China, *Agricultural Statistics Yearbook* for 1990 and 2000). In 1980 primary goods formed roughly half the total exports, but by 1990 they had dropped to only about a quarter (25.6%) despite the fact that the primary exports had grown by almost two thirds in absolute amount. The proportion of people below the poverty line shrank from 28% in 1978 to 9% in 1990 (Asian Development Bank 2000). The Chinese experience illustrates how agricultural productivity growth impinges on poverty not only by directly conferring benefits on those engaged in agriculture but also by promoting industry.

India started liberalizing its trade policy in 1991. Tariffs were cut on a range of industrial goods, forcing reductions in domestic prices. Though no explicit reforms were introduced in the agricultural sector until 2001, the procurement prices for several major commodities were raised successively in the early 1990s. Mostly, this was in response to the political pressure applied by the farmers' lobby that had become quite a formidable force. The net result was an increase in the agricultural terms of trade; output prices increased and input prices decreased for agriculture in India. The resultant increase in the profitability of investment in agriculture had the desired effect. There was a boom in private investment in Indian agriculture in the 1990s.[9] Fortuitously, the high-yield variety of rice seeds had diffused to the poorest region in India (the eastern states of West Bengal, Bihar, and Orissa). Rural growth in this region had a significant impact on the number of people below the poverty line. An interesting aspect of this episode is that a reduction in industrial tariffs is likely to have played a part in poverty reduction by inadvertently improving the profitability of investment in agriculture. Though tariff reduction certainly caused some disruption in Indian industry, overall the number of people below the poverty line in rural (urban) India declined by 7% (7.9%), from 37.2% (32.6%) in 1993–1994 to 30.2% (24.7%) in 1999–2000 (Deaton 2001). This indicates that an increase in the price of agricultural produce relative to that of industrial output had a beneficial impact on the poor in India, as it did in China.

The price of food, however, is a double-edged sword. The poor, as we have already seen, spend a considerable part of their household income on food. A 20% rise in food prices would reduce their food intake by nearly 20%, unless their wages also rose.[10] How a given policy affects the well-being of the poor will depend on how the wage rate responds to the enhanced opportunities. If the increased profitability of agriculture results in a surge of investment, the productivity of workers will increase, and so will the wage rate. If the wage rate increases by a greater amount than the price, the poor will benefit. The question is under what circumstances this is likely to obtain. To answer this question, we need to discuss the determinants of agricultural growth.

THE DETERMINANTS OF AGRICULTURAL GROWTH

The agricultural productivity growth that is relevant to labor-abundant countries takes one of two forms: crop-yield increases and a shift in crop choice toward more lucrative crops.[11]

An example of yield-increasing technology is the high-yield variety (HYV) of wheat developed by Norman Borlaug and his team in Mexico and adapted for South Asia in the 1960s, heralding what was dubbed the "green revolution."[12] Later, higher-yield seeds for rice and other grains were developed in the same way. Overall, these new seeds increased labor demand and employment for the following reasons. First, typically the new seeds had a shorter crop cycle—a highly beneficial characteristic that enabled farmers to harvest more crops per year. Second, the new seeds required much more meticulous maintenance, including weeding and water control. Third, the higher yields meant higher labor demand for harvesting. The HYV technology thus had the potential to improve the productivity of land and also to increase wages by increasing the demand for labor. In most cases the potential was realized.

The HYV technology, however, is very intensive in some inputs (such as fertilizers and pesticides). The net result is that this technology requires greater cash outlays on inputs than the traditional technology and therefore increases the need for credit. Furthermore, the HYV technology requires a steady supply of water. As a result, rich farmers—those with access to credit and to water (through tube wells)—prospered and those without languished. The new technology also increases the premium on primary education, since literate farmers manage to adopt the new technology more readily. For all these reasons, the green revolution increased income inequality in relative terms. An important lesson from this is that public investment in appropriate irrigation schemes, the development of credit institutions, and primary education are essential to ensuring an equitable distribution of the gains from agricultural productivity growth.

Efforts are currently under way to bring about yet another green revolution, this time in Africa, where it is needed the most. Unlike Asia, where there are only two staples (wheat and rice), Africa has eight or ten major staples. Yet there are already significant improvements in the yields of corn (30%) and sorghum (50%). Private companies have sprung up to undertake the delivery of hybrid seeds in time. In experimental settings, the yields of corn, sorghum, wheat, and cassava have been shown to increase two- or threefold. Hybrid corn and sorghum are thriving and spreading rapidly. A continuation of this trend promises unprecedented hope for this poorest continent. Like many new technologies, hybrid seeds come with some risks. The possible risks are much higher with genetically modified seeds, but their higher yields, pest resistance, and herbicide tolerance make them very promising instruments in the war against poverty.

Let us now discuss growth through a change in crop choices. There are many instances of rural growth being triggered by the arrival of a new infrastructural input, such as an irrigation channel or a road link to an urban market.[13] Land can have many uses, and what use it is put to depends upon the availability of complementary inputs. A piece of land capable of growing sugarcane may be sown with sorghum because there is little water. But if an irrigation channel becomes available, the farmer would switch to sugarcane and earn a much higher income. Typically, farmers sense new, lucrative market opportunities and change their crop choices. Market opportunities thus help to create a "vent for surplus" or a window of opportunity to generate higher income from a resource. The availability of complementary inputs and access to markets allow a farmer to exploit his land's unique advantage. The result is a higher level of specialization in agricultural production and higher incomes. What is crucial for being able to utilize the existing resources most profitably is that access to markets remains available so that the production pattern is not constrained by local demand. Agricultural productivity growth and linkages with outside markets go hand in hand.

The WTO Agreement on Agriculture will bring about many changes. The changes with the greatest impact will be ones in those developed countries offering the highest level of protection to agriculture. In Europe and Japan, the average levels of producer support in 1999 were 44% and 60% of the value added, respectively. For certain goods, such as dairy products, sugar, and rice, they are extraordinarily high. If this level of support to farmers in developed countries is reduced, the international prices of many commodities that the OECD countries produce, including food grains, will rise. Will that help or hurt the developing countries? First, note that a subsidy given to European farmers can be considered a gift from European taxpayers to European farmers as well as to the consumers in the rest of the world. If developed countries want to offer subsidized food to the rest of the world, it should benefit the poor in poor countries. They should move their labor to manufacturing and import cheap food. In the very long run, it would indeed make sense for land-abundant countries to produce most of the food and for labor-abundant countries to produce most of the manufactures. But, as explained earlier, the process of industrialization cannot get under way unless developing countries can import technology and machinery from developed countries and initially finance these imports by exporting primary goods, including agricultural commodities. Overall, it is fair to say that if the intransigence of developed countries in dismantling agricultural protection continues, it will present a significant obstacle to poverty reduction across the world.

The implementation of the WTO agreement will also reduce the level of protection in developing countries. The net effect on domestic prices will vary across commodities and countries. For example, oilseed prices in India (which protects its oilseed sector heavily) will collapse, and the farmers now growing oilseeds will have to cultivate other crops. But the prices for rice, dairy products, sugar, and horticultural items will rise in India, and more land will be used to cultivate these crops. In short, there will be reallocation of land to a different set of crops, and how well the farmers in a particular country do will depend on how easily they can reallocate. The primary responsibility of policy makers is to enable farmers to adjust to and take advantage of market opportunities. First, farmers should be free to grow and sell what they choose. Second, various controls (e.g., export controls, bans on interregional trade, nuisance regulations against agroprocessing) enacted during the regimes with extreme urban bias should be removed. In fact, getting rid of these irrational controls may be the highest payoff of the WTO agreement for many developing countries. Third, infrastructure such as roads, ports, railroads, primary education, and irrigation should be improved.

One serious drawback of being integrated with the world trading system is that international prices tend to be much more volatile than domestic prices in any given country. This volatility can create a lot of hardship for the poor, since they have little to cushion themselves against sudden price increases. In fact, a great deal of animosity toward trade liberalization arises precisely because of this volatility. Unless a proper safety net is put in place before large-scale deregulation is carried out, the liberalization program runs the danger of going aground before it starts paying dividends.

To sum up, it is ironic, and therefore not well appreciated, that agricultural productivity growth alleviates poverty by rendering nonagricultural activities more profitable. This is how it moves labor off land and helps a country industrialize. It spawns a productive service sector and thereby makes domestic industry more competitive. It can help finance the imports of machinery and technology through agricultural exports in the initial stages of industrialization. Agricultural growth itself goes hand in hand with the expansion of markets, infrastructure, and producer services, so that land and labor can be shifted continuously toward their most profitable uses. Given that a vast majority of the poor in the world live off agriculture in developing countries, the process of agricultural growth also helps tap the enormous but latent entrepreneurial pool in these countries. As new productive activities become available, people find niches for their intrinsic talents and generate new ideas to sustain the process. Improving the productivity of agriculture is the single most important step a developing country can take to reduce poverty.

NOTES

1. This notion, and the analysis that follows, is spelled out in Eswaran and Kotwal (1993).

2. In the 1850s, Ricardo had argued for repealing the Corn Laws on the ground that imports of cheap wheat would facilitate industrialization.

3. Bureau of the Census (1975); Urquhart and Buckley (1965); Leacy (1993).

4. Matsuyama (1992) makes this argument.

5. The argument made here is drawn from Eswaran and Kotwal (2002).

6. Lipton (1993) introduced this term and was one of the most influential tracts on the subject that blamed the persistence of poverty on "urban bias."

7. In some countries (e.g., India), farmers have formed an effective political lobby to make a greater claim on the public treasury through various subsidies, virtually canceling out the discrimination through urban bias.

8. Rawski and Mead (1998) is the source for these numbers.

9. The percentage growth rate of agricultural output in India from 1992 to 1996 was 6.1, 3.3, 4.9, and 2.4, respectively. Asian Development Bank (1996).

10. As Sen has shown in his work on famines in the twentieth century, it was

literally the rise in the price of rice that triggered events leading to the death of hundreds of thousands.

11. In explaining the cross-state differences in the trend rates of rural poverty reduction, Dutt and Ravallion (1998) found that differences in the trend growth rate of average farm yields (agricultural output per acre) was a key variable.

12. The plant was selectively bred to convert fertilizer into grain much more efficiently. But in order to be able to carry more grain without buckling over, the stalk of the plant had to be rendered shorter and thicker through selective breeding.

13. This paragraph draws on Kotwal and Ramswami (1998).

BIBLIOGRAPHY

Agricultural Department of China. *China Agricultural Statistics Yearbook.* Chinese edition. Beijing: Agricultural Press, 2000.

Asian Development Bank. *Country Economic Review: India.* Manila: The Bank, 1996.

Bureau of the Census. *Historical Statistics of the United States, Colonial Times to 1970.* Washington, D.C.: Bureau of the Census, 1975.

Deaton, Angus. "Adjusted Indian Poverty Estimates for 1999–2000." Mimeo, Department of Economics, Princeton University, 2001.

Development Research Center of the State Council of the People's Republic of China. *Almanac of China's Economy.* Chinese overseas edition. Beijing: Almanac of China's Economy Press, 2000.

Dutt, Gaurav, and Martin Ravallion. "Why Have Some Indian States Done Better Than Others at Reducing Rural Poverty?" *Economica* 65 (257) (1998): 17–38.

Eswaran, Mukesh, and Ashok Kotwal. "A Theory of Real Wage Growth in LDCs." *Journal of Development Economics* 42 (1993): 243–269.

Eswaran, Mukesh, and Ashok Kotwal. "The Role of the Service Sector in the Process of Development." *Journal of Development Economics* 68 (2002): 401–420.

Kotwal, Ashok, and Bharat Ramswami. "Economic Reforms of Agriculture and Rural Growth." *Policy Reform* 2 (1998): 369–402.

Leacy, F. H. *Historical Statistics of Canada.* 2nd ed. Ottawa: Statistics Canada and Social Science Federation of Canada, 1993.

Lipton, Michael. *Why Poor People Stay Poor: Urban Bias in World Development.* Cambridge, Mass.: Harvard University Press, 1977.

Matsuyama, Kiminori. "Agricultural Productivity, Comparative Advantage, and Economic Growth." *Journal of Economic Theory* 58 (1992): 317–334.

National Bureau of Statistics of China. *China Statistical Yearbook.* Beijing: China Statistics Press, 2001.

Rawski, Thomas, and Robert Mead. "On the Trail of China's Phantom Farmers." *World Development* 26 (5) (May 1998): 767–781.

Urquhart, M. C., and K. Buckley. *Historical Statistics of Canada.* Cambridge: Cambridge University Press, 1965.

9

Fertility and Income

T. Paul Schultz

Fertility is often higher in poorer families within a society, and across countries those with higher average fertility tend to have lower average income. Do these associations imply that high fertility causes poverty among family members, or that poverty contributes to higher fertility, or both? Is the direct association between fertility and poverty a basis for assessing the value of policy interventions that reduce fertility by subsidizing the voluntary adoption of birth control, or by imposing on parents a quota of children which penalizes excess births, such as implemented by China?

It is hypothesized in this essay that some sources of family income encourage, and other sources discourage, fertility, because different sources of family income modify the economic opportunities parents must sacrifice to have another child, or the price of children in terms of parental time and market goods (Mincer 1963). For example, if an increment in family income is due to the rising value of women's time, this source of income not only expands income opportunities of the family but also raises the effective price of children to the family. Because it is empirically observed that higher values of women's time are associated with lower levels of lifetime fertility, it is inferred that the price effect of women's wages outweighs its income effect on fertility. In contrast, if an increment in total family income is due to an increase in the returns to physical assets—financial assets, business assets, land, and natural resources, such as oil—these income sources add to family endowments while not necessarily affecting the relative opportunity cost of children to parents, in which case these income sources are expected to be associated with higher fertility, other things being equal (P. Schultz 1981, 1994).

The effect of fertility on family income may differ depending on whether the variation in fertility is due to parent reproductive choices (i.e., behavioral demands) or reproductive endowments (biological supply). Reproductive demands are likely to be coordinated with other family time and resource allocations, and reflect not only socioeconomic constraints on parent choice but also parents' heterogeneous preferences among various goals and outcomes. Reproductive supplies vary because of genetic differences in a couple's fecundity (reproductive capacity), and to a first approximation will be distributed randomly across a population. In other words, the supply is a form of biological endowment over which parents exercise no choice, but which they can influence to some extent, primarily with costly and uncertain birth control (Rosenzweig and Schultz 1985).

Figure 9.1 plots country observations in 1960 (circles) and in 2000 (pluses) for a sample of ninety-six countries in which real income and fertility are reported.[1] Income is expressed in logarithms (proportionately) of real gross domestic product (GDP) per person over age fifteen (i.e., productivity per adult), and fertility is measured by the total fertility rate (TFR) that sums the age-specific birthrates for all women aged fifteen to forty-nine. The TFR thus represents the number of children a woman would be expected to have if she survived to age fifty and experienced the current age-specific birthrate at each age. The solid line is the linear fit to the 1960 observations, and the dashed line is the linear fit to the 2000 observations. From this linear

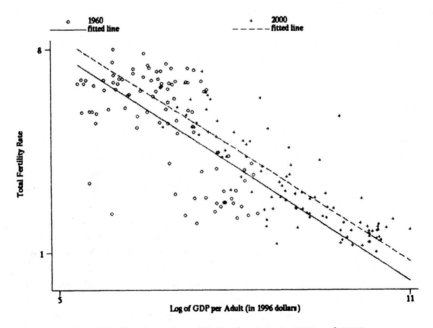

Figure 9.1 Total Fertility Rates by Adult Productivity in 1960 and 2000

pattern in the data it appears that a 10% increase in a country's GDP per adult is associated with a 13% lower TFR in both 1960 and 2000. Does this relatively stable and statistically significant association across countries accurately forecast how income and fertility changed within countries during this time? Not very well, because log income per adult increased by 2.14 in forty years, implying a compounded rate of growth of about 5.3% per year, while TFR decreased by two fifths, declining by about 1% per year.[2] If the cross-country relationship in either 1960 or 2000 had been used to forecast fertility, an even steeper decline in fertility would have been expected.

To assess the slope of the relationship between household income per adult and the number of children a woman bears over her lifetime, I will later examine a national representative survey of households. This 1997 Welfare Monitoring Survey of Kenya asks respondents about household income and consumption, and fertility. One approximation for the total income of households in poor countries is the consumption of all household members. Fertility is commonly measured by the number of children ever born to women who have completed their reproductive period, say older than forty-four; but to include younger women whose fertile period may not yet be complete, adjustments must be made for the age of the women as it affects fertility as well as household income per adult. In statistically fitting this relationship to household data, the association between log consumption per adult and fertility for women aged twenty-five to forty-four is represented by a less steeply negative slope, suggesting that a 10% increase in income is associated with a 1% decrease in fertility. Although the slope of the relationship at the household level has a smaller negative value than the slope across countries, both relationships are statistically very significant. In other words, the absolute value of the correlation exceeds what is likely to occur between two random variables. But the general argument advanced in this essay is that associations between two outcomes that are affected by coordinated family behavior should not immediately be interpreted as a causal relationship. Only if additional information is available on distinguishable sources of "outside" variation in income or in fertility that are plausibly independent of factors affecting the other variable, or that arise from processes occurring outside of the family, is it possible to infer whether such "outside" shocks to income or to fertility are causally affecting the other family outcome variable.

To isolate the factors that have caused the demographic transition, it is important to describe briefly some of the underlying developments that are often used to explain the exceptional characteristics of our era of modern economic growth. Long-run growth in factor productivity in the twentieth century, given the inputs of labor hours and capital, has been attributed mainly to the growing stock of productive knowledge and its global diffusion, which may especially enhance the productivity of educated workers, thus strengthening the financial incentives to invest privately and publicly in education. Possibly as a result of this increased productive return to schooling, the difference in years of education attained by men and women virtually vanished in high-income countries during the twentieth century, and became much smaller in much of Latin America and East Asia. However, this equalization in educational attainment between young women and men has not advanced as rapidly in many of the countries in Africa, and South and West Asia, and these patterns of education of women and men account for much of the variation in fertility observed across countries (P. Schultz 1997, 2001).

Birth control technology improved markedly in the early 1960s, when techniques were developed that could be used by women independently of sexual intercourse, in the form of the pill (oral steroid) and the IUD (intrauterine device). These "best practice" methods were adopted in high-income countries along with irreversible sterilization, and their dissemination was subsidized for women in Asia and Latin America, and then in Africa, as demands for birth control emerged (National Research Council 2000). With the recognition by 1990 of the threat of the HIV/AIDS epidemic, traditional condoms for men and reconfigured condoms for use by women were reemphasized in health and family planning programs. But these widening technological options may have encouraged women to plan more than their family size, helping them to invest in careers producing both in the home and outside of their family. Women's increasing education, access to new family-planning technologies, and accumulation of work experience outside of the home have increased the share of women's earnings in total family income. Studies suggest that this redistribution of economic power (from men) to women is associated with a reallocation of family expenditures toward children, while helping women with dependent children to head their own households if necessary, and further strengthening women's incentives to have fewer children over their lifetime because they expect to bear more of the cost of children (Becker 1981; P. Schultz 2001).

THE DEMOGRAPHIC TRANSITION AT THE NATIONAL LEVEL AND AT THE FAMILY LEVEL

In the aftermath of World War II, age-specific mortality rates declined, and population growth consequently increased in most low-income countries. Some observers expected economic pressures to reduce fertility in these low-income countries because of the rising costs of children in urban settings, and the individualistic desires of parents to promote the health and education of their children (Notestein 1945). The more common reaction to this "population explosion" followed the reasoning of Malthus ([1789] 1993), who expected fertility to remain at relatively high levels and rapid population growth to stifle improvements in the standard of living. The continuing decline in infant and child mortality in the 1960s caused the proportion of children in these low-income populations to increase. This rise in the dependency ratio (the ratio of the young and old to those in the prime working ages of fifteen to sixty-five) was expected to depress the rate of private and public savings, curb investment in physical capital, and thereby slow eco-

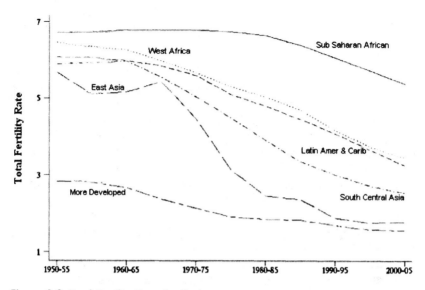

Figure 9.2 Total Fertility Rates by Region

nomic development, unless new policies were able to bribe or coerce parents to curb their fertility (Coale and Hoover 1958; Enke 1960; Erhlich 1968). After a half-century, the empirical record shows crude period birthrates have declined rapidly in most parts of the low-income world, starting in the 1960s, and eventually the number of children born per woman has fallen by at least half in most countries. Sub-Saharan Africa entered only in the last decade or two into its phase of sharply declining child mortality and the beginning of its fertility transition (National Research Council 2000). Total fertility rates for several regions of the world are plotted in Figure 9.2 from 1950–1955 through the median variant of the United Nations projections for 2000–2005 to illustrate these trends in fertility by region (United Nations 2003, vol. 1).

AGGREGATE POPULATION GROWTH AND DEVELOPMENT

This essay focuses only on the relationship between fertility and welfare at the individual family level, and does not deal with the difficult-to-measure indirect spillovers from fertility at the societal level. In other words, if having an additional birth affects the economic well-being of others than the parents or their children, these spillovers are not considered in this essay. I think it is fair to say there is no consensus on how to assess the magnitude or even determine the direction of these spillover effects of fertility and population growth on social welfare. One recent review of the evidence concluded that population growth in excess of 2% per year might constitute a significant handicap limiting economic development in an impoverished country with a weak government (National Research Council 1986). By about 1990 there appears to be a negative correlation between a country's rate of population growth and rate of economic growth in per capita income (Kelley and Schmidt 1994), but this regularity was less evident in the 1960s, 1970s, and 1980s. Simon Kuznets (1967) has noted, as did the classical economists, that early periods of rapid population growth are often periods when per capita economic growth is above average (Smith [1776] 1961; Malthus [1789] 1993). This cross-country negative pattern emerging in the 1990s may thus be a peculiar reflection of the fact that the countries for which population growth exceeds 2% per year are increasingly concentrated in sub-Saharan Africa, the one region that has experienced slow or negative rates of economic growth since the 1970s. The current cross-country inverse pattern between population and economic growth may, therefore, not be specifically due to population growth, but rather to other factors that are unusually common in Africa today, such as communicable diseases including malaria, TB, and HIV/AIDS, and prolonged disruptive wars and civil conflict (Bloom and Sachs 1998). By concentrating on observations at the family level rather than observations at the country level, I can set aside some of these unresolved issues involving the determinants of aggregate economic growth, and focus on other questions—of disentangling causal effects between fertility and income at the family level.

FAMILY-LEVEL MEASURES OF WELFARE

At the level of the family, do higher levels of parents' economic prosperity lead parents to have a smaller number of children, and does lower fertility lead to improved developmental outcomes for children in those families? Interfamily welfare comparisons are often based on total expenditures per household in a given time period, such as a year. To these market expenditures are then added home production, such as food that is produced and consumed in the home, and the imputed value of the consumer services that the household derives from its physical assets, predominantly in the form of owner-occupied housing and consumer durables. This measure of total market-purchased and home-produced consumption is a widely used approximation for "permanent income," or the present discounted value of average lifetime income opportunities, which is expected to influence the welfare of household members in the long run. In contrast, "current income" is heavily affected by temporary fluctuations in income that households are expected to try to smooth over time into their current flow of consumption, by adding to or drawing down life-cycle savings (debt). Lifetime expected income is therefore the family resource variable that should be related to lifetime fertility, and this lifetime income constraint is approximated by examining total household consumption.

This consumption is then divided by the number of adults in the household who share the consumption, to arrive at a measure of average consumption opportunities or, from the perspective of production, average adult productivity.[3] Because one objective of this essay is to examine the relationship between economic income and fertility, it is inappropriate to measure income as the household's per capita consumption, allowing explicitly for the "needs" of children in the household. The convention of measuring parents' consumption opportunities in per capita terms explicitly introduces parents' reproductive choices inversely into the measure of parents' consumption opportunities. If my goal is to estimate the causal relationship between parents' economic opportunities and their fertility, dividing consumption opportunities by the number of children they choose to have will interject a spurious negative partial correlation into the measured relationship. Consequently, household welfare is measured here by consumption per adult.[4]

SOURCES OF FERTILITY VARIATION: REPRODUCTIVE SUPPLY AND BEHAVIORAL DEMAND

To understand how fertility is determined and how economic opportunities and constraints might be causally related to fertility outcomes, a simple model is needed in which the supply of births can be distinguished from the demand for births. Demographers distinguish between the proximate determinants of fertility, or the sequence of biological events that occur to produce a birth, and the variations in behavior that modify the occurrence of these proximate determinants (Bongaarts and Potter 1983). To model fertility behavior as an economic resources-constrained choice, one may assume each couple is assigned a reproductive endowment (supply) that is affected by a random fecundity shock, and the couple then practices birth control or modifies other behavior related to fertility in order to better realize the number of births they want (demand) (Rosenzweig and Schultz 1985). Although a couple does not initially know their supply, they may learn over time from experience.[5] Since we lack good proxies in a survey for the fecundity of couples, we assume this reproductive endowment to be persistent over time and is approximated by the past fertility "success" of the couple, holding constant for their past practice of birth control, which is itself selected by the couple in light of their fertility goals and evolving information about their reproductive endowment (M. Rosenzweig and Schultz, 1985, 1987).

Within this supply-demand framework there are two sources of variation in observed fertility. The first component is related to genetic and random differences in fecundity. The second component includes the effect of systematic behavioral changes, notably including the adoption of birth control. But fertility is also affected by many other choices, such as age at marriage and duration of breast-feeding, which delays the resumption of ovulation. One way seemingly random supply variation among couples may impact their fertility is through their likelihood of having twins. Behavioral variation in fertility may respond to different perceived costs and benefits of children, including the pecuniary and psychic costs of using birth control. The former genetic variation in fertility supply may be thought of as an unanticipated shock, whereas the latter behavioral variation in fertility demand could respond to parents' perceived net benefit to having additional children, due either to observable factors (i.e., prices, wages, or wealth) or to unobserved preferences (i.e., tastes) of parents for children relative to other uses of their lifetime resources. In the case of the genetic variation in fertility supply, this source of fertility is not expected to be correlated with the parents' preferences or other unobserved behavioral constraints that could also modify family opportunities. The genetic variation in fertility would therefore operate like a randomized experiment.[6] If fertility is initially greater than parents want—in other words, if fecundity supply exceeds demand and birth control is costly—positive shocks of greater fertility associated with the arrival of twins, for example, would cause a welfare loss to parents.[7] Families would then need to reduce and reallocate their expenditures in response to the unwanted fertility shock, shifting resources away from activities that substitute for children, and shifting resources into activities that complement their additional children.[8] In contrast to this random genetic variation in fertility supply associated with the occurrence of twins, behavioral variation in fertility demand would be coordinated with other lifetime choices. Consequently, the association observed between this behaviorally determined fertility and other forms of family consumption or labor supply is not prescribed by any general economic models of family choice, or readily interpreted as an indicator of the economic consequences of an additional child or sibling on an average parent or their child, respectively.

Whether fertility is a substitute or a complement for other family activities is an important distinction, which can be inferred by estimating how random shocks to fecundity affect other family choices. Many models of family behavior assume that parents view the number of children they have (quantity) and the human capital they invest on average in each of their children (child quality) as substitutes (e.g., Becker and Lewis 1974). If child quantity and quality are in fact substitutes, which empirical studies seem to confirm, then policies that raise the price of child quantity, such as those providing subsidies for birth control in a family-planning program, can be expected to help parents lower their fertility and to also foster their demand for more child quality. Conversely, reducing the cost of child quality, which societies might do by subsidizing schooling for children, would lead parents to invest more in the schooling of their children and reduce their fertility (P. Schultz 1981, 1997).

Economic theories of the allocation of time and physical wealth of families among production and consumption activities suggest additional potential connections between the economic opportunities and constraints facing a couple and their demands for children. Let me review a few of the predictions of the household demand framework, which help to interpret cross-sectional differences in fertility and changes over time:

1. Increasing the productive value of women's time, typically measured by their wage rate outside the home or by their schooling, raises the opportunity cost of childbearing, and leads parents to want and have fewer children, despite the offsetting effect coming from an increase in their incomes (Mincer 1963; P. Schultz 1981, 1985, 1997).

2. Increasing the family's nonearned income from physical capital is not expected to affect the costs of children relative to other goods, and may in some settings raise the value of child labor to the parents, and is generally associated with higher fertility (P. Schultz 1981, 1994).

3. Increasing the returns from goods and services that are substitutes for children, such as the human capital of their children (quality), old-age pensions, health care of the elderly, and improved intergenerational capital markets, is expected to reduce fertility (Becker 1981).

4. Improving birth-control techniques reduces pecuniary and psychic costs of effective control. This fourth factor reduces fertility and uncertainty regarding the timing of births, and thereby assists women in planning their families, careers, and vocational training (Gertler and Molyneaux 1994; P. Schultz 1997).

5. As the levels of women's labor productivity and wages relative to men's increase, the opportunity costs of having children increase, thus strengthening women's influence over family resources and raising the share of household expenditures allocated to each child (Becker 1981; P. Schultz 1985, 2001).

Empirical counterparts for these theoretical price, income, technology, environment, and policy constraints, which are expected to influence lifetime fertility, have been imperfectly measured in many settings in both industrially advanced and low-income countries. They are found, in combination, to explain much of the variation in fertility, thus increasing our confidence that the household demand approach to fertility determinants offers a promising explanation for the fertility differences across a society or over time (P. Schultz 1994). The key empirical regularity is that where the productivity or schooling of women increases relative to men, fertility is likely to fall, especially if the most productive activities open to women are outside the home and thus cannot be readily combined with her traditional child care activities. Empirical studies are largely engaged in accounting for fertility differences across women in a single society, though some studies deal with populations at all stages of economic development or with subregions of a specific country over time (e.g., P. Schultz 1985).

MEASURING THE HOUSEHOLD CONNECTIONS BETWEEN FERTILITY AND INCOME IN KENYA

Sub-Saharan Africa is the last region of the world to benefit fully from health advances that have reduced child mortality from more than 20% to less than a few percent. Kenya is one of the first African countries in which fertility has declined markedly, starting probably in the early 1980s (Brass and Jolly 1993). While comprehensive economic and demographic household surveys from Africa that permit an examination of the relationships between fertility and family income are rare, the Kenyan Welfare Monitoring Surveys II and III, conducted in 1994 and 1997, allow exploration of some of the issues discussed above (P. Schultz and Mwabu 2003). The fraction of a woman's completed pregnancies (parities) that resulted in a multiple birth is one supply variable that should vary independently of family preferences and choices.[9] The effect of this "per pregnancy probability of having twins" on the woman's total number of births will be positive, but presumably less than 1.[10] The association between one additional birth when twins are born and family income expresses the impact expected from a "thought experiment" that randomly increases an average person's fertility by one birth. In reality, however, the extra child resulting from the birth of twins might constitute a minor inconvenience for some parents who want many children and who have twins from an early pregnancy and subsequently can easily adjust their use of birth control to achieve their lifetime reproductive goal. The arrival of twins could be a major setback for other parents who want few births and are thus more likely to have twins from a pregnancy that was intended to be their last; this second group of parents has little recourse but to have more children than they wanted because they had twins.

Population policies, however, more commonly seek to reduce fertility by helping couples avoid "unwanted births" through encouraging the diffusion of new, more effective family-planning methods. These population policies will thus have the opposite-signed effect on family welfare from what was inferred here from the study of the consequences of twins. As with the "twin shock," the exogenous improvement in birth control may be expected to benefit different parents differently. For parents who want few children, the provision of more effective birth control is a greater benefit than for parents who want more children, other things being equal.

Kenyan women between the ages of twenty-five and forty-four, for whom fertility is known, are analyzed, forming a sample of 5,400 women in 1994 and 4,528 in 1997. Having twins appears to increase a woman's number of children by .74 in 1994 and by .89 in 1997, suggesting that the average Kenyan couple is able to offset, through birth control and other compensating behavior, between 26% and 11% of the effect of the unanticipated birth of twins, as it affects their cumulated fertility at the time of the survey. All of the "associations" reported are estimated after controlling for the schooling of mother and father, their ages, rural/urban residence, and five regions of Kenya. The fertility increase associated with the occurrence of twins is not significantly correlated across women with their household's consumption per adult. But having one more child is significantly related to diminished consumption per adult, −1.9% per birth in 1994 and −2.5% in 1997, confirming the impression stated at the outset of this essay: higher fertility is associated with lower consumption and greater poverty. But it is notable that this negative association is not evident with respect to the random variation in fertility due to twins, suggesting that consumption is not lower if the increase in fertility occurs randomly. Unobserved factors that influence the decisions of people to have more (or fewer) children are also factors that are associated with being poorer (or richer), and among these factors I would expect the diversity of preferences for children and of productive capabilities to be important.

Household consumption per adult, my initial indicator of parent income, is significantly positively associated with the ownership of land, and the receipt of agricultural and nonagricultural rents. These three physical asset sources of income are generally positively related to fertility in Kenya. A 10% increase in household consumption per adult, arising from these asset sources of income, is associated with an increase in fertility of .19 child in 1994 and .17 child in 1997, where the average fertility in the survey samples is about four children. But a 10% increase in household consumption per adult from sources other than the three asset variables is negatively related to fertility, reducing fertility by .20 child in 1994 and by .18 child in 1997. In other words, the estimated effect of increasing assets is to increase fertility, whereas increasing other sources of income, such as labor earnings, decreases fertility, and both relationships are highly significant in both surveys.[11] An increase in the mother's schooling attainment by one year is associated with her household consumption per adult rising by 4.1% in 1994 and by 4.9% in 1997, and these effects are larger than those associated with the schooling of the father. If the household consumption effect of the woman's schooling is held constant, each additional year of her schooling has an additional effect of reducing her fertility by .12 child in both 1994 and 1997. These estimates underscore how different sources of income and human capital exhibit markedly different partial associations with fertility. It is important, therefore, to distinguish among the different sources of income in order to understand the impacts of economic development on fertility and the timing of the demographic transition in a particular society.

A second indicator of family outcome is drawn from the survey's reports on the height and weight of children under five years of age. A common anthropometric indicator of the health and nutritional status of children from ages six to sixty months is the ratio of a child's weight to height (W/H).[12] One more child born to a Kenyan woman is associated with a −.032 standard deviation change in the W/H of her young children in 1994 and a −.037 standard deviation change in 1997. This anthropometric indicator tends to be positively associated with the child's chances of survival, later health status, subsequent performance in school, and eventual productivity as an adult worker. Thus, a decline in W/H associated with a rise in fertility suggests that an additional child may involve a real cost in terms of child health. But when one focuses only on the fertility variation associated with twins, the child nutrition effect is much larger: $-.11$ and $-.20$ standard deviation in 1994 and 1997, respectively.[13]

The purpose of distinguishing between the random event of a birth of twins and other sources of behaviorally influenced fertility variation is to show that the supply and demand components of fertility are related differently to one widely used measure of child welfare, W/H. The estimated overall association of fertility to W/H is negative, but a small fraction of that associated with the random supply shock of twins. Evidently, the distinction between the behavioral demand and random genetic supply variation in fertility is critical. If we want to assess the impact of how a population policy is likely to affect the health and nutritional welfare of a woman's children, or her household's consumption, it is important to understand the source of the change in fertility. A national family-planning program that reduced the effective cost of birth control sufficiently to reduce the average number of births among Kenyan women by 1 would, according to these estimates, raise the W/H of the next generation of Kenyan children by .1 to .2 standard deviation, and increase overall consumption opportunities per adult in the average Kenyan household.

CONCLUSIONS

Forecasting the consequences of economic development on Kenyan fertility is complicated. First, one must know the sources of that economic growth. If growth is achieved by increasing the income returns from land, for example, it is likely that Kenyan fertility will remain high, perhaps because parents view land and the labor of children as complementary factors in their meager production. If economic growth is stimulated by extending additional education to women, the resulting relative rise in the price of children will favor a continuing decline in fertility, as observed in many studies within a low-income country and estimated across countries and over time (P. Schultz 1994, 1997).

Most parents benefit from an improvement in birth control that allows them to avoid unwanted births at less cost. Analogously, a policy that could miraculously reduce the incidence of twins not only would reduce fertility but also might raise family income, as measured in Kenya by consumption per adult, and improve child nutrition and health status, as measured by W/H, which in turn should enhance the child's productivity as an adult. However, a policy that reduces the level of fertility by constraining parents' demands for children, such as by implementing quantitative restrictions and tax penalties for out-of-plan births, as in China, may not advance family welfare, and could diminish it.

Fertility and income are caused by many factors. To account for the impact of fertility on society, it is useful to distinguish between genetically determined variation in the supply of births that is more or less random, and behavioral variation in the demand for births that is coordinated with many other choices parents make over their lifetimes. In the case of economic development and the growth in income, social scientists should distinguish among the various sources of modern economic growth that do not appear to have the same effects on fertility. In particular, income that flows from the human capital of the mother and father, and income that flows from stocks of physical capital, land, and other natural resources, are not likely to contribute to similar behavioral responses in fertility.

NOTES

1. I have included all ninety-six countries for which Penn World Tables (PWT) 6.1 provides estimates of GDP per adult in purchasing power parity 1996 dollars for both 1960 and 2000, and I could obtain the proportion of the population age fifteen or over from World Development Indicators of the World Bank, and their total fertility rates from the U.N. Population Division database.

2. TFR in the world declined about 46% from 1960 to 2000, from 4.97 to 2.69 (UN 2003), but growth in real income in the world is more difficult to measure; it may have grown by 4–5% per year, when the incomes of countries are weighted by their populations (P. Schultz 1998).

3. Studies of household expenditure patterns frequently define welfare by deflating observed household consumption by the consumption "needs" of the household members. Consumption needs for several demographic groups are derived in equivalent units, where the needs of male adults are typically used as a benchmark and set to 1 (Deaton 1997). Because food consumption is a large share of total consumption in a low-income country, on the order of 70% in Kenya in 1994 (Kenyan Central Bureau of Statistics 1996, 152), and about 60% in India in 1983 (Thomas 1986, 237), estimated nutritional requirements determined initially by average weight of different demographic groups—such as adult males, adult females, and children—may approximate the household's overall consumption requirements. Of course, this approximation of equivalent caloric "needs" for men and women to maintain their body weight ignores individual differences in weight within distinguished groups, as well as individual differences in the strenuousness of work (caloric demands of labor, childbearing, and breast-feeding) and the burdens of disease (fighting infection consumes calories). Moreover, as the food share of total expenditures declines with economic development, these demographic consumption units based on body weight and calorie requirements become even less satisfactory (Thomas 1986).

4. There are many reasons that consumption per adult does not perfectly measure the welfare opportunities of the parents. For example, in low-income countries, children may be important contributors to household income through their labor. Thus the causality could flow from fertility back to household consumption per adult. Nonetheless, consumption per adult is better for my purposes than consumption per capita or per adult equivalent, including children.

5. An implication of this framework is that those with greater fecundity are more likely to adopt more effective methods of birth control at a smaller family size, holding

constant for the environmental conditions that are expected to influence their demand for children (Rosenzweig and Schultz 1987).

6. Twins tend to occur in 1–3% of pregnancies, but with the recent developments in drug treatments to deal with infertility problems, the frequency of multiple births has increased and would no longer be expected to occur randomly in some high-income populations. Small variations in the probability of twins are observed according to the mother's parity and age, but these are neglected here, given the size of the samples later examined.

7. If fertility supply is lower than demanded by parents, the arrival of twins may increase welfare.

8. If we could ignore the welfare loss associated with the fertility shock (i.e., the income effect), the sign of the cross-effect of the genetic fertility variation on the other forms of family behavior would signal whether the other form of behavior was a substitute (negative) or complement (positive) for children in the parents' utility function. This implication of random rationing of the provision of a household good (children), regardless of the demand for that good, was analyzed by Tobin and Houthakker (1950–1951), and applied by Rosenzweig and Wolpin (1980). Their study confirmed that the birth of twins led Indian rural families to retrench on the schooling of their children, suggesting that numbers of children and their schooling are substitutes, neglecting the income loss associated with unanticipated twins.

9. It would be preferable to consult a pregnancy roster for each older woman who has completed her childbearing, and analyze the number of children she has ever borne and the number of twins she has had over her entire reproductive lifetime. Unfortunately, the Kenyan surveys did not collect this information, and our calculations are based on the number of surviving children of the woman enumerated as members of her household. The ages of women analyzed are restricted to between twenty-five and forty-four to minimize the likelihood that some of their children would have left the household. Control variables for age and age squared of the mother and father are included to reduce the problems of younger women not having completed their childbearing. In 1994 is it possible to compare these survey enumerated measures of surviving children with the responses of women to the question of how many live children they have ever borne and how many have died. Within the sample of women ages twenty-five to forty-four, the observed and ever-borne measures of fertility are correlated at .97 or higher. A second measurement problem arises from the nonuniform distribution of the probability of the birth of twins, which is concentrated at points such as 0, .50, .33, .25, .20, .16, .66, and .40. We use a transformation called a polyfraction exponential approximation to smooth this distribution and avoid statistical bias due to its nonsymmetric form. If we had a sufficiently large sample and the full roster of each woman's pregnancy history, we could have focused only on the effect of twins-on-first-parity, which is a better measure because it includes all women with at least one child, each one time (Olsen 1980; Royston and Altman 1994).

10. The first study I know of to examine the effect of twins on fertility and family outcomes was based on a rural Indian survey from 1971 (Rosenzweig and Wolpin 1980), in which twins are associated with a mother having .8 more children, and with the woman's other children having a significantly lower educational attainment, presumably due to the twins. Other studies have shown that fertility variation that is not explained by birth-control practices and socioeconomic controls is negatively asso-

ciated with child health and schooling in Malaysia (Rosenzweig and Schultz 1987). Studies of high-income countries have examined the consequences of twins on decisions regarding marriage and receipt of public assistance (Bronars and Grogger 1994).

11. This procedure of including the asset-identified income and the residual income among the explanatory variables in the fertility equation is analogous to the Hausman (1978) specification test in which one rejects the exogeneity of income as a determinant of fertility.

12. This variable is transformed into a Z score, defined as a deviation of the child's W/H from the median value in a reference population of children of the same age and sex, and divided by the standard deviation of W/H in each age and sex category. The World Health Organization's (1986, 1995) recommended strategy is to compare the child's growth with a population of healthy children, and a common standard is provided by the Centers for Disease Control and Prevention in Atlanta, based on large samples of U.S. children. Alternatively, we used the Kenyan survey itself to provide a smoothed estimate by gender of the age curve for W/H and its standard deviation, since we are more interested in relative ranking of nutritional status among the Kenyan children than in comparing Kenyan children against an international standard derived from a relatively well-nourished population. Both standardized indicators of W/H, based on the U.S. and Kenyan populations, yielded very similar results, though not precisely the same across genders or rural-urban differences.

13. For example, the effect of a twin on W/H would approximately offset the substantial gains associated with a mother having completed five additional years of schooling, according to the estimates based on the 1997 Kenyan survey.

BIBLIOGRAPHY

Becker, Gary. *A Treatise on the Family.* Cambridge, Mass.: Harvard University Press, 1981.

Becker, Gary, and Gregg Lewis. "Interaction between Quantity and Quality of Children." In *The Economics of the Family,* edited by T. W. Schultz. Chicago: University of Chicago Press, 1974.

Bloom, David, and Jeffrey Sachs. "Geography, Demography, and Economic Growth in Africa." *Brookings Papers on Economic Activity* 2 (1998): 207–273.

Bongaarts, John, and Robert G. Potter. *Fertility, Biology, and Behavior.* New York: Academic Press, 1983.

Brass, William, and Carole L. Jolly, eds. *Population Dynamics of Kenya.* Washington, D.C.: National Academy Press, 1993.

Bronars, Stephen, and Jeff Grogger. "The Economic Consequences of Unwed Motherhood: Using Twin Births as a Natural Experiment." *American Economic Review* 84 (5) (1994): 1141–1156.

Coale, Ansley, and Edgar Hoover. *Population Growth and Economic Development in Low-Income Countries.* Princeton, N.J.: Princeton University Press, 1958.

Deaton, Angus. *The Analysis of Household Surveys.* Baltimore: Johns Hopkins University Press, 1997.

Ehrlich, Paul. *The Population Explosion.* New York: Simon and Schuster, 1964.

Enke, Stephen. "The Economics of Government Payments to Limit Population." *Economic Development and Cultural Change* 8 (4) (1960): 339–348.

Gertler, Paul, and John Molyneaux. "How Economic Development and Family Planning Programs Combined to Reduce Indonesian Fertility." *Demography* 31 (1) (1994): 33–63.

Hausman, Jerry. "Specification Tests in Econometrics." *Econometrica* 46 (6) (1978): 1251–1271.

Kelley, Allen, and Robert Schmidt. "Population and Income Change: Recent Evidence." World Bank discussion paper 249, Washington, D.C., 1994.

Kenyan Central Bureau of Statistics. *Welfare Monitoring Survey II, 1994. Basic Report.* Nairobi: Ministry of Finance and Planning, Republic of Kenya, 1996.

Kuznets, Simon. "Population and Economic Growth." *Proceedings of the American Philosophical Society* 111 (3) (1967): 170–193.

Malthus, Thomas. *An Essay on the Principle of Population.* 1789. Reprint, Oxford: Oxford University Press, 1993.

Mincer, Jacob. "Market Prices, Opportunity Costs and Income Effects." In *Measurement in Economics,* edited by C. Christ et al. Stanford, Calif.: Stanford University Press, 1963.

National Research Council. *Population Growth and Economic Development: Policy Questions.* Washington, D.C.: National Academy Press, 1986.

National Research Council. *Beyond Six Billion.* Washington, D.C.: National Academy Press, 2000.

Notestein, Frank. "Population—The Long View." In *Food for the World,* edited by T. W. Schultz. Chicago: University of Chicago Press, 1945.

Olsen, R. J. "Estimating the Effects of Child Mortality on the Number of Births." *Demography* 17 (4) (1980): 429–444.

Rosenzweig, Mark, and Paul Schultz. "The Demand and Supply of Birth: Fertility and Its Lifecycle Consequences." *American Economic Review* 75 (5) (1985): 992–1015.

Rosenzweig, Mark, and Paul Schultz. "Fertility and Investment in Human Capital: Estimates of the Consequences of Imperfect Fertility Control in Malaysia." *Journal of Econometrics* 36 (1987): 163–184.

Rosenzweig, Mark, and Kenneth Wolpin. "Testing the Quality–Quantify Fertility Model." *Econometrica* 48 (1) (1980): 227–240.

Royston, P., and D. G. Altman. "Regression Using Fractional Polynomials of Continuous Covariates." *Applied Statistics* 43 (3) (1994): 429–467.

Schultz, Paul. *Economics of Populations.* Reading, Mass.: Addison-Wesley, 1981.

Schultz, Paul. "Changing World Prices, Women's Wages and the Fertility Transition." *Journal of Political Economy* 93 (1985): 1126–1154.

Schultz, Paul. "Human Capital, Family Planning and Their Effects on Population Growth." *American Economic Review* 83 (1994): 255–260.

Schultz, Paul. "The Demand for Children in Low-Income Countries." In *Handbook of Population and Family Economics,* edited by M. R. Rosenzweig and O. Stark. Amsterdam: North-Holland, 1997.

Schultz, Paul. "Inequality in the Distribution of Personal Income in the World." *Journal of Population Economics* 11 (3) (1998): 307–344.

Schultz, Paul. "Women's Roles in the Agricultural Household: Bargaining and Human Capital Investments." In *Handbook of Agricultural Economics,* edited by B. Gardner and G. Rausser. Amsterdam: North-Holland, 2001.

Schultz, Paul, and G. Mwabu. "The Causes and Consequences of Fertility in Contemporary Kenya." Unpublished paper, Yale University, 2003.

Schultz, Theodore W. "Fertility and Economic Values." In *Economics of the Family*, edited by Theodore W. Schultz. Chicago: University of Chicago Press, 1974.

Smith, Adam. *The Wealth of Nations*. 1776. Reprint edited by E. Cannon. London: Methuen, 1961.

Thomas, Duncan. "The Food Share as a Welfare Measure." Ph.D. dissertation, Princeton University, 1986.

Tobin, James, and Hendrick Houthakker. "The Effect of Rationing on Demand Elasticities." *Review of Economic Studies* 18 (1950–1951): 140–153.

United Nations. *World Population Prospects: The 2002 Revision*. Vol. 1. New York: United Nations, 2003.

World Health Organization. "Use and Interpretation of Anthropometric Indicators of Nutritional Studies." *Bulletin of the World Health Organization* 64 (6) (1986): 929–941.

World Health Organization. *Physical Status: The Use and Interpretation of Anthropometry*. WHO Technical Report Series no. 854. Geneva: World Health Organization, 1995.

10

Fertility in Developing Countries

Mukesh Eswaran

Rapid population growth blights the lives of a large proportion of the world's people and condemns them to poverty. Many countries still have population growth rates in excess of 2% per annum, a rate that would double the population in thirty-five years. All the developed countries of today have made the transition (the "demographic transition") from the phase of high fertility, high mortality, and high population growth to a phase of low fertility, low mortality, and low population growth. Their growth from poverty to riches has been facilitated by this transition. This essay will discuss some important aspects of high fertility in the developing countries of today and suggest approaches that will hasten their demographic transition. It will also address some disturbing, related problems that are accompanying this transition in some developing countries.

High fertility usually implies rapid population growth. This typically lowers the rate of growth of per capita income and, in addition, has serious consequences for the distribution of income across different classes of people. The growth in per capita income is retarded partly because some production inputs, such as agricultural land, are fixed in supply. Higher populations would mean that each agricultural worker, now having less land to work with, is less productive. And lower productivity implies lower per capita income. If workers also use capital in production, the total capital stock of the country has to rise faster in the face of population growth in order to maintain the amount of capital per worker. If it does not, once again productivity will fall because each worker has less capital to work with than before. In other words, in the face of population growth, the nation's savings rate has to be higher if income per capita is to be maintained. Thus, even if

143

the production inputs other than labor are not fixed but can be accumulated over time, rapid population growth will impede the elimination of poverty. Population growth also has adverse effects on the environment: Forests are depleted for fuel, groundwater is exhausted, agricultural land is overused, and so on. All of these inputs, which can be interpreted as various forms of capital, contribute to the productivity of labor. Depletion of these through rapid population growth is tantamount to reducing the future productivity of labor and, therefore, the standard of living of those who constitute the poor.

The income distribution consequences of high fertility follow from the fact that the owners of production inputs other than labor typically benefit from population growth. Landlords receive higher land rent, since the productivity of a hectare of agricultural land increases when it is worked by more labor. Likewise, the return on capital increases to the extent that a larger labor force renders capital more productive. Therefore, if everything else is constant, accompanying population growth will be a declining wage rate, an increasing rental rate on land, and an increasing return to capital. Capitalists and landlords will become richer even as workers become poorer. Since the poor in developing countries are typically those without any assets, by skewing the income distribution against the poor, rapid population growth will result in poverty persisting longer than it otherwise would.

Of course, technical progress, which increases the amount of output that can be produced from given amounts of inputs, may come to the rescue. However, the demands on technical progress will be that much greater when population is growing rapidly. It has been proposed that larger populations would induce faster technical progress because there will be more new ideas generated when there are more people.[1] Ideas are public goods: their use by one person does not preclude their use by others. Consequently, an idea can serve an entire population just as well as it can serve a single individual. Alternatively, if production requires firms to incur substantial fixed costs, the cost per unit of output would decline as the output increases—giving an advantage to large populations because they consume more output in total. However, in the populous developing countries of today, it is highly unlikely that these benefits would outweigh the negative effects outlined above. On balance, by slowing down the rate of growth of per capita income, we would expect population growth to retard the alleviation of poverty.

Empirical assessment of the intuitively simple logic outlined above has proven remarkably difficult to conduct because the attempts are plagued by various statistical problems. Kelley and Schmidt (1994) have examined the effect of population growth on the growth rate of per capita income and on the productivity of labor, using compatible data from eighty-nine countries over the period 1960–1990.[2] They found that while population growth had an insignificant effect in the first two decades, in the decade beginning in 1980 it adversely affected the growth rate of per capita GDP. The effect was particularly strong in developing countries. To bring home this point, they conducted the hypothetical exercise of assuming that the population growth rate of the median developing country fell from 2.54% in 1980 to 2.34% in 1990, in contrast to the historical constancy of this rate over the three decades. They found that this assumed decline of 0.20 percentage point in the population growth rate would have increased the growth rate of per capita GDP of the median developing country by 0.41 percentage point. The observed negative impact in the 1980s of population growth also held for the growth rate of labor productivity.

It has been argued that high fertility is a cause of poverty. However, the causation often goes in the opposite direction as well. Poverty encourages high fertility for reasons having to do with old-age security (an issue that is dealt with at length in this essay), and this increases future poverty. Using data on fifty-nine (mostly) developing countries, Eastwood and Lipton (1999) present evidence on the relationship between fertility and poverty and the direction of causation.[3] If poverty were more strongly correlated with lagged values of fertility (e.g., fertility ten years earlier) than with current values, one might infer that the causation goes from fertility to poverty; if the reverse is true, then the inference would be that the causation goes from poverty to fertility. Their finding is that while poverty is correlated with both measures, the correlation with lagged fertility measures is much stronger. They estimate that had the 1980 median country in their sample experienced the median fertility reduction actually seen in their sample during the decade, its poverty level would have fallen from approximately 19% to 14%.

While many factors influence fertility, this essay will focus only on ones that are most relevant to contemporary developing countries. Child labor, a ubiquitous institution in many of the poorest countries, is a particularly relevant factor. When child mortality rates are high, the existence of this institution strongly influences fertility for various reasons. Legislation that bans child labor is virtually unenforceable in the midst of poverty. Therefore, one cannot seriously set about resolving the problem of high fertility in developing countries without concurrently addressing the problem of child labor. Since children's work in developing countries comes at the expense of the education of children to a large extent, compulsory education—if enforced—could have significant effects on fertility.

While the argument (and some evidence) on the link between child labor and fertility will be discussed later in the essay, it may be mentioned here that, in a prescient paper, the demographer Caldwell (1980) identified universal education as having significantly hastened the demographic transition in the now developed countries. Among other things, the laws for compulsory education raised the cost of children to parents and thus lowered marital fertility. In England, for example, the Education Act of 1870 started the move toward compulsory education, which became law in 1880. As Caldwell points out, marital fertility began to fall in England and Wales between 1871 and 1881. The timing is uncanny, especially when we note that per capita income had been rising in England for nearly a century before that (as a result of the Industrial Revolution), and that had resulted, by the standards of the day, in rapid population growth. Other European countries saw fertility transitions that were synchronous with laws making education compulsory. Weiner (1991, chap. 6) has observed that even if laws banning child labor exist, they can really be enforced only when education is mandatory. Then, the authorities only need peruse the school registers in order to identify potential child laborers.

As noted, many developing countries have rapidly growing populations and exhibit no perceptible approach to the demographic transition. Others, such as the East Asian countries, are rapidly undergoing this fertility transition but are exhibiting a most disturbing feature: a biased sex ratio of children at birth.[4] This, as we shall see, is due to discrimination against females, and discrimination cannot get more extreme than where their very survival is jeopardized.

Table 10.1, using a handful of countries by way of examples, conveys how fertility correlates with some pertinent economic measures. We see that even populous countries tend to have high rates of population growth. (China is an exception, because of the one-child-per family policy implemented in 1979.) The child mortality rates are also largest in the poorer countries. Enrollment in educational institutions not only is low in poor countries but also is skewed against girls, especially in South Asia. Likewise, the economic activity of women outside the home—a measure of the autonomous influence women are likely to have in household decision making—is low in the poorer countries, again especially in South Asia. These impressionistic statistical "facts," presented here in a rough-and-ready manner, are also confirmed by comprehensive empirical studies. For our purposes, Table 10.1 is adequate to highlight the essential ingredients of the discussion to follow.

This essay outlines why fertility is high in many developing countries; why it declines with economic development; why the institution of child labor facilitates high fertility; and why high fertility is intimately tied to the extent of female autonomy in decision making. It then discusses the reasons for the biased sex ratio at birth alluded to above. Finally, the essay concludes with suggestions for policy measures that will address the problems identified here.

CHILDREN AS ASSETS

Before we can determine what can be done about rapid population growth in developing countries, we have to understand what motivates people to have many children. Policy measures that merely increase the number of family-planning clinics and disburse free contraceptives, while useful, could be misguided supply-side responses to the problem. They fail to account for why there is a demand for large families in the first place. Although the opinions of researchers on the effectiveness of family-planning programs are not uniform, the evidence is that they are useful when the desired fertility rate has been lowered but the means to implement it are not readily avail-

Table 10.1 Demographic and Economic Indicators across Selected Countries

	Total Population (Millions) 1999	Population Growth Rate (% p.a.) 1975–99	Mortality for Children under 5	Combined Primary, Secondary and Tertiary Enrollment (%)	GDP per Capita (PPP US$) 1999	Female Economic Activity rate (as % of Male Activity) 1999	Life Expectancy at Birth Females (males) 1999
United States		1.0		99	31, 872	80	79.7
	280.4		8	(91)			(73.9)
Canada		1.1		98	26,251	81	81.4
	30.5		6	(96)			(75.9)
Japan		0.5		81	24,1898	67	84.1
	126.8		4	(83)			(77.3)
Germany		0.2		93	23,742	69	80.6
	82.0		5	(95)			(74.3)
Rep. Korea		1.1		85	15,712	69	78.4
	46.4		5	(95)			(70.9)
Argentina		1.4		86	12,277	45	77.0
	36.6		22	(80)			(69.9)
Chile		1.6		77	8,652	48	78.5
	15.0		12	(78)			(72.5)
Mexico		2.1		70	8,297	47	75.8
	97.4		33	(71)			(69.8)
Brazil		1.1		80	7,037	52	71.8
	168.2		40	(79)			(63.9)
Columbia		2.0		73	5,749	60	74.6
	41.4		31	(73)			(67.8)
Philippines		2.4		84	3,805	61	71.1
	74.2		42	(80)			(67.0)
China	1	1.3		73	3,617	86	72.5
	264.8		41	(73)			(68.3
Egypt		2.3		72	3,420	44	68.5
	66.7		52	(80)			(65.3)
Indonesia		1.8		61	2,857	67	67.7
	209.3		52	(68)			(63.9)
India		2.0		49	2,248	50	63.1
	992.7		98	(62)			(62.4)
Pakistan		2.8		28	1,834	41	59.5
	137.6		12	(51)			(59.8)
Bangladesh		2.4		33	1,483	76	59.0
	134.6		189	(41)			(58.9)
Uganda		3.1		41	1,167	88	43.8
	22.6		31	(49)			(42.5)
Nigeria		2.9		41	8	56	51.7
	110.8		87	(49)	53		(51.3)
Ethiopia		2.6		19	628	67	44.9
	61.4		76	(26)			(43.3)
Tanzania		3.1		32	501	93	52.2
	34.3		41	(33)			(50.0)

Source: Compiled from various tables in *The Human Development Report 2001: Making New Technologies Work for Human Development*, By UNDP, Oxford University Press, New York.

able.[5] In other words, while they can be very effective in averting unwanted pregnancies at the onset of the demographic transition, they are not equipped to bring about a reduction in the desired number of children.

A very important source of the demand for large families in developing countries is the fact that old-age security for parents comes from children. This is particularly true in South Asia, which is a region of considerable population growth. (It comprises about a quarter of the world's population but accounts for a third of the annual increase in the world's population.) In poor countries—especially in the rural countryside, where the bulk of the population resides—there are few financial assets available for transferring income from one's working life to one's retirement. Parents view children as vehicles for ensuring security in old age. Even when financial instruments are available, they are rarely deemed to be substitutable for children. Adult children can potentially provide security in the innumerable contingencies that can arise in old age. Jensen (1990) has provided compelling evidence for the old-age security hypothesis. Using Malaysian data from a survey conducted in 1982, he examined the decisions of couples to use contraceptives. He found that old-age security concerns were very important: Only couples who had satisfied their perceived old-age security needs opted for contraception.

While security in old age may provide the motivation for having children, it does not follow that the fertility will be more than what would be deemed optimal for the society. Indeed, if a benevolent social planner had the power to impose a fertility level on each family, she would need to consult the fertility preferences of typical parents. If an imbalance arises between the private optimal fertility of a typical couple and that deemed optimal for the society, there must be some mismatch between the benefits and/or costs that a social planner would account for and those for which individual couples would. What are the sources of such a discrepancy?

An important source of socially harmful fertility behavior is that while parents may altruistically consider the well-being of their children, they do not weight it equally with their own. The mechanism, which was first proposed by Neher (1971), runs as follows. Consider a poor country where children are the only assets. An additional child imposes a cost on his parents when young. When the child becomes an adult, he generates income in excess of his own consumption and is therefore a benefit to parents. When the offspring reaches retirement, his consumption again exceeds income and needs to be subsidized by his children. Thus an additional child is a net cost in childhood, a net benefit in adulthood, and again a net cost in retirement. Parents incur the offspring's cost in childhood and reap a benefit in adulthood. But when their offspring again becomes a cost to society in retirement, the parents most likely will be dead. It is therefore very likely that, in contemplating additional children, parents will either ignore or underestimate the cost that their offspring will impose on subsequent generations in their retirement. However, a benevolent social planner who weights future generations on par with the present one will not. Thus, parents who are not completely altruistic will overestimate the benefits of children relative to the costs imposed on society. As a result, privately chosen fertility levels will be too high relative to what is optimal for society.

ECONOMIC DEVELOPMENT AND FERTILITY

The role played by economic development in eliminating the wedge between private and social net benefits of children can now be readily seen. With economic development come capital markets, offering various financial instruments for saving. Along with these, private firms begin to offer pension plans and the government may offer social security. These greatly reduce the need for parents to use children as vehicles for transferring income from their working life to retirement. Thus, on these grounds alone, one would expect to see declining fertility with economic development.

There are other, equally compelling reasons why economic development results in fertility decline. One of these has to do with the cost of the time of women. Galor and Weil (1996) have proposed that as the capital stock of a nation increases, it impinges differentially on the wages of men and women. While both engage in manual and nonmanual work, men have a relative advantage in manual work and women in nonmanual work. If the increase in the capital stock (through saving) raises productivity of nonmanual labor more than it does of manual labor, the wage rate of women will rise faster than that of men. As a couple becomes wealthier, it may want more children. However, whether, and how many, children women bear depends on their wage rate relative to the couple's income, since that determines the income women forgo by opting out of the labor market during and after pregnancy. The relative increase in the wage rate of women leads to an increase in the participation of women in the labor market and a decline in fertility.

Given the arguments outlined above, the reader might infer that no special measures need be taken with regard to excessive population growth in developing countries if they are showing respectable economic growth. The emergence of financial instruments for saving and the higher cost of children in terms of income forgone will reduce fertility. In the words of a popular quip of the 1970s: "Economic development is the best contraceptive."

Such an inference, however, would be premature. The growth rates of the GDP of many developing countries with high population growth rates are very low. Indeed, as we have seen, part of the reason why per capita GDP grows slowly is that population growth is outpacing the rate at which capital is accumulating through savings. Thus, waiting for economic growth to dilute the incentives of couples to have many children may indefinitely postpone fertility reduction.

THE EFFECT OF CHILD MORTALITY

There are good, additional reasons for the governments of developing countries to be more proactive with regard to population problems. A statistical relationship that demographers have long focused on is the decline in a country's infant or child mortality rate and the population rate of growth.[6] As the country's child mortality rate declines, the population rate of growth subsequently declines. In fact, it is not hard to see that there is a causal connection between the two: all else constant, reductions in child mortality rates are responsible for declines in the rates of population growth.

The reason for this causal connection is that the possibility of the death of children exposes parents to considerable risk. There are likely few things that parents fear more than the possibility of losing their children. This is true also in developed countries, where old-age security concerns do not motivate fertility choice; it is true with even greater force in developing countries, where they do. Faced with the possibility of child mortality, parents with an old-age security motive overcompensate for child mortality.

Suppose the desired number of children for a typical couple is four if all children are assured of survival. When the child mortality rate is 25%, one of the four children, on average, will not survive to adulthood. If parents were merely to compensate for this expected loss, they would increase their fertility to five, and the population rate of growth would stay the same. However, quite apart from the fact that only four out of five children can be expected to survive, on average, there is uncertainty introduced by child mortality. The possibility that they may lose more than one child—and possibly all of them—invariably leads parents to overcompensate for the possible loss by increasing fertility to more than five. In other words, parents tend to "hoard" children to protect themselves against the contingency of being left without support in old age. The extent of the "excess" fertility will naturally depend on the child mortality rate. When the child mortality rate declines, it takes some time before the new level becomes apparent to the populace. Sooner or later, parents perceive a reduction in the need for excess fertility, and thus the population rate of growth declines.[7]

To garner empirical evidence on the effect of child mortality on fertility, one needs to separate out the behavioral response of parents, discussed above, to anticipated children's deaths from the biological response to actual deaths. The latter refers to the fact that, in the case of infants, a death may increase fertility by reducing the sterile period of the mother, and to the fact that birth order may impinge on an infant's health. In a careful investigation, Rosenzweig and Schultz (1983) sought to isolate these effects by analyzing American data for the years 1967–1969. They found that "the average number of children per mother would increase by one-sixth of a child if an infant mortality rate of 0.1 were anticipated." This, it must be noted, is the estimated effect of increased child mortality in a highly developed country where parents do not expect their children to provide old-age security. In a developing country where parents do, one would expect the response to be even stronger.

THE ROLE OF CHILD LABOR

High child mortality rates in developing countries can induce high levels of fertility for an additional reason that works through the institution of child labor.[8] Although this is hardly a concern anymore in the developed countries, in a developing country investment in a child's education depends on the child mortality rate, for two reasons. First, when child mortality is low, off-spring are expected to live long, and so the return on their educational investment is high. Parents will opt to send their children to school and thereby forgo their income from child labor. Where child mortality rates are high, parents will not choose this option (when child labor is a socially accepted institution). Second, not only does high child mortality reduce the rate of return to education, it also renders educated children more risky "assets" than uneducated ones. For both these reasons, people who are poor would rather put their children to work. Among the poor, child labor is promoted by high child mortality rates. In such a scenario, the poor will not educate their children even if credit is made available to them. The rich, on the other hand, do not need the income from child labor, and they can reduce child mortality by expending resources privately on health care. In effect, high child mortality rates encourage high fertility rates, and when child labor laws are either nonexistent or unenforceable, they also increase the incidence of child labor.

Thus reductions in child mortality, apart from directly lowering fertility, would have the additional salutary effect of reducing child labor and increasing the skill level of the labor force of the next generation. Furthermore, since educated parents tend to educate their children, improvements in the health of one generation of children can permanently increase the skill level of the labor force and move the economy out of poverty. And affluence, as we have seen, brings about an independent reduction in fertility rates. When children become expensive—because child labor income is lost to parents and, instead, they need to incur educational expenditures—couples will naturally have fewer children. Parents will then opt for "quality" rather than "quantity" with regard to children. In most of the developed countries of today, the introduction of compulsory education for children was accompanied by a decline in fertility for this reason.

Strictly speaking, the argument made above refers to children who have successfully lived through childhood but die as adults (when they would be of use to parents for old-age security). In developing countries, we would expect the probability of death among young adults to be correlated with mortality rates during childhood—because the predominant cause of both is the prevalence of infectious diseases. It is possible to obtain a rough idea of the magnitude of the relevant probability. For India over the period 1970–

1983, the proportion of fifteen-year-old males (females) who did not survive until they were sixty was 32.8% (29.4%).[9] In other words, around one in three children in India who lived long enough to be able to go through school died before providing old-age security for his parents for the entire length of their retirement.

When parents are imperfectly altruistic, in the sense that they put less weight on their children's well-being than on their own, it is not surprising that the decision on whether to send children to work might differ from that of a social planner. Baland and Robinson (2000) have formally demonstrated that child labor can be socially inefficient even when parents are perfectly altruistic (that is, they assign as much weight to their children's well-being as to their own). It might be construed that if parents leave bequests for their children, then the decisions regarding their children's work/schooling trade-off would be also a social planner's. For if schooling contributes to a child's future earnings, then parents would send the child to school but leave behind a smaller bequest. But this is not so when parents are so poor as to leave no bequest to begin with. Furthermore, even if parents do leave bequests, child labor may be socially inefficient if capital markets are imperfect. Parents who wish to transfer some income from their retirement period to the present may find it expedient to use child labor to effect this transfer when credit markets do not extend them sufficient credit. It must be noted, however, that the formal model of Baland and Robinson generates an ambiguous relationship between child labor and fertility. This link, then, becomes an empirical issue.

Some evidence on the effect of child labor on fertility is provided by Cigno and Rosati (2001), who analyze data gathered in 1994 by the Human Development of India Survey. The data cover around 35,000 rural households in over 1,700 villages drawn from 16 Indian states. Apart from income and other economic variables pertaining to adults, the data contain information on children's work/study status and their health, nutritional, and education status. Cigno and Rosati use the average survival rate at the village level as a measure of the probability of children surviving to age six. They set up two possible theoretical scenarios in which parents choose the fertility, the expenditures that impinge on child mortality, and the work/study decisions of their children. In one scenario, the parents are altruistic, in that they give full weight to their children's well-being; in the other (nonaltruistic) one, they are concerned only with their own well-being. Cigno and Rosati found that, holding income constant, an increase in the number of school-age children increases the probability that the children will work. The probability of an additional birth was also seen to increase with the probability that a child will work when older. Furthermore, they found that when the village-level survival rate increases, so does the probability that children will be engaged in full-time study—which is consistent with the scenario positing nonaltruistic parents (but not with that of altruistic ones). This finding is also consistent with the arguments made above on the beneficial effect of reduced child mortality on education.

THE IMPORTANCE OF FEMALE AUTONOMY

The role of female autonomy in decision making is increasingly being acknowledged as an important factor impinging on fertility. Dyson and Moore (1983), were the first to discuss this factor in relation to the demographics of Indian states. There is considerable difference in the demographics of the northern and southern states of India. The northern states, characterized by low female autonomy due to kinship arrangements that minimize support to married women, display high fertility and high child mortality rates. Women in these states typically marry relative strangers from other villages and after marriage retain almost no ties with their natal families. In the southern states, women have considerable autonomy: marriages tend to occur within the village to grooms who are not relative strangers, and women maintain considerable contact with their natal families after marriage. Female autonomy is important because it determines the relative bargaining power of women in the household.

Even in developed countries, the relative bargaining power within couples is skewed in favor of males; in developing countries, the disparity is far greater. This asymmetry has many causes. Males are more likely to work in the labor force, and even if the wife earns, the husband's income is likely to be higher. Ownership of property—in particular, land—is vested in the male. Therefore, any credit that may be available to the household is accessible only to the male. Adding to this is the considerable weight of religious, cultural, and social norms that put women in a weak bargaining position relative to men. As remarked above, kinship systems are important cultural and social determinants of female autonomy.

The relative bargaining powers of males and females have considerable influence over a couple's fertility and resource allocation within the household. Child mortality rates depend, to a significant degree, on the extent of discretionary spending on children's nutrition and health care. Child mortality rates are observed to be much lower when mothers exercise control over household resources. Empirical research has sought to identify how a household's expenditures on various goods vary with the identity of the income earner. Hoddinott and Haddad (1995) found that in the Ivory Coast, an increase in the wife's share of cash income significantly increases the share of expenditure on food and reduces the shares of alcohol and cigarettes. In Brazil, Thomas (1990) found that unearned income accruing to the mother has a far greater effect on the family's health than that accruing to the father. In fact, the effect on child survival probabilities is twenty times larger in the former case.

There is a simple economic reason why mothers devote more resources to the nutrition and health care of children.[10] Since mothers bear a greater proportion of the costs of children, they prefer to have few children and ensure their survival by devoting resources to them. Fathers, on the other hand, prefer to have many children and to devote little by way of resources to each of them. Fathers and mothers, in other words, prefer to be at different points in the quality-quantity trade-off with regard to children. When bargaining power shifts in favor of mothers, the couple will have fewer but healthier children.

There is an additional benefit to society that accrues from the empowerment of women. When child mortality falls, the lower risk and higher expected return from the education of children elicits more resources for the education of children. Thus, an increase in the relative bargaining power of mothers not only results in fewer and healthier children, but it also generates a more educated labor force. These various benefits with regard to fertility alone render the empowerment of women as an important influence on the speed of the demographic transition.

The move toward fewer children as a result of greater female autonomy is also in line with what would be optimal from the point of view of society at large. As we have seen, whenever those who make the decisions share in the benefits, but do not bear a commensurate share of the costs, the decisions are unlikely to be optimal from society's point of view. Since in patriarchal societies, males have decision making power in excess—often vastly in excess—of the burden of the consequences of their decisions, the decisions pertaining to fertility and expenditures on the nutrition and health care of children are unlikely to be optimal.

TRENDS IN SEX RATIOS

A significant aspect of fertility in South and East Asia is the desired sex composition of children: there is a strong preference for male children. Economically and culturally, males are deemed to be of greater value than females. In South Asia, old-age security is expected only from male children. Female children, in contrast, are often seen as economic burdens because they have to be married off with dowries that are worth several years' incomes of their parents. In East Asia, old-age security may not be the overriding reason for the biased sex ratio at birth. Nevertheless, sons are much more valued because, culturally, sons apparently enhance the emotional and spiritual goals of their parents, and they also perpetuate the family name.

Preference for children of a particular sex tends to increase fertility. Suppose every couple's primary desire is to have two male children. Couples whose first two children happen to be males will cease to have more children. Couples with one or two female children will continue to reproduce. This will naturally increase the average fertility relative to a population of couples who desire two children but have no gender preference.

Since male children die slightly more frequently than female children in the first year of their lives, evolutionary forces have led nature to compensate for this by making the sex ratio at birth slightly larger than 100. As a result, even in developed countries with no discernible preference for children of a given sex, this ratio is around 106. There is a disturbing trend in the sex ratio at birth in many developing countries: it is often observed to be highly skewed against girls. This is particularly true in South Asia (India, Pakistan, Bangladesh) and East Asia (China, Taiwan, Korea). The proximate cause of this biased sex ratio at birth is sex-selective abortion—female fetuses detected by amniocentesis and ultrasound techniques are often aborted—or, in some countries, female infanticide. The numbers are alarming. In 1990, this ratio was 111.7 in China, 112.5 in South Korea, and 109.1 in Taiwan.[11]

As a result of a strong parental preference for male children, girls often do not receive the same medical attention to alleviate illnesses as boys do. In India, for example, in the event of an illness boys are, on average, twice as likely to be taken to a doctor than are girls. This "benign neglect"—an egregious euphemism—results in a biased sex ratio not just at birth but also for the population at large. Since, on average, women outlive men in the developed countries, this ratio is slightly less than 100 in the developed world (e.g., 97 for the United Kingdom and the United States, 98 for Canada). The sex ratio for the population at large in developing countries remains higher than 100 (e.g., in the year 2000: 106 for China, 106 for India, 101 for South Korea).[12]

In cultures with a strong preference for sons, one would also expect that discrimination against female children would increase with the birth order (parity) of the daughters. There would be greater discrimination against the second daughter than against the first, greater against the third daughter than against the second, and so on. This is indeed observed.[13]

There are reasons why fertility decline may exacerbate discrimination against female infants and children. Suppose the autonomy of adult women and/or the cost of their time increases because of better employment opportunities. This will lead, naturally enough, to a reduction in fertility. However, if cultural biases persist, it may be the case that old-age security still can be expected only from male children. Parents with, say, only two children will perceive that they can ill afford to have one or both of them be female. Thus discrimination against female children will increase. The education of all children, and females in particular, may alleviate this problem but will not necessarily eliminate it. To the extent that cultural values dictate which institutions promote one's self-interest, education may prove ineffective— except when it manages to dislodge deleterious cultural norms.

The argument outlined above suggests that the serious problems of high fertility and of the changing sex composition of families are separate issues. The suspicion that the solution to the former may exacerbate the latter is supported by recent data. High fertility arises from the low worth of women's time and the fact that old-age security is provided by children. The problem of changing sex composition of the family arises when parents perceive that security of various kinds is provided mostly by male children. Since males and females are not culturally assessed to have such disparate values in Africa, African countries, despite their poverty, display sex ratios that are remarkably free of the bias observed in South and East Asia.

The commendable performance in recent decades with regard to fertility and child mortality reduction of the southern Indian state of Kerala lends support to the view that old-age security expectations are responsible for the differential treatment of male and female children. Kerala is unique in that it has had a history of matriarchy among a substantial proportion of its population. Furthermore, in sharp contrast to the strongly patriarchal societies of the rest of India (especially in the north), where women are excluded from the line of inheritance, women in Kerala tend to inherit and hold land and other assets. In 1991, the female literacy rate in Kerala was 87% (as opposed to an all-India average of 39%). One would expect that in such a society, women would have considerable autonomy. In recent decades, the sex ratio for the population at large, the population growth rate, and the infant mortality rate in Kerala have all been vastly different from the respective Indian averages, and approach those in the developed countries.

The social consequences of biased sex ratios at birth are not hard to see. Over decades, an increasing disparity between the numbers of males and females of marriageable age will cause a serious shortage of brides. Since most cultures are averse to polyandry, this will condemn a significant proportion of marriageable men to remain without mates. This will certainly generate intense competition between males for mates. There will likely be escalating violence between males and an increase in forceful abductions of marriageable females. Over the long haul, the scarcity value of females will induce parents to look more favorably on female children and the sex ratio at birth will fall. The problem will ultimately sort itself out, though with considerable upheaval in the intervening decades.

The developed countries did not have to make any special efforts to reduce their fertility rates: fertility declined as a matter of course with development. However, the developing countries of today can hardly afford to passively wait for the higher opportunity costs of children or the emergence of better means of saving to drive down fertility. Feasible actions are urgently needed, and there are several avenues that can be pursued.

POLICY

The arguments outlined in this essay provide a strong case for government intervention to hasten the demographic transition. The traditional policy espoused by demographers for fertility reduction is still a powerful and reliable one: reduction in child mortality rates. This will bring about a more than commensurate decline in fertility. Establishing medical clinics in the rural countryside will prevent the death of children from illnesses and diseases that are easily treated, such as diarrhea, malaria, typhoid, gastroenteritis, cholera, sleeping sickness, and river blindness. Easy and universal access to health care can drastically reduce child mortality rates even in the absence of rapid growth of GDP. An egalitarian distribution of access to health care can achieve fertility reductions that might otherwise take decades to achieve through economic growth. Kerala is a prime example of how this strategy has been responsible for partly inducing a demographic transition in a state that has even lower per capita income than the all-India average.

Furthermore, as we have seen, when child mortality rates are high, the institution of child labor encourages high fertility levels and leads to a poverty trap. By lowering child mortality rates, governments in developing countries could persuade the poor that the education of children is an acceptable risk. The higher cost of educated children will also reduce fertility.

Improving the bargaining power of women vis-à-vis their husbands induces lower fertility and child mortality rates. How is the bargaining power of women within the household to be increased? There are several avenues, obvious in principle but perhaps not so easy to implement in practice. One is to facilitate greater ownership of land by women. Requiring by law the equal division of inheritance among all of one's children, regardless of gender, is a measure that would help. Providing a greater subsidy for the education of daughters rather than sons is another. Empirically, the education of women is seen to be the single most important factor in the reduction of child mortality.[14] Educated women provide better nutrition, are better able to identify serious health conditions in their children, and are better able to respond to them. Easing access to credit is yet another measure for empowering women, because this enables them to increase their contribution to the household income. This is what the well-known Grameen Bank has sought to do in Bangladesh, with considerable success. Facilitating greater political participation of women would also help.

Empowering women would undoubtedly reduce fertility in developing countries but, as we have seen, it would not address the serious problem of biased sex ratios at birth. When old-age security is provided mostly by male offspring, a reduction in fertility may result in a more blatant discrimination against female children, as is witnessed in China, Korea, and parts of India. Given long-entrenched cultural norms, it is unlikely that women will readily be accepted as equals of men as providers of old-age security. A feasible way to confront this problem is to render both male and female offspring irrelevant for old-age security purposes. Implementation of a national social security system would go a long way toward eliminating the need for children (of either sex) to perform this function. In one stroke, it would reduce fertility and, to a significant degree, also reduce the asymmetry in the treatment parents mete out to male and female children. Using data from around fifty developing countries, Entwisle and Winegarden (1984) found strong evidence indicating that state-sponsored pension programs reduce fertility.[15]

In the manner of their operation on fertility problems, the broad policy proposals suggested above are complementary to the working of an increase in affluence. The latter, with its attendant increase in the time cost of women and the cost of providing children with the human capital they will need in an increasingly modern world, would automatically reduce fertility, but only in the long run. The former proposals are measures that would work in the relatively short run, and would in fact contribute to the arrival of the regime where affluence can have its salutary effect on fertility problems. Furthermore, policy measures along these lines would also address other goals that are important in their own right, such as reduction in child mortality and an improvement in the status of women.

NOTES

I thank Ashok Kotwal and, especially, Roland Benabou for comments on an earlier draft.

1. This has been proposed by Kremer (1993).

2. They also summarize the voluminous literature on this issue and discuss the statistical problems confronting the empirical investigations.

3. The measure of poverty they use is the proportion of the population with consumption less than U.S.$1 a day (at 1985 prices).

4. This sex ratio is defined as the number of male children born for every 100 female children born.

5. See, for example, Bongaarts (1997) for a useful discussion of this debate.

6. The infant (child) mortality rate is defined as the average number of 1,000 infants (children) born today who will die before they are one year (five years) old.

7. For a general demonstration of how reductions in mortality rates can induce a demographic transition, see Eswaran (1998).

8. This link is examined in Eswaran (2000). Standard references on child labor are Basu and Van (1998), and Baland and Robinson (2000).

9. Computed by Murray et al. (1992, Table 2–6), using mortality tables. The corresponding proportion for a developed country is considerably lower; for instance, for Canada in the period 1983–1987, it was 14.3% (7.7%) (Table 2–4).

10. The arguments made in this and the following two paragraphs are drawn from Eswaran (2002).

11. See Park and Cho (1995).

12. Data from the United Nations Population Division.

13. See Das Gupta and Mari Bhat (1997) for data on select states in India, and Hull (1990) for data on China.

14. See Schultz (1997) for evidence on this.

15. Interestingly, they also found strong evidence of reverse causation: countries with reduced fertility levels are more likely to implement pension plans.

BIBLIOGRAPHY

Baland, Jean Marie, and James A. Robinson. "Is Child Labor Inefficient?" *Journal of Political Economy* 108 (2000): 663–679.

Basu, K., and P. M. Van. "The Economics of Child Labor." *American Economic Review* 88 (1998): 412–427.

Bongaarts, John. "The Role of Family Planning Programmes in Contemporary Fertility Transitions." In *The Continuing Demographic Transition*, edited by G. W. Jones, R. M. Douglas, J. C. Caldwell, and R. M. D'Souza. Oxford: Clarendon Press, 1997.

Caldwell, John. "Mass Education as a Determinant of the Timing of Fertility Decline." *Population and Development Review* 6 (1980): 225–255.

Cigno, Alessandro, and Furio C. Rosati. "Why do Indian Children Work, and Is It Bad for Them?" Mimeo, University of Rome, 2001.

Das Gupta, Monica, and P. N. Mari Bhat. "Fertility Decline and Increased Manifestation of Sex Bias in India." *Population Studies* 51 (1997): 307–315.

Dyson, Tim, and Mick Moore. "On Kinship Structure, Female Autonomy, and Demographic Behavior in India." *Population and Development Review* 9 (1983): 35–60.

Eastwood, Robert, and Michael Lipton. "The Impact of Changes in Human Fertility on Poverty." *Journal of Development Studies* 36 (1999): 1–30.

Entwisle, Barbara, and C. R. Winegarden. "Fertility and Pension Programs in LDCs: A Model of Mutual Reinforcement." *Economic Development and Cultural Change* 32 (1984): 331–354.

Eswaran, M. "One Explanation for the Demographic Transition in Developing Countries." *Oxford Economic Papers* 50 (1998): 237–265.

Eswaran, M. "Fertility, Literacy, and the Institution of Child Labour." In *Institutions, Incentives, and Economic Reforms in India*. Edited by S. Kahkonen and A. Lanyi. New Delhi: Sage, 2000.

Eswaran, Mukesh. "The Empowerment of Women, Fertility, and Child Mortality: Towards a Theoretical Analysis." *Journal of Population Economics* 15 (2002): 433–454.

Galor, Oded, and David N. Weil. "The Gender Gap, Fertility, and Growth." *American Economic Review* 86 (1996): 374–387.

Hoddinott, John, and Lawrence Haddad. "Does Female Income Share Influence Household Expenditures? Evidence from Côte d'Ivoire." *Oxford Bulletin of Economics and Statistics* 57 (1995): 77–96.

Hull, T. H. "Recent Trends in Sex Ratios at Birth in China." *Population and Development Review* 16 (1990): 63–83.

Jensen, Eric R. "An Econometric Analysis of the Old Age Security Motive for Childbearing." *International Economic Review* 31 (1990): 953–968.

Kelley, Allen C., and R. M. Schmidt. *Population and Income Change: Recent Evidence.* Washington, D.C.: World Bank, 1994.

Kremer, Michael. "Population Growth and Technological Change: 1,000,000 B.C. to 1990." *Quarterly Journal of Economics* 108 (1993): 681–716.

Murray, Christopher, G. Yang, and X. Qiau. "Adult Mortality: Levels, Patterns, and Causes." In *The Health of Adults in the Developing World*, edited by Richard Feachem, Tord Kjellstrom, Murray, Christopher, Mead Over, and Margaret Phillips. New York: Oxford University Press, 1992.

Neher, Philip A. "Peasants, Procreation, and Pensions." *American Economic Review* 61 (1971): 380–389.

Park, C. B., and N.-H. Cho. "Consequences of Son Preference in a Low-Fertility Society: Imbalance of the Sex Ratio at Birth in Korea." *Population and Development Review* 21 (1995): 59–84.

Rosenzweig, Mark R., and T. P. Schultz. "Consumer Demand and Household Production: The Relationship Between Fertility and Child Mortality." *American Economic Review* 73 (1983): 38–42.

Schultz, T. Paul. "Demand for Children in Low Income Countries." In *Handbook of Population and Family Economics*, edited by M. R. Rosenzweig and O. Stark. Amsterdam: Elsevier Science, 1997.

Thomas D., Jr. "Intra-Household Resource Allocation: An Inferential Approach." *Journal of Human Resources* 25 (1990): 635–664.

Weiner, Myron. *The Child and the State in India*. Princeton, N.J.: Princeton University Press, 1991.

11

Corruption and Development

Jean-Jacques Laffont

Corruption is a particularly serious issue in developing economies. Susan Rose-Akerman (1999), an expert on the subject, observes: "High levels of corruption limit investment and growth and lead to ineffective government. Developing countries and those making a transition from socialism are particularly at risk, but corruption is a worldwide phenomenon."

This essay asks why corruption is so widespread in developing countries. It is organized in three sections. First, I argue that a theory of corruption is needed in order to answer this question. Second, I sketch a theory linking corruption and development. Third, I empirically document the correlation between development and corruption.

THE NEED FOR A THEORY OF CORRUPTION

Corruption is an endogenous phenomenon of organizations and societies. In order to target the right level of corruption in a society, it is essential to design a proper cost/benefit analysis, and therefore to build a good understanding of the mechanics of corruption.

The Origin of Corruption

Corruption opportunities arise from the need for delegation in complex societies. Let me illustrate this through an example, that of a benevolent chief in a traditional village. The chief (the principal) can directly monitor the behavior of the members of the village (the "agents"), and has the authority to inflict the penalties required to eliminate rational misbehavior. He can also directly collect the taxes needed to fund the community's public goods.

As the village grows and becomes a city, though, the chief needs to delegate the monitoring of behavior to a police force, the levy of taxes to tax collectors, and so forth. Through delegation, the chief loses control and now suffers from asymmetric information with respect to these "intermediaries" who carry out the tasks he formerly carried out himself. The police, when observing misbehaviors, have discretion as to whether to report these misbehaviors. The tax collector similarly has discretion as to whether to report attempts at tax evasion.

The fundamental point is that delegation in general creates discretion, and thereby scope for side contracting between the intermediary and the agents, to the detriment of the "principal" (the chief in this illustration). The intermediary can offer not to report the misbehavior in return for a bribe. The stake of collusion is the size of the penalty for misbehavior.[1]

Clearly, the chief may not be benevolent, and may himself be corrupt, but this does not change the main idea. Indeed, the general point carries over once when considering that the "principal" in the relationship is not the chief or the government, but the people who delegate (through an incomplete contract defined by the constitution and the electoral process) the design of social and economic policies to politicians. Politicians, too, are intermediaries, and have discretion that they can use to their own benefit, very much like the lower-level intermediaries considered above.

Responses to Corruption

The scope for corruption is thus created by the asymmetry of information between principal and intermediary, and calls for a regulatory response. In order to avoid side contracting, the principal must give the intermediary some incentive to report misbehaviors that the latter will value more than the potential bribe. The required incentive depends on the nature of the intermediary's information (verifiable or not), on the morality and risk aversion of the intermediary, and also on the probability of being caught engaging in such a side contract.[2] When the design of the intermediary's contract is not constrained, and under conditions that have been extensively studied in the literature (in particular, perfect information about the intermediary's preferences), a "collusion proofness" principle holds: the optimal policy can be designed so as to completely deter the formation of collusion.[3] But satisfying this constraint requires costly payments to the intermediary or other costly policies. An optimal policy must take this additional cost into account.

While corruption should be reduced through appropriate policies, including incentives for intermediaries as discussed above, it should not in general be eradicated at any cost: the zero-corruption level is observed nowhere, and therefore is probably not the optimal level under a wide range of institutional arrangements prevailing for a wide range of societies. One reason for this is that the principal may not be well-informed about the intermediary's propensity for corruption—namely, about the conditions (nature of information, morality and risk aversion, and probability of being caught) that determine his willingness to misreport information to the principal. Put differently, some intermediaries can be corrupted by small bribes; others, only by very substantial ones. Making sure that corruption never occurs requires making very high payments to the intermediary. It is in general cheaper to make smaller payments and accept occasional corruption.

The Limits to Regulatory Solutions

When the intermediary is a regulatory agency, a new set of issues arises. Consider the case of a regulatory agency whose task is to partially bridge the information gap between the government and the regulated firm. The stake of collusion is then the decrease in the firm's information rent brought about by the report of the agency's information. A high-powered incentive scheme (such as a fixed-price or price-cap contract) creates scope for much larger informational rents for the regulated firm than the old cost-of-service/cost-plus contracts. Reducing the stake of collusion then requires adopting less powerful incentives. In sum, incentives are likely to be less powerful than would be advisable in the absence of concern about collusion between the regulator and the firm.[4]

A SKETCH OF A THEORY LINKING CORRUPTION AND DEVELOPMENT

I have argued that very primitive societies exhibit fewer opportunities for corruption and that as societies become more complex, more delegation is needed and more opportunities for corruption develop. At an early stage of development, though, it is rather difficult to fight corruption because

- The auditing resources (human and technical) are scarce.
- Financial resources to reward the intermediary are scarce.
- Economic agents being poor, financial penalties for corrupt activities are limited.

In such a society the costs of avoiding corruption are high, and consequently the optimal level of corruption per transaction open to corruption is also high. As development occurs, the number of transactions potentially affected by corruption increases, and therefore the amount of corruption should increase even if per transaction corruption is stable, or even decrease due to an increase in the resources that can be mobilized to fight corruption.

Institutional innovation is another source of corruption. New institutions undergo *tatonnement* processes, in which the various new features, including the incentives put in place to deter the emergence of corruption, are refined over time. Thus, as new institutions are added, new opportunities for corruption arise that can be fought only once they are well understood. This idea is consistent with the increase of corruption when large institutional changes occur, such as the transition from socialism to capitalism.

As development continues to progress, though, the government has more and more resources to fight corruption, and since agents are richer, it is easier to threaten them with high penalties (rarely used at equilibrium), so it becomes less costly to fight corruption. The corruption per transaction decreases rapidly, and the volume of corruption may also decrease.

The caveat to this last point is that the benefits from a decrease in the opportunity cost of fighting collusion are reaped only if the government is reasonably keen on curbing corruption. This in general requires a well-functioning democracy that enables the people to control the politicians.

Summing up, this reasoning suggests that corruption per transaction decreases with development, and that there is an inverted U-shaped relationship between development (say per capita GDP) and the amount of corruption, possibly with a role for the quality of democracy to strengthen the decrease of corruption. Next, we explore this correlation with cross-country data.

CORRELATIONS

A large number of measures of corruption are available. What do these data really measure? They are in general obtained from surveys of businessmen who are active in sample countries. Thus these evaluations are likely to measure the gravity of corruption per transaction. Let COR be such a measure. We should expect this measure to decrease with the level of development. The amount of corruption in a country can then be approximated by the level of activity open to corruption multiplied by the level of corruption. The variable "per capita GDP" is a rough measure of the activity open to corruption if we assume that the share of transactions open to corruption is a constant share of per capita GDP. Multiplying this variable by the level of corruption COR, we obtain a measure of the per capita amount of corruption; the prediction is that this measure should first increase, and then decrease with development.

To test these conjectures, we first need measures of these variables for some sample countries.[5] For the level of corruption, the measure chosen is given by an index obtained by Kaufmann et al. (1999), called COR(K). For the level of development, following standard procedures, per capita GNP is used as a proxy variable. After gathering such information and plotting on a graph the total corruption (COR multiplied by per capita GNP) against per capita GNP for each country in the sample, we can empirically establish more about the relationship between amount of corruption and development.

It is important to note that although our primary interest is how development affects corruption, there are some additional characteristics in each country that are also relevant in explaining corruption. For example, it can be shown that the openness of the country reduces the level of corruption, while a high level of exports of natural resources or a high level of ethnic diversity increases it. Another important variable that explains the level of corruption is the legal system a country has. The way in which rights are established and enforced is closely related to the amount of corruption in a society. Different legal arrangements result in different incentives, and ultimately agents will respond to them. Countries' legal systems can be grouped according to their legal tradition. In commercial law, for instance, we can find two major families of legal traditions: common law and civil law, with origins in England and Rome, respectively. Civil law countries can be further subdivided into French, Scandinavian, and German traditions. Scandinavian law countries have the best record of enforcing the rights established by law, and the French law ones have the worst quality in terms of enforcement.[6] Hence, it is expected that when comparing two countries with the same level of development, the country that has a Scandinavian law tradition will have a lower amount of corruption than a country with any other type of legal tradition. Henceforward, whenever looking to the observed relation between corruption and development, we have to take into account the legal system of the country.

Figure 11.1 portrays the result obtained after fitting a third-degree polynomial of total corruption in GNP per capita for all the countries in our sample. The upper line represents the relationship between the amount of total corruption and development in the sample of countries that have an English, French, or German law tradition. The figure reveals the expected inverted U-shaped relationship described earlier. For low levels of development, as the per capita GNP increases, total corruption also increases. However, after the country attains a certain level of development (a sufficiently high GNP per capita), the level of corruption decreases. The lower line in Figure 11.1 represents the best-fitting curve for Scandinavian law tradition countries. As can be seen, these countries also exhibit an inverted-U relationship between corruption and the level of development. However, as expected, for every level of development the measure of total corruption is lower in Scandinavian law tradition countries than in the other law tradition countries.

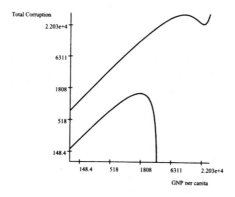

Figure 11.1 Total Corruption and GNP per Capita

ACKNOWLEDGMENTS The ideas developed in this chapter were later developed and refined by the author in chapter 4 ("Enforcement, Regulation, and Development") of his 2004 book. There Jean-Jacques Laffont considers a broader set of responses to the threat of collusion, analyzing how the enforcement system and the rule of law are determined by the level of development. He develops a theory of how the strength of institutions affects the possibility of renegotiation by a regulated firm facing financial hardship, and ultimately incentives of the firm with regard to productivity improvement. In related empirical work on the renegotiation of concessions in Latin America, he shows that, as predicted by his theory, renegotiation is more likely when the concession is run by a price-cap contract, when corruption is high, and when the concession holder has a local partner.

Jean-Jacques Laffont passed away on May 1, 2004. He wrote the draft for this essay in June 2002. This revised version was prepared by Antonio Estache, Patrick Rey, Patricia Meirelles, Catherine Rodriguez, and Jean Tirole, to all of whom we are deeply grateful. The revisions include some stylistic changes, and complete the presentation of the empirical results.

The reader is referred to Jean-Jacques Laffont's book for a broader treatment of the themes developed in the chapter.

NOTES

1. When the intermediary is a judge, whose task is to look for evidence needed to implement a contractual obligation by a supplier, say, the stake of collusion may be the difference between the expected costs for the supplier of abiding by this obligation and that incurred when the obligation is not enforced.

2. See Tirole (1986); Laffont (2000).

3. See, e.g., Laffont and Rochet (1997).

4. An exception arises when the regulator's task consists in measuring/auditing the firm's cost for cost-reimbursement purposes. A low-powered incentive scheme, by raising the fraction of the firm's cost that is reimbursed, raises the stake of collusion.

5. For further details on the sample used in this empirical exercise, refer to Laffont (2003).

6. For further information about legal traditions, refer to La Porta et al. (1998).

BIBLIOGRAPHY

Kaufmann, Daniel, Aart Kraay, and Pablo Zoido-Lobaton. "Aggregating Governance Indicators." Mimeo, World Bank, 1999.

Laffont, Jean-Jacques. *Incentives and Political Economy.* Oxford: Oxford University Press, 2000.

Laffont, Jean-Jacques. "Enforcement, Regulation and Development." *Journal of African Economies* 12 (2) (2003): 193–211.

Laffont, Jean-Jacques. *Regulation and Development.* Cambridge: Cambridge University Press, 2004.

Laffont, Jean-Jacques, and Jean-Charles Rochet. "Collusion in Organizations." *Scandinavian Journal of Economics* 99 (1997): 485–495.

La Porta, Rafael, Florenzio Lopez-de-Silanes, Andrei Schleifer, and Robert Vishny. "Law and Finance." *Journal of Political Economy* 106 (6) (1998): 1113–1155.

Rose-Ackerman, Susan. *Corruption and Government.* Cambridge: Cambridge University Press, 1999.

Tirole, Jean. "Hierarchies and Bureaucracies." *Journal of Law, Economics, and Organization* 2 (1986): 181–214.

12

Ethnic Diversity and Poverty Reduction

Edward Miguel

Many popular and academic authors have made the case that ethnic divisions lead to slow economic growth and persistent poverty in less-developed countries, noting numerous instances where ethnic divisions have led to violent conflict and set back poverty alleviation efforts—in Rwanda and the former Yugoslavia, for example. This essay first discusses the recent social science literature on the impact of ethnic, racial, and religious divisions (which I refer to simply as ethnic divisions from now on), and then proposes a set of policies I believe less-developed countries should follow to help them overcome ethnic conflict.

Specifically, I advocate the adoption of "nation-building" policies that foster the development of a common national identity. The case of Tanzania, and the contrast of Tanzania with its East African neighbor Kenya, is the focus of this essay. I believe that Tanzania's serious approach to forging a common national identity attractive across ethnic groups—which takes the form of extensive linguistic, educational, and institutional reforms, described below—offers a model for other less-developed countries that inherited ethnic divisions in the post-independence period. I also present an overview of empirical evidence, based on original field data collection, that this nation-building approach has allowed ethnically diverse communities in rural Tanzania to achieve considerable success in local fund-raising for primary schools, while ethnically diverse Kenyan communities have largely failed in this task.

The bottom line is that good economic policies alone may be insufficient to reduce poverty in countries with deep social divisions. The standard "Washington Consensus" approach to public policy reform in poor countries advocated by the international financial institutions—the International Monetary Fund and World Bank—has encouraged poor countries to rapidly implement broad economic policy reforms—for example, price liberalization, trade liberalization, and state-owned enterprise privatization—while largely ignoring the fundamental nation-building and institutional issues that I focus on in this essay. Although the "Consensus" approach may (or may not) promote short-run economic growth, I believe that in the long run any serious package of public policy reform in ethnically diverse countries must address social divisions head-on, with nation-building taking a place at the top of government policy agendas.

It may take many years for nation-building policies to show concrete results, but they can be a critical investment in long-run economic growth in many less-developed countries, and a key to overcoming persistent global poverty, especially in Africa—the world's most ethnolinguistically diverse continent. The Tanzanian case provides evidence that this approach can in fact succeed.

ETHNICITY IN ECONOMICS

Economists have been slow to explore the role of ethnic divisions in economic development, in part due to our reluctance to abandon methodological individualism as the organizing principle of research. This reluctance has also traditionally led the discipline to ignore other important group-level phenomena—including issues of social capital, identity, and social networks—preventing economists from fully appreciating the important role social factors play in perpetuating poverty. Fortunately, in recent years many economists have embraced methodologies and issues typically associated with other social science disciplines, and have finally begun contributing to the debate on ethnic divisions and economic development. This growing interest in ethnicity is also related to a broader trend within economics of renewed interest in the deep, underlying causes of persistent global poverty—including geography, disease, social institutions, and colonial history—rather than just the proximate policy causes.[1]

The seminal research article on ethnic diversity in economics is Easterly and Levine (1997). In their article, the authors explore how ethnic diversity affected growth rates across countries during the postwar period, using a data set on national ethnolinguistic diversity compiled by Russian anthropologists during the 1960s. The continent with the greatest number of ethnolinguistically diverse countries, according to this measure, is Africa, which contains nine of the ten most ethnolinguistically diverse countries (the one non-African exception being India). Kenya and Tanzania, for example, each have dozens of major ethnic groups and are both among the world's ten most diverse countries.

Easterly and Levine find two striking patterns in the cross-country data.

First, ethnically diverse countries had significantly lower per-capita economic growth rates than homogeneous countries during the postwar period. Of course, this pattern does not imply that all diverse societies are cursed with poor economic performance. In fact, some of the world's most diverse regions—including northern California, where I live—have had spectacular economic growth rates in recent decades. But, on average, diverse societies were more likely to have experienced slow economic growth.

Second, Easterly and Levine find that diverse countries exhibited poor public policy performance along a range of dimensions, including greater foreign exchange rate distortions, slow financial development, poor schooling outcomes, and less physical infrastructure investment, and use this evidence to argue that diversity led to slow growth through poor policy choices. They then work through some quantitative exercises which suggest that much of the difference in economic growth between sub–Saharan Africa and East Asia during the postwar period was attributable to the negative impact of ethnic diversity.

Since Easterly and Levine's article was published, applied microeconomists have documented many specific instances where ethnic diversity produces poor economic outcomes, and for the remainder of this essay, I focus on the growing microeconomic evidence on ethnicity at the level of communities and organizations.[2]

To illustrate, Peruvian microcredit groups have higher loan default rates when members are from different cultural backgrounds than when they are largely from similar backgrounds. U.S. municipalities with higher levels of racial diversity collect considerably less funding for local public goods. In a related finding, U.S. Civil War military desertion rates were higher in Union Army units characterized by greater age and occupational diversity. Finally, in my own work with Mary Kay Gugerty (forthcoming), rural Kenyan communities with greater ethnolinguistic diversity—or diversity across "tribes," as they are called in East Africa—have considerably less primary school funding, worse school facilities, and inadequate well maintenance. I highlight the findings of this last paper below because they figure in my main argument and because local public investments in education, health, and sanitation are critical for improving the welfare of the poor in rural Africa.

Although it has become increasingly accepted within economics that ethnic diversity often produces poor institutional performance, there is less of a consensus regarding the underlying theoretical mechanisms generating these poor outcomes in diverse settings, and two sets of theories have emerged. Although distinct mechanisms are found to be more salient in particular settings, these two sets of theories are not mutually exclusive, and both probably capture certain aspects of reality in most cases.

The first theories are what I call *taste explanations* for negative ethnic diversity effects. There are several common variants, mainly developed in research on the United States. For example, some authors have claimed that individuals from different ethnic groups prefer distinct types of public goods—roads versus libraries, for instance—so that there is less consensus on public goods choices in diverse areas, and thus lower funding. Other authors have claimed that, for the most part, individuals from different groups simply dislike mixing across ethnic lines, and this drives the poor collective action and organizational outcomes in diverse areas. Finally, there is recent empirical evidence that individuals prefer to fund public goods that benefit their own ethnic group over others, in which case once again public goods funding is lower in diverse areas. Unfortunately, none of these explanations provides a theory of where these ethnic taste differences come from, nor how they can be affected through public policy, so this body of work does not directly address our central concern in this essay—how to deal with ethnic divisions.

The second set of theories emphasizes the important role community *social sanctions* play in sustaining collective action, and shows how sanctions may be ineffective in diverse settings. Observers of less developed countries have long noted the importance of community pressure, based on dense social ties, in sustaining good collective outcomes, and the recent empirical studies from less-developed countries tend to emphasize this mechanism. The basic idea is that it becomes difficult to sustain social sanctions across ethnic groups in areas where members of different groups do not have frequent or intimate social interactions. For example, Miguel and Gugerty (forthcoming) focus on the difficulties in mobilizing diverse communities in rural Kenya, and present quantitative evidence from primary school committee meeting records that significantly fewer social sanctions are imposed in ethnically diverse areas. Other recent work comes to similar conclusions regarding the importance of informal social sanctions in sustaining loan repayment in ethnically homogeneous Peruvian microcredit groups.

RECONCILING ETHNIC DIVERSITY AND POVERTY REDUCTION

The next question is what to do about the negative impact of ethnic diversity on collective action and poverty reduction. Though few economists have directly examined these issues, there is a large literature in political science on how institutions can mitigate the negative impact of ethnic diversity, which I briefly survey below.

One possible institutional reform in diverse societies is to promote *power-sharing* across ethnic groups within governments or other organizations. In such a system, ethnic minorities are assured some minimum influence over policy choices, possibly including veto power over certain policies.

Although intuitively attractive, it is unclear whether power-sharing actually overcomes the underlying causes of negative ethnic diversity effects in practice, and I am not optimistic about its successful application in most settings. In fact, at the same time that power-sharing structures the formal rules of competition among ethnic groups in the political arena, it institutionalizes political conflict across groups rather than reducing or eliminating it. Rigid power-sharing rules that take ethnic classifications as fixed also reify existing ethnic divisions and may hinder the development of new social identities—or political coalitions—that cut across preexisting divisions. The system provides strong political incentives for ethnic community leaders to maintain these rigidly distinct identities, since they earn benefits ("rents," in economics jargon) from representing a separate ethnic constituency. Extensive veto powers for small minority groups may provoke a backlash in the majority group, and thus inflame divisions.

A second approach—which I find more promising—advocates promoting dialogue and interaction among the leaders of distinct ethnic communities, who are then able to coordinate their responses to violations of intergroup cooperation norms. One variant would have group leaders agree to punish violators from within their own ethnic group, the so-called *within-group policing* approach. For example, if there is a violent attack on a member of ethnic group A by members of group B, leaders of group B should publicly sanction the perpetrators, making organized retaliation by group A unnecessary and thus avoiding a violent downward spiral (Fearon and Laitin 1996). A closely related form of elite coordination is the establishment of formal *associational bonds across ethnic groups*. It has recently been argued that the density of cross-group associational ties is a critical determinant of interreligious peace in Indian cities during episodes of communal violence. Varshney (2002) highlights the case of Bhiwandi, near Bombay, where a determined effort to create interreligious peace committees in the 1980s paid off, successfully averting communal violence in the aftermath of the 1992 Ayodhya mosque attack while nearby cities were engulfed in anti-Muslim pogroms.

However, a weakness of approaches predicated on cooperation across ethnic group leaders is that it is not clear how this cooperation comes about in the first place. In fact, such cooperation is a manifestation of better ethnic relations as much as it is a cause, and thus it is difficult to draw strong causal claims about how the existence of cross-group associational links actually affects interethnic relations.

One promising approach for encouraging the formation of such links is for governmental and nongovernmental organizations to work to promote local interethnic ties—by subsidizing the formation of interethnic community groups, for example—although such activities have not been rigorously evaluated, to my knowledge. Another approach, which I elaborate on below, is a policy of central government-led nation-building. In the next section I compare two East African countries to bring attention to an instance where nation-building has successfully promoted interethnic cooperation, cooperation that may facilitate the within-group policing and associational links discussed above.

A NATION-BUILDING CASE STUDY: KENYA VERSUS TANZANIA

Geographic and Historical Commonalities between Kenya and Tanzania

Kenya and Tanzania are a natural paired comparison, with similar geography and histories, but they have followed radically different nation-building policies since independence. Joel Barkan writes that

> Comparison between Kenya and Tanzania [is] ... appealing because of their resemblances with respect to a number of variables that impinge upon the developmental process and that could be held constant or nearly constant in an examination of the countries. Both are populated mainly by small peasant households of similar cultures. ... Both experienced British colonial rule and inherited a common set of political, administrative, and economic institutions, as well as a common market with a single currency and a common infrastructure of rail, port, and telecommunications facilities. As adjacent countries, they share a common climate and have similar natural resource endowments. (1994, p. 7)

In the immediate post-independence period in the mid-1960s, Koff and von der Muhll (1967) wrote that in terms of attitudes toward ethnicity and a range of other political issues, "There is an often startling similarity between the responses given by Kenyan and Tanzanian students. ... The cross-national similarities are so constant as to raise questions about the significance of the nation state as a differentiating variable"—which probably should not be surprising, given the arbitrary nature of African national boundaries drawn by European imperial powers during the late nineteenth century (McEwan 1971, p. 50).

The two districts where I conducted my fieldwork—Busia, Kenya, and Meatu, Tanzania—are the sites of field offices for the nongovernmental organization ICS Africa, and were originally chosen by the NGO as particularly poor districts in need of development assistance. Although Meatu district is somewhat more arid and less densely populated than Busia, the two districts are similar along a range of important characteristics. They are located relatively near one another, on opposite sides of Lake Victoria, and both are overwhelmingly rural and share the same staple crops (including corn, sorghum, and cassava). The areas were part of a shared precolonial historical universe with extensive migration across what is today the Kenya-Tanzania border.

The total 1989 population of Busia was 401,658, and the 1998 population of Meatu was 201,981, according to government publications. The two districts have similar ethnic compositions, with majority Niger-Kordofanian (Bantu) populations and substantial Nilo-Saharan minorities: the dominant Luhya ethnic group comprises 70% of the population in the Kenyan district and the majority Sukuma ethnic group constitutes roughly 85% of the Tanzanian district. Though armed conflict associated with cattle raids was common during the precolonial period in both areas, neither district has experienced widespread ethnic violence during the colonial or post-independence periods. Another similarity between the two areas lies in the realm of precolonial language use: unlike many other regions of Tanzania, Meatu district had minimal trade ties with Swahili speakers from the East African coast during the nineteenth century, so few residents of the area spoke fluent Swahili upon independence in the 1960s; nor was Swahili widely spoken in western Kenya during the precolonial period.[3]

Parents play leading roles in local public school finance in both countries, through school committees in Kenya and village councils in Tanzania, so it is possible to compare local fund-raising across the two districts, as discussed below.

Post-Independence Divergence in Nation-Building Policies

Despite the geographical, historical, and institutional commonalities in western Kenya and western Tanzania, central governments in the two countries have pursued radically different public policies toward ethnicity during the postcolonial period, and I argue that this has had a major impact on current levels of interethnic cooperation.

Some of these policy differences can be attributed to the personalities and philosophies of Kenya's and Tanzania's respective independence leaders, Jomo Kenyatta and Julius Nyerere. Inspired by a Pan-Africanist and socialist political philosophy, Tanzanian leader Julius Nyerere forcefully downplayed the role of ethnic affiliation in public life after independence and instead emphasized a single Tanzanian national identity. A founding principle of Nyerere's ruling TANU political party was "to fight tribalism and any other factors which would hinder the development of unity among Africans" (Abdulaziz 1980). Barkan (1994) writes that "Whereas ethnic identification has formed the basis of politics and political organization in Kenya for more than thirty years [since independence], in Tanzania it has not. . . . The potential for [ethnic] conflict in Tanzania has . . . been muted by the near universal use of Kiswahili, which replaced English as the country's official language in the mid-1960s and has evolved its own political idiom, nurturing the development of a national political culture" (p. 10).

The Tanzanian regime pushed for total "Swahilization" in government administration, and established the National Swahili Council to promote that language's use in all spheres of public life. Swahili is an indigenous African language that originated on the Indian Ocean coast of East Africa through contact between Africans and Arab traders, and it is seen as largely ethnically "neutral" in both countries.

The public school curriculum has also been aggressively employed as a nation-building tool in Tanzania: the curriculum stresses common Tanzanian culture, history, and values as well as Pan-Africanism, and it inculcates students with a strong sense of national identity. Moreover, during the 1970s all individuals studying to become teachers were required to serve in the paramilitary National Service Organization, which served to indoctrinate future teachers in the national ideals of the Tanzanian regime and its socialist revolution.

The role of the central government could not be more different in Kenya. The first two post-independence presidents, Jomo Kenyatta and Daniel arap Moi, are perceived as "tribalists" within Kenya, political opportunists who have thrived on the politics of ethnic division. Ethnicity has become the primary cleavage point of political life in Kenya—as in many other African countries—and the Moi regime was widely implicated in arming and financing violent ethnic militias before national elections in 1992 and 1997, fomenting ethnic clashes that left hundreds dead (Ndegwa 1997).

Although Swahili has long been widely spoken in Kenya as a lingua franca, it competes with English and "vernacular" languages (including Kikuyu, Luhya, Luo, and others) in official settings, including political forums and schools. Local vernaculars, rather than Swahili, serve as the principal medium of primary school instruction through the fourth grade, while after fourth grade English is the medium of instruction. Unlike Tanzania, the central government in Kenya has not used the primary school curriculum to promote a coherent national linguistic or ideological identity: the official Kenyan geography, history, and civics curriculum does not include Kenyan national issues until grade 5, instead focusing on the village, the division (an administrative unit), the district, and the province in grades 1 through 4, respectively. This focus on provincial geography and history probably serves to exacerbate regional and ethnic divisions, especially among the many Kenyans who drop out of primary school before grade 5, and thus never study national history in detail.

The construction of a common national identity may have affected interethnic cooperation in Tanzania in a variety of ways. First, as particular ethnic identities gradually lose out to the broader national identity, the taste explanations for negative diversity outcomes described above become less important, as individuals increasingly identify with all of their fellow citizens rather than just their own tribe, and are thus willing to fund public goods that benefit "other" groups. If nation-building policies also increase informal social interactions with members of other ethnic groups in schools, community groups, and civic gatherings, this can also increase the scope for community social sanctions across ethnic groups, reducing free-riding and improving local collective action.

Another key component of the reform package carried out during the Tanzanian socialist period—roughly from 1967 to 1982—was the complete overhaul of local government institutions with the aim of strengthening elected local village councils and abolishing the post of traditional tribal chief. By contrast, in Kenya the colonial-era system of centrally appointed chiefs has been retained to the present day.

Preliminary Empirical Results

I found striking differences in the impact of ethnic diversity on local collective action across the two districts.[4] While local ethnic diversity is strongly negatively associated with local school funding and facilities, and with well maintenance in Busia, Kenya, as discussed in Miguel and Gugerty (forthcoming), there is no significant relationship between village ethnic diversity and local public goods funding in the Tanzanian district. It can also be shown statistically that ethnic diversity has a *significantly* more negative effect on school funding in the Kenyan district.[5] These empirical relationships are robust to the inclusion of socioeconomic and geographic control variables, to the exclusion of outliers, and to different econometric specifications. This statistical analysis uses data at the level of the village in Tanzania (66 villages), and at the level of the primary school (84 schools) and wells (667 wells) in Kenya.

Although the nation-building policies chosen in Kenya and Tanzania, and the characteristics of their post-independence leaders, may have been related to the nature of ethnic relations at the *national* level in both countries, all that is necessary for a valid comparison of the impact of nation-building policies in Busia, Kenya, and Meatu, Tanzania, is that the choice of such national policies was not directly related to (or "endogenous to," in economics jargon) ethnic relations in these two small and politically marginal western districts, which is plausible.

The basic primary school funding results are graphically presented in Figures 12.1 and 12.2, and some additional empirical issues are discussed below. For clarity, the graphical analysis in Figures 12.1 and 12.2 presents aggregated county-level patterns (called "zones" in Kenya and "wards" in Tanzania).

Even though western Kenya and western Tanzania were similar with respect to important social, economic, and political dimensions upon independence in the 1960s, within only thirty years these regions had diverged sharply. Ethnic diversity currently plays a much more prominent role in local public life in western Kenya than in western Tanzania, with negative consequences for local public goods provision, including primary school funding, which may affect future human capital accumulation and income levels.

Evidence from interviews is consistent with the statistical findings, and sheds light on how nation-building policies have allowed communities to overcome ethnic divisions in Tanzania.

The case of Matumbai Primary School in Kenya illustrates how low interethnic cooperation in Kenya leads to reduced school investment. Matumbai is one of the most ethnically diverse schools in the Kenyan study district. The headmaster of Matumbai stated in a June 2000 interview that ethnic "rivalry over ownership" of the school and over which group "will take control of the school" was the central challenge facing Matumbai. Most parents had refused to participate in community fund-raisers or in school meetings

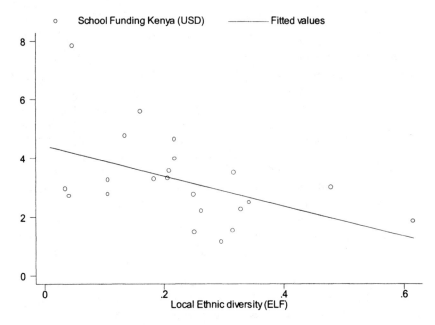

Figure 12.1 Total Local School Funds per Pupil (2001 U.S. Dollars) in 1995 versus Residential Ethno-Linguistic Fractionalization in the Geographic Zone.

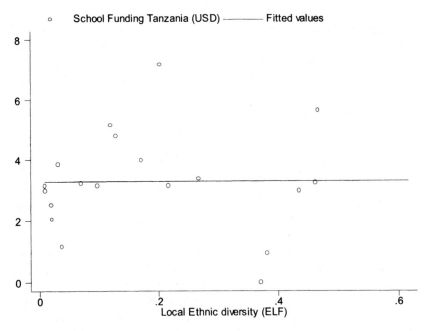

Figure 12.2 Total Local School Funds per Pupil (2001 U.S. Dollars), per Year Between 1997–2001 (Ward Average) versus Residential Ethno-Linguistic Fractionalization in the Geographic Zone.

in recent years due to a general lack of trust across ethnic groups, and the absence of a feeling of "ownership" for the school. As a result, per-pupil local school funding in the 1996 survey was one-third of average local funding in Busia and no classrooms had been constructed at the school, so all classes took place under a tree—which meant that school was canceled when it rained. Many other headmasters reported similar ethnic divisions in western Kenyan schools, in the absence of an overarching national identity to bind different groups together.

Miguel and Gugerty (forthcoming) collected information from Kenyan primary school records on the number of times school committees had imposed sanctions on parents late with their school fees—for instance, embarrassing "free-riders" by announcing the names of parents late with school payments at village meetings, or sending a local chief to their home to pressure them to pay their fees. Miguel and Gugerty found that there were significantly fewer sanctions imposed in ethnically diverse villages in the Kenyan district, and the interview evidence mentioned above provided a possible explanation why: in diverse Kenyan villages, where community cohesion and trust are low, informal sanctions imposed across ethnic lines are usually ineffective methods of pressuring individuals to contribute to the public good.

In sharp contrast, ethnic divisions were reported to be minimal in the Tanzanian study district. Primary school committee members in Imalaseko village were puzzled at the suggestion that ethnic divisions could play a role in local school funding decisions. In fact, ethnicity played such a minor role in Imalaseko that the committee had difficulty assigning an ethnic affiliation (Sukuma or Nyiramba?) to an absent committee member. A schoolteacher responded to a question about possible ethnic divisions on the school committee in a November 2000 interview by stating flatly: "This is Tanzania— we do not have that sort of problem here." In an August 2002 interview, an official in Mwamishali village explained that there was good cooperation across ethnic groups because "we are all Tanzanians," and an elder in Mwambiti village responded similarly, suggesting good ethnic relations resulted from the fact that "they [village residents] simply live as Tanzanians" ("*Wanaishi kama waTanzania tu,*" author's translation from Swahili).

The bottom line from the interviews is that while local politics in Busia are characterized by ethnic "us versus them" appeals, such arguments are considered illegitimate and downright "un-Tanzanian" in Meatu. The elimination of ethnic appeals from acceptable political discourse may be the most important legacy of the Tanzanian nation-building program. Tanzanian nation-building policies foster trust across ethnic groups, and a strong sense of identification with members of other groups as fellow Tanzanians; these emotional bonds—together with frequent village meetings and active local government institutions—have allowed diverse Tanzanian communities to thrive where diverse Kenyan communities fail.

Moving to the national context, Tanzanian economic growth rates were substantially higher than Kenyan rates during the 1990s, according to World

Bank figures, and national elections were considerably less violent. Although we should not read too much into the national differences—which are the product of many factors—these broad patterns are consistent with beneficial long-run impacts of nation-building in Tanzania. On a less formal level, visitors to Kenya and Tanzania—including myself—are routinely struck by the strikingly different popular attitudes toward ethnicity common in the two countries, and the far greater degree of attachment to the nation, to national ideals, and to the Swahili language in Tanzania.

Methodological Issues

The main methodological weakness of the comparison presented above is the small sample size of two districts, which limits our ability to generalize the results to other contexts. However, this is a drawback of much microeconomic empirical research and is perhaps impossible to overcome, given the lack of comparable data from other African settings on ethnic policies, historical patterns of ethnic relations, and current interethnic cooperation and local public goods funding. Another weakness is the lack of data on preindependence collective action outcomes in the two districts; an extensive search of secondary sources has unfortunately failed to yield any such information.

An examination of the twentieth-century history of western Kenya and western Tanzania indicates that differences in current levels of interethnic cooperation across Busia, Kenya, and Meatu, Tanzania, are in fact likely to be due to their strikingly different nation-building policies during the postcolonial period, rather than to divergent economic policies or preexisting differences.

Economic policies in Kenya and Tanzania since the financial crisis of 1982 have been largely parallel. Ndulu and Mwega (1994) write that "there were strong similarities in the nature of and responses to the [1982] crisis in each country . . . [and] the ongoing efforts at economic reform and structural adjustment in both countries are similar in many respects" (p. 101).

The period of really significant economic policy divergences between Busia, Kenya, and Meatu, Tanzania, occurred between 1974 and 1982, when the regional government forced residents of Meatu district to live in Ujamaa villages. However, if anything, the policies of this period appear more likely to have enflamed ethnic tensions rather than to have promoted cooperation. From August 1974 through 1977, the Shinyanga regional government pursued a policy of "forced villagization" in which over 340,000 rural residents were compelled to leave their homes, sometimes by force—including the burning of resisters' homes—and move to nearby villages to engage in collectivized farm production.[6] The minority Taturu and Hadzabe groups were particularly hard-hit by forced villagization, since it curtailed their traditional seminomadic lifestyles. To the extent that ethnic relations are currently better in western Tanzania than in western Kenya, it is unlikely to be due to the arbitrary and violent policies of the Ujamaa period.

POTENTIAL DRAWBACKS TO NATION-BUILDING IN DIVERSE SOCIETIES

There are many legitimate sources of concern regarding nation-building policies like those pursued in Tanzania after independence because, as with most policy reforms, nation-building can create losers as well as winners.

First, the creation and imposition of a single national identity through coordinated language and educational policies may have serious negative costs for communities that do not fit neatly into the prevailing national vision, as well-known European examples illustrate. The construction of a British identity from distinct English and Scottish identities in the seventeenth and eighteenth centuries was forged around common Protestant religious traditions and the English language, but no comparable compromise was reached for integrating Catholics or Celtic-language speakers into the mainstream of British public life. The process of nation-building in France also entailed the loss of numerous regional linguistic identities.

As a result, the fear remains real in many societies that the construction of a national identity will accelerate the erosion of some indigenous cultures and languages, and perhaps lead to a backlash from those who perceive these policies as a threat to their way of life. Nation-building policies could also be employed by opportunistic ethnic majority leaders to repress the legitimate political aspirations of minority group members—under the guise of benign nation-building reform. In societies with pronounced ethnic divisions, the process of nation-building that I advocate may be slow and painful, such that in the short term other solutions—including extensive decentralization, or even the secession of regions dominated by ethnic minority groups—may actually lead to less conflict and greater poverty reduction.

Nonetheless, even if nation-building policies should not be applied everywhere, the Tanzanian case suggests that nation-building can succeed in an African context without jeopardizing indigenous cultures and languages. Vernacular languages—such as the Sukuma language in the region where I have conducted fieldwork—continue to thrive in nonofficial contexts in Tanzania decades after independence, coexisting with Swahili in homes and markets. I feel that one key to the success of the Tanzanian program is that the central government never made efforts to "stamp out" vernacular languages or most indigenous cultural practices, nor to deny the existence of distinct ethnic groups.[7]

Another reasonable concern about nation-building is that while it binds people together within a society—reducing the likelihood of domestic civil strife—it may provoke nationalistic impulses that lead to war with neighboring countries. However, once again, this fear has not materialized in Tanzania. In fact, Tanzania has been an excellent neighbor, accepting millions of refugees fleeing armed conflicts in the region, and Tanzanian leaders have worked tirelessly for negotiated settlements to several African civil wars, most recently in Burundi. Internal tranquillity and international peace have gone hand in hand for Tanzania, perhaps as a result of the Pan-Africanist ideals at the heart of Julius Nyerere's political philosophy.

WHERE DO WE GO FROM HERE?

The recent academic literature in economics has forcefully made the case that ethnic, racial, religious, and other social divisions are a major source of poor institutional performance and persistent global poverty. Social scientists have proposed a range of reforms to address these divisions in less-developed countries, and of these, I believe that nation-building policies in language and education are the most promising. The comparison between nearby districts in Kenya and Tanzania presented above suggests that concerted central government efforts to build a coherent national identity—centered around a common language, compelling political ideals and symbols, and the abolition of traditional tribal authorities—can successfully promote interethnic cooperation in sub–Saharan Africa, the world's most ethnolinguistically diverse and poorest region, and the region with the slowest economic growth since the 1970s. These policies may also be viewed more generally as investments in social capital (Putnam, 1993).

Promoting nation-building policies will require a dramatic restructuring of cultural, educational, and language policies in many countries, and the centralized nature of this restructuring runs against current "Washington Consensus" thinking about economic development, which regards the promotion of strong central governments in less-developed countries with suspicion. Nation-building in less-developed countries is also likely to be opposed by powerful politicians in the global north, concerned that increasingly nationalistic—and assertive—less-developed countries will promote antinorthern and antiglobalization views.

Nonetheless, despite the likely opposition of the global north and the fact that benefits may take decades to materialize, I believe that nation-building should move onto government policy agendas, especially in sub–Saharan Africa. The articulation of new national political institutions and identities has been under way in many African countries since the democratization wave of the early 1990s reopened the debate on the nature of politics and the state in Africa. Now is an ideal time for progressive African political leaders to adopt elements of the Tanzanian nation-building model as investments in long-run social stability and poverty reduction in their countries.

ACKNOWLEDGMENTS I thank Melissa Gonzalez-Brenes, Michael Kremer, David Laitin, and Dan Posner for useful conversations related to this article. See Miguel (2004) for the academic version of this chapter.

NOTES

1. For two recent examples, see Acemoglu et al. (2001) and Bloom and Sachs. (1998).

2. For a review of this literature, see Costa and Kahn (2002). This paper surveys recent research on ethnicity in economics, including the articles I refer to but do not directly cite in this piece. There also exists a distinct literature on ethnic divisions and national political economy issues that I largely ignore in this chapter, due to space constraints.

3. For discussions of language policy and use, see Abdulaziz (1971) and Gorman (1974).

4. I would like to acknowledge the contributions of my research collaborators in Kenya (Mary Kay Gugerty, Michael Kremer, and Sylvie Moulin) and Tanzania (Elizabeth Beasley and Melissa Gonzalez-Brenes), and the unfailing cooperation of ICS Africa and local government officials in both countries, for making this research possible.

5. Identification of the causal impacts in Kenya relies on the relatively exogenous determination and stability of ethnic settlement patterns, an issue that is discussed at length in Miguel and Gugerty (forthcoming). Historical ethnic land settlement patterns were determined by a series of migrations and wars in the Kenyan region in the nineteenth century, were subsequently frozen by the British colonial regime, and have remained largely stable since then. Although there was some migration associated with the Tanzanian villagization program of the 1970s, villagization did not significantly alter local ethnic composition because individuals seldom moved more than a few miles from their original homes, and preliminary evidence from recent household surveys indicates that local residential patterns have been largely stable in Meatu district since the 1970s.

6. For a contemporary account, refer to Volter (1975).

7. One partial exception to this generalization about the inclusiveness of the Tanzanian approach is the small but wealthy South Asian community, who were never entirely welcome within Nyerere's Pan-Africanist and socialist vision.

BIBLIOGRAPHY

Abdulaziz, Mohamed H. "Tanzania's National Language Policy and the Rise of Swahili Political Culture." In Language Use and Social Change, edited by Wilfred Whiteley, 160–178. London: Oxford University Press, 1971.

Abdulaziz, Mohamed H. "The Ecology of Tanzanian National Language Policy." In Language in Tanzania, edited by Edgar C. Polomé and C. P. Hill. Oxford: Oxford University Press, 1980.

Acemoglu, Daron, Simon Johnson, and James Robinson. "Colonial Origins of Comparative Development: An Empirical Investigation." American Economic Review 91 (5) (2001): 1369–1401.

Barkan, Joel D. "Divergence and Convergence in Kenya and Tanzania: Pressures for Reform." In Beyond Capitalism versus Socialism in Kenya and Tanzania, edited by Joel D. Barkan. Boulder, Colo.: Lynne Rienner, 1994.

Bloom, David, and Jeffrey Sachs. "Geography, Demography, and Economic Growth in Africa." Brookings Papers on Economic Activity 2 (1998): 207–295.

Costa, Dora L., and Matthew E. Kahn. "Civic Engagement and Community Heterogeneity: An Economist's Perspective," paper prepared for the Conference on Social Connectedness and Public Activism, Harvard University, May 2002.

Easterly, William, and Ross Levine. "Africa's Growth Tragedy: Policies and Ethnic Divisions." Quarterly Journal of Economics 112 (4) (1997): 1203–1250.

Fearon, James D., and David D. Laitin. "Explaining Interethnic Cooperation." *American Political Science Review* 90 (4) (1996): 715–735.

Gorman, Thomas. "The Development of Language Policy in Kenya with Particular Reference to the Educational System." In *Language in Kenya*, edited by W. H. Whiteley. Nairobi: Oxford University Press, 1974.

Koff, David, and George von der Muhll. "Political Socialization in Kenya and Tanzania—A Comparative Analysis." *Journal of Modern African Studies* 5 (1) (1967): 13–51.

McEwan, A. C. *International Boundaries of East Africa*. Oxford: Clarendon Press, 1971.

Miguel, Edward A. "Tribe or Nation? Nation-Building and Public Goods in Kenya versus Tanzania." *World Politics* 56 (3) (2004): 327–362.

Miguel, Edward A., and Mary Kay Gugerty. "Ethnic Diversity, Social Sanctions, and Public Goods in Kenya." *Journal of Public Economics*, forthcoming.

Ndegwa, Stephen. "Citizenship and Ethnicity: An Examination of Two Transition Moments in Kenyan Politics." *American Political Science Review* 91 (3) (1997): 599–616.

Ndulu, Benno J., and Francis W. Mwega. "Economic Adjustment Policies." In *Beyond Capitalism versus Socialism in Kenya and Tanzania*, edited by Joel D. Barkan. Boulder, Colo.: Lynne Rienner, 1994.

Putnam, Robert. *Making Democracy Work*. Princeton, N.J.: Princeton University Press, 1993.

Varshney, Ashutosh. *Ethnic Conflict and Civic Life: Hindus and Muslims in India*. New Haven, Conn.: Yale University Press, 2002.

Volter, Juma Mwapachu. "Operation Planned Villages in Rural Tanzania: A Revolutionary Strategy for Development." *Mbioni* 7 (11) (1975): 5–39.

PART II

HOW SHOULD WE GO ABOUT FIGHTING POVERTY?

13

Redistribution toward Low Incomes in Richer Countries

Emmanuel Saez

During the twentieth century, most developed countries have adopted extensive government-managed income support programs for low-income families and individuals. For example, the United States launched income support programs such as Social Security for the old, unemployment compensation for those who lose their jobs, and Aid for Families with Dependent Children (AFDC) for low-income families during the Roosevelt administration in the 1930s.[1] Today, most developed countries devote significant means and effort to redistribution to those with low incomes. However, both the level of generosity and the structure of the programs vary substantially from country to country. Northern European and Commonwealth countries have developed substantially more generous programs than Southern European countries and the United States. Levels of generosity have steadily increased in Europe while there has been a cutback in the United States since the 1980s. The United States targets aid to specific groups, such as the disabled, single-parent families, and the old, and often imposes tight limits on the duration of benefits,[2] whereas many European countries have developed almost universal welfare programs covering most individuals with low incomes,[3] and the duration of welfare payments and unemployment insurance is often much longer.

Redistributive programs toward the poor generate substantial controversy among policy makers and economists. At the center of the controversy is an equity–efficiency trade-off. On the one hand, governments value redistribution and want to transfer resources from the middle- and high-income earners toward low-income individuals. On the other hand, such transfers are generally costly in terms of economic efficiency. First, raising taxes to finance the income transfer programs may reduce labor supply or savings incentives among the middle- and high-income earners who have to pay the extra taxes. Second, transfer programs may also reduce labor supply incentives of the low-income recipients. As a result, these adverse labor supply effects may substantially raise the cost of improving the living standards of the poor. The equity–efficiency trade-off is reflected in the political debate. Liberals emphasize the redistributive benefits of transfer programs and their important role in raising the welfare of the most needy individuals and families. Conservatives emphasize the efficiency costs, especially at the low-income end, blaming the welfare system for creating dependence and loss of economic self-sufficiency (see, e.g., Murray 1984, for such a point of view on the U.S. experience).

The problem of redistribution is tackled in two steps in economics research. The first step is a positive analysis in which economists develop models of individual behavior to understand how individuals or families respond to various transfer programs along various margins, such as labor supply, education, and human capital investment choices, or family and fertility decisions. The central part of the positive analysis is the empirical estimation of the models of individual behavior in order to assess the quantitative magnitudes of behavioral responses. In the United States and the United Kingdom, there is an enormous literature trying to estimate the size of the behavioral responses to most government transfer programs (see, e.g., Bane and Ellwood 1994; Blundell and MaCurdy 1999; and Krueger and Meyer 2002 for recent surveys). The literature in other countries is smaller but growing quickly. The second step is the normative analysis or optimal policy analysis. Using models developed and estimated in the positive analysis, the normative analysis investigates the structure and size of the transfer program that should be implemented to maximize social welfare. The social welfare criterion used by the government defines the redistributive tastes of the government. Presumably, a liberal government would use a more redistributive criterion than a conservative government. The normative analysis is crucial for policy-making because it shows how programs should be set or reformed in order to best attain the goals of the policy maker. In particular, the normative analysis allows separate assessments of how changes in the redistributive tastes of the government and changes in the size of the behavioral responses to taxes and transfers affect the optimal redistributive program.[4]

The discussion in this essay is organized as follows. The second section briefly describes the positive and empirical analysis (for which numerous good surveys are available) and focuses mostly on the normative analysis. The third section starts with a discussion of the optimal structure of cash transfer programs, depending on the nature and size of labor supply responses. We then extend the analysis of optimal transfer programs along various new dimensions. First, we discuss whether programs should be universal or targeted to specific groups, such as single mothers or the disabled. Second, we review whether in-kind transfers, such as food or shelter, or workfare programs, in which low-income individuals are required to perform some tasks for the government in order to receive public assistance, may be preferable to cash transfers. Last, we briefly analyze the issue of time limits. Is it preferable to have unlimited programs or to impose tight limits on the duration of benefits? The analysis of the third section is based on the standard assumption in economics that individuals do what is in their best interest. However, there are strong reasons to suspect that, in many cases, individuals may not realize how beneficial a training program could be, or how detrimental for skills a long unemployment spell could be. The fourth section discusses how the results of the third section might be affected in those situations where individuals may not be able to make the best choices for themselves. Finally, the fifth section provides a conclusion and an educated (as well as personal) view on what should be done for redistribution toward low incomes.

It is important to note that while some of the problems described in this essay have been investigated in depth and relatively robust answers have been established, a number of situations reviewed here have received much less attention. In these cases, the discussion presented here is more speculative and should be taken as an encouragement to research rather than as a collection of solidly established results.

OPTIMAL TRANSFER PROGRAMS

Market economies generate substantial levels of income inequality. Because earning and work abilities are very unequally distributed among individuals, without government intervention many individuals would end up with small or even no incomes. The existence of poverty in a developed economy is generally considered a bad market outcome that ought to be corrected to some extent. Surveys carried out in Western countries show that a very large majority favors some level of redistribution (see, for example, Alesina and La Ferrara 2001). Therefore, a government representing its constituents would like to transfer resources from those with high earnings abilities to the disadvantaged who have low earnings abilities or skills.

It is central to note that if earnings abilities were immutable and observable by the government, the government could base transfers directly on earning ability. Such transfers would be independent of investment in human skill or work effort choices, and thus would not create negative incentives.[5] However, earnings abilities cannot be observed directly, and can be inferred only indirectly, through market outcomes such as actual earnings. Thus, the government has to base redistribution on market outcomes, earnings being the most obvious one. Therefore, we first consider the benchmark case where transfers are based on income only, and we discuss below whether using other observable characteristics, such as family or disability status, can be useful to improve redistribution.

Cash Transfer Programs

Most welfare programs are means-tested in the sense that benefits are reduced when earnings increase. For example, TANF, as well as disability benefits and Supplemental Security Income for the old in the United States, or the French *revenu minimum d'insertion* are designed as means-tested programs. Such a transfer schedule relating pretransfer income (horizontal axis) to after-transfer income is depicted in Figure 13.1a. Absent any transfer program, pretransfer and after-transfer incomes would be identical, and thus the budget constraint would be the 45-degree line (the dashed line with slope 1 on the figure). The budget constraint with the transfer program is the solid line on Figure 13.1a: a guaranteed income is given to those with no earnings, and benefits are phased out as earnings increase until the break-even point, at which benefits are lost altogether. The phasing-out effectively reduces the slope of the budget constraint: for each extra dollar of earnings, the after-tax income increases by less than a dollar due to the reduction in benefits. In actual programs, the phasing-out rate is in general high, often equal to one in which case benefits are lost one-for-one as earnings increase. This

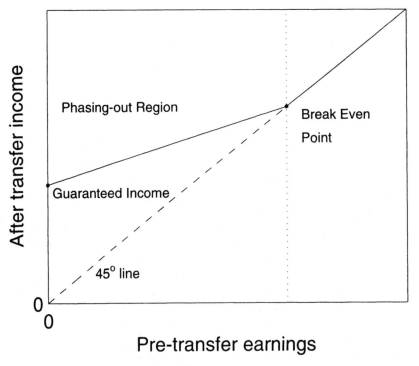

Figure 13.1a Pre-Transfer versus Post-Transfer Incomes in Traditional Welfare Programs

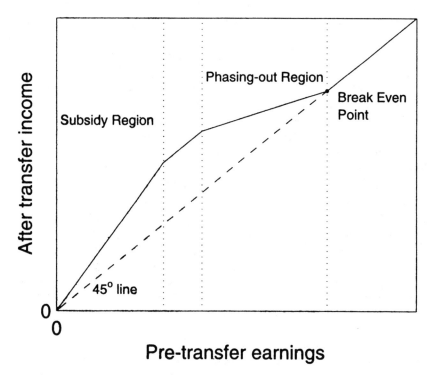

Figure 13.1b Pre-Transfer versus Post-Transfer Incomes with Earned Income Tax Credit (EITC)

type of program provides the largest benefits to those who have the lowest earnings, and hence are the most in need of income support. However, these redistributive virtues come at a potentially high efficiency cost. The introduction of such a program clearly induces recipients to work less, because the benefits provide extra income (income effect) and because recipients get to keep a much lower share of their earnings (substitution effect due to the phasing-out rate). A number of empirical studies surveyed in Krueger and Meyer (2002) have shown that these programs indeed have negative effects on labor supply, although the reductions in hours of work are typically fairly small for those who are in the labor force.

The normative analysis of the optimal shape of the transfer program (size of the guaranteed benefit and the phasing-out rate) was first investigated by Mirrlees (1971). He considered a simple model in which individuals adjust their labor supply along the intensive margin (i.e., individuals adjust the intensity of work on the job, measured, for example, by the number of hours worked, when taxes or transfers change). In that situation, Mirrlees showed that the optimal transfer program is characterized by a guaranteed benefit for those with no earnings (which depends positively on the strength of government redistributive tastes) and a positive phasing-out rate of the benefit as earnings increase. Numerical simulations performed in Saez (2001), calibrated using empirical labor supply estimates, show that the guaranteed benefit may be as high as 40% of average earnings even for moderate redistributive tastes and that the phasing-out rate is very high, typically around 70–80% (as depicted, for example, in Figure 13.1a). Such a schedule is desirable because it targets benefits to the most needy individuals in the economy and concentrates the labor supply disincentives to individuals with low earnings ability. These reductions in labor supply incentives at the bottom are not very costly because the beneficiaries would not have had very high earnings even in the absence of the program. Therefore, the Mirrlees model provides a clear answer to an important welfare policy question. It is better to target the program to low-income earners with a high phasing-out rate rather than having a lower phasing-out rate that would reduce incentives to work for a much larger number of individuals.

This suggests that many existing programs with very high phasing-out rates may actually be close to the optimum predicted by the Mirrlees (1971) model. However, such programs have often been held responsible for the low working rates among welfare recipients in the United States (see, e.g., Murray 1984). This has led politicians to advocate programs that would make work sufficiently attractive to reduce the need for income support. In the early 1990s, the Earned Income Tax Credit (EITC) program in the United States was substantially increased, and is now the largest cash transfer program for the poor. The EITC schedule, shown in Figure 13.1b, is fundamentally different from a traditional means-tested program (Figure 13.1a). The EITC does not provide any income support for individuals with no earnings, but all earnings below a given threshold are partially matched by the government, creating a strong incentive to enter the labor force and work. As a result, the slope of the budget constraint in the phasing-in range (depicted in Figure 13.1b) is higher than 1: an extra dollar of earnings translates into more than a dollar in after-transfer income.[6] Empirical studies have shown that the expansion of the EITC in the United States successfully induced low-skilled single mothers to enter the labor force (see, e.g., Meyer and Rosenbaum 2001). The United Kingdom has introduced and expanded a similar program (Working Family Tax Credit). Many other European countries have started implementing such programs on a more modest scale or are contemplating introducing such programs (see Gradus and Julsing 2001).

The key feature missing in the Mirrlees (1971) model is the labor supply decision along the extensive margin, that is, the decision to enter the labor force. Empirical studies (see, e.g., Heckman 1993) have shown that the extensive margin response (choosing whether or not to enter the labor force) is much more elastic than the intensive response margin (choosing how many hours to work once one has decided to enter the labor force). The main reason why this is the case is the fixed costs of working: search costs of finding a job, transportation costs, child care expenses, and so on. Moreover, most jobs, including part-time jobs, require a minimum and regular number of hours per week. As a result, very few people report working less than twenty hours per week. Saez (2002) shows that a subsidy for low-skilled workers is optimal when labor supply responses are concentrated along the extensive margin. The intuition is as follows: introducing a subsidy for low-skilled workers is good for redistributive purposes and also induces some individuals to enter the labor force, and thus allows the government to save on welfare money. In contrast, in a model with intensive margin responses, a subsidy for low-skilled workers would induce some higher-skill workers to work less in order to take advantage of the subsidy, and would thus increase the cost of the program. That is why such subsidies are not optimal in the Mirrlees (1971) model. Therefore, a government contemplating an increase of incentives for low-skilled workers must precisely weigh the positive effect on work participation and the negative intensive labor supply effect for higher-skilled workers. Saez (2002) presents simulations of this optimal transfer model using empirical estimates of the intensive and extensive elasticities of labor supply. Since the extensive elasticity appears to be much larger than the intensive elasticity, the simulations show that the optimal program should have lower guaranteed benefits (perhaps around 20% of the average earnings in the economy) but that the phasing-out rate should close to zero on the first $6,000 of earnings, so as to make work pay and not deter labor force participation. The benefits should then be phased out at substantial rates for earnings between $6,000 and $15,000. A high phasing-out rate in that earnings range creates only moderate reduction in labor supply because effort on the job (intensive margin) is not very sensitive to incentives.

The transfer programs we have described here are individually based and not family based. However, in practice, transfer programs are often family based.[7] The main reason for using the family is that welfare is better measured by family income than individual income. For example, the nonworking spouse of a high-income husband has no earnings but is not in need. However, the empirical literature has shown that labor supply of secondary earners is much more sensitive to incentives than labor supply of primary earners (see, e.g., Killingsworth and Heckman 1986). Therefore, basing transfers on family income can create perverse incentives for the secondary earner. For example, the EITC in the United States may deter the secondary earner from entering the labor force because the primary earner's income is enough to push family income into the phasing-out range, where the second earner's earnings are implicitly taxed (see Eissa and Hoynes 1998 for such an analysis). Therefore, even though carefully calibrated numerical simulations have not yet been done, it seems that incentives considerations outweigh redistributive considerations, and that transfer programs for low-income persons should be based to a large extent on individual income rather than family income.

Universal versus Targeted Transfers

In the previous subsection, we considered cash transfer programs based solely on earnings. However, as described above, basing transfers on earnings creates negative work incentives. As we discussed at the beginning of the section, it would be more efficient to base redistribution on characteristics that are immutable and related to work ability. For example, disabled people cannot work, and therefore targeting transfers specifically to disabled people should not create negative labor supply incentives for those who can work. Akerlof (1978) made the important theoretical point that tagging welfare programs to observable types such as the disabled can enhance redistributive efficiency. There are two important points to note on this issue.

First, tagging will enhance efficiency the most in situations where the characteristic used for targeting is less easily manipulable. In principle, disability status is not easily manipulable and thus should be an efficient way to target welfare. However, the empirical literature on the U.S. disability insurance system has shown that disability is measured with substantial error, and there is a controversial debate among researchers on whether those on disability insurance are really unable to work (see Bound 1989; Parsons 1991). If disability status is easily manipulable, then a special program targeted to disabled people will create efficiency costs and the gain relative to a universal program will not be great. A characteristic such as age is clearly not manipulable, and therefore, adopting special transfers for the elderly who are in need and who can no longer work, as done in most countries, may be desirable (see Kremer 1997 for a formal analysis).[8]

Second, the characteristic used to target welfare should be closely related to need for support. Therefore, in practice, targeted programs are always means-tested, potentially creating some efficiency costs such as those discussed above. Related to this point, targeting welfare to specific groups such as the disabled or the old may leave large numbers of those in need outside the welfare net, and thus may create unequal treatment of individuals in equal need of support. The U.S. transfer programs target specific groups such as the disabled, the old, and single mothers, and provide almost no support to able adults without children. On the other hand, a number of European transfer systems have a strong universal component.

In sum, optimal redistributive programs should do some targeting, especially using characteristics not easily manipulable and related to earnings abilities. However, it is clearly hopeless to design a program with no efficiency costs because all characteristics related to being in need of support are manipulable to some extent. An optimal program should also provide some support to those with very low incomes but no observable disability. While these theoretical considerations are well understood, it is an interesting and still open research question as to whether the optimal level of targeting should be closer to the U.S. situation or to the European situation.

Cash versus In-Kind Transfers

So far, we have considered only transfers taking the form of cash. While cash programs form the bulk of transfers, most countries have also adopted non-cash transfer programs such as health care provision, education and training programs, public housing, or food and shelter support for the homeless. If we assume that individuals make the best choices for themselves, then receiving cash is better than receiving an equivalent amount in-kind.[9] However, as shown by Nichols and Zeckhauser (1982), even for rational individuals it might be optimal for the government to provide in-kind transfers instead of cash because in-kind transfers might be valued differently by different people. For example, suppose that a shelter program is offered freely. Obviously, shelter is of no value for well-off individuals who want high-quality housing, and thus only individuals in need will take advantage of the program. As a result, and in contrast to a cash transfer that is universally desirable, an in-kind transfer allows the screening of individuals and hence endogenously targets redistribution toward the needy. Therefore, a formal analysis shows that introducing an in-kind transfer program can, in some cases, improve the redistributive power of the government and should be part of an optimal transfer structure. The analysis of workfare by Besley and Coate (1992) is based on the same idea. Workfare provides support but requires individuals to perform some time-consuming task in order to receive the support. Even if the task is completely unproductive, requiring it might be desirable because it allows the screening of recipients, since those in need presumably have a much lower opportunity cost of time.

While the theoretical advantage of in-kind transfers is well understood, it is still an open research question in regard to what extent those types of transfers should be used and how much improvement they would allow the government to make over and above pure cash transfer programs. We believe that this improvement would be small because the efficiency gains of screening come at the welfare cost of providing less desirable transfers. In any case, the theory clearly shows that in-kind transfers cannot completely replace cash transfers but should be used as a complement to cash transfers.

Time Limits for Benefits

Our discussion so far has considered static models with no time dimension. Introducing the time dimension in the optimal transfer problem raises important and interesting questions that have not been studied very extensively. In practice, the government can vary the duration of benefits. This issue is especially important in the case of unemployment insurance benefits for those who are temporarily unemployed and where the problem is dynamic by nature. Before the important welfare reform of 1996 in the United States, traditional welfare programs had no time limits. These programs were blamed for creating despondency and promoting a culture of welfare dependence because recipients had no incentives to find work and could rely on welfare benefits for very long time periods (see, e.g., Murray 1984). Careful empirical analysis has shown that the culture of welfare dependency is much less pervasive than the conservative view suggests, and that most welfare recipients use it for short periods of time (see, e.g., Bane and Ellwood 1994). In many European countries, the long duration of unemployment benefits has been blamed for keeping unemployment rates at high levels.[10] The 1996 U.S. welfare reform imposed a tight five-year limit on the duration of welfare benefits over a lifetime. Indeed, the number of families on welfare in the United States declined from over 5 million in 1994 to about 2.2 million in the early 2000s. Empirical research (see, e.g., the extensive review by Grogger and Karoly 2005) has shown that most of the decline is due to the expansion of the Earned Income Tax Credit and welfare reform, with the improving economy playing a more modest role.[11] Although employment levels of single mothers (those most likely to have benefited from welfare) rose sharply during the period, the main concern was that the loss of welfare might not have been fully compensated for by increased earnings for a number of very low-income families. Meyer and Sullivan (2004) show, however, that the material well-being of single mothers at the bottom of the distribution actually improved slightly during the 1990s.

The duration of benefits can be seen conceptually as another dimension of the generosity of benefits that also creates a classical equity–efficiency trade-off. Limiting the duration of benefits improves incentives to find work and leave welfare or unemployment before benefits end. However, imposing a limit on benefits harms those who cannot find work quickly enough and thus are the most in need of support. The optimal duration of benefits should be set so as to weigh these two considerations. A number of studies have tried to calibrate such theoretical dynamic models, using estimates from the empirical literature in order to assess how long benefits should be set in practice. Most of studies have adopted the standard dynamic model in which individuals can self-insure against future unemployment spells with savings. In that context, it has been found that the size of government-provided unemployment insurance should be rather modest because self-insurance with savings is a powerful tool to insure against short-term income loss due to unemployment (see, e.g., Werning 2002). However, empirical studies such as Gruber (1997) have shown that, in contrast to the prediction of the standard dynamic optimization model, consumption falls sharply during unemployment spells. This suggests that the standard model fails to capture important aspects of the problem, and that if individuals fail to save enough against unemployment risk, government-provided unemployment insurance might be a valuable and desirable program.

THE CASE OF MYOPIC INDIVIDUALS

Our analysis has so far considered only situations where individuals are rational and able to make the best choices for themselves. There are important reasons for believing that individuals may not always be able to make the best choices, especially when the time dimension is introduced. For example, it is very difficult to make an accurate assessment of the future benefits of investing in human capital now. Therefore, there is a concern that individuals may not realize how beneficial education is, and hence invest too little in education for them or for their children. In that situation, the optimal program should logically provide more incentives for work and invest in education than in the situation where individuals are fully rational. This element would be an additional reason to favor EITC-type programs that promote work over traditional welfare programs that discourage labor force participation.

The notion that individuals may not make the best choices for themselves raises difficult conceptual issues. Individuals may be fully rational and just happen to have a high preference for the present, which causes them to prefer not to invest in human skills today instead of investing and getting more earnings later in life. In that case, a government intervention would be a clear case of paternalism—the government wants to impose its own views over and above the preferences of citizens. That view of the government has been fiercely denounced by libertarian economists from the Chicago school.

However, the growing field of behavioral economics has shown that, in important situations, individual decisions involving the time dimension, such as investment and savings, cannot be accounted for with purely rational preferences.[12] For example, many studies have documented that individuals tend to have inconsistent time preferences that may explain behaviors such as underinvestment in education or procrastination. In those situations, government interventions may be desired by those individuals because it may help them overcome some of the shortcomings of their own behavior. (See, for example, Diamond and Koszegi 2003 for such an analysis in the case of retirement programs for the old when individuals have hyperbolic discount rates). In those situations, individuals do not have standard preferences, and thus it is not clear how the government should evaluate their utility; thus the question of defining a social welfare criterion becomes complicated. Substantial research effort is currently, and will continue to be, devoted to these new research questions in the future. (See Bernheim and Rangel 2004 for a recent exposition of some of the issues of defining a welfare concept in nonstandard situations).

There is a large literature in labor economics evaluating the costs and benefits of training programs for low-skilled and low-income earners (see, e.g., Heckman et al. 1999 for a recent comprehensive survey). Such programs are designed to improve future earnings of the trainees, and thus can be justified only if trainees are myopic (and do not realize the full benefits of being trained) or are credit constrained (and hence not able to borrow to pay for their training). The empirical literature has shown that in general training has a positive impact on future earnings, but is of modest size in most cases. Thus the gains in earnings rarely cover the training costs. However, the benefits of those programs are very heterogeneous across groups and particular programs. For example, Ifcher (2004) shows that the job placement assistance program set in place by New York City in 1999 for its welfare recipients had a very strong effect on the probability of finding a job and leaving welfare permanently, and thus was cost-effective. Therefore, this suggests that subtle variations in the way those training programs work or small differences in the environment in which they take place can have a dramatic impact on their success. Indeed, the empirical behavioral literature has shown that in a number of contexts, differences in the environment which should be irrelevant for a standard rational economic agent can have very large impacts on actual economic decisions.[13] Therefore, it is plausible to think that such framing effects might also be very important in the context of transfer programs. An important challenge for future research is to understand precisely under which circumstances such programs can be successful in helping low-income earners.

CONCLUSION

This essay has presented a critical overview of the findings of economic research on the problem of redistribution toward low incomes. There are a number of important conclusions that emerge. First, the behavioral labor supply responses to transfers, even though significant, are not so large that the costs of redistribution necessarily outweigh the benefits. Given the size of empirical behavioral responses, substantial transfers could be carried out that would greatly improve the welfare of the poorest families and individuals in American society at a reasonable cost for middle- and higher-income earners. Therefore, the difference in the size of redistribution between the United States and Northern Europe might be due to differences in the redistributive tastes and political processes of those societies.

Second, since empirical studies have found that the labor supply response is concentrated along the participation margin, it would be desirable to structure welfare programs so as to encourage work participation of beneficiaries.[14] A valuable way to do this is to lower the welfare payments for those who do not have any earnings but allow welfare recipients to keep their full earnings in addition of welfare payments up to a limit. The level of welfare payments should of course depend on the number of dependents (in particular children) but should also cover single individuals with no dependents in order not to leave out of support a significant number of persons in need of assistance as in the United States. Furthermore, in the case of two-parent low-income families, it is very important to structure the program so as to preserve incentives to work for both earners.

Third, tagging special groups, such as the disabled or the old, for assistance, as well as providing in-kind benefits instead of cash or extending workfare (i.e., provide benefits conditional on work requirements), could help to improve redistribution on the margin, but it is very doubtful that such schemes could replace cash transfers to a large extent. Recent studies suggest that many individuals may not take full account of the future benefits of current actions, such as work and investment in human capital. Therefore, this reinforces the idea we developed that redistributive programs should be structured so as to encourage work.

ACKNOWLEDGMENTS I thank Roland Benabou for useful comments. Financial support from NSF grant SES-0134946 and the Sloan Foundation is gratefully acknowledged.

NOTES

1. The AFDC was renamed TANF (Temporary Assistance for Needy Families) following the welfare reform of 1996.

2. For example, welfare payments to single parents are now limited to five years within a lifetime, and unemployment insurance benefits are in general limited to only six months.

3. For example, the guaranteed minimum income (*revenu minimum d'insertion*) in France is a monthly payment for all families or individuals above age twenty-five with no time limits and subject only to a means test.

4. In actual policy debates, these two elements, which are conceptually distinct, are often confused. Conservative policy makers rarely state explicitly that they have little taste for redistribution per se; rather, they justify their lack of taste for redistribution because they believe negative behavioral responses to redistributive programs are large. Conversely, liberals emphasize the redistributive virtues of transfer programs and often ignore negative incentive effects.

5. This general principle is known as the Second Welfare Theorem in economics. It states that any feasible and desirable outcome, no matter how redistributive, can be obtained using appropriate transfers based on immutable characteristics.

6. In 2003, the matching rate of the American EITC was 40% for families with two or more children for the first $10,500 of annual family earnings (corresponding roughly to a single full-time, full-year, minimum-wage salary). The credit is equal to $4,200 for earnings between $10,500 and $14,700. The EITC is then phased out for earnings between $14,700 and $34,700 at a rate of 21%.

7. For example, the EITC in the United States is based on family earnings.

8. This result in favor of old-age support is weakened when one recognizes that poverty in old age might be due to savings decisions taken earlier in life which might be distorted by a generous old-age program.

9. See the final section for a discussion of the case where this rationality assumption does not hold.

10. See, for example, Nickell (1997) for a cross-country empirical analysis. Empirical work in the United States has shown convincingly that the duration of unemployment benefits significantly affects unemployment spells (see Meyer 1990).

11. This finding is confirmed by the fact that welfare rolls hardly increased during the recession of 2001–2002.

12. See, for example, the survey by Frederick et al. (2002).

13. Perhaps the most striking example is the study of Madrian and Shea (2001), showing that a change in the default option for enrollment in an employer-provided pension plan had an enormous impact on enrollment and pension contribution decisions.

14. The United States made such a move with the expansion of the EITC in 1993.

BIBLIOGRAPHY

Akerlof, George. "The Economics of Tagging as Applied to the Optimal Income Tax." *American Economic Review* 81 (1978): 8–19.

Alesina, Alberto, and Eliana La Ferrara. "Preferences for Redistribution in the Land of Opportunities." NBER Working Paper no. 8267, 2001.

Bane, Mary Jo, and David Ellwood. *Welfare Realities.* Cambridge, Mass.: Harvard University Press, 1994.

Bernheim, Douglas, and Antonio Rangel. "Behavioral Public Economics: Welfare Economics When Individuals Can Make Mistakes." Mimeo, Stanford University, 2004.

Besley, Timothy, and Stephen Coate. "Workfare versus Welfare: Incentive Arguments for Work Requirements in Poverty Alleviation Programs." *American Economic Review* 82 (1992): 249–261.

Blundell, Richard, and Thomas MaCurdy. "Labor Supply: A Review of Alternative Approaches." In *Handbook of Labor Economics.* Vol. 3A. Edited by O. Ashenfelter and D. Card. Amsterdam: North-Holland, 1999.

Bound, John. "The Health and Earnings of Rejected Disability Insurance Applicants." *American Economic Review* 79 (1989): 482–503.

Diamond, Peter, and Botond Koszegi. "Quasi-Hyperbolic Discounting and Retirement." *Journal of Public Economics* 87 (2003): 1839–1872.

Eissa, Nada, and Hilary Hoynes. "The Earned Income Tax Credit and the Labor Supply of Married Couples." *Journal of Public Economics* 88 (9–10) (2004): 1931–1958.

Frederick, Shane, George Loewenstein, and Ted O'Donogue. "Time Discounting and Time Preference: A Critical Review." *Journal of Economic Literature* 40 (2) (2002): 351–401.

Gradus, R. H. J. M., and J. M. Julsing. "Comparing Different European Income Tax Policies Making Work Pay." Mimeo, OCFEB, Erasmus University, Rotterdam, 2001.

Grogger, Jeffrey, and Lynn A. Karoly. *Welfare Reform: Effects of a Decade of Change.* Cambridge, Mass.: Harvard University Press, 2005.

Gruber, Jonathan. "The Consumption Smoothing Benefits of Unemployment Insurance." *American Economic Review* 87 (1) (1997): 192–205.

Heckman, James. "What Has Been Learned about Labor Supply in the Past Twenty Years?" *American Economic Review* 83 (1993): 116–121.

Heckman, James, Robert J. LaLonde, and Jeffrey Smith. "The Economics and Econometrics of Active Labor Market Programs." In *Handbook of Labor Economics,* Vol. 3A. Edited by O. Ashenfelter and D. Card. Amsterdam: North-Holland, 1999.

Ifcher, John. "Leaving Welfare and Joining the Labor Force: Does Job Training Help? Evidence from an Innovative Intervention in New York City." Ph.D. dissertation, University of California, 2004.

Killingsworth, Mark, and James Heckman. "Female Labor Supply: A Survey." In *Handbook of Labor Economics,* Vol. 1. Edited by O. Ashenfelter and R. Layard. Amsterdam: North-Holland, 1986.

Kremer, Michael. "Should Taxes be Independent of Age?" Mimeo, Harvard University, 1997.

Krueger, Alan, and Bruce Meyer. "Labor Supply Effects of Social Insurance." In *Handbook of Public Economics*. Vol. 4. Edited by A. Auerbach and M. Felstein. Amsterdam: North-Holland, 2002.

Madrian, Brigitte, and Denis Shea. "The Power of Suggestion: Inertia in 401(k) Participation and Savings Behavior." *Quarterly Journal of Economics* 116 (2001): 1149–1187.

Meyer, Bruce. "Unemployment Insurance and Unemployment Spells." *Econometrica* 58 (1990): 757–782.

Meyer, Bruce, and Daniel Rosenbaum. "Welfare, the Earned Income Tax Credit, and the Labor Supply of Single Mothers." *Quarterly Journal of Economics* 116 (2001): 1063–1114.

Meyer, Bruce, and James X. Sullivan. "The Effects of Welfare and Tax Reform: The Material Well-being of Single Mothers in the 1980s and 1990s." *Journal of Public Economics* 88 (7–8) (2004): 1387–1420.

Mirrlees, James A. "An Exploration in the Theory of Optimal Income Taxation." *Review of Economic Studies* 38 (1971): 175–208.

Murray, Charles. *Losing Ground: American Social Policy, 1950–1980.* New York: Basic Books, 1984.

Nichols, A., and Richard Zeckhauser. "Targeting Transfers through Restrictions on Recipients." *American Economic Review* 72 (1982): 372–377.

Nickell, Stephen. "Unemployment and Labor Market Rigidities: Europe versus North America." *Journal of Economic Perspectives* 11 (3) (1997): 55–74.

Parsons, Donald. "The Health and Earnings of Rejected Disability Insurance Applicants: Comment." *American Economic Review* 81 (1991): 1419–1426.

Saez, Emmanuel. "Using Elasticities to Derive Optimal Income Tax Rates." *Review of Economic Studies* 68 (2001): 205–229.

Saez, Emmanuel. "Optimal Income Transfer Programs: Intensive versus Extensive Labor Supply Responses." *Quarterly Journal of Economics* 117 (3) (2002): 1039–1073.

Werning, Ivan. "Optimal Unemployment Insurance with Unobservable Savings." Working Paper, MIT, 2002.

14

Transfers and Safety Nets in Poor Countries: Revisiting the Trade-Offs and Policy Options

Martin Ravallion

The conventional wisdom in mainstream development policy circles is that transfers to the poor are at best a short-term palliative and at worst a waste of money. They are not seen as a core element of an effective long-term poverty reduction strategy.

What is this conventional wisdom based on? One commonly heard view is that the poor are roughly equally poor in the poorest countries, and there are so many of them and resources are so limited, that these policies are a nonstarter. However, while the extent of poverty and the resource limitations are both clear enough, it is now well established from household survey data that even in the poorest countries, the differences in levels of living among the poor can be sizable.[1] A high incidence of poverty does not diminish the equity case for targeting limited resources to the poorest first.

Another long-standing critique of this class of policies has potentially more weight. This says that leakage of benefits to nontarget groups and adverse incentive effects on the labor supply and savings of transfer recipients create a serious trade-off against efficiency and growth, which is seen to be crucial to rapid poverty reduction. For example, an article on redistribution in Britain in *The Economist* stated that "Redistribution may sound like a lovely bit of fair-mindedness, but the only sure way to get there is through more poverty, not more wealth" (*The Economist* 2003, p. 34). Even the more supportive assessments of this class of policy interventions that one finds in the literature have seen their redistributive role as solely a matter of equity. For example, Barr (1992) describes the "inequality reduction" role of these policies as "almost entirely an equity issue" (p. 746).

These views are starting to be questioned at two levels. First, careful evaluations have pointed to a number of success stories. Yes, there are programs that claim to be targeted to the poor but whose benefits are captured by others, and there are programs that concentrate their benefits on poor people but have such low coverage that they achieve little impact overall. However, assessments of a number of programs have been quite positive—debunking claims that targeted programs in poor countries are inevitably plagued by leakage and high administrative costs.[2] Limited redistribution appears to be possible by this means.

Second, the presumption of an overall trade-off between redistribution or insurance (on the one hand) and growth (on the other) has come to be questioned. It is known that a market economy can generate too much risk and inequality, judged solely from the viewpoint of aggregate output.[3] This theoretical possibility has given a new lease on life to targeted transfers as the main instruments for publicly provided "social protection" in poor countries, which is seen as being good for pro-poor growth (meaning growth that reduces poverty) by providing insurance or helping credit-constrained poor people be productive workers or take up productive opportunities for self-employment.[4]

This essay revisits the role of targeted transfers in poor countries in the light of the new theories on the social costs of unmitigated inequalities and uninsured risks. Recognizing that the policy implications depend crucially on whether there is good empirical evidence to support the theoretical arguments, the bulk of the first half of the essay discusses the evidence. The essay then takes up a key question for policy: Can the potential for efficient redistribution be realized in practice using targeted transfers, given the constraints faced in poor countries?

REVISITING THE EQUITY-EFFICIENCY TRADE-OFF

The presumption that there is an aggregate trade-off between the twin goals of economic growth and lower inequality can be questioned for a number of reasons. Unless a person can initially assure that her basal metabolic rate (BMR)—the food energy intake needed to support bodily functions at rest—is reached, there can be no productive activity of any sort. This "threshold effect" can mean that an economy generates massive involuntary unemployment under one distribution of assets, while a more equitable distribution yields full employment and high output (Dasgupta and Ray 1986).

Credit market failures also entail that some people are unable to exploit growth-promoting opportunities for investment in (physical and human) capital. Aggregate output is the sum of the individual outputs, each depending on own capital, in turn determined by own wealth, given the credit market failure. Then aggregate output depends on the distribution of wealth (Galor and Zeira 1993; Benabou 1996; Aghion and Bolton 1997, among others). The output loss from the market failure is also likely to be greater for the poor, notably when there are diminishing returns to capital, so that the productivity of investment is highest for those with least capital, who are likely to be the poorest. The higher the proportion of poor people, the more unexploited investment opportunities there will be and (hence) the lower the economy's aggregate output.

This is not the only argument as to why high inequality can be inefficient. Distribution-dependent growth can also be generated by the political economy, notably the way that the initial income or asset distribution influences the balance of power over public spending (Alesina and Rodrik 1994; Persson and Tabellini 1994). Inequality can also make it harder to achieve efficiency-enhancing cooperation among people, such as providing public goods or achieving policy reform (Bardhan et al. 2000 review these arguments).

A further set of reasons to question the existence of an aggregate trade-off stems from the way market failures can create a link between spatial inequalities and growth. This can arise from externalities whereby living in a well-endowed area means that a poor household can eventually escape poverty, while an otherwise identical household living in a poor area sees stagnation or decline (Jalan and Ravallion 2002). For this to be sustained, there must be impediments to factor mobility, such that the productivity of capital and labor comes to depend causally on location. Then policies to redress spatial inequalities can compensate for the underlying factor market failures and thus stimulate pro-poor growth.[5]

These arguments are fine in theory, but what does the evidence suggest? Compilations of aggregate data on growth and distribution suggest that countries with higher initial inequality tend to experience lower rates of growth, controlling for other factors including initial income, openness to trade, and the rate of inflation.[6] Indeed, very high inequality can stifle progress against poverty; it has been estimated that this is the case for about one fifth of the date-country combinations in a data set for developing countries (Ravallion 1997b).

There are a number of concerns about the data and methods used in testing for an aggregate equity-efficiency trade-off, and the biases can go either way. There are measurement errors in both the levels and the changes in measured income inequality, including comparability problems between countries and over time arising from errors in survey data (both sampling and nonsampling errors) and heterogeneity in survey design and processing.[7] There are also concerns about the presence of unobserved factors influencing the growth process—factors that might be correlated with initial inequality, thus making it hard to say whether higher inequality is really the cause of lower growth. The latter concern can be dealt with by allowing for country-specific effects, and then the adverse impact of inequality on growth has not been robust (Li and Zou 1998; Barro 2000; Forbes 2000). Essentially this deals with the problem by comparing changes in growth with changes in inequality. However, this method can perform poorly when there is consid-

erable measurement error in the changes in inequality over time, as is likely
to be the case with the inequality measures found in existing cross-country
data sets, making it hard to detect the true relationship.

Another concern is that spurious inequality effects can arise from aggregation, given credit market failures. For example, consistent aggregation
across microunits can require that we use the mean of log incomes in the
aggregate growth regression. However, the data are logs of means. The difference between the two is a measure of inequality, which can be significant
purely because of inconsistent aggregation. Empirical results for rural China
(Ravallion 1998) indicate that regional aggregation across the underlying mi-
crogrowth process hides the adverse effect of inequality on growth.

The choice of control variables in identifying the relationship is also open
to question. For example, past tests of the effect of inequality on growth have
controlled for the human capital stock, yet reducing investment in human
capital is presumably one of the ways that inequality matters to growth.
Inequality may have little or no adverse effect on growth at a given level of
aggregate human capital, but a large indirect effect via human capital accumulation.

The validity of the common assumption that initial inequality has a linear
effect on aggregate growth is also questionable: Banerjee and Duflo (1999)
argued on empirical grounds that changes in income inequality are bad for
growth, whichever direction the changes go. If that is so, then policies that
prevent rising inequality may well be good for growth, yet those which reduce
current inequality are not also good for growth. A deeper understanding of
such nonlinearities is needed.

Given the concerns about tests using country-level data, it is promising
that these theories also have some testable implications for microdata. The
microempirical literature on development offers support for the view that
high inequality can be inefficient. A classic case stems from the observations
that farm yields (output per acre) in poor countries tend to be lower the
larger the landholding; Binswanger et al. (1995) review the evidence on this
negative correlation, and discuss alternative explanations. To some extent the
negative correlation reflects unobserved differences in land quality (whereby
larger plots tend to have lower yields per unit area). However, there is a
reasonable presumption and some evidence suggesting that the negative correlation stems from factor market failures due to asymmetric information
(Binswanger et al. 1995). Then inequality-reducing redistributions from large
landholders to smallholders will raise aggregate output.

Supportive evidence can also be found in empirical work on micropanel
data that has tested a key implication of theoretical models based on credit
market failures, namely, that individual income or wealth at one date will be
an increasing function of its own past value, but the relationship becomes
flatter as wealth rises. Then the recursion diagram (giving current income or
wealth as a function of its lagged value) is said to be concave. Using panel
data (in which the same households are tracked over time), Lokshin and

Ravallion (2004) found such a nonlinearity in household income dynamics for Hungary and Russia, and Jalan and Ravallion (2004) found the same thing in panel data for rural China.[8] In all three countries, the recursion diagram was found to be concave, indicating that the growth rate of mean household income will be lower, the higher the initial inequality. Depending on the model specification, the results for rural China imply that inequality in current incomes lowers the mean in the following year by 4–7% at given current mean income (Jalan and Ravallion 2004). (This is based on a simulation in which all incomes are replaced by the mean; naturally, this is an upper bound that is unlikely to be attainable in practice.) These figures are lower than those obtained by Lokshin and Ravallion for Russia and Hungary, where inequality appears to be more costly to growth; inequality accounts for one fifth of mean current income in Hungary and about one tenth in Russia.

Some of the theories based on credit market failures also predict that the adverse impact of higher inequality on growth will be transmitted through the occupational structure of an economy (Banerjee and Newman 1993). In testing this link, Mesnard and Ravallion (2005) find evidence of nonlinearity in the wealth effect on business start-ups among return migrants in Tunisia, such that wealth inequality attenuates the aggregate level of self-employment.

There is also empirical support for another link between inequality and growth, via the incidence of undernutrition. This is likely to lower aggregate productivity. For example, it has been found that undernourished farmworkers in poor countries tend to be less productive (Strauss 1986; Deolalikar 1988). Also, malnutrition in children is thought to have adverse long-term consequences for their learning, and hence their future incomes; supportive evidence can be found in Bhargava (1999) (for Kenya), Glewwe et al. (2001) (for the Philippines), and Alderman et al. (2002) (for Zimbabwe); in the latter case, the authors directly link the poor nutritional status of children to a drought. Higher income inequality is also likely to raise the incidence of undernutrition; Dasgupta and Ray (1986) show how this can happen in theory, and there is supportive evidence in Ravallion (1992), using microdata for Indonesia.

Yet another link that has been studied empirically is through crime. Bourguignon (2001) discusses the theory and evidence suggesting that higher poverty and inequality can promote crime, which is surely costly to aggregate efficiency. Using microdata, Demombynes and Özler (2004) find evidence from South Africa that greater consumption inequality within and between neighborhoods leads to higher crime rates.

There is also supportive evidence from microdata on the costs of spatial inequalities. Using a six-year panel of farm household data for rural southern China in the 1980s, Jalan and Ravallion (2002) regress consumption growth at the household level on geographic variables, allowing for unobserved individual effects in the growth rates. They find that indicators of geographic capital have divergent impacts on consumption growth at the microlevel,

controlling for household characteristics. Their interpretation is that living
in a poor area lowers the productivity of a farm household's own investments, which reduces the growth rate, given restrictions on capital mobility.
The results suggest that there are areas in rural China that are so poor that
the consumptions of some households living in them were falling even while
otherwise identical households living in better-off areas enjoyed rising consumption. The geographic effects are strong enough to imply poverty traps.

One specific source of externalities is the composition of local economic
activity. In the same setting in rural China, there is evidence that the composition of local economic activity has nonnegligible impacts on consumption growth at the household level (Ravallion 2005). There are significant
positive effects of local economic activity in a given sector on income growth
from that sector. And there are a number of significant cross effects, notably
from farming to certain nonfarm activities. The sector that matters most as
a generator of positive externalities turns out to be agriculture.

There is also microevidence pointing to the importance of other mem-
bership-based inequalities. For example, van de Walle and Gunewardena
(2001) argue that market failures entail that ethnic identity influences living
standards in Vietnam independently of observable household characteristics,
and in ways that are suggestive of a self-reinforcing mechanism that perpet-
uates ethnic inequalities. Again, market failures appear to play a crucial role.

Many of the arguments cited above relate more directly to wealth inequality than to income inequality. For example, the theoretical arguments
based on credit market failures point to the importance of asset inequality,
not income inequality per se. For data reasons, much of the empirical evidence has related to income inequality rather than asset inequality. However,
the studies that have used wealth data have found evidence of adverse effects
of asset inequality on growth; examples are Birdsall and Londono (1997) and
Deininger and Olinto (2000)—both using cross-country data—and Ravallion (1998), using subnational (county-level) data for China. Before turning
to the implications of all this for targeted transfers, another strand of recent
literature needs to be brought into the picture. This concerns the possibility
that uninsured risk can inhibit growth and poverty reduction in the longer
term.

REVISITING THE INSURANCE-EFFICIENCY TRADE-OFF

By one view, publicly provided insurance encourages longer-term behaviors
that promote continuing poverty. The classic example is a generous unemployment benefit system, which is thought by some observers to discourage
personal efforts to find work. Similarly, public provision of old-age pensions
might discourage savings. These are examples of how moral hazard generates
an insurance-efficiency trade-off.

There are reasons to question the insurance-efficiency trade-off in poor
countries. If there were such an aggregate trade-off, then one would expect

poor people to be relatively well insured. That is plainly not the case. From what we know, it is difficult to argue that poor people in the world are typically *overinsured* from the point of view of making them less poor. Indeed, there is now a body of microempirical work demonstrating a high exposure to uninsured risk, notably in rural areas.[9] There is supportive evidence for the view that the poor are more vulnerable to uninsured risk from the results of Jalan and Ravallion (1999) on the sensitivity of household consumption in rural southwest China to income shocks.

Recent literature has also pointed to various ways that uninsured risk can be a cause of *chronic* poverty. One argument postulates threshold effects in consumption giving rise to a "dynamic poverty trap." To see what this means in the context of a simple example, consider a worker who cannot borrow or save, and derives income solely from labor. The worker's productivity depends on past consumption, and only if consumption is above some critical level is it possible to be productive and hence earn any income. Beyond this threshold, diminishing returns set in, meaning that extra current consumption raises future productivity but at a declining rate as consumption rises. In this type of model, permanent destitution can stem from transient shocks and people can escape even extreme poverty with only temporary income support. These features arise from the possibility of multiple solutions for the income or wealth of a given family. There can be a high-income solution and a low-income one, both of which are stable, in that income will return to its initial value after a transient shock. Between these two solutions, one can expect to find an unstable third solution, below which incomes tend to fall toward the low-income solution, while above which they rise to the high-income solution. Thus, a household at the high-income solution that suffers a sufficiently large negative shock will see its income decline until it reaches the lowest income. And a household at the low-income solution will be able to escape poverty after even a transient income gain—but only if that gain is large enough to get past the unstable solution.

This is an example of a "dynamic poverty trap." It implies that there will be large long-term benefits from institutions and policies that protect people from transient shocks or provide temporary support for the poorest. Likewise, the absence of an effective safety net emerges as a cause of long-term poverty.

Are such arguments plausible? The very existence of a positive BMR means that a consumption threshold must exist, which is one requirement for the dynamic poverty trap described above, whereby uninsured risk can create longer-term poverty. Unless a person can initially assure that BMR is reached, there can be no productive activity of any sort. A threshold effect can also stem from the fact that in almost all societies one must be housed and adequately clothed if one is to participate in most social activity, including work. Low consumption creates social exclusion. For example, advocates of a proposed (untargeted) transfer program in South Africa claimed that the grant would be productive by allowing people to travel to find work and to buy clothes to wear to job interviews (*Washington Post Foreign Service*, July 9, 2002).

However, the case for intervention rests on believing that the threshold effect exists in the absence of intervention. That is less clear. There will be a high return to private coinsurance when there is a threshold effect. One can readily grant that (market or quasi-market) credit and risk-sharing arrangements do not work perfectly, given the usual problems of asymmetric information. Yet they may still work well enough to make dynamic poverty traps a rarity.

The panel data studies by Lokshin and Ravallion (2004) and Jalan and Ravallion (2004) discussed above also tested for the existence of dynamic poverty traps. Household income or consumption was allowed to be a nonlinear function of its own lagged value with corrections for measurement errors and hidden sources of heterogeneity in the data. On calibrating the model to a six-year, household-level set of panel data (in which the same households are tracked over time) for rural southwest China, Jalan and Ravallion (2004) did not find evidence of threshold effects in the dynamics (though they did find nonlinearity, as discussed above).[10] The same is true of Lokshin and Ravallion (2004), using data for Russia and Hungary. The results for all three countries suggest that people tend to bounce back from transient shocks. However, all three studies found that the speed of income adjustment to a shock is lower for the long-term poor (those with low steady-state income).[11] This can generate a process of income dynamics that might look like a poverty trap but is not.

If one takes it as given that without a (formal or informal) safety net there will be a low-level threshold effect on productivity, then these results suggest the existence of a roughly binding consumption floor achieved by existing (public and private) safety nets. Of course, that can still leave considerable uninsured risk, which is found to be the case in the same settings.[12] And the dynamics might be quite different for highly covariate risk, since the informal safety net arrangements may then break down, leaving the threshold exposed.

Other evidence of longer-term costs of uninsured risk can be found in Dercon's (2003) study using panel data for rural Ethiopia. Dercon finds that rainfall shocks have lasting impacts on consumption—well beyond the time period of the shock. In Dercon's model specification, there is only one (household-specific) long-run solution for consumption, so this is not strictly a test for dynamic poverty traps. However, his empirical results are strongly suggestive that the long-run consumption depends on the history of past uninsured shocks in this setting.

Uninsured risk can also perpetuate poverty via production and portfolio choices. A number of empirical studies have found costly behavioral responses to income risk in poor rural economies.[13] Outmoded agricultural technologies can persist because they are less risky (see, for example, Morduch 1995). Risk can induce poor credit-constrained households to hold high levels of relatively unproductive liquid wealth. If borrowing is not an option when there is a sudden drop in income, then liquid wealth will be needed to protect consumption. For example, Indian farmers have been found to hold livestock as a precaution against risk even though more productive investment opportunities were available (Rosenzweig and Wolpin 1993).

Whether it is the poor who incur the largest costs of uninsured risk is not as obvious as is often claimed by casual observers. Jalan and Ravallion (2001) tested for portfolio and other behavioral responses to idiosyncratic risk in the same rural areas of southwest China. They confirmed other findings that wealth is held in unproductive liquid forms to protect against idiosyncratic income risk. However, consistent with expectations from their theoretical model, they found that neither the poorest quintile nor the richest appears to hold liquid wealth because of income risk; it is the middle-income groups that do so. It appears that the rich in this setting do not need to hold precautionary liquid wealth, and the poor cannot afford to do so.

Other potentially costly responses to risk include adverse effects on human capital. Jacoby and Skoufias (1997) find seasonal effects of income risk on schooling in semiarid areas of India. But here, too, the evidence is mixed. Jalan and Ravallion (2001) find in their data for rural China that schooling is quite well protected from the income and health risks faced by the household. Schady (2002) finds that schooling increased during Peru's macroeconomic crisis of 1988–1992, which he attributes to lower forgone income from attending school during the crisis.

Some of the evidence suggests large long-term costs to the poor from uninsured risk, but some does not. Of course, there are still short-term welfare costs of uninsured risks facing poor people; a case for insurance remains even if risk is not a cause of longer-term poverty.

EFFICIENT REDISTRIBUTION THROUGH TARGETED TRANSFERS

Efficient redistributions help alleviate the constraints arising from the market imperfections discussed above. This has a number of implications for policy. One implication is that the common focus on the direct and static incidence of transfers—how much goes directly to the poor versus the nonpoor—may miss important dynamic benefits from such policies, as argued by Holzmann (1990). Another implication is that efficient redistributions may require more attention to asset redistribution rather than income redistribution. A case for switching the focus to asset redistribution is made by Bowles and Gintis (1996), who argue that asset redistribution should take priority when the concern is with efficiency and growth, while state-contingent income redistributions would be more relevant for social insurance.

Finding that inequality and uninsured risk are harmful to growth does not imply that any policy to reduce inequality or risk will enhance growth and reduce poverty. Even accepting that high inequality in the command over key productive assets, such as land, reduces aggregate output, it does not follow that redistributive land reforms will be efficient (as well as equitable) in the presence of other markets or governmental failures that restrict the access of the beneficiaries to credit and new technologies (see, for example, Binswanger et al. 1995). Indeed, the impact on aggregate output could well be negative if the redistributive policy intervention is at the expense of other factors that matter to growth. Reducing inequality by adding further distortions to external trade or the domestic economy will have ambiguous effects. By the same token, the best role for policy may not be to reduce current inequality, but rather to attenuate its adverse impacts, such as by alleviating the market failures that make inequality matter.

These observations call for caution in drawing lessons for redistributive policy from the existing theory and evidence on the efficiency costs of inequality. However, as this section will argue, this new literature does hold some insights for policy. The following discussion will not try to identify the best programs in the abstract, which is probably futile; recent evidence on the heterogeneity in the performance of the same program across different settings, and the lack of heterogeneity in the performance of different programs in the same setting, points to the importance of *context* and the weak power of generalizations about what works and what does not.[14] However, there is scope for generalizations about the principles for guiding the design of effective interventions in specific settings.

Objectives and Constraints

Poverty reduction is typically seen to be the objective of targeted transfers in poor countries. "Poverty" is typically defined as the inability to afford specific consumption needs in a given society. There is a large literature on how this can be measured (for an overview, see Ravallion 1994). The present discussion will focus on some key issues that arise in the context of targeted transfers.

Firstly, aggregate poverty is taken to be a population-weighted aggregate of individual poverty levels. Group memberships may still be causally relevant to poverty and figure prominently in targeted policies (as discussed further below), but only insofar as those groups have high concentrations of individual poverty or group memberships influence other constraints on policy-making, such as political economy constraints (whereby certain groups have disproportionate influence). Such "individualism" in defining the welfare objectives of policy is standard practice, though it can be questioned (see, for example, Kanbur 2000). Further research is called for on how identity influences the prospects of escaping poverty.

Second, while targeting is a potential instrument for enhancing program impact on poverty, the most targeted program need not be the one with the greatest impact on poverty (van de Walle 1998). This can happen when finer targeting undermines political support for the required taxation (Besley and Kanbur 1993; Gelbach and Pritchett 1997; De Donder and Hindriks 1998) or when targeting generates deadweight losses (Ravallion and Datt 1995).

Third, there is an issue of how impact on poverty today should be weighed against that in the future. Theories of efficient redistribution point to the importance of reaching those who are locked out of credit and insurance, leading to underinvestment in physical and human capital and, hence, higher future poverty. It is often assumed that this is the same set of people as the currently "poor," but that is questionable. For example, while household poverty is correlated with children's school attendance, there are nonnegligible numbers of poor children at school, and plenty of children from non-poor families not at school.[15] The currently poor need not be the same set of people as those vulnerable to future poverty.

Finally, it should not be forgotten that the scope for efficient redistribution and insurance is constrained by the information available and administrative capabilities for acting on that information. Problems of information and incentives are at the heart of policy design.[16] Informational constraints are particularly relevant in underdeveloped economies. In rural sectors and the urban informal sector, policies such as a progressive income tax are seldom feasible (though of course such policies are themselves second-best responses to information constraints even in rich countries). Means tests pose similar problems.

We now see how the policies found in practice deal with these constraints.

Indicator Targeting

The problems of observing incomes and the incentive effects of means testing have led to various schemes that make transfers according to covariates of poverty, such as living in a poor area, age (both children and the elderly), and landlessness in rural areas. Everyone with the same value of the indicator is treated the same way. Tools exist for finding optimal allocations to minimize a poverty index based on such poverty proxies and for measuring the maximum impact on poverty (Ravallion 1993). Naturally, the more information is available (relaxing the informational constraints), the better indicator targeting works. For example, Elbers et al. (2004) demonstrate that considerably greater impacts on poverty for a given budget are feasible with finer geographic targeting.

Policy makers often seem to have overoptimistic views on how well they can reach the poor by administrative targeting based on readily observable indicators. Here there are some sobering lessons from empirical research. Even using a comprehensive, high-quality survey, one can rarely explain more than half the variance in consumption or income across households. And while household consumption is probably not a random walk, it is difficult to explain more than one tenth of the variance in future changes in consumption by using current information in a panel survey.[17] Add to this the fact that one must base targeting on observations for the whole population—not just a survey sample—and that there will be incentives to distort the data when it is known why it is being collected. One must expect potentially large errors in practice when using indicator targeting to fight transient poverty. This has been confirmed by empirical evidence using panel data to assess how responsive transfers have been to changes in household circumstances (Ravallion et al. 1995; Lokshin and Ravallion 2000; van de Walle 2004).

But it can also be argued that the benefits of indicator targeting are often underestimated. Past work has typically viewed targeting as a static, nonbehavioral problem; for example, location is simply one of the proxies used to indicate poverty. The possibility of poverty traps arising from market failures offers a different perspective, pointing to the potential for dynamic efficiency gains. Targeting poor areas or minority ethnic groups—that would otherwise be locked out of economic opportunities—may well have greater impact than suggested by the role of these characteristics as a purely statistical indicator of poverty would suggest.

The evidence to support that claim is still scant and often inconclusive. Some observers have pointed to evidence that a share of the transfers received by the poor is often saved or invested as indicating that the transfers reduce chronic poverty.[18] However, this could just as well reflect recipients' perceptions that the transfers are transient; there can be saving from a short-term transfer even when it has no impact on long-term income.

Panel data can offer more convincing evidence. A household panel data set collected over six years was used to study the consumption impacts of a large antipoverty program targeted to poor areas in China. It was found that the program raised long-term consumption growth rates, implying quite reasonable rates of return (Jalan and Ravallion 1998b). In another example, Garces et al. (2002) studied panel data spanning twenty-seven years for the United States and found longer-term gains in schooling and earnings from a preschool program targeted to poor families.

Productivity effects have been emphasized in schemes that redistribute between landholding classes. Landless households in rural areas tend to have a high incidence of poverty (in South Asia particularly). Ravallion and Sen (1994) studied the effects of redistribution using transfers between landholding classes in rural Bangladesh, allowing for the higher productivity (output per acre) of smaller holdings. They found that these effects do increase the poverty-reducing impact of land-based targeting, though the extra impact is not large, given that land holding is not by any means a perfect poverty indicator, even in rural Bangladesh.

Specific demographic groups (both children and the elderly) have also been targeted, and here, too, there can be efficiency benefits.[19] For example, South Africa has a pension scheme that gives cash transfers to the elderly; Duflo (2000) finds positive external benefits to child health within recipient families.

Finding that transfers based on indicators of current poverty can bring long-term benefits, given factor market imperfections, does not mean that transfers are the best policy option for this purpose. Policies to increase factor mobility can also have a role. Incentives to attract private capital into poorly endowed areas, and/or encourage labor migration out of them, could well be more poverty-reducing than targeted transfers. There has been very little work on these policy choices, and one often hears overstated claims by advocates. For example, it is far from clear that policies of out-migration from poor areas are highly substitutable with transfers to those areas that can be crucial to fostering out-migration in the longer term, such as by promoting better schooling or making livelihoods less vulnerable to temporary labor shortages.

Securing the efficiency gains from transfers targeted to indicators of poverty will often require complementary public programs or policy reforms. This has often been emphasized in the context of redistributive land reforms, where persistent impediments to access to credit and technologies can severely constrain the efficiency gains (Binswanger et al. 1995; Deininger 2003). Recognition of the need to combine transfers (of specific assets or incomes) with other initiatives to help foster the productivity of the poor has prompted recent interest in a class of conditional transfers to which we now turn.

Conditional Transfers

In the 1990s, a number of new transfer programs emerged that combine indicator targeting, often using community groups, with explicit attempts to enhance capital accumulation by the poor. One class of these programs combines transfers with schooling (and sometimes health care) requirements.[20] An example is Bangladesh's Food for Education (FFE) Program, which relies on community-based targeting of food transfers that aim to create an incentive for reducing the cost to the poor of market failures. FFE was one of the earliest of many school-enrollment subsidy programs now found in both developing and developed countries. Other examples are Progresa in Mexico and Bolsa Escola in Brazil; in these programs, cash transfers are targeted to certain demographic groups in poor areas, conditional on regular school attendance and visits to health centers.

If one were concerned solely with current income gains to participating households, then one would clearly not want to use school attendance requirements, which impose a cost on poor families by inducing them to withdraw children or teenagers from the labor force, thus reducing the (net) income gain to the poor. This type of program is clearly aiming to balance a current poverty-reduction objective against an objective of reducing future poverty. Given the credit market failure, the incentive effect on labor supply of the program (often seen as an adverse outcome of transfers) is now judged to be a benefit—to the extent that a well-targeted transfer allows poor families to keep the children in school rather than sending them to work. Notice, too, that concerns about distribution *within* the household underlie the motivation for such programs; the program's conditionality makes it likely that relatively more of the gains accrue to children.[21]

There is evidence of significant gains from Bangladesh's FFE program in terms of school attendance with only modest forgone income through displaced child labor (Ravallion and Wodon 2000). The program was able to appreciably increase schooling, at modest cost to the current incomes of poor families. Mexico's Progresa program has also been found to increase schooling, though the gains appear to be lower than for FFE (Behrman et al. 2001; Schultz 2001). This is probably because primary schooling rates are higher in Mexico, implying less value added over the (counterfactual) schooling levels than would obtain otherwise. There is evidence that there would have been greater efficiency gains (through higher schooling) from Progresa if the program had concentrated on children less likely to attend school in the absence of the program, notably by focusing on the transition to secondary school (Sadoulet and de Janvry, 2002; Todd and Wolpin, 2003; Attanasio et al., 2004).

Relying on administrative targeting based on poverty indicators naturally constrains performance. Even the best indicators available are far from perfect predictors of poverty at one date, and are typically far worse at predicting changes in welfare ex ante. Administrative inflexibility further constrains the scope for effective insurance by these means. Next we will consider some ways that developing country governments have tried to improve performance at reaching the poor within prevailing informational constraints.

Community-Based Programs

In recent times, community participation in program design and implementation has been a popular means of relieving the informational constraint. The central government delegates authority to presumably better-informed community (governmental or nongovernmental) organizations, while the center retains control over how much money goes to each locality. The main concern has been capture by local elites; the informational advantage of community-based targeting may well be outweighed by an accountability disadvantage. Good evidence on performance is still scant.[22] Reliable generalizations are also likely to be illusive, given that there are good reasons to expect heterogeneity across communities in the impacts of the same program. Relevant sources of heterogeneity identified in the theoretical literature include local asset inequality (Bardhan and Mookerjee 2000; Benabou 2000) and the extent of interlinkage in local social networks (Spagnolo 1999).

In the design of Bangladesh's FFE program, economically backward areas were supposed to be chosen by the center, leaving community groups— exploiting idiosyncratic local information—to select participants within those areas. Galasso and Ravallion (2005) use survey data to assess FFE incidence within and between villages. Targeting performance was measured by the difference between the realized per capita allocation to the poor and the nonpoor. The study found that targeting performance varied greatly between villages. Higher allocations from the center to a village tended to yield better targeting performance, but there was no sign that poorer villages were any better or worse at targeting their poor.[23]

The results also suggest that inequality within villages matters to the relative power of the poor in local decision-making. Galasso and Ravallion

(2005) found that villages more unequal in terms of the distribution of land are worse at targeting the poor—consistent with the view that greater land inequality comes with lower power for the poor in village decision-making. This suggests a mechanism whereby inequality is perpetuated through the local political economy; the more unequal the initial distribution of assets, the better positioned the nonpoor will be to capture the benefits of external efforts to help the poor.

Self-Targeting

The informational constraints on redistributive policies in poor countries have strengthened arguments for using self-targeting mechanisms. The classic case is a workfare program, in which work requirements are imposed on welfare recipients with the aim of creating incentives to encourage participation only by the poor and reducing dependency on the program.[24]

An example is the famous Employment Guarantee Scheme (EGS) in Maharashtra, India. This aims to assure income support in rural areas by providing unskilled manual labor at low wages to anyone who wants it. The scheme is financed domestically, largely from taxes on the relatively well-off segments of Maharashtra's urban populations. The employment guarantee is a novel feature of the EGS, which helps support the insurance function, and also helps empower poor people. In practice, however, most workfare schemes have entailed some rationing of the available work, often in combination with geographic targeting.

Workfare schemes generally have a good record in screening the poor from the nonpoor, and providing effective insurance against both covariate and idiosyncratic shocks.[25] They have provided protection when there is a threat of famine (Drèze and Sen 1989; Ravallion 1997a) or in the wake of a macroeconomic crisis (Jalan and Ravallion 2003 for Argentina; Pritchett et al. 2002 for Indonesia; both in the late 1990s). Design features are crucial, notably that the wage rate is not set too high. For example, Ravallion et al. (1993) provide evidence on how the EGS responds to aggregate shocks, and on how its ability to insure the poor was jeopardized by a sharp increase in the wage rate.

There are other ways to use incentives in program design to assure self-targeting of the poor. For example, the rationing of food or health subsidies by queuing can also be self-targeting (Alderman 1987), as can subsidizing inferior food staples or packaging in ways that are unappealing to the nonpoor.

Self-targeted schemes can face a sharp trade-off between targeting performance (meaning their ability to concentrate benefits on the poor) and net income gains to participants, given that these programs work by deliberately imposing costs on participants. Self-targeting requires that the cost of participation is higher for the nonpoor than the poor (so that it is the poor who tend to participate), but it may not be inconsequential to the poor.

A potentially important cost to workfare participants in developing countries is forgone income. This is unlikely to be zero; the poor can rarely afford to be idle. An estimate for two villages in Maharashtra, India, found that the forgone income from employment on public works schemes was quite low— around one quarter of gross wage earnings; most of the time displaced was in domestic labor, leisure, and unemployment (Datt and Ravallion 1994). By contrast, for a workfare program in Argentina—the Trabajar program—it was estimated that about one half of gross wage earnings was taken up by forgone incomes.[26] In the Trabajar program, the income lost to participating workers was probably compensated by indirect gains to the poor as residents of the neighborhoods in which the work was done, which typically involved the creation and maintenance of valued local infrastructure. Calculation of the cost-effectiveness of this program suggests that it still only costs about $1.00 to $1.50 to transfer $1.00 to the poor, even taking account of the deadweight loss due to costs of participation.[27] However, workfare programs have traditionally underemphasized the potential value to the poor of the assets created, which appear often to benefit mainly the nonpoor or to be of little value to anyone (see, for example, Gaiha 1996, writing about Maharashtra's EGS).

The Trabajar program illustrates the potential for a new wave of workfare programs that emphasize asset creation in poor communities. The program's design gave explicit incentives (through the ex ante project selection process) for targeting the work to poor areas, again compensating for the market failures that help create poor areas in the first place. There is typically much useful work to do in poor neighborhoods—work that probably would not get financed otherwise.

In macroeconomic or agroclimatic crises, it is to be expected that the emphasis will shift to current income gains, away from asset creation—implying, for example, more labor-intensive subprojects on workfare programs (for further discussion, see Ravallion 1999b). However, the appropriate trade-off between the objective of raising current incomes of the poor versus reducing future poverty will never be a straightforward choice.

Sustainability and Political Economy

While theory points to efficiency gains from permanent redistribution, the implications of short-term redistributions are less clear. The insurance gains from targeted transfers also depend on the sustainability of programs across different states of nature, including coverage across groups facing different risks. In these respects the record is mixed. Some programs, such as the EGS, have been sustained over long periods, and appear to have provided effective insurance. This can help assure sustainability, since (given that there is idiosyncratic risk) the potential set of beneficiaries is much larger than the actual set at any one date. It clearly also helps if the nonpoor see benefits from effective social protection, such as in attenuating migration to cities in times of stress in rural areas. However, other designs for targeted transfer schemes have been more short-lived. Sustainability depends on having broad political support, which can be at odds with fine targeting. Thus there may well be a trade-off between sustainability and the extent of redistribution by this means.

Political economy clearly looms large in this area of policy-making. The fact that inequality is inefficiently high need not mean that there will be an effective political response to lower it. Benabou (2000) has demonstrated theoretically that an economy with persistently high inequality, and little effort to reduce it, can coexist with one that is otherwise identical in fundamentals but in which active redistribution keeps inequality low. External agents, including the international financial institutions, may well have an important role in using their allocative choices and dialogues on country policy to promote efficient redistributive policies, particularly in high-inequality countries, where adoption appears less likely. Similarly, there is a role for the central government in promoting efficient redistribution in high-inequality communities.

CONCLUSIONS

Transfers to the poor have often been motivated by inequality or risk aversion with expectations that there will be a trade-off with aggregate output. A body of recent theoretical and empirical work has questioned whether there is such a trade-off. This new research has argued that there can be too much uninsured risk and inequality, when judged solely from the viewpoint of aggregate output. For example, credit market failures can mean that it is the poor who are unable to exploit new economic opportunities; the more poor people, the fewer the opportunities that get exploited, and thus the lower the rate of growth. Persistent concentrations of poverty in poor (natural and man-made) environments can also arise from market failures, given geographic externalities whereby living in a poor area is a cause of poverty.

This body of theory and evidence offers a new perspective on social protection policies in poor countries, suggesting that there is scope for using these policies to compensate for the market failures that help perpetuate poverty, particularly in high-inequality settings. There have been a number of seemingly successful transfer schemes that reflect such an emphasis. However, in drawing implications for future policy there are a number of caveats. Not all the evidence has been supportive of the theories, or suggestive of large potential gains, even when the theory is supported qualitatively by the data. It is also difficult to prejudge the best policy instruments for achieving efficient redistribution. For some purposes of antipoverty policy—"helping those who cannot help themselves"—there is no obvious alternative to targeted transfers, barring unacceptable neglect. But, more generally, it is not clear that targeted transfers dominate other options. These may include direct efforts to make factor markets work better for the poor (such as by fostering new institutions for credit provision, or by better enforcement of property rights), supply-side interventions in schooling and health care, or even untargeted transfers. And the way transfers are financed in practice will clearly matter. In theory there can be potential Pareto improvements from transfers financed out of the subsequent income gains to poor recipients; but finding a feasible means of such cost recovery is another matter.

While acknowledging these caveats, this tour of the new arguments and evidence on efficient redistribution and insurance points to a confident rejection of the generally negative stereotype of this class of interventions that has been around in mainstream development policy discussions for some time. The trade-off against efficiency has probably been exaggerated, and the record on performance is better than some (seemingly widely held) perceptions would suggest. It is time for a pragmatic and open-minded approach to this class of interventions, recognizing the potentially important role they can play but using careful design and evaluation to assure that the potential is realized.

ACKNOWLEDGMENTS For helpful comments, I am grateful to Roland Benabou, Nancy Birdsall, Alain de Janvry, Quy-Toan Do, Francisco Ferreira, Emanuela Galasso, Robert Holzman, Alice Mesnard, Rinku Murgai, Berk Özler, Elisabeth Sadoulet, Dominique van de Walle, and participants at the World Bank, the North-Eastern Universities Development Conference (2002), Williams College, and the Chronic Poverty Research Center, University of Manchester (2003). The support of the World Bank's Social Protection Board is gratefully acknowledged. The views expressed here should not be attributed to the World Bank.

NOTES

1. For example, Smith and Subbarao (2002) give data for low-income countries indicating that the consumption of the poorest decile is generally 30–40% lower than that of the next poorest.

2. Compilations of evidence on targeting performance can be found in Grosh (1995) and Coady et al. (2004). The latter compiles evidence on the targeting performance of over one hundred programs; for the majority, the share of program benefits going to the "poor" exceeded their population share. Of course, the quality of the data and methods varies considerably; the hope is that the differences average to zero.

3. A number of excellent surveys are now available of this literature, notably Aghion et al. (1999); Bardhan et al. (2000); Broadway and Keen (2000); and Kanbur (2000). Specific papers that have fueled this questioning of the aggregate equity-efficiency trade-off include Dasgupta and Ray (1986); Dasgupta (1993); Galor and Zeira (1993); Bowles and Gintis (1996); Benabou (1996, 2002); McGregor (1995); Hoff and Lyon (1995); Hoff (1996); Aghion and Bolton (1997); Aghion et al. (1999); Piketty (1997); and Bardhan et al. (2000).

4. Policy-oriented discussions can be found in Holzmann and Jorgensen (1999); Bourguignon (2000); World Bank (2000, 2001); and Smith and Subbarao (2002), among others.

5. This can be thought of as an example of a more general class of models in which memberships influence socioeconomic outcomes (Durlauf 2001).

6. Papers reporting this result include Persson and Tabellini (1994); Alesina and

Rodrik (1994); Birdsall et al. (1995); Birdsall and Londono (1997); Clarke (1995); Perotti (1996); Deininger and Squire (1998); Deininger and Olinto (2000); and Knowles (2001). Evidence using subnational (provincial) data for China can be found in Ravallion and Chen (2004).

7. For further discussion of the data problems, see Bourguignon (2000) and Kanbur (2000).

8. The dynamic panel data models in these studies were estimated by methods that allowed for the endogeneity of lagged income, latent individual effects, and endogenous attrition.

9. Overviews of the theory and evidence can be found in Deaton (1992) and Besley (1995).

10. Possibly the threshold effect takes longer than six years, though it is difficult to see why a sign of the productivity cost of low initial consumption would not be apparent over this time period.

11. The steeper the slope of the relationship between current income and lagged income, the slower the speed of adjustment to a shock. Concavity of the recursion diagram implies that the speed of adjustment for a given household will be lower when it receives a negative shock than a positive shock. However, here we are concerned with differences in the speed of adjustment between households at different steady-state incomes. In all three countries, the speed of adjustment (evaluated in a neighborhood of the steady-state solution) was found to be slower for households with lower steady-state incomes.

12. See Jalan and Ravallion (1998a) for China, and Lokshin and Ravallion (2000) for Russia.

13. Examples include Paxson (1992); Rosenzweig and Binswanger (1993); Rosenzweig and Wolpin (1993); Alderman (1996); Dercon (1998); and Fafchamps et al. (1998).

14. For an example of the diverse performance of one program in a single country, see Galasso and Ravallion (2005); for an example of how different programs can perform similarly in the same setting, see Pritchett et al. (2002).

15. See, for example, the evidence for Mexico in Sadoulet and de Janvry (2002).

16. Overviews of the arguments and evidence can be found in Besley and Kanbur (1993); Lipton and Ravallion (1995, sec. 6); van de Walle (1998); Kanbur (2000); and Coady et al. (2004).

17. For a direct test of the random walk property (as implied by the permanent income hypothesis under certain conditions), see Bhargava and Ravallion (1993), using panel data from rural India.

18. See, for example, Devereux (2002), using data for transfer programs in Mozambique, Namibia, and Zambia.

19. Here, too, measurement problems loom large. Allowing for scale economies in consumption can readily reverse the common finding that larger households tend to be poorer, based on consumption or income per person (Lanjouw and Ravallion 1995).

20. The term "conditional transfers" is widely used in recent policy-oriented discussions to refer exclusively to such programs. However, this is rather odd usage, given that it would seem that all transfer programs in practice have eligibility conditions of some sort.

21. On the arguments in favor of conditionality requirements, based on their

implications for intrahousehold distribution, see Martinelli and Parker (2003) and Das et al. (2004). Also see McGregor (1995), who provides a theoretical analysis of the policy choice between a pure transfer policy versus schooling plus transfers, suggesting that the latter option is likely to dominate.

22. For excellent surveys of the arguments and evidence on community-based targeting, see Conning and Kevane (1999) and Mansuri and Rao (2004).

23. On the theoretical arguments linking targeting performance to poverty, see Ravallion (1999a).

24. Besley and Coate (1992) provide a formal model of the incentive arguments.

25. See, for example, Ravallion and Datt (1995); Subbarao (1997); Teklu et al. (1999); Jalan and Ravallion (2003); Chirwa et al. (2002); Coady et al.(2004).

26. This is the estimate obtained by Jalan and Ravallion (2003), using matched comparisons of participants and nonparticipants in a single survey. Ravallion et al. (2005) obtained a similar estimate using the "difference-in-difference" on panel data, following up participants after they left the program.

27. These are the author's calculations, using the methods outlined in Ravallion (1999b).

BIBLIOGRAPHY

Aghion, Philippe, and Patrick Bolton. "A Trickle-Down Theory of Growth and Development with Debt Overhang." *Review of Economic Studies* 64 (2) (1997): 151–162.

Aghion, Philippe, Eve Caroli, and Cecilia Garcia-Penalosa. "Inequality and Economic Growth: The Perspectives of the New Growth Theories." *Journal of Economic Literature* 37 (4) (1999): 1615–1660.

Alderman, Harold. "Allocation of Goods Through Non-Price Mechanisms: Evidence on Distribution by Willingness to Wait." *Journal of Development Economics* 25 (1987): 105–124.

Alderman, Harold. "Saving and Economic Shocks in Rural Pakistan." *Journal of Development Economics* 51 (1996): 343–366.

Alderman, Harold, John Hoddinott, and Bill Kinsey. "Long-term Consequences of Early Child Malnutrition." Mimeo, IFPRI and the World Bank, 2002.

Alesina, Alberto, and Dani Rodrik. "Distributive Politics and Economic Growth." *Quarterly Journal of Economics* 108 (1994): 465–490.

Attanasio, Orazio, Costas Meghir, and Ana Santiago. "Education Choices in Mexico: Using a Structural Model and a Randomized Experiment to Evaluate PROGRESA," Working Paper EWP04/04, Centre for the Evaluation of Development Policies, Institute of Fiscal Studies London, 2004.

Banerjee, Abhijit, and Esther Duflo. "Inequality and Growth: What Can the Data Say?" Mimeo, Department of Economics, MIT, 1999.

Banerjee, Abhijit, and Andrew F. Newman. "Risk-Bearing and the Theory of Income Distribution." *Review of Economic Studies* 58 (1991): 211–235.

Banerjee, Abhijit, and Andrew F. Newman. "Occupational Choice and the Process of Development." *Journal of Political Economy* 101 (2) (1993): 274–298.

Banerjee, Abhijit, and Andrew F. Newman. "Poverty, Incentives and Development." *American Economic Review, Papers and Proceedings* 84 (2) (1994): 211–215.

Bardhan, Pranab, Samuel Bowles, and Herbert Gintis. "Wealth Inequality, Wealth Constraints and Economic Performance." In *Handbook of Income Distribution,* Vol.

1. Edited by A. B. Atkinson and F. Bourguignon. Amsterdam: North-Holland, 2000.

Bardhan, Pranab, and Dilip Mookherjee. "Capture and Governance at Local and National Levels." *American Economic Review, Papers and Proceedings* 90 (2) (2000): 135–139.

Barr, Nicholas. "Economic Theory and the Welfare State: A Survey and Interpretation." *Journal of Economic Literature* 30 (1992): 741–803.

Barro, Robert. "Inequality and Growth in a Panel of Countries." *Journal of Economic Growth* 5 (2000): 5–32.

Behrman, Jere, Piyali Sengupta, and Petra Todd. "Progressing through Progresa: An Impact Assessment of a School Subsidy Program." Mimeo, University of Pennsylvania, 2001.

Benabou, Roland. "Inequality and Growth." In *National Bureau of Economic Research Macroeconomics Annual*, edited by Ben Bernanke and Julio Rotemberg, 11–74. Cambridge, Mass.: MIT Press, 1996.

Benabou, Roland. "Unequal Societies: Income Distribution and the Social Contract." *American Economic Review* 90 (1) (2000): 96–129.

Benabou, Roland. "Tax and Education Policy in a Heterogeneous-Agent Economy: What Levels of Redistribution Maximize Growth and Efficiency?" *Econometrica* 70 (2) (2002): 481–517.

Besley, Timothy. "Savings, Credit and Insurance." In *Handbook of Development Economics*. Vol. 3. Edited by Jere Behrman and T. N. Srinivasan. Amsterdam: North-Holland, 1995.

Besley, Timothy, and Steven Coate. "Workfare vs. Welfare: Incentive Arguments for Work Requirements in Poverty Alleviation Programs." *American Economic Review* 82 (1992): 249–261.

Besley, Timothy, and Ravi Kanbur. "Principles of Targeting." In *Including the Poor*, edited by Michael Lipton and Jacques van der Gaag. Washington, D.C.: World Bank, 1993.

Bhargava, Alok. "Modeling the Effects of Nutritional and Socioeconomic Factors on the Growth and Morbidity of Kenyan School Children." *American Journal of Human Biology* 11 (1999): 317–326.

Bhargava, Alok, and Martin Ravallion. "Does Household Consumption Behave as a Martingale? A Test for Rural South India." *Review of Economics and Statistics* 75 (1993): 500–504.

Binswanger, Hans, Klaus Deininger, and Gershon Feder. "Power, Distortions, Revolt and Reform in Agricultural and Land Relations." In *Handbook of Development Economics*. Vol. 3. Edited by Jere Behrman and T. N. Srinivasan. Amsterdam: North-Holland, 1995.

Birdsall, Nancy, and Juan Luis Londono. "Asset Inequality Matters: An Assessment of the World Bank's Approach to Poverty Reduction." *American Economic Review, Papers and Proceedings* 87 (2) (1997): 32–37.

Birdsall, Nancy, David Ross, and Richard Sabot. "Inequality and Growth Reconsidered: Lessons from East Asia." *World Bank Economic Review* 9 (3) (1995): 477–508.

Bourguignon, François. "Can Redistribution Help Growth and Development?" Paper presented at the Annual Bank Conference on Development Economics, Paris, 2000.

Bourguignon, François. "Crime as a Social Cost of Poverty and Inequality: A Review

Focusing on Developing Countries." In *Facets of Globalization*, edited by Shahid Yusuf, Simon Evenett, and Weiping Wu. Washington, D.C.: World Bank, 2001.

Bowles, Samuel, and Herbert Gintis. "Efficient Redistribution: New Rules for Markets, States and Communities." *Politics and Society* 24 (4) (1996): 307–342.

Broadway, Robin, and Michael Keen. "Redistribution." In *Handbook of Income Distribution*. Vol. 1. Edited by Anthony B. Atkinson and François Bourguignon. Amsterdam: North-Holland, 2000.

Chirwa, Ephraim W., Evious K. Zgovu, and Peter M. Mvula. "Participation and Impact of Poverty-Oriented Public Works Projects in Rural Malawi." *Development Policy Review* 20 (2) (2002): 159–176.

Clarke, George R.G. "More Evidence on Income Distribution and Growth." *Journal of Development Economics* 47 (1995): 403–428.

Coady, David, Margaret Grosh, and John Hoddinott. "Targeting Outcomes Redux." *World Bank Research Observer* 19 (1) (2004): 61–86.

Conning, Jonathan, and Michael Kevane. "Community Based Targeting Mechanisms for Social Safety Nets." Mimeo, Williams College, 1999.

Das, Jishnu, Quy-Toan Do, and Berk Özler. "A Welfare Analysis of Conditional Cash Transfer Schemes: Implications for Policy." *World Bank Research Observer* 20 (1) (2005): 57–80.

Dasgupta, Partha. *An Inquiry into Well-Being and Destitution*. Oxford: Clarendon Press, 1993.

Dasgupta, Partha. "Poverty Traps." In *Advances in Economics and Econometrics: Theory and Applications*, edited by David M. Kreps and Kenneth F. Wallis. Cambridge: Cambridge University Press, 1997.

Dasgupta, Partha, and Debraj Ray. "Inequality as a Determinant of Malnutrition and Unemployment." *Economic Journal* 96 (1986): 1011–1034.

Datt, Gaurav, and Martin Ravallion. "Transfer Benefits from Public Works Employment: Evidence from Rural India." *Economic Journal* 104 (1994): 1346–1369.

Deaton, Angus. *Understanding Consumption*. Oxford: Clarendon Press, 1992.

De Donder, Philippe, and Jean Hindriks. "The Political Economy of Targeting." *Public Choice* 95 (1998): 177–200.

Deininger, Klaus. *Land Policies for Growth and Poverty Reduction*. New York: Oxford University Press, 2003.

Deininger, Klaus, and Pedro Olinto. "Asset Distribution, Inequality and Growth." Policy Research Working Paper 2375, World Bank, 2000.

Deininger, Klaus and Lyn Squire. "New Ways of Looking at Old Issues: Inequality and Growth." *Journal of Development Economics* 57 (2) (1998): 259–287.

Demombynes, Gabriel, and Berk Özler. "Inequality, Property Crime, and Violent Crime in South Africa." *Journal of Development Economics* 76(2) (2005): 265–92.

Deolalikar, Anil. "Nutrition and Labor Productivity in Agriculture: Estimates for Rural South India." *Review of Economics and Statistics* 70 (1988): 406–413.

Dercon, Stefan. "Wealth, Risk and Activity Choice: Cattle in Western Tanzania." *Journal of Development Economics* 55 (1998): 1–42.

Dercon, Stefan. "Growth and Shocks: Evidence from Rural Ethiopia." Mimeo, Department of Economics, Oxford University, 2003.

Devereux, Stephen. "Can Social Safety Nets Reduce Chronic Poverty?" *Development Policy Review* 20 (5) (2002): 657–675.

Drèze, Jean, and Amartya Sen. *Hunger and Public Action*. Oxford: Oxford University Press, 1989.

Duflo, Esther. "Grandmother and Granddaughters: The Effects of Old Age Pension on Child Health in South Africa." Working paper, Department of Economics, MIT, 2000.

Durlauf, Steven N. "The Memberships Theory of Poverty: The Role of Group Affiliations in Determining Socioeconomic Outcomes." In *Understanding Poverty*, edited by Sheldon H. Danziger and Robert H. Haveman. New York: Russell Sage Foundation, 2001.

Easterly, William, and Sergio Rebelo. "Fiscal Policy and Economic Growth: An Empirical Investigation." *Journal of Monetary Economics* 32 (3) (1993): 417–458.

Elbers, Chris, Tomoki Fujii, Peter Lanjouw, Berk Özler, and Wesley Yin. "Poverty Alleviation through Geographic Targeting: Does Disaggregation Help?" Policy research working paper, World Bank, 2004.

Economist. "Gordon Hood." *The Economist*, Apr. 5, 2003, pp. 11–34.

Fafchamps, Marcel, Christopher Udry, and Katherine Czukas. "Drought and Saving in West Africa: Are Livestock a Buffer Stock?" *Journal of Development Economics* 55 (1998): 273–306.

Forbes, Kristin J. "A Reassessment of the Relationship between Inequality and Growth." *American Economic Review* 90 (4) (2000): 869–887.

Gaiha, Raghav. "How Dependent Are the Rural Poor on Employment Guarantee Schemes in India?" *Journal of Development Studies* 32 (5) (1996): 669–694.

Galasso, Emanuela, and Martin Ravallion. "Decentralized Targeting of an Anti-Poverty Program." *Journal of Public Economics* 85(April) (2005): 705–727.

Galor, Oded, and Joseph Zeira. "Income Distribution and Macroeconomics." *Review of Economic Studies* 60 (1) (1993): 35–52.

Garces, Eliana, Duncan Thomas, and Janet Currie. "Longer-Term Effects of Head Start." *American Economic Review* 92 (4) (2002): 999–1012.

Gelbach, Jonah, and Lant Pritchett. "Redistribution in a Political Economy: Leakier Can Be Better." Mimeo, World Bank, 1997.

Glewwe, Paul, Hanan Jacoby, and Elizabeth King. "Early Childhood Nutrition and Academic Achievement: A Longitudinal Analysis." *Journal of Public Economics* 81 (3) (2001): 345–368.

Grosh, Margaret. "Toward Quantifying the Trade-Off: Administrative Costs and Incidence in Targeted Programs in Latin America." In *Public Spending and the Poor: Theory and Evidence*, edited by Dominique van de Walle and Kimberly Nead. Baltimore: Johns Hopkins University Press, 1995.

Hoff, Karla. "Market Failures and the Distribution of Wealth: A Perspective from the Economics of Information." *Politics and Society* 24 (4) (1996): 411–432.

Hoff, Karla. "Beyond Rosenstain-Rodan: The Modern Theory of Underdevelopment Traps." Paper presented at the World Bank Annual Bank Conference on Development Economics, World Bank, Washington, D.C., 2000.

Hoff, Karla, and Andrew B. Lyon. "Nonleaky Buckets: Optimal Redistribution Taxation and Agency Costs." *Journal of Public Economics* 58 (1995): 365–390.

Holzmann, Robert. "The Welfare Effects of Public Expenditure Programs Reconsidered." *IMF Staff Papers* 37 (1990): 338–359.

Holzmann, Robert, and Steen L. Jorgensen. "Social Protection as Social Risk Management: Conceptual Underpinnings for the Social Protection Sector Strategy Paper." *Journal of International Development* 11 (1999): 1005–1027.

Jacoby, Hanan G., and Emmanuel Skoufias. "Risk, Financial Markets and Human Capital in a Developing Country." *Review of Economic Studies* 64 (1997): 311–335.

Jalan, Jyotsna, and Martin Ravallion. "Transient Poverty in Post-Reform Rural China." *Journal of Comparative Economics* 26 (1998a): 338–357.

Jalan, Jyotsna, and Martin Ravallion. "Are There Dynamic Gains from a Poor-Area Development Program?" *Journal of Public Economics* 67 (1) (1998b): 65–86.

Jalan, Jyotsna, and Martin Ravallion. "Are the Poor Less Well Insured? Evidence on Vulnerability to Income Risk in Rural China." *Journal of Development Economics* 58 (1) (1999): 61–82.

Jalan, Jyotsna, and Martin Ravallion. "Behavioral Responses to Risk in Rural China." *Journal of Development Economics* 66 (2001): 23–49.

Jalan, Jyotsna, and Martin Ravallion. "Geographic Poverty Traps? A Micro Model of Consumption Growth in Rural China." *Journal of Applied Econometrics* 17 (2002): 329–346.

Jalan, Jyotsna, and Martin Ravallion. "Estimating the Benefit Incidence of an Anti-Poverty Program by Propensity-Score Matching." *Journal of Business and Economic Statistics* 21 (1) (2003): 19–30.

Jalan, Jyotsna, and Martin Ravallion. "Household Income Dynamics in Rural China." In *Insurance Against Poverty*, edited by Stefan Dercon. Oxford: Oxford University Press, 2004.

Kanbur, Ravi. "Income Distribution and Development." In *Handbook of Income Distribution*. Vol. 1. Edited by Anthony B. Atkinson and François Bourguignon. Amsterdam: North-Holland, 2000.

Knowles, Stephen. "Inequality and Economic Growth: The Empirical Relationship Reconsidered in the Light of Comparable Data." Paper prepared for the WIDER Conference on Growth and Poverty. Helsinki, 2001.

Lanjouw, Peter, and Martin Ravallion. "Poverty and Household Size." *Economic Journal* 105 (1995): 1415–1435.

Li, Hongyi, Lyn Squire, and Heng-fu Zou. "Explaining International and Intertemporal Variations in Income Inequality." *Economic Journal* 108 (1998): 26–43.

Li, Hongyi, and Heng-fu Zou. "Income Inequality Is Not Harmful to Growth: Theory and Evidence." *Review of Development Economics* 2 (3) (1998): 318–334.

Lipton, Michael, and Martin Ravallion. "Poverty and Policy." In *Handbook of Development Economics*. Vol. 3. Edited by Jere Behrman and T. N. Srinivasan. Amsterdam: North-Holland, 1995.

Lokshin, Michael, and Martin Ravallion. "Welfare Impacts of Russia's 1998 Financial Crisis and the Response of the Public Safety Net." *Economics of Transition* 8 (2) (2000): 269–295.

Lokshin, Michael, and Martin Ravallion. "Household Income Dynamics in Two Transition Economies." *Studies in Nonlinear Dynamics and Econometrics* 8(3) (2004).

Mansuri, Ghazala, and Vijayendra Rao. "Community-Based and-Driven Development." *World Bank Research Observer* 19 (1) (2004): 1–40.

Martinelli, Cesar, and Susan Parker. "Should Transfers to Poor Families Be Conditional on School Attendance? A Household Bargaining Perspective." *International Economic Review* 44 (2) (2003): 523–544.

McGregor, Pat. "Economic Growth, Inequality, and Poverty: An Analysis of Policy in a Two Period Framework." *Journal of International Development* 7 (4) (1995): 619–635.

Mesnard, Alice, and Martin Ravallion. "The Wealth Effect on New Business Startups in a Developing Economy" *Economica*, forthcoming, 2005.

Morduch, Jonathan. "Income Smoothing and Consumption Smoothing." *Journal of Economic Perspectives* 9 (3) (1995): 103–114.

Paxson, Christina. "Using Weather Variability to Estimate the Response of Savings to Transitory Income in Thailand." *American Economic Review* 82 (1) (1992): 15–33.

Perotti, Roberto. "Growth, Income Distribution and Democracy: What the Data Say." *Journal of Economic Growth* 1 (2) (1996): 149–187.

Persson, Torsten, and Guido Tabellini. "Is Inequality Harmful for Growth?" *American Economic Review* 84 (1994): 600–621.

Piketty, Thomas. "The Dynamics of the Wealth Distribution and the Interest Rate with Credit Rationing." *Review of Economic Studies* 64 (1997): 173–189.

Piketty, Thomas. "Theories of Persistent Inequality and Intergenerational Mobility." In *Handbook of Income Distribution*. Vol.1. Edited by A. B. Atkinson and F. Bourguignon. Amsterdam: North-Holland, 2000.

Pritchett, Lant, Sudarno Sumarto, and Asep Suryahadi. "Targeted Programs in an Economic Crisis: Empirical Findings from Indonesia's Experience." Mimeo, Kennedy School, Harvard University, 2002.

Ravallion, Martin. "Does Undernutrition Respond to Incomes and Prices? Dominance Tests for Indonesia." *World Bank Economic Review* 6 (1) (1992): 109–124.

Ravallion, Martin. "Poverty Alleviation through Regional Targeting: A Case Study for Indonesia." In *The Economics of Rural Organization: Theory, Practice and Policy*, edited by Karla Hoff, A. Braverman, and Joseph E. Stiglitz. Oxford: Oxford University Press, 1993.

Ravallion, Martin. *Poverty Comparisons*. Chur, Switzerland: Harwood Academic Publishers, 1994.

Ravallion, Martin. "Famines and Economics." *Journal of Economic Literature* 35 (Sept. 1997a): 1205–1242.

Ravallion, Martin. "Can High Inequality Developing Countries Escape Absolute Poverty?" *Economics Letters* 56 (1997b): 51–57.

Ravallion, Martin. "Does Aggregation Hide the Harmful Effects of Inequality on Growth?" *Economics Letters* 61 (1) (1998), 73–77.

Ravallion, Martin. "Are Poorer States Worse at Targeting Their Poor?" *Economics Letters* 65 (1999a): 373–377.

Ravallion, Martin. "Appraising Workfare." *World Bank Research Observer* 14 (1) (1999b): 31–48.

Ravallion, Martin. "Growth, Inequality and Poverty: Looking beyond Averages." *World Development* 29 (11) (2001), 1803–1815.

Ravallion, Martin. "Who Is Protected? On the Incidence of Fiscal Adjustment." *Journal of Policy Reform* 7(2) (2004a): 109–22.

Ravallion, Martin. "Externalities in Rural Development: Evidence for China." In *Spatial Inequality and Development*. Edited by Ravi Kanbur and Anthony Venables. Oxford: Oxford University Press, 2005.

Ravallion, Martin, and Shaohua Chen. "China's (Uneven) Progress against Poverty." *Journal of Development Economics*, forthcoming, 2005.

Ravallion, Martin, and Gaurav Datt. "Is Targeting through a Work Requirement Efficient?" In *Public Spending and the Poor: Theory and Evidence*, edited by Dominique van de Walle and Kimberly Nead. Baltimore: Johns Hopkins University Press, 1995.

Ravallion, Martin, Gaurav Datt, and Shubhum Chaudhuri. "Does Maharashtra's Employment Guarantee Scheme Guarantee Employment? Effects of the 1988 Wage Increase." *Economic Development and Cultural Change* 41 (1993): 251–275.

Ravallion, Martin, Emanela Galasso, Teodoro Lazo, and Ernesto Philipp. "Do Workfare Participants Recover Quickly from Retrenchment?" *Journal of Human Resources* 40 (2005): 208–230.

Ravallion, Martin, and Binayak Sen. "Impacts on Rural Poverty of Land-Based Targeting: Further Results for Bangladesh." *World Development* 22 (6) (1994): 823–838.

Ravallion, Martin, Dominique van de Walle, and Madhur Gaurtam. "Testing a Social Safety Net." *Journal of Public Economics* 57 (2) (1995): 175–199.

Ravallion, Martin, and Quentin Wodon. "Does Child Labor Displace Schooling? Evidence on Behavioral Responses to an Enrollment Subsidy." *Economic Journal* 110 (2000): C158–C176.

Rosenzweig, Mark R., and Hans Binswanger. "Wealth, Weather Risk and the Composition and Profitability of Agricultural Investments." *Economic Journal* 103 (1993): 56–78.

Rosenzweig, Mark R., and Kenneth I. Wolpin. "Credit Market Constraints, Consumption Smoothing, and the Accumulation of Durable Production Assets in Low-income Countries: Investments in Bullocks in India." *Journal of Political Economy* 101 (1993): 223–245.

Sadoulet, Elisabeth, and Alain de Janvry. "Alternative Targeting and Calibration Schemes for Educational Grants Programs: Lessons from PROGRESA." Mimeo, University of California, Berkeley, 2002.

Schady, Norbert R. "The (Positive) Effect of Macroeconomic Crisis on the Schooling and Employment Decisions of Children in a Middle-Income Country." Policy Research Working Paper 2762, World Bank, 2002.

Schultz, T. Paul. "School Subsidies for the Poor: Evaluating the Mexican Progresa Program." Mimeo, Yale University, 2001.

Smith, James, and Kalanidhi Subbarao. "What Role for Safety Net Transfers in Very Low Income Countries?" In *Social Safety Net Primer*. Washington, D.C.: World Bank, 2002.

Spagnolo, Giancarlo. "Social Relations and Cooperation in Organizations." *Journal of Economic Behavior and Organization* 38 (1) (1999): 1–25.

Strauss, John. "Does Better Nutrition Raise Farm Productivity?" *Journal of Political Economy* 94 (1986): 297–320.

Subbarao, K. "Public Works as an Anti-Poverty Program: An Overview of Cross-Country Experience." *American Journal of Agricultural Economics* 79 (2) (1997): 678–683.

Teklu, T., and S. Asefa. "Who Participates in Labor-Intensive Public Works in Sub-Saharan Africa? Evidence from Rural Botswana and Kenya." *World Development* 27 (2) (1999): 431–438.

Todd, Petra, and Kenneth Wolpin. "Using a Social Experiment to Validate a Dynamic Behavioral Model of Child Schooling and Fertility: Assessing the Impact of a School Subsidy Program in Mexico," Penn Institute for Economic Research Working Paper 03–022, Department of Economics, University of Pennsylvania, 2002.

Van de Walle, Dominique. "Targeting Revisited." *World Bank Research Observer* 13 (2) (1998): 231–248.

Van de Walle, Dominique. "Testing Vietnam's Safety Net." *Journal of Comparative Economics* 32(4) (2004): 661–79.

Van de Walle, Dominique, and Dileni Gunewardena. "Sources of Ethnic Inequality in Vietnam." *Journal of Development Economics* 65 (2001): 177–207.

World Bank. *World Development Report: Attacking Poverty.* New York: Oxford University Press, 2000.

World Bank. *Social Protection Sector Strategy: From Safety Nets to Springboard.* Washington, D.C.: World Bank, 2001.

15

Poverty Persistence and Design of Antipoverty Policies

Dilip Mookherjee

The experience of teaching the section on poverty in a public economics or development economics course is usually quite a letdown. After admitting the great importance of the topic, the typical course starts by devoting a substantial amount of discussion to different ways of measuring poverty. This is followed by a review of statistical estimates of poverty. Finally some policy issues are discussed: the scope and coverage of safety nets, whether transfers should be cash or in-kind, targeting and problems of work disincentives. This reflects not just the typical textbook treatment but also most existing research on poverty by economists.[1] Conspicuous by its absence is a coherent analysis of what causes poverty in the first place, its implications for the functioning of the economy, and the persistence of poverty into the future. The key questions seem never to be posed. What are the mechanisms by which people get trapped in chronic, long-term poverty? What kinds of policies might affect the nature of dynamics in and out of poverty? The discussions of measurement and policy seem to operate in a theoretical vacuum, with no emphasis on understanding mechanisms of causation. They tend to take as given the current distribution of assets and capabilities and figure out how to measure the extent of deprivation (in terms of consumption or income outcomes) and how to relieve it in the short run, ignoring possible implications for the future evolution of poverty.

Whatever little analytical content there is, concerns discussions of work disincentive effects and targeting in the design of antipoverty policies. The underlying analytical framework is a Mirrlees (1971) optimal income tax model. Each agent in the economy is characterized by a given income earning capability, and selects a work effort. The government can monitor only achieved incomes, which depend on the conjunction of ability and effort. Low-ability individuals would hardly be able to earn any income despite the application of effort, and thus fall into poverty (defined by some income threshold). An antipoverty policy would provide income support for these households, financed by taxes on higher-ability households. By their very nature, the benefits provided must be phased out as household incomes rise and cross the threshold, thereby creating a work disincentive. The more comprehensive the coverage at the bottom end, the higher the taxes needed and the steeper the benefit phaseout must be, weakening incentives of the poor to raise their incomes and escape poverty on their own. This is the fundamental trade-off, the resolution of which depends on labor supply elasticity, the distribution of abilities, and societal inequality aversion. Mirrlees's own calculations, based on British data, suggested that a substantial part of the population may be induced not to work at all in the optimal policy, even with relatively low inequality aversion.

Whatever support is provided to the poor, this framework suggests, should be in the form of cash rather than in-kind transfers because cost-effective design of an antipoverty policy entails raising the utilities of the poor as far as possible at given fiscal cost. Hence, given the assumption of consumer sovereignty—whereby poor households would be the best judges of how to spend money to enhance their well-being—giving them the cash equivalent of any in-kind-bundle would raise their welfare. By reducing the extent of paternalism, it would simultaneously enhance their independence and self-respect. Endorsements of the negative income tax from economists as diverse as Friedman and Tobin have additionally been based on the need to rationalize the overall effect of multiple, uncoordinated in-kind transfer programs; minimize resulting work disincentives; and reduce the humiliating dependence of the poor on a large welfare bureaucracy. Recent proposals for welfare reform in some developing countries (such as Mexico) are motivated by similar concerns. Proposals for "basic income" in Europe go further and seek to remove any means-tested element from the program.[2]

Yet this approach encounters significant objections from noneconomists and popular opinion, particularly in the United States, precisely over the question of conditionality of transfers. Lynn (1980) provides a detailed account of the political difficulties encountered in the efforts to introduce a negative income tax in the United States by Caspar Weinberger, secretary of health, education, and welfare in the second Nixon administration. The public concern about lack of a work requirement for welfare recipients snowballed subsequently, and formed a very significant impetus for the 1996 Welfare Reform Act during the Clinton administration. Issues of welfare dependency fostered by the welfare state have surfaced frequently in Europe as well, though public opinion there has been far more favorable to the idea of a significant segment of the population permanently on the welfare rolls.

Philosophical differences among economists about the desirability of cash versus in-kind transfers have also arisen. Thurow (1974) presented some of the arguments against cash transfers that are voiced when we depart from some of the standard assumptions. If the purpose of an antipoverty system is to respond to an externality arising from social altruism, cost-effective design depends on the precise nature of such altruism: whether it is based on consumption of particular goods and services constituting basic needs of the poor, rather than on their own sense of well-being. Additional arguments for in-kind transfers are based on the notion of universal rights to satisfaction of basic needs and acquisition of fundamental capabilities as a form of positive freedom (argued also by Sen 1984, 1985). Other arguments regarding in-kind transfers are based on a critique of consumer sovereignty, alleging limited ability of poor, uneducated households to manage their finances and make appropriate decisions on behalf of their children.

In this essay I will argue that economists have ignored a crucial dimension of poverty: its intrinsically dynamic characteristic of being locked into a low-level trap of asset (or capability) deprivation, resulting in exclusion from social and economic life on a par with the rest of society. Long-term poverty is fundamentally self-perpetuating. Hence poverty alleviation in the long run must address incentives for the poor to acquire capabilities and assets that will enable them (or their children) to escape poverty in the future. In the Mirrlees model, for instance, the income-earning capability of every household is exogenously given—hence the root causes of current poverty are not addressed. A dynamic extension of this framework would be needed to include investment decisions by households, which would affect the evolution of their future abilities. I will argue that such a framework more directly addresses some of the general public concerns concerning the tendency of comprehensive welfare systems to breed long-term dependence. At the same time, the argument for superiority of cash over in-kind transfers ceases to be valid, even within the conventional utilitarian framework where consumer "rationality" is not questioned.

IMPORTANT ATTRIBUTES OF POVERTY

One first needs to distinguish between antipoverty policy and policies of social insurance. The latter involve providing shelter to those suffering a temporary adverse shock in their earnings or needs. Poverty involves deprivation of crucial assets and capabilities, the debilitating effect of which is hardly temporary. The conceptual separation is important, despite the statistical difficulties of disentangling the two from observed income profiles. Alleviating poverty, from this point of view, requires a strategy of encouraging long-term investments in assets by those currently deprived of such assets, whereas social insurance involves buffering temporary shocks suffered by those both with and without assets.[3]

It is also important to conceptually separate poverty from inequality. One view of poverty—based especially on notions of relative deprivation—is that it simply represents the bottom tail of the income distribution, and thus is subsumed within the general notion of inequality. While I think there is some merit to viewing deprivation in relative terms, I would phrase this dimension in more functional terms. I find it more appropriate to view poverty as failure to acquire a basic minimum set of capabilities that excludes people from participating in social and economic activity in some "normal" manner on par with the rest of society. These capabilities include nutrition, education, clothing, and housing needs, which are preconditions for participating in labor and credit markets, and functioning as a social and political citizen.

This perspective lays emphasis on two key dimensions that are linked: poverty as asset deprivation resulting in exclusion and poverty as a self-perpetuating phenomenon. Thinking about poverty as a self-perpetuating phenomenon is almost definitional if one has a long-term perspective: if some households currently lack certain assets but come to acquire them within a reasonably short span of time, they would be only temporarily poor. The real concern is with those who are unlikely to acquire requisite assets within a reasonable time frame. This is a matter of special concern because it entails not just low levels of current income and consumption, but also an inability to function on par with the rest of society. Their current exclusion may in turn be a key cause of the perpetuation of their deprivation in the future, because all their current resources are consumed in the act of survival and they have no energy, knowledge, or capital available to build on. The entrapment goes hand in hand with vulnerability to adverse shocks, despair, and lack of hope. At the same time there is a social loss from their exclusion: society is denied the benefits that would flow from their participation. For instance, much of the energy and drive behind processes of growth in cities in both developing and developed countries stem from the integration efforts of immigrants who have recently arrived from countries where they had been trapped in poverty.[4]

We now have a variety of economic models that help us understand the phenomenon of exclusion. Efficiency wage models explain how undernourishment may lead to exclusion from even the most unskilled labor markets. Models of moral hazard and costly enforcement explain how the poor may be excluded from credit markets. With few exceptions, these models are mainly static, explaining exclusion as a result of current asset deprivation. There are a few explorations of their dynamic implications, starting with the well-known work of Galor and Zeira (1993) and Banerjee and Newman (1993).[5] This early literature showed how self-perpetuation of asset deprivation could result from the existence of indivisible investment thresholds, allied with mechanical behavior rules concerning the fraction of current income devoted to asset accumulation.

The more recent literature on poverty dynamics examines a wider range of settings and possible self-perpetuating mechanisms.[6] Incorporating strategic saving–investment choices by households is important, since this is central to understanding economic incentives to escape poverty. For instance, one frequently observes the poor responding to employment opportunities in distant locations by embarking on migrations that are both costly and risky.

One set of models focuses on asset dynamics of each household in isolation from the rest of society (going back to the earlier literature on optimal growth, such as Dechert and Nishimura 1983 or Majumdar and Mitra 1982), seeking possible sources of low-level poverty traps. Many of these models are based on indivisibilities inherent in the nature of various investments, such as substantial costs for acquiring a college degree or starting a new business. The empirical significance of these indivisibilities is a matter of debate, though relatively little systematic empirical work has been devoted to it. McKenzie and Woodruff (2002), for instance, do not find significant evidence for such indivisibilities for Mexican entrepreneurs. In most instances of capital accumulation—whether human capital or entrepreneurial capital—it is possible to build up asset stocks little by little.

This motivates explorations of barriers to investment for the poor that arise from other sources, such as allocation of bargaining power (as in Mookherjee and Ray 2002) or processes of economic and social interaction across agents. The latter include dependence of investment returns on market prices (Matsuyama 2000, 2002; Mookherjee and Ray 2003), neighborhood externalities in schooling or investment (Benabou 1996a, 1996b; Durlauf 1996), fertility (Kremer and Chen 1999; Moav 2001), and dependence on environmental resources (Dasgupta 1997). An even broader form of social interaction and history dependence can be embodied in political processes, wherein anti-poor government policies result from lack of political participation of the poor (e.g., in historical explanations of effects of colonialism on development, as in Acemoglu et al. 2001; Engerman et al. 1999; or Galor and Moav 2004).

With the theory of poverty dynamics in its relative infancy, it is not surprising that empirical studies are few and far between. The problem is aggravated by lack of suitable long-range longitudinal panels of income and asset dynamics. The paucity is particularly acute in developing countries. Estimating the pattern of returns to long-term investments in assets and how poor households react to them is hard enough; even harder is identifying externalities or the impact of policies on these patterns. Yet understanding these dynamic processes is central to understanding the fundamental causes of long-term poverty.[7]

REVISITING WELFARE POLICY DESIGN ISSUES

A dynamic perspective is likely to yield quite different implications for policy. This is exemplified by Ghatak et al. (2001), who examine a two-period model with credit market imperfections. In a static setting the existence of moral hazard and enforcement problems with loan repayments may cause talented poor people to be excluded from the credit market, with obvious losses of productive efficiency. Financial liberalization or public supply of subsidized credit to poor households may therefore enhance efficiency in a static setting. In a dynamic setting, Ghatak et al. point out, relieving credit market imperfections may affect incentives for poor households to save while they are young. For part of the incentive of young households to save arises from the very existence of credit market imperfections: savings augment their ability to self-finance and expand access to future credit. This motive applies an important pressure for upward mobility. Ghatak et al. show that the static gains from reducing credit market imperfections (expanded credit access among older entrepreneurs) may be offset by the reduced incentive for upward mobility among the young.

In similar vein, static welfare gains from a more comprehensive welfare system may be offset by reduced incentives for the young to accumulate assets and escape dependence on the welfare system later in their lifetimes or for their children. Checchi et al. (1999) compare mobility patterns between Italy and the United States, and find greater upward mobility in the United States despite more uniform and equal provision of education in Italy. They explain this apparent paradox by the stronger incentives for American parents to educate their children that results from a more differentiated and less equitable provision of educational opportunity. Higher education is more attractive in the United States because parents know that if their investment in their children's education is successful, it will allow their children to invest more in their own children in turn (i.e., in the parents' grandchildren). By contrast, in the Italian public system educational investments are centrally determined, independent of parental income.

This trade-off between short-run and long-run poverty may also motivate a replacement of cash by in-kind transfers to the poor. Let me illustrate this in the context of the model of educational investments with missing credit markets, based on Ljungqvist (1993), Maoz and Moav (1999), and Mookherjee and Ray (2003). Suppose there are two occupations: skilled and unskilled. To be skilled, one's parents must have invested in an education that costs a fixed amount. Educational loan markets are absent because parents cannot take loans on their children's behalf. Hence educational investments must come at the expense of parental consumption. Lowering consumption standards of parents causes the same investment to involve a larger sacrifice, so the poorer the parents, the more difficult it is for them to send their children to school. Parents are motivated to undertake these investments by altruism toward their children: they care about their own consumption as well as the future prospects of their children. To keep matters simple, abstract from any uncertainty with regard to ability or incomes. The wages of the skilled and the unskilled in any given generation then depend only on the proportion of skilled individuals among adults of that generation. Suppose also that all households have perfect foresight regarding the future sequence of wages in the economy.

Clearly, an increase in the proportion of skilled individuals in the economy will cause the unskilled wage to rise and the skilled wage to fall, leading to a reduction in wage inequality. Both occupations are essential to production activities in this economy: if there are too few individuals in any given occupation, then the wages of that occupation become arbitrarily high. To provide some parents in the economy with the incentive to educate their children, there must be a sufficient wage premium for the skilled occupation relative to the unskilled one. Hence skilled individuals must earn higher incomes than unskilled at every date. Since investment in children's education comes at the expense of parental consumption, which is subject to increasing marginal sacrifice, skilled parents will have a greater incentive to educate their children than unskilled parents.

In the absence of any uncertain shocks to technology, preferences, or earnings, a steady state in this economy will involve a stationary skill proportion, in which there is zero mobility: only the children of skilled parents will be educated. This is due to the capital market imperfection: the utility sacrifice for skilled parents in educating their child is lower because they must finance it at the expense of their own consumption out of their own incomes. Since skilled parents have greater incentives to invest than unskilled parents, for the economy to reproduce its skill ratio over time, it must be the case that all skilled parents (and no unskilled parents) invest in their children's education. Of course this extreme lack of mobility arises from the absence of any random shocks to children's abilities or parents' incomes. But it helps to clarify the argument to abstract from such sources of mobility.

Such an economy is characterized by many possible long-run equilibria (or steady states), with historical endowment of the economy determining which equilibrium outcome is actually realized. To illustrate this, consider an economy that started historically with a small fraction of skilled households. Then it would historically have been characterized by greater inequality of wages between the skilled and unskilled. The greater poverty of the unskilled would then have limited their ability to invest in the education of their children. On the other hand, the benefits of education—the satisfaction unskilled parents would derive from the prospect of their children escaping poverty—would have been greater. It is entirely possible that the former outweighed the latter, in which case unskilled households would not invest in their children. The low skill ratio in the economy and the high inequality would then be perpetuated, and so would the poverty of the unskilled. Children of unskilled parents would remain unskilled persistently, with no prospect of escape.

Consider now a negative income tax or a means-tested cash transfer program, which awards a cash subsidy to all those below the poverty line (i.e., the unskilled), funded by a tax on those above the poverty line (i.e., the skilled). Assume the subsidy is not large enough to reduce the net after-tax income of the skilled below that of the unskilled. The requirement of fiscal sustainability actually requires this to be true: since the skilled always have the option of working in an unskilled occupation, no one would work in a skilled occupation otherwise. Subject to this condition (besides the assumption that everyone works, the only issue is in which occupation), in this world there is no work disincentive effect operating at the margin. All the relevant incentive effects are dynamic, pertaining to educational investments.

Consider the effects of the negative income tax program on educational incentives. By expanding the disposable income of the poor, the welfare system lowers the sacrifice entailed in educating their children. This enhances incentives for education and upward mobility among the poor. On the other hand, it also reduces the benefit parents perceive their children will obtain from becoming skilled, for a combination of two reasons. An educated child will have to pay the taxes that fund the welfare system, while an uneducated one will receive payments from the system. The very same safety net that protects currently poor parents then reduces their incentive to invest in the ability of their children to escape poverty, a perverse welfare dependence effect.

The overall impact of all these different effects on investment incentives of parents is, then, ambiguous. It is not hard to construct examples where the welfare dependence effect dominates. It is thus entirely possible that the policy expands the long-run poverty rate and lowers per capita income.

While this may be viewed simply as a dynamic counterpart of the work disincentive effect in the Mirrlees model, there is one important distinction. Suppose we replace the cash transfers to the poor with a universal public education subsidy (i.e., the transfer is paid only to parents who educate their children). In contrast to the unconditional cash system, the conditional transfer always causes the eventual (steady-state) poverty head count rate to fall and, consequently, long-run per capita income to rise.

The reason is simple. In the long run, only skilled parents educate their children: hence the requirement of fiscal balance implies that they end up financing the cost of their own education subsidy. The benefit of educating one's child is now exactly the same as in the absence of a welfare system, since the after-tax incomes of both skilled and unskilled households are left unchanged. In particular, it does not give rise to the unfortunate welfare dependence effect induced by the negative income tax. On the other hand, it becomes less costly for unskilled parents to educate their children, owing to the education subsidy. This causes greater upward mobility and convergence of the economy to a lower poverty rate and higher per capita levels of human capital and income. A simple extension of this argument applies to education subsidy programs restricted only to the poor, as in Mexico's Progresa system.[8]

Cash and in-kind transfers thus have dramatically different effects on upward mobility and the proportion of the population that remains poor in the long run. A welfare system that takes the form of investment subsidies rather than cash payments generates stronger incentives for the currently poor to exert the effort that enables their descendants to escape poverty. But it does so at the cost of not providing any support to those currently poor who do not invest, which might cause the current poverty gap to widen. In the long run, however, the greater upward mobility in the society increases the scarcity of unskilled workers and thus raises their wages through a "trickle-down" mechanism. In-kind transfers may thus dominate cash transfers with regard to their long-term effectiveness in narrowing poverty gaps as well as lowering the head count rate. Nevertheless, in the short-to-medium run there is likely to be a difficult trade-off between more comprehensive forms of coverage for the poor and the need to provide them with stronger incentives to escape poverty. Needless to say, the extent of these trade-offs will ultimately be an empirical issue. One hopes that such aspects of the dynamics in and out of poverty will receive more attention in future research.

NOTES

1. For excellent overviews, see Atkinson (1998); Danziger and Weinberg (1986); and Wolff (1997).

2. See Atkinson (1998) and van Parijs (1991).

3. The two are of course linked: lack of insurance may encourage the poor to select "safe" options and occupations rather than risky ones that provide prospects of breaking out of poverty. But in a world without temporary shocks the insurance problem will disappear, unlike the poverty problem.

4. Berman and Rzakhanov (2000) provide theoretical arguments and empirical evidence in support of the proposition that migrations are motivated by high levels of intergenerational altruism within families, which can explain why the growth of their incomes frequently overtakes that of nonimmigrants within a few years of their arrival.

5. See also Bandyopadhyay (1993); Freeman (1996); Ljungqvist (1993); and Ray and Streufert (1993).

6. See, for instance, Aghion and Bolton (1997); Freeman (1996); Maoz and Moav (1999); Moav (2002); Piketty (1997); and Mani (2001).

7. For some interesting recent empirical work on these issues in transition and developing economies, see Lokshin and Ravallion (2000) and Jalan and Ravallion (1999).

8. This is due to the fact that by its very nature, in a long-run equilibrium unskilled parents do not invest in the education of their children (otherwise the proportion of skilled households in the economy would rise over time). Since the subsidy is conditional on sending their children to school, the poor cannot avail themselves of the subsidy in any long-run equilibrium. This implies that there is no need to tax the skilled in the long run, since there are no subsidy costs that need to be covered. Hence investment incentives in the long run are not affected at all by the education subsidy. In the short run, where some of the poor do invest, of course, it does have an effect, which is more benign than under an unconditional welfare support scheme.

BIBLIOGRAPHY

Acemoglu, Daron, Simon Johnson, and James Robinson. "The Colonial Origins of Comparative Development: An Empirical Investigation." *American Economic Review* 91, (December 2001), 1369–1401.

Aghion, Philippe, and Patrick Bolton. "A Theory of Trickle-Down Growth and Development." *Review of Economic Studies* 64 (Apr. 1997): 151–172.

Atkinson, Anthony Barnes. *Poverty in Europe.* Yrjo Jahnssen Lectures. Oxford: Black-well, 1998.

Banerjee, Abhijit, and Andrew Newman. "Occupational Choice and the Process of Development." *Journal of Political Economy* 101 (2) (1993): 274–298.

Benabou, Roland. "Equity and Efficiency in Human Capital Investment: The Local Connection." *Review of Economic Studies* 63 (Apr. 1996a): 237–264.

Benabou, Roland. "Heterogeneity, Stratification, and Growth: Macroeconomic Implications of Community Structure and School Finance." *American Economic Review* 86 (Apr. 1996b): 584–609.

Berman, Eli, and Zaur Rzakhanov. "Fertility, Migration and Altruism." National Bureau for Economic Research Working Paper no. 7964, February 2000.

Chechhi, Daniele, Andrea Ichino, and Aldo Rustichini. "More Equal but Less Mobile? Education Financing and Intergenerational Mobility in Italy and in the U.S." *Journal of Public Economics* 74 (3) (1999): 351–393.

Danziger, Sheldon, and Daniel Weinberg, eds. *Fighting Poverty: What Works and What Doesn't.* Cambridge, Mass.: Harvard University Press, 1986.

Dasgupta, Partha. "Poverty Traps." In *Advances in Economic Theory. Proceedings of the Tokyo 1995 World Congress of the Econometric Society,* edited by D. Kreps and K. Wallis. Cambridge: Cambridge University Press, 1997.

Dechert, R., and Kazuo Nishimura. "A Complete Characterization of Optimal Growth Paths in an Aggregated Model with a Non-Concave Production Function." *Journal of Economic Theory* 31 (1983): 332–354.

Durlauf, Steven. "A Theory of Persistent Income Inequality." *Journal of Economic Growth* 1 (1996): 75–93.

Engerman, Stanley, Stephen Haber, and Kenneth Sokoloff. "Inequality, Institutions and Differential Paths of Growth Among New World Economies." Working paper, University of Rochester, 1999.

Freeman, Scott. "Equilibrium Income Inequality Among Identical Agents." *Journal of Political Economy* 104 (5) (1996): 1047–1064.

Galor, Oded, and Omer Moav. "From Physical to Human Capital: Inequality in the Process of Development." *Review of Economic Studies* 71 (October 2004): 1001–1026.

Galor, Oded, and Joseph Zeira. "Income Distribution and Macroeconomics." *Review of Economic Studies* 60 (1) (1993): 35–52.

Ghatak, Maietreesh, Massimo Morelli, and Tomas Sjostrom. "Occupational Choices and Dynamic Incentives." *Review of Economic Studies* 68 (2001): 781–810.

Hubbard, Glenn, Jonathan Skinner, and Stephen Zeldes. "Expanding the Life-Cycle Model: Precautionary Saving and Public Policy." *American Economic Review* 84 (2) (1994): 174–179.

Hubbard, Glenn, Jonathan Skinner, and Stephen Zeldes. "Precautionary Saving and Social Insurance." *Journal of Political Economy* 103 (2) (1995): 360–399.

Jalan, Jyotsna, and Martin Ravallion. "Determinants of Transient and Chronic Poverty: Evidence from Rural China." Working paper, Development Research Group, World Bank, 1999.

Kremer, Michael, and Daniel Chen. "Income Distribution Dynamics with Endogenous Fertility." Mimeo, Department of Economics, Harvard University, 1999.

Ljungqvist, Lars. "Economic Underdevelopment: The Case of a Missing Market for Human Capital." *Journal of Development Economics* 40 (Apr. 1993): 219–239.

Lokshin, Michael, and Martin Ravallion. "Short-Lived Shocks with Long-Lived Impacts? Household Income Dynamics in a Transition Economy." Working paper, Development Research Group, World Bank, 2000.

Lynn, Laurence, Jr. "Caspar Weinberger and Welfare Reform." In *Designing Public Policy: A Casebook on the Role of Policy Analysis*, compiled by Laurence Lynn Jr. Santa Monica, Calif.: Goodyear, 1980.

Majumdar, Mukul, and Tapan Mitra. "Intertemporal Allocation with a Non-Convex Technology: The Aggregative Framework." *Journal of Economic Theory* 27 (1982): 101–136.

Mani, Anandi. "Income Distribution and the Demand Constraint." *Journal of Economic Growth* 6 (2001): 107–133.

Maoz, Yishay, and Omer Moav. "Intergenerational Mobility and the Process of Development." *Economic Journal* 109 (Oct. 1999): 677–697.

Matsuyama, Kiminori. "Endogenous Inequality." *Review of Economic Studies* 67 (2000): 743–759.

Matsuyama, Kiminori. "The Broken Symmetry and Theories of Endogenous Agglomerations, Fluctuations, and Distributions." *American Economic Review, Papers and Proceedings* 92 (May 2002): 241–246.

McKenzie, David, and Christopher Woodruff. "Is There an Empirical Basis for Poverty Traps in Developing Countries?" Mimeo, Department of Economics, Stanford University, 2002.

Mirrlees James. "An Exploration in the Theory of Optimal Income Taxation." *Review of Economic Studies* 38 (1971): 175–208.

Moav, Omer. "Cheap Children and the Persistence of Poverty." Mimeo, Department of Economics, Hebrew University, Jerusalem, 2001.

Moav, Omer. "Income Distribution and Macroeconomics: The Persistence of Inequality in a Convex Technology Framework." *Economics Letters* 75 (April 2002): 187–192.

Mookherjee, Dilip, and Debraj Ray. "Persistent Inequality." *Review of Economic Studies* 70 (2) (Apr. 2003): 369–394.

Mookherjee, Dilip, and Debraj Ray. "Contractual Structure and Wealth Accumulation." *American Economic Review* 92 (4) (Sept. 2002): 818–849.

Piketty, Thomas. "The Dynamics of the Wealth Distribution and the Interest Rate with Credit Rationing." *Review of Economic Studies* 64 (2) (1997): 173–189.

Ray, Debraj, and Peter Streufert. "Dynamic Equilibria with Unemployment Due to Undernourishment." *Economic Theory* 3 (1993): 61–85.

Sen, Amartya. *Resources, Values and Development*. Cambridge, Mass.: Harvard University Press, 1984.

Sen, Amartya. *Commodities and Capabilities*. Amsterdam: North-Holland, 1985.

Thurow, Lester. "Cash Versus In-Kind Transfers." *American Economic Review, Papers and Proceedings* 64 (2) (1974): 190–195.

Van Parisjs, Philippe. "Why Surfers Should Be Fed: The Liberal Case for an Unconditional Basic Income." *Philosophy and Public Affairs* 20 (1991): 101–131.

Wolff, Edward. *Economics of Poverty, Inequality and Discrimination*. Cincinnati, Ohio: Southwestern College, 1997.

16

Child Labor

Christopher Udry

Child labor is an insidious evil. Leaving aside pathological cases of child abuse and abandonment, it exists because it is the best response people can come up with to intolerable circumstances. It is particularly dangerous because it involves the sacrifice of a child's future welfare in exchange for immediate benefit, and difficult to combat because it involves questions of agency and power within households.

Some forms of child labor amount to direct abuse. There are children who work in dangerous conditions, in the sex industry, or in forced labor. But the vast majority of working children are engaged in less extreme activities, often on their own family's farm or business. For these children, the primary cost of child labor is the associated reduction in investment in their human capital. This occurs chiefly because child labor interferes with schooling. Not all work by children has this effect; I exclude such work from consideration in this essay and define child labor as the sacrifice of the future welfare of the child in exchange for additional current income. Although there are important challenges associated with empirically distinguishing child labor from the unproblematic light work that is an important component of rearing a child, we will see below that it is possible to design programs that specifically target child labor.

Many economists argue that child labor is a symptom of poverty and that its reduction can most effectively be accomplished through the alleviation of poverty. It is surely correct that child labor is a symptom of poverty; rarely do well-off parents sacrifice their children's education by sending them to work. However, child labor is also a cause of future poverty, so direct measures to move children from work into school can make an important contribution to poverty alleviation and to development in general.

In order to construct effective policies to address the problem of child labor, it is necessary to understand the circumstances that lead parents to send their children to work. That is the purpose of this essay. I make no attempt to survey the economic literature on child labor; Basu (1999) already provides an excellent review.

In the second section, I briefly describe some of the main features of child labor in developing countries. Poverty and child labor are mutually reinforcing; because their parents are poor, children must work and therefore remain out of school. As a consequence, these children grow up to be poor as adults, and the cycle continues. In the third section, I discuss the first of two features of child labor that give it a central place in a vicious cycle of poverty. This is the fact that the primary costs of child labor are realized so far in the future. When financial markets are poorly developed, the separation in time between the immediate benefits and long-delayed costs of sending children to work can result in too much child labor. The second feature is that the costs and benefits of child labor are not only separated in time; they are borne by different people: the child suffers the main consequences, while other household members benefit. This problem of *agency* is discussed in the fourth section. Finally, the fifth section concludes with a discussion of child labor policies.

PATTERNS OF CHILD LABOR

The International Labour Office (2002) estimates that about 210 million children between the ages of five and fourteen were working in 2000, about half of them working full-time. That implies that approximately one in ten of the world's children were working full-time. At the same time, UNESCO estimates that about one of every five primary school-aged children were not enrolled in school. The absolute numbers of children working are largest in Asia, but the incidence of child labor seems to be highest in Africa; the ILO estimates that about one third of children are economically active in Africa, about one sixth working full-time.

Child labor is overwhelmingly a rural and agricultural phenomenon. For example, in Pakistan, 70% of working children are employed in agriculture (Pakistan FBS 1996). Boys are more likely to work than girls, and older children are much more likely to be employed than their younger siblings (Grootaert and Patrinos 1999).

Our concern focuses on child labor that involves the sacrifice of a child's future welfare in exchange for a current benefit to the household. This is clearly the notion that motivates most child labor policy, and lies behind ILO Convention number 138.[1] The benefits to the household of sending a child to work are the wages of that child (or, equivalently, the increased production on the family farm) and the reduced education expenditures from not sending her to school. The primary costs of child labor are the lower future earnings of the child when she enters the adult labor market with lower educational attainment. In addition, there is very strong evidence of important nonmarket returns to education in child rearing: the children of well-educated parents, particularly mothers, are healthier. The sacrifice of these returns should also be counted as a cost of child labor. Finally, there are benefits to education, and thus costs to child labor, that extend beyond the immediate family. Educated coworkers may improve the productivity of everyone, and a well-educated populace provides a vital foundation for a vibrant society. These benefits that accrue to people outside of the household should also be counted as part of the cost of child labor, but I will for the most part ignore them in this essay. The primary thrust of my argument is that there are reasons to expect child labor to be "too high" among poor families in developing countries, even apart from the benefits of education for the broader public. Taking these into account would only strengthen the argument.

There are certain well-established empirical regularities about child labor that should inform our discussion. First, it is clear that child labor overwhelmingly reflects the poverty of the households in which the children live. Fallon and Tzannatos (1998) review a variety of studies that indicate a strongly negative relationship between the incidence of child labor and household income, but this relationship is less marked in more affluent developing countries. Ray (2000) finds a strong negative correlation between household income and child labor, and a positive relationship between household income and school enrollment in Pakistan, but no such relationship in relatively wealthier Peru.

It is important to note that the strong empirical evidence that child labor declines and school enrollment increases with household income does *not* imply that increases in wages necessarily reduce child labor. When a household becomes better off, it tends to increase the school enrollment of its children. Economists call this a positive "income effect." The children in a household made better off through, for example, an unconditional government grant will tend to work less and attend school more. However, when the additional income comes from an increase in wages, a countervailing force also exists. Wages of adults and children tend to move together, and an increase in child wages increases the effective cost to the household of sending a child to school rather than to work. Each hour the child spends in school (and thus not working) reduces the household's current consumption by more when the child's wage is higher. This "substitution effect," therefore, tends to increase the incidence of child labor. If this negative substitution effect is sufficiently strong, it could outweigh the positive effect of the household's increased income on child schooling. Whether it does or not depends on circumstances. For example, Kruger (2002) shows that child labor increases and school attendance decreases as coffee prices—and thus the returns to child labor—increase in Brazil. In contrast, Edmonds and Pavcnik

(2002) show that in Vietnam, increases in rice prices were strongly associated with declines in child labor.

It is also clear that child labor has important detrimental effects on schooling attainment, and thus on the future income of children. As already noted, not all work by children has this effect. Ideally, such benign work by children (occasional light work on the family farm, or limited household work) is excluded from data collection on child labor. An important question to resolve is the extent of work by children that does interfere with schooling and thus future earnings. How many of the ILO's 210 million working children are sacrificing their education? This is inherently a difficult question to answer, because child labor and school enrollment influence one another. Is a child not in school because she is working? Or is she working because there are no good opportunities for her to be schooled? Or is she sacrificing leisure to both work and attend school? However, the existing evidence is strong. For example, Psacharopoulos (1997) shows much lower educational attainment by children who work in Venezuela and Boliva. Using a very different methodology, Boozer and Suri (2001) find similar results for child labor and school attendance in Ghana.

Households that are very poor are much more likely to send their children to work, and child labor contributes to poverty in the next generation by reducing schooling attainment. This circular pattern of positive feedback between poverty and child labor may lead to a vicious cycle of poverty, in which the descendants of the poor remain poor because they were poorly educated. This cycle can be the foundation of a classical "poverty trap." However, if the cycle can be broken, the same positive circular causation can contribute to a takeoff into sustained growth. If schooling attainments can be improved, then the next generation's income is higher and their children can in turn become yet better educated. It is essential, therefore, to understand the specific mechanisms that can trap people in the awful equilibrium of persistent poverty, excessive child labor, and low education over generations.

The crucial mechanisms are, first, an inability to seize advantageous long-run investments in children's human capital because of credit market constraints and, second, problems of agency within households. These two mechanisms operate simultaneously and can interact in important ways.

IMPERFECT FINANCIAL MARKETS, CHILD LABOR, AND INVESTMENT IN HUMAN CAPITAL

I begin by abstracting from any problems associated with agency, and assume that parents fully internalize the costs of sending their children to work. From the point of view of society, what is the appropriate level of child labor? Suppose, to start, that the costs of working and the benefits of schooling are entirely private; that is, they are limited to the increased productivity, and therefore income, of better-educated adults. For now, therefore, we are ignoring the benefits of well-educated individuals for the rest of society. The benefit of child labor is the current wage earned by the child (and the reduced cost of schooling). These benefits are realized immediately, so no discounting is required. The costs of additional child labor are the lower wages that the child receives when she grows up less well-educated because she worked as a child. These costs are realized in the far future, so for cost–benefit analysis we calculate the present discounted value of these costs. For a given absolute cost, a higher interest rate implies a lower present discounted value of the cost.

From a social point of view, it is efficient to increase child labor and reduce schooling up to the point at which the present discounted value of future costs of additional child labor are just balanced by the current benefit to the household of that additional child labor. It need not be the case that the socially efficient level of child labor is zero; this will depend upon the productivity of child labor, the degree to which schooling improves future productivity, and the interest rate at which future earnings are discounted. For example, if a child already has sufficient schooling so that further years of education have a relatively small impact on her future income, and if she could generate a lot of income by working, and if interest rates are relatively high, then the immediate benefit of having the child work might be sufficiently large to offset the present discounted value of her future lower earnings as a less well-educated adult. On the other hand, if further schooling for the child would greatly increase her future income, and if the current income she could earn by working is relatively low, and if interest rates are low, then the immediate benefit of the child working would not be sufficient to outweigh the present discounted value of her future higher income from attending school, and from a social point of view she should stay in school.

If financial markets operate smoothly and there are no issues of agency, this is precisely the calculus that will guide the decisions of parents regarding work and school for their children. In this case, even if parents are poor, perfect credit markets permit them to borrow to finance the education of their children, confident in their ability to repay the loan out of the increased earnings of their well-educated adult children. These private decisions will be socially optimal.

Obviously, if the rest of society benefits from children's improved education, then these benefits will not be fully taken into account by parents as they invest in their children's schooling. In this case, from a social point of view the level of child labor will be too high, and the level of schooling too low even if financial markets operate smoothly. The existence of these social benefits from schooling is an important element in the traditional argument for subsidization of education and public schooling.

However, even if these social benefits are unimportant, in the real world financial markets are not sufficiently well developed to support the optimal calculus described in the first three paragraphs of this section. A parent who is unable to smoothly transfer income from the far future into the present by borrowing will choose too high a level of child labor. Consider a very simple example, in which the parent can borrow, but only at an interest rate that is higher than is relevant for social decision-making. This would occur, for example, if the parent can borrow only from a monopolistic money-lender. At this higher interest rate, the present discounted value to the household of the future costs of child labor are lower than they are to society as a whole, and so the child works more and attains a lower level of schooling.

This reasoning holds a fortiori when the parents have no or only constrained access to credit. In this case the parents trade off the (far) future costs of child labor against the immediate benefit of child labor to the household, without the possibility of easing that trade-off by transferring resources from the future. If the household is too poor, the value of the immediate return from the child's working trumps the future higher wages the child could earn if she stayed in school, and the child is sent to work.[2]

There is little doubt that inadequate access to financial markets is a barrier to investment in education and a force pushing the children of many poor households into the labor market. In conversation parents testify to their importance. To this, economists have added quantitative evidence. However, to be persuasive, they must go beyond the well-established correlation between poverty and child labor. To see why, consider two families who are similar, except that one is poorer than the other. In particular, each has a twelve-year-old boy who could earn $1/day in a local business, or who could go to school. Suppose we see that the child of the less poor family is in school, while the child of the poorer family is working. This is certainly consistent with the argument that the poorer family has inadequate access to financial markets, and faces a higher interest rate than does the better-off family. At that higher interest rate, the present discounted value of the future gain to income by sending the child to school might not offset the $1/day he can earn now. On the other hand, there could be many other differences between these two families. For example, the better-off family might have social connections that increase the value of schooling to them. Or the poorer family might have access only to a lower-quality school. Broadening our vision beyond the narrow focus on monetary costs and benefits, one family might be better off because the parents are better-educated themselves, and their education leads them to place a higher value on schooling. The point is that there are many reasons why we might see a correlation between low income and a high incidence of child labor. Navigating the causal pathways is difficult.

This is a general problem in the social sciences. The strategies that economists have used to attempt to distinguish various causal explanations for this particular correlation provide useful examples of the general principle.[3] In this case, some of the more persuasive evidence comes from a series of studies that relate both school attendance and child labor to transitory income shocks afflicting households that can be attributed to random events outside the control of the household. The importance of the last two phrases is that these studies aim to identify households that are temporarily poor (or rich) for no particular reason—it was just an act of God. If this can be done, we can argue that the *only* difference between households that have a temporary good shock and those that have a temporary bad shock is that (on average) those with a good shock are relatively well off.

To understand the importance of such evidence, consider a hypothetical household engaged in farming in a developing country. Like all farmers, this family is subject to random, transitory shocks that affect its income (think of shocks such as a localized flood). An important consequence of well-developed financial markets is that this family's decisions regarding the education and labor force participation of its children would be entirely unaffected by the realization of such transitory shocks. The present discounted value of the future costs of child labor are unaffected by any temporary production shock. The immediate benefits are unaffected as well, as long as the shock is sufficiently localized that the wage for child labor does not change.[4] Therefore, if this family has access to smoothly operating credit markets, it will simply borrow (or draw down its savings) to maintain its base level of consumption despite the adverse shock, and the schooling and labor status of its children would remain unchanged.

This conclusion no longer holds when the family cannot borrow and does not hold savings over the long term. Now, faced with an adverse transitory shock, a poor household is forced into a stark choice: maintain the school enrollment of the children and face a decline in an already inadequate level of consumption, or try to protect the family's current living standard by relying on increased child labor. Moreover, if we are convinced that these adverse shocks are distributed randomly through the population, and that the only effect of these shocks is to temporarily lower income, then we can be confident that the causal connection truly does run from income to schooling and child labor.

Beegle et al. (2002) provides a good example of this approach. They find that rural Tanzanian children work more when their family farms have experienced adverse events such as fires or loss due to insects or rodents. The survey they use followed households over three years, so they can also show that this effect is temporary: children work more when their household is poorer as a consequence of suffering from these events, then they work less when the household recovers. Finally, they show that the sensitivity of child labor to these shocks is greatest for poorer households with fewer assets that can serve as collateral, thus providing further support for the hypothesis that imperfect financial markets play a central role in determining the amount of child labor in rural Tanzania. In a complementary paper, Jacoby and Skoufias (1997) find that school attendance drops among children in three Indian villages when their households' income temporarily drops. This is not simply a rural phenomenon, however. Duryea et al. (2003) show that urban children in Brazil are much more likely to enter the workforce when their father becomes unemployed. For example, the probability of a sixteen-year-old girl in São Paulo entering the labor force in the next year jumps from 22% to 35% if her father loses his job; simultaneously, her probability of continuing in school drops from 70% to 60%.

Child labor can be seen as a draconian choice made by poor households faced with severely limited options. Even if the parents are fully altruistic toward their children, in the sense that they treat the future costs to the children of current child labor symmetrically with current benefits to the household, poorly functioning financial markets can induce too much child labor and too little schooling. The benefits of child labor are realized immediately. Without access to credit markets, poor households may find it too difficult to sacrifice these immediate benefits in order to reduce the far future costs associated with child labor. It bears emphasizing that this is not a consequence of impatience or an unwillingness on the part of poor households to plan for the future; rather, it is a reflection of poverty and inadequate access to capital markets.

AGENCY

Decisions regarding child labor and schooling are generally made by parents. This raises issues of agency, because decisions are being made by individuals who do not necessarily themselves experience the full implications of these decisions. Even if parents are altruistic toward their children—and surely this is the case for the vast majority of families—issues of bargaining and negotiation within households, and the difficulty of making commitments that bind over generations, may make it difficult to achieve optimally low levels of child labor.

First, consider a case in which agency causes no deviation from the socially efficient levels of child labor and schooling, in the spirit of the classic "rotten kid" theorem of Becker (1974). Suppose that the parent feels altruistic toward the child, in the sense that the parent's welfare increases when the child's welfare increases, and that the parent has access to perfect financial markets. In addition, suppose that the parent expects to leave a positive bequest to the child. In this case, the parent will choose to set the level of child labor to the socially optimum level, as described above. The argument is quite simple: the parent would like to help the child achieve a particular level of welfare, and the parent has two tools available to do so: the parent chooses the amount of child labor (and thus determines the level of schooling for the child), and the parent can give the child a bequest. The parent will choose the minimal-cost means of achieving any given level of child welfare; to do otherwise would waste resources that could be used to achieve higher welfare for the child, the parent, or both. If the parent chooses a level of child labor greater than is socially optimal, he will be wasting resources. He can reduce child labor a bit, reduce the future bequest left to the child to compensate, and have money left over to increase everyone's welfare. Therefore, a parent who cares about the welfare of his child *and* who plans to leave a positive bequest to that child would ensure that the child's labor force participation matches the socially efficient level.

However, suppose that the parent plans to leave no bequest. This is most likely to occur in a poor family, particularly in a family in which the parent's generation is especially poor relative to future generations. Child labor in this circumstance will be inefficiently high and schooling attainment too low, because once bequests have been reduced to zero, this is the only instrument available to the parents to transfer resources from the next generation to support current welfare (Baland and Robinson 2000). A potential way to reduce child labor would be for the parent to borrow to finance current consumption, with the child committing herself to pay back the loan from her future higher earnings. However, such intergenerational contracts are not enforceable.

Therefore, even when financial markets operate perfectly smoothly (at least within generations) and parents are altruistic toward their children, agency problems can induce too much child labor and too little investment in education. The source of the problem is that poor parents who plan to leave no bequest to their children use child labor to support the current consumption of the household.

Agency problems become even more salient when they occur in the typical environment of imperfect financial markets. If the household cannot borrow (and does not plan to save), then decisions regarding child labor and educational investments cannot be made by balancing the current financial gain and discounted future financial cost of child labor. Instead, decisions are made by balancing *subjective* welfare costs and benefits. Parents balance the benefit in terms of current welfare of increasing child labor (and reducing schooling) against the current subjective cost of the child's future reduced welfare.

The immediate question, of course, is *whose* subjective welfare determines the child's education and labor force participation? The two parents might hold divergent views about these costs and benefits. In fact, there is mounting evidence that this is so, and that these divergent opinions can have important effects on child welfare.

Until fairly recently, economists had ignored issues of agency within households, relying on what has come to be called the "unitary household model." This model assumes that the choices made in households can be treated as if they were made by a single individual. There was never much of a theoretical justification for this assumption; it was made for convenience, driven by the fact that data (particularly from official statistical agencies) tends to come in household-sized chunks.

An important implication of the unitary household model is that income is pooled. Whether extra income comes from the husband or the wife is irrelevant for decisions regarding expenditure or investment in children; it's all just extra income for the household. When this implication is examined using data, it is almost universally rejected. For example, Duflo (2003) finds that the nutrition of girls in South Africa is dramatically improved when their grandmothers receive old-age pensions, but is entirely unaffected when the pension is received by their grandfathers. This and much additional evidence implies that the unitary household model is an inappropriate building block for thinking about decisions within the household regarding investment in their children. Parents may have divergent preferences regarding such investments, so that shifts in bargaining power within the household could have important effects on child labor.

Economists are far from a general understanding of intrahousehold bargaining processes. In fact, the dominant successor model to the unitary household model is deliberately agnostic regarding these negotiations, assuming only that the household efficiently uses all the resources available to it.[5] However, some general patterns have emerged from a fairly lengthy sequence of empirical studies. In particular, researchers have found that extra income in the hands of mothers is associated with higher levels of investment in child human capital (see Haddad et al. 1997).

LESSONS FOR POLICIES THAT CAN MOVE CHILDREN FROM WORK TO SCHOOL

Child labor should be understood as the consequence of people coping with extreme circumstances. It is a result of current poverty, and a cause of continued poverty for the children who sacrifice their education in order to work. It is a particularly insidious problem because its primary costs are long-delayed and realized by the child, while the benefits are immediate and directly affect decision-makers within the household.

We know that the ultimate instrument for the elimination of excess child labor is the alleviation of poverty. The evidence is indisputable: child labor as a mass phenomenon disappears when the population moves out of poverty. While this is a sure solution, we're not willing to wait.

The obvious response is an outright ban of the practice of child labor. The first difficulty is that it is by no means clear that developing country governments have tools available to enforce such a ban. The task would be extremely difficult, because most child labor is in agriculture, much of it on family farms. Where bans have been imposed, it is not clear that they have been effective. Moehling (1999) shows that there is little evidence that child labor laws contributed to the dramatic decline in child labor in the nineteenth-century United States. This decline was driven instead by changes in technology, immigration, and the rise in the real wage.

Even if governments could effectively ban child labor, the consequences could be dire for those poor households (and their children) who are resorting to child labor out of desperation. These children are working to help the household make ends meet. An effective ban on child labor would make these households and these children worse off. Therefore any legal restrictions on child labor in developing countries should be focused on those cases in which there is evidence of pathology, of parents or guardians who do not take into account the interest of the child. This is most likely in the case of the most odious of forms of child labor, including working under hazardous conditions or as bonded laborers.

A closely related issue is developed-country trade policy. Many have argued for an international labor standards policy that requires the elimination of child labor for access to developed country markets.[6] In some cases, this argument is simply a smoke screen providing cover for standard-issue protectionism. However, it is often motivated by a genuine concern for the welfare of children in developing countries. If this is indeed the motivation, the implementation of trade sanctions to enforce an international standard against the use of child labor is likely to have perverse consequences. Except in unusual cases, which are discussed in Basu (1999, sec. 8), effective sanctions would make the families of child workers worse off. If sanctions are effective, they will generally have the consequence of lowering the price of the good produced with child labor. This reduction in the price would lower the value of workers to the employer, and thus lead to lower wages for child workers. Those children who remained in the labor force would be worse off because they would be paid less.

As a consequence of the lower wage, some children *will* stop working and go to school. That would seem to be a good thing! However, if child labor is indeed a means of coping with desperate poverty, families are sending children to work only when the current value of the income they earn is greater than the (discounted value) of the future benefits of education. Lowering the wage of child labor to induce the family to send the child to school makes the family worse off.

Trade sanctions are a particularly inappropriate tool for dealing with the challenge of child labor. As noted above, there is a legitimate case for bans on particular forms of child labor. If there is to be any developed-country intervention in these cases, it would be more appropriate in the form of diplomatic pressure and more general rewards and punishments to encourage government action to avoid the adverse effects of trade sanctions on the very children they are meant to help.

We have seen that dysfunctional financial markets are an important cause of child labor. Child labor would be dramatically reduced if parents could finance their children's exit from the labor force and entry into schooling from the increased future earnings of the child. Unfortunately, extremely well-functioning credit markets are required to make this kind of transaction feasible. The lag between the investment in child education and the return to that investment in the adult labor market is measured in decades, not months. There is little immediate prospect for improvements in financial markets accessible to the poor in developing countries of the order of magnitude required for such long-term transactions.

How, then, to reduce child labor?

The most effective way to draw children out of damaging work is to encourage school attendance. One way of doing so would be to improve school quality, and therefore increase the gain from attending school. Handa (2002), for example, argues that school enrollment in Mozambique is quite sensitive to the number of trained teachers. This is an important tool that is available to reduce child labor. However, it has the significant disadvantage of influencing outcomes in the distant future, when the higher quality of schooling leads to higher wages as an adult. The influence of these changes on future outcomes of current decisions regarding work and schooling is scaled down by credit constraints and agency problems.

The most promising tool yet developed for reducing child labor is a targeted subsidy to families sending their children to school. In such a program, a grant is provided to the family of any child who is enrolled in school. The particular value of this intervention is that it addresses the root causes of child labor. It overcomes the problems associated with imperfect or nonexistent financial markets by balancing the current cost of moving a child out of the labor force and into school with a current grant. It addresses the main agency problem by providing current resources, thus reducing the importance of intergenerational transfers. For a priori reasons, then, we can expect subsidies for school enrollment to be a useful tool in the effort to reduce child labor. A number of such programs have been implemented in recent years.

The flagship program of this type is the innovative Progresa poverty program in Mexico (the name of the program has recently been changed to Oportunidades). Progresa provides mothers of enrolled students in rural Mexico with grants that have a value slightly less than the wage that would be earned by the child if she were working full-time. With remarkable foresight, the Progresa program was introduced (in 1998) in a randomized sequence. This randomization, combined with systematic data collection, makes it possible to measure with great confidence the impact of the program on both school enrollment and child labor force participation. Schultz (2004) estimates that the program has resulted in an increase in schooling of about two thirds of a year (from a baseline attainment of 6.8 years), and that child labor correspondingly falls. The most dramatic effects are for secondary school girls, whose broad labor force participation is estimated to drop by almost fifty percentage points upon enrollment in school.[7]

Inspired by the Progresa example, Nicaragua instituted the Red de Protección Social (RPS) in 2000. This program also provides grants for children aged seven to thirteen who attend school that are approximately as large (as a proportion of household expenditure) as those of Progresa. Maluccio and Flores (2004) analyzes the pilot phase of this program, in which (like Progresa) it was implemented in a randomly selected group of communities. Where it has been implemented, RPS has had a massive impact. Maluccio estimates that the effect of the program is to increase enrollment rates by twenty-two percentage points (from a base enrollment rate of 69%). The effects on child labor are large for older children (ten to thirteen years old);

younger children were unlikely to work even before the program. The program's impact was to reduce the proportion of children working by almost nine percentage points (from a base of 27%).

The Food for Education program in rural Bangladesh is similar in spirit to the other two programs. The monthly payment is smaller; 15–25% of average monthly earnings for working children. Nevertheless, Ravallion and Wodon (1999) estimate that the FFE program moved primary school enrollment from approximately 75% to over 90%. Child labor force participation dropped as well (by about 30% for boys and by about 20% for girls).

Child labor can effectively be reduced by subsidies for school enrollment. This tool dominates alternatives because it directly addresses the tragic circumstances that impel families to send their children to work instead of school. An effective subsidy program is not unreasonably expensive because the costs are tied to the low wages earned by child workers. Therefore, while more careful cost–benefit analyses should be completed on an urgent basis, the expansion of targeted education subsidies into areas of developing countries with high rates of child labor force participation is an extremely promising strategy.

ACKNOWLEDGMENTS I thank Amalavoyal Chari for valuable research assistance and Roland Benabou, Markus Goldstein, Barbara O'Brien, and Tavneet Suri for comments. I am grateful to the MacArthur Foundation Network on Inequality and Economic Performance, to the Pew Charitable Trust through its Project on Moral and Social Dimensions of Microeconomic Behavior in Communities, and to the NSF (grant 0079115) for financial support. Current versions of this essay can be found at www.econ.yale.edu/~udry/.

NOTES

1. See www.ilo.org/public/english/standards/norm/whatare/fundam/childpri.htm.
2. Ranjan (1999, 2001), Hazan and Berdugo (2002), and Baland and Robinson (2000) provide superb and simple theoretical models of the relationships between imperfect financial markets and child labor.
3. Manski (1995) is a superb treatment of the general problem.
4. When the wage does change, the "substitution effect" may dominate the "income effect" and child labor may decrease. Boozer and Suri (2001) show that agricultural shocks which decrease the productivity of labor are associated with declines in child labor and increases in school attendance in Ghana.
5. This is the collective household model, as in Chiappori (1988). Even this minimal assumption is somewhat controversial. I found evidence against it in Burkina Faso (Udry 1996) and, with Duflo, in Côte d'Ivoire (Duflo and Udry 2003).
6. Brown (2000) provides a very useful review of the large literature on this topic.
7. Preliminary cost–benefit analysis of the Progressa program by Schultz (2004) indicates a real rate of return of approximately 8%. The costs of the program are relatively easy to measure; Schultz limits the benefit calculation to the private market return to education. If there are important externalities or nonmarket returns to schooling, this is an underestimate.

BIBLIOGRAPHY

Baland, Jean Marie, and James Robinson. "Is Child Labor Inefficient?" *Journal of Political Economy* 108 (4) (2000): 663–679.

Basu, Kaushik. "Child Labor: Cause, Consequence and Cure, with Remarks on International Labor Standards." *Journal of Economic Literature* 37 (1999): 1083–1119.

Becker, Gary. "A Theory of Social Interactions." *Journal of Political Economy* 82 (1974): 1063–1094.

Beegle, Kathleen, Rajeev Dehejia, and Roberta Gatti. "Do Households Resort to Child Labor to Cope with Income Shocks?" Working paper, World Bank, 2002.

Boozer, Michael, and Tavneet Suri. "Child Labor and Schooling Decisions in Ghana." Working paper, Yale University, 2001.

Brown, Drusilla. "International Trade and Core Labor Standards: A Survey of the Recent Literature." Working paper, Tufts University, 2000.

Chiappori, Pierre-Andre. "Rational Household Labor Supply." *Econometrica* 56 (1) (1988): 63–90.

Duflo, Esther. "Grandmothers and Granddaughters: Old Age Pension and Intra-Household Allocation in South Africa." *World Bank Economic Review* 17 (1) (2003): 1–25.

Duflo, Esther, and Christopher Udry. "Intrahousehold Resource Allocation in Côte d'Ivoire: Social Norms, Separate Accounts and Consumption Choices." Working paper, Yale University, 2003.

Duryea, Suzanne, David Lam, and Deborah Levison. "Effects of Economic Shocks on Children's Employment and Schooling in Brazil." Population Studies Center Research Report 03–541, University of Michigan, Ann Arbor, 2003.

Edmonds, Eric. "Is Child Labor Inefficient? Evidence from Large Cash Transfers." Working paper, Dartmouth College, Hanover, N.H., 2002.

Edmonds, Eric, and Nina Pavcnik. "Does Globalization Increase Child Labor? Evidence from Vietnam." Working paper, Dartmouth College, Hanover, N.H., 2002.

Fallon, Peter, and Zafiris Tzannatos. "Child Labor: Issues and Directions for the World Bank." Mimeo, World Bank, 1998.

Grootaert, Christiaan, and Harry Patrinos. *The Policy Analysis of Child Labor: A Comparative Study.* New York: St. Martin's Press, 1999.

Haddad, Laurence, John Hoddinott, and Harold Alderman, eds. *Intrahousehold Resource Allocation in Developing Countries: Models, Methods and Policy.* Baltimore: Johns Hopkins University Press, 1997.

Handa, Sudhanshu. "Raising Primary School Enrollment in Developing Countries: The Relative Importance of Supply and Demand." *Journal of Development Economics* 66 (1) (2002): 103–128.

Hazan, Moshe, and Binyamin Berdugo. "Child Labor, Fertility, and Economic Growth." *The Economic Journal* 112 (2002): 810–828.

International Labour Office. *Every Child Counts: New Global Estimates on Child Labour.* Geneva: ILO, 2002.

Jacoby, Hanan, and Emmanuel Skoufias. "Risk, Financial Markets and Human Capital in a Developing Country." *Review of Economic Studies* 64 (3) (1997): 311–335.

Kruger, Diana. "The Effects of Coffee Production on Child Labor and Schooling in Brazil." Working Paper, University of Maryland, College Park, 2002.

Moehling, Carolyn. "State Child Labor Laws and the Decline of Child Labor." *Explorations in Economic History* 36 (1999): 72–106.

Maluccio, John, and Rafael Flores. "Impact Evaluation of a Conditional Cash Transfer Program: The Nicaraguan *Red de Proteccion Social*" Food Consumption and Nutrition Division Discussion Paper 184, International Food Policy Research Institute, Washington, D.C., 2004.

Manski, Charles. *Identification Problems in the Social Sciences.* Cambridge: Harvard University Press, 1995.

Pakistan Federal Bureau of Statistics. *Summary Results of Child Labour Survey in Pakistan.* Islamabad: Federal Bureau of Statistics, 1996.

Psacharopoulos, George. "Child Labor Versus Educational Attainment: Some Evidence from Latin America." *Journal of Population Economics* 10 (1997): 377–386.

Ranjan, Priya. "An Economic Analysis of Child Labor." *Economics Letters* 64 (1999): 99–105.

Ranjan, Priya. "Credit Constraints and the Phenomenon of Child Labor." *Journal of Development Economics* 64 (2001): 81–102.

Ravallion, Martin, and Quentin Wodon. "Does Child Labor Displace Schooling? Evidence on Behavioral Responses to an Enrollment Subsidy." Working paper, World Bank, 1999.

Ray, Ranjan. "Child Labor, Child Schooling, and Their Interaction with Adult Labor: Empirical Evidence for Peru and Pakistan." *World Bank Economic Review* 14 (2) (2000): 347–367.

Schultz, Paul. "Education Investment and Returns." In *Handbook of Development Economics*, Vol. 1. Edited by H. Chenery and T. N. Srinivasan. Amsterdam: North-Holland, 1995.

Schultz, Paul. "School Subsidies for the Poor: Evaluating the Mexican Progresa Poverty Program." *Journal of Development Economics* 74 (1) (2004): 199–250.

Udry, Christopher. "Gender, Agricultural Production and the Theory of the Household." *Journal of Political Economy* 104 (5) (1996): 1010–1047.

17

Policy Dilemmas for Controlling Child Labor

Kaushik Basu

THE DIMENSIONS OF THE PROBLEM

Since the early nineteenth century, when Britain began to experiment with
policies to curb child labor, we have learned a lot about policy interventions
for controlling child labor. At the same time, the fact that child labor continues to be a major problem suggests that we may not have learned enough.
The purpose of this essay is to show that this is one area where seemingly
reasonable policy interventions can easily backfire. Hence, policy interventions cannot be left at the level of broad-brush statements but need to be
crafted carefully. The general possibility of pathological reactions to policy
interventions will be discussed, and one particular pathology will be spelled
out in some detail because this is a problem that seems not to have been
discussed in the literature and also because it provides a generic illustration
of the hazard of using standard instruments for curbing child labor.

Thanks to improved data collection we now have a fair idea of the nature
and extent of child labor in the world. According to data recently released
by the ILO (2002), in the year 2000, there were 211 million children below
the age of fifteen years who were "economically active." Of these, 73 million
were below the age of ten; and the total number goes up to 352 million if
we consider children up to the age of seventeen years. The ILO distinguishes
"child labor" from "economically active children" by asserting that a child
above the age of twelve who does light, part-time work that is not hazardous
may be economically active but is not to be counted as a child laborer. By
making this adjustment, and treating a child as someone below the age of
fifteen, we find that in the year 2000 there were 186 million child laborers
the world over.

Evidently, the problem is large. And there are researchers who claim that it is larger than the ILO statistics suggest. For one thing, the ILO finds that boys are more likely than girls to be laborers. This is quite consistent with official data from around the world and from nineteenth-century Britain, but in the few cases where data were collected with special effort to include domestic work, as was done in India (see Cigno and Rosati 2000), it was found out that girls do more work than boys. Hence, it is arguable that the amount of girls' work estimated by the ILO falls short of the true figure. Then there is the problem of "intermittent employment." Analysts have long suspected, and now we have formal statistics from Brazil showing, that children are much more prone to being in and out of work than adults (Levison et al. 2002). Hence, if we try to find out how many children are working simply by tracking their work status during the previous week, as the ILO did, we get an underestimate of the *number* of children who do some work. Admittedly, this does not mean an underestimate of the *amount of work* done by children.

No matter which indicator one uses to describe the magnitude of labor performed by children, it must, by now, be amply clear that the phenomenon of child labor presents us with a staggeringly large policy problem.[1]

THE POLICY PROBLEM

In crafting policy in the domain of child labor, one has, first of all, to be careful to guard against what is best described as the "fallacy of single-mindedness." While it is undoubtedly bad for a child to have to work, it is easy for us to forget that worse things can happen to a child than having to work. Hunger, serious illness, malnutrition, abandonment by family, and prostitution are all states of being or activities from which a child would readily switch to regular labor. Thus, when we try to eliminate child labor, we must be careful not to achieve this by driving children to these worse alternatives. Policy makers and even academics at times make the mistake of being so single-minded in their aim to control child labor that they do not mind if this is achieved at the expense of the welfare of the very children whom the intervention is intended to help.

Basu and Van (1998) have warned against this risk and have shown that while there may indeed be occasions when a legal ban on child labor is called for, this is not always the case. In most people's minds, an economist's argument that we must not use legislative intervention somehow gets translated into the prescription that we must not use intervention. But that is a fallacy. There are economists and historians who have argued that child labor ought not to (and some believe it cannot) be removed by direct state intervention, and that we will have to wait instead for the benefits of growth to trickle down and eventually eliminate child labor (e.g., Nardinelli 1990). But to resist legal intervention (as I would in certain contexts) is not the same as resisting intervention. Indeed, I would argue that the state has a great responsibility to improve the quality of schooling, give incentives such as school meals, and improve adult labor market conditions, all of which are known to have a negative impact on the incidence of child labor (see, for instance, Ravallion and Wodon 2000; Bourguignon et al. 2003; Grootaert and Patrinos 1999). When child labor is removed via interventions of this kind, we can generally be sure that this happens while enhancing the welfare of the child. Legal interventions, on the other hand, even when they are properly enforced so that they do diminish child *labor,* may or may not increase child *welfare.* This is one of the most important lessons that modern economics has taught us and is something that often eludes the policy maker.

Child labor policy turns out to be intricate because of the somewhat unusual factors that cause child labor in the first place. Child labor is intricately linked to poverty. Of the 186 million child laborers in the world, virtually all are located in poor countries. In the same developing country where lots of children work, one would rarely find the child of a doctor, lawyer, professor, or any middle-class person working. The evidence is overwhelming that poverty is a major cause of child labor (see, for instance, Edmonds 2001).[2]

When this is true, policies can have counterintuitive effects (see, for instance, Basu 2000; Jafarey and Lahiri 2002; Singh 2003). The policy with which I shall illustrate the risk of pathological reaction is one where a firm is fined a certain amount if it is found to be employing children. India's Child Labour (Prohibition and Regulation) Act (1986) has such a clause. Section 14 of this act requires the government to levy a fine between Rs. 10,000 and Rs. 20,000 upon a person or firm found employing children in contravention of the provisions of the act (see Government of India 1986).

At first sight it appears that such a policy must cause child labor to decrease, since firms will now be reluctant to employ children. However, it will be shown in this essay that in certain situations exactly the opposite is true. Imposing a fine for using child labor or raising an existing fine can increase the amount of child labor. What is interesting is that this argument carries over to a larger range of policies. This will be obvious as soon as the intuition behind the result is spelled out. This is done in the next section.

NOTES ON POSSIBLE PATHOLOGIES

Is there hard evidence that imposing a fine for employing children can exacerbate the problem of child labor? No. But nevertheless there are two reasons to be interested in this question. First, we do not have evidence of the opposite (that is, the proposition that fines for employing child labor curb child labor) either. What we have is simply a *presumption* that this must be so. And I want to show that a simple analysis, based on straightforward assumptions for which we *do* have empirical evidence, shows that the presumption is faulty. Thus this analysis demonstrates the need for future empirical analysis. The second reason is that there is considerable informal evidence that child labor is a hard problem to solve. Repeated interventions, since 1802 in Britain, have met with resistance and a failure to buck the problem. The evidence, which I briefly discuss below, suggests that policies for controlling child labor may not be as obvious as they seem. The possibility of "pathological" reaction to seemingly obvious interventions cannot, offhand, be ruled out.

Serious attempts to combat child labor began with Robert Peel's Factories Act of 1802 in Britain. Subsequently, progressively tougher laws were ushered in, but the incidence of child labor remained high, seemingly impervious to the interventions. According to the census of England and Wales, in 1861 the labor participation rate for boys aged ten to fourteen years was 36.9%, and for girls of the same age group it was 20.5%. This is comparable with some of the poorest developing countries today.

In the United States the attempt to legally control child labor began in 1837 in Massachusetts. Yet the incidence of child labor began declining noticeably only after 1880. For the United States, 1880 to 1910 was the period of rapid decline of child labor. This was also the period during which legislation against child labor was enacted with greater intensity. It is therefore easy to presume that child labor declined *because* of the law. But a detailed study by Moehling (1999), which made use of the fact that different states in the United States had laws of differing stringency against child labor,[3] showed that the law had very little effect on the incidence of child labor.

While there is need for formal empirical analysis of the effect of law on child labor, the broad evidence suggests that the effect may not be what people take it to be at face value. Indeed, it can be shown that when it comes to the use of a fine for employing children, the effect can be the opposite of what we may expect.

The reason why imposing a fine on firms for employing children can cause child labor to increase is intimately connected to the fact that poverty is a major cause of child labor. To see the intuition behind this, take the extreme case where a household chooses to send its children to work in order to escape extreme poverty or starvation.[4] When child labor is the product of trying to reach a target (such as a subsistence consumption), any policy that makes child labor a less effective instrument in reaching such a target will result in a more intensive use of this instrument. Now if there is a new law whereby firms are fined whenever they are caught using child labor, clearly this will cause the wage rate for child labor to drop. This is because children are now a less attractive input from the point of view of firms. But this in turn will mean children will have to work even harder to be able to earn the target minimum income that they are after.

The full analysis is a bit more complicated. Note that if the fines are made so big that the firms no longer wish to employ any children, of course child labor will fall (whether this is desirable from a welfare-consequentialist point of view is another matter). The general result that is established here is that as the fine for using child labor is increased, child labor will first rise and then fall.

The larger policy implications of this result will be discussed after I have established it formally. The result that I am about to prove can be derived under fairly general conditions but, since I wish to prove it without complex algebra, I shall use some strong simplifying assumptions for reasons of expositional convenience. The assumptions that are (more than mere simplifying ones and) central to my analysis are that (1) children are made to work only so as to achieve a certain target minimum consumption for the household and (2) child and adult laborers are substitutes, subject to, possibly, an adult equivalency correction. Even these assumptions are overstated for simplicity. We know, for instance, that when a relatively poor household comes to own more land (and this may be coincident with becoming a little richer), it tends to make its children work more (Bhalotra and Heady 2003). This indicates that while poverty is an important cause of child labor, it is not the sole cause. For instance, the ease with which a child can be employed, which no doubt increases as the household's landownership increases, can influence the incidence of child labor (Basu and Tzannatos 2003). While it is possible to take these complications on board and still derive the result I am about to derive, I shall work with the more extreme assumptions embodied in (1) and (2) in order to get the main argument across simply. Fortunately, there is now plenty of hard evidence supporting assumption (1) (see, for instance, Grootaert and Patrinos 1999; and Edmonds 2001), and though (2) has not been studied much, what little evidence there is, seems to support it (see Levison et al. 1998).

Consider a labor market in which there are several households with each household consisting of one adult and several children. In the labor market, adults and children are perfect substitutes. We could assume that a child can do only a fraction of what an adult does, but this complication would leave the results that this essay is focusing on unchanged and so is unnecessary. I shall assume that the adult always supplies labor perfectly inelastically, whereas children work only to the extent that this is necessary to achieve a subsistence level of consumption for the household. Let s be the amount of consumption that the household needs to subsist.

From these assumptions it immediately follows that children will work only when the adult wage is below s. Let w be the adult wage in the economy. If w exceeds s, subsistence consumption is achieved without requiring that the children work. Note next that, given the above assumptions, if the adult wage is w, the wage rate for a child laborer must also be w, since children and adults are perfect substitutes. If we allow for the fact that children are less productive than adults, the child wage would be a fraction of w.

Let us now bring government into the picture. Suppose the government announces that each time a firm is found employing a child, the firm will be fined D rupees, as under India's Child Labour (Prohibition and Regulation) Act (1986). For every child employed by a firm, let p be the probability of the firm's being caught. In that case, for every child employed, the firm has an expected punishment cost of pD. Hence, unless the child wage is less than the adult wage by pD, it does not make sense for a firm to employ children. It follows that the child wage must now be equal to $w - pD$. Or, equivalently, the adult wage is equal to the child wage plus the expected penalty cost of employing a child.

Therefore, the child wage tends to move in tandem with the adult wage. As long as the legal regime remains unchanged (that is, p and D are unchanged), any change in the adult wage will always be matched by the same change in the child wage.

Next note that if w falls short of s, the household will send the children out to work. Let e be the number of children sent out to work. Since households send children to work only so as to be able to reach subsistence, it must be the case that e will be chosen so as to just achieve this target.[5]

It follows from this condition that as the adult wage drops, the household will send more children to work (that is, as w drops, e will rise). Of course, this cannot go on endlessly, since after some time the household will run out of children. From then on, as w drops, there will be no further increase in supply of child labor, since all children are already working. But the general point is now amply clear—there will be a segment of the supply curve that is backward-bending.

Many of the peculiarities of the child labor market with which the literature has been concerned, such as the possibility of multiple equilibria (Basu and Van 1998; Basu 2002; Swinnerton and Rogers 1999; Bardhan and Udry 1999; Lopez-Calva 2003), can easily be constructed by using this kind of supply characterization. But that is not the direction I wish to pursue here. To stay away from that, let me consider the case where (the demand curve is sufficiently elastic so that) there is only one equilibrium, and at this equilibrium there is some child labor.

My concern here is with policy interventions and to show how there can be an adverse reaction to certain seemingly reasonable interventions. Consider the case where the government, starting from the equilibrium where there is some child labor, decides to raise the fine for employing children. (We could also think of a switch from no fines [that is, $D = 0$] to some positive fine.) This will mean that employing children will be more expensive for the firms, because with each child employed there is the risk of being caught and having to pay the larger fine to the government. Hence, as the penalty for employing children rises, the market will make sure that the child wage will drop. Otherwise, no firm will demand children. But once the child wage drops, each household will be forced to send more children to work to meet the subsistence consumption target. And herein lies the essence of the pathology: an increased fine for employing children could raise the level of child labor. Indeed, this result obtains so naturally that it is not clear that it should be thought of as pathology at all.

If, however, the government continues to raise the penalty for employing children (D) and/or the probability (p) of catching firms that employ children, the above result will cease to hold. To see this, suppose a government keeps raising D. This will cause the child wage to fall. In the extreme, the child wage will drop to zero. That is, child employment is so risky for the firm that a firm will agree to employ a child only if it does not have to pay a wage. But when this happens, raising the child labor supply will not fetch the household any extra income. Thus the child labor supply will drop to zero. In other words, there will be no child labor in the economy.

To sum up, a small punishment for child labor may have quite the opposite effect of a large punishment, because the relation between the size of the penalty for employing children and the amount of child labor may be an inverted U. A small penalty raises child labor but a large one puts an end to it. It will indeed be interesting to check this result out empirically.

It is worth emphasizing that here I have not evaluated policy from the point of view of child *welfare* but have simply studied its effect on the *incidence* of child labor. And, as I have cautioned above and elsewhere in my writings, a decline in child labor need not always coincide with a rise in child welfare.

Before moving on, I must attend to one seeming difficulty with the above analysis. Since, as we have just shown, in some cases the child labor problem is made worse by the imposition of a fine for employing children, it seems natural to wonder if the problem of child labor can be mitigated by subsidizing firms for employing children. The answer is no. A subsidy does not work like the reverse of a tax or a penalty. Thus it would clearly be wrong policy to reward firms for employing children.

To see this, we must understand something that was handled above by not talking about it. Suppose that a firm decides to use C units of child labor. Clearly it can do this by employing different numbers of children. It can, for instance, employ $2C$ children with each child doing half-time work or C children with each child working full-time, and so on. In most models of economics, it does not matter how the total is broken up, and it is implicitly assumed that firms make each worker do full-time work, so that for C units of labor it uses C laborers. In the above model, with a penalty for every child that is found working in the firm, a firm will have a clear preference for employing as few children as possible, since each child brings with him or her a possible penalty.

The trouble with a subsidy for employing children is that this implicit assumption (which is valid when there is a *fine* associated with child labor) breaks down. In the presence of a *subsidy* for each child employed, it will be in the interest of the firms to get the same volume of labor from many children, then take these children to the local government office as proof of child labor and collect the subsidy. In other words, announcing a subsidy would cause a fiscal crisis, with firms making notional use of child labor and collecting money.

CONCLUDING REMARKS

There has been a lot of discussion in the literature on what should be the right agency for controlling child labor. Should it be the national government or should it be some global body, such as the WTO or the ILO? Or should it be ordinary consumers who discourage child labor by boycotting products made with child labor? There are indeed a number of complex issues involved in answering these questions, many of them mired in intricate matters of political economy and international law (see, for instance, Fung et al. 2001). Economists such as Bhagwati (1995) have rightly worried about empowering agencies such as the WTO, to which poor countries have inadequate access and which can quickly be converted to an instrument of northern protectionism. Likewise, I would hesitate to turn this matter over to consumers in industrialized nations to exercise control through product boycotts, since this can also be an instrument of protection and because we know—and Arthur Miller has immortalized this in drama—how witch hunts come easily, with a little egging on by interested lobbies (Basu 2001).

But even apart from these larger questions of political economy, we need to contend with narrow questions concerning the kinds of instruments (whoever implements them) that ought to be used. Should we try to control child labor by offering free meals to children who go to school? Or should we control child labor by, instead, creating better schools?[6] Should we try to curb child labor by punishing those who employ children or parents who allow their children to work? And if we decide to do either, what should the punishment be? Policy makers, governments, and international organizations often pay no attention to these details in exhorting us to act. What this essay has tried to show is that such exhortations, without closer analysis of exactly *how* we should act, may not be of much value and can even be counterproductive.

ACKNOWLEDGMENTS Some of the ideas expressed here were part of a lecture given at the third MULTI conference in Bergen, Norway, on May 24, 2002. The essay has benefited from the comments of Abhijit Banerjee, Hyejin Ku, Per Boltof Maurseth, and Dilip Mookherjee. I am also grateful to the Centre for Studies in Social Sciences, Kolkata, where a part of this work was done.

NOTES

1. In Basu (1999) I have discussed how the magnitude of child labor in today's world compares with the situation in nineteenth-century Britain. For detailed analyses of the historical evidence, see Moehling (1999) and Humphries (2003).

2. It must be clarified that to say that poverty causes child labor is not to deny that child labor can have other causes, such as greater opportunity for child work, lack of schooling opportunity, or parental illiteracy (see, for instance, Emerson and Souza 2002; Bhalotra and Heady 2003), just as a fire being caused by a carelessly discarded cigarette stub does not preclude the spilled kerosene on the floor from being a cause.

3. This would change in 1938, when the Fair Labor Standards Act brought the entire nation under a uniform code of labor standards.

4. The analysis in this essay is not predicated on households taking the decision concerning child labor. The results go through even if child labor is an autonomous decision of the child, which is empirically not as remote as some may have assumed (see Iversen 2002).

5. Formally, $e(w - pD) = s - w$. Recall that $w - pD$ equals the child wage. Hence the term on the left is the total income earned by the children of the household. And this is equal to the gap between subsistence need and adult income.

6. This is the dilemma addressed by Jafarey and Lahiri (2005).

BIBLIOGRAPHY

Bardhan, Pranab, and Christopher Udry. *Development Microeconomics*. Oxford: Oxford University Press, 1999.

Basu, Kaushik. "Child Labor: Cause, Consequence and Cure with Remarks on International Labor Standards." *Journal of Economic Literature* 37 (1999): 1083–1119.

Basu, Kaushik. "The Intriguing Relationship between Adult Minimum Wage and Child Labor." *The Economic Journal* 110 (2000): C50–C61.

Basu, Kaushik. "Compacts, Conventions and Codes: Initiatives for Higher International Labor Standards." *Cornell International Law Journal* 34 (2001): 487–500.

Basu, Kaushik. "A Note on Multiple General Equilibria with Child Labor" *Economics Letters* 74 (2002): 301–308.

Basu, Kaushik, and Zafiris Tzannatos. "The Global Child Labor Problem: What Do We Know and What Can We Do?" *World Bank Economic Review* 17 (2003): 147–173.

Basu, Kaushik, and Pham Hoang Van. "The Economics of Child Labor." *American Economic Review* 88 (1998).

Bhagwati, Jagdish. "Trade Liberalization and 'Fair Trade' Demands: Addressing the Environmental and Labor Standards Issues." *World Economy* 18 (1995).

Bhalotra, Sonia, and Christopher Heady. "Child Farm Labor: The Wealth Paradox." *World Bank Economic Review* (2003).

Bourguignon, François, Francisco H. G. Ferreira, and Philippe G. Leite. "Conditional Cash Transfers, Schooling, and Child Labor: Micro-Simulating Brazil's Bolsa Escola Program." *World Bank Economic Review* 17 (2003): 229–254.

Cigno, Alessandro, and Furio Rosati. "Why Do Indian Children Work and Is It Bad for Them?" Mimeo, University of Florence, Faculty of Political Science, 2000.

Edmonds, Eric. "Does Child Labor Decline with Improvements in Economic Status?" Dartmouth College working paper #01–09, 2001. *Journal of Human Resources*, forthcoming.

Emerson, Patrick, and Andre P. Souza. "Is There a Child Labor Trap? Intergenerational Persistence of Child Labor in Brazil." *Economic Development and Cultural Change* 51 (2002): 375–398.

Fung, Archon, Dara O'Rourke, and Charles F. Sabel. "Stepping Up Labor Standards." *Boston Review* 26 (Feb. 2001): 4–10.

Grootaert, Christiaan, and Harry Patrinos. *The Policy Analysis of Child Labor*. New York: St. Martin's Press, 1999.

Government of India. Child Labour (Prohibition and Regulation) Act, 1986. Available online at http://www.vakiln01.com/bareacts/childlabouract/childlabouract.htm.

Hazan, Moshe, and Binyamin Berdugo. "Child Labor, Fertility and Economic Growth." *The Economic Journal* 112 (2002): 810–828.

Humphries, Jane. "Child Labor: Lessons from the Historical Experience of Today's Industrial Economies." *World Bank Economic Review* 17 (2003): 175–196.

ILO. *Every Child Counts: New Global Estimates on Child Labor.* Geneva: IPEC/ILO, 2002.

Iversen, Vegard. "Autonomy in Child Labor Migrants." *World Development* 20 (2002): 817–834.

Jafarey, Saqib, and Sajal Lahiri. "Will Trade Sanctions Reduce Child Labor? The Role of Credit Markets." *Journal of Development Economics* 68 (2002): 137–156.

Jafarey, Saqib, and Sajal Lahiri. "Food for Education and Funds for Education Quality." *Canadian Journal of Economics,* forthcoming.

Levison, Deborah, Richard Anker, A. Ashraf, and Sandhya Barge. "Is Child Labor Really Necessary in India's Carpet Industry?" In *Economics of Child Labor in Hazardous Industries of India,* edited by Richard Anker et al. Baroda: Centre for Operations Research and Training, 1998.

Levison, Deborah, Jasper Hoek, David Lam, and Suzanne Duryea. "Implications of Intermittent Employment for Child Labor Estimates." Mimeo, University of Minnesota, Minneapolis, 2002.

Lopez-Calva, Luis Felipe. "Social Norms, Coordination and Policy Issues in the Fight against Child Labor." In *International Labor Standards: History, Theories, and Policy Options,* edited by Kaushik Basu, Henrik Horn, Lisa Román, and Judith Shapiro. Oxford: Blackwell, 2003.

Moehling, Carolyn. "State Child Labor Laws and the Decline of Child Labor." *Explorations in Economic History* 36 (1999): 72–106.

Nardinelli, Clark. *Child Labor and the Industrial Revolution.* Bloomington: Indiana University Press, 1990.

Ravallion, Martin, and Quentin Wodon. "Does Child Labor Displace Schooling? Evidence on Behavioral Responses to an Enrollment Study." *The Economic Journal* 110 (2000): C158–C175.

Singh, Nirvikar. "The Impact of International Labor Standards: A Survey of Economic Theory." In *International Labor Standards: History, Theories and Policy Options,* edited by Kaushik Basu, Henrik Horn, Lisa Román, and Judith Shapiro. Oxford: Blackwell, 2003.

Swinnerton, Kenneth A., and Carol Ann Rogers. "The Economics of Child Labor: Comment." *American Economic Review* 89 (1999): 1382–1385.

18

The Primacy of Education

Anne Case

EDUCATION, HUMAN CAPITAL, AND HUMAN CAPABILITIES

Many economists, pressed to list the keys to economic development, would turn first to education. Beliefs regarding the primacy of education in the development process stem both from the fundamental role of education in income generation and from the many other ways in which education is thought to promote and sustain development and, in turn, to enhance quality of life.

The first section of this essay highlights what we know about the role of education in three interrelated areas: income generation, health status, and fertility. Perhaps surprisingly, given the great amount of attention that the subject has enjoyed, estimates of the extent to which education causes earnings to rise, or promotes better health and longer life, remain the subject of lively debate in economics. We discuss reasons why measuring the impact of education is difficult, and present the best current estimates we have for the effects of education in these important areas.

In bringing education to people in the developing world, an understanding of which school inputs are most effective, and at what levels of education, is paramount. The second half of the essay discusses why we know very little about which inputs are most effective, and contrasts different approaches to assessing the impact of school inputs. We end with a discussion of programs that promise to be more successful in helping governments and policy makers decide how best to invest in human capital.

Education and Income Generation

In both developing and developed countries, better-educated workers earn higher wages on average than do less well-educated ones. This may be true for a host of reasons, which complicates attempts to quantify the causal effects of schooling on earnings. In developing countries, wealthier families can afford to educate their children, and can aid them in finding superior jobs. Untangling which part of earnings is due to education, and which part to (say) the quality of family connections, is often far from straightforward. Years of completed schooling may also reflect a person's abilities, and those who are more able would be expected to earn higher incomes, regardless of schooling. Further complications arise because schooling is of uneven quality, so that, among children in South Africa, for example, having completed six years of schooling in rural KwaZulu-Natal may be very different from completing the same number of years in Durban. More broadly, this last point highlights the problems caused by the rather noisy measures of schooling we generally have available for analysis: not only does schooling vary in quality, but people misremember the number of years they have obtained, and (perhaps more often) their schooling is misremembered by the "knowledgeable household member" chosen to act as the family's informant in many household surveys.

Since the 1970s, much has been learned about the relationship between education and earnings, largely due to marked improvements in the quantity and quality of data collected, and to the attention paid to the measurement issues raised above by both economic theorists and applied economists.[1] Several strategies have been suggested to quantify the impact of education on earnings. For example, some researchers have looked at differences in earnings between siblings and have correlated these with differences in their educations. To the extent that siblings have the same access to family resources and contacts, the differences in earnings between them may be attributable to the differences in their educational attainment. While such a strategy may succeed in neutralizing the role of families, it doesn't explain why siblings differ in their years of schooling. If these differences are due to differences in ability, then this sort of strategy could end up magnifying the bias caused by unobserved ability.

A second tack in analyzing returns to schooling has been to focus on those differences in years of completed schooling that can be attributed to institutional differences, between places or over time. Differences in proximity to a school, enforced minimum school leaving ages, or restrictions on child labor may lead some children to attend school longer. Differences in completed schooling that can be attributed to such institutional arrangements may meet the statistical requirements necessary for them to be useful in estimating returns to education. For example, in recent work Duflo (2001) analyzes the impact of a massive school-building program in Indonesia where, between 1973 and 1978, 61,000 primary schools were built, targeted in those areas in which children were least likely to have been enrolled prior to the building program. Children young enough to benefit from the new schools, who were living in areas targeted for school building, completed more years of schooling on average. Observing these children as working adults, Duflo estimates an economic return to an extra year of schooling of roughly 10%.

This work broadly confirms the findings of Psacharopoulos (1994), who provides a comprehensive set of estimates on the profitability of investments in education around the world. Psacharopoulos concludes that primary schooling remains "the number one investment priority" for developing countries. He also finds the return to an additional year of education is marginally higher for girls (increasing earnings by 12.4% on average) than for boys (11.1%), and that the returns to education follow the same rules as other sorts of investments, declining as the investment is expanded.

In regions in which there are payoffs to learning—due to the introduction of new technologies or to changes in market conditions, for example—investment in education can yield a large return. However, in order for returns to education to be positive, either there must be economic opportunities that take advantage of the skills embodied in education, or investment in education must induce innovation. Rosenzweig (1995) makes this point through an example of differences in the returns to primary education between regions of India during the green revolution. In those areas agroclimatically suited to the use of the new higher-yielding variety seeds, returns to primary schooling rose: those farmers who had been to school were apparently more skillful in adopting the new seeds. However, those areas unsuited to the new seeds saw no change in the returns to primary schooling.

Recognition that better-educated workers need opportunities, if incomes are to be enhanced by schooling, is especially important when large changes in education policy are under consideration—changes, for example, such as the enforcement of compulsory schooling laws or extensive school-building programs. Duflo (2004), in a follow-up to her original work on the Indonesian school-building program, finds that while the program led to large increases in the proportion of primary school graduates in the labor force in those parts of the country that undertook the largest building efforts, this resulted in slower wage growth in the earnings of older workers—a result that would be expected if (for whatever reason) physical capital wasn't increased in response to the increase in human capital. It may be the need for different vintages of human capital, rather than physical capital, that holds down returns to education. Kremer and Thomson (1998) posit that older and younger workers are imperfect substitutes, having comparative advantages in different, complementary tasks, which may explain why many African countries witnessed marked increases in educational attainment but little improvement in economic growth.

Countries have also been observed reaping the benefits of earlier investments in education, but only after economic reforms are introduced. Drèze and Sen (2002) contrast the differences in economic performance in China and India before and after market reforms enacted in China in 1979. China had invested much more heavily in education than had India through the 1970s, with the result that literacy rates among adults in China (51% for women, and 79% for men) were markedly higher than those in India (26% and 55% percent, respectively) by the early 1980s. However, Drèze and Sen note that until the Chinese market reforms of 1979, India and China had similar economic growth rates. It took market reform, in combination with higher literacy rates in China, to sustain rapid economic expansion there in the 1980s and 1990s.

Moreover, once there is tangible evidence that human capital investments yield a handsome return, couples may choose to limit the number of children they raise, in order to offer each child more education. Lucas (2003) argues that the phenomenon of children leaving the family farm, where all necessary skills are acquirable through on-the-job training, for work that requires additional skills learned at school, where there is a substantial return to this investment, may result in fertility declines. In this way, improved opportunities—brought on by technological change or the opening of markets—blazes a trail from fertility reduction and increased educational attainment to sustained economic growth.

Education and Health Status

In both developed and developing countries, a strong correlation exists between schooling and good health, whether measured using mortality rates, morbidity rates, or self-reported health status. Each additional year of schooling for men in the United States is associated with an 8% reduction in mortality, a result consistent with those found in many European countries.[2] In surveys run in both the developed and the developing world, people with greater levels of schooling report themselves to be significantly healthier (Case 2002).

There are many ways in which education may affect health. Not only does education lead to higher income and to less risky choices of occupation, but education also increases people's understanding of sanitation and hygiene, improves their ability to read labels of all sorts, encourages their use of health care systems, and, in countless other ways, acts to protect and promote their health (Caldwell 1986).

Health disparities between better- and less well-educated people often increase when a new health technology is introduced. If better-educated people understand the importance of a health innovation more quickly, or are able to change their behaviors more rapidly to take advantage of health advances, we would expect to see differences in health status between better- and less well-educated people widen, at least in the medium run, until those with less education are able to catch up with the new technologies. Preston (1996) presents evidence on this, using data from U.S. censuses conducted around the beginning of the twentieth century. He argues convincingly that until the germ theory of disease was advanced in the late 1800s, the mortality rate for the children of schoolteachers was no better than the national average. However, by the early 1920s, when knowledge of how to protect against germs was spreading, the mortality of teachers' children fell to 40% below the national average.

As was true of income, there are many other reasons why a correlation might exist between education and health, which makes it difficult to quantify the impact of education in this domain. Healthier people may be better able to succeed in the classroom, leading to a channel from better health to additional schooling. Healthier people may anticipate a longer life, and thus greater lifetime returns to education, which may also lead them to choose more years of schooling. (The extent to which the shadow of HIV/AIDS will affect schooling decisions in the developing world is not yet well understood, but it seems likely that the specter of premature death will influence investment choices.) In addition, there may be determinants of health and education that lead to a spurious correlation between them. People with more self-control, for example, may invest more in both their health and their education. Evidence along these lines comes from creative work showing that although there is a strong, negative relationship between smoking and completed schooling at age twenty-four, this can be explained by differences in smoking behavior at age seventeen, when all of the individuals under study were still in the same grade (Farrell and Fuchs 1982). Since future schooling cannot reach back and cause smoking at age seventeen, the association between smoking and education is more likely attributable to third factors that drive them both.

New evidence on the causal effect of education on longevity comes from innovative work that exploits differences in years of schooling that grew out of changes in compulsory schooling laws in the United States. Lleras-Muney (2005) finds that differences between states in these laws in the early part of the twentieth century are strong predictors of completed education for individuals raised in the 1920s and 1930s, and she uses the variation in years of completed education that can be attributed to differences between states in their compulsory schooling laws to identify the impact of schooling on mortality. She finds that, in 1960, an additional year of education increased life expectancy at age thirty-five by as much as 1.7 years. This work is the most convincing work to date on the causal impact of education on health, since compulsory laws are not expected to influence health outcomes except through their impact on years of completed education.

Education and Fertility

There are many reasons why we would expect increased education to have a causal effect on fertility, and many researchers have documented the close articulation between education and fertility decline. Complementary to the arguments made by Lucas—that enhanced opportunities for educated workers act as a catalyst for fertility transition—Caldwell (1982) hypothesizes that, in the developing world, schools serve to advance the values of the Western middle class, leading to a restructuring of family relationships and a reversal in the flow of household resources (in favor of children). Prior to the onset of mass education, children worked inside and outside the house, doing chores and contributing time and money to the household resource base. Once children are in school, not only do they have less time for work, but their status as students also tends to lower the household's expectations about their work. And, given that the education of children has a public good component, society also invests in children's educations, raising expectations generally that children's families will protect that investment. Thus, while Lucas emphasizes the increased return to investment in education as leading to fewer children, Caldwell focuses on the increased costs of raising a child and diminished expectations of the lifetime return to parents from that child—both consequences of schooling—as setting off a fertility transition.

Other researchers have focused on the relationship between women's education and fertility decline, arguing that a woman's education reduces her desired family size, changes the relationship between her desired number of children and planned number of births, and improves her ability to achieve her desired family size.[3] Education increases the opportunity cost of women's time, because the skills learned at school find a return in the marketplace. Better-educated women may have higher aspirations for their children, which may cause them to weigh "quality" more heavily in a "quality vs. quantity" trade-off with regard to their children. Declines in fertility and infant mortality move hand in hand, and women's education may also have an indirect effect on fertility through the role it plays in reducing infant mortality. Better-educated women are more likely to know about hygiene and nutrition, and are more likely to act on this knowledge.[4] Education is apt to give women more voice in household decisions, allowing them to stand up to men in general. If women are the protectors of the needs of small children, then children are apt to benefit indirectly in this way from mothers' schooling.

These arguments on the impact of mass education in reversing intergenerational resource flows, and of women's education in reducing total fertility, are all sensible. Unfortunately, it is difficult to find evidence that education has a causal effect on fertility, evidence that would allow us to reject the view that the association between increased education and reduced total fertility rates is due to some third factor. Girls in developing countries who are educated beyond primary school may be a highly motivated, very select group, who may have lower total fertility for other reasons.[5] It may not be women's education per se that causes fertility to decline, but that educated women are more likely to marry educated men, and these men may have strong preferences for lower fertility. Young women who have had children may find it difficult to return to school—because of the demands placed on them at home and because many schools discriminate against young mothers returning to school. All of these factors would lead us to find a connection between women's education and fertility but not one that was causal.

Even keeping these third factors in mind, some researchers argue that the evidence supports a causal impact of education on fertility. Caldwell (1982) notes that fertility declines in the countries of nineteenth-century Europe followed immediately after increases in mass education in these countries and that, within a decade of the introduction of compulsory schooling, fertility was declining for all occupational groups. However, this is far from settled territory. It may be that fertility declined as a result of the mortality decline that Europe witnessed in the late nineteenth century, and the mortality declines were responsible for increased schooling. This, then, would put the timing of schooling increases and fertility declines in close proximity.

A second piece of evidence comes from India. Drèze and Murthi (2000) find that women's education is the most important correlate of fertility decline, both across districts and within districts over time. Because they are following districts from decade to decade, these researchers can estimate the impact of education on fertility solely using differences in these variables over time within each district. Doing so allows them to rule out some of the "third factor" explanations for the relationship between education and fertility by eliminating differences between districts that remain fixed over time. Drèze and Murthi find large effects of women's education: a ten percentage point increase in female literacy is associated with an expected decline in the total number of children born to women during their lifetimes of 0.2 child. To understand the magnitude of this estimate, it is interesting to compare it with the impact of religion on fertility: a ten percentage point increase in the proportion of the population in the district that is Muslim is associated with an increase in total fertility of 0.2 child.

EDUCATIONAL PRODUCTION

Taking as given that education plays an important role in development, we are led to a second set of questions: How should countries deploy school resources to increase educational attainment? Is it more important for a school with a fixed budget to reduce class sizes or to increase teachers' salaries? Do student outcomes respond more to the availability of textbooks or to enhanced teacher incentives? Understanding the impact of school inputs is indeed an important goal, one that has spawned a very large literature devoted to measuring the impact of school inputs. Unfortunately, most papers in this literature attribute a causal effect to the association between school inputs and student performance, which is not appropriate if resource allocation responds to students' needs, as will almost always be the case. Schools and parents can and do respond to the academic readiness of their children by moving the levers they have available—setting class sizes and allocating teachers' aides and classroom resources, for example. That schools respond to children's academic readiness makes it difficult to evaluate the relative merits of different inputs, and adds much confusion to the debate over resource effectiveness.

School Inputs as Choice Variables

This point is addressed thoughtfully in a paper by Lazear (1999), who builds on the idea that, at any point during the schoolday, there is some chance that any given student will be "disruptive," initiating behavior that temporarily stops other students in the class from learning. "Disruptive" behavior includes misbehavior, as well as asking questions to which other students in the class already know the answer. A prerequisite for learning to take place at a point in time is that all children in the class are nondisruptive at that moment. If p is the probability that a student is not being disruptive at a given point in time, then the probability that no student in the class of size n is being disruptive at a point in time is p^n. Lazear notes that we would expect children to behave most of the time but, even if $p = 0.98$, in a class of twenty-five students, disruptions would occur 40% of the time: $(1 - 0.98^{25} = 0.40)$. Learning per student decreases with increases in class size, and increases with the probability that children are behaving.

As Lazear notes, by itself this tells us little about optimal class size. Answers to questions about optimal class size depend on several factors. We also need to know the value of education to the students, for which (as discussed above) estimates exist. In addition, we need to know the cost of providing teachers and classrooms. With this information, working under the assumption that any given child is disruptive $(1- p)$ fraction of the time, we can calculate the optimal class size.

Lazear makes several related points about the relationship we should observe between class size and student outcomes if class size has been set optimally. He stresses that because class size is a choice variable, we should expect to find only small, or possibly perverse, class size effects in cross-sectional data. We should expect to see fewer disruptive students in larger classes and, if class size varies primarily because of differences in student behavior, then we should expect to find larger classes with better students and better outcomes, leading to a perverse relationship between class size and educational output.

This provides an explanation for the sometimes small and insignificant effects of class size on student outcomes reported in the literature. Surveys by Hanushek (1986, 1995), for example, argue that school facilities have little effect on outcomes, particularly on test scores (although, for developing countries, the results are quite mixed, with some research finding large and significant effects of school inputs).

One reason researchers analyzing developing country data find significant effects of school inputs, while those analyzing industrialized country data do not, may be because schools in developing countries are less responsive in general to the needs of students. Lazear also notes that his results are consistent with the fact that researchers find large and significant effects of school inputs in those cases where variation in inputs is due to some sort of experiment—that is, to some identifiable factor thought to influence input choice but not otherwise influence student outcomes.

Experiments and Quasi Experiments

There have been very few true experiments designed to evaluate the merits of school inputs. Some researchers argue that this is not an accident. Experiments offend the sensibilities of those who were trained in schools of education, and who view schools as complex social organizations that can be better served by management consultants than by social scientists running experiments (Cook 2001).

There are many questions, however, where evidence based on experiments may offer insight that would otherwise be lost. Glewwe et al. (2004), for example, analyze retrospective data on the presence of flip charts in Kenyan primary schools and their impact on children's test scores. When looking just at the association between flip charts and test scores, they find a large and significant effect, with the presence of flip charts increasing student test scores by 20% of a standard deviation. Such results might cause schools to place the small amount of discretionary funds they have available on flip charts. However, when these same authors ran controlled trials, in which flip charts were given to a randomly selected set of schools, whose test scores were later compared with those in a set of control schools that did not receive the flip charts, these authors found no effect of flip charts on test scores— suggesting that their earlier findings were due to some other factor correlated with both the presence of flip charts and students' test results.

Experiments designed to help us better understand the role of different school inputs are currently being run in many developing countries (Kremer 2003). However, until they are well established, our best hope of quantifying the impact of school resource allocation on student achievement comes from *natural experiments*—that is, from identifiable factors that affect school inputs, but whose only connection with the outcomes under study comes via their influence on inputs used.

Variation in school inputs that comes from such factors allows us to avoid the pitfalls discussed above—that schools' input choices reflect deliberate responses to students' needs—that prevent us from estimating the causal effects of inputs on student achievement. There is a second pitfall that natural experiments also often help us avoid. School administrators are not the only actors influencing the quality of a child's education. Parents who care about education may move to be close to good schools and may be willing to pay higher housing prices to do so. They may fight to increase local school funding and quality. Such parents may also instill in their children a strong desire to learn, and they may spend time and effort at home helping children with their studies. In such cases, a positive relationship between school resources and outcomes for children may be due to unobserved parental tastes for education, and it may not be possible to disentangle the effects of such tastes from those of school inputs. Natural experiments may allow us to do so. In the following subsections, we present results of studies on schooling in Israel and South Africa, in which school inputs were allocated in a manner that may allow us to quantify the impact of school resources.

Results from Israel: Maimonides' Rule

Angrist and Lavy (1999) examine the impact of Maimonides' Rule (a twelfth-century biblical dictum governing class size) on student test scores. Maimonides' Rule states that a class size is allowed to rise until there are forty students in a given class. When the forty-first student enters, the class is cut in half, so that instead of one class of forty-one, there are now two classes—one with twenty students and one with twenty-one students. Angrist and Lavy use the nonlinear relationship between the local number of students and the class size predicted by Maimonides' Rule to estimate the impact of class size on student performance, and to evaluate the effect of being just below the number of students for whom an additional teacher would be required, and of being just above that number. Maimonides' Rule yields highly irregular patterns in class size that are precisely mirrored in student test scores, with students in smaller classes scoring significantly higher on tests. Here, the important part of the identification strategy is that otherwise identical children are being treated differently. Their treatment depends on the number of children who are to be served locally. Angrist and Lavy find that a reduction in predicted class size of ten students is associated with a 0.25 standard deviation increase in fifth graders' test scores.

Results from South Africa

Case and Deaton (1999) use variation in school quality between magisterial districts in South Africa to estimate the impact of school quality on children's progress through school. Under apartheid, blacks were severely limited in their residential choice. Black parents were forced to send their children to black schools, whose funding decisions were made in Pretoria, by white-controlled entities on which blacks were not represented and over which they had no control. Over time, large differences evolved in average class sizes, with some districts averaging twenty children per teacher in black schools and others averaging upwards of eighty children per teacher. Controlling for household background variables—which themselves have powerful effects on outcomes, but have no effect on pupil-teacher ratios in South Africa—they find strong and significant effects of pupil-teacher ratios on enrollment, on educational achievement, and on test scores for numeracy. The striking result—that variables such as the mean schooling of parents in a community are uncorrelated with pupil-teacher ratios—provides support for the view that black families in the past had little control over the quality of the schools in their communities.

Interpreting Nonexperimental Evidence (Shoe Leather versus Technical Fixes)

Where school quality is thought to vary either because school administrators allocate resources systematically, according to student need, or because parents sort themselves according to their tastes for education, it is essential to have evidence from experiments or quasi experiments with which to judge the impact of school resources. Some researchers, grappling with these issues, have tried to minimize the estimation bias caused by the behavior of administrators and families, either by controlling directly for all available school and family variables, or by instrumenting school quality variables on variables thought to be correlated with school quality but not otherwise correlated with student achievement.

Neither of these approaches can solve the fundamental identification problem: such data do not have the information in them, and cannot be made to disgorge it by "technical fixes," such as sample selection corrections or instrumental variables.[6] It is unlikely that the complete set of variables that jointly determine school inputs and children's outcomes will ever be available to researchers. Even if they were, they cannot estimate the causal effect of school inputs: all are as much determined by achievements as by determinants of them. For this reason, calls in the literature for very expensive data collection—based on surveys that would collect information on every aspect of school production (class size, teacher incentives, textbooks, teacher autonomy, and so on) and every child and household characteristic (cognitive skills, attitudes toward school, aspirations, family background)—are misplaced. These variables are all determined jointly: students' attitudes toward school depend on their cognitive skills, which depend in turn on the students' attitudes toward school. Both of these depend upon (among many other things) class size, and class size will likely depend on students' cognitive skills and attitudes toward school. The point is not that researchers in education lack the "tools" that other social science researchers have in their toolboxes for disentangling the causal effects of each on the rest. The point is that such tools do not exist. Researchers could have at hand every variable related to school quality and to children's abilities and their households' characteristics, but they will not be able to use these data to settle disputes on the magnitude or significance of school inputs or operating style.

Estimation in which researchers identify variables that could be used as instruments for school inputs when estimating their impact on student outcomes is equally unlikely to yield meaningful results, unless there is a genuine experiment or quasi experiment where some individuals get treated in a way that affects their education—for example, by being just above or below Maimonides' cutoff for an additional class. On average, parents with more education often work to improve the quality of schools their children attend. But parents' education also has a direct effect on children's achievements, and therefore is not eligible for use as an instrument. The same is true of household income, distance to the better school, and most other variables thought to influence school quality.

Evaluating outcomes between schools that are operating under different rules in order to assess features of school operating systems is also generally not advisable. The phenomenon addressed by Lazear—that schools make choices based on the conditions they face (quality of the student body and faculty, attentiveness of parents, and so on)—comes into play here as well. To take a concrete example, the World Bank and many governments are interested in knowing whether school decentralization improves student outcomes. Decentralized schools give more control to the local decision makers, who may have superior information and may be better equipped to monitor the functioning of the schools. Evaluation of some countries' experiences with decentralization is made difficult, however, when schools are chosen by the government to participate in the decentralization program, or are allowed to volunteer for the program. Schools that choose to participate (or are "volunteered" by the government) differ in observable and unobservable ways from those that do not. The "treatment" and "control" terminology that researchers sometimes use when contrasting outcomes between two groups can obscure the fact that the choice to innovate may be related to features of the school that have their own effects on student achievement.

PROPOSALS FOR FUTURE RESEARCH

In spite of all the papers written on the relationship between school inputs and educational outcomes, almost everything is still unknown. We know that differences in the underlying conditions (pupil readiness, the value of education, the opportunity cost of teachers' time) should affect optimal allocations. We have argued above that our ignorance on the effectiveness of different policy interventions is likely to remain, unless governments or international organizations are prepared to do the hard (and sometimes expensive) work of documenting the impact of different policies. This idea is far from new. Newman et al. (1994) provide a thoughtful discussion of randomized control designs for the evaluation of social programs in developing countries, arguing not only that the results of experimental (randomized control) evaluations are the most robust, but also that they can make a virtue of necessity. Often resource constraints dictate that a program cannot begin everywhere at once. Those are often cases in which randomized control design can be built into a program's introduction at low cost.

We end by contrasting two different large-scale school intervention programs, one in which evaluation has been built in, the other in which evaluation is largely absent. Policy makers can learn lessons from both when forming a working agenda on education research.

India's District Primary Education Program (DPEP)

DPEP began in 1994, as a collaborative effort between the government of India and the World Bank, the European Commission, and the Department for International Development (DFID, U.K.). According to Aggarwal (2000), DPEP was designed to help poor areas, and was targeted to reach areas in which female literacy was especially low. Under DPEP, districts are given a high degree of discretion in developing strategies to provide access to primary education for all children and reduce primary dropout rates, equalize enrollment across genders and social strata, and improve test scores. However, the first districts chosen for treatment were selected "on the basis of their ability to show success in a reasonable time frame" (Pandey 2000, p. 14) and, within districts, the areas with the lowest female literacy were avoided. As a result, it is not possible to answer important questions—such as, on average, how effective is DPEP expected to be? That the program was intended to reach areas where female literacy was low, but program rollout was avoided in such areas, does little to aid our understanding of whether this is a program that will effectively equalize enrollment by gender!

In addition to the problems of evaluation caused by the nonrandom selection of initial sites for intervention, evaluation of DPEP is not based on the differences that develop between the DPEP and non-DPEP districts. Aggarwal notes in passing that "[t]here is a group of professionals who advocate that the progress of DPEP districts should be compared with non-DPEP districts to have more realistic assessment of the DPEP gains. While there is some justification in the argument, this provision does not form part of the proposed [monitoring and evaluation] mechanisms. . . . Comparison between DPEP and non-DPEP districts will not be adequate to measure the differential impact of DPEP since the base conditions in both areas are different in terms of many other inputs" (Aggarwal 2000, p. 36). But without data from non-DPEP districts, it is not possible to evaluate DPEP properly, which deprives educators, governments, parents, and students of a chance to understand clearly which of the many DPEP changes are working, and which ones only reflect changes in the country that are occurring in all (DPEP and non-DPEP) schools.

Mexico's Progresa Program

In contrast, school interventions in Mexico have been evaluated carefully. Mexico's Progresa (now Oportunidades) program is a large-scale poverty alleviation program designed to increase human capital. Under Progresa, parents are given transfers if their children attend school regularly. The program couldn't be initiated everywhere at once, and the decision was made to evaluate the difference in outcomes between groups who were treated and similar groups (randomly chosen) who were not.

Results of the intervention are powerful, with findings suggesting that the program has been successful in reducing the age of school entry, in decreasing the extent of grade repetition, and in reducing dropout rates (Behrman et al. 2001). This sort of evaluation, based on differences between treatments and controls, need not be as rare as is currently the case, and suggests an important way forward.

ACKNOWLEDGMENTS I thank Angus Deaton for helpful discussions and comments on an earlier draft.

NOTES

1. See the discussion provided in Card (1999).

2. See Elo and Preston (1996) for evidence from the United States, and Valkonen (1989) for estimates from Europe.

3. See Murthi et al. (1995).

4. Caldwell (1986) presents evidence that the interaction between mothers' education and access to an adequate health facility is a powerful combination in increasing child survival in Nigeria.

5. See Bledsoe et al. (1999) for a discussion on this point.

6. See Freedman (1991) for the seminal contribution here.

BIBLIOGRAPHY

Aggarwal, Y. "Monitoring and Evaluation Under DPEP, Measurement of Social Impact." Mimeo, National Institute of Educational Planning and Administration, India, 2000.

Angrist, Joshua D., and Victor Lavy. "Using Maimonides' Rule to Estimate the Effect of Class Size on Scholastic Achievement." *Quarterly Journal of Economics* 114 (1999): 533–575.

Behrman, Jere, Piyali Sengupta, and Petra Todd. "Progressing Through PROGRESA: An Impact Assessment of a School Subsidy Experiment." Mimeo, University of Pennsylvania, 2001.

Bledsoe, Caroline H., J. A. Johnson-Kuhn, and John G. Haaga. "Introduction." In *Critical Perspectives on Schooling and Fertility in the Developing World*, edited by Caroline H. Bledsoe, J. B Casterline, J. A. Johnson-Kuhn, and John G. Haaga1–22. Washington, D.C.: National Academy Press, 1999.

Caldwell, John C. *Theory of Fertility Decline.* London: Academic Press, 1982.

Caldwell, John C. "Routes to Low Mortality in Poor Countries." *Population and Development Review* 12 (1986): 171–220.

Card, David. "The Causal Effect of Education on Earnings." In *Handbook of Labor Economics*, edited by Orley Ashenfelter and David Card. Amsterdam: Elsevier Science, 1999.

Case, Anne. "Health, Income and Economic Development." In *Annual World Bank Conference on Development Economics 2001/2002*, edited by B. Pleskovic and N. Stern, 221–241. Washington, D.C.: World Bank, 2002.

Case, Anne, and Angus Deaton. "School Inputs and Educational Outcomes in South Africa." *Quarterly Journal of Economics* 114 (1999): 1047–1084.

Cook, Thomas D. "Reappraising the Arguments Against Randomized Experiments in

Education: An Analysis of the Culture of Evaluation in American Schools of Education." Mimeo, Northwestern University, 2001.

Drèze, Jean, and Mamta Murthi. "Fertility, Education and Development." Development Economics Discussion Paper Series, no. 20. Suntory and Toyota International Centres for Economics and Related Disciplines, London School of Economics, 2000.

Drèze, Jean, and Amartya Sen. "India and China." In *India, Development and Participation*, edited by Jean Drèze and Amarty Sen. 2nd ed. Oxford: Oxford University Press, 2002.

Duflo, Esther. "Schooling and Labor Market Consequences of School Construction in Indonesia: Evidence from an Unusual Policy Experiment." *American Economic Review* 91 (2001): 795–813.

Duflo, Esther. "The Medium Run Effects of Educational Expansion: Evidence from a Large School Construction Program in Indonesia." *Journal of Development Economics* 74 (2004): 163–197.

Elo, Irma T., and Samuel H. Preston. "Educational Differentials in Mortality: United States, 1979–85." *Social Science and Medicine* 42 (1996): 47–57.

Farrell, Phillip, and Victor R. Fuchs. "Schooling and Health: The Cigarette Connection." *Journal of Health Economics* 1 (1982): 217–230.

Freedman, David A. "Statistical Models and Shoe Leather." *Sociological Methodology* 21 (1991): 291–313.

Glewwe, Paul, Michael Kremer, Sylvie Moulin, and Eric Zitzewitz. "Retrospective vs. Prospective Analyses of School Inputs: The Case of Flip Charts in Kenya." *Journal of Development Economics* 74 (2004): 251–268.

Hanushek, Eric A. "The Economics of Schooling: Production and Efficiency in Public Schools." *Journal of Economic Literature* 24 (1986): 1141–1177.

Hanushek, Eric A. "Interpreting Recent Research on Schooling in Developing Countries." *World Bank Research Observer* 10 (1995): 227–246.

Kremer, Michael. "Lessons from Randomized Evaluations of Educational Programs in Developing Countries." *American Economic Review, Papers and Proceedings* 93 (2003): 102–106.

Kremer, Michael, and James Thomson. "Why Isn't Convergence Instantaneous? Young Workers, Old Workers and Gradual Adjustment." *Journal of Economic Growth* 3 (1998): 5–28.

Lazear, Edward P. "Educational Production." *Quarterly Journal of Economics* 116 (1999): 777–803.

Lleras-Muney, Adriana. "The Relationship Between Education and Adult Mortality in the U.S." *Review of Economic Studies* 72 (1) (2005): 189–222.

Lucas, Robert E. "The Industrial Revolution Past and Future." *The Region*. Federal Reserve Bank of Minneapolis, 2003. Available online at http://www.minneapolisfed.org/pubs/region/04–05/essay.cfm.

Murthi, Mamta, Anne-Catherine Guio, and Jean Drèze. "Mortality, Fertility and Gender Bias in India: A District-Level Analysis." *Population and Development Review* 21 (1995): 745–782.

Newman, John, Laura Rawlings, and Paul Gertler. "Using Randomized Control Designs in Evaluating Social Sector Programs in Developing Countries." *World Bank Research Observer* 9 (1994): 181–201.

Pandey, R. S. "Going to Scale with Education Reform: India's District Primary Education Program, 1995–99." World Bank Country Studies, Education Reform and Management Publication Series, Vol. 1 (4). 2000. Available online at: http://www .worldbank.org/education. Accessed Oct 10, 2005.

Preston, Samuel H. "American Longevity: Past, Present and Future." Policy Brief no. 7. Center for Policy Research, Syracuse University, 1996.

Psacharopoulos, George. "Returns to Investment in Education: A Global Update." *World Development* 22 (1994): 1325–1343.

Rosenzweig, Mark R. "Why Are There Returns to Schooling?" *American Economic Review* 85 (1995): 153–158.

Valkonen, Tarmo. "Adult Mortality and Level of Education: A Comparison of Six Countries." In *Health Inequalities in European Countries*, edited by J. Fox, 142–162. Aldershot, U.K.: Gower, 1989.

19

Public Goods and Economic Development

Timothy Besley & Maitreesh Ghatak

Effective provision of public goods is a key determinant of quality of life. Conventional approaches to poverty measurement look only at private goods, but this view is too narrow. Access to safe drinking water, sanitation, transport, medical care, and schools is essential both as a direct component of well-being and as an input into productive capability.

The rich have the option to seek private alternatives, lobby for better services, or, if need be, move to a different area. The poor frequently do not. This accentuates deprivation that is measured on a more conventional private consumption basis. Households that appear to enjoy very similar levels of private consumption may in reality enjoy very different standards of living once public goods are taken into account. Mechanisms for effective delivery of public goods and services are therefore central to any credible poverty reduction strategy. This is increasingly recognized by development policy makers. For example, the U.N. Human Development Index, published since 1990, is an attempt to take a broader perspective by including indicators such as life expectancy and literacy. The World Bank's *World Development Report* of 2004 was devoted to the topic of improving public service delivery to the poor.

There are two broad categories of public goods that are needed to strengthen the position of the poor in developing countries:

Market-supporting public goods, those state interventions that make it feasible for the poor to participate in markets and hence benefit from gains from trade;

Market-augmenting public goods, which deal with cases where even a well-functioning market will not provide the correct level of the public good.

In both cases, it is well known that uncoordinated private actions will lead to underprovision of public goods. The main issue is what institutional arrangements have a comparative advantage in dealing with this underprovision.

The traditional view in economics was to equate public goods with government provision. The state was viewed as an actor that stands above the market and is able to correct failures without introducing any new distortions. Also, in this view, nonstate nonmarket institutions, such as voluntary and community organizations, either were ignored entirely or were thought to be transitional phenomena in the development process whose functions would eventually be displaced by state or market activity.

We will argue that this view is now defunct. When it comes to public-goods provision, traditional boundaries between the state and the private sector do not provide a very useful analytical basis. It is now widely appreciated that government failure may be as important as market failure, and the mere existence of the latter does not necessarily justify government intervention. To the extent government intervention is called for, this does not automatically mean direct involvement of the state in economic activity, and could entail an indirect involvement through partnership with the private sector and the "third sector" consisting of voluntary and community organizations.

Despite the overwhelming evidence that a large fraction of government expenditure in developing countries on the provision of public goods does not reach the intended beneficiaries, public policy debates often continue to revolve around "how much" (i.e., how much money) is spent by the government on some particular public good.[1] Clearly, the question to ask is "how" (i.e., designing effective mechanisms for the delivery of public goods). This is the main theme of this essay. It is organized as follows. In the next section, we discuss different kinds of public goods that are vital to the poor and the evidence we have on their value. In the third section, we discuss spontaneous or voluntary private provision of public goods by the beneficiaries. In the fourth section we discuss formal provision of public goods where the government or some other organization is in charge of providing the public good, with special emphasis on institution design issues.

TYPES OF PUBLIC GOODS

Market-Supporting Public Goods

The key market-supporting public good is the provision of law and order. The Weberian view of the state puts the monopoly of force as the sine qua non of state structures. This can be justified on public-good grounds: competitive provision in the presence of externalities implies suboptimal private provision. Indeed, where we see private provision, it is frequently through social networks for enforcing contracts. However, this leads to restriction of potential trade to those within the network. From the point of view of the economy as a whole, this is suboptimal. It would be better to permit trade with those outside the network.

Inadequate law and order is one of the principal symptoms of state failure throughout the developing world—the state is too weak in some dimensions and overbearing in others. It is too weak in failing to stand up to strong vested interests while failing to guarantee legal remedies to those with legitimate claims. It is overbearing when it exercises arbitrary authority and overrides judicial independence.

While law and order is often seen as a preoccupation only of businessmen and conservative politicians, the poor have much to gain from an efficient and transparent legal system, whether it is in the form of the ability to get a loan without huge collateral requirements, protection from unlawful eviction, or seeking recourse from exploitative behavior of unscrupulous moneylenders and employers.[2] The judicial system in developing countries often suffers from a shortage of resources, which results in slow and/or ineffective resolution of disputes.[3] On top of this, since access to the legal system is often governed by an individual's wealth or influence, the poor suffer disproportionately from failures of the legal system. There is strong evidence that improving property rights can enhance the possibilities for the poor to participate in markets. For example, Field (2003) examines a land titling program in Peru and shows that there is a significant gain in labor market participation by households that gain access to land titles.

Law and order is far from being a homogeneous public good. Around the world we see two broadly competing systems of law: the civil law system and the common law system. These differ both in terms of the implementation of laws and in the relationship between the political and legal systems. Glaeser and Shleifer (2002) have argued that there are important economic consequences for economic prosperity resulting from the choice of a legal system. They argue that civil law systems are more vulnerable to abuse by bad governments, leading to insecure property rights and poor governance in general.

If the legal system is weak, then goods that would normally be considered private goods can effectively become public goods. For example, consider the extreme case where formal property rights cannot be enforced at all. Then what an individual produces on his or her farm is essentially a public good, since other people can expropriate it. In this case, improving property rights and the legal system has extremely high payoffs in terms of improving investment incentives.[4]

There is also mounting macroeconomic evidence that weak legal systems discourage investment and adversely affect economic development. For example, the score of average protection against expropriation risk compiled by Political Risk Services is significantly positively correlated with GDP per capita in a large cross section of countries.[5]

Market-Augmenting Public Goods

Market-augmenting public goods are much closer to the standard list from economics textbooks, such as health and education, whose provision can bring benefits to society beyond the benefits to individuals. They also include some kinds of infrastructure investments, such as electricity, transport, and telecommunications.

In general, economists have become much more circumspect about the case for state provision in all these cases. This is mirrored in practical experience. Infrastructural services, such as postal and telecommunication services and rail and air transportation, have been privatized in many countries, and in many others, private providers coexist and compete with public agencies (Dixit 2002). Public agencies routinely subcontract road construction and repair work to private agencies. Whether private solutions are viable will depend on the nature of the legal system and the possibility for effective regulation.

In all cases, it has become evident that only some parts of the sectors in question have substantial public-good components. For example, electricity distribution may have important network externalities while electricity generation is not really a public good. Public health interventions, such as clean water and vaccination, have much stronger public-good components than some kinds of curative treatments. In universities, research is a public good that generates externalities that travel far beyond the campus, but teaching is not a public good in this sense. This should lead to solutions for provision that reflect the degree to which private action fails to serve the social good.

Spontaneous Provision of Public Goods

The canonical model of private provision of public goods is founded on the importance of free-rider problems in affecting individual incentives. The central proposition is that in the absence of coordination, cooperation, or coercion, a group of independent individuals is unlikely to be able to provide public goods at the socially optimal level even if they care about the level of public goods provided. Their private incentives to voluntarily contribute toward provision will be inadequate because they will receive only a fraction of the total benefit but bear the full cost. If we allow for altruism, things are more promising. But the general prediction is that things will fall short of the first best, as described by the Lindahl-Samuelson rule.

Recent research in economics has studied spontaneous collective action in response to this problem. It is important to understand when conditions favor collective action. The main insights from recent theoretical models in economics are that this is more likely when (1) interactions are more likely to be repeated because those who refuse can more easily be punished; (2)

when information is good, so that individuals' actions to assist in public-good provision can be observed; and (3) when there is a strong social structure that can be used to ostracize individuals or to withdraw other forms of cooperation.

These conditions are most likely to be satisfied in traditional societies where social ties and communities are strong. It is an irony of the development process that it sows the seeds of destruction for the basis of collective action by voluntary means, necessitating the creation of more formal institutions to provide public goods. That said, there is now plenty of evidence that collective action based on social ties can remain strong for many forms of activities, even those in developed economies where trust is important.

Social networks are a key part of the fabric for the private provision of public goods. This is true for market-supporting public goods. For example, McMillan and Woodruff (2002) discuss the provision of contract regulation in networks. However, since these networks are restricted to small groups that are socially connected, they clearly are very imperfect substitutes for formal legal enforcement. Networks are equally important for market-augmenting public goods. For example, Wade (1988) describes the importance of social networks in the regulation of water distribution in India.

However, networks tend to lead to a patchy solution to public-goods provision; those outside the network receive less access to public goods. Network provision could therefore be a source of inequality. Networks may also constitute a brake on mobility because individuals are reluctant to lose the benefits of network membership. Nonetheless, inequality of access may also be a feature of formal provision, depending on the way in which the political process allocates public goods.

Recent research on spontaneous collective action is making the role of inequality in public-good provision more apparent. The basic model of free-riding may suggest that income or wealth inequality should favor public-good provision if the rich are more likely to step in and provide the public good on behalf of the whole community. This is likely to be case if the marginal benefit from the public good is increasing wealth; for example, a rich farmer has the most to gain from a well-functioning irrigation canal.

However, there are reasons to doubt this neofeudal vision of a patrician class on whom the poor are dependent. There are a number of good reasons to think that inequality can reduce incentives for spontaneous collective action. First, it may be that there are reasons to think that heterogeneity of any kind creates greater social distance that weakens the use of social ties. For example, Miguel and Gugerty (2002) find evidence that social sanctions, which are an important mechanism for sustaining collective action, work less effectively in ethnically diverse communities. Second, the assumption of decreasing returns, a standard one in most economic contexts, implies that the more scarce an input is in a given production unit, the higher is its marginal return. As a result, one would expect a more unequal distribution of this input across production units to reduce efficiency.[6]

These theoretical possibilities are now borne out by empirical studies suggesting that inequality and population heterogeneity are impediments to public-goods provision. In a study of forty-eight irrigation communities in south India, Bardhan (2000) finds that the degree of inequality in landholding among the irrigators has a significant negative effect on cooperation on water allocation and field channel maintenance. Similar results have been reported by Dayton-Johnson (2000) from his analysis of fifty-four farmer-managed surface irrigation systems in central Mexico.

Formal Provision of Public Goods

There are two main kinds of formal institutions for provision of public goods: governments and nongovernmental organizations (NGOs). The latter are private organizations funded by private donors and governments that are typically run on a nonprofit basis. Whether provision is public or private, incentive problems abound in formal provision of public goods. These concern how projects are selected and employees are motivated to provide goods with wider social benefits. These issues have received only limited attention in existing analyses. But recognizing this may go to the heart of what form of provision is optimal.

We discuss formal provision of public goods in two steps. One key set of issues concerns the determinants of the level and composition of public-goods provision. Next, we discuss how to organize provision, taking the funding level as given.

Determinants of the Level and Composition of Public-Goods Provision

To study the financing and distribution of public goods, one cannot ignore the political system that governs how policy makers are chosen, and what kinds of policies are adopted. There is little doubt that the state has been, and will remain, a central player in public-goods provision. As long as it monopolizes coercion, it has the only viable way of raising significant revenues needed to fund ambitious programs of public-good provision. The earlier economics literature somewhat naïvely assumed the state to be some sort of planner that was interested in maximizing social surplus. The new political economy literature has put politics back at the heart of policy choice.

Economists have recently become sanguine about the use of constitutional engineering in improving government. This is partly motivated by an improved understanding of the way in which incentives work under different rules. For example, Persson and Tabellini (1999, 2003) argue that proportional representation systems and parliamentary systems provide better incentives for provision of public goods. They also find evidence for this proposition in cross-national data.

Another interesting possibility, which has been tried in India, is the use of political reservation. A certain proportion of seats are reserved for disadvantaged groups, such as low-caste groups or women. This boosts their political power. It can make the political system more representative of their interests, and hence the bundle of public goods provided by the state can be better targeted to their interests. There is mounting evidence (see Besley et al. 2004; Chattopadhyay and Duflo 2004; and Pande 2003) that this can change the priorities of government.

It is also becoming clear that a variety of complementary institutions are needed to support the state in delivering its functions effectively. Key among these are the media. If voters are uninformed about policy and politicians, they have little means of disciplining incumbents for poor performance. Agency problems on the part of politicians can be mitigated by effective media. Besley and Burgess (2002) argue that states in India with greater newspaper circulation also have governments that are responsive to shocks affecting the rural sector, such as droughts and floods.

A number of recent empirical studies suggest complex interactions over time between the economic environment and political institutions that affect a country's current economic condition, as well as the level and composition of public-goods provision.

For example, Iyer (2003) argues that there is a persistent effect on public-goods provision from patterns of colonial settlement in India. She finds that areas that were annexed by the British during the colonial period have lower levels of public goods such as schools, health centers, and roads in the post-independence period compared with areas that were ruled by native kings.

Countries in the Caribbean islands or Spanish America, such as Argentina, Brazil, and Cuba, were much richer than the United States or Canada until at least the beginning of the nineteenth century. Their fortunes were based on a plantation economy that employed slaves from Africa or the native population. This implied that the initial distribution of human and physical capital was very unequal. The elites in these countries, mostly of European descent, enjoyed a political hegemony and chose institutions (such as rules about landownership) to perpetuate their power. In contrast, the northern United States and Canada had neither a climate favorable to plantation economy nor a substantial endowment of native or slave labor. Thus the population consisted largely of people of European descent with similar levels of human and physical capital. Most operated as independent proprietors. Engerman and Sokoloff (2000) argue that this affected their relative progress toward democracy and in turn affected public policy. This was the case especially in the development of public primary schools, in which the United States and Canada performed exceptionally well compared with the Caribbean islands and Spanish America.

A parallel set of studies shows that ethnically diverse societies tend to provide fewer public services. According to calculations by Easterly (2001), most ethnically diverse societies have half the schooling, one thirteenth the telephones per worker, nearly twice the electric power losses, and less than half the share of paved roads compared with most ethnically homogeneous societies. What could be the mechanisms that lead to this? If externalities are limited to within ethnic groups, then the total demand for public goods, such as roads and education, that benefit all groups will be less. For example, if ethnic groups are separated geographically, there will be little demand for interregional travel. Similarly, if the different ethnic groups speak different languages and have different cultures, they will be less willing to support investment in public education.

INSTITUTION DESIGN ISSUES

We now discuss aspects of institution design that are critical in understanding public-goods provision. Thus, we abstract from funding issues and ask how public goods can be provided effectively at a given funding level. We focus on four issues: how incentives work in organizations charged with providing public goods; the scope for private provision via NGOs and contracting out to for-profit firms; the case for decentralized provision; and the role of competition.

Incentive Design for Public-Goods Provision

Whether provided by state or private organizations, individuals need to be motivated to provide goods that achieve collective benefits. The traditional model of state provision assumes away incentive problems, believing that the government can stipulate and enforce a level of provision. It implicitly assumes that individuals who work in the public sector need little direct motivation to pursue the social good. Rewards therefore depend little on performance. The implicit assumption is that teachers, health care professionals, and bureaucrats are public-spirited and that this is enough (see LeGrand 2003).

Under the title of the New Public Management, there is now much more attention paid to incentives in the public sector. The two central propositions are (1) that beneficiaries need to be given more say in the provision of public goods and services, and (2) that incentives for public servants need to be more high-powered, explicitly linking outputs and inputs. At some level, this is compelling. After all, it seems to mirror the model that prevails in the private sector. Beneficiaries or consumers have the right to choose among different providers, and workers and managers receive bonuses for generating higher profits.

But before embracing this new paradigm, it is important to remember where it came from. It was born out of efforts, most notably in the United Kingdom under Margaret Thatcher, to decrease the amount of public finances going to public goods and services while preserving service levels. The prevailing view was that the public sector was getting rents that could be extracted and converted to better service levels.

There are some important differences between public and private goods which imply that incentive issues are somewhat different and that a mechanical application of what is efficient in the private sector is likely to be misleading. Also, it is important to note that this has nothing to do with who owns or operates the organization that provides the public good, be it public, private for-profit, or nonprofit. These issues are fundamental to the technology of public-goods production and consumption.

First, in many cases the goods are complex, and as a result the objectives of the relevant organizations are somewhat imprecise. For example, the objective of a school is to provide good education, but this is much harder to define compared with, say, production of rice or provision of banking services or even some public services, such as garbage removal or power supply. This means that in these cases it would be hard to find good performance measures.

Second, such goods are complex because they involve several dimensions. For example, good education involves students being able to achieve high scores on standardized tests but also encourages a spirit of creativity and curiosity and inculcates values. The former is easy to measure, but if teachers are rewarded solely on the basis of the performance of students on tests, this might lead to an excessive focus on test-taking skills at the expense of the other components of a good education. This makes provision of incentives hard when employees have to perform multiple tasks (Holmstrom and Milgrom 1991). Similarly, if hospitals are given incentives to cut costs, they are going to sacrifice quality by refusing to treat certain types of illnesses or being excessively selective in using expensive medical procedures.

Third, individuals who choose to work in an organization that supplies public goods may be motivated not just by money, but also by the "cause." There are a number of different explanations for this. Individuals could be altruistic, caring about the benefits that they achieve for others. They could also be ideological, believing that their private actions fulfill some wider objective (religious or political). Outside of economics, this is given the general label of public service motivation (François 2000). Behavioral economists have urged going beyond the narrow conception of a self-interested economic agent and have emphasized the importance of the motive to reciprocate and the desire for social approval (Fehr and Falk 2002). The role of incentives is to harness these feelings and to apply them to the social good in an efficient manner.

Fourth, there may be many competing views on the right way to provide public goods—not just on the optimal level of provision but also on crucial aspects of project design. For example, should a school run by a nonprofit be allowed to teach religious material or just science and mathematics? This affects the extent to which agents working together to produce public goods and the beneficiaries have congruent objectives. What do these considerations imply about how agents providing public goods should be rewarded?

In terms of standard incentive theory, it is well known (see, for example, Dixit 2002) that in these environments, low-powered incentives are likely to be optimal. If performance measures are noisy, then making rewards very sensitive to performance does not give effective incentives, and imposes unnecessary risk on the employee. If the employee has to do several tasks, and some of these have good performance measures and others do not, then making her pay sensitive to the good performance measures will cause her to substitute effort away from the other tasks, and could result in a loss of efficiency.

The fact that providers may be motivated is also very important. This may reinforce the tendency toward low-powered incentives. If the employee receives a nonmonetary reward for doing her job well, then clearly she can be paid a lower wage and her pay does not have to be made very sensitive to her performance. Of course, the incentive structures offered for providing public goods may affect who chooses to work within the public-goods-producing sector. Lower wages may act as a screening device, attracting only those workers who have a desire to achieve the social good.

However, there are important caveats to this strategy. First, there may be a trade-off if individuals differ in their abilities. With lower wages and low-powered incentives, the public sector may end up being a haven for well-meaning but incompetent individuals. There may also be an adverse selection problem if there are some dishonest individuals who will use the public sector to pursue private ends. Besley and McLaren (1993) refer to the strategy of paying ultralow wages because these agents are expected to take bribes as capitulation wages. Under this strategy the public sector may end up being a haven for dishonest individuals.

The general point here is that a system of organization and remuneration for the provision for public goods will have to take into account not only how on-the-job incentives affect how those who work in the sector, but also who is attracted to work there. In this context, it is important to note that even if individuals are value-driven, whether they choose to exert extra effort may depend on whether the organization is run for profit (François 2000). In similar vein, Besley and Ghatak (2003, 2005) suggest an approach to public-goods provision that emphasizes the importance of mission formation in galvanizing effective organizations. Such missions serve to match individuals to organizations on the basis of their mission preferences. This also lessens the need for formal incentives.

Public-Sector Provision versus Contracting to Private For-Profits and NGOs

In the developing world, NGOs have been increasingly involved in the provision of relief and welfare, social services, and various development projects (e.g., agricultural extension, microlending) either directly or in partnership with the government.[7] This raises questions about alternative organizational forms of public-goods provision.

That the government should bear some responsibility for financing public-goods provision is quite uncontroversial. However, as to whether the government should provide it directly, through the public sector, is the subject of active policy debate in developed as well as developing countries. Organizational alternatives include contracting out to private for-profit firms or NGOs and public-private partnerships.

The advantage of government or NGO provision stems from the fact that no one is a residual claimant. This dulls incentives for the manager of such an organization to minimize waste. In contrast, if provision is through a for-profit firm (which is subsidized by the government because the good in question is a public good), the manager or the owners have strong incentives to run the operation in as cost-effective a manner as possible. The trouble is, sometimes this can be at the expense of quality, especially when it is hard to contract on. For example, a school run by a for-profit firm may be cost-efficient, but it may be unwilling to admit students from disadvantaged backgrounds or take extra care of students with learning disabilities. To the extent these things can be contracted on, the government may try to create incentives for these schools to admit such students. But if that is not the case, the choice of organizational form of delivery would depend on whether cost-cutting or quality maintenance is more important.[8]

A key issue in the choice between government provision and provision through NGOs is noncontractible aspects of project design. As we discussed in the previous subsection, people who may have the same valuation of a public good (e.g., dedicated teachers) may have very different views on the right way to provide it (e.g., importance of religion in the curriculum). NGOs may attract more motivated workers by providing a better match between the mission of the organization, its workers, and the beneficiaries. To the extent government policy is driven by electoral concerns, this may result in some public servants having to carry out policies they do not necessarily believe in, which will undermine motivation. However, the flip side of this is that contracting out to NGOs may involve project design that does not reflect the preferences of the median voter or may lead to a society polarized along religious or ethnic lines. To the extent these elements cannot be regulated, the government may decide to provide public goods in-house, even when contracting to an NGO would have saved money or ensured greater motivation on the part of employees.

Another key issue in the government versus NGO choice is that of accountability of NGOs. The prevailing view of public-goods provision by NGOs has transferred the traditional model of the public sector as staffed by highly motivated personnel to the private sector. Just as public sector workers were thought to be beyond incentives, so now it is the NGO workers. However, one has to be careful about the possibility of opportunistic behavior by NGOs. In countries with high unemployment and bad job prospects in the private sector, NGOs often become an instrument for rent-seeking activity at the expense of donors. The weak accountability structures of NGOs become worryingly apparent in this context. Unless there are many NGOs operating in the area, the beneficiaries are not in a position to vote with their feet. The same is true of government provision. But NGOs do not have to worry about getting elected. This can be a good thing in some respects, but it also means they are not accountable to their beneficiaries.[9]

A related but distinct question is, even when the government decides to collaborate with NGOs, what form should that collaboration take? Should the government retain the ownership of the public good (say, a school) and ask an NGO to run it, or should it finance or subsidize a school that is owned by an NGO?

The property rights approach, pioneered by Grossman, Hart, and Moore (see Hart 1995), studies this questions in the context of private goods where the allocation of ownership affects incentives to undertake noncontractible relationship-specific investments. Because these investments are not contractible, there is ex post bargaining over the surplus that they generate. Ownership positively affects bargaining power because the owner can always threaten to fire the other party after investments have been sunk. Therefore, the owner can extract a higher share of the surplus of the project, and this improves his investment incentives. However, by the same token, it reduces the investment incentives for the other party. Therefore, according to this theory, the party whose investment is more important for the project should be the owner. In particular, if one party has no useful investment to make, he should never be the owner, since that will only undermine the incentives of other parties.

Besley and Ghatak (2001) develop a theory of ownership in public-goods provision. They show that how much a party values a project is critical for who should own the project, irrespective of whose investment is more important. In particular, even if a party has no useful investment to make, he could optimally be the owner if he values the public good the most. This result reflects a key property of public goods—even if a party is fired after investments are sunk, he continues to care about the outcome of that project. This is never the case with private goods. Because of this property it is efficient to give ownership of the project to the party that values it most highly, since it gives the best investment incentives to that party, as well as to others. This reinforces the message that when public goods are being considered, the motivation of providers matters.

Decentralization

One of the key issues is the extent to which the responsibility of public-goods provision should reside with local or central government. Clearly, where public goods have national repercussions, as with defense, local solutions are likely to have spillovers across jurisdiction boundaries, and this would make local provision inefficient.

There are two main arguments for decentralization in public-goods provision. The first is based on the importance of exit options as citizens vote with their feet. Long ago, Tiebout described a quasi-market mechanism for public-goods provision that worked on this basis. However, it is arguably of limited relevance in the context of developing countries, where mobility costs are high due to pure infrastructure and segmented markets.

Arguments for decentralization have, therefore, for the most part hinged on improved accountability, due either to improved information being brought into the political process or to a better reflection of local preferences in the supply of public goods.

There is emerging evidence that decentralization does have an impact on local government performance. For example, Foster and Rosenzweig (2001) analyze Indian states which vary in terms of how decentralized they are, and find that more decentralized states produce a mix of public goods that more closely reflects the interests of the local population.

However, some areas may lack the preconditions for effective accountability due to the power of entrenched elites and poor political competition. If economic and political power is concentrated in the hands of the local elite, then there is a danger of elite capture in decentralized governments.[10] The local elites not only may be indifferent to the general promotion of local public services but may even obstruct it to prevent the empowerment of disadvantaged groups.[11]

The Role of Competition

Another key organization design issue concerns the role of competition. The well-known effect of competition in the context of private goods is that in order to retain existing consumers or attract new ones, an organization has to either cut costs or to improve quality. To the extent that cutting costs or increasing quality is at the expense of monopoly rents, consumers are better off, even though owners and employees of the organization can be worse off because they lose a quiet life, to borrow Hicks's phrase. Cutting costs can be at the expense of quality. Competition works best when consumers are well-informed. If this is not the case, poor quality organizations can survive for long periods even with competition. To the extent that being informed is correlated with being educated or affluent, this may lead to both inefficient and inequitable outcomes. This calls for appropriate regulatory institutions and legal protection.

Can these arguments in favor of competition for the provision of private goods be borrowed in the context of public goods? According to some advocates of school competition and vouchers, such as Hoxby (2001), the answer is yes. Competition from private organizations can induce public organizations to get their act together in order to hold on to funding and to their clientele—competition is a tide that raises all boats.[12] Hoxby draws the parallel between this and the effect of entry of Federal Express and DHL into the package delivery market in the United States, which forced the U.S. Postal Service to improve quality, cut costs, and offer new products such as Express Mail. Opponents argue that competition will lead to cream-skimming. New schools will attract students from higher income and education groups. As these students leave, taking with them the per capita government funding, poorer students in old schools will be strictly worse off. However, this is not an argument against competition per se. It merely calls for "smart" vouchers whose value depends on the socioeconomic background of the student, so as to make them attractive to new schools.

Also, competition in the context of public goods can take interesting forms. For example, Besley and Ghatak (2003, 2005) argue that schools can be viewed as competing by picking different kinds of curriculum and attracting teachers who are most motivated to teach according to that curriculum. One element of the curriculum could, for example, be whether religious instruction is included. Well-matched schools can forgo incentive pay and rely exclusively on agents' motivation. This explains why some schools (such as Catholic schools) can be more productive by attracting teachers whose mission preferences are closely aligned with those of the school management. More generally, a decentralized schooling system in which missions are developed at the school level will tend to be more productive (as measured in our model by equilibrium effort) than a centralized one in which a uniform curriculum (mission) is imposed on schools by government.

CONCLUSION

We have argued in this essay that the standard public-private dichotomy is of limited use in thinking about institution design for public-goods provision. The following news that hit the headlines recently highlights this starkly.[13] On July 16, 2004, an illegal thatched roof of a popular private school caught fire in the small town of Kumbakonam in the southern Indian state of Tamil Nadu. Around ninety young children between the ages of six and eleven died. This was a private school subsidized by the government. Its popularity, especially among working-class parents, came from the fact that local government schools were of poor quality. As part of receiving government aid, the school was supposed to be inspected every three years to ensure that it met government fire, health, and safety standards. Those inspections were never carried out.

This ghastly tragedy dramatically highlights the need to come out of the private-versus-public or government-versus-market dichotomy in thinking about public-goods provision. First, this was a hybrid school: privately owned and run, but receiving government funds. Second, the event underscores the fact that private (or hybrid) schools need to be regulated—being private is no guarantee of quality. However, this does not mean that we should get rid of private schools and supply education only through government schools. There were government schools in this town to which the parents of pupils attending this school could have sent their children but chose not to because of poor quality. Also, similar incidents regarding government schools are regularly reported in the media. Finally, a big part of the fault lies with government regulators. If they were doing their jobs, this tragedy could have been avoided.

How an organization performs, depends on its internal design, the competitive environment it faces, the regulatory environment in that sector, and the overall institutional environment of the economy (flow of information, efficiency of dispute resolution and contract enforcement, etc.). These elements are all important. If the regulatory environment is slack, then competition is no guarantor of success. However, the case for government monopoly is also often weak.

If a strict regulatory regime enforcing quality and safety standards is present, then it is fairly uncontroversial to say that greater choice and greater competition are good. However, the ground reality of developing countries is that regulatory bodies do not do what they are supposed to do and do everything that they are not supposed to do (e.g., demand bribes, harass firms as well as workers and consumers). However, even in this environment competition in other forms can act as a disciplinary device. Competitive media will expose regulatory lapses. A competitive polity will punish underperforming administrations. Competition and choice are ideas that are far too important to be left to champions of unregulated markets. They can and should be used to empower the poor.

ACKNOWLEDGMENTS The authors thank Markus Goldstein, Dilip Mookherjee, and Inger Munk for helpful comments.

NOTES

1. For example, for some government schemes targeted to the rural poor in India, the "leakage" of funds is as high as 70% (Farrington and Saxena 2004). Also, doctors and nurses in government medical centers and teachers in public schools do not regularly show up to work. Banerjee et al. (2004) report that on average 36–45% of medical personnel are absent from the health care centers they studied in rural Rajasthan. Since some of these centers are staffed by only one nurse, this high absenteeism means that these facilities are often closed, which drives the poor to unregulated and mostly unqualified private providers. Kremer et al. (2004) report an average absenteeism rate of 25% of teachers in government primary schools in India.

2. Hernando de Soto (2000) has argued that the poor accumulate huge assets in their shanty homes and small businesses, but because they have no legal protections, they cannot access credit, nor can they safely invest. If the owner tries to obtain a title, he will spend years doing it. Worse, he will risk having the property condemned and torn down.

3. Djankov et al. (2003) present evidence on the time it takes to collect a bounced check in various countries. For example, in the United States it takes 54 days; in the United Kingdom, 101 days; and in Pakistan, a year.

4. Besley (1995) provides evidence on the positive effect of property rights on investment incentives.

5. See, for example, Acemoglu et al. (2001).

6. See Bardhan et al. (2002) for a formal treatment of this trade-off.

7. According to the UNDP (1993), there are more than 50,000 NGOs working at the grassroots level in developing countries, and their activities have affected the lives of more than 250 million individuals.

8. See Hart et al. (1997).

9. It seems that the time is ripe to insist on greater transparency in NGOs, which would include a much greater use of evaluation studies of their actions. While this is beginning, and NGOs have sometimes been on the frontier in promoting evaluation of interventions, there are cases that are shrouded in mystery, with myth triumphing over measurement. A glaring example of this is microcredit provision by NGOs, which is crying out for randomized evaluation.

10. See Bardhan and Mookherjee (2000).

11. See Drèze and Sen (1995).

12. See Hoxby (2001).

13. See Rohde (2004).

BIBLIOGRAPHY

Acemoglu, Daron, Simon Johnson, and James A. Robinson. "The Colonial Origins of Comparative Development: An Empirical Investigation." *American Economic Review* 91 (5) (2001): 1369–1401.

Banerjee, Abhijit, Angus Deaton, and Esther Duflo. "Wealth, Health, and Health Services in Rural Rajasthan." *American Economic Review, Papers and Proceedings,* 94 (2) (2004): 326–330.

Bardhan, Pranab. "Irrigation and Cooperation: An Empirical Analysis of 48 Irrigation Communities in South India." *Economic Development and Cultural Change* 48 (4) (2000): 847–865.

Bardhan, Pranab, Maitreesh Ghatak, and A. Karaivanov. "Inequality, Market Imperfections, and the Voluntary Provision of Collective Goods." Working paper, London School of Economics, 2002.

Bardhan, Pranab, and Dilip Mookherjee. "Capture and Governance at Local and National Levels." *American Economic Review* 90 (2) (2000): 135–139.

Bardhan, Pranab, and Christopher Udry. *Development Microeconomics.* Oxford: Oxford University Press, 1999.

Basu, Kaushik. *Analytical Development Economics.* Cambridge, Mass.: MIT Press, 1997.

Besley, Timothy. "Property Rights and Investment Incentives: Theory and Evidence from Ghana." *Journal of Political Economy* 103 (5) (1995): 903–937.

Besley, Timothy, and Robin Burgess. "The Political Economy of Government Responsiveness: Theory and Evidence." *Quarterly Journal of Economics* 117 (4) (2002): 1415–1451.

Besley, Timothy, and Maitreesh Ghatak. "Government versus Private Ownership of Public Goods." *Quarterly Journal of Economics* 116 (4) (2001): 1343–1372.

Besley, Timothy, and Maitreesh Ghatak. "Incentives, Choice and Accountability in Public Service Provision." *Oxford Review of Economic Policy* 19 (2) (2003): 235–249.

Besley, Timothy, and Maitreesh Ghatak. "Competition and Incentives with Motivated Agents." *American Economic Review,* 95 (3), (2005): 616–636.

Besley, Timothy, and John McLaren. "Taxes and Bribery: The Role of Wage Incentives." *The Economic Journal* 103 (1) (1993): 119–141.

Besley, Timothy, Rohini Pande, Lupin Rahman, and Vijayendra Rao. "The Politics of Public Good Provision: Evidence from Indian Local Governments." *Journal of the European Economics Association* 2 (2–3) (2004): 416–426.

Chattopadhyay, Raghabendra, and Esther Duflo. "Women as Policy Makers: Evidence from an India-Wide Randomized Policy Experiment." *Econometrica* 72 (5) (2004): 1409–1443.

Dayton-Johnson, J. "The Determinants of Collective Action on the Local Commons: A Model with Evidence from Mexico." *Journal of Development Economics* 62 (1) (2000): 181–208.

De Soto, Hernando. *The Mystery of Capital: Why Capitalism Triumphs in the West and Fails Everywhere Else.* New York: Basic Books, 2000.

Dixit, Avinash. "Incentives and Organizations in the Public Sector: An Interpretive Review." *Journal of Human Resources* 37 (4) (2002): 696–727.

Djaankov, Simeon, Rafael La Porta, Florencio Lopez de Silanes, and Andrei Shleifer. "Courts: The Lex Mundi Project." *Quarterly Journal of Economics* 118 (2) (2003): 453–512.

Drèze, Jean, and Amartya Sen. *India: Economic Development and Social Opportunity.* Delhi: Oxford University Press, 1995.

Easterly, William. *The Elusive Quest for Growth: Economists' Adventures and Misadventures in the Tropics.* Cambridge, Mass.: MIT Press, 2001.

Engerman, Stanley L., and Kenneth L. Sokoloff. "History Lessons: Institutions, Factors Endowments, and Paths of Development in the New World." 14(3) (2000): 217–232.

Farrington, John, and N. C. Saxena. "Protecting and Promoting Livelihoods in Rural India: What Role for Pensions?" *Opinion* 12 (2004). Overseas Development Institute. Available at http://www.odi.org.uk/publications/opinions/index.html.

Fehr, Ernst, and Armin Falk. "Psychological Foundations of Incentives." *European Economic Review* 24 (2–3) (2002): 687–724.

Field, Erica. "Entitled to Work: Urban Property Rights and Labor Supply in Peru." Working paper, Harvard University, 2003.

Foster, Andrew, and Mark Rosenzweig. "Democratization, Decentralization, and the Distribution of Local Public Goods in a Poor Rural Economy." Working paper, Brown University and University of Pennsylvania, 2001.

François, Patrick. "Public Service Motivation as an Argument for Government Provision." *Journal of Public Economics* 78 (2000): 275–299.

Glaeser, Edward, and Andrei Shleifer. "Not-for-Profit Entrepreneurs." *Journal of Public Economics* 81 (1) (2001): 99–115.

Glaeser, Edward, and Andrei Shleifer. "Legal Origins." *Quarterly Journal of Economics* 117 (4) (2002): 1193–1230.

Grossman, Sanford, and Oliver Hart. "The Costs and Benefits of Ownership: A Theory of Vertical and Lateral Integration." *Journal of Political Economy* 94 (4) (1986): 691–719.

Hart, Oliver. *Firms, Contracts and Financial Structure.* Oxford: Clarendon Press, 1995.

Hart, Oliver, Andrei Shleifer, and Robert Vishny. "The Proper Scope of Government: Theory and an Application to Prisons." *Quarterly Journal of Economics* 112 (4) (1997): 1119–1158.

Holmstrom, Bengt, and Paul Milgrom. "Multi-Task Principal-Agent Analysis: Incentive Contracts, Asset Ownership, and Job Design." *Journal of Law, Economics, and Organization* 7 (spec. iss.) (1991): 24–52.

Hoxby, C. M. "Rising Tide." *Education Next* 1 (4) (2001): 69–74.

Iyer, Lakshmi. "The Long-Term Impact of Colonial Rule: Evidence from India." Typescript, Massachusetts Institute of Technology, 2003.

Kremer, M., K. Muralidharan, N. Chaudhury, J. Hammer, and H. Rogers. "Teacher Absence in India." Working paper, World Bank and Harvard University, 2004.

LeGrand, Julian. *From Knight to Knave, from Pawn to Queen.* Oxford: Oxford University Press, 2003.

McMillan, John, and Christopher Woodruff. "The Central Role of Entrepreneurs in Transition Economies." *Journal of Economic Perspectives* 16 (3) (Summer 2002): 153–170.

Miguel, Edward, and Mary Kay Gugerty. "Ethnic Diversity. Social Sanctions, and Public Goods in Kenya." Working paper, Department of Economics, University of California, Berkeley, 2002.

Pande, Rohini. "Minority Representation and Policy Choices: The Significance of Legislator Identity." *American Economic Review* 93 (4) (2003): 1132–1151.

Persson, Torsten, and Guido Tabellini. "The Size and Scope of Government: Comparative Politics with Rational Politicians." *European Economic Review* 43 (1) (1999): 699–735.

Persson, Torsten, and Guido Tabellini. *The Economic Effect of Constitutions: What Do the Data Say?* Cambridge, Mass.: MIT Press, 2003.

Ray, Debraj. *Development Economics.* Princeton, N.J.: Princeton University Press, 1998.

Rohde, David. "In Fire, Striving Town Finds Dangers on Path to Modernization." *The New York Times,* July 18, 2004, International News, Section 1, 1.

United Nations Development Program. *Human Development Report.* New York: Oxford University Press, 1993.

Wade, Robert. *Village Republics: Economic Conditions for Collective Action in South India.* Cambridge: Cambridge University Press, 1988.

20

Intellectual Property and Health in Developing Countries

Jean Tirole

THE DEBATE

Few issues are as controversial as the impact of intellectual property on health in developing countries. Activists and poor countries' governments have, for example, long claimed that patents on antiretroviral (ARV) drugs make AIDS treatments unaffordable in Africa and other low-income areas. Pharmaceutical companies have argued, to the contrary, that the problem is elsewhere, and that rich countries' governments should take the responsibility if vaccines and drugs are to be brought to the poor. Rich countries' governments, unsurprisingly, have not been keen on committing funds to promote health in Third World countries.

Finger-pointing with regard to the AIDS problem is but one of the many symptoms of the overall tension over intellectual property rights (IPRs) between high-income countries, on the one hand, and middle- and low-income ones, on the other hand. More generally, IPRs are the focus of intense interest to developing countries, which express particular concerns for health, plant breeders' rights, traditional knowledge, and education and research.

The WTO TRIPS agreement[1] requires that all WTO members put in place some minimal protection of IPRs by 2006, with a more recent option for the least developed countries to extend the transition period to 2016. Of particular relevance for this chapter, about fifty developing members of WTO that did not provide patent protection for pharmaceutical products will now have to do so, although they will still be able to impose price controls on medicines and in "emergencies" (a concept left broadly undefined at the WTO consultation in Doha in 2001) resort to compulsory licensing.

This essay focuses on the impact of IPRs on low- and middle-income countries' health care. Many fine contributions have been made to this topic, and the essay aims only at taking stock of where we stand and at listing what we need to give further thought to.

It is widely recognized that there are two different reasons why poor countries may not have access to needed vaccines and drugs.

In the case of *global diseases,* such as diabetes or cancer, patents may hinder the diffusion of pharmaceuticals. IP owners are often reluctant to offer drastically lower prices to poor countries because they fear that rich countries will balk at tiered pricing (witness the shameful statements of some American politicians to the effect that drugs invented in America should not be available at much lower prices elsewhere,[2] and the more insidious use of reference price controls, a benchmarking procedure that ties prices in a rich country to prices abroad, and therefore discourages the use of discounts in poorer countries). Pharmaceutical companies may further be concerned that low prices in poor countries will lead to massive parallel imports in rich countries, their natural income base[3] (although this concern has been partly alleviated by the August 30, 2003, WTO decision on the implementation of Paragraph 6 of the Doha Declaration).

But even if pharmaceutical companies ignore these linkages and, as business judgment would command, practice price discrimination in favor of poor countries, much of the population of these poor countries may still not have access to the drugs for several reasons. First, profit maximization may lead pharmaceutical companies to target the elite and the middle class, not the insolvent poor. Second, and as the rich countries' protagonists (pharmaceutical companies, governments, activists) all agree, patents are at most part of the issue, for two reasons.

First, other costs may be added on top of royalties. Royalties are only part of the financial cost of medicines; manufacturing and monitoring costs may also be significant.

While most medicines' marginal cost is very small, it may be nonnegligible for some. In particular, the lowest cost of ARV triple therapies treatment is often estimated at $200–$300 per person per year by producers of cheap copies in India and elsewhere, and used to be much higher. This is still an enormous amount of money for low-income countries with average per capita health expenditures of $23.[4]

The monitoring of treatments by medical personnel can be extremely important for treatments such as those for ARV, for which a proper monitoring brings the cost to about $1,100 per capita per year.[5] The medical infrastructure is also crucial for prescriptions; estimates for India indicate a 50% rate of unnecessary or contraindicated drug prescriptions.[6] More generally, the health infrastructure is often so underdeveloped that diseases whose treatment or vaccine is off patent and cheap to produce are still widespread.[7] A related problem is that treatments are not always available in poor countries in which IP owners do not bother to take patents. A widely cited study by Attaran and Gillespie-White (2001) looks at fifteen ARV drugs in fifty-three countries. Of the resulting 795 potential patents, only 172 (21.6%) actually exist. While the actual picture is more complex[8] (patent owners tend to patent in relatively high-income and populous or highly infected countries, such as South Africa; patents may not reflect IP importance; etc.), this number makes it clear that patents cannot be the end of the story.

Still another reason why royalties are only part of the cost is that some countries impose tariffs and taxes on pharmaceuticals.

Second, populist sentiments may deter politicians in rich and poor countries, as well as multilateral organizations, from trying to find solutions. I have already mentioned the equivocal stance of rich countries, which argue in favor of low prices for poor countries while being unwilling to foot the bill and opposing tiered pricing. Poor countries' leaders sometimes do not help either, as when they express nationalistic preference for locally produced cures, or when President Mbeki of South Africa expresses doubts about the link between HIV and AIDS. Populist sentiments also deter multilateral organizations such as the WHO from recommending vaccines that have not been approved in developed countries because of their side effects; such side effects may be relevant in countries in which the vaccine is of little use, but, for lack of anything better, second-order in others in which the disease is pandemic. Yet health authorities may balk at recommending such vaccines for fear of a (misguided) political backlash.

The second set of issues relates to *neglected or tropical diseases*, such as malaria, tuberculosis, and leishmaniasis, that are of primary concern to developing countries, or more generally to diseases for which revenues from rich countries do not suffice to attract R&D funding. The corresponding vaccines or drugs are not developed because of low profitability due to the poverty of potential customers (perhaps combined with the fear of compulsory licensing). There are several illustrations of the shortage of research in the area: limited work on malaria and tuberculosis, and virtually none on sleeping sickness.[9] A widely circulated statistic is that since 1975, only 11 of 1,300 newly developed drugs relate to developing countries' diseases, and five of them are by-products of veterinary research. The (off-patent) drugs against sleeping sickness date back to 1917, 1939, and 1949 (a dangerous arsenic derivative) and also include an inadvertent by-product of cancer research.[10] More indirect evidence that there is little R&D on poor countries' diseases is the observation that there is much less research on vaccines than on drugs, despite the fact that the former have an important advantage over the latter in poor countries, in that they are much less dependent on a good health care delivery system.[11]

It is of course hard to draw a clear line between global and neglected diseases. AIDS, for instance, stands in between. While it is a global disease, most of the research has focused on the strain that is most common in rich countries. But it is useful to keep in mind this taxonomy, since the solutions for global and neglected diseases are likely to differ.

As might be expected, the wide consensus around the insufficient access of poor countries to vaccines and drugs disappears when it comes to attributing responsibilities and duties for helping the poor bridge their health gap with the rich world. Candidate policies include

- Donations and acquiescence to low prices in LDCs by the industry;
- Unilateral actions by poor countries' authorities, in the form of compulsory licensing;
- Unilateral actions by rich countries' governments, such as aid to health programs in poor countries; or, in countries with an innovative pharmaceutical industry, tax credits for R&D on neglected diseases or matching programs when the pharmaceutical industry donates or sells vaccines and drugs to nonprofit or multilateral organizations dealing with poor countries;[12] and research on neglected diseases in national laboratories;
- Multilateral efforts by rich countries, including conferring on the WHO a role of certification similar to that of the U.S. Food and Drug Administration;[13] pull and push programs aimed at encouraging research on neglected diseases; or the development by the WTO of a set of precise guidelines for the compulsory licensing of drugs.

TOWARD A GLOBAL SOCIAL CONTRACT FOR HEALTH

Intervention in the marketplace always requires a prior analysis of the source of failure and an identification of what goals one is trying to pursue.

In the context of health, one must first understand why health and pharmaceuticals (as opposed to poverty) are such controversial issues. For example, no one would think that the poor's lack of access to Sony's Trinitron tube patented system for color TV is a serious issue (as opposed to the poor's being poor). So why is health different? Curiously, and for all our intuition about the matter, the answer is not completely obvious, and requires some thinking. In the mid-1970s, two economists, Tony Atkinson and Joe Stiglitz, derived a result that still confounds the advocates of targeted policy interventions. They showed that under some conditions,[14] all redistribution among economic agents should operate through a redistribution of income. That is, however redistribution-minded the government is, it should refrain from subsidizing some goods and taxing others. For example, governments should not "force" consumers to consume electricity or local telephone services (often subsidized services) by offering them low prices. The message and logic behind this result are straightforward: make the distribution of income more equal,[15] and let the consumers decide what they want to consume. This result is useful for what it really is: a benchmark that serves as a warning against unmotivated paternalistic preferences of governments, and for which departures are vindicated by well-documented failures of the assumptions. One of the strong assumptions underlying the sufficiency of income taxation is the perfect verifiability of income; in practice, income tax is evaded in legal (perks, loopholes) and illegal ways, which suggests taxing goods and services mostly demanded by the rich more heavily.

To see why health is different from other goods and services, let us first take a look at rich countries. There are several reasons why using health-related policies to redistribute may actually make sense despite the Atkinson and Stiglitz result (these reasons by and large also apply to education, which may explain why health and education are the two pillars of social democracy). First, health is an input into the production of income (this will be particularly so for poor countries). An alternative to income taxation as a means of redistributing income—and one that is less distortive of labor supply—is to make sure that access to health services is not too unequal. Second, decisions relative to health are, in the case of children, made on behalf of the person, and not by the individual himself/herself; there is thus a concern that some children are denied access to the treatments that they should receive. Third, there are, in the case of vaccines, externalities.

Lo and behold, even the more market-oriented economies heavily regulate health care. Price caps on medicines are widespread (with substantial variations, though; for example, prices of on-patent drugs in the United States are about twice the French or Italian level).

To be certain, the real motivation behind these regulations is often unrelated to the normative considerations just discussed; rather, they reflect two less avowable political economy considerations. First, the pharmaceutical industry has high fixed costs and low marginal costs, a situation that makes expropriation of investment through low prices, once the fixed costs have been sunk, quite tempting. Second, and more specific to the international context, innovations are global public goods, and thus individual countries do not benefit from promising "fair prices" even if they can commit to them. Indeed, each country has a private incentive to free-ride on other countries and pay as little as possible for these global public goods.[16] Price regulation of patented drugs is a simple way to obtain this free ride.

An interesting case in point is the fall 2001 Cipro saga in the United States. In the midst of the anthrax scare, Health and Human Services Secretary Tommy Thompson threatened Cipro manufacturer Bayer with compulsory licensing[17] and forced it to slash prices (ironically, in the same way South Africa forced Merck, Bristol-Myers, and others to cut prices on AIDS treatments, generating a protest from the American government). While everyone will agree that something would have gone wrong if the anthrax threat had proved to be widespread and if Bayer had jacked up prices so as to make Cipro unaffordable to a fraction of the American population, the U.S. government's intervention raises questions about the pharmaceutical industry's incentive to develop vaccines and drugs for future bioterrorism attacks. Low-probability events require large rewards to justify R&D expenditures. (To be sure, the problem is not specific to the pharmaceutical industry. Take the power industry, in which prices may, even in the absence of exercise of market power, jump by a factor of 20 or 100 during peak time—a few hours or days during the year. Price caps aimed at limiting economic rents during these peak hours are widely perceived as a disincentive to install or maintain peaking production facilities that operate optimally only a few days a year.)

To sum up:

- There is a legitimate (normative) argument in favor of using the health care system in order to redistribute. And, given limited budgets, there is also a case for regulating drug prices so as to allow a more democratic access to drugs, although it must be recognized that such policies come at the cost of a lower innovation rate.
- While price controls are probably better explained by the unavowable motives of (a) opportunistically expropriating pharmaceuticals once R&D has been sunk and (b) free-riding on other countries, the normative side is still a key ingredient in these positive explanations, to the extent that it can explain why governments are given much larger discretion in the realm of pharmaceuticals than for other products under the TRIPS and other multilateral agreements.

The case for redistribution through health policies is stronger internationally. Income redistribution is less developed across than within countries. This of course is due to the selfishness of rich countries, which redistribute hardly anything to poor countries. Selfishness, to be certain, is only part of the story. First, the fight against poverty is itself a global public good, and so even a country with altruistic preferences may still prefer other countries to provide the global public good. Second, it is by no means easy to ensure that income transfers reach the right people.[18] Third, means-tested aid, like any other form of assistance, creates moral hazard. Yet it is a safe bet that even if a multilateral agreement could be reached concerning rich countries' contributions to world economic development and if solutions to the delivery problem could be found, rich countries' generosity would still show its limits.

Historically, a substantial, although not very visible, share of the redistribution from rich to poor countries has operated through free (or low-price) IP transfers. Technologies developed in rich countries reach poor countries, after a delay, when they go off-patent. And on-patent technologies have in the past not been covered by IP protection, a situation that is modified by the TRIPS agreement, although, as we have noted, countries can still threaten compulsory licensing in order to obtain very favorable deals from IP owners. It is perhaps unsurprising that substantial transfers have occurred in-kind through the IP system while there have been very few in cash. For one thing, knowledge transfers are much less dependent on the cooperation of rich countries' governments. And they don't confront quite the same delivery problems as cash transfers. But the fact that IP transfers are an important source of redistribution to low- and middle-income countries in a world desperately in need of worldwide redistribution does not imply that existing transfers are fair or efficient, as we will observe.

A global social contract for global diseases should differentiate prices so as to reflect the health-related needs of countries and, for neglected diseases, design new mechanisms that will boost private incentives to develop vaccines and drugs. The final two sections of the essay accordingly investigate two (complementary) policy interventions: compulsory licensing and health-related aid.

RULE-BASED COMPULSORY LICENSING

This section argues that compulsory licensing should keep playing an important role for low- and middle-income countries, although definitely not in its current form. Before we take up the argument, let us step back and return to some basic economics of compulsory licensing. (Many of the issues discussed below are also relevant for the discussion of the prize mechanism studied later in this paper, since the issue of the "right prices" arises there as well.)

General Considerations about Compulsory Licensing

As is well understood in industrial organization, the problem of encouraging innovation is akin to that of regulating a natural monopoly. Both setups involve substantial returns to scale, and thus pricing at marginal cost does not allow firms to cover their total cost. Somehow, fixed costs have to be recouped through sizeable "taxes," "contributions," or "markups" above marginal costs.[19]

A "Ramsey social planner" (as it is called in the economics literature) must, in order to maximize social welfare:

- Design an overall reward or price level that allows the firm to receive a fair rate of return on the fixed cost of producing the "facility" or the patent (*price level challenge*);
- Allocate the markups on the different uses made of the "facility" or patent so as to minimize the social deadweight loss (*relative prices challenge*).

The economist's answer to the latter challenge is the well-known Ramsey rule. Lower markups should be applied to those segments with the highest elasticities of demand (which often coincide with segments populated with low-income consumers), so as to minimize the value loss incurred when high prices deter potential users from consuming. It turns out that this Ramsey principle is in tune with private incentives, since it is also in the interest of a private monopoly to tailor prices across segments as a function of what each market segment can bear; this observation is indeed one of the justifications for price caps, which decentralize the choice of relative prices to the regulated firm in network industries such as the telecommunications, electricity, gas, rail, and postal sectors.[20] (A caveat here: the elasticities of demand reflect not only the consumers' true demand function and their income, but also the availability of substitute products—the so-called bypass opportunities. Ramsey pricing may be constrained by these bypass options, but ideally would eliminate them so as to achieve unconstrained Ramsey pricing. More on this later.)

The price-level challenge poses more complex issues. To provide the firm with a fair rate of return on investment, the Ramsey social planner must have an estimate of the investment cost. In regulated industries, regulators' permanent and specialized staffs collect substantial amounts of data about the firms' costs in regulated segments and further try to insulate regulated segments from cross-subsidization in favor of unregulated ones. In the case of a patent, the regulator—the authority that orders and monitors the compulsory license—has little knowledge about the actual cost incurred by the pharmaceutical company in developing the particular medicine.

Another informational obstacle in the case of a compulsory license comes from the fact that R&D is a very risky activity. A project that costs $100 million and has a 10% chance of success should engender $1 billion in income (ignoring interest and risk premiums) in order for the pharmaceutical company to be willing to undertake it. A regulator's attempt at regulating the rate of return on a medicine must therefore also estimate the ex ante probability that this medicine will succeed. The "fair income" is highly sensitive to the subjective estimate of this probability (for example, it is multiplied by 4 when the probability of success moves from 20% to 5%).

The implications are clear. Even in the simple context envisioned here, a proper implementation of compulsory licensing is no easy task, even for a benevolent regulator. It is no surprise, then, that courts routinely commend "licensing at a fair and reasonable price" when they order compulsory licenses but rarely specify what it means. Things get worse if the regulator behaves opportunistically; in contrast to the case of regulated network industries, in which the firm can appeal what it perceives to be a taking by relying on regulatory evidence on cost data, there is no such natural benchmark to substantiate the appeal in the case of a patent.

Application to Medicines for Global Diseases

I heartily subscribe to the view that the cost burden of medicines for global diseases should be shared unequally across countries. Low-income countries should pay less than medium-income countries, which in turn should pay less than rich countries. Unfortunately, current practice associated with the threat of compulsory licensing[21] hardly delivers such a Ramsey structure. Until recently, compulsory licensing was credible only if the country had a reasonable domestic capacity for competitive production of copies. With some exceptions (India being the most prominent one), such countries are rarely low-income countries.[22] Sub-Saharan African countries are unlikely to take advantage of compulsory licensing unless they purchase copies from third countries, in contravention of international agreements. Another issue is that compulsory licensing is a unilateral initiative that rewards countries with little (to) fear and penalizes (relatively) those who are afraid of reprisals.

A normatively satisfactory pricing system would not reflect the bargaining positions of the countries (whether they result from bypass opportunities or other considerations), but rather their needs. The current setting certainly does not obey this principle.

A more satisfactory and fairer system would probably reflect the following desiderata:

- Rule-based compulsory licensing rather than unilateral actions by individual countries,
- Expedient procedures administered by a politically independent agency (so as to avoid constant political pressure from influential countries),
- Means-tested conditions,
- Strict prohibition of parallel imports/exports, and
- Some other forms of conditionality.

Let me briefly discuss a few of these desiderata. First, the prohibition of parallel imports or exports is of the utmost importance. The medicines manufactured for Bangladesh or Botswana should not reach the United States, France, or Saudi Arabia, for this would destroy the whole edifice. Developing countries must understand that they have a lot to lose from parallel imports. This is not to say that the system created by the TRIPS agreement, in which compulsory licenses are primarily for domestic production, is a good one. It was motivated partly by the fear that medicines would turn footloose, thereby undermining the tiered-pricing system; but, as we observed, it did not allow the vast majority of poor countries to have access to the needed products.

One should therefore create a monitoring body (to which pharmaceutical companies could be associated, so they would gain some reassurance and would thereby be co-opted into the scheme) in order to license producers of copies and control flows of medicines. Thus, Botswana could procure a medicine from India if it failed to reach a *production* agreement with the patent owner for the supplies needed (it is important to conceptually separate IP ownership and production, even though in practice the patent owner already has facilities and expertise, and is often a serious candidate supplier).

While the principle of means-tested conditions is straightforward, its application is not. Per capita income is certainly a key component, but it is not the only one. One difficult issue, for example, is the treatment of countries with high income inequalities (that is, relatively rich countries with a sizable fraction of destitute inhabitants).

As in the case of other multilateral agreements, the benefits of being part of the scheme could go together with some forms of conditionality regarding minimum standards for health information, tariffs and taxes on pharmaceuticals, and so forth.

Probably the thorniest issue concerns the compensation under a compulsory license. One aspect is its structure: Should this be a lump sum paid by the country to the pharmaceutical company for basically unlimited access to the medicine at marginal cost—possibly from producers of copies? Or, as is most often proposed, a royalty of 3% or 4%[23] of the sales price of the medicine?[24]

Still another, more market-oriented scheme that could be considered is the purchase by each country (or an international organization or foundation on its behalf) of an unlimited licensing right for domestic consumption. Although this scheme could be transaction-cost-intensive (but see the discussion below), here is how the mechanism could operate. The pharmaceutical company could be instructed to spin off an entity with the exclusive right to distribute the product in the country (or group of countries) in question. The market price for this entity would presumably be the monopoly profit to be made in the country. The entity could be taken over through a tender process by the buyer (again a foundation, such as the Gates Foundation, a multilateral organization, the country itself, or a combination of the three),[25] which could then sell the medicine at a negligible price or donate it. This procedure would have several benefits:

- The pharmaceutical company would de facto be allowed to keep its profit (the new entity's shareholders would turn down a tender price below this profit).
- At the same time, monopoly prices would not prevail. That is, the medicine would no longer be targeted to the elite of the country.
- Country differentiation would obtain. Richer countries would pay more for control over the medicine.

This mechanism has costs as well. As mentioned above, doing this for all medicines and countries would be infeasible. Grouping countries and/or medicines would be required. On the other hand (and as for compulsory licensing), the procedure could just be a default point on which negotiation would most often converge (and so the procedure itself would rarely be invoked). Another potential difficulty, as in any purchase funding proposal (see below), is the availability of the money. We therefore have in mind that such a scheme would apply primarily to poor countries. For rich countries, the sums at stake might be too large to attract funding.

Little economic research has investigated the trade-offs, and certainly much remains to be done in the area.

PURCHASE FUNDS FOR NEGLECTED DISEASES

The previous discussion of a market-oriented scheme for the purchase of licenses for global diseases brings us to the purchase fund proposal for neglected diseases. I'll be brief both because many of the difficulties faced by these proposals are similar to those, discussed earlier, faced by compulsory licensing (both approaches involve an ex post purchase, using taxpayer money in the case of aid, and user money under actual compulsory licensing practice, in order to compensate the innovator), and because the benefits of and obstacles faced by purchase funds policies have been discussed with much lucidity by Michael Kremer (2001a, 2001b, 2002).

The prize system, in which the innovator receives a lump sum for delivering an invention with specified characteristics, and thereby forfeits any IPR, has a long history but was not employed much through the nineteenth and twentieth centuries. Lately, though, its principle has made a comeback with proposals by the World Bank, the WHO, and the Clinton administration.

In theory, the prize mechanism is quite appealing since it allows an unlimited diffusion of the knowledge created by the inventive act. In practice, though, it is very difficult to define in advance the characteristics of an innovation, which raises the issue of the ex post assessment of its value. The patent system, for all its flaws, has the major benefit that its market-based reward approach is not subject to the two rocks that bureaucratic procedures usually strike: capture and overpayment, and opportunistic expropriation and underpayment.

Kremer offers the design for a prize mechanism for neglected diseases based on, among other things:

- A list of specifications to be satisfied by the vaccine or drug (efficacy, length of protection, side effects, sensitivity to improper usage, and monitoring . . .);
- A technical approval process by an independent agency (which keeps in mind that the medicine may be the only hope for poor countries);
- A market-based test that uses copayments by countries, which would then supply yet another signal about the medicine's efficacy.

Kremer also discusses the (complex) design of prizes in a world with sequential innovations.

It is clear that this approach is partly dependent on rich countries being willing to contribute to the purchase funds. If experience with international aid in general, and with health-related aid in particular,[26] unfortunately does not invite much optimism, economists and political scientists should nonetheless attempt to design multilateral processes that alleviate the free-rider problem.

In the matter of neglected diseases, as for global diseases, economic research that can help guide policy is scarce, and further research in this area as well is most welcome.

NOTES

1. Agreement on Trade Related Aspects of Intellectual Property (1994). The TRIPS agreement has homogenized the (minimum standard for) protection of novel, non-obvious, and useful inventions, including pharmaceuticals, to twenty years for all members of the WTO. The protection of IPRs should naturally be defined broadly,

not solely through the lens of formal laws but also considering the extent of their enforcement (see, e.g., Combe and Pfister 2002, for survey evidence of corporate perceptions of the relative importance of the legal IP framework and its enforcement).

2. Kettler and Collins (2002), 6.

3. This fear has been growing with the development of the Internet (Lanjouw 2001, pp. 6–7). Much of the parallel importation at this stage occurs between developed countries (e.g., Canada and the United States).

4. Commission on Intellectual Property Rights (2002), 31.

5. Kremer (2002), 80.

6. Phadke (1998).

7. For example, WHO's Expanded Programme of Immunization, while a clear success, still fails to reach many children despite the low cost of vaccines—less than $1 for a polyvalent vaccine (Commission on Intellectual Property Rights 2002, p. 35).

8. Lybecker (2003).

9. Médecins Sans Frontières (2001), 12.

10. Moran, in Session 6 (2002).

11. Kremer (2001a, 2001b). Note that this argument differs from the standard one (unrelated to the quality of the health infrastructure), according to which vaccines are undersupplied in a market economy because people don't internalize the reduced risk of contagion for others when they choose whether to be inoculated. See Kremer and Snyder (2003) for an interesting analysis of comparative biases in the provision of vaccine and drug research.

12. The United States has such a tax deduction for donations, but it is rather small because it is computed on the basis of the medicine's production cost.

13. Kremer (2002), 86.

14. For the technically minded reader, these conditions are (1) economic agents differ in their ability to earn money (say, their hourly wage); (2) their incomes (but not their ability to earn money) are perfectly verifiable by tax authorities; (3) their preferences are perfectly separable between their labor input, on the one side, and a basket of consumption goods and services, on the other side (that is, their relative preference for two goods is independent of the amount of their labor); and (4) there are no consumption externalities.

15. How much more equal depends on both the government's preference for equality and the incentive effect of income taxation on the supply of production factors such as labor.

16. Under the constraint linked to the fact that manufacturers can threaten not to market the drug in the national market in question.

17. There are other motivations than emergencies for compulsory licensing in the United States and other developed countries. First, competition authorities and courts may order licensing because they deem that a piece of IP is a "unique path" that cannot be bypassed by producers of follow-up innovations or of downstream products, and that the piece of IP allows its owner to command a rent incommensurate with the investment cost. A special case of this situation may arise when a patented technology becomes a standard, and thereby an "essential facility" for the industry. Second, compulsory licenses are often requested when a merger reduces competition. For instance, in the Ciba-Geigy-Sandoz 1997 merger into Novartis (which also controlled Chiron), the U.S. Federal Trade Commission required the merged entity to license a number of products to Rhône Poulenc Rorer and to offer nonexclusive licenses of Cytokine (at, at most, 3% of the net sale prices) to all requesters. Last,

there are a number of exemptions to the free exercise of ownership of IP, as when other inventors are entitled to a free use of patented IP for experimental purposes.

18. The World Bank and other multilateral organizations increasingly resort to NGOs in the delivery of services to poor countries, in an effort to bypass potentially corrupt national and local governments. While this policy is to be applauded, one should also recognize its limits, both in terms of the need to enlist the cooperation of local officials for the provision of complementary services, and of the observation that NGOs, as they secure bigger and bigger budgets and become (unelected) governments, will attract more opportunistic (and less idealistic) types.

19. See Crampes and Hollander (2003) and Jack and Lanjouw (2003) for Ramsey theoretic frameworks of pharmaceuticals' pricing. Crampes and Hollander develop a detailed analysis of the impact of parallel imports on the world price structure of pharmaceuticals.

20. Roughly, price caps impose an average-price-level constraint. For the link between price caps and Ramsey pricing, see Laffont and Tirole (2000), chap. 2.

21. Under Article 31(f) of the TRIPS agreement, a licensee under a compulsory license must produce primarily for the domestic market of the member granting the license. (There are a number of other conditions, such as the necessity of prior negotiations with the patent owner and the subjection to independent review. See Scherer and Watal 2001.) Article 31(h) of the TRIPS agreement provides that "the rights holder shall be paid adequate remuneration in the circumstances of each case, taking into account the economic value of the authorization." See Abbott (2002), 35, for an interpretation of this article.

22. Brazil and India are the best-known producers of copies. For data on India, see Lanjouw (1998), and on Brazil, Commission on Intellectual Property Rights (2002), 43. Other countries with competitive producers of copies include Argentina, Chile, Italy, Turkey, South Korea, Egypt, and Lebanon. See Maskus (2000) for more details.

23. From 1923 through 1992, Canada had an extensive compulsory license policy. In the 1970s and 1980s, it mostly employed a royalty rate of 4% of the licensee's price.

24. The choice between these two policies probably would not affect the final price much, especially for those medicines with low production costs; 4% on a competitive price (competition among licensees bringing prices close to marginal cost) would not have much impact on the diffusion. The benefit of a lump-sum payment is that it allows for more differentiation between low-income countries (which presumably would pay a very low amount) and medium-income countries; on the other hand, the royalties could be differentiated according to income, but with the drawback that medicine prices would depart much more from marginal cost for middle-income countries. Other relevant considerations are that proportional (price-based) payments better reflect the "size of the market" for a particular pharmaceutical (for example, how widespread the disease is in the country), but are too sensitive to the magnitude of marginal production costs (which may differ widely across medicines).

25. The standard free-riding problem would not occur because it would be as if the entity were taken private. The idea of a takeover was first proposed by Cohen (2000), who suggests a takeover of the firm, followed by a spin-off of unwanted entities.

26. For example, the U.S. National Institutes of Health spent only 0.8% of its 1999 budget on tropical diseases (Lanjouw 2001, p. 23). Similar figures apply to European countries.

BIBLIOGRAPHY

Abbott, Frederick. "WTO TRIPS Agreement and Its Implications for Access to Medicines in Developing Countries." In Study Paper 2b, Commission on Intellectual Property Rights, London, U.K., 2002.

Atkinson, Anthony Barnes, and Joseph Stiglitz. "The Design of Tax Structure: Direct and Indirect Taxation." *Journal of Public Economics* 6 (1976): 55–75.

Attaran, A., and L. Gillespie-White. "Do Patents for Antiretroviral Drugs Constrain Access to AIDS Treatment in Africa?" *Journal of the American Medical Association* 15 (2001): 1886–1892.

Cohen, Daniel. "Sida et médicaments: Que faire?" Mimeo, CEPREMAP, Paris, 2000.

Combe, Emmanuel, and Etienne Pfister. "The Effectiveness of Intellectual Property Rights: An Analysis on French Survey Data." In *Multinational Firms and Impacts on Employment, Trade and Technologies: New Perspectives for a New Century*, edited by R. Lipsey and J. L. Mucchielli. London: Routledge, 2002.

Commission on Intellectual Property Rights. "Health." In *Integrating Intellectual Property Rights and Development Policy.* London: Commission on Intellectual Property Rights, 2002.

Crampes, Claude, and Abraham Hollander. "The Pricing of Pharmaceuticals Facing Parallel Imports." Mimeo, IDEI and University of Montreal, 2003.

Jack, William, and Jean Lanjouw. "Financing Pharmaceutical Innovation: How Much Should Poor Countries Contribute?" Mimeo, Georgetown University and Brookings Institution, 2003.

Kettler, Hannah, and Chris Collins. "Using Innovative Action to Meet Global Health Needs Through Existing Intellectual Property Regimes." In Study Paper 2b, Commission on Intellectual Property Rights, London, 2002.

Kremer, Michael. "Creating Markets for New Vaccines. Part 1: Rationale." In *Innovation Policy and the Economy.* Vol. 1. edited by A. Jaffe, J. Lerner, and S. Stern. Cambridge, Mass.: MIT Press, 2001a.

Kremer, Michael. "Creating Markets for New Vaccines. Part 2: Design Issues." In *Innovation Policy and the Economy.* Vol. 1. Edited by A. Jaffe, J. Lerner, and S. Stern. Cambridge, Mass.: MIT Press, 2001b.

Kremer, Michael. "Pharmaceuticals and the Developing World." *Journal of Economic Perspectives* 16 (4) (2002): 67–90.

Kremer, Michael, and Christopher Snyder. "Why Are Drugs More Profitable Than Vaccines?" NBER working paper 9833, 2003.

Laffont, Jean-Jaques, and Jean Tirole. *A Theory of Incentives in Procurement and Regulation.* Cambridge, Mass.: MIT Press, 1993.

Laffont, Jean-Jacques, and Jean Tirole. *Competition in Telecommunications.* Cambridge, Mass.: MIT Press, 2000.

Lanjouw, Jean. "The Introduction of Pharmaceutical Product Patents in India: 'Heartless Exploitation of the Poor and Suffering'?" NBER working paper 6366, 1998.

Lanjouw, Jean. "A Patent Policy Proposal for Global Diseases." Mimeo, Yale University, 2001.

Lanjouw, Jean. "Intellectual Property and the Availability of Pharmaceuticals in Poor Countries." *Innovation Policy and the Economy.* Vol. 2. Edited by A. Jaffe, J. Lerner, and S. Stern. Cambridge, Mass.: MIT Press, 2002.

Lybecker, Kristina. Review of "Do Patents for Antiretroviral Drugs Constrain Access to AIDS Treatment in Africa?," by A. Attaran and L. Gillespie-White, 2003. Available online at http://www.researchoninnovation.org/tiip/.

Maskus, Keith. *Intellectual Property Rights in the Global Economy.* Washington, D.C.: Institute for International Economics, 2000.

Médecins sans Frontières. "Fatal Imbalance: The Crisis in Research and Development for Drugs for Neglected Diseases." Brussels: MSF, 2001. Available online at http://www.msf.org/source/access/2001/fatal/fatal.pdf.

Phadke, Anant. *Drug Supply and Use: Towards a Rational Policy in India.* New Delhi: Sage, 1998.

Scherer, Mike, and Jayashree Watal. "Post-TRIPS Options for Access to Patented Medicines in Developing Countries." Commission on Macroeconomics and Health Working paper W64, Harvard University, 2001.

"Session 6: Medicines and Vaccines." Conference "How Intellectual Property Rights Could Work Better for Developing Countries and Poor People." Royal Society of London, Feb. 21–22, 2002. Transcript.

21

Public Policies to Stimulate Development of Vaccines for Neglected Diseases

Michael Kremer

In 2003, 5 million people were newly infected with HIV, 3 million of whom live in sub-Saharan Africa (UNAIDS 2004). Worldwide, almost 3 million people died of HIV/AIDS in 2003 (UNAIDS 2004). In 2002, 300 million clinical cases of malaria resulted in over 1 million deaths, and almost 2 million people died of tuberculosis (WHO 2002a, 2002b). Almost all of these deaths occurred in developing countries (WHO 2000b, 2000c). Yet relative to these enormous numbers, very little research is directed toward these diseases. Potential developers of vaccines appropriate for poor countries fear that they will not be able to sell enough of their product at a sufficient price to recoup their research and development (R&D) investments. This is both because these diseases primarily affect poor countries, and because vaccine markets are severely distorted. This essay examines the reasons for under-investment in R&D and the potential of various public policies, including committing in advance to purchase needed products, if and when they are developed, to address the problem.

The first section of this essay provides background information on malaria, HIV, and tuberculosis, and discusses the dearth of R&D investments in vaccines for these diseases. The second section discusses distortions in the markets for vaccines and vaccine research. The third section examines the potential roles of what are called "push" and "pull" programs in encouraging research and improving access to vaccines once they are developed. The fourth section compares alternative "pull" programs. The fifth section discusses how a purchase commitment (one type of "pull" program) could be made credible and outlines a possible process for determining vaccine eligibility. The sixth section discusses the appropriate size of the commitment as well as the cost effectiveness of the program. The seventh section argues that purchase commitments are most needed and would be easiest to implement for vaccines, but that the approach could be adapted for other products needed by developing countries. The eighth section discusses how national governments, international organizations, and private foundations could participate in a purchase commitment program.

BACKGROUND ON HIV, MALARIA, AND TUBERCULOSIS

The burden of infectious disease is huge and is concentrated in poor countries. More than 42 million people are infected with HIV worldwide, and over 95% of them live in developing countries (UNAIDS 2004). Almost all cases of malaria are in developing countries, and almost 90% are in Africa (WHO 2000c). More than 98% of deaths from tuberculosis occur in developing countries (WHO 2000b).

The spread of resistance poses a threat to developed as well as developing countries (WHO 1997): resistance to the major drugs used for treating malaria and for providing short-term protection to travelers is spreading (Cowman 1995), and up to 17% of tuberculosis infections are resistant to all five major antitubercular drugs (WHO 1997). The existing BCG (Bacillus of Calmette-Guérin) vaccine, which is widely distributed, provides short-run, imperfect protection against tuberculosis, but a more effective vaccine providing longer-term protection is lacking.[1] There are currently no vaccines for malaria and AIDS.

However, vaccines have proved effective against many other infectious diseases, and provide the best hope for long-run, sustainable solutions to malaria, tuberculosis, and HIV/AIDS. The potential of vaccines is illustrated most vividly by the success of the smallpox vaccination program, which led to the eradication of the disease in 1980. Currently, about 70% of children in low-income countries receive a standard package of cheap, off-patent vaccines through the World Health Organization (WHO)'s Expanded Programme on Immunization (EPI), and these vaccines are estimated to save 3 million lives worldwide each year (Kim-Farley 1992).[2]

Little research is oriented toward tropical diseases. Although the difficulty of developing vaccines against HIV/AIDS, tuberculosis, and malaria may have contributed to the reluctance among firms to invest in the necessary research, it is probably not the main reason, since many scientists are optimistic about the long-run scientific prospects for vaccine development.[3] A much more plausible explanation for the dearth of R&D is that the potential market for these vaccines is very small.[4] Pecoul et al. (1999) report that of the 1,233 drugs licensed worldwide between 1975 and 1997, only 13 were for tropical diseases. Of these, five came from veterinary research, two were modifications of existing medicines, and two were produced for the U.S. military. Only four were developed by commercial pharmaceutical firms specifically for tropical diseases of humans.[5] The private sector in particular performs remarkably little research on the diseases of poor, tropical countries. According to the WHO (1996), 50% of global health research and development in 1992 was undertaken by private industry, but less than 5% of that was devoted to diseases specific to less-developed countries.

FAILURES IN THE MARKETS FOR VACCINES AND VACCINE RESEARCH

One reason for the paucity of research on vaccines for malaria, tuberculosis, and strains of HIV common in Africa is simply that the countries affected by these diseases are poor, and cannot afford to pay much for vaccines. If this were the only reason, however, there would be no particular reason to target aid expenditures to vaccines or vaccine research, rather than to other goods needed in poor countries, such as food, or public goods such as roads. However, distortions in the research market destroy incentives for private firms to conduct research that would be cost-effective for society as a whole, even by the stringent cost-effectiveness standards used to evaluate health interventions in poor countries. Moreover, distortions in the markets for vaccines lead them to be underconsumed even relative to the incomes of the poor.

The private returns for developing products to fight diseases of developing countries are likely to be a tiny fraction of the social returns to these products. Economists have estimated that the social returns to research and development are typically twice the realized returns to private developers (Nadiri 1993; Mansfield et al. 1977). To take an example, consider a hypothetical malaria vaccine. A standard way to assess the cost-effectiveness of a health intervention is the cost per disability-adjusted life year (DALY) saved, which takes into account not only the lives lost through disease but also the number of years of disability caused (Murray and Lopez 1996a, 1996b). A common cost-effectiveness threshold for health interventions in the poorest countries is $100 per DALY.[6] At this threshold, a malaria vaccine would be cost-effective even at a price of $45 per immunized person (Glennerster and Kremer 2001) but, based on the historical record of vaccine prices, the developer of a malaria vaccine would be lucky to receive payments of one tenth or one twentieth of that amount. With the expectation of such prices, private developers lack incentives to pursue research on socially valuable projects.

At least two other factors also contribute to the reluctance of pharmaceutical firms to invest in R&D on diseases that primarily affect developing countries: first, intellectual property protection is often lacking, implying that the potential revenue from product sales is far smaller than the sum of customers' willingness to pay; and second, there is a tendency for governments to force down prices after firms have sunk their R&D costs.

Facing a trade-off between providing access to critical medicines and rigorously enforcing patent protection, many developing countries have historically provided little protection for intellectual property rights. There may be some advantages to this decision, but it reduces incentives for R&D on products needed in these countries. Pharmaceutical R&D is what economists call a "global public good," meaning that it benefits individuals who do not themselves finance the R&D expenditures or commit to protect intellectual property rights. The global public good problem implies each country has an incentive to "free-ride" on research financed by the governments of other countries or induced by other countries' greater commitment to protect intellectual property rights. Small countries, such as Uganda, can assume that individually their actions will have little effect on total research incentives. However, if all African countries act this way, there will be little incentive for firms to invest in developing a malaria vaccine. It is not clear whether the World Trade Organization (WTO) will lead to effective intellectual property rights enforcement in developing countries, especially since the Doha Agreements explicitly left open several provisions that provide potential escape hatches. For instance, countries can impose compulsory licensing in national emergencies, the definition of which is deliberately not stated (WTO 2001). Recent events suggest that national emergencies may be interpreted liberally, and whatever the overall benefits of these decisions, there is little doubt that pharmaceutical developers see the weakening of patent protection as a precedent that could be used to obtain vaccines and drugs at low prices in the future.

The high initial R&D costs, combined with the low costs of producing additional vaccines once the R&D has been completed, create what economists call a "time consistency" problem for governments. Once pharmaceutical firms have made their R&D investments and vaccines have been developed, governments have an incentive to set prices at or near the cost of producing additional vaccines (what economists call the "marginal cost"). After vaccine developers have invested the R&D necessary to develop vaccines, governments are in a strong bargaining position because they are often the primary purchasers of vaccines, as well as the regulators of pharmaceuticals and enforcers of intellectual property rights. If firms anticipate low prices, they will be reluctant to invest. In repeated interactions between nations and pharmaceutical producers, this time consistency problem could potentially be overcome through building credible reputations of governments.[7]

These global public-good and time consistency problems are exacerbated by political conditions in many developing countries that make vaccines a low priority. In particular, since vaccines deliver a widely distributed benefit, they tend to receive less political support than expenditures that benefit more concentrated and politically organized groups, such as salaries for health workers.

Overcoming the global public-good and time consistency problems requires creating incentives that both encourage new pharmaceutical development and provide the poor with access to these new pharmaceuticals once they have been developed. Because of the free-riding problems facing individual countries, solutions will have to come from entities with broader mandates—such as international organizations, bilateral aid programs, or private foundations.

THE ROLES OF "PUSH" AND "PULL" PROGRAMS IN ENCOURAGING VACCINE R&D

Programs to encourage R&D can take two broad forms. "Push" programs subsidize research inputs—for example, through grants to researchers or R&D tax credits. "Pull" programs reward research outputs—for example, by committing in advance to purchase a specified amount of a desired product at a specified price.

While push programs are important for basic scientific research, they also often encounter a number of problems. Because funders cannot perfectly monitor the actions of grant recipients, the latter may have incentives to devote effort to pursuing general scientific research or preparing their next grant application rather than focusing on development of the desired product. In contrast, under a pull program researchers will not receive payment unless a usable product is delivered, so they have incentives to focus on developing the desired product.

Because push programs pay for research inputs rather than results, decisions must be made about where to commit funds before any product is actually developed—and the authority for these decisions often lies in the hands of administrators who frequently rely on advice from those with vested interests in the decisions. Research administrators or their ultimate employers—the public and their elected officials—may not be able to determine which research projects in response to certain diseases are worth pursuing, nor which diseases should be targeted. Decision makers may therefore wind up financing ideas with only a minute probability of success or, worse, failing to fund promising research because they do not have confidence that its backers are presenting objective information on its prospects. In contrast, under a pull program, in which developers are rewarded only if they successfully produce the desired product, there is a strong incentive for firms considering research investments to assess prospects for success realistically. For instance, if a tuberculosis vaccine is feasible, but a malaria vaccine is not, developers will pursue the tuberculosis vaccine under a pull program.

When governments allocate research spending up front, they may also base decisions partly on political, rather than scientific, considerations. For example, there may be political pressure to allocate research expenditures to particular regions or countries, developing countries in particular. With pull programs, in contrast, the sponsors promise to pay for a viable vaccine wherever it is developed. In addition, even if push programs select research projects that appear to be appropriate at the outset but ultimately prove not to be, the original judgments are unlikely to be revised. If results on a particular research project that initially appear promising later turn out to be disappointing, a private firm is likely to shut the project down. A publicly funded entity, on the other hand, may acquire its own bureaucratic momentum, which can lead governments to throw good money after bad.

A centralized push program may prevent a situation where private firms competing for a patent inefficiently duplicate each other's activities. However, in the case of research on malaria, tuberculosis, and even HIV/AIDS vaccines, the world is far from a situation in which developers are overinvesting in R&D or inefficiently duplicating each other's work. Moreover, while decentralization may lead to some duplication of effort, it also ensures that mistakes by a single decision maker will not block progress toward a vaccine.

The problems that plague push programs are illustrated by the U.S. Agency for International Development's (USAID) 1980s program to develop a malaria vaccine. During the USAID program, external evaluators suggested that additional funding should not be provided to two of the three research teams. However, USAID provided substantial new resources to all three teams and was sufficiently confident that vaccines would be developed that it even arranged to purchase monkeys for testing a vaccine. Two of the three researchers diverted grant funds into their private accounts and were later indicted for theft and criminal conspiracy. The project director received kickbacks from the contract to purchase monkeys and eventually pleaded guilty to accepting an illegal gratuity, filing false tax returns, and making false statements. Before the indictments, the agency claimed that there had been a "major breakthrough in the development of a vaccine against the most deadly form of malaria in human beings. The vaccine should be ready for use around the world, especially in developing countries, within five years" (Desowitz 1991, p. 255). That was in 1984. Today, the world is still waiting for a malaria vaccine. By the end of the project, USAID had spent $60 million but had obtained few results. While the example is extreme, it vividly illustrates the problems with push programs.

As an alternative to push programs that directly finance research, some have proposed R&D tax credits targeted to private research on vaccines needed by developing countries. However, such tax credits are subject to similar problems. Firms would have an incentive to relabel as much of their R&D as possible to have it be eligible for the targeted credit. For example, if there were an R&D tax credit for a malaria vaccine, researchers might focus on a vaccine that would likely provide only temporary protection suitable for travelers and military personnel (who spend only short times in developing countries) but not for residents of these areas. To take another example, firms would have every incentive to state that work on an adjuvant intended for an ineligible vaccine was actually for a malaria vaccine, so as to claim a tax credit. Finally, R&D tax credits will not improve access to vaccines once they are developed.

In contrast, under pull programs, the public pays nothing unless a viable vaccine is developed. Pull programs give researchers incentives to self-select projects with a reasonable chance of yielding a viable product and to focus on developing a marketable vaccine. Several historical precedents, such as the Orphan Drug Act, suggest that pull-like mechanisms can be effective tools for spurring product development.[8] Moreover, appropriately designed pull programs can help ensure that if new vaccines are developed, they will reach those who need them. For example, if developed countries or private foundations committed to purchase malaria vaccine at $15 per immunized person, if and when it was developed, they could then make it available to developing countries either for free or in return for a modest copayment.

A key limitation of pull programs is that they require specifying the output in advance. A pull program could not have been used to encourage the development of the Post-It Note or the graphical user interface, because these products could not have been adequately described before they were invented. Similarly, pull programs may not work well to encourage basic research, because it is typically difficult to specify the desired results of such research in advance. Simply rewarding the development of applied products is not a good way to stimulate basic research, since a program that tied rewards to the development of a specific product would encourage researchers to keep their results private as long as possible, in order to have an advantage in the next stage of research. A key objective of basic research is to provide information to other researchers rather than to develop products, and grant-funded academics and scientists in government laboratories have career incentives to publish their results quickly. In contrast to unanticipated inventions or to basic research, it is comparatively easier to define what is meant by a safe and efficacious vaccine, especially since existing institutions, such as the U.S. Food and Drug Administration (FDA) or its European counterpart, the European Agency for the Evaluation of Medicinal Products (EMEA), are already charged with making these determinations.

Both push and pull approaches have important roles in encouraging R&D on products needed by developing countries. While both push and pull incentives are already in place for pharmaceutical products needed in high-income countries, the world lacks a pull system for diseases that primarily affect low-income countries.

PULL PROGRAM OPTIONS

Pull programs that reward successful vaccine research can take several different forms, including commitments to purchase vaccines, patent buyouts, and extensions of patent rights on other products. Given the huge disparities between private and social returns to research, it is likely that any program that is committed to providing compensation to developers of vaccines needed by poor countries would be an improvement on the status quo. However, purchase commitments are likely the most attractive option for a pull program to encourage such R&D.

Patent buyouts are economically similar to purchase commitments, but purchasing products provides a clearer link between payments and product quality. For example, suppose that a vaccine received regulatory approval, but was later found to have side effects. This was the case with the Wyeth-Ayerst rotavirus vaccine, which was withdrawn from the U.S. market following evidence that it causes intussusception in rare cases. If a patent buyout had been made at the date of regulatory approval, it might be difficult to recover the money. Vaccine purchases, on the other hand, could be suspended as soon as there was evidence of unacceptable side effects. Though in theory patent buyouts lead to free competition in manufacturing, because biologicals are difficult to produce, a patent buyout might leave the developer with an effective monopoly due to trade secrets, even without the patent. In this case, the public would effectively pay twice: once for the patent and again for the vaccine.

Another proposed design for a pull program is to reward developers with extensions of patents on other pharmaceuticals. This approach would inefficiently and inequitably place the entire burden of financing development on patients who need these other pharmaceuticals. For example, giving a patent extension on Prozac for developing an HIV vaccine could prevent some people from getting needed treatment for depression.

THE CREDIBILITY AND DESIGN OF PURCHASE COMMITMENTS

The effectiveness of a purchase commitment at inducing new research depends crucially on its credibility to investors and its design. Potential developers must believe that once they have sunk money into producing a vaccine, it will be purchased at a price that covers their risk-adjusted costs of research as well as their manufacturing costs. Courts have held that similar public commitments to reward contest winners or to purchase specified goods constitute legally binding contracts, and that the decisions of independent parties appointed in advance to adjudicate such programs are binding. For example, in the 1960s the U.S. government pledged to purchase, at a minimum price, domestically produced manganese. After the world price of the commodity fell, the General Services Administration (GSA), the U.S. agency in charge of administering the program, attempted to renege, but U.S. courts forced the GSA to honor the commitment (Morantz and Sloane 2001).

The more binding the commitment is, the stronger the incentives for potential developers. In general, there is a trade-off between flexibility and credibly committing to pay for a desired product. While general eligibility and pricing rules could be set out, some degree of discretion in interpreting these rules would be needed once candidate products have been developed and tested. Delegating decisions regarding eligibility and pricing to a committee that included some members who had worked in the industry and insulating the adjudicators from political pressure through long terms of service could increase potential developers' confidence that the committee would not impose unreasonable conditions after they developed a vaccine.

The eligibility conditions set for candidate products will also be a key determinant of the success of a purchase commitment in encouraging research. A purchase commitment would, for instance, need to minimize the possibility that misspecified eligibility and pricing rules divert research incentives away from appropriate products. For example, it would be important to make clear that the commitment would not cover a hypothetical malaria vaccine that interfered with the development of natural immunity and provided only temporary protection. At the same time, it is important not to set specifications so stringently that they would discourage pharmaceutical firms from following promising leads. For example, it would be a mistake to require a vaccine that achieved 90% efficacy against all strains of the disease, since in this case potential vaccine developers might not pursue a candidate vaccine that would be likely to yield 99% protection against most strains, but only 85% protection against others, even if this candidate vaccine were the best available research opportunity. If developers had sufficient confidence in the program adjudicators, some flexibility in the technical requirements would not substantially decrease research incentives.

The eligibility conditions would likely include some minimal technical requirements that could outline specific characteristics an eligible vaccine must have. Determination of vaccine eligibility might also require either clearance by a regulatory agency, such as the U.S. FDA, or a waiver of regulatory approval in developed countries for products that would pass a cost-benefit analysis for use in developing but not developed countries. Some of the key technical issues that would need to be considered in determining vaccine eligibility and pricing include

- Vaccine efficacy, or the reduction in disease incidence among those receiving the vaccine.
- Efficacy might vary in different circumstances. For example, a vaccine could potentially be better suited to some geographic areas than others.
- The number of doses required, the efficacy of the vaccine if an incomplete course is given, and the ages at which doses must be taken. If too many doses are required, fewer people will bring their children in to receive the full course of immunization. If the vaccine can be given along with vaccines that are already widely administered, delivery will be much cheaper.
- Vaccine side effects. Side effects also could differ for different subpopulations.
- The time over which the vaccine provides protection, and whether booster shots could extend this period.
- What level of rigor would be required in the field trials. For example, how many separate studies in different regions would need to be conducted to assess efficacy against different varieties of the disease?

- The extent to which vaccines would lose their effectiveness over time. Presumably, some ongoing monitoring of vaccine effectiveness in the field would be required, and if it appears that resistance to the vaccine is spreading, vaccine purchases would have to be reassessed.

Products that meet the technical requirements could then be subject to a market test: nations wishing to purchase vaccines might be required to provide a modest copayment tied to their per capita income, so that countries would have an incentive to carefully investigate whether candidate vaccines are appropriate for their local conditions. This provision would also help to assure that limited donor funds are allocated well and would increase incentives for developers by increasing the payment offered to the successful developer. On the other hand, a copayment requirement could reduce the confidence of potential vaccine developers in the program by increasing the uncertainty of future vaccine demand in poor countries. A purchase commitment could also include a system of bonus payments for products that exceed the minimum technical requirements.

PRODUCT PRICING AND COVERAGE

After suitable eligibility requirements have been set and credibility has been established, the key determinant of research incentives for potential vaccine developers will be the total discounted revenue generated by a product. It is very expensive to conduct R&D, but once research is complete, it is typically fairly cheap to produce additional doses. For a fixed amount of total revenue, product developers will therefore be almost as happy to produce a high volume at a low price as a low volume at a high price.

This implies that, at least as a first approximation, prices should be set per person immunized or treated, not per dose. There is little reason to pay more per person immunized if more doses are required to provide immunity than if a single dose is required. In fact, the vaccine is more valuable if only a single dose is required to provide immunity, since this reduces delivery costs and is likely to increase patient compliance. Moreover, the purchase program would not save money by excluding large countries from coverage, or excluding countries if vaccination is cost-effective at the marginal cost of production but not at the average price paid under the program. Such exclusions would be a false economy. Because potential developers will need a fixed amount of revenue to induce them to conduct research, if fewer doses are purchased, the price per person immunized will need to be greater in order to induce the same amount of research.[9]

The total market promised by a purchase commitment should be large enough to induce substantial effort by vaccine developers, but less than the social value of the vaccine. Because potential developers know that their research may fail, in order to have incentives to conduct work on needed vaccines, they must expect to more than cover their research expenses if they succeed. For example, if potential biotechnology investors expect that a candidate product has one chance in ten of succeeding, they will require at least a tenfold return on their investment in the case of success to make the investment worthwhile.

The larger the market offered under a purchase commitment, the more firms will enter the field, the more research leads each firm will pursue, and the faster a product will be developed. Given the enormous burden of diseases such as malaria, tuberculosis, and HIV/AIDS, it is important to provide sufficient incentive for many researchers to enter the field and to induce major pharmaceutical firms to pursue several potential leads simultaneously, so that products can be developed quickly. There is little risk that payments made as a result of a purchase commitment could exceed the cost of saving the equivalent number of lives using existing approaches.

Prior work by the author and others suggests that an annual market of $500 million or more in years with peak sales is needed to motivate substantial research (Kettler 1999; Berndt et al. 2005; Mercer Management Consulting 1998). Berndt et al. (2005) estimate that the total vaccine purchase commitment size that would be necessary to create a "market" comparable to markets of existing pharmaceutical products would be approximately $3.1 billion (in 2004 dollars).

A condition of participation in the program could be agreement among developing firms to license the products to producers in developing countries after a certain pre-set number of doses of the vaccine have been sold. Potential developers are likely to heavily discount sales after, say, ten years, in part because in more normal circumstances developers are likely to assume that competing products are apt to emerge after ten years in any case, thus driving down prices of their product.[10]

It is useful to consider the cost-effectiveness of a commitment to guarantee a price of $15 (in 2004 dollars) for the first 200 million people immunized against malaria in exchange for a commitment that, after the initial purchases, the price would drop to $1 per person—which is still more than the current price of many EPI vaccines. The exact cost-effectiveness depends on a variety of assumptions.[11] But to get an idea of the magnitudes, consider a case in which (a) the contract covers all countries with a per capita income of less than $1,000 per year with sufficient disease prevalence to make vaccination worthwhile; (b) countries adopt the vaccine over seven years at rates consistent with those of the EPI program; (c) the vaccine is deliverable with the EPI vaccines; and (d) the vaccine is 60% effective and protects against infection for ten years. Under this fairly conservative set of assumptions, the cost—including incremental delivery costs—per discounted DALY saved over a fifty-year horizon would be about $15 (in 2004 dollars). Under similar assumptions, a commitment to guarantee a price of $15 for the first 200 million people immunized against HIV would cost about $17 per DALY saved, and a commitment for a tuberculosis vaccine would cost about $25 per DALY saved.[12]

It is thus clear that purchases under a vaccine commitment would save more lives than almost any alternative use of funds.[13] A commitment of 3 billion 2004 dollars in net present value of sales (as would be generated by the scenario described in the previous paragraph) would certainly be appropriate. The larger the commitment, the more firms will enter the search for a vaccine, and the faster a vaccine is likely to be developed. Since malaria kills 3,000 people every day, erring on the side of parsimony does not seem wise.

SCOPE OF A PURCHASE COMMITMENT

This essay focuses on purchase commitments for vaccines for malaria, HIV, and tuberculosis. Potentially, purchase commitments could be used to encourage research not only on vaccines, but also on other techniques for fighting disease, including drugs, diagnostic devices, and insecticides against the mosquitoes that transmit malaria. Given a sufficient budget, it might be appropriate to commit in advance to purchase vaccines or drugs developed against other diseases that primarily affect developing countries. However, if funding is tightly limited, it may be appropriate to target the most deadly diseases. Table 21.1 shows the number of deaths caused annually by various diseases for which vaccines are needed.

Including some easier-to-develop vaccines in a purchase commitment for a range of diseases, perhaps maintaining separate funds (or making separate financial commitments) for different diseases, would enable the program to build up a reputation for fair play and for fulfilling promises. It also may be useful to first experiment with purchase commitments for a few vaccines or drugs and then consider modifying or extending the program based on the resulting experience. Of course, it is likely to require time and experimentation to refine this new tool, just as it took time for institutions such as the patent system or the peer review process to evolve into their current forms. The institutions that today are integral in supporting our systems of innovation required both time and trial-and-error to develop. The first step in developing price guarantees as a tool for encouraging R&D would be to try the system in a few cases where current R&D incentives are inadequate and where the pull approach seems well suited to fill the gap.

IMPLEMENTING A PURCHASE COMMITMENT

A vaccine commitment has considerable appeal across the ideological spectrum as a market-oriented mechanism that brings the resources and inventiveness of the private sector to the fight against diseases disproportionately killing some of the world's poorest people. To move forward, it will be necessary for institutions with sufficient resources (such as national governments, international organizations, or private foundations) to launch a legally binding commitment program. A host of policy leaders and organizations

Table 21.1: Deaths from Diseases for Which Vaccines Are
              Needed

Diseases	Deaths (000)[a]	%
AIDS	2285	27.47
Tuberculosis	1498	18.01
Malaria	1110	13.34
Pneumococcus[b]	1100	13.22
Rotavirus	800	9.62
Shigella	600	7.21
Enterotoxic E. coli	500	6.01
Respiratory syncy-tial virus[c]	160	1.92
Schistosomiasis[d]	150	1.80
Leishmaniasis	42	0.50
Trympanosomiasis	40	0.48
Chagas disease	17	0.20
Dengue	15	0.18
Leprosy	2	0.02
Total deaths	8319	100.00

Source: Children's Vaccine Initiative, CVI Forum 18, July 1999, p. 6.
[a]Estimated, World Health Report, WHO, 1999
[b]A pneumococcus vaccine was just approved for use in the United States,
but it needs to be tested in developing countries, and perhaps modified
accordingly.
[c]The Jordan Report, NIAID, 1998
[d]R. Bergquist, WHO, personal communication

have endorsed the concept of vaccine commitments. The Clinton administration proposed a pull program for HIV, tuberculosis, and malaria vaccines,
and Secretary of the Treasury Larry Summers was a key advocate. Legislation
incorporating these provisions was introduced in Congress by Senators Bill
Frist and John Kerry and by Representatives Nancy Pelosi and Jennifer Dunn.
An Institute of Medicine committee has also recommended pull programs
for vaccines in the United States (IOM 2003). The Bush administration's
Project Bioshield, intended to improve vaccines and drugs that protect
against chemical and biological warfare, uses a spending authority intended
to function as a pull program. However, a key weakness of Project Bioshield
is that the government is not committed to paying specific prices for new
therapies, so developers still run the risk that, after the fact, the government
will offer terms that do not cover the fixed costs. The G-8 Group of Nations
has also strongly supported the idea of advance purchase commitments. Fol-

lowing its June 2005 Summit, the G-8 asked Italy to study the issue and to come up with more concrete proposals by the end of the year.

In February of 2000, then World Bank president James Wolfensohn, indicated that the institution planned to create a $1 billion fund to help countries purchase specified vaccines if and when they are developed (*Financial Times* 2000), though the World Bank has not acted on this commitment. The Gates Foundation, with $22 billion in assets and a focus on children's health in developing countries and on vaccines in particular, also would be well placed to forward a vaccine purchase commitment. While continuing to fund its other priorities, such a foundation could simply pledge that if a product were actually developed, the foundation would purchase and distribute it in developing countries.

Any of several organizations—including the World Bank, national governments, and organizations such as the Gates Foundation—thus would have the ability and the opportunity to create a credible purchase commitment to stimulate research on vaccines needed in developing countries. If such a commitment fails to induce the development of the needed vaccines, no funds would be spent. If it succeeds, millions of lives would be saved each year at remarkably low cost.

ACKNOWLEDGMENTS This chapter draws in part on the deliberations of the Pull Mechanisms Working Group of the Global Health Policy Research Network, a program of the Center for Global Development that is supported by the Bill and Melinda Gates Foundation. I am particularly grateful to Rachel Glennerster and Ruth Levine for extensive discussions, and would also like to thank Daron Acemoglu, Philippe Aghion, Martha Ainsworth, Susan Athey, Amir Attaran, Abhijit Banerjee, Amie Batson, Peter Berman, Ernie Berndt, Nancy Birdsall, David Cutler, Sara Ellison, Sarah England, John Gallup, Gargee Ghosh, Chandresh Harjivan, John Hurvitz, Eugene Kandel, Hannah Kettler, Jenny Lanjouw, Sendhil Mullainathan, Ariel Pakes, Ok Pannenborg, Leighton Reid, Sydney Rosen, Jeff Sachs, Andrew Segal, Raj Shah, Scott Stern, Larry Summers, Wendy Taylor, Jean Tirole, Adrian Towse, David Weber, and Georg Weizsäcker for comments and discussions on these issues. Radu Ban, Marcos Chamon, Andrew Francis, Fabia Gumbau, Amar Hamoudi, Jane Kim, Jean Lee, Ben Olken, Kathy Paur, Margaret Ronald, Courtney Umberger, Heidi Williams, and Alix Peterson Zwane provided excellent research assistance.

NOTES

1. The BCG vaccine has been much more effective in some trials than others: trials in Britain suggest effectiveness up to 80%, while those in the southern United States and southern India suggest close to zero efficacy (WHO 1999). A widely accepted explanation is that exposure to environmental mycobacteria, often found in warmer climates, reduces the protection provided by BCG.

2. However, more than a quarter of children worldwide and over half of children in some countries do not receive the EPI vaccines, and 3 million lives are lost annually as a result (World Bank 2001). Only a small fraction of children in poor countries receive newer hepatitis B and Haemophilus influenzae b (Hib) vaccines, which are still on patent and hence significantly more expensive at a dollar or two per dose.

3. Recent advances in immunology, biochemistry, and biotechnology have provided new tools for understanding the immune responses to these diseases, and genetic sequencing of HIV and the organisms causing tuberculosis and malaria is complete. Although some scientists are more pessimistic about the prospects for a malaria vaccine, Moorthy et al. (2004) argue that "although exact predictions are not possible, if sufficient funding were mobilized, a deployable, effective malaria vaccine is a realistic medium-term to long-term goal." Recent results from a GlaxoSmithKline (GSK) vaccine trial in Mozambique offered some evidence that the development of an effective malaria vaccine may be possible: they suggest the vaccine reduced the risk of falling sick from malaria by nearly 30%, and halved the risk of contracting a severe case of malaria. Candidate vaccines have been shown to induce protection against tuberculosis infection and HIV in animal models and, for HIV, to induce immune responses in humans.

4. For example, Africa now generates less than 1% of pharmaceutical sales (PhRMA 2005).

5. Note, however, that the definition of tropical disease used in their assessment was narrow, and that many of the other drugs licensed in this period were useful in both developing and developed countries.

6. Others have suggested using a cutoff equal to a country's per capita GNP (WHO, Regional Office for South-East Asia 2002), and several have noted that the World Bank may use this as a rule of thumb (GAVI 2004; WHO 2000c). For comparison, health interventions are considered cost-effective in the United States at up to 500 to 1,000 times this amount: $50,000–$100,000 per year of life saved (Neumann et al. 2000).

7. Indeed, one reason why developed countries are developed may be that they were able to establish good reputations in a variety of areas, including research incentives. Developed countries typically have more stable governments that are more likely to invest in reputation formation for the long run.

8. On the effect of market size on innovation in the pharmaceutical industry, see Acemoglu and Linn (2004) and Finkelstein (2004). Acemoglu and Linn exploit variations in market size for pharmaceuticals linked to demographic changes, and estimate that a 1% increase in the potential market size for a drug category leads to a 4%–6% increase in the number of new drugs in that category. Finkelstein investigates the private response to health policies that, in attempting to increase immunization rates, also increased the expected profits from new vaccines, and argues that a 1993 Medicare policy helped stimulate the R&D responsible for the approval (in 2003) of the first new flu vaccines since 1978.

9. Excluding countries that would have bought vaccines, in the absence of a program, at prices greater than or equal to the price paid by the program, would, however, increase incentives to develop products.

10. The life of a patent is twenty years. However, a vaccine would reach the market only several years after the date of application for a patent. The effective life of a patent is the number of years remaining from the time that it is first brought to market. Shulman et al. (1999) report that the average effective patent life for new drugs and biologicals is 11.2 years under the Waxman-Hatch Act, which granted extra protection to inventors to partially make up for loss of patent life during regulatory review. Without the act, patent life would be 8.2 years. The act covers the United States only, and there is no reason to believe that developing countries will offer similar patent protection.

11. A more detailed description of our data and assumptions on the burden of disease, fertility, and delivery costs, and the benefits of vaccination can be found in "A Vaccine Price Guarantee: Preliminary Cost-Effectiveness Estimates and Pricing Guidelines." This is available at http://post.economics.harvard.edu/faculty/kremer/vaccine.html.

12. For HIV, the calculation assumes that ten-year-olds will be vaccinated at a higher cost of delivery than newborns, and also considers a twenty-year vaccine rather than a five-year vaccine. The calculation for tuberculosis also considers a vaccine that protects for twenty years after immunization.

13. Indeed, commitments would remain cost-effective under a wide range of assumptions about vaccine efficacy, level and speed of vaccine adoption, and the amount of money spent for vaccines. On the whole, there is a large range of values under which a vaccine commitment would be sufficient to stimulate substantial research, yet still be extremely cost-effective. See http://post.economics.harvard.edu/faculty/kremer/vaccine.html.

BIBLIOGRAPHY

Acemoglu, Daron, and Joshua Linn. "Market Size in Innovation: Theory and Evidence from the Pharmaceutical Industry." *Quarterly Journal of Economics* 119 (3) (2004): 1049–1090.

Berndt, Ernst, Rachel Glennerster, Michael Kremer, Jean Lee, Ruth Levine, Georg Weizsacker, and Heidi Williams. "Advance Purchase Commitments for a Malaria Vaccine: Estimating Costs and Effectiveness," National Bureau of Economic Research, Working Paper #11288, 2005.

Cowman, A. F. "Mechanisms of Drug Resistance in Malaria." *Australia and New Zealand Journal of Medicine* 25 (6) (1995): 837–844.

Desowitz, Robert S. *The Malaria Capers: More Tales of Parasites and People, Research and Reality.* New York: Norton, 1991.

DiMasi, Joseph, et al. "Cost of Innovation in the Pharmaceutical Industry." *Journal of Health Economics* 10 (2) (1991): 107–142.

Elliott, Larry, and Mark Atkinson. "Fund to Beat Third World Disease." *Guardian,* Feb. 23, 2001. Available online at http://www.guardian.co.uk/globalisation/story/0,,441883,00.html. *Financial Times.* "Discovering Medicines for the Poor." Feb. 2, 2000, 7.

Finkelstein. Amy. "Health Policy and Technological Change: Evidence from the Vaccine Industry." *Quarterly Journal of Economics* 119 (2) (2004): 527–564.

GAVI (Global Alliance for Vaccines and Immunizations). "Health, Immunization, and Economic Growth. Research Briefing #2: Vaccines Are Cost-Effective. A Summary of Recent Research." 2004. Available online at http://www.vaccinealliance.org.

Glennerster, Rachel, and Michael Kremer. "A Vaccine Purchase Commitment: Cost-Effectiveness Estimates and Pricing Guidelines." Mimeo, Harvard University, 2001.

G8 Finance Ministers' Conclusions on Development, London, June 10–11, 2005. Available online at http://www.g8.gov.uk/servlet/Front?pagename=OpenMarket/Xcelerate/ShowPage&c=Page&cid=1078995903270&aid=1115146455234.

Herfkens, Eveline. "Strategies for Increasing Access to Essential Drugs: The Need for Global Commitment." Presentation at the Conference for Increasing Access to Essential Drugs in a Globalised Economy, Amsterdam, Nov. 25–26, 1999.

IOM (U.S. Institute of Medicine). *Financing Vaccines in the 21st Century: Assuring Access and Availability.* Washington, D.C.: National Academy Press, 2004.

Kettler, Hannah E. *Updating the Cost of a New Chemical Entity.* London: Office of Health Economics, 1999.

Kim-Farley, R., and the Expanded Programme on Immunization Team. "Global Immunization." *Annual Review of Public Health* 13 (1992): 223–237.

Kremer, Michael. "Creating Markets for New Vaccines—Part I: Rationale." In *Innovation Policy and the Economy.* Edited by Adam B. Jaffe, Josh Lerner, and Scott Stern. Cambridge, Mass.: MIT Press, 2001a.

Kremer, Michael. "Creating Markets for New Vaccines—Part II: Design Issues." In *Innovation Policy and the Economy.* Edited by Adam B. Jaffe, Josh Lerner, and Scott Stern. Cambridge, Mass.: MIT Press, 2001b.

Mansfield, Edwin, et al. *The Production and Application of New Industrial Technology.* New York: Norton, 1977.

Mercer Management Consulting. "HIV Vaccine Industry Study, October-December 1998." World Bank Task Force on Accelerating the Development of an HIV/AIDS Vaccine for Developing Countries, 1998.

Mitchell, Violaine S., Nalini M. Philipose, and Jay P. Sanford, eds. *The Children's Vaccine Initiative: Achieving the Vision.* Washington, D.C.: National Academy Press, 1993.

Moorthy, Vasee, Michael Good, and Adrian Hill. "Malaria Vaccine Developments." *Lancet* 363 (2004): 150–156.

Morantz, Alison, and Robert Sloane. "Vaccine Purchase Commitment Contract: Legal Strategies for Ensuring Enforceability." Harvard University, 2001. Mimeo.

Murray, Christopher J. L., and Alan D. Lopez. *Global Health Statistics: A Compendium of Incidence, Prevalence, and Mortality Estimates for Over 200 Conditions.* Cambridge, Mass.: Harvard School of Public Health/WHO, 1996a.

Murray, Christopher J. L., and Alan D. Lopez, eds. *The Global Burden of Disease: A Comprehensive Assessment of Mortality and Disability from Diseases, Injuries, and Risk Factors in 1990 and Projected to 2020.* Cambridge, Mass.: Harvard School of Public Health/WHO, 1996b.

Nadiri, M. Ishaq. "Innovations and Technological Spillovers." NBER working paper 4423, 1993.

Neumann, Peter J., Eileen Sandberg, Chaim A. Bell, Patricia Stone, and Richard H. Chapman. "Are Pharmaceuticals Cost-Effective? A Review of the Evidence." *Health Affairs* (Mar.–Apr. 2000).

Pecoul, Bernard, Pierre Chirac, Patrice Trouiller, and Jacques Pinel. "Access to Essential Drugs in Poor Countries: A Lost Battle?" *Journal of the American Medical Association* 281 (4) (1999): 361–367.

PhRMA. "PhRMA Industry Profile 2005." 2005. Available online at http://www.phrma.org/publications/publications/17.03.2005.1142.cfm.

PIU (Performance and Innovation Unit, U.K. Cabinet Office). "Tackling the Diseases of Poverty: Meeting the Okinawa/Millennium Targets for HIV/AIDS, Tuberculosis, and Malaria." London, May 8, 2001. Available online at http://www.strategy.gov.uk/downloads/su/health/recommendations/default.htm.

Shulman, Sheila, Joseph DiMasi, and K. I. Kaitin. "Patent Term Restoration: The Impact of the Waxman-Hatch Act on New Drugs and Biologics Approved 1984–1995." *Journal of BioLaw and Business* 2 (4) (1999): 63–68.

UNAIDS. *2004 Report on the Global AIDS Epidemic.* Geneva: UNAIDS, 2004.

Wellcome Trust. "An Audit of International Activity in Malaria Research." 1996. Available online at http://www.wellcome.ac.uk/doc%5Fwtd003221.html.

WHO (World Health Organization). *Investing in Health Research and Development: Report of the Ad Hoc Committee on Health Research Relating to Future Intervention Options.* Geneva: WHO, 1996.

WHO. *Anti-Tuberculosis Drug Resistance in the World.* Geneva: WHO, 1997.

WHO. *Issues Relating to the Use of BCG in Immunization Programmes.* By Paul E. M. Fine et al. Geneva: WHO, 1999.

WHO. *Anti-Tuberculosis Drug Resistance in the World: Report No. 2.* Geneva: WHO, 2000a. Available online at http://www.who.int/csr/resources/publications/drug resist/WHO_CDS_TB_2000_278/en/.

WHO. *Global Tuberculosis Control 2000.* Geneva: WHO, 2000b. Available online at http://www.who.int/docstore/gtb/publications/globrep00/index.html.

WHO. *World Heath Report 2000.* Geneva: WHO, 2000c.

WHO. *WHO Global Tuberculosis Control Report.* Geneva: WHO, 2002a.

WHO. *World Heath Report 2002.* Geneva: WHO, 2002b.

WHO, Regional Office for South-East Asia. "Prevention of Hepatitis B in India: An Overview" New Delhi: WHO, Aug. 2002.

World Bank. *Disease Control Priorities in Developing Countries,* edited by Dean T. Jamison et al. New York: Oxford University Press, 1993a.

World Bank. *World Development Report 1993: Investing in Health.* New York: Oxford University Press, 1993b.

World Bank. *World Development Indicators.* 2001. CD-ROM.

WTO. (World Trade Organization). *Fact Sheet: TRIPS and Pharmaceutical Patents.* Geneva: WTO, 2001. Available online at http://www.wto.org/english/tratop_e/trips_e/factsheet_pharm00_e.htm.

22

Microinsurance: The Next Revolution?

Jonathan Morduch

Managua is a city of gaps. City blocks are scattered across the terrain as if they had been dropped from an airplane and had then broken into pieces upon hitting the ground. A block of buildings is followed by an open field, and then more buildings, and then a stretch of grass and dirt, more buildings, another field . . . and on it goes. The topography is a product of the earthquake of 1972, which killed six thousand people and toppled 80% of Managua's buildings. Neither the right-wing president Anastasio Somoza Debayle, nor the leftist Sandinistas, nor subsequent governments have patched the city together again. The scattered blocks are an ongoing reminder to residents of both the power of nature and the limited means they have to respond.

The most recent reminder of nature's vast power came in 1998 when Hurricane Mitch sat over Nicaragua for ten days. Three thousand people are reported to have died, and 20% of the population suffered directly. Even today, the hurricane is cited to explain disrepair and dislocation. While Mitch was particularly devastating, hurricanes course through the Caribbean with regularity. Nevertheless, most citizens and businesses cannot buy insurance against weather-related risks; as in much of the developing world, insurance markets are thin and public responses are limited. Health insurance, life insurance, property insurance—all are unobtainable for average citizens in most of the world, and this is doubly so for the poorest.

Below, I describe why this is so and how new ideas can change things. Others have so far focused mainly on how to build strong institutions that can provide insurance. In this essay my focus is instead on designing products that can most help poor customers deal with the risks that life throws before them.

THE INSURANCE CHALLENGE

My calculations from a 1998 survey of areas affected by Hurricane Mitch show the implications of missing insurance markets. For 21% of households, the main response to the hurricane was not to draw on insurance, nor to use savings, nor to borrow funds; it was a drastic reduction in consumption. As a "second most important response" another 18% report drastically reduced consumption. Most households in the survey (89%) reported receiving no assistance at all after Mitch, and for those who did report getting assistance, NGOs—not the government nor private insurers—were the largest single provider.[1]

Development experts are recognizing how intimately the lack of insurance and the persistence of poverty are related. When World Bank staff set out to define a new agenda on reducing poverty for the Bank's 2000/2001 *World Development Report,* addressing risk and vulnerability was pushed to top billing alongside traditional concerns such as spurring economic growth and creating jobs. Indeed, Ravi Kanbur, a Cornell economist on leave as the report's director, resigned his World Bank post rather than demote concern with risk (as well as concern with political "voice" and "empowerment") as bank higher-ups had requested he do.[2] In the end, the report still forcefully makes the case for addressing risk. The International Labour Organisation followed suit by taking the reduction of risk as a unifying theme in its work on social safety nets (as does the Bank's own Social Protection Strategy Paper), and the UNDP has also jumped on board.

The challenges in reducing risk are great. The lack of insurance markets has not happened through inattention, and hundreds of doctoral dissertations and other scholarly studies explain in careful detail why insurance markets remain so problematic. Despite the generally strong markets of the United States, for example, 44 million poorer households had no health insurance in late 2004. And insurance for U.S. farmers exists largely because taxpayers have subsidized it at a rate of about $5 of subsidy for every $1 of insurance provided (Yaron et al. 1997).

Around the world, most poor people are farmers, and crop insurance faces the same fundamental difficulties as in the United States. In the early 1990s, I spent parts of several summers in villages in Shandong province in northern China, investigating how poor households were coping with risk after the dramatic rural reforms that had started in 1978. The short answer to the question was "not too well." While on average incomes were growing at 8% per year, a quarter of the population in any given year was suffering losses of about 20% (Morduch and Sicular 2001). This was mainly due to fluctuations in agriculture as households battled a range of plagues with biblical echoes: drought, floods, hail, pest infestation, and livestock disease. The state-owned People's Insurance Company had been revived in the 1980s, but it provided agricultural insurance purely to appease policy makers, and the company's lack of enthusiasm translated into miserly insurance coverage. Farmers could not buy coverage against infestation of cotton by boll worms, for instance, despite their frequent appearance and destructiveness, and the maximum coverage for losses was 70 yuan per mu, although the cost of production was roughly 200 yuan per mu from planting to harvest.[3] All the same, the company still suffered losses on its agricultural lines.

The Chinese experience has parallels globally; experts whom I have canvassed have difficulty naming even one truly successful small-scale crop insurance program anywhere (i.e., one that serves the poor, makes profits, and meaningfully reduces the largest risks). To make profits, insurers must pay out less than they take in as revenues, but Hazell (1992) finds the ratios of costs to revenue all well above break-even levels (i.e., 1 or below) in his studies of Brazil (4.6), Costa Rica (2.8), Japan (4.6), Mexico (3.7), and the United States (2.4). Most crop insurance, such as the People's Insurance Company's agricultural lines, is both subsidized and relatively ineffective.

Why do farmers have difficulty finding effective insurance? The problems are several, and a handful of Nobel Prizes in economics have been given to those who generated the key insights. First, "moral hazard" is omnipresent; once insured, farmers are less likely to apply the extra fertilizer, labor, and other inputs needed to maximize chances of success: the very fact of being insured raises the probability of losses. Second, "adverse selection" arises since farmers in the riskiest situations are naturally the most eager to purchase insurance. When insurers cannot tell beforehand who is most risky, they have to charge everyone the same price for insurance, but often that only ends up pushing "safer" farmers farther away. If insurers lowered prices, they might be able to attract a better pool of clients, but profit margins will fall if the improvement in clients is less than proportional to the price drop. This problem could be solved by charging different prices to different types of farmers, but the insurance company (at least at the outset) has little to go by when distinguishing the best prospects from the worst. The third issue is analytically less interesting (and thus receives less attention from academics), but it is often critical in practice: it's hard for insurers to provide crop insurance in a cheap way, since contracts are generally for small amounts and damages have to be assessed by insurers on an individual basis; scale economies are thus limited.

This all sounds grim: transactions costs are high and information problems are ubiquitous—not to mention that clients have limited cash flows and may not be literate or numerate, and that enforcement mechanisms are limited. Private-sector insurers naturally look elsewhere for profits, leaving state-subsidized companies as the main players—and even they are having a rough time of it.

But is it really as hopeless as it sounds? Despite the woeful litany, the characterization sounds a lot like the situation facing the "microfinance" industry in the 1980s—the early pioneers such as Muhammad Yunus of Bangladesh's Grameen Bank also faced great skepticism when arguing that it is possible to lend profitably to the poor. Credit markets in poor regions, like insurance markets, are also characterized by similar problems of high transactions costs, moral hazard, adverse selection, limited cash flows, low education levels of clients, and weak enforcement mechanisms. And in the case of credit, too, the main "formal" lenders also had too often been bloated, subsidized, ineffective state-owned companies.

But today, thanks to a series of clever innovations, microfinance is booming, and the Grameen Bank served 3.4 million clients in early 2004 (which is perhaps one quarter of all microfinance clients in Bangladesh); a 2003 tally puts the global total at over 80 million served—with rapid growth predicted by some advocates (Daley-Harris 2004). Marguerite Robinson (2001) has described an international "microfinance revolution." Can the "microinsurance revolution" be far behind? Is it possible to find ways to sell small-scale insurance to low-income clients—profitably and on a wide scale?

Several promising innovations are described below: credit life insurance, health insurance partnerships, and weather insurance. Each was created to serve populations that were previously unserved, and workable institutional solutions are emerging. I argue that the next step must be to shift from the question of what creates workable institutions to the question of how to refine designs to best serve low-income populations. In doing so, current approaches must be reassessed in order to most improve clients' lives—and to avoid doing unintended harm.

WHAT WE DON'T KNOW (AND WHY IT SHOULDN'T STAND IN THE WAY)

The prospects are exciting, but much remains unknown. The expanding gaggle of microinsurance advocates is ahead of the available evidence on insurance impacts. Microinsurance advocates argue that selling insurance to the poor will give households new freedoms to pursue profit without fear. They argue that incomes will rise as a result and that poverty will fall substantially. (They thus argue that their projects should be generously funded by donors.) The advocates may be right, at least in the long term, but it is impossible to point to a broad range of great evidence on which to base that prejudice.

The problem is not that empirically inclined academic economists are not interested in risk. Quite the opposite. But they have not had much usable data from low-income countries with which to work, and academic economists have (understandably) stuck close by the questions that they can answer most precisely. The precise answers that they yield are not yet the stuff on which revolutions can be built. Taken together, though, the scattered studies make it clear that the poor have some protections but, in general, remain highly vulnerable to risk. The evidence is still far from perfect, but it's adding up.

The problem for researchers is that to gauge the role of fluctuations, they need economic data on the same households over many years. Typical surveys, though, are done only once; some are done twice on the same households; and only a very few offer a longer time dimension. The longest suitable series that exists covers eight years for roughly 120 households in three villages in south India (see Walker and Ryan 1990). The questionnaire is rich, and over fifteen years, a series of excellent studies have been based on the data. But, at the end of the day, the survey still covers just three villages in the semiarid tropics. Researchers ideally want more than ten years of data on a much broader range of people and regions.

A second issue for researchers is that households are enormously resourceful. This means that not only do households take pains to protect consumption in the face of a period of unusually low income, but they will also have taken steps long beforehand to make sure that future income declines are limited in the first place—for instance, through crop and labor diversification, choice of technology, and risk-reducing input use. Because the ways that this is done are so varied (and often partial and overlapping), researchers have had limited success in calculating how costly these protective measures are (and thus we do not have good estimates of gains from replacing the measures with market-based insurance). A few estimates exist (again, mainly from rural south India), but we don't have anything very solid yet that, by itself, can justify major investments.[4]

A third issue is that the results we have, particularly those from rural south India, have been too frequently misinterpreted by readers eager for confirmation of their particular hunches. Some readers have been quick to conclude that (1) in the absence of formal insurance, villages brim with informal substitutes (such as the reciprocity-based gift-giving to those in need described by Besley 1995a); (2) informal insurance is principally cooperative as communities come together to help each other out; and (3) given all this activity within villages, policy makers should concentrate on regionwide risks. While there is variation, of course, my reading is that the three propositions are most often more wrong than right.[5]

Part of the confusion can be traced to interpretations of an important and clever paper by the University of Chicago economist Robert Townsend. He asks whether community-based informal insurance arrangements in the three south Indian villages might in fact be so effective that the poor can do a very good job of protecting their consumption levels against unusual swings in income—that is, he asks whether points 1, 2, and 3 in the preceding paragraph hold in the data. To do this, he shows that if "perfect insurance" occurs, then villagers will effectively pool their resources so that unusual losses are compensated for and unusual gains are contributed to the communal pot. I will help you today, the logic goes, if you promise to help me when I need it. This is not socialism: the pot is not necessarily split evenly for all; the goal is only to smooth away idiosyncratic ups and downs. To everyone's surprise, Townsend finds that in these poor, isolated villages, this kind of "perfect insurance" is a "near miss."

If the result is right, community-based informal sharing must be strong, the village can be seen as a "natural insurance unit," and policy makers can stop worrying about the vagaries of risk facing individual villagers. Instead, policy makers can turn attention fully to "aggregate," covariant risks that villages as entities cannot deal well with on their own: droughts, floods, price swings, disease epidemics, and the like.

But the work after Townsend's initial research shows the picture to be more complicated (Townsend 1995). In my doctoral dissertation I returned to the ICRISAT data and found weaker evidence of insurance, using a somewhat different statistical formulation (Morduch 1991, 2004). Nor could I find much evidence of risk-sharing within caste groups, arguably an even more "natural" insurance unit.[6]

Youngjae Lim and Robert Townsend (1998) have written an especially illuminating follow-up study. Townsend's 1994 study had shifted attention from individual coping mechanisms (as studied fruitfully by, for example, Mark Rosenzweig 1988) to how the mechanisms add up when taken together. Thus immediate concern was only with whether consumption was protected from income swings, but not how this was achieved. Lim and Townsend (1998) instead sift through the data to find the specific ways that households are actually coping. The biggest part of the answer is that the action is not via informal community-based sharing after all. It is through individuals building up grain reserves and drawing them down as needed (a sort of in-kind saving). It is self-insurance. And this, coupled with the new evidence on imperfect informal insurance, radically changes the policy picture. It suggests the need to pay attention to idiosyncratic risk along with regionwide risk, and it points to the strengthening of opportunities to save as an important policy area.

Interpreting results on imperfect insurance is not easy. Townsend (1994) had asked a sharp question and gotten a sharp answer (even if it proved not to be entirely robust), but subsequent analyses are open to multiple interpretations. Take the interesting result of Jalan and Ravallion (1999) from China, for example; they show that on average 40% of idiosyncratic income shocks are translated into consumption shocks for the poorest households in a large longitudinal survey conducted between 1985 and 1990. This is an important result, confirming the vulnerability of the poor in a large non-Indian data set. But the average is hard to parse, and the result admits various possibilities. Is it that all poor households are vulnerable to 40% of shocks? Or can, say, half in fact fully insure while the other half suffers 80% of the loss? Or is it something in between? Are positive shocks handled very differently from negative shocks? Are protections achieved through borrowing and saving? Through community-based informal insurance?

Perhaps more important, the studies after Townsend, including those from

China, don't tell us about how well households deal with aggregate risk. Putting concern back onto the idiosyncratic risks of individual villagers was a step forward, but researchers are now at risk of losing track of aggregate, regionwide risks in the process (Townsend's method remains mute on the impact of shocks facing an entire region). We have bits of evidence on the impacts of droughts and floods and other major disasters, but studying periods of upheaval, with its attendant migration and dislocation, is hard in practice; it is also difficult to separate out the impact of an aggregate shock from other contemporaneous changes.

So, where should researchers go? From a policy perspective, ideally we would like to know probabilities that losses will occur (and how great they will be)—whether they are due to aggregate or idiosyncratic forces—within a given number of months or years. This is exactly what Gisele Kamanou, a Berkeley-trained statistician at the United Nations, and I set out to do in defining a framework to measure vulnerability in a way that might guide policy in Africa, but we quickly ran up against data issues (Kamanou and Morduch 2004). We used the data set with the greatest coverage of people (a World Bank survey from the Ivory Coast), but it tracked households for just two successive years. With two years of data, forecasting risk thus became impossible without heroic assumptions. But to see how far we could get, we pushed on. As we did so, however, the data proved to be noisy in ways that were particularly pernicious: measurement error was impossible to disentangle from actual fluctuations in income and consumption. The very poorest households as judged in the first year had huge increases in income by the second (+50%), and the very richest in the first year had what seemed like big losses (−30%). Perhaps we were seeing a spectacular case of what statisticians and geneticists call "reversion to the mean," but it seemed more likely that we were seeing a spectacular case of measurement error. The pattern we saw was consistent, for example, with the income of the "poorest" in the first year being severely undercounted (making for a big jump to a more accurate figure in year 2), while that of the "rich" was severely overcounted at first. To understand how vulnerable households really are, we need longer, cleaner data series. But policy makers should not hold their breath while waiting.

The experience with microfinance suggests that there is no need to despair. Muhammad Yunus, for example, did not wait until he had all the answers before he set up the Grameen Bank of Bangladesh. But once it was set up, the introduction of the bank provided a way to learn about credit markets by comparing outcomes in places served by Grameen versus outcomes in control villages (Morduch 1998). As a result, we are now learning about the nature of credit markets in ways impossible before microfinance was established. So too, I expect, with microinsurance. The best hope is that microinsurance implementers will forge ahead with pilot projects, and that, if they are carefully rolled out (with an eye to evaluations), a great deal about risk, vulnerability, and poverty can be learned in the process.

THINKING ABOUT LIFE INSURANCE

Let's return to the scene on the ground. Before getting to crop insurance and health insurance, take a moment to consider life insurance. If you support a family, one of the greatest fears is that one day you will no longer be alive to do so. From your family's perspective, your death will surely bring emotional and economic loss—and, more immediately, high funeral costs. Demand for life insurance among the poor is thus considerable. Neither moral hazard nor adverse selection is nearly as problematic here as it is for crop and health insurance (Would you be more likely to walk to the very edge of a precipice or to take up a pack-a-day smoking habit just because you have a life insurance policy in the drawer?), and verifying the loss is straightforward: either there was a death or there wasn't. (To further allay moral hazard, insurers typically exclude death from suicide, driving while intoxicated, and illegal activity.) So here, at least, we would expect to see private insurance companies jostling their way into the market. But we don't, at least not yet.[7]

Instead, to the extent that we see any action, it is informal, community-based arrangements without legal status, operating below the radar screen of the formal economy. Stuart Rutherford (2000), for example, describes burial societies in the fishing communities of Cochin, India. The societies are typically based around a church, temple, mosque, or social club, and each involves 300 people or more. In a typical fund, each member contributes at least 2 rupees per week (about 4 cents). For each rupee per week contributed, the society guarantees that if a member of the contributor's family dies within the year (with exclusions for infants and partial exclusions for young children), the family gets Rs. 500 (about $10) from the fund. Since the fund is taking in at least Rs. 600 per week (or about Rs. 300,000 over fifty weeks), the fund can cover deaths of at least thirty people. If each family has four adults (or their equivalent), there are at least 1,200 individual lives being insured, and the fund covers costs as long as no more than 5% of participants die in any given year; in typical years surpluses are generated and redistributed to members, but in other years extra collections are made.

This kind of burial society can be found worldwide, but the security comes at a high price for relatively healthy households. Each family puts in at least Rs. 100 rupees over the year (two rupees per week over fifty weeks), and the family gets Rs. 1,000 if an adult dies. To be a "fair" bet, the family would thus have to reckon that there is a 10% chance that an adult in their family will die in any given year (assuming that the fund exactly breaks even). If the probability is much lower, the family would be better off simply putting the money into the bank. To put the probability in perspective, the 10% figure implies that participants believe there is roughly a 30% chance that an adult in the family will die within three years—and roughly a 50% chance that an adult will die within six years. For a household with elderly members, these odds may not be far off, but for a young family (absent the threat of killers such as AIDS), the odds are wildly unfavorable. Nevertheless, burial societies remain widely popular.

Partly their popularity comes from the fact that most people have a hard time thinking straight about probabilities. This was most famously demonstrated by the experimental psychologists Daniel Kahneman and Amos Tversky, who found that attitudes toward risk depend critically on how questions are framed (Kahneman et al. 1982). Hospital patients will show more interest in undergoing radical surgery when told that there is, say, an 80% survival rate versus when told that there is a 20% chance of dying—even though the two scenarios are, of course, just different ways of saying the exact same thing. And even if people think consistently, there is typically a lot of uncertainty about survival probabilities, not to mention the fact that calculations can get complicated quickly (to check the calculations for the simple example in the preceding paragraph, I used a computer spreadsheet program). On top of it all is uncertainty about one's general economic situation in the future, the ability to get public handouts and private charity, and so on. Add in emotional elements, and it becomes clear why even young, healthy families seem highly risk averse when they take "bets" on life insurance. The continuing mystery, again, is why private companies don't edge their way into this market. Compared with operations attached to the local church or mosque, private companies have far better opportunities to diversify risks and to offer a range of products, helping to cut effective costs and to increase quality for clients.

Here, the example from Cochin helps to make another point that gets us closer to the answer; burial societies handle a lot of small change: the equivalent of 4 cents a week, collected from each of three hundred families. Burial societies can operate this way because they are based out of local institutions where people already gather weekly; the societies can thus collect small payments as part of other activities. But an insurance company, coming from outside, lacks that advantage (not to mention lacking a reputation that insurees can trust). Insurance companies typically collect insurance premiums one-by-one, and given the costs of record-keeping and staff salaries, 4 cents a week per household looks like very small change indeed.[8]

In China, the People's Insurance Company cleverly addressed the small-change problem by setting up deposit accounts for purchasers of certain kinds of insurance—but instead of receiving interest, the depositors got insurance coverage. The PIC was able to do this because farmers were already used to having savings deposits and most were experiencing fast income growth. But consider the Cochin case again. If the insurance company earns, say, 5% per year on its deposits, depositors would need to put in Rs. 2,000 to generate Rs. 100 of annual premiums for the insurer. While Rs. 2,000 is just $40, it is a lot of money for a poor household to have up front and to tie up in a "nonproductive" investment (bearing in mind that the insurance payout in the event of death is just $10). The deposit-cum-insurance scheme deserves wider application, but it will likely be a hard sell in the poor neighborhoods of Cochin.

Another option is to have insurees pay premiums less frequently (16 cents per month? 50 cents per quarter?), and this will work if the insurer's cost structure is low enough and insurees can save up reasonably well. Saving is not so easy, though, and if the solution was really as simple as collecting premiums less frequently, my guess is that we would currently see a lot more private life insurance. Stuart Rutherford, the founder and chairman of Dhaka's SafeSave cooperative, has written a helpful volume, *The Poor and Their Money*, which describes the ubiquity of savings difficulties through example after example of informal attempts to overcome them (Rutherford 2000); the theme of savings constraints is developed as a main theme of Armendariz de Aghion and Morduch (2005).

One hope is to pay local agents a small commission to collect funds and check claims. As microfinance institutions are starting to recognize, they are often already in this niche, and the emerging microinsurance movement is closely allied to the established microfinance movement. The most popular insurance product offered by microfinance institutions is credit life insurance. For a percentage of each loan, the bank will pay off any debt outstanding in case of death (plus, often, a bit extra for the family). This insurance mainly helps the lenders, and it turns out to be profitable, given the infrequency of death. As of several years ago, FINCA Uganda, for example, charged an additional interest rate of 0.5% per month for credit life insurance, with a $630 payout in the event of accidental death; FINCA's partner, the American Insurance Group, was enjoying a profit rate of 30% at these prices. Of course, access is permitted only if you're in a microfinance program. The ongoing challenge here is to provide wider access to life insurance, as well as to health, property, and crop insurance.

HEALTH INSURANCE: FOCUSING ON THE BIGGEST RISKS

There is a movement afoot to provide health insurance, and the model of the Self-Employed Women's Association (SEWA) of Ahmedabad, India, is one of the most discussed. SEWA has been ambitious in the health care that it provides its members, who are typically poor women working in the informal sector, but it has had difficulty covering costs. The problem with providing health insurance is that both moral hazard and adverse selection are rife. NGO practitioners pushing forward here are finding two problems. First, the risks can be sizable, so a large, established partner is invaluable to provide reinsurance. Second, historical data on health risks are inadequate to yield insurance premiums with much accuracy. Microinsurers thus see the value of their new endeavors at the same time they see how easily they could lose their shirts if they've guessed wrong about risk levels and costs.

As a result, putting caps on coverage is nearly universal, as is excluding coverage of particularly expensive health conditions. FINCA Uganda's health plan, for example, covered a range of in-patient and out-patient services but chose to exclude ongoing coverage of AIDS-related illnesses. The impulse to cap payouts is understandable: it reduces the insurer's exposure to risk, and this will surely calm jittery accountants.

The other fairly common practice is to cover expenses starting with the first dollar spent.[9] It is popular with clients, but can lead to lots of costly, small claims that insurees could typically handle without insurance. More-over, to reduce moral hazard, economic theory tells us that insurers should insist on sizable copayments and deductibles. Coverage from the first dollar spent too easily leads to wasteful overuse.

The use of caps also does not sit particularly well with the economic theory of the household. To make insurance most valuable, the theory sug-gests that an enlightened manager would want to do the opposite: to cover the expenses that are really big and exclude the small items. The priority ought to be on costs that would cripple a household—that is, priority should go to insurance against "catastrophic" events.

So why isn't economic theory more persuasive? The microinsurers that I have spoken to suggest that if they don't give "first dollar" coverage, people will wait until their problems become severe before going to the doctor. This hardly makes sense, unless clients are very ill-informed about the nature of their problems. If that's so (and Das and Das 2001 provide interesting evi-dence from India suggesting that it's not far-fetched), it is possible that first-dollar coverage actually saves money by encouraging preventive treatment. A better solution, though, would be to improve public information about health conditions and the importance of prevention.

Another often-heard defense of "first dollar" coverage is that clients want to get something back for the money they spend on insurance. At the end of the year, for example, new clients sometimes demand their money back if they haven't had to use a doctor within the year. This is a marketing problem, and should not be used to justify the dubious practice of "first-dollar" coverage. On the other hand, the idea of rebating some money to clients who have made no claims within a period isn't bad (in fact, that's the way some U.S. insurers create positive incentives for clients).

Another issue is reinsurance. Catastrophic events are costly but usually rare, and an unexpected cluster of large claims can wipe out an insurer (whereas it may be able to handle a steady stream of small claims capped at low levels on its own). Moving to insurance against catastrophic events re-quires that the insurer have a way to handle potentially large losses. The best way to do that is by reinsuring through arrangements with other insurers (paying another company to share some of the risk). This requires some sophistication, but it is not conceptually difficult and there are signs that reinsurers are becoming interested in relationships in low-income countries (partly to diversify their own portfolios of activities).

Another set of issues arises with the ability to pay for health insurance. If households suffered only from a clear set of readily identifiable and insurable risks, designing appropriate coverage could follow textbook rules. But a major problem for the poor is that (1) many risks are not insurable (such as the risk that farmers will suffer falling crop prices) and (2) bad news tends to come in waves.

This has two implications. First, customers may be particularly price-sensitive when it comes to buying insurance. Not because they ignore health problems, but because they don't want to tie up scarce funds by paying insurance premiums. This makes the ability to save an important way to self-insure, and I come back to this at the end of the essay.

The second implication is that uninsurable risks may drag households down, pushing them to the point at which it's impossible to keep paying premiums for health insurance. Most programs cut off coverage for households not in good standing, which means that even after paying premiums regularly for years, the household is left to fend for itself once it gets behind in its payments. If a household then faces a health crisis, it is doubly hit since it must contend both with the original (uninsurable) loss and the fact that its health problems are no longer covered. One way to address this problem is to create an emergency loan and grant fund that is earmarked for households with a history of reliable insurance payments but a current demonstrated emergency.

The bottom line is that providing health insurance (particularly against catastrophic events) can reduce the vulnerability of low-income households in important ways, just as it does for higher-income households. But in this population especially, insurance may not be enough on its own. Coupling insurance with health education and an emergency fund to cover temporary nonhealth crises can make insurance more effective for clients and providers alike.

INSURING RAINFALL: A NEW SOLUTION TO AN OLD PROBLEM

Providing life and health insurance will help reduce vulnerability, but when it comes to rural risk, agriculture is where it's at. Existing microfinance institutions, though, focus mainly on urban or rural nonagricultural enterprises—conspicuously not on agricultural ones. Microfinance participation may reduce risk for farm households by allowing them to diversify their income sources (evidence showing this is presented in Morduch 1998), but microfinance institutions are far from being in a position to do much about crops and rural risks directly.

Falling crop prices can hit poor farmers hard, as can bad weather. We turn here to the latter problem. Insuring farmers against generic crop losses has turned out to be full of difficulties for reasons cited already (high transactions costs, moral hazard, and adverse selection). Recently, though, policy makers are rethinking their options. Why not abandon trying to insure against bad crop yields and instead insure against bad weather directly?

While Hurricane Mitch brought too much rain, a more common fear in Central America is in fact the opposite: drought. So why not create a product that pays out in the case of drought, irrespective of actual crop yields? The beauty of such drought insurance is that the insurance company pays clients when rainfall (as measured at a local weather station) fails to reach specified targets (see Hazell n.d.; Skees et al. 2004). Since rainfall is determined by higher powers than those commanded by the typical client, client behavior and client characteristics have no bearing on the probability of adverse events. Insurance executives can thus sleep at night without worrying about moral hazard and adverse selection. The insurer's problem is simplified to setting prices appropriate for the specified weather patterns. With short data series, this is an imprecise science, but at least it is mainly a technical exercise.

The other beauty of rainfall-linked insurance is that in principle the market is open to everyone. With crop insurance, only farmers are clients. But with rainfall insurance, the local cobbler or tailor can insure as well, and in that way gain a bit of protection from weather-related demand and supply fluctuations.

Another advantage of rainfall insurance is that it is simple to administer— and this may speed up the time between the experience of the drought and the disbursal of funds. After Hurricane Mitch hit Nicaragua in October 1998, for example, the Swedish aid agency SIDA set up a program in the hills of Matagalpa to rebuild infrastructure and assets. But money for the program was not allocated by SIDA until seven months after the hurricane, and the first disbursement to farmers was not for another two months; the final disbursement was in July 2000, one year and nine months after the hurricane.[10] In contrast, one of the most promising aspects of rainfall insurance is that it offers the possibility of very speedy initial disbursements, free of the usual politics and bureaucracy.

But rainfall insurance also faces practical hurdles, two of which are often noted. First, reinsurance, once more. On its own, an insurance company will likely have difficulties handling claims made for events (such as regional drought) that affect a great many people at the same time. A large company can diversify its portfolio by selling contracts in very different climatic zones, but possibilities are limited in a relatively small place like Nicaragua. Selling part of the portfolio to an international reinsurer provides local insurers with a way to limit their risk to acceptable levels. The downside is that the local insurer must do the administrative legwork involved in collecting premiums and disbursing payments, must conform to the wishes of the reinsurer in terms of types of coverage, and then must split a share of profits with the reinsurer. The bigger, practical tension is that the need for reinsurance necessitates scale and sophistication. Unlike microfinance, say, it's not practical to start very small and slowly scale up, village by village; here, the local insurer must start fairly big if it is to entice an international reinsurer to be interested.

The second well-recognized problem is "basis risk." Driving from Lake Managua up through the hills of Matagalpa, one can immediately sense how variations in elevation translate into continually changing microclimates. The frequency of microclimates adds to the idiosyncrasy of rainfall patterns even within small regions of Nicaragua, reducing the correlation between incomes and rainfall as measured at the local rain gauge or weather station. The greater the degree of idiosyncrasy, the less useful rainfall insurance is to potential clients (although, on the other hand, an insurer's portfolio gets more diversified).

There are two forces that combine to create basis risk. First, the local rainfall gauge may simply be too far away to provide data relevant to conditions throughout the region. This can be solved in principle by putting up more rainfall gauges, but that's the easy part. The harder part is to set premiums. To do that, the insurer needs to know gauge-specific probabilities of risk, and this requires having historical data on rainfall patterns for every gauge. Lack of disaggregated historical data on rainfall patterns turns out to be an important constraint in Nicaragua, and it is not exceptional; the constraints imposed by basis risk and missing data have helped push rainfall insurance to the back burner in much of the world. The sooner efforts to collect better data can begin, the better.

In Morocco, on the other hand, a World Bank study found more promising results. Moroccan agriculture is based on cereals, and the correlation between cereal revenues and rainfall was found to be 60%–80%. Since the incidence of drought and overall GDP growth move closely in Morocco, the World Bank hopes that addressing weather risk will ultimately affect economic growth rates. Based in large part on the Morocco study, the World Bank's International Financial Corporation invested $80 million in 2002 to establish a Global Weather Risk Facility in partnership with Aquila, a Kansas City-based trader in weather-based derivatives (World Bank 2002). Rainfall insurance will now get a trial run, and we will be able to track its impacts.

RAINFALL INSURANCE: FROM THE POPULATION'S PERSPECTIVE

The establishment of the Global Weather Risk Facility provides hope for many farmers. But it is not the end of the road. First, it is mainly a pilot project. Second, the analysis of microinsurance here has mainly concerned constraints and opportunities for insurers only. But it is happy, healthy customers who are of ultimate concern, not just happy, healthy insurers. We need to step back and think about society's welfare more broadly. We have taken it as a given that more insurance is necessarily a good thing. But we need to ask whether that's in fact true for everyone in all circumstances— and if it's not, what can policy makers do about it?

Some of the most important aspects of insurance will be indirect. The first important indirect impact of rainfall insurance involves possible changes in the pattern and level of consumer prices. It's useful to turn to Amartya Sen's (1981) work on the Great Bengal Famine for an analogy. He describes how the famine resulted from price increases faced by poor households—in a situation where food availability was not low enough to create famine conditions by itself. Price increases typically particularly harm landless laborers and other net consumers.

As a result, landless laborers are often the ones worst off in droughts. Will introducing rainfall insurance improve their lots—or possibly worsen them? An advantage of rainfall insurance over crop insurance is that now landless laborers have the possibility of purchasing insurance against drought, something that's impossible when only crop insurance is being sold. If they buy rainfall insurance, landless laborers will have added purchasing power in times of crisis. This should be a great advantage.

The flip side is that landless laborers may not have access to rainfall insurance (or an equivalent); this may be because prices for premiums are too high for households with inadequate cash flows, marketing is ineffective, or, as I found in Nicaragua, insurers are reluctant to sell directly to individuals, preferring to reduce transactions costs by selling through established groups and associations. In this case, the landless poor could be made substantially worse off by the introduction of rainfall insurance. Now farmers (who are insured) will have added purchasing power to bid up prices for whatever food and services are available in the market during the drought. The price increases will further diminish the lot of the landless. The landless can thus be made worse off relative to a world without rainfall insurance.

In short, rainfall insurance has very positive elements, but if it is not accompanied by other measures for the poor, it can exacerbate losses for some of the most vulnerable populations. The magnitude of costs and benefits of rainfall insurance is an empirical question, and there is no a priori reason to assume the worst. But there is an a priori reason to be careful about distributional effects.

Let's also go back to the initial claim that rainfall insurance banishes concerns about moral hazard and adverse selection. This is certainly so from the perspective of the provider of rainfall insurance. But, if we look closer, it's not so from a global perspective; introducing rainfall insurance can improve or worsen moral hazard and adverse selection in other markets.

For example, provision of rainfall insurance could make other informal risk-sharing arrangements work less well. Consider, say, neighbors agreeing to help each other out in times of need. Informal insurance in this example is characterized by the inability to write binding, enforceable long-term contracts. Instead, the arrangements stay together only as long as the expected value of staying true to the arrangement exceeds the value of reneging and facing risk alone (i.e., self-insuring). The arrangements weaken when the self-insurance option improves.[11] Rainfall insurance can hurt by improving the fallback position for those who renege on their obligations and are thus left to their own devices (which, lucky for them, would now include buying rainfall insurance). Of course, partially displacing informal arrangements by introducing rainfall insurance here could, on net, be a good thing, but there will inevitably be winners and losers (Morduch 1999a).

There is no empirical evidence yet that speaks to the magnitude of these kinds of spillovers, but they are there in principle, and we should be mindful. As rainfall insurance moves into view, it's important to see what it can do and what it can't. No one thinks it's a panacea, but it is promising. Still, failure to take into account the broader perspective of social welfare can lead to programs that can increase the vulnerability of some populations, despite the best of intentions.

CONCLUDING THOUGHTS

The poorest citizens of the poorest countries are typically exposed to the greatest risks. Earthquakes, floods, drought, disease, crime all tend to hit the poor hardest. Vulnerability and poverty go hand in hand, but microinsurance holds out the promise of breaking a part of the cycle that ties them together. The aim is to create sustainable, professionally run insurance programs that protect poor households from the most debilitating losses.

The task is tall, and reading the academic literature on insurance—strewn with well-documented accounts of why and how insurance markets fail—should be enough to force most observers to abandon hope. But knowing the main pitfalls is a first step toward finding workable innovations, and important new ideas are emerging. The past decade has seen renewed possibilities for life insurance, health insurance, and rainfall insurance that can substitute for crop insurance. The products and processes are mainly small-scale and imperfect, but they hold promise.

One early and critical lesson is that the constraints on building better insurance programs include more than the information asymmetries on which economists have focused most sharply. To be workable, solutions will have to address a set of very practical issues. The first is the need for reinsurance, the second is having data on which to base premiums, and the third is the ability to cut the costs of dealing with many small transactions. The parallel to the "microfinance revolution" offers cause for encouragement, but establishing widespread insurance will require more detailed regulatory architecture than the microfinance pioneers ever needed.

More than anything else, though, it will be important to keep the clients' views in mind. And doing that may mean taking a broad view of what providing "insurance" entails. Much vulnerability can be reduced through mechanisms that don't involve insurance per se. As with health insurance and rainfall insurance, both efficiency and equity may be enhanced by providing public education about the nature of risks, creating emergency funds to help households falling behind in their premium payments, and combining for-profit insurance provision with subsidized provision for poorer populations.

Being well-insured also often means having a cushion of savings on which to fall back. Researchers have shown that villagers in south India were mainly easing risks through individual savings behavior (implemented by adjusting buffer stocks of grain). In Chinese studies, too, savings offered the main form of protection. In Bangladesh, Stuart Rutherford is piloting new savings products in Dhaka's slums, and is generating much interest. In Indonesia, savings facilities are in high demand by the poor (Robinson 2001). Having savings allows households to manage their affairs more flexibly, and it cushions against losses that are fundamentally uninsurable. Economists have long argued that the poorest households are simply too close to subsistence levels to save much. That idea is right in principle, but in practice even households substantially below the poverty line are eager to stash away something for later—if given an appealing way to do so.[12] The new microinsurance initiatives bank on the proposition that the same holds for insurance.

NOTES

1. These results parallel Morris et al.'s (2002) account of Hurricane Mitch's impact in Honduras.

2. See Wade (2001) for a lively account focusing on the U.S. Treasury's behind-the-scenes machinations with regard to World Bank policy, and Kanbur (2001) for his take on the disagreements.

3. One mu is 1/15 hectare or 1/6 acre; households commonly held three to four mu per family member. The 1990 official exchange rate was 4.77 yuan per $1, but purchasing power parity–adjusted exchange rates were roughly six times as high.

4. The issues and evidence are discussed in greater length in Morduch (1991, 1995).

5. For more on the issues here and below, see Morduch (1999a).

6. Ravallion and Chaudhuri (1997) similarly find additional evidence of imperfections, as do others; see Deaton (1997) and Morduch (2004).

7. There are of course exceptions, such as Delta Life's Gono Bima (People's Insurance) of Bangladesh, but closer inspection shows it to be effectively a lending institution in the guise of a life insurance company, and it has been doing poorly at that (Matin 2002).

8. Delta Life's Gono Bima of Bangladesh did, though, base its life insurance program on individual weekly collections of premiums, so it is not impossible.

9. Some programs have coinsurance rates and deductibles, but these tend to be kept low.

10. Information is from an interview with the head of the SIDA-funded program, Matagalpa, August 2000.

11. For useful discussion and references, see Ray (1998); a related example of "dysfunctional crowding out" in an insurance context is provided by Arnott and Stiglitz (1991).

12. Although they lack convenient access to banks, poor women in Bangladesh whom I interviewed in December 2002 confided that they routinely sew savings into their saris for safekeeping; others give savings to neighbors to guard or stash coins and small bills in hiding places around the home. Promising pilot projects are developing new mechanisms to make such accumulation easier, but their impacts have not yet been evaluated.

BIBLIOGRAPHY

Armendáriz de Aghion, Beatriz, and Jonathan Morduch. *The Economics of Microfinance.* Cambridge, Mass.: MIT Press, 2005.

Arnott, Richard, and Joseph Stiglitz. "Moral Hazard and Nonmarket Institutions: Dysfunctional Crowding Out or Peer Monitoring?" *American Economic Review* 81 (1) (1991): 179–190.

Besley, Timothy. "Non-Market Institutions for Credit and Risk-Sharing in Low-Income Countries." *Journal of Economic Perspectives* 9 (1995a): 115–127.

Besley, Timothy. "Savings, Credit, and Insurance." In *Handbook of Development Economics,* Vol. 3. Edited by Jere Behrman and T. N. Srinivasan. Amsterdam: North-Holland, 1995b.

Daley-Harris, Sam. State of the Microcredit Summit Campaign Report 2004. Microcredit Summit, Washington, D.C., Nov. 2004.

Das, Jishnu, and Saumya Das. "Trust, Learning, and Vaccination: Case Study of a North-Indian Village." *Social Science and Medicine* 57 (2001): 97–112.

Deaton, Angus. *The Analysis of Household Surveys.* Baltimore: Johns Hopkins University Press, 1997.

Hazell, Peter. "The Appropriate Role of Agricultural Insurance in Developing Countries." *Journal of International Development* 4 (1992): 567–581.

Hazell, Peter. "Potential Role for Insurance in Managing Catastrophic Risk in Developing Countries." Draft, International Food Policy Research Institute, n.d.

Jalan, Jyotsna, and Martin Ravallion. "Are the Poor Less Well Insured? Evidence on Vulnerability to Income Risk in Rural China." *Journal of Development Studies* 58 (1999): 61–81.

Kahneman, Daniel, Paul Slovic, and Amos Tversky, eds. *Judgment under Uncertainty: Heuristics and Biases.* Cambridge: Cambridge University Press, 1982.

Kamanou, Gisele, and Jonathan Morduch. "Measuring Vulnerability to Poverty." In *Insurance against Poverty,* edited by Stefan Dercon. Oxford: Oxford University Press, 2004.

Kanbur, Ravi. "Economic Policy, Distribution and Poverty: The Nature of Disagreements." *World Development.* 29 (6) (2001): 1083–1094.

Lim, Youngjae, and Robert Townsend. "General Equilibrium Models of Financial Systems: Theory and Measurement in Village Economies." *Review of Economic Dynamics* 1 (1) (1998): 59–118.

Matin, Imran. "New Thinking and New Forms of Microfinancial Services in Bangladesh: A Comparative Study of ASA, SafeSave, and Gono Bima." IDPM working paper, University of Manchester, 2002.

Morduch, Jonathan. "Risk and Welfare in Developing Countries." Ph.D. dissertation, Department of Economics, Harvard University, 1991.

Morduch, Jonathan. "Poverty and Vulnerability." *American Economic Review* 84 (May 1994): 221–225.

Morduch, Jonathan. "Income Smoothing and Consumption Smoothing." *Journal of Economic Perspectives* 9 (3) (1995): 103–114.

Morduch, Jonathan. "Does Microfinance Really Help the Poor? New Evidence on Flagship Programs in Bangladesh." Draft paper, Princeton University, 1998.

Morduch, Jonathan. "Between the State and the Market: Can Informal Insurance Patch the Safety Net?" *World Bank Research Observer* 14 (2) (1999a): 187–207.

Morduch, Jonathan. "The Microfinance Promise." *Journal of Economic Literature* 37 (4) (1999b): 1569–1614.

Morduch, Jonathan. "Consumption Smoothing Across Space." In *Insurance Against Poverty*, edited by Stephan Dercon: Oxford: Oxford University Press, 2004.

Morduch, Jonathan, and Terry Sicular. "Risk and Insurance in Transition: Perspectives from Zouping County, China." In *Communities and Markets in Economic Development*, edited by Masahiko Aoki and Yujiro Hayami. Oxford: Oxford University Press, 2001.

Morris, Saul, Oscar Neidecker-Gonzales, Calogero Carletto, Marcial Munguia, and Juan Manuel Medina. "Hurricane Mitch and the Livelihoods of the Rural Poor in Honduras." *World Development* 30 (1) (2002): 49–60.

Newbery, David, and Joseph Stiglitz. *The Theory of Commodity Price Stabilization*. Oxford: Oxford University Press, 1981.

Ravallion, Martin, and Shubham Chaudhuri. "Risk and Insurance in Village India: Comment." *Econometrica* 65 (1) (1997): 171–184.

Ray, Debraj. *Development Economics*. Princeton, N.J.: Princeton University Press, 1998.

Robinson, Marguerite S. *The Microfinance Revolution: Sustainable Finance for the Poor.* Vol. 1. Washington, D.C.: World Bank, 2001.

Rosenzweig, Mark R. "Risk, Implicit Contracts, and the Family in Rural Areas of Low Income Countries." *Economic Journal* 98 (Dec. 1988): 1148–1170.

Rutherford, Stuart. *The Poor and Their Money*. Delhi: Oxford University Press, 2000.

Sen, Amartya. *Poverty and Famines: An Essay on Entitlement and Deprivation*, chap. 6. Oxford: Clarendon Press, 1981.

Skees, Jerry, Panos Varangis, and Donald Larson. "Can Financial Markets Be Tapped to Help Poor People Cope with Weather Risks?" In *Insurance Against Poverty*, edited by Stephan Dercon. Oxford University Press, 2004.

Townsend, Robert. "Risk and Insurance in Village India." *Econometrica* 62 (May 1994): 539–592.

Townsend, Robert. "Consumption Insurance: An Evaluation of Risk-Bearing Systems in Low-Income Countries." *Journal of Economic Perspectives* 9 (1995): 83–102.

Wade, Robert. "Showdown at the World Bank." *New Left Review* 7 (Jan.–Feb. 2001): 124–137.

Walker, Thomas S., and James G. Ryan. *Village and Household Economies in India's Semi-Arid Tropics*. Baltimore: Johns Hopkins University Press, 1990.

World Bank. *World Development Report 2000–2001: Attacking Poverty*. Washington, D.C.: World Bank, 2000.

World Bank. "IFC Invests in Weather Insurance in Emerging Markets." DevNews Media Center article. 2002. Available online at http://www.worldbank.org.

Yaron, Jacob, Benjamin McDonald, and Gerda Piprek. "Rural Finance: Issues, Design, and Best Practices." Draft paper, World Bank, 1997.

23

Credit, Intermediation, and Poverty Reduction

Robert M. Townsend

The purpose of this essay is to show how credit markets influence development and to argue that the impact of improvements in credit markets is quantitatively significant. The essay first establishes the fact that access to credit is limited, emphasizing the magnitudes. It then goes on to the potential importance of financial sector development, again quantifying the impact. Toward the end of the essay there is a discussion of the merits of different interventions.

The policy recommendations in this essay are based on estimated versions of the Thai reality, filtered through the lens of artificial environments, or what economists call models. For example, to understand the effect of financial development, we create an artificial environment that is structured to imitate key aspects of Thailand in this period, where we let financial development take place. Further, as the logic of the model is made explicit, one can trace a particular recommendation to a given set of assumptions or rules. In Thailand, where this research is being conducted, with the aid of much data gathered in field research, specific and concrete policy advice can be given.

CREDIT IS LIMITED: A QUANTIFICATION

There is strong evidence from Thailand that credit markets and institutions do not function well, that limited credit is a big constraint on the small business sector. That is, despite systematic and evident efforts on the part of the Thai government to solve the problem of imperfect and limited credit, through the joint-liability groups of the government's Bank for Agriculture and Agricultural Cooperatives (the BAAC) and through village-level institutions such as production credit groups and poverty eradication funds, for example, many rural and semiurban households still face a simple, mechanical relationship between their accumulated wealth and the amount of overall credit they have access to.

The extent of the problem, and indeed the underlying constraint that is causing the problem, may vary with wealth or region. On the very low end of the wealth spectrum, a virtual absence of credit is not a bad approximation to the survey data. More generally, in the northeast and among households with below-average wealth, the higher wealth is, the greater the magnitude of overall credit. The main determinant of lending seems to be whether the household has land and other assets, either as predictors of the magnitude of crop income or as collateral for the lenders who remain worried about eventual default—thus the low levels of wealth in this part of the sample condemn these households to an astoundingly low level of credit, and there are few formal or informal alternatives. In contrast, though still restricting attention to households in semiurban and rural areas, higher-wealth households and households in the central region are more able, apparently, to roll over loans when they face serious and genuine difficulties in repayment, either because the lender explicitly allows this to happen (perhaps because of the rather substantial level of lending from family, friends, money lenders, and the informal sector), or because formal lenders such as the BAAC and commercial banks are afraid to lose customers or to foreclose. The overall level of credit is still determined by the level of loan recovery, but the higher wealth is, the more these households invest in their own businesses, the more they bear the fruit of their own effort, and the less the overall level of credit is.

More analysis is needed to determine the underlying problem with certainty. But there is little question that credit markets are far from perfect. For business owners, collateral values average nine times the amount of the loan, and for other households, the ratio is almost twice as high, seventeen times. Restricting attention to those with the median level of education (in the sample, four years) and comparing the number of households running businesses in the lowest wealth quartile against those in the highest wealth quartile, the fraction of those in business rises from 26% to 43% in the central region and from 8% to 16% in the northeast. Similarly, controlling for demographic and geographic variables at the time of the 1997 survey, a doubling of household wealth five years prior to the interview date leads to a 21% increase in the number of households that went into business over the past five years (1992–1997).

Likewise, the presence of financial constraints implies that entrepreneurial households that are in business invest less than the optimal amount. According to our estimates, as of 1992, a doubling of wealth in the cross-sectional sample is associated with an increase in start-up investment of 40%. Likewise, under financial constraints, the returns to business investment will be high for low-wealth households and will fall as wealth increases. For the whole sample, median returns to business investment—that is, income:capital ratios—fall from a strikingly high 57% for households in the lowest wealth quartile to 16% for households in the highest wealth quartile. Entrepreneurial talent, as measured by education and whether parents were in business, does seem to facilitate business entry, and the ability to exploit relatively high marginal returns, but it also appears there are a nontrivial number of talented but low-wealth households that are constrained on these margins.

Various underlying artificial environments (models) would deliver these findings while differing radically in the proposed policy remedy. In one environment, credit markets are so limited that they can be ignored entirely, except for a relatively small fraction of the population. It is for this model that a simple, crude expansion of credit presents the most compelling case. In a second environment, households can freely borrow at interest to go into business, but only up to a multiple of their assets. Thus, if assets are limited, they will be constrained, regardless of education and talent. This is a model of simple asset-backed lending, and in this kind of model the issue is whether it is possible to find a way around collateral requirements, as with joint-liability groups, for example. In a third environment, households that borrow much will pay back much in principal and interest, leaving little incentive to work for residual profits, on their own account. This is an environment in which effort or diligence is unobserved by outside lenders, and too much insurance against nonpayment would cause the entrepreneur to shirk (economists and insurance companies refer to this as a moral hazard). This environment trades off incentives and insurance by a judicious choice of risk contingencies, that is, exceptions to repayment for prespecified events (coupled with ex post verification of those events if necessary).

Environments can also differ in what is assumed about the relationship between the returns to investment and education. One might imagine that start-up costs are high for households with little education, so that the necessary investment decreases with education. On the other hand, human capital and physical capital may be complements, so that more talented households will want to invest even more.

Each of these model environments generates a prediction about whether or not a household will go into business as a function of measured wealth and education, and as a function of the marginal productivity of capital, risk aversion, and the distribution of talent in the population. When we take each model to the data, we discover the no-credit model and asset-backed lending model fit the data better than the other models for low-wealth households and those in the northeast. In contrast, the risk-contingent credit model fits the data best among high-wealth households and those in the central region. Among the subsample of relatively wealthy households in the central region, a doubling of wealth leads to a 40,000 baht increase in savings.

This is not true in the northeast. Likewise, the moral hazard model predicts that virtually all businesses that borrow will report some degree of constraints, whereas the asset-based lending model allows low-talent households to borrow and go into business without hitting constraints. In the data we see that being constrained is strongly associated with borrowing in the central region; 73% of constrained businesses in the central region have outstanding debt, compared with only 54% of unconstrained businesses. Constrained businesses in the central region also have more debt than unconstrained businesses, a median of 50,000 baht versus 30,000 baht. That is, businesses that have managed to secure more credit are more likely to complain about persistent constraints. Neither of these relationships holds in the northeast.

The implication of some of the models that investment should increase with education and talent is strongly supported in the data, contrary to the presumption that talented households will need to invest less. Thus physical capital and human capital are complements—we should expect that more educated households will want to invest more and that, holding wealth fixed, increasing education causes more households to complain of credit constraints. Likewise, there is a positive relationship in most models between investment and wealth, and this is true in the data: if past wealth were to increase by 1 million baht, business investment would increase by 40%. Put another way, median business investment for firms in the lowest wealth quartile is 17,953 baht but reaches 30,583 baht for firms in the highest wealth quartile.

THE MACROECONOMIC AND DISTRIBUTIONAL IMPACT OF EXPANDED CREDIT AND INTERMEDIATION

Even modest improvements in the financial system of Thailand could lead to large increases in the growth of per capita income. Specifically, as noted, financial intermediation in Thailand is limited, which means that personal wealth still plays a dominant role in deciding whether to expand a business via investment, or to go into business at all. The data suggest, then, that business activity is dictated too much by wealth and too little by actual ability and underlying productivity. If some of that squandered wealth were saved in interest-bearing accounts, rather than invested in low-yield activities, and those savings were in turn lent at interest to existing businesses short of capital, and to households for business start-ups, then national income would go up. Likewise, relatively small but steady improvements over time in intermediation could lead to substantially higher per capita growth rates. Even the relatively high precrisis growth rates of Thailand would seem to be within reach.

The gains from improved financial sector policies would not be uniform in the Thai population, however. Those with the most to gain would be those who could expand existing small or medium businesses, or switch from agriculture or wage employment into business—that is, those with relatively low current wealth but relatively high entrepreneurial talent. Likewise, with a steady expansion of financial infrastructure, real wages in Thailand would likely be higher than they otherwise would be. That would benefit relatively unskilled workers. However, wage increases could harm those already in businesses, so some opposition to improved financial sector policies might be anticipated.

Rather than resorting to forecasts or simple extrapolations from the experience of other countries, however, we base these results on a firm understanding of what happened to Thailand in its past. Using a simple economic model, we can understand Thailand's remarkable growth from 1976 to 1996, at 6% on average, and much higher in the second part of this twenty-year period, a growth rate driven in no small part by expansion of financial infrastructure, that is, by improved intermediation. If, contrary to what actually happened, that expansion had been far more limited, virtually zero, then the model predicts that Thailand would not have grown much at all. The best that can be managed is a low and flat 2% per year, and that is driven by an overestimate of total factor productivity (TFP) gains in agriculture at 4% per year. The observed increase in the GDP growth rate (net of TFP growth), from the mid- to late 1980s on into the early 1990s, at 8%–10% per year, can be reconciled in the model only by imagining a domestic savings rate at astoundingly high levels.

However, if we progressively allow the population access to competitive financial intermediaries at exactly the rate observed in Thai data, with its surges from 10% with access in the mid-1980s to 20% by the mid-1990s, then we can track the upturn in the Thai growth rate reasonably well. More generally, the model is able to reproduce the movements of key macroeconomic variables such as the labor share, savings rate, income inequality, and the fraction of entrepreneurs observed in Thailand during the past two decades.

Indeed, with the understanding of Thailand's historical experience that the artificial model economy provides, we can ask who gained from the observed financial sector expansion. We address this issue by comparing two versions of Thailand's history from 1976 to 1996, the actual one and a counterfactual one with a policy distortion that limits financial intermediation. The results confirm that not everyone benefits equally from the financial expansion. In 1978, for example, the modal gain from enhanced intermediation was between 5,000 baht and 17,000 baht per household, measured in 1997 domestic currency (the numbers depend on the specific estimation procedure used). Under the former exchange rate, this is equivalent to $200 to $680 per household for that year. Relative to average income, these numbers represent a 14% to 41% increase in the levels of income in 1978, a surprisingly high increment. Moreover, relatively low-wealth households that managed to switch occupations and go into business gained the most—the welfare numbers would be even higher if we used the simple arithmetic average.

By 1996 the wage was roughly 60% higher than it would have been without the expansion. Such price movements help determine the distribution of welfare gains and losses attributable to the financial sector expansion. The bottom line is that there were still substantial winners in 1996. The modal increase in welfare was 25,000 baht, approximately 26% of 1997 average household annual income, equivalent to $1,000. With the wage increase, unskilled laborers employed by business also gained. However, that wage increase created welfare losses for those running firms: 116,000 baht each for such households, on average, roughly $4,600.

Like estimates delivered by any model, these gains and losses should be taken with a grain of salt. There needs to be a comparison with other models that have taken alternative stands on the underpinnings of the Thai economy and therefore yield potentially different distributions of gains and losses from policy interventions. Nevertheless, with this caveat, the estimates here should be taken seriously. The point is that the gains can be quantified and are large, and are not uniform in the population.

The remarkable Thai growth experience as modeled here can be better understood if it is compared with an extended artificial environment that takes into account international capital movements. We allowed foreign investment but limited the observed domestic expansion in infrastructure. This established that the miracle of growth and higher incomes was driven simply by the increased mobility of the Thai population across existing sectors, and hence by better allocation of existing domestic resources, not by globalization.

INTERVENTIONS: AN ANALYSIS OF VILLAGE-LEVEL MICROFINANCE INSTITUTIONS

Village-level and county-level financial organizations are promoted by government and nongovernment organizations in Thailand. Given the quantitative evidence that there are credit constraints and the quantitative evidence that improved financial intermediation can have relatively large impacts, it is natural to expect to find impacts of these village institutions at the local level, in microeconomic data. That is, we would expect local financial institutions to help in efforts to mobilize savings, offer credit, and reduce reliance on usurious moneylenders, enhance small household business start-ups and provide working capital, facilitate occupation shifts, reduce poverty, and provide insurance against bad times.

Such financial funds run the gamut from production savings groups that are like local savings and loans to buffalo banks, which lend cattle; rice banks, which operate as regular banks but use rice and not money; women's groups, which are associations of females engaged in improved occupation development; and poverty eradication funds administered by the government. The policies of these institutions vary: the amount of initial funding; the amount and type of training of villagers and committee members; whether savings accounts are optional, with flexible depositing and withdrawal, or are mandatory, with withdrawal limited; whether lending occurs; if lending does occur, the size of loans and interest rates; and whether emergency services are provided.

We find that institutions (varying by type and policy) have very mixed experiences; many fail within the first year or first five years, while others show growth in membership, lending, and savings services. Some of these experiences are related to chosen policies. In effect the different types of interventions are associated with positive and negative intermediation, and so we can see the effect of intermediation and policies in the microdata. As a natural and highly desirable corollary, we can see which types of funds and which policies should be pursued and which abandoned.

We find support overall for the positive impact that local financial institutions can have, under some circumstances:

- We find evidence in support of theory for positive impacts of village institutions on asset growth, especially among those institutions and policies that were associated with successful provision of intermediation services. That is, institutions which seem to succeed in membership, savings mobilization, and lending are institutions that have higher positive impact on households. In particular, cash loans are associated with the stability or expansion of services, while rice lending institutions and buffalo banks are associated with contraction or failure. Production credit groups and women's groups, institutions that typically lend cash, had positive impacts on asset growth, while buffalo banks and, to a lesser extent, rice banks appear to have had, if any, negative impacts. Also, three specific policies associated with institutional success (offering training services, savings services, and pledged savings accounts) were individually associated with faster asset growth rates. Institutions with these policies yielded 5%–6% higher annual growth in assets to their villagers.
- Institutions with certain policies can help to smooth responses to income shocks. These policies include offering emergency services, training services, and various savings-related policies. While both standard (i.e., flexible) and pledged (i.e., restrictive) savings accounts help with smoothing, flexible accounts appear to be more helpful. Households in villages with these beneficial policies were ten to twenty-nine percentage points less likely to reduce consumption/input use in a year with a bad income shock. Nevertheless, the average institution does not appear to alleviate risk and may increase the probability of having to reduce consumption, buffalo banks and perhaps rice banks in particular.
- Though the overall lack of a positive impact on alleviating risk is troubling, the fact that institutions associated with diminishing services had perverse (if any) impacts, and the policies correlated with

successful intermediation had positive impacts, is in line with what theory suggests.

- We find some evidence in support of the theories of constrained occupational choice, but more so for job mobility per se than entering into business. Women's groups do seem to increase job mobility. Pledged savings accounts (associated with successful intermediation) appear to increase the probability of switching jobs, and possibly starting a business, while traditional savings accounts (associated with diminishing intermediation) seem to have the opposite impact. Nevertheless, the evidence is not fully in harmony with the theory, since PCGs decrease the probability of switching jobs and, perhaps, the probability of starting a business, and emergency services also lower the probability of starting a business.

- The most robust result is that institutions overall help reduce reliance on moneylenders, our indirect measure of the prevalence of formal credit constraints. The effect on the average villager is to reduce the probability of becoming a moneylender's customer by eight percentage points. Our interpretation is that village institutions loosen households' constraints on formal credit, at least to credit that could be acquired alternatively from moneylenders. Other than women's groups, however, there is no strong evidence of any particular institution or policy associated with this impact.

Our overall recommendation, then, is that institutions, when established, offer training to potential village customers and to staff. They should also be encouraged to offer lending services when, by their own assessment, they are able to do so. Our advice on the provision of savings is more qualified: it depends on the local objective. Pledged savings are a surprisingly good vehicle, though the benefits may have more to do with the simplicity of administration and the minimization of transaction costs than with the nature of the pledge itself. Standard savings, with more flexible withdrawal, offer benefits similar to those of emergency services.

PART III

NEW WAYS OF THINKING
ABOUT POVERTY

24

Poor but Rational?

Esther Duflo

Modern development economics emerged with the realization that poverty changes the set of options available to individuals. Poverty thus affects behavior, even if the decision maker is "neoclassical": unboundedly rational, forward-looking, and internally consistent. The *Homo economicus* at the core of neoclassical economics ("calculating, unemotional maximizer" [Mullainathan and Thaler 2000]) would behave differently if he were poor than if he were rich. Asset market failures and preferences toward risk are sufficient to explain why asset ownership matters, why worthwhile transactions and investments may not always take place, and why the poor may remain poor as a result. The initial theoretical advances opened a new empirical agenda to mainstream economists.[1]

Prior to these advances, the debate revolved around the phrase "poor but efficient," popularized by Ted Schultz (1964). According to this concept, the poor certainly have bad lives, but there is nothing special about them; they just do the best they can under the difficult circumstances in which life has placed them and their fields are as productive as possible (Tax 1953)—they just cannot be very productive. Rejecting (or accepting) the hypothesis of "poor but efficient" meant rejecting (or accepting) all the postulates of neoclassical economics.

When the theoretical work made it clear that being poor meant being cut off from many opportunities that were available to others, the task of empirical economics shifted to providing evidence for market inefficiencies and the potential of economic policies to alleviate them. A new paradigm, "poor but neoclassical" (but not necessarily efficient) helped define an empirical agenda and structure a vision of the world, even though it often remained implicit in empirical work. While the poor (and the rich) are all perfectly rational, the markets, left to themselves, may not produce an efficient outcome. In turn, many of the predictions of this body of work have been substantiated by the data. But there are also some fundamental facts for which this view of the world does not account. Using two classic examples, which have been very fertile ground for research in development economics—insurance and agricultural investment—I will try to explore how far this agenda has led us, and what remains out of its reach.

INSURANCE

The poor, it is commonly acknowledged, face a very risky environment: the weather is uncertain, crops fail for all sorts of reasons, prices are volatile, illness strikes often, and so on. Because they are close to subsistence, risk is particularly painful to the poor. This makes insurance both more valuable and easier to implement, since the very threat of canceling someone's insurance if he is caught cheating should be very powerful. Moreover, at least some of the poor live in a close-knit environment (the village) where information flows easily, and people have the possibility of exerting sanctions against each other if they are found to be abusing the system. This should alleviate some of the common problems that insurers traditionally face: How to distinguish bona fide claims from forgery? How to prevent people who know they are insured from taking unreasonable risks, now that they are not going to pay for it? How to avoid a situation where only people who know they may encounter problems in the future sign up for insurance?

In a village, part of the risk is common to all families: if there is a really severe drought, it affects everyone. But part of the risk is specific to the circumstances of specific households; for example, someone's cow may die. This has made the village institution a fertile testing ground for one of the "poor but efficient" hypothesis: within a village, the poor should be able to insure each other against the part of the risk that is common across households.

Townsend (1994) made this point in a very influential article. Using detailed data from several Indian villages, he argued that the incomes of families within a village have ups and downs at very different times. This creates substantial scope for insurance, and Townsend argued that advantage was fully taken of this possibility. The consumption of all families within a village moves very close together: when someone has a bad year, everybody in the village suffers a little bit, and the affected family's consumption does not fall behind that of others.

This all goes to show, the article argued, that the village institution is fully efficient. The article generated very lively controversy, and the question of how well rural households cope with risk and insure each other was a focus of much of the research in development economics in the following years.

Taking stock after ten years, it appears relatively clear that the claim made in the seminal Townsend paper gave somewhat too much credit to the village institution. Subsequent work by Townsend himself (Townsend 1995a, 1995b), as well as others, recognized the incompleteness of the insurance provided in the village, and the variety of insurance arrangements across villages.

There are several reasons why insurance may be imperfect even in the village economy. First, villagers may be able to hide part of their output from others. Second, if efforts cannot be perfectly monitored, perfect insurance might result in disastrous outcomes if household members stop working in anticipation of being bailed out if and when their output is low. The villagers will thus need to balance the need for insurance with the necessity of giving people incentive to work, and as a result, will insure each other only partially. Ligon (1998) argued that the data analyzed by Townsend (1994) is actually consistent with this model.

These two explanations, however, do not do justice to Townsend's central intuition, that the village institution should be better than modern institutions in dealing with these dimensions. A third explanation draws from the specificity of the village institution. Agreements are not legally backed, and therefore cannot rely on external pressure to be honored. In other words, people cannot be coerced to stay in the system: if they are not happy with the transfers they have to make at any point in time, they can decide to walk away and operate on their own (Coate and Ravallion 1993). Worse still, several villagers may decide to walk away together and form their own insurance group (Genicot and Ray 2003). Individuals who are enjoying a good year will then continue to participate only if the transfers they have to make today are not greater than the value of the insurance in the future. This limits the extent of insurance that can be provided in the village; in particular, someone who has done particularly well in a given year may be offered the option of receiving higher net transfers from the common pool in all subsequent years. Insurance starts looking much more like credit, since future claims are linked to today's contributions to the pool. Udry (1990) finds evidence of this in Nigerian villages, where debt repayments are contingent on how well both the creditors and the debtors did in the previous year. Udry rejects the hypothesis that villagers are fully insured.

All these arguments suggest that if individuals have good information on what others are doing (so that they cannot shirk or make false claims), and have a strong reason to stay together, they should be insuring each other. One group that seems to satisfy these conditions is the family: its members know each other, expect to stay together, and should therefore be able to achieve an efficient outcome, at least among themselves. Yet insurance seems less than perfect in the family. The private consumption of household members in southern Ghana seems to be completely unrelated to the income of their partners (Goldstein 2000). Of course, this could be because, in reality, household members are effective at hiding income from each other. This seems likely, since when asked directly about their partners' income, household members seem to know very little about it. Since an individual's private consumption consists mostly of goods that can be consumed outside of the house (beverages, meals taken out, transportation, kola nuts, etc.), it is plausible that the individual is consuming part of the income on the road between the market and the home, before it reaches the house and can be put into the common pool. If family members do not observe each others' actions, they cannot fully insure each other.

Troubles do not stop here, however. In joint work with Chris Udry (Duflo and Udry 2004), we studied whether household members in Côte d'Ivoire are able to insure each other against shocks that all of them can observe. Households grow different crops, which react differently to the same rainfall. For example, men tend to grow tree crops, which are more sensitive to the previous year's rain than to this year's. Women grow vegetables, which are sensitive to current rainfall. Thus, variation in quarterly rainfall is a predictor of variation in each individual's income: a good year for the women in the household can be a bad year for the men in the household. We then asked the following question: If a particular year is good for the women of the household in a village, do we observe a shift in the type of goods that are consumed in the household in that year, relative to a good year for the men? This is exactly what we find. If the year is good for women in a particular household, more money is spent on food than in good years for men. In fact, none of the unexpected increase in the income from the male cash crops (coffee and cocoa) is spent on extra food; all of it is spent on private goods (clothing, alcohol, and tobacco). This is particularly striking, since none of the information we used in our analysis was unknown to the household members. We used only the information on the weather, which everybody in the household could observe. The household members seem not to insure each other against variation in income that they can perfectly observe. Furthermore, the household members do not seem to have an option of just leaving the household as a villager leaves the informal insurance arrangement, since they are linked by an intricate web of exchange (the women prepare food, the men bring in cash income, etc.), so that it is somewhat difficult to take as given the explanation that intrahousehold insurance arrangements are limited by the threat of walking away. And finally, household members have strong sanctions at their disposal, which could potentially help them enforce efficient transfers.

The study in Côte d'Ivoire adds one more piece of evidence that further undermines the hope of finding an explanation for household behavior in a "poor but neoclassical" framework. There is one crop in Côte d'Ivoire, yam, that is traditionally grown only by men (some specific operations cannot be accomplished by women, and property rights on yam fields and yam crops are clearly attributed to males). However, a strong social norm limits the legitimate uses of the proceeds from yams (Meillassoux 1964). Yams are supposed to be used for feeding household members and for taking care of children. We therefore treated yams as a separate group and examined how expenditure on various goods reacted to variation in yam income predicted by rainfall. Good years for yams are indeed associated with more expenditure on food, both purchased and eaten at home. Expenditures on private goods (alcohol, tobacco, ornamental clothing, and jewelry) do not respond at all to increases or decreases in yam income. Expenditure on education responds only to changes in yam income, not to changes in female or male income. Men seem to treat income from different sources differently and do not use the windfall from one source to compensate for any shortfall from the other source.

The household therefore seems to keep separate "mental accounts" (Thaler 1994), treating different types of income differently. The separation of accounts goes beyond the failure to put together money that "belongs" to different people: different sources of income are allocated to different uses depending on their origin. The fact that these accounts respond differently to observable shocks in income is difficult to reconcile with imperfect observability, moral hazard, or limits on self-enforcing insurance schemes. The complexity of intrahousehold sharing arrangements seems to resist explanations based only on information and incentives. Understanding why these norms and arrangements emerge (which problems they solve) and how they are sustained requires a deeper understanding of decision-making of individuals and groups. It will also shed some light on how important economic decisions are made and what constraints are put on the household.

AGRICULTURAL INVESTMENT

The classic articulation of the "poor but efficient" hypothesis for agricultural households is in the book by Schultz (1964), which argues that poor peasants are on the productive efficiency frontier, citing notably the study by Tax (1953), *Penny Capitalism,* which studies peasants in Guatemala.

If agricultural production is efficient, the investment, effort, and production on the land should not depend on who is tilling it: whoever is working on the land should extract the maximum from the land, and these profits should then be shared. The impact of tenancy arrangements on agricultural investment and productivity suggests that the story is more complicated. For instance, Shaban (1987) showed that in India a given farmer works 40% more and uses 20% more fertilizer on his own land than on land that he is sharecropping. Even after accounting for intrinsic differences in productivity of different plots of land, agricultural productivity is 30% higher on land farmed by the owner. Tenancy arrangements are clearly inefficient.

The notion of limited liability provides a possible unified framework to explain why sharecropping arrangements arise, and why they are inefficient (Banerjee et al., 2002). If there is a limit on how miserable someone can be (e.g., in no circumstance can someone's last bowl of food be taken away), a tenant has to be protected in bad years, and thus his payment cannot be fully dependent on how well he did. Limited liability also explains why those who do not have land cannot borrow to purchase it, and thus why there are tenants and landlords in the first place. It implies that land or wealth redistribution would increase investments and productivity. The poor are different because they are desperate (Banerjee 2001). Having nothing to lose, they cannot be made fully responsible for their actions. They thus cannot be given the same opportunities as others, and this explains the persistence of poverty.

In this world, productivity should be maximal on owner-occupied land, at least when the necessary investments are not larger than the maximum an individual can borrow. Since land can serve as collateral, maximum permissible borrowing should be related to the value of the land. Very large investments (such as digging a new irrigation well) may not take place, even if they would eventually be profitable for a single farmer,[2] but the choice of seeds, the use of fertilizer, the use of bullocks, and so forth should be efficient.

This intuition seems at odds with a number of facts sharing the feature that the technology employed on owner-occupied farms seems to be far from the most efficient. For example, Goldstein and Udry (1999) show that the rate of return to growing pineapples greatly exceeds that of growing any of the other crops that are traditionally planted by farmers: it is 531% for growing pineapple, while it is only 21% for growing traditional crops. Yet only 24.4% of male farmers, and almost none of the female farmers, grow pineapple. This is surprising, since pineapple growing requires a moderate initial investment that could easily be covered by a loan secured by the land owned by these farmers.

It is true that any new investment requires taking some risk that the poor may be wary of facing. For example, in India, Morduch (1993, 1995) documents that poor farmers are less likely than richer farmers to use the high yielding varieties of seeds. One possible explanation is that farmers are reluctant to borrow, perhaps for fear of losing their land if the investment does not pay off. They will prefer a safe strategy with a low return to a riskier strategy with a higher return. It is reasonable to think that the poorer someone is, the more he dislikes taking risks. In that case, the poor (and sometimes even more so the near-poor, who have more to lose) will tend to be more conservative than the rich, and more likely to fail to undertake efficient investments. In particular, small owners may be very reluctant to use their land to secure a mortgage. This is poverty as vulnerability (Banerjee 2001). Again, this means that the poor will tend to remain poor, while those who start with enough wealth will be able to accumulate more of it. According to Morduch, this accounts for the discrepancies in hybrid seed use across rich and poor farmers: those who have access to assets that can safeguard their consumption are more likely to use fertilizers and hybrid seeds.[3]

There remain many facts that resist either of these views of the world. To clarify the discussion, I will focus on one example that I have been studying for a few years in collaboration with Michael Kremer and Jonathan Robinson: fertilizer use in western Kenya.

Corn is one of the main staple cereals in the region, and most farmers grow it on their own fields, mainly for home consumption. There are still periodic food shortages in this region, so increasing agricultural productivity is critical. On experimental farms, chemical fertilizers have been shown to generate very large increases in yield, and are recommended by the Agricultural Ministry as part of a package including hybrid seeds, fertilizer at planting, and fertilizer at "top dressing" (when the plant is knee-high). While commercial corn farmers in other regions of Kenya all use this package, in Busia (the region we study) less than 20% of farmers use fertilizer at any point in time.

Prima facie, neither limited liability nor risk aversion seems capable of explaining such a low level of fertilizer use. Fertilizer comes in small packages, so it could be used on a very small part of the farmer's land. This would not require a large investment, so it seems implausible that the inability to borrow should be a major factor limiting investment. For example, it costs 8 shillings, less than the price of 1 kilogram of corn, to apply fertilizer on an area of 30 square meters. This is the average production of only 10 square meters of corn in a relatively bad season. Even if there is no credit market, the farmer could always save during one season to start to use fertilizer the next season. The size of the investment could be chosen so as to maintain the acceptable level of risk.

One obvious possibility is that fertilizer, while very effective on experimental farms and for commercial farmers who have access to mechanized agricultural tools, is actually not profitable for these farmers. To investigate this, International Child Support (ICS), an NGO with a long-standing presence in the area, conducted small field trials on farmers' lands. During five consecutive seasons, ICS asked a group of farmers (randomly selected from the list of parents of students in several schools) to select two or three small contiguous plots of land (each measuring 30 or 60 square meters). A field officer then randomly selected one plot to be a control plot, and the others to be subjected to different "treatments" (fertilizer at top-dressing only, or the full "package" of hybrid seeds, fertilizer at planting and top-dressing). Because the recommendations on how much fertilizer to use were conflicting, ICS also varied the quantity of fertilizer applied on a given plot from season to season. The field officer monitored fertilizer application and measured yields in treatment and control plots, but did not provide any other inputs or instructions, so that these results should reflect the profitability of using a given quantity of fertilizer under regular conditions.

The average (annualized) rate of return of applying a small quantity of fertilizer at top-dressing was very large: 231%, on average, over six seasons. With larger quantities on the same sized plot, the average rate of return went down. The experiments are too coarse to tell us what is the optimal quantity of fertilizer to use, but it seems clear that it is positive. The full package recommended by the Ministry of Agriculture, however, had low or negative returns (-86% over two seasons); the reason was that, under real conditions, hybrid seeds often do not germinate and need to be replaced. In this case, the initial investment in fertilizer at planting is lost. The experiments thus taught us that it is clearly efficient for these farmers to use some fertilizer on their land. However, they also showed that even though the technology has been around for a long time, what to use and how to use it are not necessarily effectively conveyed to the farmers.

This may open an avenue to rescue the hypothesis that lack of access to credit prevents fertilizer use. Learning about a technology requires some experimentation, which requires effort, and presumably some losses in the first years (Foster and Rosenzweig 1995). If the farmer knows that after this initial investment he will be able to use fertilizer on only a very small scale for a long period of time (because he cannot have access to the funds to do it on a large scale), he might rightly consider it worthless to make the initial investment to master the technology.

The field trials allowed us to directly evaluate the strength of this hypothesis: in essence, they constituted a particularly intensive form of agricultural extension. After the harvest, an ICS field officer visited each farmer, and discussed his experience as well as the experience of everybody who participated in the trials with him. The field officer went through detailed profit calculations, using both the farmer's own data and the average numbers. The farmers thus learned both how to use fertilizer and how profitable it really was: ICS gave the farmers a chance to learn how to use fertilizer at no cost to them. If learning how to use fertilizer was the main barrier to adoption, we might thus expect that farmers participating in the trials would have higher fertilizer use than those who did not. Since farmers were randomly selected from parents of students in a few schools, the parents of other children in the same schools formed a natural comparison group. We thus monitored the adoption of fertilizer by all farmers who had participated in ICS trials for the following seasons.

Indeed, fertilizer adoption increased in this group. On average, while 20% of the farmers who did not participate in the trial adopted fertilizer in a given season, 37% of those who did participate were using fertilizer.

The explanation in terms of fixed costs of learning may thus have some bite, but fails to explain the entire phenomenon. First, more than 60% of the farmers continued not to use fertilizer. And second, the effect of having participated seemed to diminish over time: after three seasons, only 29% of farmers who had initially participated in the trial used fertilizer.

We thus have to turn to other explanations. A possibility, which sounds plausible in view of the farmers' overwhelming explanation of why they were not using fertilizer (98% of them said they did not use fertilizer because they had no money) is that farmers find it very difficult to save even the small amount of money necessary to purchase fertilizer. We also observed that farmers seemed reluctant to use fertilizer on a very small plot. Perhaps there is a psychological cost to deviating from "business as usual." In this case, farmers need to be able to save (or borrow) a reasonable amount of money to start using fertilizer.

To test the hypothesis that the lack of savings opportunities prevented the farmers from using as much fertilizer as they would want, ICS offered farmers the option of having ICS purchase fertilizer on their behalf immediately after the harvest, when corn is relatively plentiful. ICS would either deliver the fertilizer right away, or store it until the time of top-dressing. The farmers could pay either with cash or with the equivalent value in corn.

This opportunity was offered to farmers in six different seasons, and proved very popular. In the first year, twelve out of the fifty-four farmers to whom ICS offered this opportunity purchased fertilizer in advance. The increase in fertilizer adoption occasioned by the scheme was the same as the number of people who elected to purchase fertilizer under the scheme. This suggests that all those who elected to take up the scheme were new adopters. By offering farmers a way to save for just a few weeks, ICS doubled the rate of fertilizer usage.

In the following years, the scheme was offered to farmers who had participated in the agricultural trials. Among those, the adoption of the scheme varied but was at least 30%. It was higher when farmers were asked to make a decision on the spot, and reached 80% among farmers who had sold a fraction of their corn crop to ICS for some other purpose. This simple commitment device led to a very sharp increase in adoption rate, over and above the effect of learning alone.

We are far from understanding fully why this program was so successful. Did farmers value the opportunity to commit their money to be used for fertilizer purchase because they knew that if they kept the money, they would be tempted to use it on other things before the time for purchasing and using the fertilizer occurred (Laibson 1997)? Were they protecting the cash against themselves (they knew that they needed to tie their hands), or were they worried about their families or their neighbors? Were farmers just lured by fertilizer as one possible purchase, and would they have been just as happy with a radio or some alcohol? Were farmers particularly aware of the value of fertilizer, after we had just weighed and valued the output of the two plots, and would this have lost its salience if the farmers had waited longer before having to decide whether or not to use fertilizer?

Many further experiments will be necessary to disentangle these possibilities, and, with ICS, we are currently designing and implementing some of them. What is clear, however, is that the inefficiently low level of fertilizer investment in this region cannot easily be accounted for by the "poor but neoclassical" paradigm. It is definitely the task of economists to understand this fundamental production decision. It will require a deeper understanding of the determinants of decision-making in a very poor environment than what the *Homo economicus* framework has left space for.

TOWARD A THEORY OF BEHAVIOR IN POVERTY

The "poor but neoclassical" research program systematically explores the structural constraints that poverty imposes on the decision-making of an unboundedly rational individual in an environment where information is incomplete. The two examples we just covered have shown that many important facts can be accounted for in this framework, but that other facts are resistant.

A natural tendency would then be to turn to new hypotheses, incorporating insights of psychology to better understand economic decisions. This has been the research agenda of "behavioral economics" (Mullainathan and Thaler 2000). Behavioral economists have argued that three main ways in which humans deviate from the standard economic model need to be incorporated into economic reasoning. Their ability to analyze information, compute, and remember is limited. Their willpower is also bounded; they do not always make choices that are in their best interest in the long run. Finally, they are not purely self-interested. Developing countries could then be seen as ideal testing grounds for some of these theories, since program evaluation experiments and field experiments can be combined, as in the example of the fertilizer program. There may be more to learn about human behavior from the choices made by Kenyan farmers confronted with a real choice than from those made by American undergraduates in laboratory conditions. There are a few examples of "real world" experiments that test specific hypotheses in a developed country, such as the "Save More Tomorrow" program (Thaler and Benartzi 2004), where individuals were offered the possibility of signing up for a program in which a part of their future salary increases would be saved. There are also natural experiments, such as changes in default rules for enrollment in voluntary retirement savings plans (Madrian and Shea 2002), or variation in the debt structure of a financial aid package with the same monetary value (Field 2002). Real or natural experiments, however, are rare in developed countries; in developing countries, it might be easier to collaborate with NGOs to offer programs with different rules, and different characteristics, designed to test specific behavioral hypotheses. This could be a fruitful avenue of collaboration between practitioners and academics, since it may help practitioners to design programs that effectively help improve an individual's options.

Faithfully applying the theories designed for developed countries to the analysis of the decisions of the poor in developing countries would, however, be making the same mistake as the proponents of the "poor but efficient" framework, and failing to recognize the central insight of the "poor but neoclassical" line of research. Trying to reduce the behavior of a Kenyan farmer who does not use fertilizer and that of an American employee to the same model may be as fruitless as trying to convince oneself that Guatemalan farmers are on the efficiency frontier. Being poor almost certainly affects the way people think and decide. Perhaps when choices involve the subsistence of one's family, trade-offs are distorted in different ways than when the question is how much money one will enjoy at retirement. Pressure by extended family members or neighbors is also stronger when they are at risk of starvation. Or decision making may be influenced by stress.

What is needed is a theory of how poverty influences decision-making, not only by affecting the constraints, but also by changing the decision-making process itself. That theory can then guide a new round of empirical research, both observational and experimental.

ACKNOWLEDGMENTS I gratefully acknowledge financial support from the Alfred P. Sloan Foundation.

NOTES

1. Among others, Loury (1981); Banerjee and Newman (1991, 1993, 1994); Galor and Zeira (1993); Aghion and Bolton (1997); and Piketty (1997).

2. In practice, very large investments will often benefit more than one farmer, so one other source of inefficiency is that it will be difficult to get everyone to agree on what to build and who should pay for it.

3. Note that the necessity for the poor to adopt this conservative behavior will disappear if the poor can be insured. In this world, asset redistribution is not the only way to increase efficiency and investments.

BIBLIOGRAPHY

Aghion, Philippe, and Patrick Bolton. "A Trickle-Down Theory of Growth and Development with Debt Overhang." *Review of Economic Studies* 64 (2) (1997): 151–172.

Banerjee, Abhijit V. "The Two Poverties." *Nordic Journal of Political Economy* 26 (2) (2001): 129–141.

Banerjee, Abhijit V., Paul L. Gertler, and Maitreesh Ghatak. "Empowerment and Efficiency: The Economics of Tenancy Reform." *Journal of Political Economy* 110 (2) (2002): 239–280.

Banerjee, Abhijit V., and Andrew Newman. "Risk Bearing and the Theory of Income Distribution." *Review of Economic Studies* 58 (2) (1991): 211–235.

Banerjee, Abhijit V., and Andrew Newman. "Occupational Choice and the Process of Development." *Journal of Political Economy* 101 (2) (1993): 274–298.

Banerjee, Abhijit V., and Andrew Newman. "Poverty, Incentives, and Development." *American Economic Review* 84 (2) (1994): 211–215.

Coate, Stephen, and Martin Ravallion. "Reciprococity without Commitment: Characterization and Performance of Informal Insurance Arrangements." *Journal of Development Economics* 40 (1) (1993): 1–24.

Duflo, Esther, and Christopher Udry. "Intrahousehold Resource Allocation in Côte d'Ivoire: Social Norms, Separate Accounts and Consumption Choices," NBER working paper 10498, 2004.

Field, Erica. "Educational Debt Burden and Career Choice: Evidence from a Financial Aid Experiment." Working paper 469, Princeton University, Industrial Relations Section, 2002.

Foster, Andrew D., and Mark R. Rosenzweig. "Learning by Doing and Learning from Others: Human Capital and Technical Change in Agriculture." *Journal of Political Economy* 103 (6) (1995): 1176–1209.

Galor, Oded, and Joseph Zeira. "Income Distribution and Macroeconomics." *Review of Economic Studies* 60 (1) (1993): 35–52.

Genicot, Garance, and Debraj Ray. "Group Formation in Risk-Sharing Arrangements." *Review of Economic Studies* 70 (1) (2003): 87–113.

Goldstein, Markus Paul. "Intrahousehold Allocation and Farming in Southern Ghana." Ph.D. dissertation, University of California, Berkeley, 2000.

Goldstein, Markus, and Christopher Udry. "Agricultural Innovation and Resource Management in Ghana." Final Report to IFPRI Under MP17. Mimeo, Yale University, 1999.

Laibson, David. "Golden Eggs and Hyperbolic Discounting." *Quarterly Journal of Economics* 112 (2) (1997): 443–477.

Ligon, Ethan. "Risk Sharing and Information in Village Economics." *Review of Economic Studies* 65 (4) (1998): 847–864.

Loury, Glenn C. "Intergenerational Transfers and the Distribution of Earnings." *Econometrica* 49 (4) (1981): 843–867.

Madrian, Brigitte, and Dennis F. Shea. "Preaching to the Converted and Converting Those Taught: Financial Education in the Workplace." Mimeo, Graduate School of Business, University of Chicago, 2002.

Meillassoux, Claude. *Anthropologie économique des Gouros de Côte d'Ivoire.* Paris: Mouton, 1964.

Morduch, Jonathan. "Risk, Production and Saving: Theory and Evidence from Indian Households." Mimeo, Harvard University, 1993.

Morduch, Jonathan. "Income Smoothing and Consumption Smoothing." *Journal of Economic Perspectives* 9 (3) (1995): 103–114.

Mullainathan, Sendhil, and Richard Thaler. "Behavioral Economics." NBER working paper 7948, October 2000.

Piketty, Thomas. "The Dynamics of the Wealth Distribution and the Interest Rate with Credit Rationing." *Review of Economic Studies* 64 (2) (1997): 173–189.

Schultz, Theodore W. *Transforming Traditional Agriculture.* New Haven, Conn.: Yale University Press, 1964.

Shaban, Radwan. "Testing between Competing Models of Sharecropping." *Journal of Political Economy* 95 (5) (1987): 893–920.

Tax, Sol. *Penny Capitalism: A Guatemalan Indian Economy.* Washington, D.C.: Smithsonian Institution, Institute of Social Anthropology Publication no. 16, 1953.

Thaler, Richard H. "Psychology and Savings Policies." *AEA Papers and Proceedings* 84 (2) (1994): 186–192.

Thaler, Richard H., and Shlomo Benartzi. "Save More Tomorrow: Using Behavioral Economics to Increase Employee Saving." *Journal of Political Economy* 112 (1) (2004): S164–S187.

Townsend, Robert. "Risk and Insurance in Village India." *Econometrica* 62 (4) (1994): 539–591.

Townsend, Robert. "Consumption Insurance: An Evaluation of Risk-Bearing Systems in Low-Income Economies." *Journal of Economic Perspectives* 9 (3) (1995a): 83–102.

Townsend, Robert. "Financial Systems in Northern Thai Villages." *Quarterly Journal of Economics* 110 (4) (1995b): 1011–1046.

Udry, Christopher. "Credit Markets in Northern Nigeria: Credit as Insurance in a Rural Economy." *World Bank Economic Review* 4 (3) (1990): 251–269.

25

Better Choices to Reduce Poverty

Sendhil Mullainathan

A recent theme of development economics is that institutions matter. Enforcing property rights promotes investment because people can reap the returns of what they sow (both literally and figuratively). Good courts, with judges who make speedy decisions, allow people to write the complex contracts necessary to run complex businesses. A well-developed stock market, with regulation to protect minority shareholders and promote transparency, facilitates the transfer of capital to firms that might otherwise not get it. Though there are subtle (and not so subtle) differences in why good institutions affect property rights, there is a broad theme here. Good institutions help to smooth and facilitate the interactions between people. They prevent people from reneging on contracts. They prevent one person from taking the rightful property of others. They help people transfer resources to one another with the confidence that they can get them back.

Surely anyone who has been in a country with poor institutions can sympathize with this viewpoint. A few summers ago I was in India, examining some exquisite furniture at very good prices. The seller, trying to get the sale, pointed out that he could easily ship it for me anywhere. Boston? No problem. And he reassured me that he'd been in business for quite some time and done this sort of thing for a long time. But I would have to pay in cash. He seemed honest enough, but I couldn't help thinking, "Will I ever see this furniture once I return to Boston?" The cynic in me knew that there was little I could do if the seller failed to satisfy his part of the bargain. Distance was not the only problem. My uncle lived nearby, but could he practically take the seller to court in case of nondelivery? Perhaps, but it likely would have done little good. The courts would have taken a year, or more likely many years, to review the case. And perhaps the judge might accept a bribe or be a friend of a friend of the furniture seller. To even the marginally honest seller, this could be a tempting situation. Surely, if the furniture seller had been in Virginia, which has much better enforcement, I would have worried a lot less. Now, in the end, I did buy the furniture (and actually received it). But who knows how many such transactions are hindered every day by these poorly functioning institutions?

While compelling, I think this picture—that good institutions help facilitate transactions between people—is incomplete. I think good institutions also help to reduce the problems that arise *within* a person. This kind of statement is hard to make sense of with standard economic reasoning. Individuals are rational, autonomous units with full self-control. This framework doesn't leave room for people to have problems with themselves, so what could institutions help with?

I am one of a growing set of researchers who study how to integrate psychological insights into economic reasoning (see Mullainathan 2004; Bertrand et. al. 2004). In this perspective, people sometimes make bad choices, ones that they themselves would like to improve on. This perspective is opening up new ideas, such as how good institutions, in some contexts, might help people improve their decisions. I will discuss these insights using a few choice examples. My goal here is not to tell you about concrete policies that might emerge. It is a bit early for that. Instead, it is to give you a glimpse of how radically different our policy suggestions might be in ten or twenty years as the integration of psychology and economics deepens.

ACTIVE VERSUS PASSIVE CHOICES

The standard economic model assumes all choices are decisions. Individuals weigh the benefits and costs of one action versus another and then choose the one that fits them best. In many cases this makes sense. I end up on vacation in Bermuda, rather than Jamaica, through a series of explicit and conscious actions designed to choose the locale that will give me the greatest pleasure. I read through various guidebooks and talk to friends. I try to examine the relative benefits of Bermuda (much closer) and costs (less to do), weigh them, and come to a conclusion. Perhaps I overweighted one dimension or another, but at least my decision was an active one. Economics assumes all choices occur in this conscious, active manner.

Yet many of the choices we make, even big ones, are not active ones. Why does my e-mail go unread for days (weeks! months!)? At no point did I decide this would be what is best for me (surely it isn't). Instead, it overflowed because there was never a point at which I chose otherwise. In fact, it is because I never sat down to make this decision that I ended up with a too large mailbox. Part of the reason for this is procrastination and a lack of self-control. Part is that other things got in the way. This distinction is not just a philosophical one. A growing body of research suggests that this distinction may be very important for understanding various important decisions. The idea that many decisions may be passive ones draws on a large set of psychology experiments that show we often process information automatically, without it ever entering our conscious realm. Perhaps the most salient (and certainly most fun) demonstration of this principle is the Stroop test.

Passive decision making can even affect large decisions. Consider an economically important decision such as how much to save. How do people make this decision? In the traditional model, people trade off consuming more today against consuming less in the future or when retired. They assess their assets, their future earnings (and the riskiness of those earnings), their projected Social Security payments, and their expected life span, then use these factors to decide how much they need to put away.

But all this assumes that savings is a calculated, active decision. Is this really the case? Some evidence suggests otherwise. In one survey, 76% of Americans believed that they should be saving more for retirement. In fact, 55% felt they were behind in their savings and only 6% reported being ahead (Farkas and Johnson 1997). Though they want to save, many never get around to it. Perhaps they meant to save but an appealing purchase reared its head and they lacked the self-control to resist. Perhaps other tasks simply caught their attention and they never got around to organizing their finances in such as a way as to accomplish their planned savings rate.

Madrian and Shea (2001) conducted a particularly telling study along these lines. They studied the choice to participate in a 401(k) plan. When they join a firm, people typically are given a form that they must fill out in order to participate. The 401(k)s are very lucrative, so people have a very strong incentive to participate. Nevertheless, participation rates are quite low. Standard economic models might suggest that the subsidy ought to be raised. Many firms in fact do this. But participation rates are still low, and the programs are quite expensive. Madrian and Shea study a firm that changed a very simple feature of its 401(k) program. Prior to the change, new employees received a form that said something to the effect of "Check this box if you would like to participate in a 401(k). Indicate how much you'd like to contribute." After the change, however, new employees received a form that said something to the effect of "Check this box if you would not like to have 3% of your paycheck put into a 401(k)." By standard reasoning, this change should have little effect on contribution rates. How hard is it to check off one box? After all, that's the only difference between the two conditions. In practice, however, Madrian and Shea found a large effect. When the default option was not to contribute, only 38% of those given the form contributed. When the default option was contribution, 86% contributed. Moreover, even several years later those exposed to a contribution default still showed much higher contribution rates.

These results are consistent with (and motivated) the discussion above. While we cannot be sure from these data what people are thinking, I would speculate that some combination of procrastination and passivity played a role. Surely many looked at this form and said, "Well, I'll decide this later." But later never came. Perhaps they were distracted by more interesting activities than deciding on 401(k) contribution rates (hard to believe, but there are more interesting activities). Perhaps it simply slipped their minds because other factors came to occupy it. In either case, whatever the default on the form was, they ended up with it as their choice. In fact, as time went on, they may well have justified their "decision" to themselves by saying "Five percent is what I wanted anyway," or "That 401(k) plan wasn't so attractive." In this way, their passivity made their decision for them. By making the small active choice to choose later, they ended up making a large decision about thousands of dollars.

These kinds of passive choices occur in many aspects of savings. When I teach saving to my graduate students, I often tell them that "savings is simply what you don't spend." Partly I'm being facetious, but partly I am serious about this distinction. Some people sit down with a budget and decide how much they're going to save (and some of them even stick to that decision; more on this later). For the rest of us, savings is just what is left over after we've made all our active decisions about what to buy.

This is why many of the institutions that help us save do so by simply getting to the money before it ever enters our hands. As we've seen, firms automatically deduct money for 401(k) contributions. Another example is mortgages. I often suggest to friends that they buy the biggest house they can. Most avoid doing this because they don't want to spend all their money on housing. They'd like to save some of it in other ways. While this is an eminently sensible plan, it is not what happens. Inevitably the money not put into housing finds some other way of being spent, rather than being saved. What makes the mortgage such a good savings device is that it is automatic. Each month, a payment must be made.

These insights can also help us design whole new institutions. One example is Save More Tomorrow, a program created by Benartzi and Thaler. The basic idea of Save More Tomorrow is to get people to make one active choice, but to have them make it in such a way that if they remain passive afterward, they are still saving. Think of why housing is such a good savings device. You decide once to buy it, and then forever more (well, probably only thirty years, but it certainly feels like forever), you're committed to keep putting money into it. Save More Tomorrow works on a similar principle, though without such a strong commitment. Individuals are offered a chance to participate in this program. To participate, they decide on a target savings level (and we know that people actually want to save). Once they decide on what they'd like to save, they agree to start 401(k) deductions at a small level from their paycheck *next year*. And then each year, as they receive a raise, their deductions increase until they hit their target savings level. They can opt out of the program at any time. But the genius is that if they do nothing and remain passive, they will continue to save (and even increase their savings rate).

The results have been stunning. In one firm, for example, more than 75% of those offered the plan participated in it rather than simply trying to save on their own. Of these, interestingly few (less than 20%) opted out. As a result, savings rates went up sharply. By the third pay raise (as the default increases cumulated), individuals had more than tripled their savings rates. But perhaps the greatest success has been the diffusion of this product. Many major firms and pension fund providers are thinking of adopting it, and participation in the program will likely soon number in the millions.

Save More Tomorrow is a trademark for what psychologically smart institutional design might look like in the future. It does not solve a problem between people but instead helps solve a problem within the person: not saving as much as he or she would like. It does so by harnessing a variety of psychological tools. Besides the one I've highlighted, it relies on two others. First, it asks people to save out of future raises. In that sense they are saving money that they don't have currently, money that isn't already budgeted for one thing or another. It's much easier to put future money to savings (a forgone gain) than to bear a loss now by cutting back on some valued consumption. Second, it relies on the power of defaults. Save More Tomorrow doesn't lock you in. It simply defaults you in, and being defaulted in may be far more acceptable to people than being locked in. Finally, it relies on the fact that people are far more patient about decisions impacting them tomorrow. Save More Tomorrow starts, as the name suggests, tomorrow. It's far easier to agree to a "good" thing for the future than for today.

The insights I've highlighted from this research can help speed up the process of development in many ways. One direct way is to recognize that many institutions in developing countries work well because they encourage good default behaviors. Some of these institutions can be transplanted. Automatic deduction from paychecks, for example, to a separate savings account could be a very powerful savings device. The highly regulated banks that populate developing countries are unlikely to implement innovations such as these on their own. But with effort and prodding they can, in my opinion, be transplanted. If they are transplanted, then at least for some part of the population these kinds of institutions might allow saving (rather than not saving) to become the default.

Of course many in developing countries do not have bank accounts. For the unbanked, these insights serve to strengthen or reinforce an existing policy suggestion: increase the scope of banking services. In the existing view, increasing access to banking services is good because it increases the amount of capital in the banking system and perhaps raises the return on savings for some. In work with Marianne Bertrand and Eldar Shafir, however, I've argued that a more sophisticated view of human psychology reveals numerous other advantages of a bank account. First, it takes money farther from the individual, so in many cases the passive choice or procrastination leads to not spending. When money is around, active effort is required to save it. When money is in the bank account, active effort is required to go and get it in order to spend it. Second, and relatedly, it forces people to attend to what they are actually taking out and spending.

WHAT WE WANT AND WHAT WE DO

Even when we do sit down and actively make a decision, we may not always have the willpower to carry through on that decision. I had actively decided to write this essay a year and a half ago but am writing it only now. I alluded earlier to procrastination and lack of self-control as one of the prime reasons for procrastination. That we lack full self-control is a growing part of economic discourse. The savings example has once again been the center of this discussion. Recall the survey evidence on desired savings. Surely some of the reasons people do not meet their desired savings level is that they do not have the willpower to implement their plans.

One way institutions can help solve these self-control problems is by committing people to a particular path of behavior. A common analogy here is with Ulysses, who has himself tied to his ship's mast so that he can listen to the song of the sirens but not be lured out to sea by them. While not so dramatic, commitment devices exist in everyday life. Many refer to their gym membership as a commitment device. ("Being forced to pay that much money every month really gets me to go to the gym, lest I waste it.") Christmas clubs, while less common than they used to be, were a very powerful commitment tool for saving to buy Christmas gifts. Smokers not having cigarettes around or dieters not buying appealing snacks are examples of commitment devices. Financially, pension plans, automatic drafts from checking to investment accounts, and direct debits from paychecks all at least partly help people to achieve commitment behavior.

Commitment devices for savings also appear in developing countries. For example, rotating savings and credit associations (ROSCAs) might serve as a commitment device (Gugerty 2003). In a ROSCA, a group of people meets at regular intervals. At each meeting, members contribute a prespecified amount. The sum of those funds (the "pot," so to speak) is then given to one of the individuals. Eventually, each person in the ROSCA will get a turn, and thus a return on his contributions. While ROSCAs often pay little or no interest, and the participants bear the risk that some may drop out after getting the pot, they are immensely popular. One reason for their popularity may be that they offer a commitment device. They may help to save by providing pressure to put aside money regularly (Ardener and Burman 1995). As some ROSCA participants say, "You can't save alone." The social pressure to save may bind their hands and serve as an effective commitment device to put aside regularly. Commitment devices may also appear in the guise of durable goods. People may commit themselves by saving in kind rather than in cash, which is far too tempting to spend. They may hold their wealth in jewelry, livestock, or grain because these items are harder to dip into.

What can policy do? It can provide cheaper and more efficient commitment devices than what little exists now. After all, even if saving in grain provides commitment, it is an expensive way to save. Vermin may eat the grain, and the interest rate earned on the grain could be zero or even negative. Moreover, it is important to recognize that even if people demand such commitment devices, the free market may not do enough to provide them. The highly regulated financial markets of developing countries may lead to too little innovation on these dimensions. Monopoly power may also lead to inefficient provision of these commitment devices, depending on whether a monopolistic financial institution can extract more profits by catering to the desire for commitment or to the temptations themselves. In this context, governments, NGOs, and donor institutions can play a large role by promoting such commitment devices.

Government policy can also be improved by understanding the power of temptation and the desire to avoid it. This understanding could turn some conventional logic on its head. For example, in designing saving policies, standard logic dictates that the more liquid an account, the more valuable it is. After all, liquidity allows people to free up cash to attend to immediate needs that arise. If a child gets sick, money is needed to pay for medicine. This might be especially true for the poor. Shocks that are small for the well-off can be big for the poor, and they would need to dip into real savings to address them.

Nevertheless, the poor may value illiquidity. Ashraf et al. (2003) give a stunning illustration. They offer savers in the Philippines the opportunity to participate in lockbox savings accounts. The accounts are literal lockboxes, to which the bank has the key. Individuals can put aside small amounts of cash (as they want to) into the lockbox. Every one to two weeks they deposit the box with the bank, which in turn deposits the contents of the lockbox into an account. They also test a savings vehicle in which a certain amount of money from all of an account holder's deposits are automatically set aside each month into a separate account. Money cannot be withdrawn from this account until a predefined event occurs (such as planting season or a certain target has been reached). Both savings tools are very illiquid, yet there is a large demand for them. The recognition that illiquidity can be a net good is a very important policy lesson. The creation of market institutions that increase liquidity may be a net bad, not a net good. Such caveats will force us, I feel, to reconsider the full set of financial market policies in developing countries.

Though the bulk of my examples have been from savings, I think policy in many other areas may also be affected. One salient example is potentially addictive substances, such as alcohol or the nicotine in tobacco. The economist's approach to such goods has been to treat them like any other good: people choose them willingly (or, in the extreme case, people willingly choose to be addicted to them). Yet there is some evidence that this is not the case. For example, in a recent study I did with Jon Gruber, we found that smokers are made better off by raising cigarette taxes. When states increased their taxes, we found increases in self-reported happiness of those who tend to smoke. Cigarette expenditures are a big part of total expenditures, especially for the poor, and the cigarette tax, we argue (and others have found), helps those trying to quit to actually do so. Thus the tax helps them do something they've been trying to do. Much as the lockbox puts tempting money out of reach, the taxes may put cigarettes out of (financial) reach. This is the exact opposite of the standard arguments made about taxes. When economists suggest taxes to alter behavior, it is to deal with externalities, to alter behavior that negatively affects others. In this case, behavior changes, but the benefits accrue to the individuals themselves. In other words, taxation here may (in a few cases) actually be an institution to help people solve problems with themselves.

In the developing countries, such distortions could potentially be even more severe because these expenditures would form a sizable bulk of consumption. Because the costs of alcohol and cigarettes are such a large portion of income, addiction to them could be very costly in real terms. Perhaps there is room for tax (or regulatory) policies in these cases as well.

Of course, these policies are not firm suggestions. It is too early to say that a tax on cigarettes is always good. We simply do not have enough evidence. But thinking about self-control problems and how government policies interact with them is beginning to produce some extremely interesting insights, ones that I think will eventually change the way development policy is done.

CONCLUSION

Despite the psychological evidence I cite, I am constantly surprised at some of the empirical evidence. For example, how can a simple default have such a large effect on behavior? How can the cost of checking the box be enough to drive such large decisions? I think this is one of the central messages of psychology for economics, especially when one is trying to design institutions. Small differences can affect large behaviors. Getting an institution right is partly about getting the broad theme of it correct. Psychology can help us with that, such as in thinking about commitment devices. But it is in large part about getting the microdetails right. What is the default? How are the choices framed for the person? I think psychology will revolutionize the way we redesign the institutions of developing countries and, I hope, in the process help to alleviate poverty.

BIBLIOGRAPHY

Ardener, Shirley, and Sandra Burman, eds. *Money-go-Rounds: The Importance of Rotating Savings and Credit Associations for Women.* Washington, D.C.: BERG, 1995.

Ashraf, Nava, Nathalie Gons, and Wesley Yin. "Testing Savings Product Innovations Using an Experimental Methodology." Mimeo, Princeton University, 2003.

Benartzi, Shlomo, and Richard H. Thaler. "Save More Tomorrow: Using Behavioral Economics to Increase Employee Saving." Mimeo, University of Chicago Graduate School of Business, 2001.

Bertrand, Marianne, Sendhil Mullainathan, and Eldar Shafir, "A Behavioral-Economics View of Poverty," *American Economic Review* 94 (2) (2004): 419–423.

Farkas, Steve, and Jean Johnson. *Miles to Go: A Status Report on Americans' Plans for Retirement.* Washington, D.C.: Public Agenda, 1997.

Gruber, Jonathan, and Sendhil Mullainathan. "Do Cigarette Taxes Make Smokers Happier?" Mimeo, Massachusetts Institute of Technology, 2002.

Gugerty, Mary Kay. "You Can't Save Alone: Testing Theories of Rotating Savings and Credit Associations in Kenya." Mimeo, Washington University, St. Louis, Mo., 2003.

Madrian, Brigitte, and Dennis Shea. "The Power of Suggestion: Inertia in 401(k) Participation and Savings Behavior." *Quarterly Journal of Economics* 116 (4) (2001): 1149–1187.

Mullainathan, Sendhil. "Psychology and Development." Mimeo, Harvard University, 2004.

26

Nonmarket Institutions

Kaivan Munshi

INTRODUCTION

The market is responsible for the provision of most goods and services in the U.S. economy. We visit the bank when we need a loan to buy a house or to start up a business. We buy insurance to tide over unforeseen circumstances. And we pay to settle in retirement communities when we get older. In much of the developing world, however, people simply do not have access to such market-provided services. Banks are absent, or function extremely inefficiently, and most ordinary people would never qualify for a loan. Insurance is generally unavailable, and institutionalized retirement facilities do not exist.

So how does most of the world's population survive without well-functioning markets? The answer is very simple: they survive just as they have for centuries, with the help of social ties. Nonmarket institutions exist where market institutions are absent, providing an alternative supply of goods and services. Community-based networks provide credit to their members when bank loans are unavailable. Mutual insurance arrangements and younger relatives support the individual when times are bad or when he is too old to be productive.

The pervasiveness of these nonmarket institutions in developing economies, and their persistence, demand an explanation from economists. And, indeed, there has been a great deal of research conducted on these institutions since the 1990s. My objective in this essay is to describe what has been learned about these institutions: why they emerge, why they persist, the inefficiencies that are associated with their presence, and how the presence of these institutions might affect the design of development policy. This essay does not attempt to review the rich literature on nonmarket institutions that has emerged in recent years. It is based instead, for the most part, on my own research conducted with numerous collaborators.

WHY ARE NONMARKET INSTITUTIONS SO PERSISTENT?

There are two basic explanations for the persistence of nonmarket institutions in developing countries. The first, essentially anthropological explanation is based on the idea that the structure of economic institutions reflects the underlying culture of their participants. Thus, the observation that informal credit arrangements tend to be organized commercially in the city, whereas they tend to be cooperatively organized among closely tied individuals in the village, is explained by cultural differences among the participants—individuals in the village expect to share and cooperate with each other, and the profit motive is less central in that environment. By the same reasoning, nonmarket institutions continue to be prevalent in developing countries because people there are accustomed to conducting business in a particular fashion.

In contrast, the explanation for the prevalence of nonmarket institutions that has found favor among economists in recent years is based on the idea that markets generally tend to function imperfectly in developing countries. Community ties reduce information and enforcement problems in this environment, facilitating economic activity. In this view, individuals are intrinsically the same—whether they live in the city or the village, whether they live in a developing country or an advanced economy. What determines the structure of institutions is the economic environment, which is determined by historical circumstances or other exogenous factors. I will use this basic framework to analyze a variety of nonmarket institutions and the individual decisions that surround these institutions.

A TAXONOMY OF NONMARKET INSTITUTIONS

The most basic role for the community in a developing economy is the provision of information, through what is known as social learning. Social learning describes the process through which individuals learn from their neighbors' decisions and experiences about a new technology or activity. The idea that neighbors' previous decisions and experiences play an important role in the diffusion of new technology and practices has been known to rural sociologists and communications specialists for decades. Recent theoretical advances in economics have placed social learning within the standard economic framework, giving rise to a small but growing empirical literature that attempts to test for the presence of such learning.

There is little doubt that social learning and the information networks that support it play an important role in the development process, spreading new ideas and innovations. But it is really geographical proximity, rather than social ties per se, that defines the boundaries of these networks. The information generated by decisions and experiences is an externality in the sense that the individual receives no benefit from its provision. At the same time there is no cost incurred by the provision of such information. Individuals might still end up learning from members of their own social group because members of that group happen to live close to each other. However, information from a stranger is, in principle, just as valuable to the individual.

The next level of nonmarket activity is organized through informal institutions known as social networks. Banks ration credit in developing economies because they know that by raising interest rates and allowing the market to clear, they will bring in risky borrowers. By restricting business to a few trusted customers, or those who can provide collateral, they also avoid the enforcement problem in which borrowers renege on their loans. Community-based networks relax these restrictions on the provision of credit by exploiting social ties. Information flows smoothly within the community, and thus only responsible individuals will have access to community capital. Default is also costly, since the individual can be punished by the community in the future. Individuals in a tight-knit community interact along many dimensions, so, for example, a defaulter might be punished by not being invited to social gatherings, or being excluded from future business transactions. Note, however, that while social networks may be very effective in generating capital, participation in these institutions is potentially costly: the borrower could still default on his loan. Social ties just make it less likely that such an event will occur.

Social ties are seen to avoid information and enforcement problems in the capital market, providing us with a simple explanation for the popularity and the persistence of credit networks in developing countries. We could use the same sort of approach to explain the presence of networks in the labor market or the product market. Mutual insurance arrangements and retirement assistance can also be explained in this fashion. A member of a mutual insurance arrangement is less likely to default on his obligation if he is tied to the other members of his group along other (social) dimensions. Similarly, younger relatives are more likely to discharge their duties to the elderly if they expect to receive the same service from the next generation when they are older, something only a stable community can provide.

The discussion up to this point has restricted attention to informally organized nonmarket institutions. The community can also, where appropriate, establish formal nonmarket institutions with well-specified rules governing participation and behavior within the institution. Well-known institutions of this sort include producers cooperatives, rotating savings and credit associations (ROSCAs), and credit institutions such as the Grameen Bank. Essentially the same framework that we used to understand the prevalence of social networks can be used to understand the emergence of these formal nonmarket institutions.

For example, the banking system typically functions very inefficiently in developing countries. The information and enforcement problems that we described earlier prevent most potential borrowers from receiving loans. And the rate on deposits is kept far below the shadow price of capital by the imperfectly competitive banking system, discouraging deposits in the bank. In this environment, ROSCAs, which have functioned as informal rural savings arrangements for centuries, have in some cases modified their structure to substitute for the modern banking system.

The simple ROSCA, found throughout the developing world, essentially consists of a small group of socially connected individuals who join together to save for a durable good. Imagine that ten individuals are interested in buying bicycles that cost $100, and suppose that each individual can save $10 per month. With no assistance, each individual would be able to buy a bicycle at the end of ten months. Now suppose that the ten individuals pool their savings each month, and draw lots to see who wins the $100 "pot." One member of the group will win each month, starting from the first month, and everyone is at least as well off as he would have been in autarky.

The simple organizational structure just described has been transformed in many Third World cities, to the point where the urban ROSCA starts to look like a bank. In south Indian cities, "chit funds" bring thousands of individuals together in small groups. The participants do not know each other personally, and the organizing company makes sure that individuals continue to contribute to the group after they have won the pot. Subscribers interested in earning high interest rates on their deposits match with businessmen who need working capital, and the pot is auctioned in each period to generate a competitive interest rate. The chit funds generate an interest rate that is three to four percentage points higher than the interest rate offered by the government banks, so it is not surprising that this nonmarket institution has grown enormously popular in recent years. The volume of deposits in formally registered chit funds in the south Indian states of Tamil Nadu and Kerala grew to approximately 20% of the corresponding volume in the government banks over the period 1970–1990, and if we were to include the myriad informally organized chit funds in south Indian cities, this institution would rival the banking system in size.

While urban chit funds are now commercially organized and legally registered, there is still a social aspect to this institution. Subscribers are not required to provide collateral when they win the pot, as they would when receiving a loan from the bank. Instead, they submit three guarantors who are well known in the community. Thus social ties still matter, and it is not surprising that the urban variant of the ROSCA functions only in south Indian cities. When chit funds based in Tamil Nadu set up branches elsewhere, they restrict participation to members of the expatriate Tamil community. What we are seeing here is the transformation of a nonmarket institution in response to a changing economic environment, where this transformation is constrained by the underlying social structure that is required to sustain economic activity.

The same sort of framework can be applied to understand the proliferation of microcredit institutions throughout the developing world in recent years. Perhaps the best-known of these microcredit institutions is the Grameen Bank, established in Bangladesh, which has been used as a model for such institutions throughout the world. The basic objective of the Grameen Bank is to provide credit to individuals who are excluded from the modern banking system, typically because they lack collateral to secure their loans. Participants form small groups, which are jointly responsible for any loan that an individual member receives. Thus the individual liability under the standard debt contract is transformed into joint liability by the microcredit institution, and members of a group now have an incentive to look out for each other. Members of a typical small group belong to the same community, and thus have better information about each others' attributes, and the projects that are chosen by the borrowers, than the bank does. They are also better positioned to enforce repayment, by applying social pressure when a borrower attempts to renege on her responsibilities. The microcredit institution thus harnesses the power of social ties to reduce information and enforcement problems. Indeed, the Grameen Bank is well known for achieving extremely high loan repayment rates.

The final nonmarket institution that I describe is the producers cooperative, which also is found throughout the developing world. Classic examples of successful cooperatives in India include the milk producers cooperatives, associated with the white revolution that transformed India into the world's largest milk producer in the 1980s, and the sugarcane cooperatives, which helped make India the world's largest sugar producer around the same time. A common feature of successful producers cooperatives is that the product tends to be perishable and there are increasing returns to scale in collection and processing (this is just saying that larger facilities are more efficient). For example, milk must be chilled immediately after collection. Fresh-cut sugarcane must also be crushed without delay, to avoid inversion losses by which sucrose is converted to fructose. Collection and processing of both milk and sugarcane exhibit increasing returns to scale, so if transportation delays were not costly, the efficient organization of production would be characterized by extremely large processing plants. Since transportation delays do matter for these products, the optimal configuration would trade off transportation delays with increasing returns to scale, giving rise to local monopsony—a single milk-chilling plant or sugarcane-collecting firm in each local area—as the equilibrium market structure. These local monopsonies would collect from all farmers in the local area, and so they would inevitably use their market power to push the price of milk or sugarcane below the efficient (competitive) level. The cooperatives avoid this distortion by transferring ownership of the processing facility to the producers.

The community plays a coordinating role in the cooperative by bringing the participants together. The milk cooperatives are organized at the village level and thus typically consist of a few hundred members. In contrast, each sugar cooperative covers many villages, and consists of 10,000–25,000 members. Mobilizing all these farmers to launch the cooperative is a formidable task. Subsequently, the members must commit to participating at a sufficiently high level, since there are increasing returns to scale in processing the product. There is an externality associated with the individual's participation in this setting, since he does not account for the effect of his production on the overall efficiency of the cooperative; once more the community plays an important role in ensuring that the nonmarket institution functions efficiently by using social ties to enforce participation.

INEFFICIENCIES IN NONMARKET INSTITUTIONS

Our view of nonmarket institutions up to this point has been entirely favorable. These institutions are seen to emerge when markets function imperfectly, using social ties to avoid information and enforcement problems, and to coordinate economic activity. However, ultimately there is no perfect substitute for the (well-functioning) market, and we will see below that these alternative institutions come with inefficiencies of their own.

The first source of inefficiency that I describe arises because economic activity in nonmarket institutions is confined to the community, inevitably restricting trade and mobility. Take the case of a credit network in which capital flows within the boundaries of the community. It is often the case that migrants to a business center are those individuals who have the highest ability in their community, yet the local businessmen who are not similarly selected still have preferred access to credit by virtue of their better-established networks at that location. Research on the knitted garment export industry in Tirupur, a small town in south India, shows that local businessmen invest twice as much as the outsiders who migrated from elsewhere. Yet the outsiders have a steeper output trajectory and end up selling more than the locals within five years of entering the business. When we look within either community, firms with more capital grow faster, consistent with the standard assumption that ability and capital are complements: entrepreneurs with higher ability invest more and thus grow faster for both reasons. It is only when we look across communities that a negative relationship between investment and growth is observed. This must be because locals face a lower cost of capital, allowing them to invest more, while the outsiders have so much greater ability that they grow faster despite this capital disadvantage. The community with higher ability on average ends up investing less. This mismatch between ability and capital arises entirely because the network must restrict activity within community boundaries in order to function smoothly.

A similar sort of inefficiency arises in the sugar cooperatives described earlier. Recall that these cooperatives avoided the (local) monopsony problem by transferring ownership of the processing facility to the growers. In principle, the growers share the profits from the sale of the finished product (sugar) in proportion to the amount of sugarcane they produce. However, in practice, the large growers, who typically organize the formation of the cooperative, tend to retain control of the institution once it starts to function. This disproportionate control by the large growers distorts pricing within the cooperative, resulting in a suboptimal supply of sugarcane.

To understand the source of this inefficiency, consider a simple setup in which there are two types of growers—small growers and large growers. All growers supply their sugarcane to the processing facility at harvest time, the cane is converted to sugar, and finally is sold on the (competitive) market. In a smoothly functioning cooperative, the profits from the sale of sugar would be distributed among the grower-members in proportion to the amount that they contributed. Instead, we now assume that the controlling large growers retain a fraction of the profits to be shared exclusively among themselves, distributing what remains as a sugarcane price to all growers.

Consider the representative large grower's problem: On the one hand, he would like to depress the price of sugarcane paid back to the growers as far as possible, in order to share the remaining surplus with the other large growers. On the other hand, he is also a grower, and in that role he would like to set the price at the competitive level. When all the growers in the cooperative are large growers, there is no incentive to underprice the sugarcane. But as the proportion of small farmers in the cooperative grows, the representative large grower cares less and less about his role as a farmer, and more and more about his role as a controller of the cooperative. As a consequence, the price of sugarcane will decline as the proportion of small farmers grows. In the extreme case, with a single large farmer and many small farmers, the controlling large farmer pays no attention to the sugarcane he supplies, and will set the monopsony price.

Up to this point we have assumed that control of the cooperative always stays with the large farmers. The cooperatives do have regular elections, and while the large growers may have disproportionate power within the institution, control will ultimately shift to the small farmers as their numerical strength in the cooperative grows. In the limit, in a cooperative consisting exclusively of small farmers, there will be no underpricing of sugarcane. Bringing together all the pieces of the preceding discussion, a U-shaped relationship between sugarcane price and inequality in landownership is obtained. The efficient (competitive) sugarcane price is set in homogeneous cooperatives, while maximum underpricing occurs where inequality is greatest: where there are substantial numbers of big and small farmers. Data from sugar cooperatives in the western Indian state of Maharashtra match perfectly with these predictions from theory. In addition, participation by the large farmers actually declines once the proportion of small farmers crosses a certain threshold and prices start to rise (this is the right-hand segment of the U-shaped pattern), presumably because they receive less in rents as they lose control of the cooperative.

The sort of inefficiency that I have just described is likely to be observed in many collective community-based institutions, precisely because these institutions must restrict competition in order to function effectively. Legal restrictions and social pressure prevent small farmers from "migrating" to neighboring cooperatives, which would limit the extent of underpricing. While community ties solve the coordination problem, and permit the cooperative to function at efficient scale, the trade-off in this case is that these restrictions on mobility open up the possibility of rent-seeking behavior and the abuse of power. In contrast, the composition of the membership has no effect on institutional performance, and the efficient price is always set, in a competitive market.

The networks and the formal collective institutions that I have described all exploit community ties in order to avoid information, enforcement, and coordination problems. But these alternative nonmarket arrangements are only a second-best solution. Community membership cannot be transferred, and restrictions on trade and mobility will inevitably arise within these institutions, generating a new set of inefficiencies in equilibrium. In addition, as discussed below, nonmarket institutions are associated with dynamic inefficiencies in a changing world. While community-based institutions may improve efficiency, they often must do so by placing restrictions on individual behavior. For example, mutual insurance arrangements, microcredit institutions, and credit networks all work by punishing individuals who renege on their obligations. When the economic environment changes, these same restrictions may prevent individuals from exploiting new opportunities, giving rise to a new inefficiency. A member of a mutual insurance arrangement may be prevented from migrating to the city to take advantage of new opportunities there, or a member of a credit network may be discouraged from finding a new source of employment that would reduce his participation in the network.

These sorts of restrictions may stop individuals, and entire communities, from changing their behavior for very long periods of time. Recent evidence from rural Bangladesh suggests that social restrictions may have delayed the onset of the fertility transition by an entire generation. A family-planning program was introduced in Matlab thana, in Comilla district, in 1978. Modern contraceptives were made available, free of cost, to all women. We would expect households to have welcomed the availability of this new and superior technology, but instead the family-planning program faced a great deal of hostility in its early years.

There is an externality associated with fertility decisions in a tight-knit society, since economic activity is so interconnected. It is consequently not surprising that most traditional societies have put norms into place regulating fertility. The traditional equilibrium in these villages was characterized by early and universal marriage, followed by immediate and continuous childbearing. While this may have been the optimal arrangement when the norms were first put into place, it is not at all clear that this continued to be the case when the family-planning program was introduced. Individual households apparently did want to use the modern contraceptives, but in many cases were deterred from doing so by the social pressure, ridicule, and even ostracism that they faced from the community by deviating from the traditional norm.

Gradually change did occur, and the sanctions did grow less effective over time as a greater proportion of households in the villages deviated from the norm. Contraceptive prevalence today is just over 70% in the treatment villages, but it took over twenty years for this change to occur, and there continues to be wide variation in contraception levels across villages that are otherwise very homogeneous. A particularly striking feature of this process of change is that it occurred exclusively within religious groups (Hindus and Muslims) within each village, consistent with the view that social norms were slowly breaking down within each local community.

The discussion up to this point has focused on the difficulty in changing individual behavior when social restrictions are in place. The converse inefficiency is associated with delays in the formation of new norms. Just as existing norms grow less effective as a greater fraction of the community deviates from prescribed behavior, so the formation of new norms requires a similarly high level of coordination.

One case where such coordination should have occurred, but did not, possibly with disastrous consequences, is the failure of the marriage institution to reorganize itself in sub-Saharan Africa during the HIV/AIDS epidemic. The marriage institution evolved very differently in sub-Saharan Africa, compared with the rest of the world, for historical reasons. Land was plentiful and labor was scarce, so women were valued for both their productive and their reproductive capabilities. Marriage in Africa thus came to be associated with the system of bride wealth, in which transfers flow from the man to the bride's family at the time of marriage, and the institution of polygyny, in which the man invested in multiple wives as productive assets. Polygyny, in turn, gave rise to a culture with few restrictions on extramarital sexual relationships.

This feature of African culture, which is a natural consequence of historical economic conditions, assumes great importance during the HIV/AIDS epidemic. It is well known that the vast majority of HIV/AIDS cases to date have occurred in sub-Saharan Africa. Most men in Africa, as in the rest of the developing world, are married by the age of thirty-five. Thus, if the sexual activity of married men were curtailed, this could have a significant impact on the spread of the disease. By extension, differences in the organization of the marriage institution could account for a substantial fraction of the regional differences in HIV/AIDS prevalence that we observe today.

Marriage plays an important role in facilitating exchange in traditional network-based economies. Marriage strengthens existing network ties and forges new ties, so there is an externality associated with the individual's marriage decision. It is consequently not at all surprising that strict rules regulating marriage have emerged in most societies. While marriage in sub-

Saharan Africa may not have regulated sexual activity, it did facilitate the functioning of community-based networks. Indeed, evidence from a recent survey of Luo migrants in Kisumu, Kenya, shows that marriage does increase employment, income, and remittances. Yet marriage plays absolutely no role in curtailing sexual activity, once we control for observed and unobserved differences between married and single men, despite the fact that HIV/AIDS levels are as high as 30% in Kisumu.

Why did the marriage institution not respond to the HIV/AIDS epidemic and reorganize itself in sub-Saharan Africa? Individuals continue to follow the traditional rules of marriage, and the marriage institution continues to contribute to community-based networks that regulate economic activity, even among migrants in the city. But changing the way this institution is organized is a very challenging task, since a sufficiently large proportion of the community must coordinate their actions to put a new set of rules in place. The examples of dynamic inefficiency that I have just described apply to fertility and marriage. But the same sort of reasoning would explain the rigidity of nonmarket economic institutions, such as networks, as well. Externalities associated with individual decisions give rise to social restrictions, and so the very strength of community-based institutions also makes them slow to change.

CONCLUSION

This essay has provided a mixed assessment of the benefits of nonmarket institutions. It is clear that these institutions serve a useful purpose when markets function imperfectly. At the same time, the restrictions on individual behavior within these institutions may leave the community ill equipped to respond to a changing world. This in turn suggests a role for policy, and I conclude this essay by briefly discussing how external interventions could help move the community out of its traditional equilibrium when the economic environment changes.

The first point to note is that the evaluation of any program needs to take account of the externalities that accompany individual decisions in a network-based economy. To understand the bias that could arise from a failure to account for these externalities, consider the effect of a rural education program that successfully increases wages among its (randomly selected) participants. In one scenario, these individuals would improve the quality of the networks that they belong to, generating positive spillovers within the community. In another scenario, these fortunate individuals would exit from the network, leaving the remaining members of the network worse off. By simply comparing the treatment group and a randomly selected control group, we could substantially underestimate or overestimate the true effect of the program.

Apart from program evaluation, the preceding discussion also allows us to say something about the optimal design of interventions themselves. Nonmarket institutions move the community to a preferred equilibrium, when externalities are present, by placing restrictions on individual behavior. The equilibria that are put in place are thus robust to change by construction. This is the basic source of the dynamic inefficiency that we discussed above.

As we saw in the rural Bangladesh application, coordinated action is required for norms to grow less effective and ultimately to change. A sophisticated external intervention would facilitate this change by subsidizing individual deviation from the norm, or by providing public signals that allow the community to coordinate on a new pattern of behavior. Instead, most interventions today focus on changing individual behavior, without taking account of the restrictions that regulate this behavior in a traditional society.

27

Racial Stigma: Toward a New Paradigm for Discrimination Theory

Glenn C. Loury

This essay examines interconnections between "race" and economic inequality in the United States, focusing on the case of African Americans. I will argue that it is crucially important to distinguish between *racial discrimination* and *racial stigma* in the study of this problem. Racial discrimination has to do with how blacks are treated, while racial stigma is concerned with how black people are perceived. My view is that what I call reward bias (unfair treatment of persons in formal economic transactions based on racial identity) is now a less significant barrier to the full participation by African Americans in U.S. society than is what I will call development bias (restricted access to resources critical for personal development but available only via informal social transactions that are difficult to regulate because they do not take place in a market context). By making these points in the specific cultural and historical context of the black experience in U.S. society, I hope to contribute to a deeper conceptualization of the worldwide problem of race and economic marginality.

EMBODIED SOCIAL SIGNIFICATION

A theory of racial economic disparity should begin with some account of the phenomenon of "race" itself. We need to explain why people take note of and assign significance to the skin color, hair texture, and facial bone structure of other human beings. That superficial markings on human bodies are socially significant—that agents routinely partition the field of human subjects whom they encounter into groups, with this sorting convention based on the subjects' possession of some cluster of observable bodily marks—is a universal feature of human societies.

My proposal is that we think about "race" as a social phenomenon resulting from the combination of two processes—*categorization* and *signification*. Categorization involves the sorting of persons into a cognitively manageable number of subgroups, based on bodily marks, for the purpose of differentiating one's dealings with such persons. Signification involves the mental activity of associating certain connotations or "meanings" with these categories. My argument is that, at bottom, "race" is all about "embodied social signification."

Let me dispose of a red herring at the outset. Some critics (e.g., Gilroy 2000) have suggested that social analysts should abandon the use of racial categories, since modern science has shown that there are no "races" as such. The attempt to classify human beings on the basis of natural variation in genetic endowments across what for much of human history had been geographically isolated subpopulations is controversial (Cavalli-Sforza 2000; Olson 2002). I wish to stress, however, that my use of "race" as an instance of *social cognition* is an altogether distinct enterprise from using "race" as an instrument of *biological taxonomy*. While there well may be no "races" in the biological sense, we can nevertheless adopt the linguistic convention that when saying "Person A belongs to race X," what we mean is that "Person A possesses physical traits which (in a given society, at a fixed point in history, under the conventions of racial classification extant there and then) will cause him to be classified (by a preponderance of those he encounters in that society and/or by himself) as belonging to race X."

To see this point more clearly, consider the following thought experiment. Let people believe that fluctuations of the stock market can be predicted by changes in sunspot activity. This may be because, as an objective meteorological matter, sunspots correlate with rainfall, which influences crop yields, thus affecting the economy. Or solar radiation might somehow influence the human psyche so as to alter how people behave in securities markets. Each of these accounts proposes an objective causal link between sunspots and stock prices. They can be likened to grounding one's cognizance of "race" on the validity of a race-based biological taxonomy. But let us posit that no such objective links of this kind between sunspots and stock prices exist. Still, if enough people believe in the connection, monitor conditions on the sun's surface, and act on the basis of how they anticipate security prices will be affected, then a *real* link between these evidently disparate phenomena will have been forged out of the subjective perceptions of stock market participants. As a result of this process, a belief in the financial relevance of sunspot activity will have been rendered entirely rational.

Likewise, no *objective* racial taxonomy need be valid for the *subjective* use of racial classifications to become warranted. It is enough that influential social actors hold schemes of racial classification in their minds and act on those schemes. For if a person knows that others in society will classify him on the basis of certain markers, with these acts of classification affecting his material or psychological well-being, then it will be a rational cognitive stance on his part—not a belief in magic and certainly not a *moral* error—for him to think of himself as belonging to a "race." In turn, that he thinks of himself in this way and that others in society classify him similarly provides a compelling reason for a newcomer to adopt this ongoing scheme of racial classification. Learning the extant "language" of embodied social signification is a first step toward assimilation of the foreigner, or the newborn, into any "raced" society. I conclude that "races," in the social-cognitive sense, may come to exist and to be reproduced over the generations in a society, even though there may exist no "races" in the biological-taxonomic sense.

BIASED SOCIAL COGNITION

My "new paradigm" for discrimination theory builds on the observation that, due to the history and culture peculiar to a given society, powerful negative connotations may become associated with particular bodily marks carried by some persons in that society. I claim that this is decidedly the case with respect to the marks that connote "blackness" in U.S. society. (This claim is defended at length in Loury 2002, chap. 3.) My proposal is that analysts should place more emphasis on the ways in which observers interpret social data that bear on the status of disadvantaged racial groups, as distinct from (say) their "tastes" for discrimination against such people. With my core concept—*biased social cognition*—I attempt to move from the fact that people make use of racial classifications in the course of their interactions, to some understanding of how this alters the causal accounts they settle upon for what they observe in the social world. My signature question is: When does the "race" of those subject to a difficult social circumstance affect whether powerful observers see the disadvantages experienced by such people as constituting a societal problem?

Here is a nonracial example that may help to make this point. Much evidence supports the conclusion that there is disparity in social outcomes for males and females. Consider two distinct venues where this is the case— the schools and the jails. Compared with girls, boys are overrepresented among those doing well in math and science in the schools, while men are overrepresented among those doing poorly in society at large by ending up in jail. Yet only one of these disparities is widely perceived to be a societal problem—the first. Why? One possible answer is this: it offends basic intuitions about the propriety of underlying social processes that boys and girls attain different levels of achievement in the technical curriculum, while no disquiet is stirred by gender disparities in the jails. Because we do not easily envision a wholly legitimate causal chain of events that could produce the school disparity, we set ourselves the task of solving a problem. In the face of this inequality we are inclined to interrogate our institutions—to search the record of our social practice and examine myriad possibilities in order to see where things might have gone wrong. Yet nothing like this happens for male–female disparity in the jails because, tacitly if not explicitly, we are "gender essentialists." In effect, our model of social causation posits that males and females differ—either in their biological nature or in their deep-seated acculturation—and it is this essential difference that accounts for the observed disparity. As "gender essentialists," our intuitions are not offended by the fact of vastly higher rates of imprisonment among males than among females. We do not ask deeper questions about why this disparity has come about. And so, since there is no problem perceived, no solution is sought.

Whether we are right or wrong to act as we do in these gender matters, my point is that the bare facts of disparity do not, in themselves, provide any motive for action. To act, we must marry what we observe to some model of social causation. This model need not be explicit; it can lurk beneath the surface of our conscious reflections. Still, it is the facts *plus* the model that lead us to perceive a given circumstance as indicative of some as yet undiagnosed failing in our social interactions, or not.

Now consider another example of how people's models of the world (what they take as exogenous) prevent them from seeing the social structures that may engender racial inequality. Suppose taxi drivers in a big city are reluctant to stop for young black men because they fear being robbed. That is, they calculate that the chance of robbery conditional on race (and, perhaps, other information, such as age and sex) exceeds a prudential threshold when the prospective fare is a young black man, but not otherwise. Imagine that, as a matter of the crime statistics, this surmise is objectively correct. Even so, a process of adverse selection could explain how such a racial disparity might arise.

If an agent knows taxis are unlikely to stop for him, and if he does not intend to rob the driver, then he may not want to rely on taxis for transportation because of the expected length of his anticipated wait. It is plausible to assume that waiting costs are less for someone who intends to rob the driver than for someone who does not. After all, to get in a night's work, the robber may need only one cab to stop during the night. That drivers are slow to stop for a certain group may discourage all members of that group from using taxis, but those intent on robbing will be relatively less discouraged than those who have no such intention. Thus, should the drivers begin with an a priori belief that a certain group of people is more likely to harbor robbers, and so become slow to stop for them, the result may be to create incentives for self-selection within that group such that robbers become relatively more likely to hail cabs.

This example shows that if people on one side of a transaction are inclined to make racial generalizations when forming their beliefs, if they act on those beliefs, and if they start out believing differently about people who have different racial traits, then the actions they take can indirectly produce evidence that confirms them in their views. But, being completely oblivious to such an endogenous source of racial disparity, they may mistakenly attribute the inequality to exogenous sources.

Thus, imagine that an observer (correctly) takes note of the fact that, on the average and all else being equal, black residential neighborhoods are more likely to decline. This may lead that observer to move away from any neighborhood when more than a few blacks move into it. But what if the racial composition of a neighborhood connotes decay in this manner only because, when a great number of observers act on their worst fears, the result (through some possibly complex chain of social causation) is to bring about the confirmation of their beliefs? Perhaps nonblack residents panic at the arrival of a few blacks, selling too quickly and below the market value to lower-income (black) buyers, and it is this process that promotes a neighborhood's decline. Under such circumstances observers might mistakenly attribute racially disparate behaviors to ingrained limitations of African Americans—thinking, say, that blacks take poor care of their property because they are simply less responsible people on average, when in fact there need be no racial differences in such character traits.

A mistaken causal attribution of this kind could be of great *political* consequence since, if one attributes an endogenous difference (a difference produced within a system of interactions) to an exogenous cause (a cause located outside that system), then one is unlikely to see any need for systemic reform.

Notice what is happening here: the taxi drivers' or homeowners' behaviors are creating the facts on which their pessimistic expectations are grounded. Thus, were most drivers as willing to stop for young black men as for others, the set of blacks hailing cabs might be no more threatening than the overall population average. But then it would be reasonable for drivers to pay no heed to race when deciding whether or not to stop! Clearly, once a convention employing the self-confirming racial stereotype has been established, the observing agents' beliefs and actions can be defended on the basis of reason. But the deeper conclusion—that there is an intrinsic connection between race and crime, or race and neighborhood decline—is altogether unjustified. I think it is safe to assume that this subtle distinction will elude most cab drivers, homeowners, politicians, op-ed writers, and not a few social scientists!

It is this distinction between *endogenous* and *exogenous* social causation that is, I believe, the key to understanding the difference in our reformist intuitions about gender inequalities in the schools and in the jails: because we think the disparity of school outcomes stems from endogenous sources, while the disparity of jail outcomes is tacitly attributed in most of our "causal models" to exogenous sources, we are not moved to the same extent to do something about the observed disparities. My argument is that a given instance of social disparity is less likely to be perceived as a social problem when people take the disparity to have been caused by the deficiencies of those who lag behind. My contention is that in American society, when the group in question is blacks, the risk of this kind of causal misattribution is especially great.

This kind of reflection on the deeper structure of our social-cognitive processes, as they bear on the issues of racial disparity, is what I had hoped to stimulate with my discussion of "biased social cognition." And the role of "race" in such processes is what I am alluding to when I talk about "racial stigma."

I believe the disparate impact of the enforcement of antidrug laws offers a telling illustration of the value in this way of thinking. There could be no drug market without sellers *and* buyers. (Just as there would be no street prostitution without hookers and johns.) Typically, those on the selling side of such markets are more deeply involved in crime and disproportionately drawn from the bottom rungs of society. When we entertain alternative responses to the social malady reflected in drug use (or in street prostitution), we must weigh the costs likely to be imposed upon the people involved. Our tacit models of social causation will play a role in this process of evaluation. Have bad lawbreakers who sell drugs on our city streets imposed this problem on us? Or has a bored, spoiled middle class with too much time on its hands engendered the problem in its hedonistic pursuit of a good time? How serious a given crime is seen to be by those who, through their votes, indirectly determine our policies, and how "deserved" the punishment for a given infraction, may depend on the racial identities of those involved, because the tacit causal accounts adopted by influential observers may depend on "race."

In Loury (2002) I use the theory of biased social cognition just sketched to argue that durable racial inequality can be understood as the outgrowth of a series of "vicious circles of cumulative causation" (Myrdal 1944). I have in mind a model where popular support for egalitarian policy reforms benefiting a stigmatized racial group depends on the causal explanations ordinary people are inclined to give for observed racial disparities. The tacit association of "blackness" in the public's imagination with "unworthiness" distorts cognitive processes and promotes essentialist causal misattributions. In plain English, observers will have difficulty identifying with the plight of people whom they (mistakenly) see to be simply "reaping what they have sown." In turn, this tendency to see racial disparities as *communal* rather than a *societal* problem encourages the reproduction of inequality through time because, absent some reformist interventions, the low social conditions of many blacks persist, the negative social meanings ascribed to blackness are then reinforced, and thus the racially biased social-cognitive processes are reproduced, completing the circle.

WHY NOT REPARATIONS?

Because it has its roots in past unjust acts that were perpetrated on the basis of race, present-day racial inequality on the scale to be observed in U.S. society constitutes a gross historical injustice. This much is clear. Not so clear are the implications of this observation for present-day public policy choices. In Loury (2002) I address this problem, proposing what I take to be a necessary condition for the attainment of racial justice. Specifically, I claim that past racial injustice establishes a general presumption against indifference to present racial inequality. Notice that this is a result-oriented, not a process-oriented criterion. That is, guaranteeing the unbiased treatment of blacks from this point forward, with there being no effort taken to reduce current racial disparities, would not be sufficient to secure a racially just outcome in my view. However, I do not think that the public response to this situation can or should be conceived in terms of "correcting" or "balancing" for historical violation. I conclude by briefly elaborating on this point.

A central reality of our time is the fact that a wide racial gap has opened in the acquisition of cognitive skills, the extent of law-abidingness, the stability of family relations, attachment to the workforce, and the like. I place this racial disparity in human development at the center of my analysis, and put forward an account of it rooted in social and cultural factors, not in blacks' inherent capacities. What I am saying in so many words is that even if there were no overt racial discrimination against blacks, powerful social forces would still be at work to perpetuate into future generations the consequences of a universally acknowledged history of racism in America. A corollary of this position is that combating such racism as continues to exist will be insufficient to achieve racial justice.

In stating this, I do not suggest that conventional efforts to combat discrimination be suspended, or that racism is an empty concept or a historical relic. The evidence of continuing racial unfairness in day-to-day social intercourse in this country is quite impressive. But so, too, is the evidence of a gap in acquired skills that at least partly explains racial disparities. I seek an argument for racial egalitarianism that requires neither a showing of contemporaneous discrimination nor an insistence upon some kind of transgenerational historical debt. I ground that argument on biased processes of human development deriving from the extreme social isolation of many blacks.

Whereas reparations advocacy conceives the problem of our morally problematic history in *compensatory* terms, I propose to see the problem in *interpretive* terms. That is, I seek public recognition of the severity, and (crucially) the contemporary relevance, of what has transpired. I stress that this is not merely a question of historical fact; it is also a matter of how we choose to look at the facts. My goal is to encourage a common basis of historical memory—a common narrative—through which the past racial injury and its continuing significance can enter into current policy discourse. What is required for racial justice, as I conceive it, is a commitment on the part of the public, including the political elite and the opinion-shaping media, to take responsibility for the plight of the urban black poor, and to understand this troubling circumstance as having emerged in a general way out of an ethically indefensible past. Such a commitment should, in my view, be open-ended and not contingent on demonstrating any specific lines of causality.

ACKNOWLEDGMENT This essay draws on my paper "Racial Justice: The Superficial Morality of Colour-blindness in the United States," prepared for the U.N. Research Institute for Social Development and Delivered at the World Conference Against Racism, Durban, South Africa, September 2001.

BIBLIOGRAPHY

Cavalli-Sforza, Luigi L. *Genes, Peoples and Languages.* New York: North Point Press, 2000.

Gilroy, Paul. *Against Race: Imagining Political Culture Beyond the Color Line.* Cambridge, Mass.: Harvard University Press, 2000.

Loury, Glenn. *The Anatomy of Racial Inequality.* Cambridge, Mass.: Harvard University Press, 2002.

Myrdal, Gunnar. *An American Dilemma: The Negro Problem and Modern Democracy.* New York: Pantheon, 1944.

Olson, Steve. *Mapping Human History: Discovering the Past Through Our Genes.* Boston: Houghton Mifflin, 2002.

28

Aspirations, Poverty, and Economic Change

Debraj Ray

INTRODUCTION

My aim in this short essay is to discuss a particular aspect of poverty, which is its close and brutal association with a failure of aspirations. Lest the point I am about to develop be misunderstood, let me state immediately that this is not an assertion about individuals who are poor; it is a statement about the condition of poverty itself. Poverty stifles dreams, or at least the process of *attaining* dreams. Thus poverty and the failure of aspirations may be reciprocally linked in a self-sustaining trap. The notes in this essay are meant to draw out various aspects of this theme and, in the process, to introduce and discuss an aspirations-based view of individual behavior.

The starting point, then, is a view of the individual that isn't standard in economics, but it should be: individual desires and standards of behavior are often defined by experience and observation; they don't exist in social isolation as "consumer preferences" are so often assumed to do. This simple remark has strong implications: if a person's behavior is conditioned by the experiences of other individuals in the cognitive neighborhood of that person, these experiences may be all-important in driving group interaction and group dynamics in a way quite different from what the simple aggregation of individual "preferences" would lead us to believe.

This social grounding of individual desires I will refer to by the term "aspirations." My objective is to remark on this concept of aspirations as it relates to issues of poverty (and this includes not just economic impoverishment but associated ills, such as poor health). I will argue that there is much to be learned by viewing poverty both as a (partial) result of and a (partial) cause of a failure of aspirations.

While I, and other economists, have been concerned with aspirations-based theories of individual behavior for some time,[1] the immediate source of inspiration for these notes is the work of Appadurai (see Appadurai 2004) on what he calls the "capacity to aspire." In a thoughtful and provocative sequence of arguments, Appadurai—an anthropologist—has drawn attention to this fundamental determinant of behavior. He has forcefully made the point that aspirations are socially determined, and—to complete the vicious circle—has argued that the poor may lack "the [aspirational] resources to contest and alter the conditions of their own poverty." My notes will explore some of these issues—and others—from the vantage point of an economist.

THE ASPIRATIONS WINDOW

I begin by developing the idea of an *aspirations window*. The window is formed from an individual's cognitive world, her zone of "similar," "attainable" individuals. Our individual draws her aspirations from the lives, achievements, or ideals of those who exist in her aspirations window.

Put this way, we aren't really saying much. The individuals who populate my window are the individuals who determine my aspirations—that's tautological. We really begin to put structure on the problem when we take up two issues: (a) the determinants of an aspirations window and (b) the effect of aspirations on behavior. I address (a) here and postpone (b) to the next section.

First, notice that the concept of aspirations itself may be inherently multidimensional. Individuals aspire to a better material standard of living, but there are other aspirations as well, some a bit more sinister than others: dignity, good health, recognition, political power, or the urge to dominate others on religious or ethnic grounds. Depending on one's place in the socioeconomic hierarchy, these many-faceted aspirations may complement one another, or they may be mutual substitutes.

Because aspirations and the notion of "similarity" are both multidimensional concepts, so is the aspirations window. If I am a forty-five-year-old Indian professor of economics who lives in New York City and has mainly nonacademic friends, you can count at least five dimensions that might enter my aspirations window—and just from that one line of introduction. But there are several ways in which one can narrow down the notion of similarity and give it substance.

First, it may simply be that individuals use their peers (or near-peers) to form comparisons, invidious or otherwise, because that's just the way people are. I might use the standards and achievements of other economists, or those of other Indian academics, or perhaps academics in my age group as a basis for forming my aspirations. But I'm unlikely to call on the experiences of Bill Gates or Madonna: they're just too far away from who I am. There may be a biological or evolutionary basis for this restriction, though the particular *form* assumed by the restriction may of course be highly society-specific.

Second, there may be restrictions that arise simply because of the flow of information; what people can physically observe may be limited, or communication may be circumscribed in some way. Wilson's (1987) study of role models may be a useful example: successful individuals who emigrate from the inner city are no longer there to be observed and cannot influence aspirations or behavior among the young. Munshi and Myaux's research on the Bangladesh fertility slowdown (Munshi and Myaux 2001) suggests that Hindu fertility averages had a separate and significant effect on fertility rates for a Hindu couple (likewise for the Muslim averages). There is also some ethnographic evidence that individuals set reproductive goals depending on the mortality experience of infants or children in their own locality or family (Lewis 1958; Das Gupta 1994).

Third, there may be statistical reasons. Once again, Munshi's work is relevant: in his 1999 study of adoption of high-yielding varieties, he shows that a farmer will want to look at the adoption decisions of farmers who are "close" to him—spatially, economically, perhaps even socially. Looking at the experiences of individuals similar to me is like running an experiment with better controls, and therefore has better content in informing my decisions—and, by extension, my aspirations. Likewise, in forming estimates of the rate of return to education, a poor individual might look only at the experiences of similarly poor individuals, believing (perhaps correctly) that the rate of return to education calculated from other observations may be colored by contacts and connections (this issue is logically distinct from the truncation effect discussed above, in the context of Wilson's work).

Fourth, "similarity" is contextual: it depends on how much mobility (or perceived mobility) there is in society. The greater the extent of (perceived) mobility, the broader the aspirations window. A bonded laborer may believe that there is an unbridgeable wall between him and the local shopkeeper in the village; if labor is free to move and possibly change occupations, such comparisons may well be made.

Finally, the different dimensions of aspirations are obviously connected with different facets of the aspirations window. As an economic agent who desperately seeks to escape poverty, I will emulate, imitate, and learn from the economic strategies of those in my neighborhood income or wealth group. As a Hindu Indian who is drawn to the idea that Indian Muslims should head off to Pakistan, I may emulate an entirely different set of people. More dangerously, an aspirations failure along one dimension may spur my ambitions along another.

THE ASPIRATIONS GAP AND INDIVIDUAL BEHAVIOR

Why are these considerations important? To address that question, we need to combine a theory of how aspirations are formed with a theory of how aspirations affect behavior. I now turn to a simple—perhaps simplistic—account of this.

In this account, the idea of an *aspirations gap* plays a central role. For concreteness, let me illustrate this by using material aspirations alone (the same idea can be applied, perhaps with modification, to other dimensions). The aspirations gap is simply the difference between the standard of living that's aspired to and the standard of living that one already has. I want to argue that it's this *gap*—not aspirations per se, nor one's standard of living per se—that affects future-oriented behavior.

The aspirations gap is a measure of how far one wants to go. To complete this story, one must discuss how such a gap is filled by deliberate action. The easiest way to think about it is to introduce some notion of costly investment. Such investment (in education, health, or income-generating activities) raises future standards of living. Presumably, this narrows the aspirations gap (an interesting variant of the argument that we don't consider is that the aspirations themselves will slide forward as well, as newer horizons come into view). At the same time, investment is costly to the individual. Current sacrifices will need to be made.

An economist would approach this sort of description by postulating that our individual wants to choose investment effort to maximize the difference between benefits (a reduced gap) and costs (lower current standards).[2] One implication of such an exercise is the following interesting feature: *individual investment efforts are minimal for both high- and low-aspiration gaps.*

A little reflection renders this proposition intuitively obvious. Individuals whose aspirations are closely aligned to their current standards of living have little incentive to raise those standards. However, individuals whose aspirations are very far from their current standards of living *also* have little incentive to raise standards, because the gap will remain very large before and after. A lot of investment will cover only a small part of the way: the overall journey is too long, and therefore not worth undertaking in the first place.

Thus our concept of an aspirations window, together with this description of aspirations and individual behavior, has an interesting implication. If economic betterment is an important goal, the aspirations window *must* be opened, for otherwise there is no drive to self-betterment. Yet it should not be open too wide: there is the curse of frustrated aspirations. There must be individuals in our immediate cognitive neighborhood who do better than we do, yet if they do *a lot* better, we will invest little even if such individuals remain within our cognitive neighborhood. In short, the experiences of others may have little effect on us because *either* they lie outside our aspirations window *or*, even if they are within it, their living standards (which form our aspirations) are far from ours.

SOCIAL POLARIZATION, POVERTY, AND ASPIRATIONS FAILURE

The minimal effect of an aspirations gap at both ends of the gap spectrum is crucial to the understanding of an *aspirations failure*. How might such a failure come about for the poor? To understand this, it is necessary to think about societies in which there is a substantial amount of social polarization, or stratification.

The best way to do this is to think of the opposite scenario: a *connected society*, one in which there is much (economic) diversity in every cognitive neighborhood, diversity in which every individual can justifiably think of herself as being on the attainable fringes. Crudely put, a society in which there is a chain of *observed, local* steps between the poorest and the richest will be more vibrant, in the sense that individuals not only will have aspirations but also will have the sorts of aspirations they can act upon.

In contrast, a polarized society (see, e.g., Esteban and Ray 1994; Wolfson 1994) is one in which there are few inhabitants between the poor and the rich.[3] In such a society, there are only two possibilities.

First, the poor do not include the rich in their cognitive window. This will especially be the case if economic polarization is aided and abetted by other forms of stratification: slavery, serfdom, caste, racial discrimination. Then the aspirations gap will be low, and so will individual investments for the future. This sort of aspirations failure often goes by other names, most commonly fatalism. But true fatalism—a deep belief that one's destiny is preordained and beyond control—cannot be affected by socioeconomic policy. This variant of fatalism—the one that says there is little hope of betterment, because this is the way things have always been—*can* be so affected. Faced with the diagnostic choice between true fatalism and an aspirations failure, one can only hope that it is the latter.

Second, the poor do aspire to be like the rich, but the gap is simply too large. The costs of the many steps of investment are too high, and the reward—in terms of a relative narrowing of the aspirations gap—is simply too low. This is another kind of aspirations failure. The aspirations do exist, but the feeling is widespread that such aspirations are largely unreachable. The seeming absence of class distinctions, or caste divisions, can only enhance this brand of aspirations failure, because there are no ostensible barriers to block the view of the rich from the cognitive windows of the poor. Poverty in such societies will find expression not in the "fatalism" of the previous paragraph, but in frustration and envy, much like the poor admirers of Richard Corey: "We thought that he was everything,/To make us wish that we were in his place" (Robinson 1922).

So it is not the condition of poverty alone that is responsible for an aspirations failure. It is poverty in conjunction with a lack of connectedness, the absence of a critical mass of persons who are better off than the person in question, yet not so much better off that their economic well-being is thought to be unattainable. In contrast, *inequality* isn't really the prime mover at all, though to some extent it may be correlated with polarization. It is perfectly possible for an unequal society nevertheless to be thickly populated at all points of the economic spectrum, creating local, attainable incentives at the lower end of the wealth or income distribution. Affirmative action and public education may be policy tools that help in creating this sense of local connectedness.

SOCIOECONOMIC CHANGE AND ASPIRATIONS

So far I've focused on the effect of aspirations on individual behavior. I now want to take this framework a step further by discussing the effect of social and economic change on aspirations (and therefore on behavior). In the next section I take up the question of deliberate activism to change the aspirations of the poor.

As a first example, consider the seemingly paradoxical thesis of Tocqueville ([1856] 1986) that economic development may generate social tensions and rebellions more than situations of stagnant mobility and high inequality. Tocqueville was addressing the fact that an anti-feudal revolution broke out in the one European country (France) where the feudal oppression was the lightest to start with. While I do not have the time here to go into the details, Toqueville's argument is clear: iniquities and oppressions that are cloaked with implacable inevitability can be borne.[4] Once this sense of inevitable oppression is removed by increased mobility and increased economic development (at least in aggregate terms), the aspirations window must widen. This, in turn, will increase the aspirations gap unless all *actual* standards of living can keep pace with changing aspirations. The result may very well be increased conflict, rather than less.

Tocqueville's thesis may thus be summarized in one of his own memorable lines: "The French found their position all the more intolerable as it became better." The very process that raises aspirations must also fulfill those aspirations in the not-too-distant future; otherwise, enhanced voice can all too easily turn to violent exit.[5]

My second example concerns societies (such as the United States) where an increased aspirations gap may not lead to violent exit, but to increased effort. In such societies, culture may be "constructed" to enhance impressions of economic mobility. I do not say that there's a deliberate conspiracy here (though who knows?). One "nondeliberate" source for this construction stems from the familiar "truncation bias" created by the media, which will report newsworthy "successes" (lottery winners, basketball superstars) but not mundane "failures." Notice that the truncation bias grows with the underlying inequality in that society—the truncated positive half of the distribution will mistakenly suggest an even greater rate of return to occupations.

If such constructions raise the aspirations gap—but moderately so—that might induce hard work for a large working class with no real reward. One can see how fables of economic mobility can be beneficial for worker productivity.[6] Furthermore, while the notion of illusory mobility cannot be immediately extended to developing countries, there are parallels. For instance, to what extent might relatively costless lip service, accolades, and awards for participatory collective activity by the poor directly (albeit unwittingly) serve to postpone real economic change in their living conditions? For instance, Appadurai (2002) writes, referring to a (justly celebrated) alliance of three urban NGOs in Mumbai, India:

> In June 2001, at a major meeting at the United Nations, ... the Alliance and its partners elsewhere in the world, built a model house as well as a model children's toilet in the lobby of the main United Nations Building, after considerable internal debate within the SDI and official resistance at the UN. These models were visited by Kofi Annan in a festive atmosphere which left an indelible impression of material empowerment on the world of UN bureaucrats and NGO officials present. Annan was surrounded by poor women from India and South Africa, singing and dancing, as he walked through the model house and the model toilet, in the heart of his own bureaucratic empire. It was a magical moment, full of possibilities for the Alliance, and for the Secretary-General, as they engaged jointly and together with the global politics of poverty.

I cannot help but be caught up in Appadurai's obvious enthusiasm, yet I wonder whether such "festive" activities might have the effect of staving off—rather than fostering—deep change.

Finally, one can use this sort of framework to ask whether the poor can be "hijacked" to serve other "cultures," such as the rise of religious fundamentalism. In the Gujarat genocide of 2002, the lives and livelihoods of several thousand Muslims were destroyed by rampaging Hindu mobs. Fundamentalism aside, two things appear evident: first (as in all the great communal riots), there was a strong economic component to the violence; businesses and commercial establishments were targets. Second, the poor—often not excluding tribals and Dalits who occupy the bottom of the Hindu hierarchy—joined forces with upper-class Hindus to loot and kill. There is no doubt that money exchanged hands to facilitate such alliances, but in the words of Engineer, "This does not explain the fury with which they attacked. The constant propaganda against Muslims—they are enemies and anti-nationals who must be taught a lesson—also had its effect. The Vishwa Hindu Parishad, in order to fight Muslims with the help of Dalits, expressed solidarity with them as Hindus and instilled in them a strong dose of Hinduness while deemphasising their Dalitness" (Engineer 2002). And, I might add, their poverty. The Gujarat carnage is only one example of how a failed capacity to aspire in the (direct) material sense may actually ignite other (relatively indirect) aspirational routes. The former failure, in turn, may arise from an economically polarized society.[7]

In the Indian case, there is an odd twist to the question of religious fundamentalism. I have emphasized the "push" into a distinct aspirational dimension (religion) emanating from the failure along another aspirational dimension (economic well-being). In addition, there may be "pulls." The demolition of the Babri Masjid in 1992 may have raised fundamentalist aspirations and the level of violence in its own right, in an eerie echo of Tocqueville's reading of the French Revolution.

COLLECTIVE ACTION AND ASPIRATIONS

Now let me turn to the effects that may be deliberately generated through collective action. What are the avenues of deliberate, significant influence on the capacity to aspire? I want to mention three pathways, each of which can have significant impact on aspirations and the consequent future orientation of individuals.[8]

Groups as Internal Conveyors of Information

Groups are repositories of pooled information, which they can credibly convey to every member. For instance, the simple fact that group members are saving (or are making a commitment to save) is information that can be conveyed—with good effect—to all members. The key word in this context is *pooling*: the sharing of the experience of peers. Suppose that you believe the rate of return to primary education is high, and want to convey this to a poor individual in order to get him to send his son to school. There is a simple reason why this statement will mean very little to him (see also my remarks on activism in a slightly different context): *there is no experience quite as compelling as the experience of your immediate family and, more broadly, those in your socioeconomic and spatial neighborhood.* You might say that econometricians had found a high rate of private return to investment in primary schooling in a study of nationwide panel data that had controlled appropriately for differences in characteristics within the underlying population: the terms of such a statement would mean nothing to him (and would have meant nothing to us—probably still doesn't) unless it is complemented by the immediacy of shared experience. This is why the pooling of information, of experience, among group members is of paramount importance.

Group Actions as External Conveyors of Information

Next, consider group actions that credibly communicate information to outsiders: the government, perhaps, and certainly the public at large. Such communication can have enormous impact, if for no reason other than the fact that the numerical strength of the affected party is publicly revealed, which directly (and indirectly, through public awareness) must affect overall political calculation. Thus activities such as self-surveys (carried out by the Mumbai Alliance and described in Appadurai 2002) may be capable of great instrumentalist power. If used carefully and credibly, even a survey can be an enormous lobbying force, with real economic benefits. Just the awareness of the sheer numbers of people living in a slum can possibly scuttle a relocation effort. Statistical visibility is power.

The key word here is *credibility*. A fundamental threat to the efficacy of activism is that a person listening to an activist will feel (perhaps correctly) that the activist is trying to convince him of something. One might—in deference to the other dilemmas present in game theory—call this the activist's dilemma. If I, as an activist, believe in something more than another person does, and am in possession of objective, valuable information that might bring the other person closer to, but not *fully* in line with, my beliefs, I will want to exaggerate my information (or at least will be suspected of doing so, whether I actually do so or not). All would be well if such exaggerations could be appropriately stripped away to reveal the true informational content, but a simple game-theoretic argument[9] shows that this significantly hampers the ability to communicate. More precisely, an activist may be able to credibly transmit statistical changes that are large, but lose the ability (in the strategic game) to credibly communicate more nuanced variations in the data.

Groups as Coordination Devices

Finally, an important aspect of group effectiveness can be succinctly and easily summarized in the language of "multiple equilibrium." A state x persists in society, which leads individuals in that society to take actions a. The actions a aggregate back to x, and the cycle is complete. The idea has been applied to everything under the sun: poverty traps, high-fertility regimes, persistence of social norms, business cycles, and, yes, there is place here for the aspirational trap.

If I live in a community in which the majority of my peers do not save for a better future, then my own aspirations are dulled, I do not fear a relative loss of standing among these peers, and I may not save. This equilibrium can take hold with ease (even in rich countries: witness the United States). On the other hand, if my neighbors are known to save on a regular basis, it will spur my desire to save. This is not to underestimate the sheer difficulties of saving under poverty, but as several microfinance organizations and rotating savings and credit associations (ROSCAs) have shown, the difficulties are far from insuperable. A savings group may be viewed as a *coordination device* to break such a trap. By coordinating an open, observable promise to save among a large number of similar individuals, it induces greater incentives to save for each one of them, shoring up an entirely different equilibrium. (Indeed, it is little wonder that group savings organizations are widespread among the poor in developing countries.[10])

SUMMARY

In this short essay, I have discussed an aspirations-based approach to individual behavior, and its implications for the persistence of poverty. The approach has three major components. The first is the most basic: individual aspirations are born in a social context; they do not exist in a vacuum. Other individuals—their lifestyles, their social and political norms, and their economic well-being—serve to condition and determine the goals and aspirations of any particular person. At the same time, it is only "local society"—individuals who are broadly similar to me or relevant to my experiences—that appears on my radar screen: this is the idea of the "aspirations window" developed in the essay.

With this basic component in place, we can explore two other features. First, how do aspirations affect individual behavior? I introduce here the notion of an aspirations gap: the distance between what an individual might aspire to and the conditions she currently finds herself in. The main observation here is that both a large aspirations gap and a small aspirations gap may be inimical to investment effort to better one's own conditions. The latter occurs because there is very little to aspire toward; the former, because there is too much. Both conditions may be present in a society that is polarized, either economically or socially, but the failure to invest may manifest itself in different forms in each case: the former in fatalism, the latter in frustration.

Second, how do socioeconomic conditions influence the aspirations window and, therefore, aspirations? There are several pathways discussed in the essay; in particular, I address the seemingly paradoxical thesis of Tocqueville: that economic development may generate social tensions and rebellions more than stagnant mobility and high inequality do. I study this as an example of how rapid development and increased mobility may widen the aspirations window, raising the possibility that (even positive) economic change may be associated with the potential for increased conflict. I also discuss cultures that may be constructed to enhance impressions of economic mobility. In such situations, an increased aspirations gap may not lead to violent exit, but to increased effort. I also entertain the possibility that a failure of aspirations along one dimension (such as economic well-being) may propel a move into a distinct aspirational dimension (such as religious fundamentalism).

The aspirations-based view in this essay should not detract from the possibility (an important possibility, in my opinion) that a poverty trap is very difficult to reverse, no matter how strong the drive and effort of the trapped individual. It is to suggest, however, that additional reinforcement mechanisms may be at work. In particular, as discussed, a circle of low (or frustrated) aspirations and endemic poverty may be a self-sustaining outcome.

Finally, while I have focused on poverty throughout this essay, the idea of socially determined aspirations (and its two-way interaction with individual behavior) may be relevant in other contexts as well. At the risk of appearing somewhat cryptic, one might use these ideas to explore a variety of socioeconomic issues: why relatively affluent countries destroyed by war may grow back quickly, why middle-income countries often grow faster than either their rich or their poor counterparts, why immigrants may save at extraordinarily high rates, or why polarized societies may exhibit low social mobility. But these will be the subjects of other essays.

NOTES

1. See, for example, Karandikar et al. (1998); Borgers and Sarin (2001); Bendor et al. (2001a, 2001b); Dixon (2000); Gilboa and Schmeidler (2001); and Ray (1998). More generally, the fact that individuals may use the consumption experiences of others as a basis for what they themselves might want is, of course, not a new idea in economics, though by and large it has remained outside the mainstream. The early work of Veblen (1947) and Duesenberry (1949) comes immediately to mind. But I have in mind something a bit different from conspicuous consumption, envy, or keeping up with the Joneses, issues that Veblen emphasized. Rather than envy, individuals may use the experiences of others (and perhaps their own past experiences) as the yardstick for setting goals for themselves, against which they evaluate the pleasures and pains of their own immediate experience. This is logically distinct from envy.

2. Here is a slightly more formal account. If s denotes an individual's current standard of living, and a the standard that's aspired to, then the aspirations gap is $g(a,s) \equiv \max \left\{ \dfrac{a-s}{a}, 0 \right\}$. Thus someone with extraordinarily high aspirations relative to his current standard will be "fully gapped," as it were, having an aspirations gap of 1. Someone who does not look beyond his current lot will have $a \approx s$, and the aspirations gap will be zero. Investment i raises future standards of living (say, according to some function $\sigma(i, s)$, thus narrowing the aspirations gap, but is costly to the individual. Denote this cost function by $c(i)$. An agent may be viewed as choosing i to minimize the sum (perhaps weighted) of gap and cost: $g(a, s') + c(i)$, subject to the constraint that $s' = \sigma(i, s)$.

3. Note that connectedness is a statement about observables. It is far from clear that connectedness in individual wealth, assets, or income translates directly into connectedness in observed standards of living. An example of a situation in which the two notions of connectedness are firmly linked is one in which no good is consumed for the purpose of social signaling. Then a standard set of conditions yields the continuity of consumption (or expenditure) in income, and endowment connectedness immediately translates into consumption connectedness. This equivalence fails, however, if there are "goods" (such as wedding banquets) that are "consumed" simply to convey status. Following Bernheim (1994) and others, it can be then shown that such expenditure on such items is necessarily clumped in discrete categories, even if the underlying distribution of endowments is smoothly dispersed. Such clumping helps to destroy connectedness, and can precipitate an aspirations failure.

4. Compare with Appadurai's argument that the poor display "fairly deep moral attachment to norms and beliefs that directly support their own degradation."

5. A lesser-known idea of Albert Hirschman is the "tunnel" effect (see Hirschman and Rothschild 1973). You are caught in a multilane tunnel and all traffic is jammed as far up as you can see. Suddenly the lane next to you starts to move. You're still stuck. How would you feel? The Hirschman argument is that you'd initially feel happy, for this is a signal that your lane is about to move as well. With the passage of time, however, a continuing move of the next lane and continued paralysis of your lane may lead to immense frustration.

6. Several recent studies conclude that the United States displays no higher economic mobility than its European counterparts, and along some dimensions—such as mean exit time from poverty—may display lower mobility (see, e.g., Burkhauser and Smeeding 2001, on the use of microlevel panel data, and the references contained therein).

7. This line of reasoning forms the basis of ongoing research with Joan-Maria Esteban and Rohini Pande on religious conflict in India.

8. Of course, there are other pathways. For instance, I neglect violent action. Much of this literature is connected with the group as a successful coordination device—see, for instance, Hardin (1995)—and I do say something about coordination below. I also ignore groups as negotiating devices with the law, with bureaucracy, with the police and government officials. Finally, group action may itself bestow a sense of dignity and self-respect; on these matters see Appadurai (2002).

9. Such an argument would be a simple variant of Crawford and Sobel (1982).

10. For a general discussion of microfinance in developing countries, see Morduch (1999).

BIBLIOGRAPHY

Appadurai, Arjun. "The Capacity to Aspire." In *Culture and Public Action.* Edited by V. Rao and M. Walton. Stanford, Calif.: Stanford University Press, 2004.

Bendor, Jonathan, Dilip Mookherjee, and Debraj Ray. "Aspiration-Based Reinforcement Learning in Repeated Games: An Overview." *International Game Theory Review* 3 (2001): 159–174.

Bendor, Jonathan, Dilip Mookherjee, and Debraj Ray. "Reinforcement Learning in Repeated Games." *BE Press Advances in Theoretical Economics* 1 (1) (2001): art. 3.

Bernheim, Douglas. "A Theory of Conformity." *Journal of Political Economy* 100 (1994): 841–877.

Borgers, Tilman, and Rajiv Sarin. "Naive Reinforcement Learning with Endogenous Aspirations." *International Economic Review* 41 (2000): 921–950.

Burkhauser, Richard V., and Timothy Smeeding. "The Role of Micro-Level Panel Data in Policy Research." In *Schmollers Jahrbuch*, 121–132. Berlin: Duncker and Humblot, 2001.

Crawford, Vincent, and Joel Sobel. "Strategic Information Transmission." *Econometrica* 50 (1982): 1431–1451.

Das Gupta, Monica. "What Motivates Fertility Decline?: A Case Study from Punjab, India." In *Understanding Reproductive Change*, edited by Bertil Egerö and Mikael Hammarskjold. Lund, Sweden: Lund University Press, 1994.

Dixon, Huw David. "Keeping Up with the Joneses: Competition and the Evolution of Collusion." *Journal of Economic Behavior and Organization* 43 (2000): 223–238.

Duesenberry, James. *Income, Savings, and the Theory of Consumer Behavior.* Cambridge, Mass.: Harvard University Press, 1949.

Engineer, Asghar. "Gujarat: An Area of Darkness." *Secular Perspective* (Apr. 2002): 16–30.

Esteban, Joan-Maria, and Debraj Ray. "On the Measurement of Polarization." *Econometrica* 62 (1994): 819–852.

Gilboa, Itzhak, and David Schmeidler. "Reaction to Price Changes and Aspiration Level Adjustments." *Review of Economic Design* 6 (2001): 215–223.

Hardin, Russell. *One for All: The Logic of Group Conflict.* Princeton, N.J.: Princeton University Press, 1995.

Hirschman, Albert, and Michael Rothschild. "The Changing Tolerance for Income Inequality in the Course of Economic Development; With a Mathematical Appendix." *Quarterly Journal of Economics* 87 (1973): 544–566.

Karandikar, Rajeeva, Dilip Mookherjee, Debraj Ray, and Fernando Vega-Redondo. "Evolving Aspirations and Cooperation." *Journal of Economic Theory* 80 (1998): 292–331.

Lewis, Oscar. *Village Life in Northern India.* Urbana, Ill.: University of Illinois Press, 1958.

Morduch, Jonathan. "The Microfinance Promise." *Journal of Economic Literature* 37 (1999): 1569–1614.

Munshi, Kaivan. "Learning from Your Neighbors: Why Do Some Innovations Spread Faster Than Others?" Working Paper, Department of Economics, University of Pennsylvania, 1999.

Munshi, Kaivan, and Jacques Myaux. "Development as a Process of Social Change: An Application to the Theory of Fertility Transition." Mimeo, Department of Economics, University of Pennsylvania, 2001.

Ray, Debraj. *Development Economics.* Princteon, N.J.: Princeton University Press, 1998.

Robinson, Edward Arlington. "Richard Corey." In Robinson's *Collected Poems.* New York: Macmillan, 1922.

Tocqueville, Alexis de. "L'Ancien Régime." In *Démocratie en Amérique; Souvenirs; L'Ancien Régime et la Révolution.* Paris: Robert Laffont, 1986.

Veblen, Thorstein. *The Theory of the Leisure Class.* New York: Modern Library, 1974.

Wilson, William Julius. *The Truly Disadvantaged.* Chicago: University of Chicago Press, 1987.

Wolfson, Michael. "When Inequalities Diverge." *American Economic Review, Papers and Proceedings* 84 (1994): 353–358.

Index

Boldface indicates that the topic appears in a figure or table.

Index   435

tariffs and revenue, 51–52
tortilla cartel, 100
trade liberalization, 89–91
Micawber problem, 7–8
microcredit groups, 171–172, 396. *See
    also* Grameen Bank
microfinance. *See also* banking
    and the Grameen Bank, 340
    need for, xliii–xlv
    and new growth theories, 81
    programs and life insurance in
        Uganda, 346
    in Thailand, 362–364
microinsurance. *See also* insurance
    data for, 340–341
    need for, xliv
    and the poverty trap, xxxiv
    programs for, xxxv
    prospects for, 340, 353
migration, 85, 214–215. *See also*
    immigrants
Mill, John Stuart, 20
Millennium Development Goals
    adopted, xvii
    and poverty, xvi, 3
    poverty and capabilities, 10
minimum wages, xxiv, 68. *See also*
    wages
Mirrlees theory
    critique of, xxxv–xxxvi
    and EITC, xxxii, **191–193**
    optimal income tax model, 231–232
    on poverty, xxxi–xxxii
    work disincentives, 238
mobility patterns
    among poor wage earners, 103
    and aspirations, 411, 414
    and capital market imperfections,
        237
    and decentralization of public
        services, 296–297
    and education, 238–239
    in nonmarket institutions, 394, 396
    social networks and public goods,
        289
    United States, 236
    and worker productivity, 414–415
modernization theory, xlvi
Moi, Daniel arap, 176

monopsony, 393, 394
moral hazard. *See also* insurance
    and agriculture insurance, 339–340,
        368
    and business loans, 359–360
    credit markets and poverty, 234–236
    and health insurance, 346, 347
    insurance/efficiency trade-off, 208
    and life insurance, 344
    means testing, 308
    and mental accounts in family
        insurance, 371
    and weather insurance, 349, 351–352
Morocco. *See also* Africa
    foreign investment and pollution, 107
    rainfall insurance, xliv, 350
mortgages, 383
Mozambique, 254. *See also* Africa
Mughals, India, 24, 28. *See also* India
multiple equilibrium, 417
Mumbai Alliance, 415, 416
Muslims. *See also* India
    and fertility, 275, 411
    Gujarat genocide, 415
Mwamishali village, 179

National Service Organization, 176
National Swahili Council, 175
nation-building. *See also* LDCs (less
        developed countries)
    drawbacks to, 181
    and ethnic conflict, xxx, 169
    Kenya and Tanzania, 174–176
    reasons for, 182
    research methodological issues, 180
Netherlands, 87. *See also* Europe
New Industrial Policy, 77
New Public Management, 292
New Zealand, 24, 40
NGOs (non-governmental
        organizations). *See also* government
    agricultural research in Kenya, 373–
        375
    health insurance provision, 346–347
    Mumbai Alliance, 415
    as public goods providers, 290, 294–
        296
    role of in growth and poverty
        reduction, 81

CPSIA information can be obtained at www.ICGtesting.com
Printed in the USA
BVOW042110290812

299109BV00004B/2/A